The Best Book of:

of:

RELATED TITLES

*For the retailer nearest you, or to order directly from the publisher,
call 800-428-SAMS. In Indiana, Alaska, and Hawaii call 317-298-5699.*

The Best Book of:

DOS

Alan Simpson

HOWARD W. SAMS & COMPANY

A Division of Macmillan, Inc.
4300 West 62nd Street
Indianapolis, Indiana 46268 USA

To Zeppo, a wise and faithful companion

FIRST EDITION
FIRST PRINTING—1989

International Standard Book Number: 0-672-22680-4
Library of Congress Catalog Card Number: 89-62336

Acquisitions Editor: *Richard K. Swadley*
Development Editor: *James Rounds*
Manuscript Editor: *Gary Masters*
Production Coordinator: *Marjorie Hopper*
Illustrator: *Don Clemons*
Cover Art: *DGS&D Advertising, Inc.*
Cover Photography: *Cassell Productions, Inc.*
Indexer: *Northwind Editorial Services*
Technical Reviewer: *Gary Masters*
Compositor: *Shepard Poorman Communications Corp.*
Keyboarder: *David Ann Gregson*
Prepress Assistance: *Becky Imel, Bill Hurley, Larry Lynch, Wm. D. Basham, and Lou Keglovits*

Printed in the United States of America

Overview

Contents

P   A   R   T

DOS Essentials

P   A   R   T

Managing Programs and Files

P   A   R   T

Customizing Your System   185

10. Creating and Editing Files   187

P   A   R   T

four

Programming DOS   295

13. Creating Your Own Commands   297

HOWARD W. SAMS & COMPANY

fff

Bookmark

DEAR VALUED CUSTOMER:

Howard W. Sams & Company is dedicated to bringing you timely and authoritative books for your personal and professional library. Our goal is to provide you with excellent technical books written by the most qualified authors. You can assist us in this endeavor by checking the box next to your particular areas of interest.

We appreciate your comments and will use the information to provide you with a more comprehensive selection of titles.

Thank you,

Vice President, Book Publishing
Howard W. Sams & Company

COMPUTER TITLES:

Hardware
- ☐ Apple 140
- ☐ Macintosh I01
- ☐ Commodore I10
- ☐ IBM & Compatibles I14

Business Applications
- ☐ Word Processing J01
- ☐ Data Base J04
- ☐ Spreadsheets J02

Operating Systems
- ☐ MS-DOS K05
- ☐ OS/2 K10
- ☐ CP/M K01
- ☐ UNIX K03

Programming Languages
- ☐ C L03
- ☐ Pascal L05
- ☐ Prolog L12
- ☐ Assembly L01
- ☐ BASIC L02
- ☐ HyperTalk L14

Troubleshooting & Repair
- ☐ Computers S05
- ☐ Peripherals S10

Other
- ☐ Communications/Networking M03
- ☐ AI/Expert Systems T18

ELECTRONICS TITLES:

- ☐ Amateur Radio T01
- ☐ Audio T03
- ☐ Basic Electronics T20
- ☐ Basic Electricity T21
- ☐ Electronics Design T12
- ☐ Electronics Projects T04
- ☐ Satellites T09

- ☐ Instrumentation T05
- ☐ Digital Electronics T11

Troubleshooting & Repair
- ☐ Audio S11
- ☐ Television S04
- ☐ VCR S01
- ☐ Compact Disc S02
- ☐ Automotive S06
- ☐ Microwave Oven S03

Other interests or comments: _____

_____

Name_____
Title _____
Company _____
Address _____
City _____
State/Zip _____
Daytime Telephone No. _____

A Division of Macmillan, Inc.

4300 West 62nd Street Indianapolis, Indiana 46268

22680

Bookmark

HOWARD W. SAMS & COMPANY

P   A   R   T

Five

Advanced DOS Techniques

Introduction

Most of us don't even like to read the tiny instruction pamphlet that comes with an appliance like a toaster or a mixer. So, the thought of reading a 500- or 1,000-page DOS manual is not particularly enticing. However, there is a big difference between the overwhelmingly technical DOS reference manual and this book, which has been carefully constructed to teach you DOS.

The most important difference between the two is that the technical manual merely presents information, while this book is specifically designed to make your learning experience easier, more productive, even enjoyable, and, perhaps most importantly, not confusing or bewildering. Manuals are written with the product in mind; this book was written with you in mind.

Following are the specific features that this book offers.

Who This Book Is For

You might be wondering if this book is the correct one for your computer equipment and needs. The answer is yes if your equipment and experience level match these:

■ You use or own an IBM or IBM-compatible microcomputer (such as a Compaq, Epson, Sharp, or any of the myriad IBM "clones"). All of these computers use DOS.

■ You have no computer experience whatsoever.

■ You have some computer experience, but you want to expand your knowledge of DOS so that you can master your computer and harness its true power.

Probably the only person that this book is *not* designed for is the DOS expert who already knows everything but the most advanced and technical issues. Those readers are better off consulting a more advanced book, perhaps about assembly language programming.

Versions of DOS Supported

Just as there are many different microcomputers that use DOS, there are many different versions of DOS. DOS has evolved and expanded throughout the years, and each major enhancement of the product received a new version number. Currently, there are Versions 1, 2, 3, and 4. Within these versions are sub-versions that Microsoft Corporation issued to introduce minor changes and improvements (for example, Versions 3.1, 3.2, 3.21, and 3.3 are all widely used updates of Version 3.0).

Regardless of which version of DOS your computer uses, this book will help. That's because although DOS *adds* features in newer versions, it retains compatibility with older versions by not changing the way in which old features work. If a particular feature is so new that it doesn't work in older versions of DOS, this book will let you know. In addition, the comprehensive reference in Appendix B explains exactly which versions of DOS include a particular feature.

How Much Do You Really Need to Know About DOS?

The most often asked question about DOS is simply: "What is DOS?" Chapter 1 answers that right away. The second most often asked question is: "How much do I need to know about DOS?" The answer to the second question varies. Because DOS is the "master-control" program that allows you to use other programs (such as games, graphics, spreadsheets, and word processors), you need to know at least the bare essentials of DOS to be able to run those programs.

However, if you *really* want to take control of your computer and use features such as extended and expanded memory, super-fast RAM disks (which are already built into your computer!), and other high-powered techniques, then you need to add more depth to your knowledge of DOS.

This book is designed so that you can learn quickly and effectively: You start by learning the absolutely essential techniques (such as starting DOS and using DOS to run your programs), and you continue reading only as far as your needs require. To simplify matters further, the book is divided into five separate parts, each increasingly advanced, each revealing new powers of DOS.

Part 1: DOS Essentials

Here you learn about the role that DOS plays on your computer, how to start your computer, and how to explore what's already available. This section is specifically designed for absolute beginners, regardless of whether you are using a new personal computer or a computer shared by co-workers or other students. By the time you finish this part of the book, you will be able to locate and run any program on any computer that uses DOS.

Part 2: Managing Your Computer

This section teaches you how to use DOS to manage disks and specific techniques that let you create, copy, move, erase, and even unerase programs and information stored in *files*. After you've read these chapters, you'll be fluent in the most important DOS techniques. These are the procedures you will use every day to make your work easier and more efficient.

Part 3: Customizing Your System

These chapters take you deeper into DOS and show you techniques that let you tailor your computer to your own needs and therefore simplify its use. The techniques presented here will also give you complete control of your screen displays, your printer, and the functions of the various keys of your keyboard.

Part 4: Programming DOS

Part 4 moves you into a new realm of DOS programming. Here, you'll learn how to create your own DOS commands to further simplify your work and increase your productivity. (If the term "programming" sends chills down your spine, don't worry. Step-by-step instructions guide you through every example to make the most powerful commands easy to understand.) If you decide you would rather wait to tackle this topic, merely skip to the next part; that's the way this book is designed.

Part 5: Advanced DOS Techniques

Part 5 takes you deeper into the internal workings of your computer and DOS. In these chapters, you'll learn about extended and expanded memory, communications, interfacing and networking, virus protection, and other advanced topics that add still more power and flexibility to your computer prowess.

Appendices

The Appendices present detailed technical information about DOS. In particular, you can use Appendix B as a quick and thorough reference to all the switches, options, and technical details of DOS long after you've outgrown the need for the more structured tutorials presented in the body of the book.

Features of the Book

Icons

The icons in this book identify sections that are dedicated to all users, command prompt users, and DOS 4 Shell users, as indicated below:

The *shell* icon applies only to readers using the DOS 4 Shell. If you are using an earlier version of DOS, or you prefer to use the command prompt in DOS 4, you can skip this section. (When you see this icon, skip to the next *all* or *prompt* icon.)

The *prompt* icon applies to readers entering commands at the DOS command prompt. If you are a DOS 4 user who prefers to use the DOS 4 Shell, skim through these sections until you get to the next *all* or *shell* icon. (However, many advanced DOS features discussed later in the book will require you to use the DOS command prompt.)

The *all* icon applies to all readers and all versions of DOS.

Margin Notes

Notes in the margins provide tips, warnings, reminders, and references to related topics.

End Papers

Inside the front cover of this book, all DOS users can refer to a list of common DOS operations that apply to all versions of DOS. DOS 4 users can find a quick reference to the DOS 4 Shell and File System inside the back cover of this book.

Quick Reference Card

You'll also find a quick reference card inside this book. Tear this card from the book along the perforations, and use it as a pocket dictionary to DOS commands.

Acknowledgments

Although only a single author's name appears on the cover of a book, every book is a team project. I'd like to give credit where it is due and thank the following people:

Gary Masters was instrumental in the development of this book; his careful editing and boundless knowledge of DOS vastly improved the original manuscript.

Cliff Phillip also contributed to many sections of this book, particularly to the references in Appendix B.

Many thanks to my agent, Bill Gladstone of Waterside Productions, for keeping my writing career busy and productive.

Many thanks to all the people at Howard W. Sams who supported and produced this book; they brought it from the "idea" stage into your hands.

And, of course, many thanks to my wife, Susan, and daughter, Ashley, for their support and patience through yet another time-consuming project.

Trademarks

All terms mentioned in this book that are known to be trademarks or service marks are listed below. In addition, terms suspected of being trademarks or service marks have been appropriately capitalized. Howard W. Sams & Company cannot attest to the accuracy of this information. Use of a term in this book should not be regarded as affecting the validity of any trademark or service mark.

Above Board and Intel are trademarks of Intel Corporation.
ANSI is a registered trademark of the American National Standards
Institute.
AST is a trademark of AST Research, Inc.
AT&T is a registered trademark of AT&T.
Brooklyn Bridge is a trademark of White Crane Systems.
Carbon Copy and Carbon Copy Plus are trademarks of Meridian
Technology, Inc.
Certus is a trademark of Foundation Ware.
Compaq is a registered trademark of Compaq Computer Corporation.
Concurrent DOS/386 is a trademark of Digital Research, Inc.
Connection CoProcessor is a trademark of Intel PCEO.
COPY AT2PC is a trademark of Microbridge Computers International.
Crosstalk Mark IV and Crosstalk XVII are trademarks of Crosstalk
Communications.
dBASE III, dBASE III PLUS, and dBASE IV are registered trademarks
of Ashton-Tate.
Disk Optimizer is a trademark of SoftLogic Solutions, Inc.

DOS Essentials

Chapters 1 through 5 provide a framework for understanding your computer and DOS. Because you will use the techniques presented in these chapters every time that you use your computer, the time you invest in learning this essential information will certainly be time well spent.

These chapters discuss the following essential topics:

- *The role that DOS plays with your computer, and why you must know about DOS.*

- *How to start your computer with DOS, and why you can't start your computer without DOS.*

- *How information is organized on a computer, and how to find the information you need.*

- *How to run programs on your computer.*

These chapters are written so that even an absolute beginner can follow at a comfortable pace. If you read each chapter thoroughly, you'll find that you are well on your way to understanding your computer, and that will help you use it more effectively.

Your Computer and DOS

*If you have not read
"Icons" in the Intro-
duction, do so now.*

All computers are designed to perform one basic task: Read instructions. In this sense, a computer is similar to a stereo or cassette player. If you turn on a cassette player without music (stored on a cassette tape) in it, the cassette deck does nothing. When you put in a cassette tape and press the Play button, the stereo plays whatever music the tape "tells" it to play, be it Beethoven, the Beatles, or Bon Jovi.

Similarly, if you turn on a computer without a *program* (instructions) in it, the computer does nothing. But when you "play" a program (which is usually stored on a magnetic *disk* rather than on a cassette tape), the computer does whatever the program's instructions tell it to do, such as manage your business, create graphics, or help you write a book.

If you work around people who use computers, you've probably heard the word DOS (pronounced *dawss*) mentioned repeatedly. Why are "computer people" always talking about DOS? Because DOS is a very special program that makes everything possible on the computer. Furthermore, every time you work with a computer, you are certain to use DOS.

Before you learn the specifics of using DOS, let's discuss computers in general and define some common computer terms like *hardware, software, RAM,* and *DOS.* This will make the computer (and the strange language that people use when talking about it) less mysterious and intimidating.

Computer Hardware

Computer *hardware* is the stuff you can see and touch, and would probably break if you dropped it on the floor. A microcomputer *system* usually consists of the computer itself and several *peripheral devices* (or, simply, *devices*) such as the video monitor, printer, keyboard, and perhaps others. For example, Figure 1.1 shows an example computer system that uses several peripheral devices.

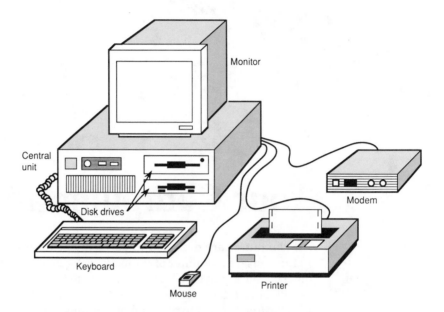

Figure 1.1. A microcomputer system that includes
several devices.

Virtually all microcomputer systems consist of a central unit (also called the system unit), a keyboard, and a video monitor. Most microcomputers also have at least one disk drive, for storing programs and information.

Other useful devices that you can attach to your computer include: a printer, which provides *hard* (printed) copies of information from the computer; a *modem* (short for modulator/demodulator) for communicating with other computers via telephone lines; and a *mouse*, an optional device that lets you interact with the computer without having to type on the keyboard.

Let's discuss the functions of these peripherals in more detail now.

The Keyboard

The keyboard lets you type information into the computer. The primary section of the keyboard is similar to a standard typewriter, except that the Carriage Return key is replaced by a key labeled Enter, Return, or the symbol ↵. (As you'll see later, the Enter key is an important one on computers.)

In addition to the standard "typewriter" keys, most computer keyboards also include a numeric keypad (similar to that on an adding machine), cursor control (arrow) keys, and function keys. Look at Figure 1.2, and identify the keyboard that most resembles you own. Note the location of the various special keys that are pointed out.

(A)

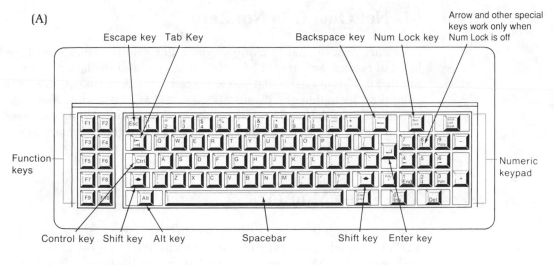

(B)

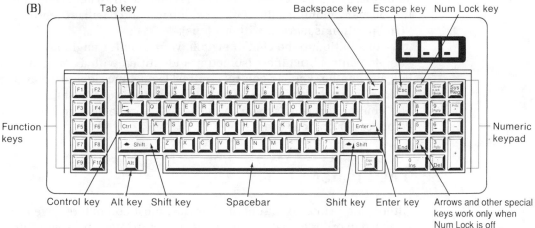

(C)

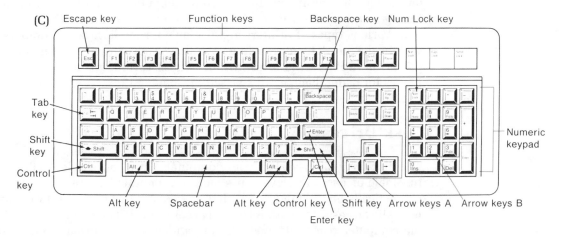

Figure 1.2. Examples of various computer keyboards.

l Is Not One, O Is Not Zero

If you are accustomed to using a typewriter, you may have developed a habit of typing the letter "l" for the number 1, and the letter "O" for the number 0. This is a habit that you will need to break when you start using a computer. Even though "l" and "1", and "O" and "0" look the same on paper, they are definitely not the same to a computer. When you need to type the number 1 or 0, use the number keys above the keyboard, or on the numeric keypad.

The Video Monitor

The video monitor (also called the *screen*, the *monitor*, the *display*, or the *VDT*) shows what you type at the keyboard and what the computer's response is. Like a TV screen, it usually has an On/Off switch. Note, however, that on many monitors, the "Off" position is marked with a 0 (zero), and the "On" position is marked with a 1 (one).

In addition to the On/Off switch, your monitor might also include a knob to control brightness (sometimes identified with a "sunburst" symbol) and another knob to control contrast (sometimes identified by a circle divided into a dark half and a light half). Use these to adjust the brightness and contrast on your screen to make text more legible and background colors easier on your eyes.

The Printer

Although a printer is an optional device, most computers have a printer attached in order to make *hard copies* (copies printed on paper rather than on the monitor) of information. If your computer has a printer attached, DOS (and this book) will help you use it to its fullest potential.

Various types of printers are available for modern microcomputers, such as the fast *dot matrix* printer, the slower *daisy-wheel* printer, and the powerful and versatile *laser* printer. These various printers, and techniques for using them, are discussed in Chapter 12.

Disk Drives

The disk drive (or drives) on your computer play a role similar to that of a turntable or cassette player on a stereo. Computer programs are stored magnetically on diskettes, in much the same way that music is stored magnetically on cassette tapes. As the drive spins the diskette within its casing, the computer reads information from and records information onto the diskettes.

Microcomputer diskettes come in two basic sizes—5.25-inch floppy diskettes (or mini-diskettes) and 3.5-inch microfloppies (or micro-diskettes). Your computer probably has at least one disk drive that is capable of handling one of these diskette sizes.

The larger of the two, the 5.25-inch diskette, is the "older model," but it is still used on most microcomputers. The smaller, sturdier 3.5-inch diskette is a newer model, used primarily on IBM PS/2 and similar computers and on most portable computers. Figure 1.3 shows both types of disks.

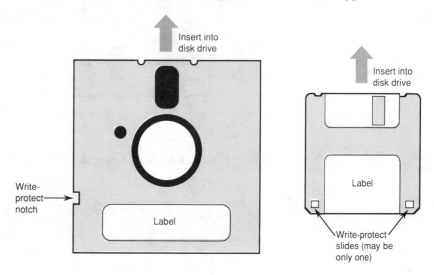

Figure 1.3. Two types of diskettes.

Notice that the 5.25-inch diskette has a *write-protect* notch, and the 3.25-inch diskette has a write-protect slide. You use these to prevent information from accidentally being erased from the diskette. We'll discuss this write-protection feature in more detail in Chapter 6.

General Care of Diskettes

Always handle diskettes with the label side up and your thumb on the label. This will help prevent you from touching the magnetic media (particularly on 5.25-inch disks where the magnetic media is exposed in a large oblong cut-out section). This procedure also ensures that you will insert the diskette into the drive correctly.

The diskette drive "in-use" light is on only when the computer is actually reading from or writing to the diskette. Simply inserting a diskette does not make the light go on.

When you remove diskettes from your computer, keep them away from extreme temperatures, dust, dirt, coffee spills, pets, young children, and—most importantly—magnets. If you use 5.25-inch diskettes, be sure to place the diskette back in its paper sleeve to keep dust and dirt off of the exposed magnetic media.

The procedures for inserting and removing 3.5-inch and 5.25-inch diskettes are somewhat different, as discussed below.

7

Inserting and Removing 5.25-inch Diskettes

If your computer uses 5.25-inch disk drives, the front of the drive will probably resemble either Figure 1.4 (a full-height drive), or Figure 1.5 (a half-height drive).

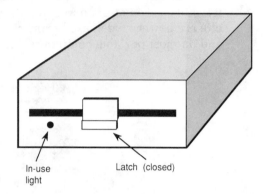

Figure 1.4. A full-height 5.25-inch disk drive.

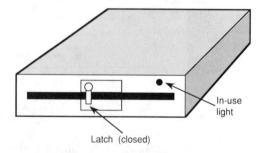

Figure 1.5. A half-height 5.25-inch disk drive.

Before you can insert a diskette into a 5.25-inch drive, you must first open the latch. To open the latch on a full-height drive, place your thumb near the top of the latch, your forefinger near the bottom of the latch, and gently push in with your thumb while pulling out with your finger.

To open the latch on a half-height drive, simply swing the latch so that it is in a horizontal position.

To insert a diskette into the drive, hold the diskette so that the label is up and toward you (the oblong hole will be facing toward the drive). Gently push the diskette all the way into the drive.

If you are using a full-height drive, close the latch by pressing it downward. To close the latch on a half-height drive, swing the lever down until it is in the vertical position. The diskette is now fully inserted and ready for use.

To remove a diskette from a full-height drive, simply open the latch and pull the diskette out. To remove a diskette from a half-height drive, first swing the latch to the open (horizontal) position. The diskette will partially pop out. Gently pull the diskette the rest of the way out.

Remember to return the 5.25-inch diskette to its protective paper sleeve when you remove it from the disk drive.

Inserting and Removing 3.5-inch Diskettes

Most 3.5-inch disk drives do not use levers or doors, and they look something like the drawing in Figure 1.6. To put a 3.5-inch diskette into a drive, hold the diskette with the label up and toward you (the metal shutter will be facing the drive). Gently push the diskette into the drive slot until you feel a slight click; that locks the diskette in the drive.

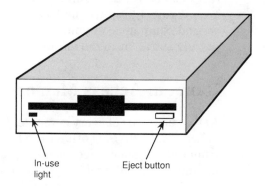

In-use
light

Eject button

Figure 1.6. A 3.5-inch diskette drive.

To remove the 3.5-inch diskette, push the eject button on the drive. The diskette will partially pop out. Gently pull the diskette the rest of the way out.

Fixed Disks

In addition to diskette drives, many computers also have a fixed disk (or *hard disk*, as it is often called). Unlike the drives that use diskettes, a fixed disk uses magnetic media that cannot be removed—it stays inside the fixed disk unit at all times.

A single hard disk can store as many programs as dozens, or even hundreds, of diskettes. Whenever you buy a new software product (a program), you copy it onto you hard disk and then store the original diskette in some safe place. In the future, when you want to use a program, such as an inventory manager or a form-letter generator, you don't need to bother with diskettes. Just select (or type in) the name of your program, and it's immediately available for use.

In addition to its great storage capacity, a hard disk drive operates at a much higher speed than diskette drives, which in turn increases your productivity.

Even though the hard disk is usually optional, some software products require your computer to have one. Also, if you work with very large volumes of data, such as a mailing list with thousands of names and addresses, a hard disk is almost a must. We'll discuss this topic in more detail later in this chapter.

Disk Drive Names

Each disk drive is assigned a "name," which consists of a single letter followed by a colon. The diskette drives are always named A: and B: (if your computer has only one drive, it is named A:). The hard disk is always named C:. Note, however, that some computers might have additional hard disks named D:, E:, F:, and so on.

Figure 1.7 shows the locations and names of various disk drives on several computers. If your computer has two diskette drives, drive A: is usually above, or to the left of, drive B:.

Random Access Memory

At the very heart of every computer is the Random Access Memory, abbreviated RAM. (RAM is often called *main memory* or just *memory*.) RAM is composed of small electrical components called *chips*. These chips are mounted inside the main system unit, and need never be removed.

When you first turn on your computer, most of RAM is empty. When you tell your computer to perform a particular job, it copies the program (instructions) required to perform that job from the disk into RAM. Once the program is in RAM, the computer reads the program's instructions, and behaves accordingly. Figure 1.8 shows an example in which a program to manage accounts receivable is currently in RAM.

Some people find this arrangement of disk drives and RAM a bit perplexing. After all, if a program is already stored on disk, why can't the computer just read the instructions directly from the disk without first copying them into RAM? There are actually a few reasons for this, but the most important is speed. Basically, RAM operates at a much higher rate of speed than the disk drives. The computer copies a program into RAM before executing its instructions to ensure that everything goes at top speed, so that your work gets done as quickly and efficiently as possible.

So, if RAM is so much faster than the disk drives, why not just store everything in RAM and forget about the disk drives? Well, there are several reasons for this too. The most important being that, while disks store information *magnetically*, RAM stores information *electronically*. As soon as you turn off the computer, or the electricity goes off, everything in RAM vanishes instantly! For this reason, RAM is said to be *volatile*.

The fact that RAM is so volatile is a bit unnerving to some beginning computerists, and is the basis for many computer "horror stories" about power outages causing huge losses of computer information. But these stories are often exaggerated, because only a *copy* of information is loaded

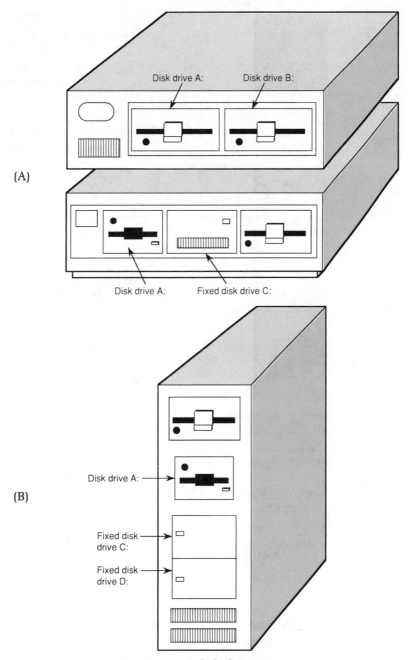

Figure 1.7. Names of disk drives on various computers.

into RAM from the disks. Even if a sudden power outage causes RAM to go blank, everything on disk remains unharmed and intact.

If all this business about loading programs into RAM and executing instructions and so forth sounds a bit intimidating to you, don't worry. As

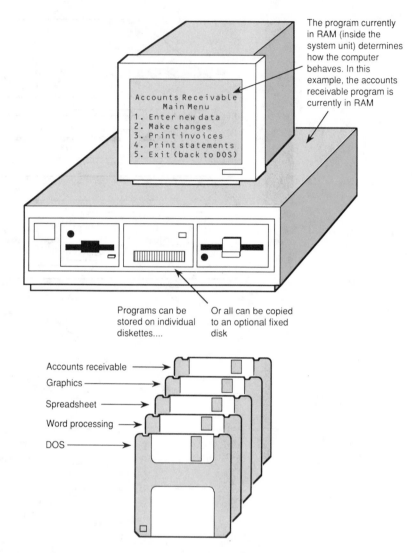

The program currently in RAM (inside the system unit) determines how the computer behaves. In this example, the accounts receivable program is currently in RAM

```
Accounts Receivable
     Main Menu
1. Enter new data
2. Make changes
3. Print invoices
4. Print statements
5. Exit (back to DOS)
```

Programs can be stored on individual diskettes....

Or all can be copied to an optional fixed disk

Accounts receivable

Graphics

Spreadsheet

Word processing

DOS

Figure 1.8. The program currently in RAM determines how the computer behaves.

you will see in coming chapters, DOS takes care of all the details for you. When you want to use a program on your computer, all you have to do is type a *command* (usually one word) or press a button. DOS takes care of the rest.

Computer Software

We've already talked about how *software* provides instructions that tell the computer how to behave. When you buy a piece of software (a program), it is stored on a diskette. To use the software, you enter a command that tells the computer to load that program into RAM and to execute its instructions.

There are literally thousands of software products available for modern microcomputers—everything from video games to accounting packages. The following sections briefly discuss the major categories of software.

Word Processing

Word processing programs turn your computer into a sort of super-sophisticated typewriter. In fact, word processing programs have virtually replaced the typewriter because they offer features that no typewriter can provide. With a word processor, you can easily move, copy, or delete words, sentences, paragraphs, or entire groups of paragraphs. You can even reformat an entire document (such as changing the margins or line spacing) with the press of a key.

Some word processors can check and correct your spelling and even suggest changes in your grammar. Most also provide capabilities for printing form letters, mailing labels, and envelopes.

Desktop Publishing

Desktop publishing programs turn your computer into a powerful typesetting machine that can produce printed pages with various print sizes and fonts, margin notes, embedded graphs, and other advanced printing features (such as those you see in this book).

Spreadsheets

If you've ever used a ledger sheet to work with financial data and had to change an entry and recalculate the entire ledger sheet with your calculator, pencil, and eraser, you're sure to love spreadsheet programs. A spreadsheet program acts much like a ledger sheet, except that when you change any individual piece of information on the ledger sheet, *all* of the calculated values on the sheet are instantly updated for you.

Many spreadsheet programs also provide a graphics capability that lets you instantly plot ledger information on a graph. Spreadsheets are great for projecting "what-if" scenarios, because you can experiment with any piece of information, such as interest rates or potential sales forecasts, and immediately see the results of your experiments.

Database Management Systems

Database management systems are designed to manage large volumes of information, such as mailing lists, customer lists, inventories, financial transactions, and scientific data. These programs let you store, change, delete, sort, search, and print large volumes of information.

Most database management systems (abbreviated DBMS) also let you develop very specific *applications* that are tailored to your own business needs. For example, a single database management system could be used to manage your company's accounting, inventory management, personnel information, sales prospects, and customer lists.

Some database management systems also provide graphics capabilities that let you see information in the form of graphs, pie charts, and other types of graphs.

Accounting Packages

Accounting packages are programs specifically designed to aid in bookkeeping and accounting. Most accounting packages are modularized so that you can buy and use only what your company requires. Accounting packages usually consist of the following modules: General Ledger, Accounts Payable, Accounts Receivable, Time and Billing, Payroll, Job Costing, Inventory Control, and Manufacturing Planning.

Operating Systems

Regardless of which types of software you use with your computer, you must have an *operating system*. This program starts your computer and manages the flow of information to and from the various components, such as the diskettes, the hard disk, the printer, and so on.

DOS, an acronym for **D**isk **O**perating **S**ystem, is such an operating system. As you'll learn in coming chapters, DOS provides many services that are absolutely essential to your computer.

Computer Capacities

Suppose a friend or a computer salesman shows you a computer, pats it gently atop the monitor, and says "This baby has an 80386 microprocessor running at 20 megahertz, with 640KB RAM, and a 30 meg hard disk." Unless you are already familiar with computer terminology, you might wonder if this person is even speaking English. Yes, this person is speaking

English, and is describing how "big" and how fast the computer is. Let's define these often-used computer buzzwords.

Kilobytes

A single character of information occupies one *byte* of storage on a computer. Hence, the word "cat" occupies three bytes, and the word "Banana" occupies six bytes. Most diskettes can store many thousands of bytes, and hence their capacities are often expressed in *kilobytes* (often abbreviated *K* or *KB*). You can think of a kilobyte as 1,000 bytes (though, actually, it's 2^8, or 1,024 bytes). Hence, a 720KB diskette can store 737,280 characters of information. Because the average typed, double-spaced page contains 2,000 characters, a 720KB diskette can store approximately 360 typed pages (i.e., 720,000/2,000 equals 360).

Megabytes

In case you insist upon absolute accuracy, I should mention that a megabyte is actually 1,024 kilobytes, or 1,048,576 bytes).

Some diskettes, and certainly all hard disks, can store millions of bytes, and their capacities are measured in *megabytes* (often abbreviated as *M* or *MB* when written, or the word *meg* when spoken). A megabyte is equal to a thousand kilobytes, or approximately one million bytes. Therefore, a 30MB (i.e., 30 meg) hard disk can hold about 30,000,000 characters, or about 15,000 typewritten pages.

RAM also stores information, and its storage capacity is also measured in kilobytes or megabytes. Remember, RAM only stores a copy of the program that you are using at the moment. Therefore, you only need as much RAM as your computer's largest program requires.

"People" Bytes

To demonstrate how kilobytes and megabytes relate to everyday work requirements, let's look at a practical example. Suppose you want to buy a computer to manage a mailing list of 100,000 customers. By "manage," you mean that you need to be able to add and delete customers, sort them into zip code order (for bulk mailing), isolate certain customers (such as those that are delinquent in payments), print form letters and mailing labels, and perhaps perform other jobs.

Your best starting point would be to select *software* that can handle such a big job—even before you start looking at computers. For the sake of this example, let's say you decide to use a large, powerful database management system to help you manage the customer list, because it can do everything you need to do.

Of course, you also need an operating system, because the computer

Most software products
list their minimum
computer requirements on
the box that the program
is packaged in; that way,
you know what's involved
before you buy the
program—or a computer.

can't run without it. So let's say you select DOS as your operating system. To determine how much RAM and disk storage capacity your computer will need, look at the minimum requirements of each software product. Let's suppose that DOS specifies the following minimum requirements:

System Requirements:
> 256KB RAM (minimum)
> One 720KB 3.5-inch disk drive or
> One 360KB 5.25-inch disk drive

Now suppose your database management program states the following minimum requirements:

System Requirements:
> 640KB RAM (minimum)
> A fixed disk with at least 4MB of space available.
> One 3.5-inch or one 5.25-inch floppy disk drive.

Here it's easy to see that the computer you buy will need at least 640KB RAM because the larger of two programs requires that much. You need at least one floppy disk (diskette) drive: either a 3.5-inch drive that can handle at least 720KB or a 5.25-inch drive that can handle at least 360KB.

You will also need a hard disk for the database management system, one that has at least 4MB of space available on it. The word *available* is important because it refers to the amount of space that remains on the hard disk *after* you store all of your other programs there.

Right off the bat, you should plan on DOS and other miscellaneous programs occupying at least two megabytes. The database management program needs at least 4MB, so that brings the total up to 6MB so far.

But, don't forget that you also need to store your 100,000 names and addresses on the disk. How much space does that require? Well, let's look at an exceptionally large name and address and determine how many bytes it requires:

> Mr. Thadeus P. Tabacopolous
> University of California at Cucamonga
> Department of Medicine
> 17047 Ocean View Drive, Bldg. C-0433
> Cucamonga, CA 92011-0433

Counting all the characters (including blank spaces between words) gives you 135 bytes. So, if you allot as much space for all 100,000 names and addresses, you'll need 13,500,000 bytes (13.5MB) for the names and addresses. So adding that to the 6MB required by DOS and the database management system, brings the total hard disk storage requirements up to 19.5MB.

You could get by with a computer that has about a 20MB hard disk.

However, it's a good idea to buy at least double the capacity of hard disk storage that you think you need, because one way or another, you'll eventually grow into it. The increase in the cost of purchasing a 40MB hard disk as opposed to a 20MB hard disk is fairly small, so you should probably spend a little extra money to buy a lot of growth potential.

Now, you might be wondering why you need at least 20MB (20,000,000 bytes) of disk storage, but only 640 KB (640,000) bytes of RAM in this example. Well, because RAM only stores one program at a time, you only need as much RAM as the largest single *program* that your computer uses. In this example, the database management program, which requires 640KB of RAM, is the largest. Therefore, the computer will need at least 640KB RAM. The names and addresses are *data* (information), not a program (instructions), so they have no bearing on the amount of RAM required. When the database management program is in RAM, it will "know" that the names and addresses (all 13,500,000 characters worth) are stored on disk, and it will manipulate and print them without bringing them all into RAM.

I should point out that this example is something of an oversimplification, designed mainly to help clarify how computer buzzwords translate to work requirements. In truth, many programs, particularly spreadsheets, store data in RAM. Furthermore, it is possible to store several programs in RAM, and useful to do so in many situations. Therefore, your best bet is to define your needs in terms of the work you want the computer to perform, then consult an expert before you invest in a computer.

Megahertz

Besides the storage capacity of a computer, *clock speed* is an important factor. All computers operate with an internal *clock*. Each time the clock "ticks," the computer does a tiny bit of work. The speed at which the clock ticks is measured is *megahertz* (abbreviated MHz). One megahertz equals one million ticks per second.

The maximum clock speed of a computer is closely related to the model number of the *microprocessor* that that computer uses. (The microprocessor, also called the Central Processing Unit or CPU, consists of components that execute instructions stored in RAM and perform operations, but we do not need to go into detail about that just now). The four microprocessors used in most modern IBM-compatible microcomputers are the 8086, the 8088, the 80286, and the 80386 models.

Often, the first two digits of the model number are dropped when discussing microprocessor models. For example, a "386 machine" is a computer that uses the 80386 microprocessor.

The first-generation microprocessor (for IBM-compatible microcomputers) was the 8088, which ran at a clock speed of 4.77 MHz. The next-generation microprocessor was the 8086, which can operate at a top speed of about 8 MHz. The next-generation microprocessor is the 80286, which can operate at speeds up to about 20 MHz. The newer 80386 model can operate at speeds in excess of 30 MHz.

To give you an idea of the differences in speed of these various microprocessors, Table 1.1 shows examples of the time required to calculate the sum of 10,000 large numbers on three different computers using various microprocessors.

Table 1.1. Time required to add 10,00 large numbers.

Microprocessor Model	Clock Speed	Time Required
8086	8 MHz	128 seconds
80286	12 MHz	32 seconds
80386	20 MHz	8 seconds

Although programs do not require a specific clock speed, some programs run only on computers that use an 80286 or 80386 microprocessor.

When purchasing software, you will never see any "minimum speed" requirements listed on the package because any program can run at any clock speed. However, a faster computer is a more productive computer, so any investment in speed is a worthwhile investment.

So Where Does DOS Fit In?

We've already mentioned that DOS is an operating system—a specialized set of programs that you use to start and operate your computer. It is DOS that actually coordinates all the components of your computer, even to the point of getting other programs into RAM and starting them running.

Much of what DOS does actually occurs automatically, "behind the scenes" where you do not have to be concerned with it. But DOS definitely lets you perform important and useful tasks, including those listed below:

- Run applications programs, such as business programs, graphics programs, word processors, spreadsheets, and any other program you want to use.
- Organize large amounts of information for quick and easy retrieval.
- Format diskettes and copy information to them to share with co-workers or for use on other computers.
- Make backups (copies) of information on your hard disk, so that if you ever accidentally erase information, you can always get it back.
- Add new components—such as a mouse, a modem, or a laser printer—as your system grows.
- Internationalize your computer for printing in foreign language alphabets.

Before you do any of these tasks, however, you need to get DOS "up and running." That's exactly what you will learn to do in the next chapter.

Summary

This chapter examined the basic components of a computer system and discussed the purpose of each element. This chapter also defined several computer "buzzwords" which you might have heard (or eventually will encounter) in your work with computers. In summary:

- Computer *hardware* is the physical components of your computer, such as the central unit, the keyboard, the monitor, and other optional devices.

- *Programs*, which tell the computer how to behave, are stored magnetically on *hard disks* and *diskettes*.

- Floppy *disk drives* allow the computer to read information from and record information on diskettes.

- A *fixed disk* (or hard disk) is an optional device that can store copies of programs and information from many dozens, or even hundreds, of diskettes.

- *RAM* (Random Access Memory) is the part of the computer that stores whatever program you happen to be using at the moment.

- *Software* is the programs (i.e., instructions) used in RAM and stored magnetically on disks.

- The amount of software that a diskette, hard disk, or RAM can store is measured in bytes (a single character, such as the letter "A"), *kilobytes* (about 1,000 bytes), and *megabytes* (about 1,000,000 bytes).

- The speed at which a computer operates is measured in megahertz, abbreviated MHz.

- DOS (an acronym for Disk Operating System) is a special set of programs that your computer needs to get started and to use all other types of programs.

Starting Your Computer and DOS

As mentioned in Chapter 1, you can't even start a computer without DOS (or some other operating system). That's because when you turn on the computer, it immediately searches the diskette in drive A: (or the hard disk, if one is available) for DOS. If the computer cannot find DOS, it has no operating instructions—so it simply does nothing.

The procedure of starting your computer with DOS is sometimes called *booting up*. This term comes from the expression "picking yourself up by the bootstraps," which is a good analogy to how a computer starts. That is, first the computer gets power, then it automatically starts searching the disk for the operating system (DOS) that actually lets itself get started.

If you already know how to start your computer and what version of DOS is installed on it, you can proceed directly to Chapter 3.

Because there are so many different types of computers and different versions of DOS, the *exact* start-up procedures for your particular computer cannot be specified here. However, this chapter will explain general start-up procedures, and show you how to determine the version of DOS that is installed on your computer. The overall procedure might seem a bit complicated at first, but rest assured that the information in later chapters will be much more direct and specific.

Installing DOS

If you experience a problem during the start-up procedure, see the Troubleshooting section near the end of this chapter for advice.

Before you can use DOS, you need to install it on your computer. Note that DOS only needs to be installed once—not every time you want to use it. So, if you are sure DOS is already installed on your computer, you can now read either the section titled "Starting DOS with a Hard Disk" or the section "Starting DOS Without a Hard Disk," as appropriate for your own computer.

If you are certain that DOS is *not* already installed on your computer, you need to install it before reading any further in this book. Appendix A

If you are learning on a computer that's also used by co-workers or other students in a class, you can safely assume that DOS is already installed.

provides basic installation guidelines, using DOS Version 4.0 and an IBM computer as the example. If you are using an earlier version of DOS or a non-IBM computer, you should first read the installation instructions that came with your version of DOS.

Starting DOS with a Hard Disk

If your computer has a hard disk and DOS has been installed to start from the hard disk, the steps for starting DOS are quite simple, as listed below:

1. Be sure that any floppy disk drives are empty. If the disk drive has a latch (or door), put it in the "open" position.

2. Turn on the computer (as well as the monitor and printer) by turning on all the appropriate knobs and switches. (If your switches are labeled 0 and 1 rather than Off and On, switch them from 0 to 1.)

3. Wait until the computer finishes its power-on tests and sounds a "beep."

4. Proceed with the section titled "Entering the Date and Time" below.

Starting DOS Without a Hard Disk

If your computer has no hard disk (or if DOS is installed so that it must be started from a floppy disk), the following steps will start DOS:

Chapter 1 shows you the location of drive A: and explains the proper way to insert a diskette.

1. Insert the DOS Startup disk in drive A:.

2. Turn on the computer (as well as the monitor and printer) by turning all of the appropriate switches to On (or from 0 to 1).

3. Wait until the computer finishes its power-on tests, and then sounds a "beep."

4. Proceed with the next section.

Entering the Date and Time

Depending on the setup of your computer and the version of DOS you are using, your screen might or might not request that you enter the current date and time before proceeding. If your computer does not have a battery-driven clock that keeps track of the date and time when the computer is off, DOS will probably ask for the current date by displaying a message similar to the one below:

```
Current date is Tue 1-01-1980
Enter new date (mm-dd-yy):
```

If you make a mistake while typing, use the Backspace key to erase the error; then make the correction.

The blinking cursor to the right of the colon (:) indicates that DOS is waiting for you to enter the current date. Type the current date using the format mm-dd-yy (e.g., 10-1-89 for October 1st, 1989). Press the Enter key (labeled as ←, Enter, or Return) on your keyboard.

Next, DOS probably displays a message similar to the one below:

```
Current time is 21:04:43.47
Enter new time:
```

Again, the blinking cursor indicates that DOS is waiting for you to enter the time. DOS expects the time to be entered in a 24-hour (military) format, where morning hours up to noon are expressed as usual (i.e., 1:00 a.m. to 12:00 noon). But after noon, each hour has 12 added to it. For example, the hour for 1:00 p.m. is 13, for 2:00 p.m. the hour is 14, and so on until 11:00 p.m., which is hour 23. Midnight is expressed as hour zero (0).

For example, if the current time is 3:30 in the afternoon, you would enter the current time by typing **15:30** and then pressing the Enter key.

What happens next depends on the version of DOS that is currently installed on your computer, as well as *how* DOS is installed. If you are using a version of DOS prior to Version 4, you will see the DOS *command prompt*, which usually appears as a single letter followed by a greater-than sign, such as A> or C>. (See Figure 2.1.) Your screen might also show additional information, such as the version of DOS in use and copyright notices.

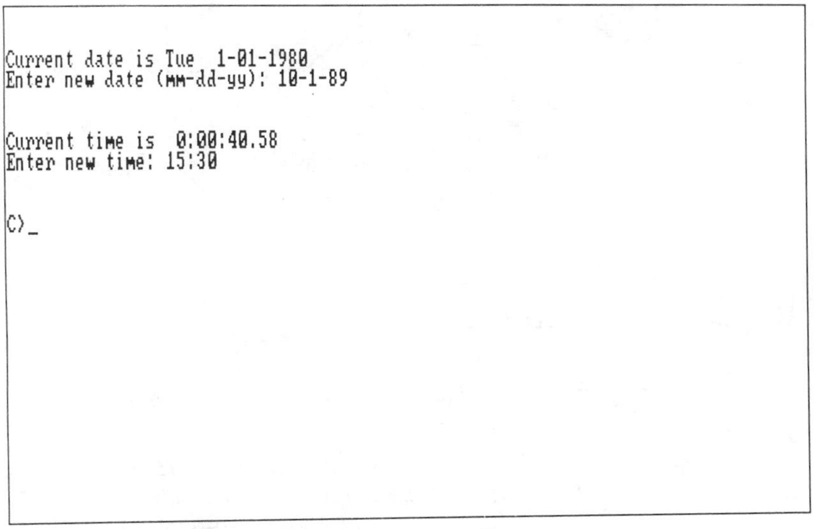

```
Current date is Tue  1-01-1980
Enter new date (mm-dd-yy): 10-1-89

Current time is  0:00:40.58
Enter new time: 15:30

C>_
```

Figure 2.1. The DOS command prompt.

If you are using DOS Version 4, your screen might show the *DOS Shell*, which displays much more information, as shown in Figure 2.2. (Your screen might not look *exactly* like Figure 2.2, the reasons for which will be discussed in the next chapter.) For the time being, let's assume that your computer is displaying the DOS prompt. The next section shows you how to determine which version of DOS is currently installed on your computer (in case it is not already displayed on your screen).

Determining Your Version of DOS

Although this book focuses on the newest version of DOS (Version 4), it also can be used with earlier versions. If your screen is now displaying the DOS prompt (for example, A> or C>) with a blinking cursor to the right, you can easily determine what version of DOS is in control. Merely type VER and press Enter.

When typing DOS commands, such as VER, you can use uppercase, lowercase, or a combination of upper- and lowercase letters.

The screen now displays a brief message similar to the one that follows:

```
DOS Version 4.xx
```

Don't be concerned if your message is worded differently; the important fact is that the correct version number appears.

What you do now depends on which version of DOS you are using. Note that the version number is displayed as a whole number followed by a decimal number (such as *Version 3.20* or *Version 4.00*). The numbers to the right of the decimal point represent minor changes within a particular major revision of DOS.

> If you are currently using Version 2 or 3 of DOS, you can skip to the section titled "Getting It Down Pat".
>
> If you are using Version 4 of DOS continue with the next section.

The DOS Version 4 Shell

If you are using Version 4 of DOS, the *DOS Shell* is probably already displayed on your screen. (If it is not, don't worry, you can display it at any time.) Figure 2.2 shows how the DOS Shell looks on your screen when it is first activated (although your particular screen might look slightly different).

The DOS Shell offers a simplified method of interacting with DOS, and it is available only in Version 4 of DOS. It is called a "shell" because, in

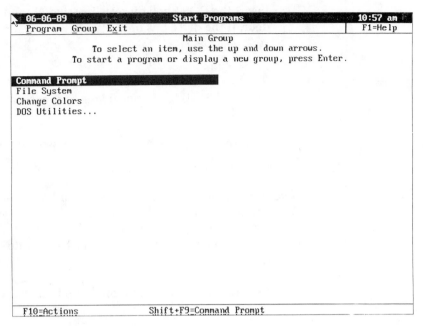

Figure 2.2. The DOS Shell when it is first activated.

a sense, it surrounds the complicated inner workings of DOS and lets you interact with DOS in a simplified, *graphical* manner. You'll learn how to use the DOS Shell in the next chapter.

If the DOS Shell is not on your screen and you are certain that DOS Version 4 is installed on your computer, refer to the appropriate section below to activate the DOS Shell.

Starting the DOS Shell from a Hard Disk

If your computer has a hard disk and you are certain that you are using Version 4 of DOS, start the DOS Shell by typing DOSSHELL and pressing Enter. The DOS Shell that appears on your screen resembles Figure 2.2, although it may look slightly different for reasons discussed in the next chapter.

Starting the DOS Shell on a Computer Without a Hard Disk

If you are certain that your computer has no hard disk and that DOS Version 4 is installed on your computer, use the following steps to start the DOS Shell:

1. Remove the Startup diskette from drive A:.

2. Insert the DOS Shell diskette in drive A:, and close the drive latch or door, if the drive has one.

3. Type DOSSHELL.

4. Press Enter.

The DOS Shell then appears on your screen.

An Alternative Startup Procedure for DOS Version 4 Users

If your computer is not equipped with a hard disk, but you are sure that DOS Version 4 *is* installed on your computer *and* your computer uses 3.5-inch diskettes (as opposed to 5.25-inch diskettes), you can use the alternative procedure described below to start DOS and the DOS Shell simultaneously:

1. Remove any diskette that might be in drive A:.

2. Insert the DOS Shell diskette in drive A:.

3. Turn on the computer (as well as the monitor) by turning all switches to On (or from 0 to 1).

The DOS Shell (similar to the one in Figure 2.2) then appears on your screen.

Getting It Down Pat

The fact that different computers and different versions of DOS require different startup procedures can be a bit confusing at first. If your startup procedure is more complicated than merely flipping on a switch, you might want to repeat this chapter while jotting down notes about the different steps for starting your computer.

Keep these notes near the computer so that you (and anyone else who uses your computer) can refer to them as necessary. Also, you might want to jot down the exact version number of DOS that is installed on your computer, as you may need to know this from time to time as you read this book.

Turning Off the Computer

You can turn off your computer any time that the DOS command prompt or the DOS Shell is displayed. However, it's good practice first to remove any diskettes from their drives before you turn off the computer.

Feel free to turn off your computer to take a break at any time as you read through this book. Now that you know how to start DOS, you should be able to pick up where you left off quite easily.

Troubleshooting

If your computer does not start, determine which of the following descriptions most accurately represents your problem, and then try the suggested solution.

■ If the screen displays the message `Non-System disk or disk error Replace and press any key when ready`, then you have inserted the wrong diskette in drive A:, or your hard disk does not have DOS installed on it. Remove any diskette that is in drive A:. Place the correct Startup disk in drive A: (even if your computer has a hard disk). If you've installed DOS Version 4, insert the copy labeled Startup. If you use DOS Version 3.3, insert the disk labeled Startup or Startup/Operating. If you are using an earlier version of DOS, use the disk labeled DOS—*not* the one labeled DOS Supplemental Programs. After you insert the disk and close the drive latch (if the drive has a latch), press any key to try starting DOS again.

■ If the computer seems to start, but nothing appears on the screen, be sure your monitor is turned on, and then rotate the brightness knob clockwise to illuminate the screen. If this does not help, turn off the computer, and be sure all the wires are properly plugged into the back of the computer and into the wall socket. Then turn on the computer again.

■ If nothing happens when you turn the power switch on the computer (for example, you cannot even hear the fan running), return the switch to the off position, and be sure everything is plugged in according to the directions in your computer's Operation manual. Then try again.

■ If all else fails, refer to both your computer's Operations manual and the DOS manual for additional startup procedures.

Summary

This chapter showed you how to start your computer with DOS and how to find out which version of DOS is installed on it. The main points of this chapter are summarized below:

■ If your computer has a fixed (hard) disk on which DOS is installed, your basic startup procedure is to remove any diskettes from the floppy disk drives, leave the drive latches (if any) in the open position, and turn the On/Off switches to On (or 1).

■ If your computer does not have a hard disk, or if DOS is not installed to start from the hard disk, you *must* first insert a DOS startup diskette into disk drive A:, and *then* turn on the computer and the monitor.

■ The DOS Shell is available only in Version 4 of DOS.

■ The DOS command prompt, which typically appears as a single letter followed by a > symbol and a blinking cursor, is available in all versions of DOS (although it might not immediately appear in Version 4).

■ A blinking cursor next to the command prompt indicates that DOS is waiting for you to type a *command* and then press the Enter key.

Exploring the DOS Shell

This chapter gives you an opportunity to practice using the DOS Shell. Note that *only* Version 4 of DOS offers the DOS Shell, so none of the information in this chapter is directly relevant to users of earlier versions of DOS.

However, if your computer does have an earlier version of DOS installed on it, you might still want to read this chapter to see what DOS Version 4 has to offer. Although you won't be able to perform the hands-on exercises, you might like what you read about. If you do decide to upgrade your current version of DOS to Version 4, refer to the section "Upgrading to DOS Version 4" near the end of this chapter for further information.

About the DOS Shell

In Chapter 2 you got your computer, DOS, and the DOS Shell "up-and-running." Figure 3.1 shows how the DOS Shell looks on a high-resolution graphics screen (such as on a computer equipped with a VGA, MCGA, or EGA display).

Figure 3.2 shows how the DOS Shell looks on a text screen (such as a computer with a monochrome or a CGA display).

Most of the figures in this book depict the DOS Shell as a high-resolution graphics screen. If you are using a text display, your screen might not always exactly match the figures. Any important differences between the text screen and the graphics screens are noted, so you needn't be concerned about any minor differences.

The main elements of the DOS Shell are labeled in Figures 3.1 and 3.2. You might want to refer to these figures from time to time as you explore the DOS Shell in the sections that follow.

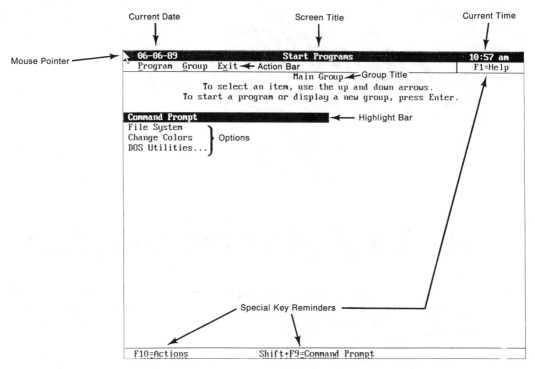

Figure 3.1. The DOS Shell on a high-resolution graphics screen.

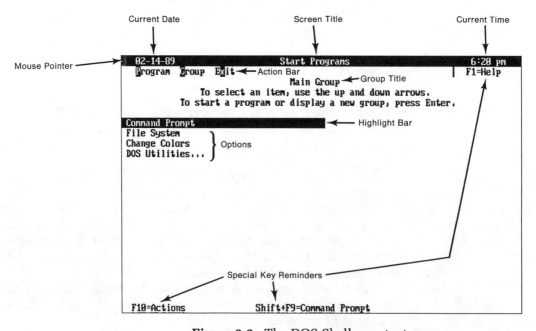

Figure 3.2. The DOS Shell on a text screen.

Using the Keyboard with the DOS Shell

You can easily use the keyboard to select options on the DOS Shell. First use the arrow keys to move the highlight bar to the option you want, and then press the Enter key to select the highlighted option.

Note that if your computer keyboard has arrow keys only on the numeric keypad, the arrow keys work *only* if the Num Lock key is in the Off position. To determine whether Num Lock is on or off, press the ↓ key now. If the computer beeps and the highlight bar does not move, press the Num Lock key once. Then press the ↓ key again. Notice that the highlight bar moves each time you press the key.

Next let's use the DOS Shell to set the computer system's date and time.

1. Use the ↓ or ↑ key to move the highlight bar to the DOS Utilities . . . "group name."

2. Press Enter to display the DOS Utilities . . . screen.

If you do not have a mouse connected to your computer, the mouse pointer always stays in the upper left corner of the screen.

Notice that the group name near the top of the screen now reads DOS Utilities . . . and that a new set of options appears. To set the current date and time, you must first select the proper option. If necessary, use the ↓ or ↑ key to move the highlight bar to the Set Date and Time option. Press Enter.

Now a *dialog box* appears and asks you to enter a new date, as shown in Figure 3.3. Type the current date using the format mm-dd-yy (for example, 1-1-90 for January 1, 1990). Note that if Num Lock is off, you must either use the numbers on the main keyboard or, if you prefer to use the numeric keypad, press the Num Lock key again.

If you make a mistake while typing the date (or anything else use the Backspace key to erase the error, and then enter. When you see the message Press any key..., this refers to any letter, number, or the Spacebar. Other keys like Ctrl, Esc, Alt, and Num Lock will have no effect.

After you type the current date in the appropriate format and press Enter, the screen asks you to enter a new time in hh:mm format, as shown in Figure 3.4. Use the 24-hour clock format to enter the current time (for example, 1:00 pm is 13:00, 2:15 pm is 14:15, and so on).

After you type the current time in the proper format and press Enter, the message Press any key to continue... appears. Press any key on the keyboard.

Now you are back to the DOS Utilities . . . screen. To return to the Main Group screen, merely press the Escape key (usually labeled Esc or Cancel on the keyboard).

Remember that if you pressed the Num Lock key to use the numeric keypad to enter the date or time, you'll need to press it again to reactivate the arrows on the numeric keypad.

Using a Mouse with the DOS Shell

If your computer is equipped with a mouse, you can use the mouse to interact with the DOS Shell. By using a mouse you can select options and per-

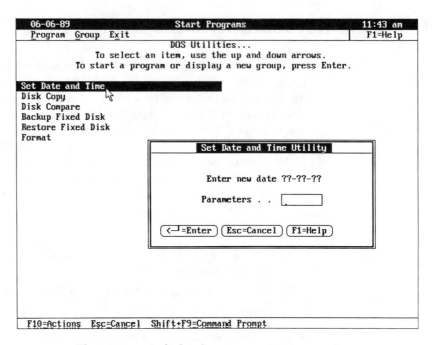

Figure 3.3. A dialog box requesting a new date.

```
06-06-89                        Start Programs                      11:44 am
 Program  Group  Exit                                              F1=Help
                               DOS Utilities...
                To select an item, use the up and down arrows.
                To start a program or display a new group, press Enter.

Set Date and Time
Disk Copy
Disk Compare
Backup Fixed Disk
Restore Fixed Disk
Format
                              ┌──── Set Date and Time Utility ────┐
                              │                                   │
                              │                                   │
                              │        Enter new time hh:mm       │
                              │                                   │
                              │        Parameters . . [_____]     │
                              │                                   │
                              │   (<──┘=Enter) (Esc=Cancel) (F1=Help) │
                              └───────────────────────────────────┘




 F10=Actions  Esc=Cancel  Shift+F9=Command Prompt
```

Figure 3.4. A dialog box requesting a new time.

A mouse will work only if it is properly installed for DOS Version 4. See Appendix A for instructions if your mouse does not work with the DOS Shell.

form operations merely by pointing at them and clicking a button. Simply roll the mouse in the direction that you want the mouse pointer to move; when the mouse pointer touches the option you want to select, click the left mouse button.

Note that if your mouse has two or three buttons, only one of the buttons is active in the DOS Shell. Typically, this is the button on the left, but you might have to try all the buttons to determine which one works on your particular mouse. This book uses the following terms for clicking the mouse button:

Click   Press the active mouse button once

Double-Click   Press the active mouse button twice in rapid succession (as quickly as possible)

Practice using the mouse by following the instructions below to set (once again) your computer system's date and time.

1. Move the mouse pointer to anywhere on the DOS Utilities . . . option.

2. Click the active button to move the highlight bar to that option.

3. Keep the mouse pointer anywhere on the highlight bar, and double-click the mouse button.

Notice that a single click simply moves the highlight bar to the option that the mouse pointer is positioned on. The double-click actually *selects* that option. This difference between single- and double-clicks is fairly consistent throughout all the options in the DOS Shell.

Notice that you are now in the DOS Utilities . . . screen and that a new set of options appears. To check and change the current date and time, follow these steps:

1. Move the mouse pointer to the Set Date and Time option.

2. Double-click.

A *dialog box* appears and asks you to enter a new date and time, as shown in Figure 3.3. Note that a small cursor appears in the box labeled Parameters. You cannot use the mouse within this box; you must use the keyboard to type the current date using the format mm-dd-yy (for example, 1-11-90 for January 1, 1990).

3. Enter today's date in the appropriate format.

4. Move the mouse pointer to the ↵ =Enter box and click once.

Notice that in this step you only had to click once to select the ↵ =Enter . That's because Enter is actually a key name (the name of a key on the keyboard), and key names are activated by only a single mouse click (just as if you had pressed the key on the keyboard).

5. A dialog box appears and asks you to enter a new time, as shown in Figure 3.4. Type the current time using the format hh:mm with the 24-hour military clock format (e.g., 15:30 for 3:30 pm).

6. Move the mouse pointer to the small box containing ↵=Enter and click once.

7. When the screen displays the message Press any key to continue..., press any key on the keyboard, except those mentioned earlier and the mouse button.

This brings you back to the DOS Utilities . . . screen. To return to the Main Group, merely move the mouse pointer to the Esc=Cancel prompt at the bottom of the screen and click once.

And now you are back to the Main Group. Note that the figures inside the back cover of this book summarize when you need to click the mouse once and when you need to double-click the mouse. Refer to those figures as needed in your work with DOS. Now let's examine some other handy features of the DOS Shell.

Using the DOS Shell Help System

Notice that the upper-right corner of your screen displays the message F1=Help. This message tells you that you can press the function key labeled F1 to get some help. You can use this help system in several ways:

- To get immediate help with either the job you are performing or the option that is currently highlighted, press F1.

- To get more general information at any time, press F1 and then press F11 (or Alt-F1) to see an index of topics.

- To get help with special keys, press F1 and then press F9.

- Some common errors that you might make when using the Shell display the F1=Help prompt. Pressing F1 describes the error and offers suggestions to correct the error.

For some hands-on practice with the help system, follow the steps below:

1. Using the mouse or the ↑ and ↓ arrow keys, move the highlight bar to Change Colors.

2. Press the Help key (F1), or move the mouse pointer to F1=Help and click once.

The screen displays a *context-sensitive help window* that provides information about changing colors, as shown in Figure 3.5. The term context-sensitive means that the help screen currently displayed refers to the option or context that was active or highlighted when you pressed F1 (Change Colors in this example).

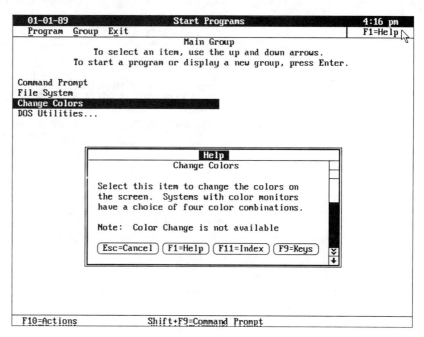

Figure 3.5. An example help window.

Typically, there is more information about a given topic than can fit in only one help window. You can read additional lines or pages of text by using the ↓ and ↑ keys to scroll line-by-line or the PgDn and PgUp keys to scroll page-by-page. For example, press the ↓ key repeatedly; notice how new lines beneath the current line scroll into view. Continue pressing ↓ until the text no longer scrolls and the computer begins beeping. (Notice that pressing ↓ no longer has any effect when no more information about the topic is available.)

Now, practice using the PgUp and PgDn keys. Press PgUp; notice that each time you press the key, the preceding "page" of information fills the help window (until you get to the top). Experiment with these keys until you feel comfortable using them.

Using the Slider Box

If your computer has a graphics screen, a *scroll bar* appears at the right border of the screen. (This scroll bar does not appear on a text screen.

If you have a mouse, but do not have a graphics display, you can scroll through the help window by clicking on the ↑ and ↓ symbols that appear next to the More: *prompt in the window.*

Instead, you'll see the word More: followed by an arrow or two.) If your computer also has a mouse, you can scroll through the text in the help window by clicking on various parts of the slider box. You can also position the mouse pointer at any key name box and click once, instead of pressing the named key. Figure 3.6 illustrates the areas in the help window (with a graphics screen) on which you can click the mouse button.

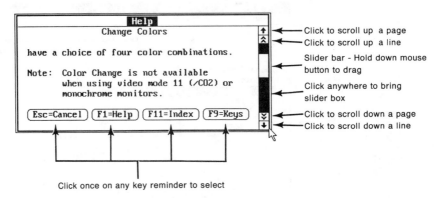

Figure 3.6. Using the slider box and key name boxes
with a mouse.

Notice (in Figure 3.6) that you also can "drag" the slider box to any location using the following steps:

1. Move the mouse pointer to the slider box.
2. Press and hold down the mouse button.
3. Move the mouse up or down (an outline of the slider box moves with the mouse pointer).
4. Release the mouse button to display both the slider box and the appropriate page of help text.

If an option is not currently available for selection with the mouse, it is shaded gray. For example, when the slider box is all the way at the top of the scroll bar, the options for scrolling up are shaded gray. If you try to select a shaded option, the computer merely beeps and ignores your request.

The scroll bar not only lets you scroll through text with a mouse, it also shows you how much information there is to scroll through. The size of the slider box within the scroll bar is proportional to the amount of text displayed in the window. The next example demonstrates this feature.

Using the Help Index

At the bottom of the display screen, the message F11=Index indicates that you can access an index of help topics by pressing the function key labeled

F11. To explore the index, either press the F11 key, or move the mouse pointer to F11=Index and click once. If your keyboard does not have a function key labeled F11, press Alt-F1 (hold down the Alt key and then press the F1 key). This displays the index shown in Figure 3.7.

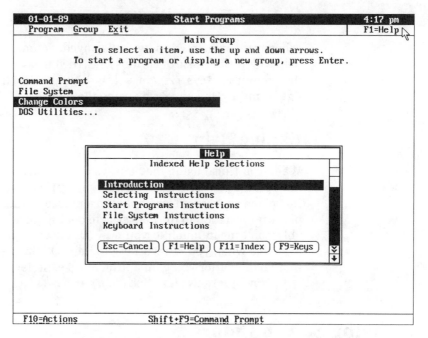

Figure 3.7. The first page of the help index.

The initial screen of the Help Index displays only five topics; however, many more topics are listed alphabetically after those first five items. (In this example, notice that the slider box is rather small, indicating that only a small proportion of all the text available in the index is displayed in the window.)

Use either the ↓, PgDn, ↑, and PgUp keys or the mouse and scroll bar to scroll through the options in the index. To get help about a specific topic, press the arrow keys until the highlight is on the correct topic, and then press Enter. (If you are using a mouse, you should scroll until the correct topic appears on the screen, and then click once on the topic.)

Practice the technique by following these steps:

1. Press PgDn about nine times (or use the mouse to scroll) until Help on Help appears on the screen.

2. Use the ↑ or ↓ keys to move the highlight to Help on Help.

3. Then press Enter (or move the mouse pointer to Help on Help and click once).

Now that the help window is displaying information about using the

DOS doesn't require you to use the help index to reach Help on Help; instead, you can take a shortcut. Simply press the F1 key whenever any help window is displayed.

DOS help system, take some time to scroll through the pages and read the help. When you finish, you can return to the Help index by pressing the F11 key again (or by clicking the mouse while the pointer is on `F11=Index`).

Getting Help with Keys

Whenever the help window is displayed, you can press the F9 key to get help with the purpose of various keys. (If you have a mouse, merely click on the prompt `F9=Keys`.) Again, scroll through these lines of text using the ↓, PgUp, and PgDn keys, or by using the mouse.

Exiting Help

In some situations you might need to press Esc more than once to exit the help system.

When you finish using the help system, you can remove the help window and resume your previous work simply by pressing the Esc key (or by clicking on the `Esc=Cancel` prompt with a mouse). I should point out that much of the information in the help system deals with advanced topics that probably don't mean much to you now. But keep in mind that help is always available when you are working in the DOS Shell—it will indeed come in more handy after you gain a little more experience with DOS.

Now, press Esc (or click once on `Esc=Cancel`) to exit the help system.

Changing Screen Colors

The Change Colors option on the Main Group screen lets you change the color scheme that the DOS Shell uses. To experiment with different colors, follow the steps below:

1. If Change Colors is not already highlighted, use the ↓ and ↑ keys (or the mouse) to move the highlight bar to the Change Colors option.
2. Press Enter (or click the mouse button twice) to select `Change Colors`.

The Change Colors screen displays examples of various color schemes, as shown in Figure 3.8. You can press the ← and → keys to scroll through four different color schemes. The number of the current color scheme appears at the upper right corner of the Change Colors title box.

Scroll through all four color schemes now, either by pressing → four times (or by positioning the mouse pointer to the → key symbol beneath the Change Colors screen title and clicking once per screen). Press or click on the → key until you find the color scheme you like the best.

After you decide on a color scheme, press Enter to return to the Main Group screen. (If you are using a mouse, you can click once on the ↵ `=Enter` option at the lower left corner of the screen.) When the Main Group screen reappears, the new color scheme will be in effect.

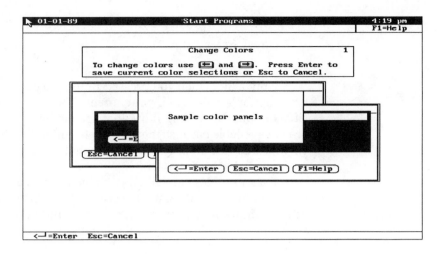

Figure 3.8. Screen for viewing different color schemes.

Using the Action Bar

The DOS Shell also contains an *Action Bar*, a feature that provides *pull-down* menus for accessing additional options. On the **Start Programs** screen, the Action Bar consists of three options: Program, Group, and Exit. Table 3.1 summarizes the keys that you can use to access the Action Bar pull-down menus.

Table 3.1. Functions of keys used with the Action Bar

Key(s)	Effect
F10	Highlights an option on the Action Bar
← →	Scrolls to the left or right, across Action Bar options.
↑ ↓	Moves the highlight up and down, through pull-down menu options.
Enter	Selects the currently highlighted Action Bar option or the currently highlighted pull-down menu option.
Esc	Cancels the most recent selection, the current pull-down menu, or the Action Bar.
F1	Provides help for the currently highlighted option.

To take a quick tour of the Action Bar, follow these steps

1. Press the function key labeled F10.

2. Press the ← and → keys a few times, and notice how the highlight moves through Action Bar options.

3. Use ← or → to move the highlight to the Program option.

4. Press Enter.

Notice that when you pressed Enter, the pull-down menu for the Program option appeared on your screen. The pull-down menu lists all possible options—including those that are currently available and those that are not available because they are irrelevant to the situation at hand. (Later examples in this book will demonstrate how the "irrelevant" options become available for selection.)

On a graphics screen, unavailable options are shaded or blurred, as shown in Figure 3.9. On a text screen, the unavailable options contain an asterisk in place of a key letter, as shown in Figure 3.10. If you attempt to select an unavailable option, the computer merely sounds a beep and ignores the request (no harm done!).

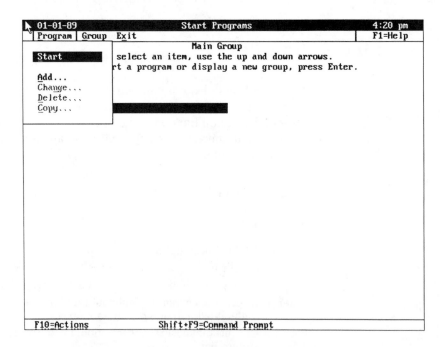

Figure 3.9. A pull-down menu on a graphics screen.

To explore the pull-down menus further, use the ↑ and ↓ keys to move the highlight from option to option. Then, use the ← and → keys to display pull-down menus for the other Action Bar options.

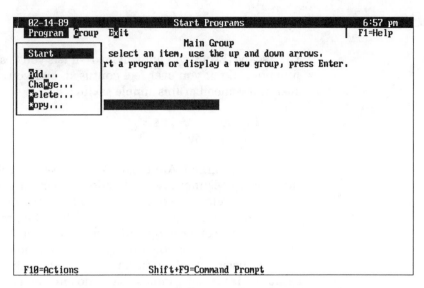

Figure 3.10 A pull-down menu on a text screen.

Canceling Menu Selections

You will soon use the pull-down menus to put DOS to work for you. However, before you do so, you need to know what to do in case you select an option by mistake. Follow these steps for a demonstration:

1. Press → or ← until the pull-down menu for the <u>G</u>roup option on the Action Bar is displayed.

2. Press ↑ or ↓ key, if necessary, to move the highlight to the Add . . . option.

3. Press Enter to select Add....

At this point a pop-up dialog box appears to allow you to add information to the current group. However, because you don't know how to use this option yet, you should probably cancel the operation. To cancel a selection, merely press Esc.

This returns you to the Main Group screen and deactivates the Action Bar and pull-down menus. Of course, you can always reactivate the Action Bar and the pull-down menus by pressing F10.

The most important point to remember from this exercise is that no matter what happens while you are using the DOS Shell—even if you are suddenly faced with a screen or a situation that you do not understand—you always have a quick and simple remedy: Merely press the Esc key. Continue pressing Esc until you return to a more familiar situation.

Escape

The Escape (Esc) key is aptly named—it lets you "escape" from unfamiliar situations. So, if you ever feel confused, and you don't know what to do next, just remember this simple saying:

> If in doubt . . .
> Escape key out!

Be forewarned: Although pressing Esc can get you out of unfamiliar situations, it cannot always "undo" an action that you've already performed. Therefore, *do not proceed with an unfamiliar menu option under the assumption that you can cancel it later.* The proper way to use the Escape key is to cancel an operation as soon as you feel uncertain about your *next* action, not after you already take that action.

The basic rule of thumb here is: Don't be intimidated by the computer, because it is virtually impossible to do any damage simply by pressing the wrong key. However, that doesn't mean that you should be reckless and assume there is an easy way out of every mistake. Before you begin exploring areas that you know nothing about, press F1 to get some help, or press the Esc key to cancel the action until you consult this book for further information. (Look inside the front cover of this book for a quick and easy reference to any action that you might need to take.)

Exiting the DOS Shell

If you are using a version of DOS prior to Version 4, the command prompt is the only method of interacting with DOS that is available to you.

As an alternative to using the DOS Shell, you can type *commands* directly at the DOS *command prompt*. Whereas the DOS Shell lets you interact with your computer through menu options and optionally a mouse, the command prompt requires that you type a command, and then press Enter to enter that command into the computer.

As you'll see later in this book, there are occasionally times when you will want to leave the DOS Shell to use the DOS command prompt. There are two different ways to leave the DOS Shell, the easiest being to press the function key labeled F3.

You'll notice that the DOS Shell disappears immediately, and only the *command prompt* is displayed on your screen. If your computer has a hard disk, the command prompt probably looks like this:

```
C:\DOS>
```

If your computer does not have a hard disk, the command prompt probably looks like this:

```
A:>
```

In either situation, you'll also see a blinking cursor to the right of the command prompt, which indicates that DOS is awaiting your next instruction. You'll learn to use the command prompt later. For now, let's see how you can get back to the Shell once you've exited and reached the command prompt.

First of all, you need to know that in order to enter a command at the command prompt, you must first type a command, and then press Enter. For example, to return to the DOS Shell right now, type DOSSHELL and press Enter.

As discussed in Chapter 9, entering the command EXIT at the command prompt will also take you back to the Shell (in some situations).

The DOS Shell will appear on your screen, and you are back in more familiar territory. Note that this exercise represents one of those situations where pressing the Esc key does *not* take you back into more familiar territory. You must specifically type in the DOSSHELL command and press Enter.

Upgrading to Version 4

If you are using an earlier version of DOS, yet you like what Version 4 has to offer, you can upgrade to Version 4 very easily and inexpensively. Contact your computer dealer, software store, or any mail-order house (many of which advertise regularly in computer magazines) for pricing information. Then refer to Appendix A at the end of this book (or to the DOS Version 4 manual) for quick-and-easy instructions on upgrading your computer to DOS Version 4.

Along these same lines, if your computer is not equipped with a mouse, but you like the point-and-click interface that the mouse offers, you can probably add a mouse to your current computer very inexpensively. Contact your computer dealer for details; then refer to the mouse's operation manual or to Appendix A in this book for instructions about installing the mouse for use with DOS Version 4.

Incidentally, if you already have a large investment in software programs that you use with an earlier version of DOS, you do *not* need to worry about "losing" those programs when you upgrade to Version 4 of DOS. You can easily upgrade to DOS Version 4 without having to upgrade or change existing programs. In fact, you do not even need to re-copy them to your hard disk after upgrading. The DOS Version 4 installation procedure lets you easily replace an earlier version of DOS without any of the complications you might expect.

Troubleshooting

If you experience problems during this chapter, locate the exact problem in the following section and then try the suggested solutions.

■ If you cannot get the DOS Shell running, then one of three things is wrong:

1. You are not using Version 4 of DOS (see Chapter 2 to determine your version of DOS).

2. The wrong diskette is in drive A: (see the section titled "An Alternative Startup Procedure for DOS Version 4 Users" in Chapter 2).

3. If your computer has a hard disk, type `CD\DOS` (be sure to use a backslash (\) rather than a forward slash (/)) at the command prompt and press Enter. Then type `DOSSHELL` and press Enter.

■ If none of the arrow keys, nor the PgUp or PgDn keys, work on your keyboard, press the key labeled Num Lock once (to "unlock" the numbers on the numeric keypad) then try the arrow keys again.

■ When you exit the DOS Shell and try to get back into it, the message `Bad command or file name` appears. In this case, you might simply have misspelled the command (for example, you typed `DOSHHEL` instead of `DOSSHELL`). Retype the command (using the proper spelling) and try again.

■ If you cannot get your mouse to work in the DOS Shell, first be sure it is properly connected, as per the instructions that came with the mouse; then refer to Appendix A for mouse installation procedures.

Summary

This chapter has provided general techniques for using the DOS Shell, a graphical system that lets you interact with DOS. The DOS Shell is available only in Version 4 of DOS. To summarize:

■ To select an option from the DOS Shell, move the highlight bar using the ↓ and ↑ keys to highlight the option you want; then press Enter.

■ If you have a mouse, you can select an option by moving the mouse pointer to it and double-clicking.

■ To get help at any time while using the DOS Shell, press the F1 key or click on the box that contains `F1=Help`.

■ To see an index of topics that are available in the help system, press the F11 (or Alt-F1) key whenever a help window is displayed.

■ For help with the meanings of special keys in DOS, press the F9 key whenever a help window is displayed.

■ For help about using the help system, press the F1 key whenever a help window is displayed.

■ To scroll through pages of text displayed in help windows, press the ↓,

PgDn, ↑, or PgUp keys. With a mouse, merely click on the up- and down-pointing arrows in the help window, or click on the scroll bar.

■ To exit help, press the Esc key. With a mouse, click in the box that contains `Esc=Cancel`.

■ To change the colors on your screen, highlight the Change Colors option and press Enter (or move the mouse pointer to the Change Colors option and double-click).

■ To access the DOS Shell Action Bar, press the F10 key; then press the Enter key.

■ When the Action Bar pull-down menus are displayed, you can move the highlight bar using the ↑, ↓, ←, and → keys.

■ To leave the Action Bar—or an accidental selection from an Action Bar pull-down menu—press the Esc key.

■ When in doubt, Escape Key out!

■ To get back to the DOS Shell from the command prompt, type `DOSSHELL` and press Enter.

Exploring Your Computer

Most computer work consists of running *programs* to manage *data* (information). As this chapter explains, programs and data are stored on computer disks as *files*, and DOS is the tool that you use to locate programs and run them.

The exact files stored on a computer vary from system to system and user to user. However, if your computer is brand new, and the only program you've installed is DOS, the files that comprise DOS will probably be the only files on your computer. If you share a computer with others in a company or a classroom, many more files might exist, because each computer user can create and save his or her own files.

This chapter focuses on specific techniques that you can use to see the names of all the files that are stored on any computer that uses DOS. At first, the techniques presented in this chapter might seem abstract because they don't directly help you solve a particular problem, such as managing an inventory. However, be assured that you will use these basic techniques in *all* your future computer work, every time that you use the computer.

Disk Files

Any program or collection of data that is stored on a computer disk is stored in a *file*. The name is actually quite appropriate: Just as a filing cabinet contains many different files (typically stored in manila folders), a computer disk also stores many different files. Figure 4.1 illustrates this simple analogy.

Unlike filing cabinets, which typically contain only printed information, computer disks can store two different types of files:

■ *Program files* (or *programs*) contain instructions that tell the computer what to do and how to do it.

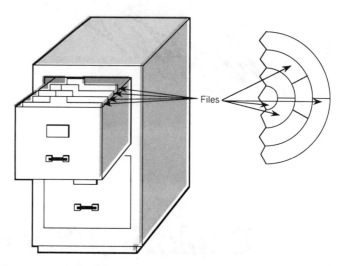

Figure 4.1. Like filing cabinets, computer disks store files.

■ *Data files* (or *text files*) contain data (information), such as names, addresses, letters, and inventory or bookkeeping data.

Every file on a disk, whether it be a program file or a data file, has a name that consists of two parts—*base name* followed by an *extension*. The base name can be one to eight characters long. The extension always starts with a period (.) and can contain as many as three additional characters. File names cannot contain blank spaces. Following are some examples of legal file names:

APPEND.EXE   IBMDOS.COM
LETTER_1.TXT   9.WKS
SALES.DAT   GRAPH.1

In the first example file name, APPEND is the base name, and .EXE is the extension. When talking about file names, experienced computers often refer to the period that separates the base name from the extension as "dot." Hence, when spoken, the file name MYLETTER.BAK would be pronounced *my-letter-dot-back*.

As a rule of thumb, the file's base name usually describes the contents of the file, and the extension usually describes the type of information in the file. You'll learn these details later; for now, merely remember that file names consist of two parts—the base name and the extension.

Disk Directories

A hard disk can store many hundreds, or even thousands, of files. To make it easier for you to manage a large number of files, DOS lets you divide the

As mentioned in Chapter 1, a hard disk cannot be removed from the hard disk drive, so you will never actually see the disk itself.

hard disk into *directories*, each of which contains its own set of related files. You might think of directories as the drawers of a file cabinet, as illustrated in Figure 4.2.

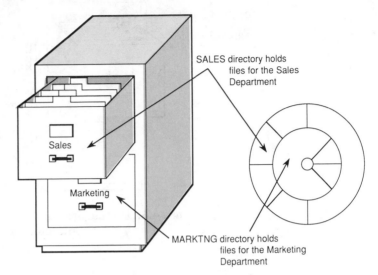

SALES directory holds files for the Sales Department

Sales

Marketing

MARKTNG directory holds files for the Marketing Department

Figure 4.2. Each directory on disk has its own set of files.

Like file names, directory names can only have as many as eight characters (which is why the directory that stores files for the Marketing department must be abbreviated in Figure 4.2). Like file names, directory names may not contain blank spaces. A directory name can have a three-character extension, but to prevent directory names from being confused with file names, people rarely use extensions with directory names.

Individual directories can be further divided into subdirectories. You might think of subdirectories as areas within a drawer (or directory) that are marked off with dividers. The example in Figure 4.3 shows that the Sales department's file drawer contains two sections (subdirectories), one for Bob's records and one for Carol's.

Subdirectory names follow the same conventions as directory names. That is, they can be as many as eight characters long, cannot contain spaces, and generally do not include an extension.

Locating a file in an office that doesn't use computers involves a simple, obvious series of steps:

1. Go to the correct filing cabinet.

2. Open the correct drawer.

3. Read through the file labels until you locate the file you want.

The process for locating a file on a computer is very similar, except that the terminology is a little different (and, obviously, there is no paper involved):

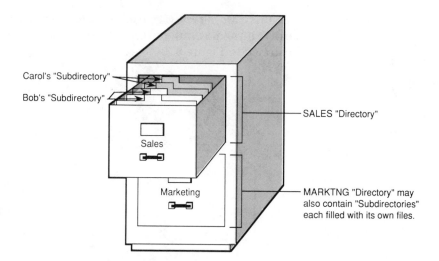

Figure 4.3. Directories can be further divided into subdirectories.

1. Insert the correct diskette into the disk drive, or access the correct hard disk drive (like going to the correct filing cabinet).
2. Access the correct directory or subdirectory (like going to the correct drawer in the file cabinet).
3. Glance through the file names on the display screen to find the right file (like thumbing through the labels on top of manila file folders).

Of course, a key factor in using a computer is knowing the correct disk drive, directory or subdirectory, and file name for a particular file. The designers of DOS realized this, and they included several tools for helping you discover this information. Even if you don't know exactly where to look for a particular file, there are techniques that you can use to "look around" and find the appropriate file.

Later, this chapter will explain these methods of searching disk drives, directories, and subdirectories to locate files. These techniques are valuable skills that you will use often in your work with DOS and your computer. But first, let's discuss the topics of directories and subdirectories in a little more detail.

The Directory Tree

The *structure* of directories and subdirectories on a disk is often referred to as the *directory tree*. Every hard disk and diskette contains an initial directory called the *root* directory. DOS automatically assigns the simple name \

Chapter 8 discusses the best techniques for organizing information on your computer's hard disk.

to this root directory. Any additional directories (and subdirectories) that you create are considered to be "below" the root directory.

To illustrate this concept, let's suppose that you are using a company's computer whose hard disk contains files organized into three directories—one for the Sales department, one for the Marketing department, and one for the Shipping department. Furthermore, individual employees in each department have divided these directories into separate, "personal" subdirectories, in which they store their own files. Each employee has used his or her first name as the name of his or her subdirectory.

The directory tree for such an organization appears in Figure 4.4. (Note that the root directory, as mentioned earlier, is always shown at the top of the hierarchy).

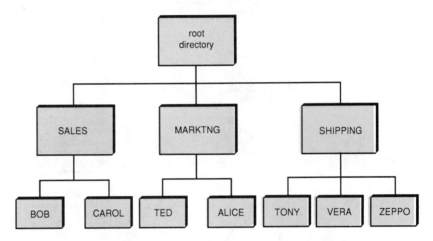

Figure 4.4. A directory tree divided into departments and further divided into employees within each department.

Keep in mind that each "box" in the hierarchy shown in Figure 4.4 represents a kind of "drawer" or "folder" that contains its own set of files. As you'll see, it's very easy to explore each "box" in the directory tree to see what files it contains.

Using the DOS 4 File System

DOS 4 offers a work area called the *File System* that lets you easily switch among directories and subdirectories, view file names, view the contents of files, and run programs. If you are using an earlier version of DOS, proceed directly to the section in this chapter titled "Managing Files and Directories from the Command Prompt." (Note, from now on, this book refers to Version 4 of DOS simply as DOS 4 and refers to Version 3 of DOS as DOS 3.)

Assessing the File System is simplicity itself. Assuming that the DOS

The File System names displayed in Figures 4.5 through 4.8 include examples that might not appear on your screen.

Shell's **Start Programs** screen is currently displayed on your monitor, use the ↑ or ↓ keys, (or the mouse) to move the highlight bar to the File System option. Then, press Enter (or double-click the mouse) to select File System.

The **File System** screen displays useful information about the disk drives, directories and subdirectories (if any), and files that are currently available on your computer. Figure 4.5 shows a sample File System display. In this example, users have already created several directories, the names of which are listed near the left side of the screen.

```
 05-08-89                        File System                    5:09 pm
 File  Options  Arrange  Exit                               F1=Help
 Ctrl+letter selects a drive.
 ▱A   ▱B   ▱C

 C:\DOS
       Directory Tree                              *.*

   C:\                              4201     .CPI      6,404    06-17-88
 ✓ ├─DOS                           4208     .CPI        641    06-17-88
   ├─SALES                         5202     .CPI        402    06-17-88
   │ ├─BOB                         ANSI     .SYS      9,148    06-17-88
   │ └─CAROL                       APPEND   .EXE     11,186    08-03-88
   ├─MARKTNG                       APPGROUP .MEU      3,552    04-18-89
   │ ├─TED                         ASSIGN   .COM      5,785    06-17-88
   │ └─ALICE                       ATTRIB   .EXE     18,247    06-17-88
   └─SHIPPING                      BACKUP   .COM     33,754    06-17-88
     ├─TONY                        BASIC    .COM      1,065    06-17-88
     ├─VERA                        BASICA   .COM     36,285    06-17-88
     └─ZEPPO                       CEMM     .SYS     64,736    06-14-88
                                   CHKDSK   .COM     17,771    06-17-88
                                   COMMAND  .COM     37,637    06-17-88
                                   COMP     .COM      9,491    06-17-88
                                   COUNTRY  .SYS     12,838    06-17-88
                                   CUSTUTIL .MEU      9,768    04-28-89
                                   DEBUG    .COM     21,606    06-17-88
                                   DISKCOMP .COM      9,889    06-17-88
                                   DISKCOPY .COM     10,428    06-17-88
                                   DISPLAY  .SYS     15,741    06-17-88
 F10=Actions   Shift+F9=Command Prompt
```

Figure 4.5. A sample File System display.

Figure 4.6 shows how the **File System** might appear on a computer with a hard disk that currently has only DOS installed on it.

Figure 4.7 shows how the **File System** screen might appear on a computer without a hard disk, but with the DOS Shell diskette in drive A:.

The File System displays a great deal of information about your computer. Let's examine this information in more detail.

What the File System Shows

Figure 4.8 shows yet another screen that the File System might display. This figure also points out the names of various areas of the screen and describes what these areas show you.

Like the **Start Programs** screen, the **File System** screen displays a top line of general information, including the date, time, and screen title. The File System also has an Action Bar and a reminder that you can press F1

```
 03-14-89                        File System                     4:01 pm
 File  Options  Arrange  Exit                                  F1=Help
 Ctrl+letter selects a drive.
 ⊞A  ⊞B  ▣C

 C:\DOS
       Directory Tree                            *.*
                                    ┌─────────────────────────────────────┐
    C:\                             │ ANSI     .SYS      9,148    06-17-88 │
    └─DOS ✓                         │ APPEND   .EXE     11,186    08-03-88 │
                                    │ ASSIGN   .COM      5,785    06-17-88 │
                                    │ ATTRIB   .EXE     18,247    06-17-88 │
                                    │ BACKUP   .COM     33,754    06-17-88 │
                                    │ BASIC    .COM      1,065    06-17-88 │
                                    │ BASICA   .COM     36,285    06-17-88 │
                                    │ CHKDSK   .COM     17,771    06-17-88 │
                                    │ COMMAND  .COM     37,637    06-17-88 │
                                    │ COMP     .COM      9,491    06-17-88 │
                                    │ COUNTRY  .SYS     12,838    06-17-88 │
                                    │ DEBUG    .COM     21,606    06-17-88 │
                                    │ DISKCOMP .COM      9,889    06-17-88 │
                                    │ DISKCOPY .COM     10,428    06-17-88 │
                                    │ DISPLAY  .SYS     15,741    06-17-88 │
                                    │ DOSSHELL .BAK        213    03-13-89 │
                                    │ DOSSHELL .BAT        256    03-13-89 │
                                    │ DOSUTIL  .MEU      6,660    06-17-88 │
                                    │ DRIVER   .SYS      5,274    06-17-88 │
                                    │ EDLIN    .COM     14,249    06-17-88 │
                                    │ EGA      .CPI     49,052    06-17-88 │
 F10=Actions  Shift+F9=Command Prompt
```

Figure 4.6. A hard disk with only the DOS directory installed.

```
 03-14-89                        File System                     4:12 pm
 File  Options  Arrange  Exit                                  F1=Help
 Ctrl+letter selects a drive.
 ⊞A  ⊞B

 A:\
       Directory Tree                            *.*
    A:\ ✓                           │ 012345   .678        109    06-17-88 │
                                    │ 09051D4D          1,892    12-29-88 │
                                    │ CHKDSK   .COM     17,771    06-17-88 │
                                    │ COMMAND  .COM     37,637    06-17-88 │
                                    │ DISKCOPY .COM     10,428    06-17-88 │
                                    │ DOS02I   .400          0    06-17-88 │
                                    │ DOSSHELL .BAK        196    12-28-88 │
                                    │ DOSSHELL .BAT        256    12-29-88 │
                                    │ DOSUTIL  .MEU      6,660    06-17-88 │
                                    │ PCIBMDRV .MOS        295    06-17-88 │
                                    │ PCMSDRV  .MOS        961    06-17-88 │
                                    │ PCMSPDRV .MOS        801    06-17-88 │
                                    │ PRINT    .COM     14,024    08-03-88 │
                                    │ SHELL    .CLR      4,438    12-29-88 │
                                    │ SHELL    .HLP     65,667    08-03-88 │
                                    │ SHELL    .MEU      4,588    08-03-88 │
                                    │ SHELLB   .COM      3,937    08-03-88 │
                                    │ SHELLC   .EXE    154,377    08-03-88 │
 F10=Actions  Shift+F9=Command Prompt
```

Figure 4.7. The File System display on a computer without a hard disk.

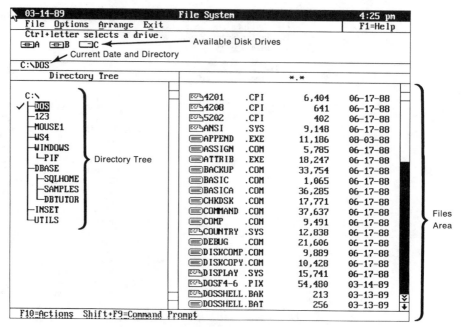

Figure 4.8. Areas of the **File System** screen.

help. The bottom of the screen reminds you that you should press F10 to access the Action Bar. (You also press F10 to leave the Action Bar.)

The Disk Drives

The names of the disk drives available on your computer appear beneath the Action Bar. In Figure 4.8, the computer contains two floppy disk drives, named A: and B:, and a hard disk, named C:, even though the File System displays only the drive letters (A, B, and C) without the colon that usually follows. Note that if your computer uses a text screen, you see only the drive names and not the small rectangular *icons* (pictures).

The Current Drive

Beneath the drive names is the "current" drive, the drive you are now using. In Figure 4.8, C: is the current drive, and DOS is the current directory, as indicated by C:\DOS. Names of files that are stored in the DOS directory of drive C: are displayed in the Files Area, at the right of the screen.

The Directory Tree

Beneath the current drive indicator is a graphical representation of the directory tree on the current drive. Notice that DOS displays the directory tree in a vertical line format, rather than the horizontal hierarchical format shown in Figure 4.3. DOS uses this format simply because it fits on the vertically oriented screen better. Subdirectory names are indented under the higher directory names. For example, in Figure 4.8, DBASE is the name of a directory, and SQLHOME, SAMPLES, and DBTUTOR are subdirectories beneath the DBASE directory.

The topmost directory in the tree is always the root directory, which DOS always names simply \. The File System also lists the drive name next to the root directory name, which is why `C:\` appears at the top of the directory tree in Figure 4.8.

The current directory (that is, the one you are now using) has a check mark next to it in the Directory Tree Area. For example, in Figure 4.8, the DOS directory is the current directory. In addition, the highlight bar is currently on the DOS directory name.

The Files Area

The right half of the **File System** screen displays the names of the individual files on the current drive and directory. On a graphics screen, files that are programs (that is, files that contain instructions that the computer can run) are indicated by a rectangular icon. Text files, which contain information rather than instructions, are marked by an icon that has its upper-right corner folded down. (These icons do not appear on a text screen, but you can still identify *program* files by their file name extension, which usually are .BAT, .COM, or .EXE).

The Files Area also displays the size of each file (in bytes) and the date that the file was created or last changed. For example, in Figure 4.8, the program file named BACKUP.COM is 33,754 bytes long, and was created (or last modified) on June 17, 1988.

Now that you know what information the File System displays, let's look at techniques for using the File System.

Keys for Navigating the File System

Look inside the back cover of this book for a summary of the keys used in the File System.

When you first enter the File System, the highlight bar appears in the disk drives section of the screen. To move the highlight bar to other parts of the screen, press the Tab key or the Shift-Tab keys. Follow these steps to experiment with these keys:

1. Press the Tab key repeatedly, and watch how the highlight bar moves around the various parts of the screen.

2. Press the Shift-Tab key (hold down the Shift key and press the Tab key) a few times, and watch how the highlight bar moves in the opposite direction around the screen.

As with the **Start Programs** screen, the F10 key activates the Action Bar options. Press the F10 key a few times, and watch how the highlight bar moves into, and out of, the Action Bar.

You can also use a mouse to move around in the File System. The examples that follow provide instructions for using a mouse.

Accessing a Disk Drive

Your computer probably has more than one disk drive available. To see the names of files on a different disk drive, you must *access* that drive. However, note that you can only access a floppy disk drive if that drive contains a diskette. (If you attempt to access an empty floppy disk drive, DOS displays an error message, such as `Drive not ready`. You then need to press Escape to cancel the request.)

Assuming that your computer has more than one disk drive and that none of the floppy disk drives is empty, you can use the following general steps to access other drives:

If you have a mouse, you can access a different disk drive by moving the mouse pointer to the new drive name and then clicking once.

1. Press the Tab key until the highlight bar is positioned in the disk drive section.
2. Press the → or ← key to move the highlight to a new disk drive name.
3. Press Enter to select the currently highlighted drive name.

After a brief pause, the screen displays a new directory tree and the names of the files on the diskette in the new disk drive.

An alternative method for assessing a different disk drive is to hold down the Ctrl key and type the drive name. (Note that this method works only when the highlight bar is in the area of the screen in which drive names are displayed). DOS reminds you of this alternative method by displaying the message `Ctrl+letter selects a drive` beneath the Action Bar.

For example, assuming that your computer has a hard disk drive named C: and that you want to access that disk drive, you merely press Tab until the highlight bar is in the disk drive section, and then type Ctrl-C (hold down the Ctrl key and type the letter C).

Should you encounter any problems while accessing hard disk or floppy disk drives, press Esc to cancel the operation, or press F1 to display a help screen. Optionally, refer to the Troubleshooting section near the end of this chapter for details.

Accessing a Directory (or Subdirectory)

The Files Area of the screen displays the names of files in the current directory only. If you or other users have previously created directories and subdirectories, you might want to see the names of the files on those directories.

To access a different directory (or subdirectory), follow these general steps:

1. Press the Tab key until the highlight bar gets to the Directory Tree Area of the screen.

If you have a mouse, you can access another directory simply by moving the mouse pointer to the directory name and clicking once.

2. Press the ↑ and/or ↓ keys to move the highlight bar to the new directory or subdirectory name.

3. Press Enter to access the currently highlighted directory name.

If your computer already contains several directories, you might want to practice changing to other directories on your own. Note how the Files Area displays the names of the files that are stored on each new directory. Later chapters will show you how to create directories and teach you practical applications for putting directories to use.

Remember that the root directory, named \, is always displayed at the top of the directory tree. To see what files it contains, you can access it using the same techniques that you use to access other directories.

Exploring File Names

The Files Area of the screen lists the names of the files on the current directory. To move the highlight bar to the Files Area, press the Tab key until the highlight bar is on a file name.

If a directory contains more files than can fit within the window, DOS activates the scroll bar (on a graphics screen) so that you can scroll up and down the list of file names. A text screen, on the other hand, displays the word **More:** followed by arrows that indicate the directions in which you can scroll. Use the same techniques that you used to scroll through help windows to scroll through file names. With the keyboard, use the ↓, ↑, PgDn, and PgUp keys. With a mouse, click on the single or double arrows, click on a darkened area of the scroll bar, or drag the slider box to a new location.

Narrowing the File Name Search

DOS offers a shortcut that eliminates the need for scrolling through a lengthy list of file names to locate a particular file: You can use DOS *wildcard characters* to locate file names that match a specific pattern. This is roughly similar to using a Rolodex file that groups information alphabetically: the letter tabs let you "flip to" the appropriate section of cards and narrow your search for a particular card.

The DOS wildcard characters are:

? Matches any single character

* Matches any group of characters

When you combine a wildcard character with "regular" characters, you create an *ambiguous file name*. For example, the ambiguous file name J*.* isolates file names that begin with the letter J, because J* matches any file name that starts with J and is followed by any other characters, and .* matches any extension.

The ambiguous file name *.LET isolates all file names that have extension .LET. The ambiguous file name QTR*.DAT isolates file names that start with the letters QTR, that are followed by any other characters, and that have the extension .DAT (for example, QTR1.DAT, QTRLY.DAT, QTR31989.DAT, and others that contain a similar pattern of letters).

The ? wildcard matches any single character. For example, the ambiguous file name QTR?.DAT isolates file names that begin with the letters QTR, that are followed by any *single* character, and that have the extension .DAT. For example, QTR?.DAT matches QTR1.DAT, QTR2.DAT, and QTRJ.DAT, but not QTR31989.DAT. The ambiguous file name JAN19??.EXP isolates file names such as JAN1987.EXP, JAN1988.EXP, JAN1989.EXP, and so on.

As a demonstration, let's assume that you are looking for a file whose exact name and extension you do not remember; however, you *do* remember that the file name begins with the letter C. Be sure the File System is displayed on your screen, and then follow the steps below to tell DOS to display only the names of files that begin with the letter C:

If you have a mouse, merely click on the Options choice in the Action Bar, and then click on Display Options once rather than performing steps 1 through 5.

1. Press F10 to activate the Action Bar.
2. Press → or ← until the Options choice is highlighted.
3. Press Enter to display the pull-down menu.
4. Press ↑ or ↓ until Display Options is highlighted.
5. Press Enter to select Display Options.

Note that DOS displays *.* in the box next to the Name: prompt. This indicates that DOS is currently displaying all of the directory's file names (any name followed by any extension). Change that to C*.* by following these steps:

6. Type C*.*
7. If you need to delete extra characters, press the Del (or Delete) key to remove characters that are ahead of the cursor, or press the Backspace key to erase characters to the left of the cursor.
8. Press Enter when the box contains C*.*, as shown in Figure 4.9.

Now the Files Area displays only those file names that begin with the letter C, as shown in Figure 4.10. (Your screen might list other file names, or it might display the message No files match file specifier if the current drive and directory does not contain any files that begin with the letter C.) Restricting the number of file names that DOS displays makes it much easier for you to locate a particular file in a drive or a directory.

Now, suppose you can't find the file that you're searching for on the current drive or directory. You can quickly check other directories or diskettes for files that begin with the letter C. If your hard disk or floppy diskette contains several directories or subdirectories, follow these general steps:

1. Press Tab until the highlight bar moves to the Directory Tree Area.

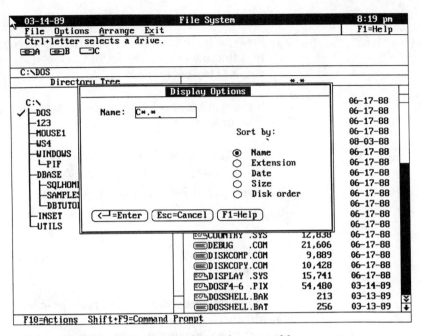

Figure 4.9. Entering the ambiguous file name C*.*.

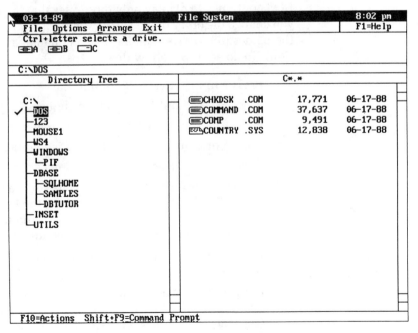

Figure 4.10 Only file names that begin with the letter
C are displayed.

2. Move the highlight to any directory (or subdirectory) name.

3. Press Enter to select it. (If a particular directory does not contain any files that begin with the letter C, DOS displays the message No files match file specifier.)

If you want to check floppy diskettes for files that begin with the letter C, follow these steps:

1. Press Tab until the highlight bar moves to the disk drive section, above the Directory Tree and Files Areas.

2. Insert the diskette you want to search into drive A:.

3. Move the highlight to the A drive option.

4. Press Enter to select drive A:.

5. Repeat steps 2 through 3 above to search as many diskettes as you wish.

Later chapters will show you more practical and powerful uses of DOS wildcard characters. For now, just remember that ? represents only a single character in a file name and that * represents any group of characters.

Redisplaying All File Names

DOS continues to display only those files that begin with the letter C until you change the entry in the Display Options back to *.*, which displays all file names (the first * matches any file name, and .* matches any extension). To do so now, follow these steps:

1. Press F10 to activate the Action Bar.

2. Press → or ← until the Options choice is highlighted.

3. Press Enter to display the pull-down menu.

4. Press ↑ or ↓ until Display Options is highlighted.

5. Press Enter to select Display Options.

6. Press the Del (or Delete) key on your keyboard to erase the leading C, so that the specifier now reads *.*. (If the Del, or Delete, key does not work correctly, press Num Lock once, and then use the Delete, Backspace, or arrow keys to make corrections.)

7. When the box contains only *.*, press Enter to return to the Action Bar.

8. Press F10 to leave the Action Bar.

Once again, the Files Area displays all the file names in the current drive and directory. Note that the ambiguous file name *.* appears at the top of the Files Area so that you always know the files DOS is displaying.

In the next chapter, you will use the File System and ambiguous file names to locate files and run programs. First, however, you need to learn how to exit the File System and return to the **Start Programs** screen.

Exiting the File System

An alternative—and easier—method of exiting the File System is simply to press the F3 key.

To exit the File System and return to the **Start Programs** screen, follow these steps:

1. Press F10 to move the highlight to the Action Bar.

2. Press ← or → to move the highlight to the Exit option.

3. Press Enter.

4. If necessary, move the highlight to the Exit File System option.

5. Press Enter.

The computer now displays the Main Group on the **Start Programs** screen.

The Optional Command Prompt

For DOS 4 users, the command prompt (discussed in the sections that follow) is simply an alternative method of using DOS. Whether or not you use it is simply a matter of personal preference. You probably should try some of the alternative techniques presented in the following sections, so that if you ever need to use a computer that has an earlier version of DOS, you will know what to do. First, you must leave the Shell and activate the command prompt by pressing the F3 key.

Remember, if at any time you decide that you would prefer using the Shell instead of the command prompt, you need only type the command DOSSHELL at the command prompt, and then press Enter. This reactivates the DOS Shell.

Managing Files and Directories from the Command Prompt

If you are using DOS 3, you need to use DOS commands to move among disk drives and directories and to view file names. Although you can't see the "graphical" presentation of disk drives, directories, and file names that the DOS 4 Shell offers, you still can find your way around the computer.

Changing Disk Drives

When the DOS command prompt appears, it usually displays the name of the current drive (without a colon) followed by a greater-than (>) sign. For example, if your screen is displaying the prompt

`A>`

you are currently accessing disk drive A:. If your screen displays

`C>`

you are now accessing hard disk drive C:.

You can change your current drive to another drive name simply by typing the new drive name (including the colon) and pressing Enter. Note, however, that you cannot access a floppy disk drive that does not have a diskette in it. If you attempt to do so, DOS displays an error message, such as `Not ready reading drive A`, and then presents the options `Abort, Retry, Ignore` (early versions of DOS) or `Abort, Retry, Fail` (Versions 3.3 and 4).

To correct the error, either insert a diskette into the drive and type `R` to retry the command, or type `A` to abort (cancel) accessing the new drive. (If you have problems accessing drives, see the Troubleshooting section at the end of this chapter.)

Suppose your computer has two floppy disk drives, but no hard disk. You would follow these steps to access disk drive B:

1. Insert a diskette (perhaps a DOS diskette other than the one currently in drive A:) into disk drive B:.
2. If the disk drive has a latch or door, be sure it is completely closed.
3. Specify disk drive B: by typing `B:`.
4. Press Enter to access the new drive.

The command prompt now displays the name of the current drive, `B>`. To again access disk drive A:, type `A:` and then press Enter.

Suppose your computer has a hard disk and one floppy disk drive named A:. To access drive A: (which, of course, must contain a diskette) simply type `A:` and then press Enter. To again access the hard disk drive C:, type `C:` and then press Enter.

Viewing Directory Names

The DOS TREE command shows you the names of directories and subdirectories on the current hard disk or floppy diskette. You can use this command to check your hard disk, or any diskette, to see if it has already been divided into directories and subdirectories. You use the TREE command like any other DOS command; type its name at the command prompt and then press Enter.

The results of the TREE command vary slightly from one version of DOS to the next. In general, though, versions prior to 4 display only sub-directory names that are beneath the current directory. Therefore, to view all the directory names on a disk, you would want to start from the highest-level directory–the root directory. To do so, you need to use the CHDIR or CD (for Change Directory) command to switch to the root directory (this command is discussed in detail in a later section of this chapter).

Let's assume that your computer has a hard disk named C:. Follow the steps below to change to the root directory of drive C: and view the names of all directories on that disk:

WARNING: The backslash (\) and the slash, or forward slash (/), are not the same characters. Be sure to type the backslash (\) character as indicated in these steps.

1. Type `C:` and press Enter to access the hard disk.

2. Type `CD\` and press Enter to change the current directory to the root directory.

3. Type `TREE` and press Enter.

If entering the TREE command produces the error message `Bad Command or File Name`, see the Troubleshooting section near the end of this chapter.

If there are no directories (or subdirectories) on the hard disk, the screen displays a message, such as `No subdirectories exist`. If there are directories (and subdirectories) on the hard disk, DOS lists their names on the screen. In versions of DOS prior to Version 4, the listing resembles the following example (with different names, of course):

```
DIRECTORY PATH LISTING FOR VOLUME

Path: \DOS
Sub-directories: None

Path: \SALES
Sub-directories: \BOB
                \CAROL

Path: \MARKTNG
Sub-directories: \TED
                \ALICE

Path: \SHIPPING
Sub-directories: \TONY
                \VERA
                \ZEPPO
```

If you are using DOS Version 4, the TREE command displays the directory in the following format:

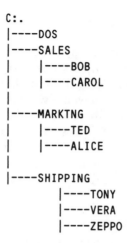

```
C:.
|----DOS
|----SALES
|      |----BOB
|      |----CAROL
|
|----MARKTNG
|      |----TED
|      |----ALICE
|
|----SHIPPING
        |----TONY
        |----VERA
        |----ZEPPO
```

Printing the Results of a Command

If the TREE display whizzes by too quickly on your screen, you can send its output to the printer. Chapter 12 covers many techniques for using your printer effectively. But for the time being, it's sufficient to know that you can send the output from any command to the printer by following the command with a blank space, the symbol >, and the letters PRN. Just think of PRN as an abbreviation for the PRiNter, and the > as an arrow pointing to the printer.

If you have a laser printer, you may need to eject the page to see the printout. See Chapter 12 for details.

Therefore, if you type the command TREE > PRN and press Enter now, the directory tree will be displayed on your printer. (You can think of the plain-English translation for TREE > PRN as being "Show me the directory tree, and send the results to the printer".).

Determining the Current Directory

On some computers, you can tell which directory is current simply by looking at the command prompt. For example, if the current directory is named DOS, the command prompt shows C:\DOS>. If the current directory is the root directory of drive A:, the command prompt shows A:\> (because the root directory is named \).

If your command prompt does not show the name of the current directory, there are two techniques that you can use to see the name of the current directory. One is to enter the CHDIR or CD command with no additional directory name. That is, simply type CD and press Enter. The names of the current drive and directory appear on your screen, and then the command prompt reappears.

Another way to view the name of the current drive and directory is to use the DOS PROMPT command to customize the command prompt. Chapter 12 discusses the PROMPT command in detail, but for the time being, suffice it to say that entering the command PROMPT PG changes the command prompt so that it displays both the current drive and directory. To try this yourself, type `PROMPT $P$G` now and press Enter.

The command prompt will continue to display the current drive and directory for the remainder of your current session (i.e., until you turn off the computer). That way, you can see which directory is current at any time by glancing at the command prompt.

Accessing a Different Directory

To access a different directory on a disk, use the CHDIR (usually abbreviated as CD) command. (Both are actually abbreviations for CHange DIRectory). When you use the commands, precede the name of the directory that you want to access with a backslash (\). The TREE command that you used earlier listed the names of directories (if any) that are available on your computer.

The simple steps below demonstrate how to change to the directory named DOS. If your computer does not contain a directory named DOS, substitute one of the directory names from your directory tree (use a directory name rather than a subdirectory name). The steps also assume that you are currently using hard disk C:.

1. If your computer has a hard disk, first type `C:` and press Enter to make drive C: current.
2. Type `CD \DOS` (or substitute the name of another directory in place of DOS).
3. Press Enter.

Your command prompt will now display the name of the new current directory. For example, after switching to the directory named DOS in the steps above, your command prompt would display `C:\DOS>`.

If you do not have a hard disk, chances are that most of your floppy disks will have all of their files stored on the root directory. If you can find a diskette with multiple directories, however, you'll be able to use the CHDIR or CD command to change directories on that diskette.

Accessing Subdirectories

To access a subdirectory, you must specify the entire *path* in the CHDIR or CD command. The "path" is the series of directory names that leads from the current directory name (or root) to the final subdirectory. Separate each directory name with a backslash (\).

For example, suppose your disk has a subdirectory named BOB beneath the SALES directory. The TREE command would display this fact in the following format in Version 3 of DOS:

```
Path: \SALES
Sub-directories: \BOB
```

or in Version 4 . . .

```
|----SALES
|    |----BOB
```

To access the BOB subdirectory, you must include both the SALES and BOB names—separated by backslashes—in the CHDIR or CD command, as in the following example. (Again, you can substitute names that are relevant to your own directory tree in place of \SALES\BOB.) First, type CD **\SALES\BOB** and then press Enter.

When you use the CHDIR or CD command to change to a different directory or subdirectory, you can move "down" one level by excluding the backslashes. For example, assuming that BOB is a subdirectory beneath the SALES directory, and SALES is the current directory, you can enter the command CD BOB to move "down" to the BOB directory. The command prompt would then show **C:\SALES\BOB>**.

Note that this technique, however, works *only* when you are moving down one level in the tree. To access the SALES\BOB subdirectory from any directory other than SALES, you would need to type in the complete *path* required to get to the subdirectory. That is, you need to enter the command CD **\SALES\BOB** which tells DOS that in order to get to the BOB subdirectory, it needs to take a path starting at the root (\), then down to the SALES directory, then down another level to the BOB subdirectory.

If your disk is already divided into directories and subdirectories, you may want to practice using the CD command on your own to switch among the various directories. (Chapter 9 will display some handy shortcut techniques.) In a moment, you'll learn how to view the names of all the files on the current directory.

Accessing the Root Directory

As you might recall, the root directory is always named \. Therefore, to change to the root directory, you type only CD \ and then press Enter. The command prompt then displays **C:\>** to indicate that the current directory is root.

Viewing File Names

The DOS DIR command lets you see the names of all files on the current directory, as well as the names of subdirectories (if any) beneath the current directory. In general, you will probably use this command to check a floppy disk, or directory, to see what files it contains.

You use the DIR command just as any other DOS command; type it in at the command prompt and press Enter. You can try it right now, regardless of what disk or directory is current, simply by typing DIR and pressing Enter.

The DIR command displays a list of file names, extensions, sizes, and the dates and times that files were created or last modified. For example, your screen might show the following file names and information:

The DIR command also displays other information, such as the number of files in the current directory and the amount of storage space remaining on the current disk.

```
UTILS          <DIR>        03-01-89   9:40a
COMMAND   COM      37637 06-17-88  12:00p
DISKCOPY  COM      10428 06-17-88  12:00p
FIND      EXE       5983 06-17-88  12:00p
```

The first item is actually a directory named UTILS, as indicated by the <DIR> label. The directory was created on March 1, 1989 at 9:40 a.m. The remaining items are program files. You know this because programs files usually have one of the following extensions: .COM (for "command"), .EXE (for "executable"), or .BAT (for "batch"). (You'll learn more about file name extensions in Chapter 7.)

The DIR command does not show the period that normally separates a file name from its extension. Instead, it aligns the file name extensions in a column to improve readability. Hence, the files displayed are actually named COMMAND.COM, DISKCOPY.COM, and FIND.EXE. Each of these was created or last edited on June 17, 1988 at 12:00 noon. The largest of the three files contains 37,636 bytes of instructions, the smallest contains 5,983 bytes.

Slowing Down the DIR Display

If there are many files on the current directory, DOS displays them too quickly for you to see. You can use the /P *switch* to make DOS pause after it lists one screenful of file names. The switch must be preceded by a blank space, and it requires a forward slash (/) rather than the back slash (\) character. For example, type in the command DIR /P and then press Enter.

If the directory contains more than one screenful of file names, the screen displays only one "page" of file names and the prompt Press any key to continue.... When you are ready to view the next screenful of file names, simply press a key. Continue paging through the file names until the DOS command prompt reappears.

Displaying File Names on a Different Drive

You need not actually change to a new disk drive to see what files are on it. Instead, merely specify the disk drive name (preceded by a space) after the DIR command. For example, suppose your current drive is hard disk drive

C:, but you want to see the names of the files on a diskette in drive A:. To do so, simply type in the command `DIR A:` and press Enter.

Displaying File Names in a Different Directory

You also can view the names of files on any directory without changing your current directory. Simply include the complete directory name in the DIR command. Be sure to precede all directory (and subdirectory) names with a backslash. For example, if you are currently accessing the DOS directory, but you want to see the names of files in the \SALES directory, you would type the command `DIR \SALES` and press Enter.

As you know, the root directory is always named \. Therefore, to view the names of the files that are stored on the root directory, you would type the command `DIR \` and press Enter.

Viewing Specific Groups of Files

You don't need to always view all of the file names on a particular diskette or directory; you can limit the display to files that match some *pattern* of characters. This is similar to using an alphabetically arranged Rolodex file, which lets you then "flip to" a smaller group of cards to narrow your search for a particular card.

To search for (isolate) file names that match a pattern, use the following DOS *wildcard characters*:

?   Matches any single character

*   Matches any group of characters

When you combine the wildcard characters with "regular" characters, you create an *ambiguous file name*. For example, the ambiguous file name M*.* isolates all file names that begin with the letter M, because M* matches file names that begin with M followed by any characters, and .* matches any extension.

The ambiguous file name, *.LET isolates only those file names that have the extension .LET. The ambiguous file name QTR*.DAT isolates file names that start with the letters QTR, that are followed by any other characters, and that have the extension .DAT (for example, QTR1.DAT, QTRLY.DAT, QTR31989.DAT, and so on).

The ? wildcard matches any single character. For example, the ambiguous file name QTR?.DAT isolates file names that begin with the letters QTR, that are followed by any single character, and that have the extension .DAT. For example, QTR?.DAT matches QTR1.DAT, QTR2.DAT, QTRJ.DAT, but not QTR31989.DAT. The ambiguous file name JAN19??.EXP isolates file names such as JAN1987.EXT, JAN1988.EXT, JAN1989.EXP, and so on.

Try using these wildcards yourself. Suppose you are looking for a file whose full name and extension you do not recall, but you do know it begins with the letter C. To display only those file names that begin with the letter C (on the current drive and directory), type DIR C*.* and then press Enter.

Your screen might display a list that resembles the one in Figure 4.11. If no file names on the current drive and directory start with the letter C, DOS displays a message, such as File not found, and then simply redisplays the command prompt so that you can enter another command.

```
C:\DOS>DIR C*.*

Volume in drive C has no label
Volume Serial Number is 201A-2C4C
Directory of  C:\DOS

COMMAND  COM     37637 06-17-88  12:00p
COUNTRY  SYS     12838 06-17-88  12:00p
COMP     COM      9491 06-17-88  12:00p
CHKDSK   COM     17771 06-17-88  12:00p
         4 File(s)   19937280 bytes free

C:\DOS>
```

Figure 4.11 Sample display from the command DIR C*.*.

Suppose that you want to see only the names of files that have the extension .BAT. In that case, you merely type the command DIR *.BAT and press Enter. If you want to see only the names of files that begin with the letters BASIC and that have the extension .COM, type the command DIR BASIC*.COM and press Enter.

Note that if the current drive and directory does not contain *any* files that match the ambiguous file name, DOS displays the message File not found; then it redisplays the command prompt and awaits your next command.

Also keep in mind that DIR displays only the names of files in the current directory (or subdirectory). Therefore, after you use CHDIR or CD to change to a new directory or subdirectory, entering another DIR command displays only the names of files on the new directory or subdirectory.

In the next chapter, you'll begin to see that ambiguous file names can be very powerful tools for managing your computer files. For the time being, however, just remember that ? represents any single character and that * represents any group of characters in an ambiguous file name.

Displaying Only File Names

Appendix B contains additional information about all DOS commands, including the important DIR command.

If you want to display only the names of files and subdirectories—without sizes, dates, and times—use the /W switch with the DIR command. The W stands for *Wide*, because this switch lists the file names in a wide horizontal format. For example, to view a wide display of the files on your current directory, type the command `DIR /W` and then press Enter.

Printing File Names

To list file names on the printer rather than on the screen, add `> PRN` (*redirection symbol* and a *device name*) next to the DIR command. For example, if your printer is connected and ready to accept output, type the command `DIR > PRN` and then press Enter. This produces a printed copy of file names on the current disk drive and directory.

If you are using a laser printer, you might need to eject the page from the printer manually. See Chapter 12 for details.

Troubleshooting

This section discusses common problems that you might encounter while exploring disk drives and directories. If you need additional information, refer to Appendix B, which discusses all DOS commands in more detail.

- ■ DOS displays the message `Bad command or file name`. This error occurs in two situations: either you misspelled a command or program name, or you attempted to run a program that is not available on the current disk drive or directory.

  1. If you simply misspelled a command (such as typing DOR rather than DIR), type the command again and press Enter.

  2. If you are certain that you typed the command properly and you still see the error message `Bad command or file name`, then you are attempting to run a program that is not available on the current disk drive or directory. Be sure the file name is in the current directory on the current drive. For example, the TREE command is actually a DOS program that DOS must find on the disk. In DOS 3, the TREE program is usually found in the root directory. So, to run the TREE command, first access the root directory by typing `CD \` and then pressing Enter. Then, type `TREE` and press Enter.

- ■ DOS displays the message `Abort, Retry, Ignore` or `Abort, Retry, Fail`. This error occurs when you type a command that the computer cannot carry out, such as when you attempt to access an empty floppy disk drive.

1. If you can determine the cause of the problem (based on the brief message that appears above the Abort, Retry, Ignore options), do so, and then press R to retry the command.

2. If you cannot correct the situation, type the letter I to select Ignore, or F to select Fail (whichever is displayed on your screen as an option). The command prompt will display Current drive is no longer valid>. You must then switch to a valid drive. For example, if you have a hard disk named C:, type C: and press Enter. If your disk drive A: contains a diskette, type A: and press Enter. The command prompt will redisplay the current drive name.

■ DOS displays the message General failure reading drive followed by a drive name (such as A). In this case, the diskette in the drive is not *formatted.* and therefore cannot be accessed yet. Try a different diskette, or see Chapter 6 for formatting techniques.

■ You type a command, but DOS does nothing. This occurs when you type a command and forget to press Enter. Typing a command merely displays it on the screen. You must press Enter to "send" the command to the computer's processor. If you forget, DOS waits indefinitely, until you press Enter.

Summary

This chapter discussed the way in which information is organized into directories and files on a computer. It also discussed techniques and commands for accessing disk drives and directories and for viewing the names of available files. These are the most fundamental (and perhaps most important) techniques for using your computer, as they permit you to use *any* program to manage *any* information contained in your computer. The summary below lists these important techniques:

■ DOS provides two handy wildcards to help you manage computer files. ?, which stands for any single character, and *, which stands for any group of characters.

■ You must enter commands to access different drives and directories and to view file names.

■ To change the current drive from the command prompt, type the new drive name (including the colon) and then press Enter.

■ To display the name of the current directory and drive in the DOS command prompt, type the command PROMPT PG and press Enter.

■ To display the names of directories and subdirectories on the current drive, type the command TREE and press Enter.

■ To access a directory or subdirectory, use the CHDIR—or CD—command, followed by the directory name (or path), and then press Enter.

■ DOS Version 4 offers the File System, which presents a graphical summary of the drives, directories, and file names available on the computer.

■ To access the DOS 4 File System from the **Start Programs** screen, select the File System option.

■ Keys and techniques that you use in the File System are summarized inside the back cover of this book.

Running Programs

So far, you've learned that your computer stores programs (instructions) and data (information) in files and that these files can be stored in separate directories and subdirectories to better organize those individual files. You have also learned how to access disk drives, directories, and subdirectories and how to view the names of files stored on the current directory or sub-directory.

Now that you know the basics of how to search for specific files, you need to learn how to use those techniques to find and run programs that put the computer to work. This chapter demonstrates techniques for running two types of programs: 1) Programs that came with your DOS package (DOS programs) and 2) Optional programs that you purchase separately (*application* programs).

DOS Programs

Although DOS, in itself, is a program, it also includes additional programs that help you perform common tasks. In this chapter, you'll use one of the simpler of these DOS programs, named CHKDSK (short for Check Disk). CHKDSK checks the storage capacity of your disk (or diskette), reports on how much RAM is available, and can even fix minor disk problems.

Application Programs

Whether you bought your computer for personal use or are using a computer that is owned by a company or a school, you probably have programs other than DOS available on your computer. As mentioned in Chapter 1, a computer is like a stereo, and programs are like albums. After you buy a stereo, you need to purchase albums to play on it. After you buy a computer, you must purchase programs to run on it.

Your computer might already have several programs installed on it, particularly if you are sharing it with co-workers or other students. For example, the hard disk on a business computer might already contain the popular WordPerfect word processing program, the Lotus 1-2-3 spreadsheet program, and the dBASE IV database management program. Because these application programs are purchased and installed separately from DOS, I have no way of knowing which particular application programs are currently installed on your computer. However, I can give you general pointers to help you locate and use any program that is available on your computer.

This chapter uses the popular Lotus 1-2-3 spreadsheet program in examples that demonstrate how to run an application program. Of course, I cannot possibly go into detail about actually *using* the 1-2-3 program; this is a book about DOS, and to fully discuss 1-2-3 would require hundreds of additional pages.

Although application programs often require you to learn different techniques for effective use, most programs provide instant help when you press the F1 key.

To effectively use an application program, such as Lotus 1-2-3, WordPerfect, dBASE IV, or any other, you need to read either the printed documentation that came with the program or a separate book that focuses on that program. Also, if you are using a computer that is used by others in a company or school, there is a very simple, non-technical technique that you can use to find out which application programs are currently installed on your computer and how to run those programs: Simply ask some who knows.

WARNING: Do not run the DOS FORMAT.COM program until you've thoroughly read Chapter 6 of this book.

Please be forewarned: although the techniques you will learn in this chapter will help you find and run any program on your computer, you should run only those programs mentioned in this chapter or those that you know something about. If you arbitrarily run programs that you know nothing about, you might inadvertently erase important information from your disk!

Running Programs from the DOS Shell

If you are using DOS 4, you can easily run DOS programs from the DOS Shell. The general technique is quite simple, as summarized below (the sections that follow, however, provide more specific examples):

▪ If your computer has no hard disk, you must remove the DOS diskette from drive A: and then insert the diskette that contains the program you want to run into drive A:.

▪ From the DOS Shell **Start Programs** screen, select the `File System` option.

■ If your computer has a hard disk, use the File System to change to the directory that contains the program that you want to run.

■ In the Files Area, highlight the program's file name and press Enter (or double-click the file name with your mouse).

■ Enter any necessary information in the dialog box that follows and/or press Enter.

The next section demonstrates how to use these steps to run the DOS CHKDSK program.

Running a DOS Program

The CHKDSK program is stored with the file name CHKDSK.COM. On a hard disk, the program is stored in the DOS directory. For computers that do not have hard disks, the CHKDSK.COM program is stored on the Shell diskette that you created during the installation process.

Assuming that you are starting from the DOS Shell **Start Programs** screen, use the following steps to run the CHKDSK program:

1. If your computer has no hard disk, be sure that the Shell diskette is in drive A:.

If you are using diskettes, and CHKDSK.COM is not on the DOS Shell diskette, use the techniques discussed in Chapter 4 to locate the CHKDSK.COM file on one of the other DOS diskettes.

2. Select the File System option from the **Start Programs** screen to switch to the File System.

3. If your computer has a hard disk, press the Tab key until the highlight is in the Directory Tree area of the screen.

4. If your computer has a hard disk, press ↑ or ↓ until the highlight is on the DOS directory name, and then press Enter to access that directory (or click the mouse once on the DOS directory name).

5. Press Tab to move to the Files Area of the screen, and then use the ↓ or ↑ key to move the highlight to the CHKDSK.COM file name.

6. When CHKDSK.COM is highlighted (as shown in Figure 5.1), press Enter. (If you have a mouse, you can avoid using the arrow keys by moving the mouse pointer to CHKDSK.COM and double-clicking.)

7. The Open File dialog box shown in Figure 5.2 appears on the screen. You don't need to add any options right now, so skip this step by pressing Enter (or by clicking once on the ↵=Enter box).

The screen now displays information about your computer's memory (RAM) and the current hard disk or diskette. (If a question appears on the screen asking if you want to convert lost clusters to chains, type the letter N and press Enter.) Figure 5.3 shows an example of the information displayed by CHKDSK. Note that your screen probably shows completely different information.

Don't be concerned about the details that CHKDSK is now displaying; the important point here is that you were able to run this program.

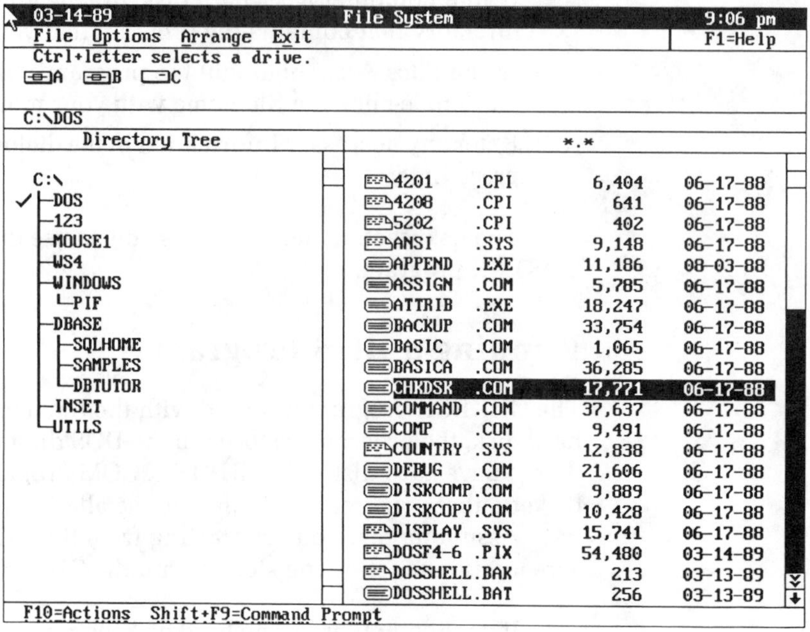

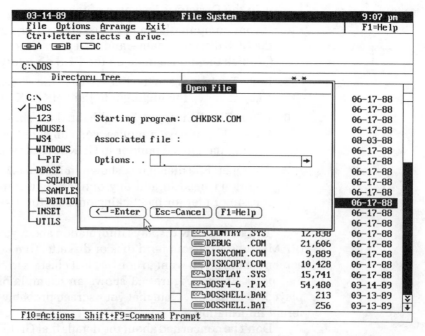

Figure 5.1. The CHKDSK.COM file name is highlighted.

Figure 5.2. The OpenFile dialog box for running a program.

```
Volume Serial Number is 201A-2C4C

33323008 bytes total disk space
   71680 bytes in 2 hidden files
   65536 bytes in 12 directories
13268992 bytes in 770 user files
19916800 bytes available on disk

    2048 bytes in each allocation unit
   16271 total allocation units on disk
    9725 available allocation units on disk

  655360 total bytes memory
  414304 bytes free




Press Enter (<─┘) to return to File System.
```

Figure 5.3. Sample output of the CHKDSK program.

(When you do want to learn more about the information that CHKDSK displays, refer to Appendix B.)

Note that, near the bottom of the screen, the prompt Press Enter (←┘) to return to File System appears. Go ahead and press the Enter key now. The CHKDSK program will end, and you'll be returned to the DOS Shell File System. If you wish to leave the File System and return to the **Start Programs** screen, press the F3 key.

Running an Application Program from the DOS Shell

The basic techniques for running application programs are essentially the same as those used to run DOS programs. The following exercise assumes that you (or someone else) has already purchased and installed the popular Lotus 1-2-3 program on your computer.

If your computer has a hard disk, the Lotus 1-2-3 manual recommends that you create a directory named 123 to store the 1-2-3 program on; it also tells you to start the program by entering the command 123 at the DOS prompt. Let's work through the exact steps required to run 1-2-3, both for computers with and without a hard disk. (Again, you cannot perform these exact steps unless you already have a copy of the 1-2-3 program installed on your hard disk or available on floppy diskettes.)

1. If your computer does not have a hard disk, remove the DOS diskette from drive A:, and insert the Lotus 1-2-3 System Disk in drive A:.

2. Select File System from the DOS 4 **Start Programs** Main Group screen.

3. If your computer has a hard disk, press Tab until the highlight is in the Directory Tree Area of the screen.

4. Use the ↑ or ↓ key to move the highlight to the 123 directory name, and then press Enter to access that directory. (If you are using a mouse, simply click once with the mouse pointer on the 123 directory name.)

5. Press Tab until the highlight is in the Files Area of the screen.

6. Use the ↑ or ↓ keys to move the highlight to the 123.COM file name. (If you are using a mouse, click once on the 123.COM file name.) Your screen now should resemble the one shown in Figure 5.4.

7. Press Enter (or double-click the mouse).

8. When the program dialog box appears, press Enter (or click on the ↵=Enter box) to run the program.

Although several files are named 123 (see Figure 5.4), you know that 123.COM is the file that contains the program, because most programs have the file name extensions .COM, .EXE, or .BAT. (On a graphics screen, program files are also represented by a rectangular icon without the upper-right corner folded down.)

```
 03-14-89                    File System                  9:09 pm
 File  Options  Arrange  Exit                            F1=Help
 Ctrl+letter selects a drive.
 ⌷A   ⌷B   ⌷C

 C:\123
      Directory Tree                              *.*

   C:\                              📄123     .CMP      135,142   07-04-86
   ├─DOS                            📄123     .CNF          265   07-04-86
 ✓ ├─123                            📄123     .COM        2,304   07-04-86
   ├─MOUSE1                         📄123     .DYN       11,157   08-05-86
   ├─WS4                            📄123     .HLP      114,362   07-04-86
   ├─WINDOWS                        📄123     .SET       34,149   03-13-89
   │ └─PIF                          📄BLOCK1  .FNT        5,732   08-05-86
   ├─DBASE                          📄BLOCK2  .FNT        9,273   08-05-86
   │ ├─SQLHOME                      📄BOLD    .FNT        8,624   08-05-86
   │ ├─SAMPLES                      📄COPYHARD.COM       40,272   08-05-86
   │ └─DBTUTOR                      📄DBF2    .XLT       36,544   08-05-86
   ├─INSET                          📄DBF3    .XLT       42,272   08-05-86
   └─UTILS                          📄DIF     .XLT       27,232   08-05-86
                                    📄FORUM   .FNT        9,727   08-05-86
                                    📄INSTALL .DVC        4,469   08-05-86
                                    📄INSTALL .EXE       50,688   08-05-86
                                    📄INSTALL .LBR      231,468   08-05-86
                                    📄INSTALL .SCR       37,353   08-05-86
                                    📄ITALIC1 .FNT        8,949   08-05-86
                                    📄ITALIC2 .FNT       11,857   08-05-86
                                    📄JZZLOTUS.XLT       17,328   08-05-86
 F10=Actions   Shift+F9=Command Prompt
```

Figure 5.4. 123.COM file name is highlighted.

After a brief pause, the Lotus 1-2-3 program spreadsheet appears on your screen, as shown in Figure 5.5. (Depending on your settings, the menu at the top of the screen might not appear immediately.)

As mentioned earlier, you won't actually use the 1-2-3 program here. You need to study a book or the documentation that comes with the Lotus 1-2-3 software package to learn how to use 1-2-3. (Lotus 1-2-3 might not look impressive when it first appears on the screen, but it is actually a very powerful and useful program for managing and analyzing business and financial information!)

However, the important point here is that you have performed the

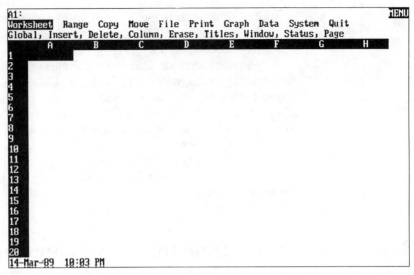

```
A1:                                                          MENU
Worksheet Range Copy Move File Print Graph Data System Quit
Global, Insert, Delete, Column, Erase, Titles, Window, Status, Page
          A        B        C        D        E        F        G        H
1
2
3
4
5
6
7
8
9
10
11
12
13
14
15
16
17
18
19
20
14-Mar-89  10:03 PM
```

Figure 5.5. Lotus 1-2-3 spreadsheet program is "in control."

necessary steps to run an application program. The general steps you used to run Lotus 1-2-3 hold true for all other application programs. However, always remember to check the documentation that comes with an application program for detailed information about running that program, such as which diskette to insert, the directory location, the name of the program file, and listings of options that you might need to enter in the Options Box.

Exiting an Application Program

Unlike the CHKDSK program, which automatically returns control to DOS when it finishes its task, most application programs stay in control of your computer until you take specific steps to exit them. Because different programs require different steps for exiting, you must always find exact instructions in the program's documentation.

If you used the preceding steps to run the 1-2-3 program on your computer, it is probably still on your screen. To exit the 1-2-3 program and return to DOS, follow these steps:

1. Press the **/** key to display a menu of options at the top of the screen.

2. Type **Q** to select Quit from that menu.

3. When given the options No and Yes, type **Y** to select Yes.

4. When the message `Press Enter (←┘) to return to the File System` appears, press Enter to return to the DOS Shell.

Now you have used the DOS Shell to run both a DOS program and an optional application program. The basic steps described in these sections work for all programs that you might use on your computer. In addition, you can customize the DOS Shell to make it easier to run programs, as discussed in Chapter 11.

The next sections discuss techniques for running programs from the command prompt, without the aid of the DOS Shell. Remember, if you are using DOS 4, the command prompt is entirely optional for the time being. Therefore, if you feel that learning an alternative technique might be confusing, you can skip to the chapter summary to review important techniques and concepts.

Also remember that if you are using DOS 4, you must press the F3 key (twice, if you are in the File System) to leave the DOS Shell and get to the command prompt.

Running Programs from the DOS Command Prompt

 The general techniques for running programs from the DOS command prompt are as follows:

- If your computer has no hard disk, you must remove the DOS diskette from drive A:, and insert the diskette that contains the program that you want to run into drive A:.

- If your computer has a hard disk, use the CHDIR (or CD) command to change to the directory that contains the program that you want to run.

- Type the file name necessary to run the program, and press Enter.

The following section demonstrates how to use these steps to run the DOS CHKDSK program.

Running a DOS Program from the Command Prompt

The DOS commands that you used in the previous chapter, such as DIR, PROMPT, CHDIR, and CD, are stored in RAM, so you don't need to change disk drives or directories to use those commands.

The DOS CHKDSK (short for Check Disk) program is stored in a file named CHKDSK.COM. Exactly where the CHKDSK.COM program is stored depends on your computer system and the version of DOS you are using. If you installed DOS on a hard disk, DOS automatically stored the CHKDSK.COM on the root directory (for DOS 3) or the DOS directory (for DOS 4). If your computer has no hard disk, the CHKDSK.COM program is stored on the DOS diskette (for DOS 3) or on the Shell diskette (for DOS 4).

To run the CHKDSK program on your computer, use the following steps:

1. If your computer has no hard disk, be sure the DOS diskette is in drive A:. (If you are using DOS 4, be sure the Shell diskette is in drive A:.)

2. If your computer has a hard disk, type CD \ and then press Enter to access the root directory. (If you are using DOS 4, type CD \DOS and then press Enter to access the DOS directory.)

3. To run a program, type its file name, without the extension. So in this case, type CHKDSK and press Enter to run the CHKDSK program.

If the current diskette or hard disk directory does *not* contain the CHKDSK.COM program, DOS displays the error message Bad command or file name. If that error occurs, you need to use the techniques discussed in Chapter 4 to search other DOS diskettes or other directories to find CHKDSK.COM. Use the command DIR C*.* on each directory or each diskette (to view file names that begin with the letter C) until you find the directory or diskette that contains CHKDSK.COM. When you find the correct diskette or directory, type the CHKDSK command and press Enter to run the program.

The CHKDSK program performs a somewhat simple task—it displays information about memory (RAM) and disk storage space. (If a question appears on the screen asking if you want to convert lost clusters to files, type the letter N and press Enter). Figure 5.3 shows an example of the information displayed by CHKDSK. Note that your screen probably shows completely different information.

Don't be concerned about the details that CHKDSK is now displaying; the important point here is that you were able to run this program. (When you do want to learn more about the information that CHKDSK displays, refer to Appendix B.)

Let's review the basic techniques you used. First, you located the file that contains the program you want to run (CHKDSK.COM in this example). Then, you simply typed the program name, which is the same as the file name without the extension (CHKDSK in this example). After typing the file name, you pressed Enter, and DOS ran the program.

After the CHKDSK program ends, it automatically returns you to DOS. When you see the DOS command prompt, this means that CHKDSK is done, and DOS is back in control. (You can now enter any DOS command that you wish.)

Running an Application Program from the Command Prompt

The basic techniques for running application programs are essentially the same as those used to run DOS programs. The following exercise assumes that you (or someone else) has already purchased and installed the popular Lotus 1-2-3 program on your computer.

If your computer has a hard disk, the Lotus 1-2-3 manual recommends that you create a directory named 123 to store the 1-2-3 program on; it also tells you to start the program by entering the command **123** at the DOS prompt. Let's work through the exact steps required to run 1-2-3, both for computers with and without a hard disk. (Again, you cannot perform these exact steps unless you already have a copy of the 1-2-3 program installed on your hard disk or available on floppy diskettes.)

1. If your computer does not have a hard disk, remove the DOS diskette from drive A: and insert the Lotus 1-2-3 System Disk into drive A:.
2. If your computer does have a hard disk, change to the 123 directory by typing in the command **CD \123** and pressing Enter.
3. Type the program name **123** and then press Enter.

After a brief pause, the Lotus 1-2-3 program spreadsheet appears on your screen, as shown in Figure 5.5. (Depending on your settings, the menu at the top of the screen might not appear when you first run the program.) You won't actually use the 1-2-3 program here. You need to study a book or the documentation that comes with the Lotus 1-2-3 software package to learn how to use 1-2-3. (Lotus 1-2-3 might not look impressive when it first appears on the screen, but it is actually a very powerful and useful program for managing and analyzing business and financial information!)

However, the important point here is that you have performed the necessary steps to run an application program. The general techniques you used to run Lotus 1-2-3 hold true for all other application programs. However, always remember to check the documentation that comes with an application program for detailed information about running that program, such as which diskette to insert, which directory to access, and the command required to run the program.

Exiting an Application Program

Unlike the CHKDSK program, which automatically returns control to DOS when it finishes its task, most application programs stay in control of your computer until you take specific steps to exit them. Because different programs require different steps for exiting, you must find exact instructions in the program's documentation.

If you used the preceding steps to run the 1-2-3 program on your computer, it is probably still on your screen. To exit the 1-2-3 program and return to DOS, follow these steps:

1. Press the **/** key to display a menu of options at the top of the screen.
2. Type **Q** to select Quit from the menu.
3. When given the options No and Yes, type **Y** to select Yes. This returns you to the DOS command prompt, which indicates that DOS is back in control. You can now use DOS to run another program.

Although the above exercises did not help you to understand or to use the Lotus 1-2-3 program, the general techniques that you used to start and exit the program are important—you will use these same general techniques to start and use *all* programs on your computer. (Again, the specific techniques that you need to run, use, and exit an optional application program are included in the documentation that comes packaged with that program.)

To recap, the basic procedure you use to start a program is as follows: First, if your computer doesn't have a hard disk, you must insert the appropriate program diskette in drive A:. If your computer has a hard disk, you must change to the appropriate directory, using the usual CHDIR (or CD) command. Then, type in the file name (without the extension) that starts the program. The required diskettes, directories, and program names are discussed in the documentation that comes with any application program that you purchase.

Summary

Regardless of whether you start a program from the DOS Shell or the command prompt, two points should be kept in mind:

- DOS programs automatically return control to DOS after they've completed their job.

- Most application programs "take over" your computer until you explicitly exit the program. When you exit an application program, DOS automatically takes control of your computer again.

The basic techniques for running programs—be they programs that came with DOS or optional *application* programs—are very similar. However, there are a few differences between DOS programs and application programs that you need to keep in mind:

- DOS programs are automatically available after you install DOS, and all are discussed in this book.

- Application programs must be purchased separately and must be installed on your hard disk or diskettes using instructions found in the program's documentation.

- The documentation that comes with an application program provides complete instructions for installing, starting, using, and exiting the program.

To run programs from the DOS command prompt, follow these general steps:

■ If your computer has no hard disk, insert the diskette that contains the program into drive A:.

■ If your computer has a hard disk, use the DOS CHDIR or CD command to access the directory that contains the program that you want to run.

■ Type the name of the file name (without the extension) required to run the program.

To run programs using the DOS Shell (available only in DOS 4), follow these basic steps:

■ If your computer has no hard disk, insert the diskette that contains the program into drive A:.

■ If your computer has a hard disk, use the DOS Shell File System to access the directory that contains the program that you want to run.

■ From the DOS Shell File System Files Area, highlight the name of the file that the program is stored in, and then press Enter. (Mouse users double-click the file name.)

■ When the Open File dialog box for running the program appears, you can press Enter (or click the mouse on the ↵=Enter box) to proceed.

Managing Programs and Files

In Part 1 of this book, you learned how to perform essential DOS operations that you will probably use on a daily basis in your work with the computer. After reading those chapters, you should be able to find your way around any DOS computer, whether it be your personal computer or one you share with co-workers or other students.

Part 2 focuses on more specific techniques for actually putting the computer to work. The techniques discussed in this section are essential to using your computer effectively; you will use them regularly as you gain experience with your computer. For example, Part 2 covers the following topics:

- How to format new diskettes for use on your computer.
- How to copy and compare diskettes.
- How to create directories and subdirectories on your hard disk and diskettes to better organize your files.
- How to perform basic file operations such as copying, erasing, moving, and protecting files.
- How to use advanced "power tips" to increase your efficiency and make your work easier.

Managing Your Diskettes

 As you know from Chapter 1, diskettes store information and computer programs. If your computer does not have a hard disk, you must use diskettes to store all your computer files. Even if your computer has a hard disk, you still need to use diskettes to copy new programs onto your hard disk and to store backup copies of hard disk files.

This chapter focuses on techniques for preparing diskettes to store information, for making backup copies of files, and for comparing diskettes. The later sections of this chapter explain the important features of modern diskettes.

Performing the Exercises in This Chapter

To do the sample exercises in this chapter, you need at least two new, blank diskettes. If you do not have any blank diskettes available, you still might want to read through this chapter in order to get an overview of the formatting procedure; then, you can do the exercises later, when you have some blank diskettes.

Formatting Diskettes

When you purchase an application program for use on your computer, the package contains a diskette (or sometimes several diskettes) with the program's files stored on it. You can use these diskettes with your computer at any time, because they are already *formatted* (prepared) for use on your computer.

On the other hand, when you purchase a box of new, blank diskettes, those diskettes are *not* ready for use on your computer. They first must be *formatted*, using the techniques described in this chapter, before you can store files on them.

Formatting is required because different computers use different types of disk drives and operating systems. Although DOS is the most widely used operating system in the world, there are other operating systems available for microcomputers, and each requires a different diskette format. The formatting procedure prepares a new, blank diskette for use with a particular type of computer and a particular operating system.

Format with Caution!

WARNING: Never reformat the diskette that contains DOS or the hard disk on which you installed DOS; doing so permanently erases all of its stored files!

Be forewarned that formatting a diskette permanently erases all information that is stored on that diskette. If you format a diskette that already contains information or programs, you will no longer be able to access that information or use those programs. They are gone forever. Therefore, you need to exercise a great deal of caution when formatting diskettes.

In some situations, you might not be sure if a particular diskette has been formatted or not. However, there is a quick and easy way to tell the difference between formatted and unformatted diskettes. Merely ask DOS to show you the names of the files that are stored on the diskette. If the diskette is not already formatted, DOS displays a message informing you of this fact, as you'll see in the exercises that follow.

Checking a Diskette Before You Format It

Let's assume that you have a blank, unformatted diskette in hand, and you are ready to format it. Before you format the diskette, however, you should always double-check it to ensure that it does not already contain files. Regardless of which version of DOS you are using, always start with the following procedure:

Chapter 1 discussed the proper method for inserting and removing diskettes from the floppy disk drives.

■ If your computer has a hard disk, put the diskette that you want to format into disk drive A:.

■ If your computer does *not* have a hard disk, but it has two floppy disk drives, place the DOS Startup diskette in drive A:, and insert the diskette you want to format into drive B:.

If you are using DOS 4, and the DOS Shell is currently displayed on your screen, use the following steps to check the diskette:

1. From the DOS Shell **Start Programs** screen, select the File System option.

2. Access the disk drive that contains the diskette to be formatted by highlighting the disk drive name (either **A** or **B**) in the disk drive

section of the screen and then pressing Enter. (With a mouse, simply click the drive name.)

If you press F1 for help while the error message is displayed, DOS tells you that the probable cause of the error is that the diskette is not formatted. Press Esc to leave the help window.

3. If your screen displays a Warning window with the message `General Error` (as shown in Figure 6.1), you know you've attempted to access an unformatted diskette. It is now safe to proceed with the formatting procedure.

4. Remove the warning message from your screen by selecting option 2, `Do not try to read this disk again`, or by pressing the Esc key.

5. Skip the next three steps that follow.

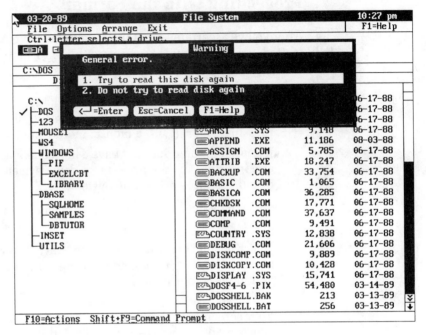

Figure 6.1. Warning message displayed when trying to access an unformatted diskette.

If you using DOS 3 (or the optional DOS 4 command prompt), use the following steps to check the diskette:

1. Use the DIR command, followed by the name of the drive that contains the diskette that you want to format, to see if the diskette contains any files. (For example, if the diskette to be formatted is in drive A:, type `DIR A:`. If the diskette to be formatted is in drive B: type `DIR B:`.)

2. Press Enter.

3. If your screen displays an error message, such as `General failure reading drive`, followed by the drive name, then the diskette is not yet formatted. Type the letter `A` to select Abort from the options that appear.

If you did not get an error (or warning) message when checking the diskette, then the diskette is already formatted and does not need to be reformatted. Furthermore, if you proceed with the formatting procedure on a diskette that already contains files, you will erase all of the files on that diskette. Instead, when you discover that a diskette has already been formatted, remove it from the drive, and replace it with a blank, unformatted diskette. Repeat the previous steps to check other diskettes until you find an unformatted diskette.

Proceeding with the Format

After you've ascertained that the diskette in drive A: or B: is indeed unformatted, you are ready to proceed with the formatting process. If you are using the DOS 4 DOS Shell, follow these steps:

If DOS displays an error message during the formatting procedure, refer to the Trouble-shooting section near the end of this chapter.

1. If your computer has a hard disk, change back to the hard disk by highlighting its name (usually C:) in the disk drives area and then pressing Enter. (With a mouse, merely click the drive name.)

2. If your computer does not have a hard disk, place the DOS Shell diskette in drive A:; then access that drive by selecting drive A from the disk drives area of the File System.

3. Press the F3 key to leave the File System and return to the **Start Programs** screen.

4. Select DOS Utilities... from the **Start Programs** screen, either by highlighting the option and pressing Enter or by double-clicking the option with your mouse.

Your screen now shows the DOS Utilities . . . screen; note that Format is the last option. You used the DOS Utilities . . . screen earlier in this book to set your computer's date and time. Now you will use this screen to format a diskette by following these steps:

5. Select the Format option, either by highlighting it and pressing Enter or by double-clicking it with your mouse.

6. When the Format Utility dialog box appears (as shown in Figure 6.2), it initially suggests a disk drive for formatting (either a: or b:).

7. If the suggested drive is *not* the one containing the diskette you want to format, simply type the name of the drive that does contain the diskette (either A: or B:). Use the Backspace, arrow, and Delete (Del) keys to make changes or corrections, as necessary.

8. Press Enter, or use your mouse to click once on the ↵=Enter box.

9. Skip the next four steps that follow.

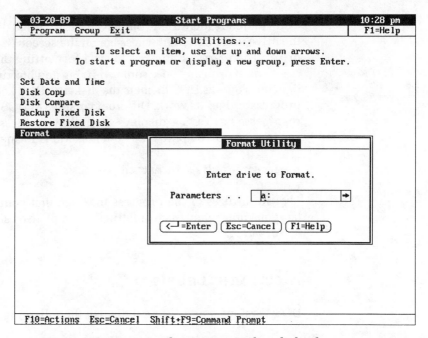

```
 03-20-89                    Start Programs                  10:28 pm
 Program  Group  Exit                                        F1=Help
                          DOS Utilities...
            To select an item, use the up and down arrows.
           To start a program or display a new group, press Enter.

 Set Date and Time
 Disk Copy
 Disk Compare
 Backup Fixed Disk
 Restore Fixed Disk
 Format
                              ┌──────────── Format Utility ────────────┐
                              │                                          │
                              │          Enter drive to Format.          │
                              │                                          │
                              │     Parameters . .  │a:              │→│ │
                              │                                          │
                              │   (<─┘=Enter) (Esc=Cancel) (F1=Help)    │
                              └──────────────────────────────────────────┘



 F10=Actions  Esc=Cancel  Shift+F9=Command Prompt
```

Figure 6.2. The Format Utility dialog box.

If you are using DOS 3 or the optional DOS 4 command prompt, follow these steps to start the formatting process:

1. If your computer has a hard disk, access the root directory by typing CD \ and pressing Enter.

2. If your computer does not have a hard disk, insert your DOS diskette in drive A:. (If you are using DOS 4, insert the DOS Shell diskette in drive A:.)

3. Type the FORMAT command followed by the name of the drive that contains the diskette that you want to format. For example, to format the diskette in drive A: type FORMAT A:. If the diskette to be formatted is in drive B:, type FORMAT B:.

4. Press Enter.

At this point, DOS displays a message similar to the one below. (Your message reflects the drive name you specified in the dialog box, in place of x.)

```
Insert new diskette for drive x
and press ENTER when ready...
```

Be sure to follow the next instruction carefully whenever you format diskettes, so that you do not inadvertently format the wrong diskette.

You've already identified your new (unformatted) diskette; now, insert it in the drive indicated in the message on the screen (if it is not already in that drive). Then, press Enter (←) to start formatting the diskette.

The drive light goes on when the disk drive is in use. Never remove a diskette when the drive light is on.

You'll probably hear some whirring and buzzing—after the disk drive light goes on—as DOS formats the diskette. DOS keeps you informed of its progress as does its work. Different versions of DOS present different progress messages. DOS 4 displays the following message (the n number advances toward 100 percent as the diskette is formatted):

`n percent of disk formatted`

Regardless of the progress message that your screen displays, DOS lets you know when the formatting is complete by showing a message such as `Format complete`.

Electronic Labels

DOS Versions 4 and 3.3 next display the following message:

`Volume label (11 characters, ENTER for none)? _`

A *volume label* (also called an *electronic label*) is simply a brief descriptive title (no more than 11 characters long) that you can store on the diskette. This label appears on your screen during certain DOS operations and is useful for reminding you of the contents of the diskette. However, the label is entirely optional, and it has no effect on your use of the diskette. For now, skip the volume label option by pressing Enter.

Available Diskette Space

Next, DOS displays the number of bytes of disk space available on the newly formatted diskette. If DOS encountered any flawed areas on the diskette while it was formatting, is disables those areas so that they cannot store files. This prevents the flawed areas from corrupting data or making certain files unreadable later.

Depending on the version of DOS you are using, your screen might also display information about *allocation units* and a *volume serial number*. You don't need to be concerned about these items now. (Chapter 15 discusses some of these "technical details.")

Finally, DOS displays the prompt:

`Format another (Y/N)?`

This last prompt lets you know that you can format another diskette merely by typing a Y. If you type N (for No) DOS knows that you are finished, and it ends the FORMAT program. For now, simply type the letter **N** (for No), and then press Enter.

If you are using the DOS Shell, the screen displays the message `Press any key to continue....` Press a key to return to the DOS Utilities . . . screen. To get back to the **Start Programs** Main Group screen, press Esc.

The new diskette is now formatted and ready for use with your computer. However, unlike the DOS Startup diskette, this new diskette can only be used to store files; it cannot be used to start your computer. It is possible to format a new diskette so that it *can* be used to start a computer, but you don't need to be concerned about this yet. (When you do need further information on this topic in the future, see the FORMAT and SYS command references in Appendix B.)

At this point, however, you've learned how to format a diskette for use with your computer. Remember, when you buy a box of new diskettes, they must be formatted before you can use them. But one last word of warning: Never format diskettes that already contain files (such as the diskettes that come with an application software package).

Copying Diskettes

As mentioned earlier in this chapter, you can use formatted diskettes to make backups (copies) of the files on a hard disk or for storing data from computers without a hard disk. Occasionally, you might also want to make a copy of an entire diskette—either as an extra (archival) backup or as a means of sharing data with co-workers.

Some application programs are stored on copy-protected diskettes to prevent users from giving away free copies of the program. These diskettes cannot be copied.

DOS provides a utility that allows you to make an exact duplicate of any diskette that is not copy-protected. This same utility can also format a new diskette (if necessary) before it makes the copy.

When you copy a diskette, DOS needs to know which drive contains the *source* diskette and which contains the *destination* (or *target*) diskette. As the names suggest, the source of the copy is the diskette that contains the files you want to copy; the destination (or target) diskette is the blank diskette that you want to copy the files to. Figure 6.3 illustrates this concept.

If you use a DOS diskette to start your computer, use the Disk Copy utility to make some extra backup copies of your startup diskette.

Note that the Disk Copy utility can only copy an entire diskette to another diskette of the same *media*. That is, you cannot use the Disk Copy utility to copy from a hard disk to a diskette or from a 5.25-inch diskette to a 3.5-inch diskette. Nor can you use the Disk Copy utility to copy files between low (or double) density, and high density, disks (see "Diskette Storage Capacities" later in this chapter for a definition of disk density). Chapter 8 discusses techniques for copying files among various types of disks.

To practice using the Disk Copy utility, select a diskette (such as one of your DOS diskettes) to copy, and get a new, unformatted diskette to store the copy on. Then, follow the next series of instructions, according to the version of DOS that you are using.

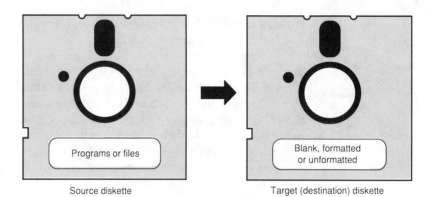

Source diskette   Target (destination) diskette

Figure 6.3. Files are copied from the source
diskette to the destination diskette.

If you are using DOS 4 and the **Start Programs** screen is currently
displayed, follow these steps to start the Disk Copy utility:

1. If your computer doesn't have a hard disk, insert your DOS Shell diskette into diskette drive A:.

2. From the **Start Programs** Main Group screen, select `DOS Utili-`
   `ties....`

3. From the DOS Utilities . . . screen, which appears next, select `Disk`
   `Copy`.

This displays a dialog box for the Disk Copy utility, as shown in Figure 6.4. The dialog box suggests possible source and destination drives, but
you can change these suggestions simply by typing over them. Use the
usual Backspace, Delete (or Del), ←, and → keys to make corrections, as
described in the next steps:

Be sure to separate the
source and destination
diskette drives with a
blank space.

4. If your computer has only one floppy disk drive (or two or more non-
   matching disk drives), change the suggested source and destination
   drives to `a: a:` by typing over the suggested drive names.

5. If your computer has two matching floppy disk drives, leave the suggested source and destination as `a: b:`.

7. Press Enter (or click the `←┘=Enter` box with your mouse).

8. Skip the next four steps.

If you are using DOS 3 or the optional DOS 4 command prompt, follow
these steps to start the Disk Copy utility:

1. If your computer does not have a hard disk drive, insert your DOS
   diskette in drive A:. (Insert the Shell diskette if you are using DOS 4.)

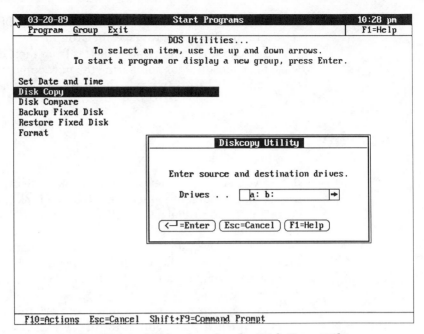

Figure 6.4. Dialog box for the Disk Copy utility.

2. If your computer has a hard disk, access the root directory by typing CD \ and pressing Enter.

3. Type the DISKCOPY command, then by the name of the drive that contains the source diskette, then the name of the drive that contains the destination diskette. Separate the two drive names with a blank space (by pressing the Spacebar). For example, if your computer has two matching floppy disk drives, type the command DISKCOPY A: B: or, if your computer has only one floppy disk drive, type the command DISKCOPY A: A:.

4. Press Enter.

Additional messages that appear on the screen depend on what type of diskette you are copying, and whether or not you are using one disk drive or two. After DOS tells you to insert the source and destination diskettes, simply follow the instructions as they appear on the screen. Always be sure to insert the source and destination diskettes into the correct drives.

If you encounter a problem during the Disk Copy procedure, refer to the Troubleshooting section near the end of this chapter.

If you are copying using a single diskette drive, you might see the messages Insert SOURCE diskette... and Insert TARGET diskette several times. Follow the instructions exactly as they appear on the screen.

When the copy procedure is done, DOS presents the message Copy another diskette (Y/N)?. Type the letter N if you do not want to copy any other diskettes. Then, as indicated on the screen, press any key. (If you are using DOS 4, you can also press Esc to leave the DOS Utilities . . . screen to return to the **Start Programs** Main Group.)

You can now remove all diskettes from their disk drives. Next, you'll learn the procedure for comparing the new copy of the Startup diskette to the original diskette—to verify that the copy was accurate.

Comparing Diskettes

You can use the COMP command, discussed in Appendix B, to compare data stored on different types of disks.

Before you store your newly copied backup diskette for safekeeping, you should take a moment to make sure that the Disk Copy program did its job correctly. To do so, you use the Disk Compare utility to compare the source and destination diskettes.

Like the Disk Copy utility, the Disk Compare utility can only be used to compare diskettes that are of the same type. That is, you cannot use Disk Compare to compare a hard disk to a diskette or a 5.25-inch diskette to a 3.5-inch diskette.

To demonstrate, we'll compare your original DOS Startup diskette to the copy you just made. Follow the next series of instructions, according to the version of DOS that you are using.

If you are using DOS 4 and the DOS Shell, follow these instructions to start the Disk Compare procedure:

1. If your computer doesn't have a hard disk, insert the Shell diskette in drive A:.

2. From the **Start Programs** Main Group screen, select `DOS Utilities....`

3. From the DOS Utilities . . . screen, select `Disk Compare`. the Disk Compare Utility (abbreviated *Diskcomp Utility*) dialog box appears on your screen, as shown in Figure 6.5. (The dialog box suggests `a: b:`, but you can change this by typing over the characters and by using the Backspace, Delete (or Del), and arrow keys.)

4. If your computer has two matching floppy disk drives, leave the dialog box suggestion at `a: b:`; otherwise, change the suggested drives to `a: a:` (making sure to separate the drive names with a blank space).

5. Press Enter or click on the `↵=Enter` box with your mouse.

6. Skip the next three steps.

1. If your computer doesn't have a hard disk, insert your DOS Startup diskette in drive A:.

2. If your computer has a hard disk, change to the root directory by typing `CD \` and pressing Enter.

3. Type the DISKCOMP command followed by the name(s) of the

drive(s) that you want to use to compare the diskettes. (Be sure to separate the drive names with a space.) For example, if your computer has only one floppy disk drive, type `DISKCOMP A: A:` or, if your computer has two matching disk drives, type `DISKCOMP A: B:`.

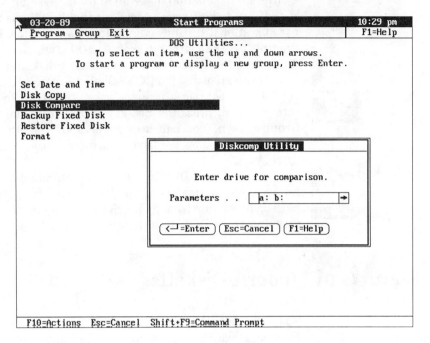

Figure 6.5. The Disk Compare Utility dialog box.

DOS initially shows some information about the type of diskette in use (which is not important at the moment); then, it presents instructions for inserting the diskettes to be compared. It refers to one of the diskettes as the FIRST diskette and the other as the SECOND diskette. Technically, it does not matter which disk you use as the FIRST, and which you use as the SECOND. But, if you consistently use the original disk as the FIRST, and the copy as the SECOND, you'll be able to tell which is which in case you have to recopy later.

If you are using a single disk drive for the comparison, DOS first asks you to insert the FIRST diskette in drive A:. After it finishes reading the data, it asks you to insert the SECOND diskette in drive A:. DOS might cycle through these prompts a few times. However, it pauses each time it asks, giving you a time to remove the diskette currently in the drive and replace it with the other diskette. To continue the comparison, press any key after you remove one diskette and insert another.

Diskette "tracks" and "sides" are discussed in Chapter 15.

If DOS finds any differences between the two diskettes, it displays the message `Compare error` followed by the track and side where the discrepancy occurs. Don't be concerned about the actual track and side numbers;

the fact that DOS displays the `Compare error` message is sufficient to let you know that the two diskettes are *not* identical. Therefore, your copied diskette will not function *exactly* like the original when you use it with your computer. You should then repeat the Disk Copy procedure (perhaps using a different destination diskette) to try to make an accurate copy.

If the diskettes are indeed identical, DOS displays the message `Compare Ok` after it finishes comparing the diskettes. DOS then displays the prompt `Compare another diskette (Y/N)?`, which asks if you want to repeat the procedure. Type `N` to stop comparing diskettes.

If you are using the DOS 4 Shell, the screen shows the message `Press any key to continue....` Press a key to return to the DOS Utilities . . . screen. Then, press the Esc key to return to the **Start Programs** Main Group screen. You can now remove all diskettes from their drives. If your computer does not have a hard disk, insert the DOS Shell diskette in drive A:.

If you started DiskCopy from the command prompt, you immediately return to the command prompt. Remove the diskettes you used in the comparison procedure from their drives. If your computer does not have a hard disk, insert the DOS diskette into drive A:.

Features of Modern Diskettes

So far, this book has discussed several terms for using diskettes with DOS. Now, let's take a moment to discuss the features of diskettes themselves in a little more detail.

Diskette Write Protection

Like cassette and VCR tapes, diskettes can be used in either of the following two modes:

Read/Write: You can format the diskette and freely store, retrieve, and erase information on it.

Write-Protected: You can only read files (information) from the diskette. You cannot reformat it, nor can you change, delete, or add new information to the diskette.

In most cases, you use diskettes in their read/write status. However, when you want to be sure that the information on a diskette is not inadvertently altered or destroyed, you can change its status to write-protected (also called *read-only* status).

You change the status of a 5.25-inch diskette to write-protected by covering the notch in the side of the disk with a small adhesive tab. (These tabs are usually included in a new box of diskettes.) Figure 6.6 illustrates the write-protect notch of a 5.25-inch diskette and shows how the adhesive tab fits over it.

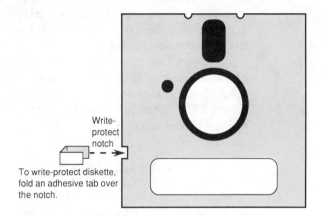

Figure 6.6. Write-protection on a 5.25-inch diskette.

The 3.5-inch diskettes usually include one or two write-protect notches that can be opened or closed by moving a sliding door. If the door is closed, the diskette has read/write status. Opening the door changes the status of the diskette to write-protected, as shown in Figure 6.7. (With diskettes that have two doors, you must open both doors to fully write-protect the disk, and you must close both doors to provide full read/write access.)

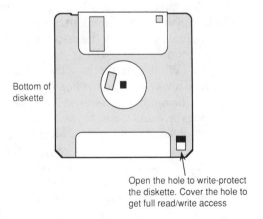

Figure 6.7. Write-protection on a 3.5-inch diskette.

Note that some diskettes, particularly those in application software packages, have no write-protect notch or door. These diskettes are "permanently" write-protected so that you can never inadvertently erase files stored on the diskette.

Diskette Storage Capacities

As discussed in Chapter 1, diskettes come in two basic sizes: 3.5-inch and 5.25-inch. In addition to the difference in physical sizes, these diskettes also differ in the amount of information that they can store. The storage capacity of modern diskettes is determined mostly by how densely (tightly) the diskette stores information.

Table 6.1 compares the storage capacities of diskettes—both in terms of the number of files that a diskette can hold and the number of bytes (characters) it can hold. Remember, KB is the abbreviation for kilobyte (about 1,000 characters), and MB is the abbreviation for megabyte (about 1 million characters).

Table 6.1. Comparison of various diskette sizes and storage capacities.

Diskette size	Density	Maximum Files	Maximum Bytes
5.25-inch	Low(or Double)	112	360KB
5.25-inch	High	224	1.2MB
3.5-inch	Low	112	720KB
3.5-inch	High	224	1.44MB

Which type of diskette you can use is determined by the disk drives you have in your computer. The physical size difference (5.25-inch versus 3.5-inch) of diskettes is obvious from looking at the diskette (as shown in Chapter 1). But you might not be sure of the capacities of your drives. If you are in doubt, check the documentation that came with the computer, or ask your computer dealer.

When you purchase blank 3.5-inch diskettes for use in your computer, be forewarned that the box that the diskettes are packaged in might be a bit confusing; this is because 3.5-inch diskettes are often sold in two sizes—1-megabyte and 2-megabyte. Note that this apparently conflicts with Table 6.1, which states 3.5-inch diskettes have either a capacity of 720KB or 1.44MB.

However, the 1-megabyte and 2-megabyte capacities printed on the package refer to *unformatted* diskettes. The required formatting procedure stores information on the diskette that occupies space, thus leaving the diskettes with reduced storage capacities.

Diskette Compatibility

Some leeway is provided in using diskettes of different storage capacities within different disk drives. The basic rule of thumb is that a disk drive can use diskettes that are equal to, or less than, the drive's own total capacity.

The 5.25-inch diskettes are also sometimes rated as single- or double-sided. However, because all IBM microcomputers (and compatibles) use double-sided diskettes, single-sided 5.25-inch diskettes are rarely sold.

That is, a high capacity drive can read both high-capacity and low-capacity diskettes. A low-capacity disk drive, however, can only use low-capacity diskettes.

However, if you use a high-capacity drive to copy files to a low-capacity diskette, you might not be able to use that diskette in a low-capacity drive. Several factors determine the compatibility between drive capacities and diskette capacities, including the version of DOS that you are using. For complete information on this topic, see the FORMAT command reference in Appendix B.

Tracks, Sectors, and Other Strange Terms

When you use DOS to format, copy, or compare diskettes, you see messages on your screen that provide information about *tracks*, *sectors*, *sides*, *allocation units*, and other terms that refer to the structure of the diskette in use. Be assured that although DOS occasionally displays such information on your screen, you don't need to be concerned about any of these terms now. They all refer to "structures" that DOS handles automatically "behind the scenes."

Why then does DOS present information about tracks, sectors, and other technical issues, if that information is not important to users? Well, the truth is—the information *is* useful, but only to a handful of computer engineers and software developers. (These people, however, probably comprise less than 1 percent of all computer users.)

Be assured that, just as you can drive a car without knowing the technical inner-workings of its transmission and voltage regulator, you can use your computer for years to come without knowing anything about tracks, sectors, and allocation units. However, the more you use your computer, the more interested you probably will become in some of these technical issues, including how your computer manages information at its most technical level. When your curiosity gets the better of you, feel free to read Chapter 15 to find out just how the computer "does it."

Troubleshooting

DOS 4 users: Remember that you can press the Help key (F1) for "instant help" whenever the error message window is displayed on the screen.

Should you encounter a problem while doing any of the exercises in this chapter, DOS probably will display one of the following error messages. Locate the error message that is displayed on your screen, and try the recommended solutions:

■ `Attempted write-protect violation`: You tried to copy data onto (or format) a write-protected diskette. If you are using 5.25-inch diskettes, remove the write-protect tab (if possible), or use a different diskette. If you are using 3.5-inch diskettes, close the write-protect slot(s)

The exercises presented in this book assume a standard organization of DOS files; however, your computer might be organized differently.

(if possible), or use another diskette. (See the section "Diskette Write Protection" in this chapter for more information.)

■ **Bad Command or File Name:** You either misspelled the command name, or the program you attempted to run is not available on the current drive or directory. If the problem is simply one of misspelling, retype the command (using proper spelling) and press Enter.

If you are sure you typed the command correctly, then the program is not available on the current drive or directory. The Format, Disk Copy, and Disk Compare utilities described in this chapter require that DOS have access to the following programs (files): FORMAT.COM, DISKCOPY.COM, and DISKCOMP.COM. Use the general techniques described in Chapter 5 to search other diskettes or hard disk directories for the appropriate files. When you locate the appropriate file, start the utility from that diskette or directory.

■ **Drive letter must be specified:** You tried to use the FORMAT utility without specifying a disk drive. Try again, but be sure to specify either **A:** or **B:** as the drive to format.

■ **Drive types or diskette types not compatible:** You tried to use incompatible disk drives or incompatible diskette types during a Disk Copy or Disk Compare procedure. Try using one diskette drive (for example, **a: a:**) rather than two (for example, **a: b:**). If that does not work, the diskettes are incompatible and cannot be copied or compared.

■ **Invalid drive specification:** You specified a disk drive that does not exist on your computer. For example, you specified drive B: with a computer that has no drive named B:, or you omitted a drive name where one is required.

■ **File Not Found:** You tried to view the names of files on a diskette that has no files stored on it, or you used an ambiguous file name that does not match any of the file names on the diskette. (Note that the diskette is already formatted for use, and you don't need to reformat it.)

■ **Parameter format not correct:** Most likely, you omitted a parameter or left out a blank space. For example, when using the Disk Copy and Disk Comp utilities, entering **a:a:** or **b:b:** produces this error because the drive names are not separated by a space. Try the command again, this time inserting the required blank space between the drive names (for example, **a: a:**, or **b: b:**).

■ **Required parameter missing -:** You did not completely specify optional parameters. For example, you must include a drive name with the Format utility, and you must provide two drive names (separated by a blank space) with the Disk Copy and Disk Compare utilities.

■ **Write protect error:** Same as **Attempted write-protect violation** above.

Summary

This chapter provided useful techniques to help you use diskettes with your computer. Following is a summary of these techniques:

- New diskettes must be formatted before you can use them on your computer. Be sure that you format *only* diskettes that do not already contain programs or other files.

- To write-protect 3.5-inch diskettes—thereby preventing files from being modified, changed, or erased—slide the write-protect door(s) to the "open" position.

- To write-protect 5.25-inch diskettes—thereby preventing files from being modified, changed, or erased—cover the write-protect notch with an adhesive tab.

- For detailed information about diskette and drive compatibilities, see the reference to the FORMAT command in Appendix B.

- To format a diskette from the DOS command prompt, enter the FORMAT command followed by the name of the drive that contains the diskette to be formatted.

- To copy a diskette from the DOS command prompt, enter the DISKCOPY command followed by the names of the source and destination disk drives.

- To compare diskettes from the command prompt, enter the DISKCOMP command followed by the names of the drives used for comparing.

- DOS 4 users can format diskettes by selecting DOS Utilities... from the **Start Programs** Main Group screen and then Format from the DOS Utilities . . . screen.

- To use the DOS Shell to make an exact copy of a diskette, select DOS Utilities...from the **Start Programs** Main Group, and then select Disk Copy from the DOS Utilities . . . screen.

- To use the DOS Shell to compare diskettes after copying to ensure that they are indeed identical, select DOS Utilities... from the **Start Programs** Main Group Screen, and then select Disk Compare from the DOS Utilities . . . screen.

Managing Your Hard Disk

 Chapter 4 discussed ways in which your computer's hard disk might already have files organized into directories and subdirectories, and it showed techniques for searching those directories and subdirectories. This chapter focuses on techniques that let you create your own directories and offers tips on how to best organize a hard disk (or high-capacity diskettes) for quick and easy access to your files.

Even though directories and subdirectories are used primarily on hard disks, they can be used on floppies as well. Therefore, even if your computer doesn't have a hard disk, you may want to experiment with some of these techniques. To do so, put a formatted diskette in drive A: or B: of your computer. Then, anywhere that you see a reference to hard disk drive C:, substitute drive A: or B:, (depending on which drive you want to use).

Naming Directories

As you might recall from Chapter 4, a directory on a disk is a place in which you can store files (like a drawer in a file cabinet). Each directory can have a name as many as eight characters long. No directory name can contain blank spaces or any of the following characters: . " / \ [ ] ; : * < > | + = , ?.

Rather than remember all the symbols that you *cannot* use in directory names, it's easier simply to limit yourself to using letters, numbers, underscores (_), and hyphens (-) in directory names.

Also, do not use any of the following names as directory names—DOS uses these as the names of *devices* (as you'll learn later in this book):

CLOCK$ CON   AUX   COM1   COM3   COM3
CON   LPT1   LPT2   LPT3   NUL   PRN

Table 7.1 lists examples of valid and invalid directory names.

Table 7.1. Examples of valid and invalid directory names.

Directory Name	Status
MYBOOKS	valid
ACCT_REC	valid
ACCTSREC	valid
GL	valid
UTILS	valid
1989_TAX	valid
ACCT REC	invalid (contains a blank space)
ACCT:REC	invalid (contains colon)
GENERAL_LEDGER	invalid (too long)
PRN	invalid (same as device name)

You can use any combination of uppercase and lowercase letters when typing in a directory name. However, when DOS displays the name, it automatically converts lowercase letters to uppercase.

A disk may also contain subdirectories, which are also places to store files. However, whereas directories branch off "root," subdirectories branch off other directories. Thus, subdirectories are "beneath" directories in the directory tree. Subdirectory names follow the same rules as directory names. However, a subdirectory name is preceded by the higher-level directory name and a backslash.

For example, ACCTSREC\QTR1 refers to a subdirectory named QTR1, which is beneath the directory named ACCTSREC. Note that the backslash *separates* the two names; it is not *part* of either name.

Simplifying the Terminology

Before you continue your exploration of directories and subdirectories, let's take a moment to simplify the terminology a bit. To begin with, the only difference between a directory and subdirectory is that a subdirectory *name* appears beneath a directory *name* on a directory tree. Other than that one small difference, directories and subdirectories are basically the same thing—a place on a disk in which you can store files.

However, referring to something like \ACCSREC\QTR1 as both a directory, and subdirectory, can be confusing. To simplify matters, DOS uses the term *path*. This is actually a very descriptive name, because the series of directory and subdirectory names actually do describe a path to follow

As you gain experience with DOS, you'll see that many messages on your screen also use the terms directory, subdirectory, and path interchangeably.

to find a particular file. For example, the path \ACCSREC\QTR1 indicates that in order to get to the QTR1 directory, DOS must follow a path that starts at the root directory (\), then go down one level to the ACCSREC directory, then down one more level to the QTR1 directory. Similarly, the path \SALES\BOB tells DOS that in order to find the BOB directory, DOS would start from the root directory (\), move down one level to the SALES directory, and then down one more level to the BOB directory.

Creating a Directory

If you get an error message while doing any of the exercises in this chapter, refer to the Troubleshooting section near the end of this chapter, or, if you are using the DOS Shell, press F1 for help.

It's very easy to create a directory on a disk. But there is one important point that you need to keep in mind when creating your own directories: *When you create a new directory, DOS automatically creates it below the current directory.*

As you know, the root directory is the highest-level directory in any directory tree. All directories that you create are below the root directory in the tree. In the exercise that follows, you will create a new directory, named PRACTICE, on hard disk drive C:. This directory will be one level beneath the root directory. Follow the appropriate steps for your version of DOS:

If you are using DOS 4 and the **Start Programs** Main Group is displayed on your screen, follow these steps to create the PRACTICE directory:

If you have a mouse, you can use the point-and-click method to perform Steps 1-7.

1. Select the `File System` option.

2. Be sure that you are accessing hard disk drive C: by selecting drive `C` from the Drives Area.

3. Press the Tab key to move the highlight to the Directory Tree Area of the screen.

4. Select the root directory by moving the highlight to `C:\` at the top of the tree and pressing Enter.

5. Press F10 to activate the Action Bar.

6. Move the highlight to the `File` option, and press Enter to pull down the File menu.

7. Highlight the `Create Directory...` option (as shown in Figure 7.1), and then select that option by pressing Enter.

8. When you see the Create Directory dialog box, type the new directory name `PRACTICE` (as shown in Figure 7.2).

9. Press Enter to complete the command to create the directory. Note that the new directory name, PRACTICE, is in the directory tree, as in the example shown in Figure 7.3.

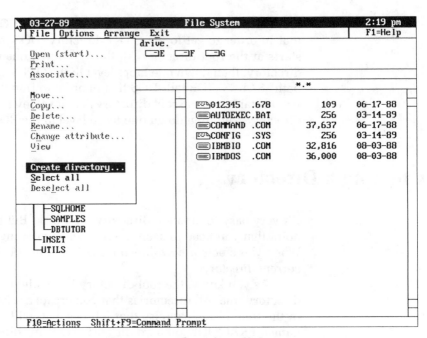

Figure 7.1. The File pull-down menu.

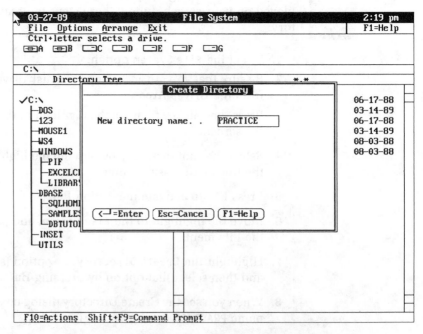

Figure 7.2. The Create Directory dialog box with
a new directory name.

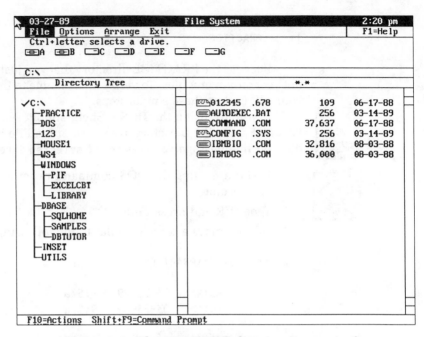

```
 03-27-89                    File System                    2:20 pm
 File  Options  Arrange  Exit                              F1=Help
 Ctrl+letter selects a drive.
   A     B    C    D    E    F    G

 C:\
       Directory Tree                            *.*

 ✓C:\                             012345  .678        109    06-17-88
  ├─PRACTICE                      AUTOEXEC.BAT        256    03-14-89
  ├─DOS                           COMMAND .COM     37,637    06-17-88
  ├─123                           CONFIG  .SYS        256    03-14-89
  ├─MOUSE1                        IBMBIO  .COM     32,816    08-03-88
  ├─WS4                           IBMDOS  .COM     36,000    08-03-88
  ├─WINDOWS
  │  ├─PIF
  │  ├─EXCELCBT
  │  └─LIBRARY
  ├─DBASE
  │  ├─SQLHOME
  │  ├─SAMPLES
  │  └─DBTUTOR
  ├─INSET
  └─UTILS




 F10=Actions  Shift+F9=Command Prompt
```

Figure 7.3. The PRACTICE directory is now in the
directory tree.

If you are using DOS 3 or the optional DOS 4 command prompt, you use the MKDIR (often abbreviated as MD) command (both are short for Make Directory) to create a new directory. To ensure that the new directory is created one level below the root directory, follow these steps exactly:

1. Be sure that you are accessing the hard disk by typing C: and pressing Enter.

2. To start from the root directory, type the command CD \ and press Enter.

3. Next, type the command MD PRACTICE and press Enter.

4. To view the new directory tree, type TREE and press Enter.

The TREE display shows the names of all the directories and subdirectories on the disk. Depending on the version of DOS you are using, DOS displays the new directory name (with all other existing directory names) either in the format:

Remember, you can enter the command TREE >PRN to print the directory tree.

```
DIRECTORY PATH LISTING...
Path: \PRACTICE
Sub-directories: None
```

or the format:

```
C:.
|-----PRACTICE
```

Because the PRACTICE directory that you just created is new, it does not yet contain any files. To verify this, change to the directory and see for yourself. Follow these simple steps:

If you are using the DOS 4 Shell, simply select the directory name PRACTICE from the Directory Tree Area of the File System. The Files Area displays the message No files in the selected directory.

1. If you are using the DOS command prompt, type CD PRACTICE and press Enter.

2. Type DIR and press Enter.

3. DOS displays a screen similar to the following:

```
Directory of C:\PRACTICE

  .           <DIR>     03-23-89    9:57a
  ..          <DIR>     03-23-89    9:57a

         2 File(s) xxxxxxxxx bytes free
```

Remember, you can enter the command PROMPT PG to make DOS show the name of the current directory.

The bottom line of the DIR command says that there are *2 File(s)* on this newly created directory, and it appears as though these are named . and .. However, . and .. are not truly files. Instead they are shortcut names for the current and parent (higher-level) directory. You will learn how to use these shortcut names in Chapter 9. But for the time being, you need not be concerned about the . and .. symbols displayed by the DIR command.

Creating Subdirectories

As mentioned earlier, DOS automatically places any new directory that you create "beneath" the current directory in the tree. Therefore, to create a subdirectory, you merely change to the *parent* directory (the one that you want to be above the new subdirectory), and follow the same steps that you did to create the PRACTICE directory, but using the new subdirectory names.

As an example, let's create a subdirectory named TEST beneath the PRACTICE directory. Follow the appropriate procedure for your version of DOS.

If you are using the DOS Shell and the File System is displayed on your screen, follow these steps:

1. If you have not done so already, change to the PRACTICE directory by selecting its name from the Directory Tree Area.

2. Press F10 to access the Action Bar.

3. Select the _File_ option by highlighting it and pressing Enter.

4. Select `Create Directory....`

5. Type the subdirectory name `TEST` and press Enter.

Note that the new directory name is indented beneath the PRACTICE directory name in the Directory Tree, as follows:

```
|
|--PRACTICE
   |---TEST
```

If you are using the command prompt, follow these steps:

1. If you have not already done so, change to the PRACTICE directory by typing `CD \PRACTICE` and pressing Enter.

2. Type the command `MD TEST` and press Enter to create the new directory.

3. To view the directory tree, type TREE and press Enter.

Depending on your version of DOS, the new TEST directory is displayed beneath the PRACTICE directory either in the following format:

```
DIRECTORY PATH LISTING...
Path: \PRACTICE
Sub-directories: TEST
Path: \PRACTICE TEST
Sub-directories: none
```

or in the format:

```
|
|--PRACTICE
   |---TEST
```

You will use the new directories that you created in this chapter to practice some file management techniques in the next chapter. However, now that you know how to create directories, there are some general tips and techniques that you should keep in mind before you start organizing your own hard disk into new directories. These general tips are discussed in the sections that follow.

Tips for Creating an Efficient Directory Tree

The whole purpose of your dividing a hard disk into directories is to organize your files for easier access. If you create directories haphazardly, your files eventually become disorganized and difficult to keep track of. To avoid making a maze of your hard disk, keep in mind the following tips as you create your directory structure.

Tip #1: Don't Clutter the Root Directory

The initial DOS installation procedure automatically creates the root directory and stores a few files on it. Because the root directory is already there when you start using your computer, you might be tempted to use it as a sort of dumping ground for all your files or, perhaps, for those "stray" files that do not seem to belong in any other directory.

However, the only files that really need to be in the root directory are AUTOEXEC.BAT, CONFIG.SYS, and a few others that DOS placed there when it was installed. (The purpose of these DOS files in the root directory is discussed in Chapters 10 and 11.)

Cluttering the root directory with extra files is like throwing manila file folders into a big, unmarked, cardboard box. After you install DOS on your computer and DOS stores its own files in the root directory, let DOS keep the root directory to itself. Before creating and storing your own files, make your own directories for related programs and files. In other words, start getting organized from the beginning. Rather than using a cardboard box, store all your information in clearly marked file drawers (that is, directories).

Tip #2: Keep All DOS Programs in a Single Directory

This tip is similar to tip #1: Once DOS stores its files in certain directories, just leave those files alone, and do not use those directories to store other files. For example, installing DOS 4 on your computer automatically creates a directory named DOS. The installation process also stores most DOS files in this directory.

There is no reason for you to move or copy DOS files from the DOS directory to other directories. Nor is there any reason for you to store other files in the DOS directory. Again, when you start creating and storing your own files, create and use your own directories.

Tip #3: Install Application Programs on the Recommended Directories

Whenever you buy an application program, the manual that comes with that program usually suggests that you create a unique disk or unique directory on your hard disk to store that program on. (In fact, the program might come with an automatic *installation program* that creates the appropriate directory for you on a hard disk.)

When installing an application program on a hard disk, use the directory name that the program's documentation recommends. Otherwise, you might find it difficult to use that program's manuals, which probably assume that you followed their recommendations.

Tip #4: Make the Directory Tree Broad and Shallow

DOS allows you to be creative when constructing a directory tree. You can create subdirectories beneath directories, sub-subdirectories beneath sub-directories, and so on. However, the "deeper" you go in this scheme, the longer the path names become.

For example, you could create a series of subdirectories with a path name DBASE\BOB\PROJECTS\UPSALES; this involves four separate directories. However, when you want to change directories at the command prompt, or when you want to identify the location of a file in UPSALES, you will often have to type this entire path name. Trust me, it won't be long before you grow tired of typing **DBASE\BOB\PROJECTS\UPSALES**.

A second reason for keeping the directory tree broad and shallow is to provide easy access to all related files. For example, let's suppose that you have purchased two application programs for use with your computer: dBASE IV (a database management program) and Lotus 1-2-3 (a spreadsheet program). You store these programs in the directories that the manuals advise—DBASE and 123, respectively.

Now, let's assume that you need to create two new directories, one for storing your accounts receivable data, and one for inventory data. You decide to name these directories ACCT_REC and INVENTRY. Let's further assume that you will use the dBASE IV program to handle some information in both accounts receivable and inventory data and Lotus 1-2-3 to handle the rest of the data.

Given all this information, you have two options for creating the directory tree. A "deep" structure would look like the tree shown in Figure 7.4, with the directories containing accounts receivable and inventory files beneath the program directories. The problem with that directory tree is that it artificially divides the accounts receivable and inventory data into four separate directories: DBASE\ACCT_REC, DBASE\INVENTRY, 123\ACCT_REC, and \123\INVENTRY.

Figure 7.5 shows a better directory tree for organizing the various programs and your business data. Notice that each directory is on the same level (that is, the tree is shallower than the one in Figure 7.4).

The shallower directory tree has the distinct advantage of organizing both the accounts receivable files and the inventory files into their own clearly-named directories. The files are not artificially divided into subdi-

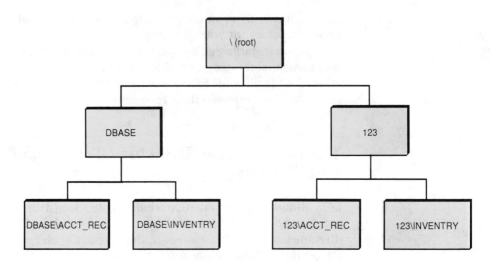

Figure 7.4. A deep directory tree.

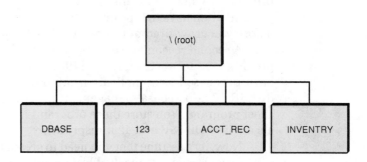

Figure 7.5. The preferred shallow directory tree.

rectories that are dependent on individual application programs. If you change inventory data, you need only do so on one directory.

Given this new tip, you might be wondering when you would ever want to create a subdirectory. Actually, using a subdirectory makes sense when all of the files on it are relevant *only* to the parent directory. For example, when you install the dBASE IV program on your computer, the installation process automatically creates several directories, including DBASE, DBASE\SAMPLES, and DBASE\DBTUTOR.

This organization makes sense because the SAMPLES and DB-TUTOR directories contain files that can be used *only* with dBASE IV. There is no artificial breakup of files, as there was in the example involving the ACCT_REC and INVENTRY directories, which were both used by the dBASE and 1-2-3 programs. Figure 7.6 illustrates this concept.

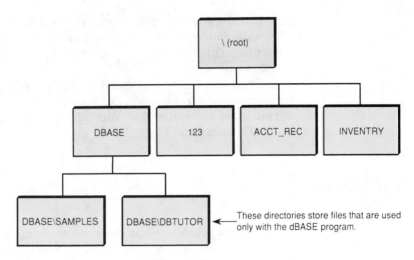

Figure 7.6. The SAMPLES and DBTUTOR directories contain files that are used *only* with dBASE IV.

Tip #5: Use the PATH Command to Simplify Access to Programs

As you already know, DOS normally requires that you access the directory that contains a program before you use that program. If you have not changed to the correct directory when you try to run a program, DOS displays the error message Bad command or File Name because it cannot find the file that contains the program. This can indeed be an inconvenience.

Fortunately, DOS provides a simple and elegant way around this problem—the PATH command. In a nutshell, the PATH command tells DOS, "If you cannot find my program on *this* directory, check these other directories." For example, referring back to the shallow directory tree in Figure 7.5, suppose that you are currently accessing the INVENTRY directory, but you want to run the 1-2-3 program to manage your inventory data.

If you try to run 1-2-3 (or dBASE, for that matter) from the INVENTRY directory, DOS merely displays the Bad command or file name error because that program is not in the INVENTRY directory. However, if you first enter the command PATH C:\123; C:\DBASE at the command prompt, DOS "knows" that it also needs to check the directories named 123 and DBASE on drive C: before ending its search for the program. Hence, you'll be able to run your 1-2-3 and dBASE IV programs from any directory on the hard disk.

Once entered at the command prompt, the PATH command stays in effect for the entire current session (that is, until you turn off the computer). As an alternative to typing in the appropriate PATH command for your directory tree each time you turn on your computer, you can have DOS automatically enter the command for you as soon as you start the computer. This is by far the preferred method for using the PATH command.

Chapter 11 discusses specific steps for setting up a PATH command for your computer. For now, just keep in mind that this option is available to you. (Also, remember that Appendix B provides a complete reference to the PATH command.)

Troubleshooting

If you have a problem while creating, or changing to a directory, you will probably see one of the error messages below. Try the suggested solution for each error message.

■ `Access denied`: If you see this error message while trying to create a new directory from the DOS Shell, the directory name already exists. You cannot create two directories with the same name, so you cannot proceed with the command. (Press the Esc key to cancel the operation.)

■ `Directory already exists`: You tried to create a directory that already exists. DOS returns you to the prompt and doesn't allow you to proceed with the command.

■ `Invalid directory`: You tried to access a directory that does not exist or that does not exist beneath the current directory. Perhaps you merely misspelled the directory name in the command line. Try re-entering the command with the directory name spelled properly. If the problem persists, review Chapter 4, or study the CHDIR command reference in Appendix B.

■ `Invalid switch`: Most likely, you used a forward slash (/) rather than a backslash (\) in the command. Try again, this time using the correct backslash (\) character.

■ `Unable to create directory`: DOS displays this message when any one of the following errors occurs: 1) The directory that you tried to create already exists; 2) You tried to create a directory beneath a non-existent directory; or 3) You specified a directory name that contains invalid characters or has the same name as a reserved device.

Check the existing directory tree structure, using either the DOS 4 File System or the DOS 3 TREE command, to determine which error occurred in your situation. (If necessary, you might also want to refer to the MKDIR and CHDIR commands in Appendix B for more details.)

Summary

This chapter taught you specific techniques for creating directories and presented some general tips on how to best organize your own computer's directory tree.

- A directory name can be as many as eight characters long, cannot contain blank spaces or reserved device names, and should contain only letters, numbers, hyphens (-), and underscores (_).

- The terms *directory* and *subdirectory* are often used interchangeably, because each term refers to an area on the hard disk in which you store files. *Path* refers to the "route" (through various levels of directories) to files in subdirectories.

- When you create a new directory, DOS places that new directory beneath the current directory in the tree structure.

- To create a directory that is one level below the root directory, always begin by changing to the root directory.

- To create a new directory from the command prompt, first change to the parent directory, and then type MKDIR or MD followed by a blank space and the name of the new directory. Then, press Enter. (See the MKDIR reference in Appendix B for other optional methods.)

- To create a directory using the DOS Shell, first access the **File System** screen, and then change to the appropriate drive and parent directory. Then, press F10 to access the Action Bar, and select the Create Directory... option from the File pull-down menu. Type the name of the new directory and press Enter.

Managing Files

This chapter discusses how to manage your files by viewing, copying, erasing, moving, renaming, and protecting them. These general file management techniques will be useful in all your future work with your computer and DOS; in fact, you'll probably use some of these techniques every time you sit down at the keyboard.

If DOS 4 is installed on your computer, you can use the DOS Shell to perform file management operations. The basic procedure is as follows:

1. Access the File System.
2. Select a file (or files) for the operation.
3. Select the appropriate operation from the File pull-down menu.

Figure 8.1 illustrates the general procedure (discussed in more detail with each operation).

DOS 3 users (and, of course, DOS 4 users who prefer the command prompt) can use several built-in DOS commands for these operations, including COPY, RENAME, ERASE, and TYPE. Remember, "built-in" commands are available in DOS at any time, so you can perform these operations on any disk drive and in any directory.

Remember, if you have any problems when doing these exercises, you can refer to the Troubleshooting section near the end of the chapter. DOS 4 users can also press the F1 key for help whenever the F1=Help option is displayed on the screen.

Rules on Naming Files

When you start creating, copying, and renaming files, remember that DOS imposes certain restrictions on file names, and that all file names must abide by these rules. This holds true even if you create files with an application program, such as a spreadsheet, a database management system, or a word processor.

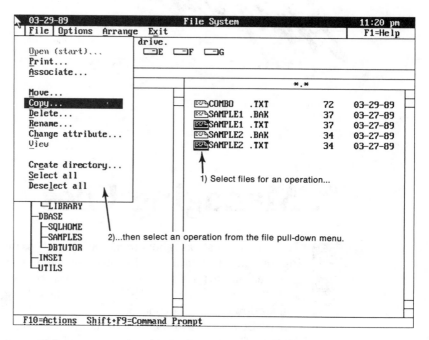

Figure 8.1. Performing file operations with the DOS 4 Shell.

The basic rules for creating files names (described briefly in Chapter 4) are as follows:

- The base name for the file can be no more than eight characters long and may not contain blank spaces.

- You can include an optional three-letter extension—preceded by a period—with any file name.

- You should restrict file names to only letters, numbers, hyphens (−), and underscores (_). (Use the period only to separate the base name from the extension.) The following characters can *never* be used in a file name: " . / \ [ ] : * < > | + : , ?

- Do not use any of these reserved device names as file names: CLOCK$ CON AUX COM1 COM2 COM3 CON LPT1 LPT2 LPT3 NUL PRN.

- Try to use *meaningful* file names that describe the contents of the file. For example, rather than assigning the file name X.DAT to your first-quarter 1990 data file, use the more meaningful file name QTR1-90.DAT.

- As much as possible, try to use a similar pattern of file names for related files. (For example, you might use QTR1-90.DAT,

QTR2-90.DAT, QTR3-90.DAT, and so on for files that store quarterly data.) This helps make it easier for you to manage the files as groups when copying, moving, or erasing them later.

■ Avoid using the file name extensions .BAT, .COM, and .EXE, as these are reserved for programs. (You'll learn how to create your own .BAT program files in Chapter 13.)

Examples of valid and invalid file names are presented in Table 8.1.

Table 8.1. Examples of valid, and invalid, file names.

File Name	Status
ACCT_REC.DAT	valid
X.ABC	valid (but not very descriptive)
LEDGER.WKS	valid
ABC-CO.LET	valid
1990SUMM.TXT	valid
READ.ME	valid
PRNT.TXT	valid
GENERAL-LEDGER.DAT	invalid (base name is too long)
MY LETTER.DOC	invalid (contains a blank space)
MY.LET.DOC	invalid (contains two periods)
PRN.TXT	invalid (PRN is a DOS device name)

File Name Extensions

You can assign any extension to a file name when you create a file. However, many application programs automatically assign their own extensions to file names. Some examples of commonly used file name extensions, and the types of information that those files hold, are listed in Table 8.2.

Table 8.2. Examples of commonly used file name extensions.

Extension	Contents
.BAT	A DOS "batch" program (discussed in Chapter 13)
.COM	A program that DOS can run
.EXE	A program that DOS can run
.TXT	Written text
.DOC	A document (written text)
.BAK	A backup (copy) of another file
.BAS	A BASIC program

Table 8.2. (cont.)

Extension	Contents
.WKS	A Lotus 1-2-3 (version 1) spreadsheet
.WK1	A Lotus 1-2-3 (version 2) spreadsheet
.XLS	A Microsoft Excel Spreadsheet
.MSP	A Microsoft Paint picture
.DBF	A dBASE database
.DB	A Paradox database
.OVL	An overlay file (discussed in Chapter 15)

Creating Sample Files

To perform some of the file management techniques in this chapter, you need to create a few simple practice files, named SAMPLE1.TXT and SAMPLE2.TXT. There are many ways to create files on your computer. I'll demonstrate a somewhat primitive technique in this chapter, only because the sample files are small and the technique is simple. As you gain experience with your computer, you'll probably want to use a word processor or the Edlin program (discussed in Chapter 10) to create larger text files and programs.

If your computer has a hard disk, place these practice files in the PRACTICE directory. If your computer does not have a hard disk, place the sample files on a blank, formatted diskette. To create these files, follow the appropriate steps for your particular computer:

1. If you are using DOS 4, press the F3 key until the Shell disappears and the command prompt appears.

2. If your computer has a hard disk, type C: and press Enter to access the hard disk. Then type CD \PRACTICE and press Enter to change to the PRACTICE directory.

3. If your computer does not have a hard disk, place a blank, formatted diskette in drive B:. Then, type B: and press Enter to access drive B:.

4. Type the command COPY CON SAMPLE1.TXT and press Enter.

5. Type the sentence This is the first sample text file. (Use the Backspace key to make corrections, if necessary.)

6. Press Enter after typing the sentence.

7. Press Ctrl-Z (hold down the Ctrl key and press the letter Z) or press F6. This displays a ^Z on your screen.

8. Press Enter again.

After DOS displays the message 1 File(s) copied, the command prompt reappears. DOS has copied the sentence you typed on the screen into a file named SAMPLE1.TXT. To create the second sample file, follow these steps:

1. Type `COPY CON SAMPLE2.TXT` and press Enter.
2. Type the sentence `I am the second sample text file`. (Again, use the Backspace key to make corrections, if necessary.)
3. Press Enter after typing the sentence.
4. Press Ctrl-Z (or F6) and then press Enter.

You have now created the two practice files you will use in later examples in this chapter. You did so by COPYing text from the CONsole (screen) to a file. But, don't be concerned about memorizing this technique, because you'll learn a more practical method for creating files in Chapter 10.

 If you are using DOS 4, return to the familiar DOS Shell now. If you have a hard disk, merely type the command `DOSSHELL` and press Enter. If you do not have a hard disk, be sure your Shell diskette is in drive A:; then, type `A:` and press Enter to access that drive. When the A> command prompt appears, type the command `DOSSHELL` and press Enter.

Selecting Files for Operations in DOS 4

*Remember, to get to the File System from the **Start Programs** screen, merely select the* `File System` *option. .*

If you are using DOS 4, you often need to select files from the Files Area before you perform an operation. Therefore, let's review the general techniques that you can use to select file names. As with all DOS 4 operations, you can use either the keyboard or a mouse to select file names, as summarized below:

■ To select a file using the keyboard, press the Tab key until the highlight moves to the File Area of the **File System** screen. Then use the ↓, ↑, PgUp, or PgDn keys to move the highlight bar to the file you want to select. Press the Spacebar to select the file.

■ If you have a mouse, you can select a file by moving the mouse pointer to the name of the file in the Files Area, and then clicking once.

On a graphics screen, a *selected* file is displayed with its icon in reverse video (that is, white-on-black rather than black-on-white). For example, in Figure 8.1, the files SAMPLE1.TXT and SAMPLE2.TXT are currently selected. On a text screen, selected files are represented by a right-pointing triangle to the left of the file name.

If you want to "deselect" a selected file, use exactly the same process you used to select it. That is, highlight the selected file and press the Spacebar (or click the mouse once with its pointer on the file name). In other words, the basic procedure for selecting files acts as a "toggle"—it is a "switch" that alternately selects a "un-selected" file and "deselects" a selected file.

Note that if you accidentally press Enter rather than the Spacebar, or you double-click rather than single-click your mouse when selecting a file name, DOS assumes that you are attempting to *run* the file as though it were a program. This minor (and common) mistake causes DOS to display the Open File dialog box, as shown in Figure 8.2.

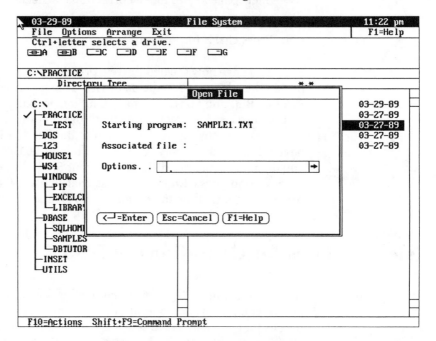

Figure 8.2. The Open File dialog box.

If you happen to make this mistake, merely press the Escape key to cancel the accidental request. When DOS redisplays the File System, press the Spacebar or click once with your mouse to properly select the file name. (If you should inadvertently proceed with the Open File dialog box by pressing Enter instead of Escape, you still will have no problems with the files used in this chapter. DOS will just display the Bad command or File Name error message and tell you to press any key to continue. When you press a key, DOS will return to the **File System** screen.)

Viewing the Contents of a File

DOS contains a built-in command that lets you look at the contents of any file. However, the contents of many files (particularly programs) might appear on the screen as strange characters or cause the computer to "beep," because they contain instructions that only the computer can read. The

SAMPLE1.TXT and SAMPLE2.TXT files you just created, however, contain text, so you can easily view their contents. Follow the steps below:

1. From the **Start Programs** Main Group screen, select File System.

2. If your computer does not have a hard disk, select B from the Drives Areas to access drive B:.

3. If your computer has a hard disk, change to the PRACTICE directory by selecting PRACTICE from the Directory Tree Area.

A quick reference guide to basic File System operations appears inside the back cover of this book. You can use either the keyboard or mouse techniques throughout this chapter.

The Files Area of your screen now shows the names of the SAMPLE1.TXT and SAMPLE2.TXT files. To view the contents of a file, you must first *select* a file (as described earlier in this chapter) and then select the View option from the File pull-down menu. Let's perform the exact steps necessary to view the contents of the SAMPLE2.TXT file:

1. Press Tab until the highlight moves to the Files Area.

2. Press ↓ until the highlight is on SAMPLE2.TXT.

3. Press the Spacebar to select the file.

4. Press F10 to access the Action Bar.

5. Use the ← or → keys to move the highlight to the File option.

6. Press Enter to pull-down the File menu.

The View option is available on the File pull-down menu only when a single file name is selected in the Files Area.

7. Select View.

Your screen now changes to display the contents of the SAMPLE2.TXT file, as shown in Figure 8.3. Because the SAMPLE2.TXT file is so small, you can see its entire contents. However, when viewing larger files, you might need to use the PgDn and PgUp keys to scroll through the file, as the message at the top of the screen indicates. Notice in the second line of the File View window that DOS tells you that you are currently viewing the SAMPLE2.TXT file stored in the PRACTICE directory of drive C: (via the message Viewing file: C:\PRACTICE\SAMPLE2.TXT).

After viewing the contents of the file, press Esc to return to the **File System** screen.

If you are using an earlier version of DOS or the optional DOS 4 command prompt, you must use the TYPE command to view the contents of a file. Let's use this method to look at the contents of the SAMPLE2.TXT file.

Because DOS *always* requires that you press Enter after typing a command, from now on I'll merely use the term *enter* to mean "type the command and then press Enter.") For example, when I say "Enter the command TYPE SAMPLE1.TXT," that means you should type the command TYPE SAMPLE1.TXT and press the Enter key.

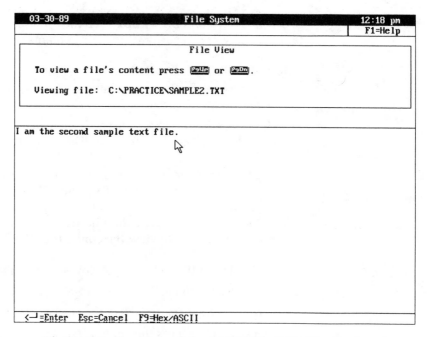

Figure 8.3. Contents of the SAMPLE2.TXT file displayed.

1. If your computer doesn't have a hard disk, be sure to access drive B: by entering the command **B:**.
2. If your computer has a hard disk, be sure to change to the PRACTICE directory by entering the command **CD \PRACTICE**.
3. Enter the command **DIR** to verify that the SAMPLE2.TXT file is on the current drive and directory.
4. Enter the command **TYPE SAMPLE2.TXT**.

After DOS shows the contents of the file, it redisplays the command prompt, as shown in Figure 8.4. (Your screen might also show preceding commands.)

Use the basic techniques discussed above to view the contents of other files. Note, however, that if you attempt to view the contents of a program, your screen will display strange symbols and might "beep" repeatedly. However, this does not harm the file; the information is merely stored as codes that only the computer can "read."

Copying Files

Much of your work with DOS involves the copying of files. You make these copies for any or all of the following reasons:

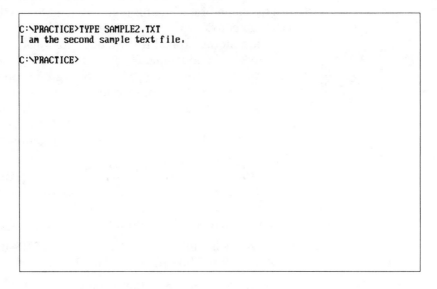

```
C:\PRACTICE>TYPE SAMPLE2.TXT
I am the second sample text file.

C:\PRACTICE>
```

Figure 8.4. Contents of the SAMPLE2.TXT file are displayed.

- To backup important files.
- To use the same set of files on more than one computer.
- To transfer files between the hard disk and diskettes.

When making copies, you always specify (either explicitly or implicitly) the *source* and the *destination* of the copy. There are a few details you must keep in mind when copying files:

- If no drive is specified, DOS uses the current drive.
- If no directory is specified, DOS uses the current directory.
- If no file name is specified for the destination, DOS uses the source file name.
- You can place the wildcard characters ? and * in file names when you use the command prompt.

The sections that follow examine specific techniques for copying files.

Making Multiple Copies

Occasionally you might want to make multiple copies of files in the same directory; this ensures the safety of your data in case you inadvertently erase or change the original file. However, because no two files in one directory can have the same name, the copy must have a different name from the original. The easiest way to keep track of originals and backups is to use the same first name for both files, but to use the extension .BAK for the backup copy.

The general procedure for copying files using the DOS Shell is straightforward and simple. First, use the File System to access the drive (or directory) that contains the files you want to copy. Select all of the files that you want to copy, and then select Copy from the File pull-down menu. Finally, specify the destination for the copy in the dialog box that appears. Let's use this procedure to copy SAMPLE1.TXT to a file named SAMPLE1.BAK. Here are the exact steps to follow:

1. At the DOS Shell **File System** screen, first be sure that the SAMPLE1.TXT and SAMPLE2.TXT file names are displayed in the Files Area. (If they are not, use the usual techniques to access the appropriate drive and directory.)

2. Move the highlight to the SAMPLE1.TXT file name in the Files Area, and press the Spacebar to select that file name.

3. Press F10 to move to the Action Bar, and then press Enter to pull down the File menu.

4. Select `Copy....`

5. When the dialog box appears, press the End or → key to move the cursor to the end of the suggested destination.

6. Type `\SAMPLE1.BAK` so that the dialog box looks like Figure 8.5. (You must use the backslash to separate the file name from the directory name.)

7. Press Enter to perform the copy.

DOS 4 users can copy several files in a single operation by using the command prompt COPY command.

When DOS is finished copying, it lists the SAMPLE1.BAK file name in the Files Area. Repeat the general procedure outlined in steps 1 through 7 above, but this time copy SAMPLE2.TXT to a file named SAMPLE2.BAK. When you finish making this second copy, your screen should look like Figure 8.6. (Use the View option on the File pull-down menu to verify that the copied files match the originals.)

To make copies from the command prompt, use the COPY command followed by the source file name (the original) and the destination file name (the copy). To store copies of SAMPLE1.TXT and SAMPLE2.TXT in files names SAMPLE1.BAK and SAMPLE2.BAK, you *could* use the following two separate COPY commands (remember to press Enter after typing each command):

```
COPY SAMPLE1.TXT SAMPLE1.BAK

COPY SAMPLE2.TXT SAMPLE2.BAK
```

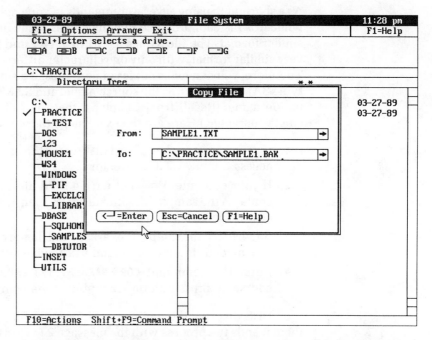

Figure 8.5. SAMPLE1.TXT will be copied to SAMPLE1.BAK.

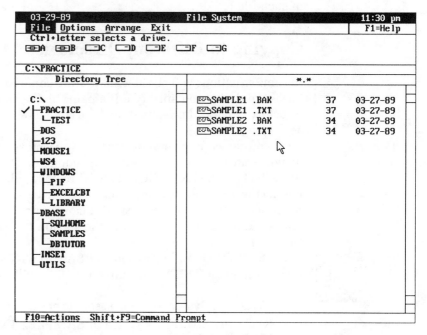

Figure 8.6. SAMPLE1.BAK and SAMPLE2.BAK in the
Files Area.

As a shortcut to using several commands to copy multiple files, you can use wildcards instead, provided that the names of the files being copied have a similar format. The file names SAMPLE1.TXT and SAMPLE2.TXT have a very similar format, with only one character differentiating the two names. Therefore, you can make copies of both files in a single operation by specifying SAMPLE?.TXT as the source name, and SAMPLE?.BAK as the destination name. (Recall from Chapter 4 that the ? character stands for *any* single character.) Here are the exact steps to follow:

1. If your computer has a hard disk, enter the command CD \PRACTICE to access the PRACTICE directory.

2. If your computer does not have a hard disk, insert the diskette that contains the sample files into drive B:; then, enter the command B: to access the diskette in drive B:.

3. Be sure that the sample files are indeed on the current drive and directory by entering the command DIR to view all file names.

4. Enter the command COPY SAMPLE?.TXT SAMPLE?.BAK. (Be sure, of course, to press Enter after typing in the command.)

DOS displays the name of each original file as it makes the copies; then, it ends the process with the message 2 File(s) copied. To verify that you now have two new files named SAMPLE1.BAK and SAMPLE2.BAK, enter the DIR command. (Also, verify that the copies contain exactly the same text as the originals by using the TYPE command to view the contents of each file.)

Copying to Different Directories

In some situations you might want to store copies of files in multiple directories. To do so, you specify a file name as the source of the copy and a directory name as the destination. (The copied file will have the same name as the original file.)

You can copy several files to a new directory in a single operation. To demonstrate this procedure, let's store copies of SAMPLE1.TXT and SAMPLE2.TXT on the PRACTICE\TEST directory (which is currently empty). Follow the appropriate steps below for your version of DOS. (If your computer does not have a hard disk, you can create these files and directories on a diskette, or you can skip to the section "Copying to Different Disk Drives.")

To use the DOS Shell to copy the SAMPLE1.TXT and SAMPLE2.TXT files to the PRACTICE\TEST directory, follow these steps:

1. At the **File System** screen, be sure to access the PRACTICE directory.

2. Select the SAMPLE1.TXT and SAMPLE2.TXT file names by highlighting each and pressing the Spacebar (or by clicking each once with your mouse).

3. Press F10 and then Enter to access the File pull-down menu.

4. Select Copy....

5. Press End and type \TEST to change the suggested destination to C:\PRACTICE\TEST as shown in Figure 8.7. (You must use the backslash to separate the directory names.)

6. Press Enter to perform the operation.

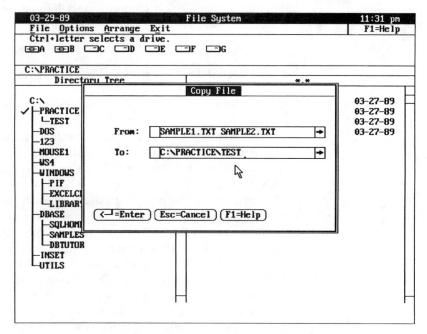

Figure 8.7. Dialog box to copy files to the PRACTICE\TEST directory.

When the operation is complete, the dialog box disappears. To verify that the PRACTICE\TEXT directory now contains copies of SAMPLE1.TXT And SAMPLE2.TXT, move the highlight to the Directory Tree Area and select the TEST directory name. Note the names of the two copied files in the Files Area of the screen.

To copy files to a new directory using the command prompt, specify the name of the file (or group of files, using wildcard characters) as the source, and specify the drive and directory name as the destination. For example, to copy SAMPLE1.TXT and SAMPLE2.TXT to the TEST directory (beneath the PRACTICE directory), follow these steps:

1. Enter the command CD \PRACTICE to access the PRACTICE directory.

2. Enter the command COPY SAMPLE?.TXT C:\PRACTICE\TEST. Don't forget to press Enter.

DOS displays the names of the files as they are copied, and then it ends the operation with the message 2 File(s) copied. To verify that the TEST directory indeed contains these new files, change to the directory by entering the command CD TEST, and then enter the DIR command to view the names of files stored there.

Note that both the PRACTICE and PRACTICE\TEST directories contain copies of the SAMPLE1.TXT and SAMPLE2.TXT files. Even though the files share the same name and content, they are completely independent of each other. Hence, changing or deleting these files on one directory has no effect on the copies on the other directory.

Copying to Different Disk Drives

Some application programs are copy-protected with a structure that enables them to be used on only one computer. Although DOS can copy such programs, the copies will not work on different computers.

Copying files from one disk (or diskette) to another is one of the most common types of copying. If your computer has a hard disk, you use this basic procedure to copy application programs from their original diskettes onto your hard disk. You also use this technique to copy files from your hard disk to diskettes, an operation that lets you store extra backups or use files on other computers.

If your computer doesn't have a hard disk, you use this procedure to copy files from one diskette to another so that you can store the copies in a safe place as backups. Or, you copy files from one diskette to another so that you can use the same files on multiple computers.

To copy a file from one disk drive to another, specify the file(s) that you want to copy as the source, and specify the disk drive that you want to copy to as the destination. You can also specify a directory on the destination disk drive, but it must be a name of an existing directory. (DOS will not automatically create a new directory while copying files.) If you do not specify a directory on the destination drive, DOS places the copies in the root directory.

To practice this procedure, let's copy the SAMPLE1.BAK and SAMPLE2.BAK files to a new diskette. To do so, you need a blank, formatted diskette (in addition to the one you might have used in earlier exercises). To prepare for the procedure, set up the diskettes as follows:

■ If your computer does *not* have a hard disk, insert the source diskette (the one with SAMPLE1.BAK and SAMPLE2.BAK on it) in drive B:, and insert the blank, formatted diskette in drive A:.

■ If your computer has a hard disk, insert the blank, formatted diskette in drive A:.

Now, follow the appropriate steps for your computer:

1. From the DOS Shell **File System** screen, access the directory or the drive that contains the files you want to copy (that is, PRACTICE on a hard disk, or drive B: if you have no hard disk).

2. Select the file names SAMPLE1.BAK and SAMPLE3.BAK from the Files Area by highlighting them and pressing the Spacebar, or by clicking once with your mouse.

3. Press F10 and then Enter to access the File pull-down menu.

4. Select Copy....

5. Hold down the Del (or Delete) key until the suggested destination is completely erased; then, type the new destination A:, as shown in Figure 8.8.

6. Press Enter.

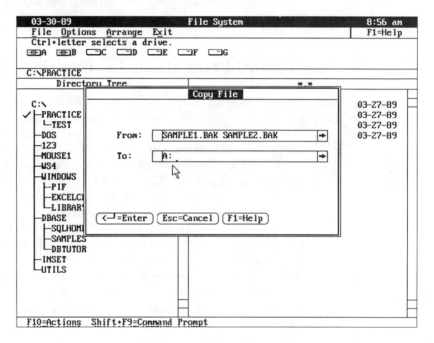

Figure 8.8. Dialog box to copy SAMPLE1.BAK and SAMPLE2.BAK to drive A:.

When the copying is complete, the dialog box disappears from the screen. To verify that the copy was accurate, first press Esc to cancel the pull-down menu. Press Tab; then, select drive A: from the Drives Area to access disk drive A:. Note the names SAMPLE1.BAK and SAMPLE2.BAK in the Files Area of the screen.

After verifying the copy, return to the hard disk (if you have one) by selecting C from the Drives Area of the File System. If you do not have a hard disk, remove the backup diskette from drive A:, and replace the Shell diskette in drive A:. To update the Files Area, select A from the Drives Area of the screen.

1. If you have a hard disk, enter the command **CD \PRACTICE** to change to the PRACTICE directory, or, if you do not have a hard disk, access drive B: by entering the command **B:**.

2. Enter the command **COPY SAMPLE?.BAK A:** to copy the sample backup files to the diskette in drive A:.

DOS displays the names of the files as they are copied, and it ends the operation with the message **2 File(s) copied**. To verify that the diskette in drive A: now contains the copied files, enter the command **DIR A:** at the command prompt. (If you are using a system without a hard disk, remove the diskette from drive A:, and re-insert the DOS diskette after you verify the copy.)

General Precautions for Copying Files

Before you start copying files on your own, keep in mind this important point: *If you copy a file to a disk drive or directory that already contains a file of the same name, the copied file replaces the original file.* For example, let's suppose that a directory named ACCT_REC contains a file named CUSTLIST.DAT that lists 1,000 customer names and addresses. Now, let's say you create another file named CUSTLIST.DAT in a directory named INVENTRY, but this file lists only two customer names and addresses.

Finally, let's suppose you decide to copy the CUSTLIST.DAT file from the INVENTRY directory to the ACCT_REC directory. If you do so, the 1,000 names and addresses in CUSTLIST.DAT will be lost forever because DOS will *overwrite* (replace) the original CUSTLIST.DAT file on the ACCT_REC directory with the copy from the INVENTRY directory.

DOS 4 somewhat protects users from potential problems of this type. Whenever you copy a file using the DOS Shell File System, DOS first checks the destination drive or directory to see if it already contains a file with the same name as the one it's about to copy. If DOS finds a file on the destination with the same name, it presents the warning shown in Figure 8.9.

As you can see, the warning displays the message **Filename already exists** and the name of the files that will be overwritten (CUSTLIST.DAT in this example). You have two options: **1. Skip this file and continue** or **2. Replace this file.** If you select the first option, the file is not copied, and DOS proceeds to copy other files (if any). If you select the second option, DOS replaces the file on the destination with the new copy, and then proceeds to copy other files (if any).

When you work at the command prompt (in any version of DOS), DOS gives no warning when a copy procedure is about to replace an existing file—DOS simply replaces the file! Because of this, you should always check the destination directory (or drive) to see if it already contains a file that has the same name as the one you are about to copy. (Use the DIR command to do so.)

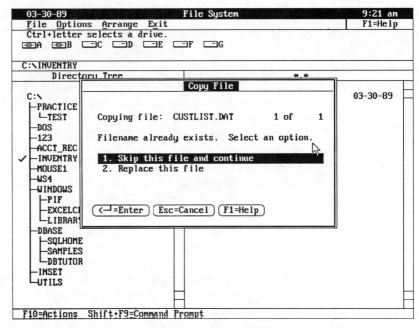

Figure 8.9. DOS 4 warning before overwriting an existing file.

For example, let's say that you are planning to copy CUSTLIST.DAT from the INVENTRY directory to the ACCT_REC directory. (Because your computer probably does not have these directories, you cannot try this out right now; this is merely a hypothetical example.) Before you rush into the copy procedure, you decide to check the destination directory to see if it already contains a file with this same name. You enter the command `DIR C:\ACCT_REC\CUSTLIST.DAT`.

Now, suppose DOS informs you that there is already a file named CUSTLIST.DAT on the ACCT_REC directory, and it displays the file name and the following information:

```
Directory C:\ACCT_REC
CUSTLIST    DAT       35000     03-15-90     3:22p
```

The question you must now ask yourself is: "Should I proceed with this copy, thus overwriting (replacing) the CUSTLIST.DAT file's contents with the CUSTLIST.DAT file on the INVENTRY directory?"

To answer this question, you would first look at the basic file information for CUSTLIST.DAT on the INVENTRY directory. To do so, you would enter the command `DIR CUSTLIST.DAT` (you don't need to specify the drive and directory if you are already accessing the INVENTRY directory), and DOS might show you the following information about that file:

```
Directory C:\INVENTRY
CUSTLIST      DAT           50      06-20-90      8:00a
```

In this example, you would be very wise *not* to copy CUSTLIST.DAT from the INVENTRY directory to the ACCT_REC directory for one very important reason: As you can see in the two directory displays, the CUSTLIST.DAT file in the ACCT_REC directory contains 35,000 bytes (characters), while the CUSTLIST.DAT file in the INVENTRY directory contains only 50 bytes. If you were to proceed with the copy, you would lose the 35,000 characters in the CUSTLIST.DAT file in the ACCT_REC directory. This could, indeed, be a rather unpleasant loss (particularly if you had no backups of the file being replaced).

Remember, even if you are planning to copy a group of files with a single COPY command, you can check the destination directory to see if it already contains files with the same names as the files being copied. For example, suppose that you plan to copy `*.TXT` (all files with the extension .TXT) from the PRACTICE directory to the PRACTICE\TEST directory. To preview the current (PRACTICE) directory to see what files will be copied, enter the command `DIR *.TXT`. To check the destination directory for files with similar names, enter the command `DIR C:\PRACTICE\TEST\*.TXT`.

Renaming Files

As you gain experience using your computer and DOS wildcards, you'll notice what an advantage it is to name related files with file names that have a similar pattern. For example, let's suppose you store quarterly data for your business in separate files. If you were to name these files in a haphazard manner, such as 1990QTR1.DAT, QTR2-90.INF, and 90-3-QTR.TXT, you could not use ambiguous file names to perform operations on these files as a group. However, if you renamed the files using a consistent format, such as QTR1-90.DAT, QTR2-90.DAT, and QTR3-90.DAT, you could more easily display or manage these related files using the ambiguous file names QTR?-90.DAT or QTR*.DAT.

It's easy to use DOS to rename a file, and you don't need to worry about accidentally replacing an existing file with a new one, because DOS will never allow you to do so. When you change the name of a file, the new name must be unique in the current directory. If the new name is not unique, DOS displays a warning message and refuses to continue the operation.

You can use the usual DOS wildcard characters ? and * to simultaneously rename several files. To demonstrate, let's rename both the SAMPLE1.BAK and SAMPLE2.BAK files on the PRACTICE directory to SAMPLE1.OLD and SAMPLE2.OLD. Use the following steps for your version of DOS:

1. If your computer has a hard disk, select the PRACTICE directory from the Directory Tree Area of the **File System** screen.

2. If your computer does not have a hard disk, be sure that disk drive B: contains the diskette that has the SAMPLE1.BAK and SAMPLE2.BAK files on it; then, select **B** from the Drives Area.

3. Select the SAMPLE1.BAK and SAMPLE2.BAK file names from the Files Area by highlighting each and pressing Enter (or clicking each file name with your mouse).

4. Press F10 and press Enter to pull down the File menu.

5. Select Rename....

The Rename File dialog box appears on your screen, as shown in Figure 8.10. Notice that the box displays the current name for the file, a blank box for entering a new name for the file, and a counter that keeps you informed of the number of operations you are performing. (In Figure 8.10, for example, SAMPLE1.TXT is 1 of 2, the first of two files that you are going to rename.)

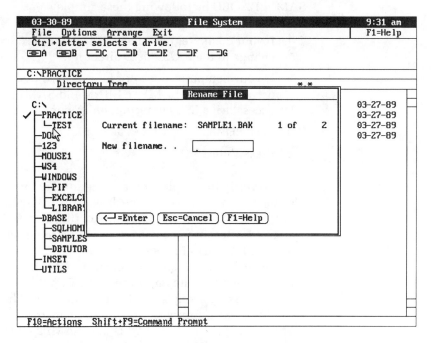

Figure 8.10 The Rename File dialog box.

You must remember to enter a complete file name for each file. After you type the new file name and press Enter, DOS prompts you to rename the next file, until you've provided a new name for each selected file. (If you decide not to rename a particular file, press the Enter without typing a new name.) As usual, you can also press F1 for help, or press Esc to cancel the entire request.

To proceed with the renaming exercise, follow these steps:

6. Type `SAMPLE1.OLD` and press Enter.

7. Type `SAMPLE2.OLD` and press Enter.

The Files Area of your screen now displays the two files with the new names you provided.

To rename files from the command prompt, use the RENAME command followed by the current name, a blank space, and the new name, as shown in this general format:

`RENAME currentname newname`

You can use wildcard characters to rename a group of files, but you need to exercise a little caution when doing so, as demonstrated later. For now, let's rename SAMPLE1.BAK and SAMPLE2.BAK to SAMPLE1.OLD and SAMPLE2.OLD by following these simple steps:

1. If your computer has a hard disk, enter the command `CD \PRACTICE` to change to the PRACTICE directory.

2. If your computer does not have a hard disk, be sure the diskette in drive B: has the SAMPLE1.BAK and SAMPLE2.BAK files on it, and access drive B: by entering the `B:` command.

3. Type `RENAME SAMPLE?.BAK SAMPLE?.OLD`.

4. Press Enter.

To verify the results of the procedure, enter the `DIR` command to display the new files names. As the directory display shows, DOS renamed the SAMPLE1.BAK and SAMPLE2.BAK files to SAMPLE1.OLD and SAMPLE2.OLD. Because you used the ? wildcard character, both files were included in the renaming operation.

In the future, when you rename groups of files using wildcard characters, keep in mind one important rule: Don't shorten the names of two or more files using a single RENAME command. The reason for this rule is straightforward. Suppose you attempt to rename SAMPLE1.OLD and SAMPLE2.OLD to SAMP1.OLD and SAMP2.OLD using the single command `RENAME SAMPLE?.OLD SAMP?.OLD`.

The problem here is that DOS does not "know" that the last character in the file name (i.e., 1 or 2) is the one that makes each file name unique. So, it renames the first file to SAMPL.OLD. Then, it also attempts to name the second file SAMPL.OLD. When DOS sees that the file name SAMPL.OLD is already in use, it displays the error message `Duplicate file name or file not found` and cancels the renaming of the second file. (If you then entered the DIR command to see the names of files, you would see that only one of the files was renamed.)

If you want to shorten the names of several files, you must rename each file individually. Hence, in this example, rather than using the command RENAME SAMPLE?.OLD SAMP?.OLD, you would need to enter the following two commands:

```
RENAME SAMPLE1.OLD SAMP1.OLD
RENAME SAMPLE2.OLD SAMP2.OLD
```

Also keep in mind that you *cannot* provide a new drive or directory location for a file while renaming it. For example, the seemingly logical command RENAME C:\PRACTICE\SAMPLE1.TXT A:SAMPLE1.BAK merely displays the error message Invalid parameter, because the command attempts to rename a file in the PRACTICE directory while at the same time trying to move the file to the diskette in drive A:. Such operations are simply not allowed with the RENAME command. (However, the command COPY C:\PRACTICE\SAMPLE1.TXT A:SAMPLE1.BAK *would* work; it would leave SAMPLE1.TXT intact on the PRACTICE directory, while also putting a copy of that file—with the name SAMPLE1.BAK—on the diskette in drive A:.)

Deleting Files

From time to time, you probably will want to delete (or *erase*) files to make room for new ones or to unclutter your disks. However, you need to be very careful when deleting files because once you do, there is no turning back. That is, as soon as you erase a file, it is permanently gone! And DOS erases a file very quickly; so, even if it took you days, weeks, or even months to create a file, DOS will "zap" it into oblivion before you can say "whoops."

As with the other basic file operations discussed in this chapter, you can erase several files during a single operation. However, when doing so, you must exercise extreme caution to ensure that you do not inadvertently erase more files than you intended. Techniques that illustrate caution are built into the following exercises, which show you how to safely erase the SAMPLE1.OLD and SAMPLE2.OLD files.

The basic technique for using the DOS Shell to erase files is the same as it was for other operations, except that you must be absolutely sure that you've selected *only* the files that you want to erase. You do this by first "deselecting" all files, as discussed in the following steps:

1. Be sure that you are still accessing the PRACTICE directory if you are using a hard disk, or, if your computer has no hard disk, that your current drive is drive B:.

2. With the **File System** screen displayed, press F10 and Enter to pull down the File menu.

3. If the last option `Deselect All` is available, select it. (If the option is shaded and unavailable, then there are no selected files, so you can press the Esc key to close the menu.)

4. Now that you know that there are no selected files (which you might have otherwise overlooked), press Tab (or use your mouse) to move to the Files Area of the screen.

5. Select the SAMPLE1.OLD and SAMPLE2.OLD files using the usual technique (position the highlight and press the Spacebar, or click each file name with your mouse).

6. Press F10 and Enter to pull down the File menu.

7. Select `Delete....`

8. DOS displays the Delete File dialog box, which contains the names of the files to delete. Press Enter to proceed.

The next dialog box provides options that permit you to skip the current file (that is, don't erase it) or to delete the file, as shown in Figure 8.11. DOS displays these options for each file that you previously selected for deletion. (This is an added precaution in case you forget to "deselect all" files before selecting new files for this operation.)

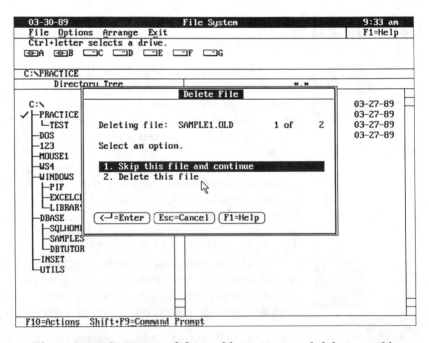

Figure 8.11 Options to delete a file or to cancel deleting a file.

To delete the file whose name is shown next to the `Deleting file:` prompt, select the second option either by pressing the number `2`, by clicking the option with your mouse, or by highlighting the option and pressing Enter. To complete this exercise, proceed with the following steps:

9. Select **2. Delete this file** to delete SAMPLE1.OLD.

10. When the options appear for SAMPLE2.OLD, select option **2** again to delete the file.

After DOS erases both files, it redisplays the **File System** screen. Note that SAMPLE1.OLD and SAMPLE2.OLD are no longer listed in the Files Area, as Figure 8.12 shows.

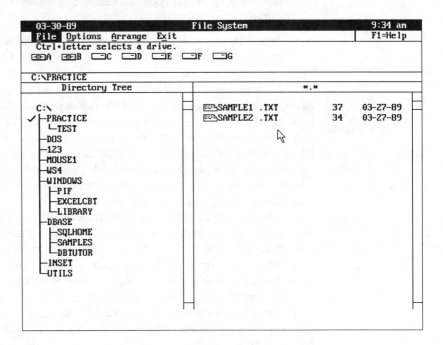

Figure 8.12. SAMPLE1.OLD and SAMPLE2.OLD have been deleted.

DOS 4 users have some additional protection options when using the ERASE command at the command prompt. See the ERASE (also DEL) command reference in Appendix B for details.

To erase files from the command prompt, use the ERASE (or DEL, for delete) command followed by the name of the file you want to erase.

You can also use ambiguous file names to erase multiple files. For example, to erase SAMPLE1.OLD and SAMPLE2.OLD or the identical command DEL SAMPLE?.OLD, you could use the command **ERASE SAMPLE?.OLD**. But before you do so, let's look at some precautionary steps you can take so that you don't accidentally erase other files:

1. If your computer has a hard disk, be sure to change to the PRACTICE directory by entering **CD \PRACTICE**. If your computer does not have a hard disk, be sure that the diskette containing SAMPLE1.OLD and

SAMPLE2.OLD is in drive B:, and access the drive by entering the **B:** command, if necessary.

2. Before erasing SAMPLE?.OLD, first enter the command **DIR SAMPLE?.OLD** to see exactly which files fit this ambiguous file name pattern.

3. In this case, you should see only two file names, SAMPLE1.OLD and SAMPLE2.OLD (in addition to the usual information that the DIR command provides).

4. Because SAMPLE1.OLD and SAMPLE2.OLD are indeed the two files you want to erase, type the command **ERASE SAMPLE?.OLD** and press Enter.

5. Type **DIR** to see the names of remaining files, which will not include the deleted SAMPLE1.OLD and SAMPLE2.OLD files.

As mentioned at the beginning of this section, you need to exercise caution when erasing files, because once you do, the file is gone forever (which, of course, is also a very good reason for always making backup copies of important files!). However, at a deeper, more technical level, the file is not *really* deleted. Instead, DOS merely changes the first character in the file name to make the file "invisible" and ready to be replaced by a new file. When you save a new file in the future, DOS *then* overwrites the "invisible" file with the new file's contents.

You can also protect files from being accidentally erased, as discussed in the section "Protecting Files" later in this chapter.

Although DOS (oddly enough) does not provide any built-in feature to locate and recover these invisible files, several optional software products do. Therefore, it is possible to "unerase" an accidentally erased file, provided that you have one of these optional products available.

You should seriously consider purchasing one of these products for your computer. Do so now, before an accident actually occurs, because you can only recover an erased file if DOS has not already replaced it with a new file. In other words, you need to use the unerase program right away, before saving any new files on your hard disk or on the diskette that contains the deleted file.

Most of the unerase packages also provide additional tools to extend the power of DOS. There are several programs available, as listed below. For more information, contact the manufacturers. (Note that this is only a partial list of programs that I happen to be familiar with; your software dealer might be able to provide additional options.)

The Mace Utilities
Paul Mace Software
400 Williamson Way
Ashland, OR 97520
(800) 523-0258

Professional Master Key
RPG Software Farm
P.O. Box 9221
Columbus, MS 39705-9221

The Norton Utilities
Peter Norton Computing, Inc.
2210 Wilshire Blvd.
Santa Monica, CA 90403
(213) 453-2361

PC Tools Deluxe
Central Point Software, Inc.
9700 S.W. Capitol Hwy. #100
Portland, OR
(503) 244-5782

Remember, even if you own an unerase program, up-to-date backup copies of files are still the best way to protect yourself from accidentally losing files.

Combining Files

You can copy and combine (merge) several individual text files into a single new file. This can be handy when, for example, you've created several files containing names and addresses, and you want to create a larger file combining all of the names and addresses. The DOS 4 Shell does not provide any means of combining files, but all versions of the DOS command prompt do.

Don't forget to press Enter after typing each DOS command.

The basic technique for combining files is to use the COPY command. As the source of the copy, you must list the names of files to be combined, separated by a plus (+) sign. As the destination, you must provide a new, unique file name. Let's look at an example that combines the SAMPLE1.TXT and SAMPLE2.TXT files:

1. If you are using the DOS 4 Shell, press the F3 key until the Shell disappears and the command prompt appears.

2. Be sure to access the correct drive or directory; enter the command `CD \PRACTICE` if you have a hard disk, or enter `B:` if you don't have a hard disk.

3. Type the command `COPY SAMPLE1.TXT+SAMPLE2.TXT COMBO.TXT`. (Note the plus sign that joins the source files and the blank space in front of the new file name COMBO.TXT.)

4. To verify that the command worked, enter the command `DIR` to view the file names.

5. To view the contents of the new COMBO.TXT file, enter the command `TYPE COMBO.TXT`.

The TYPE command displays the contents of the COMBO.TXT files as follows:

```
This is the first sample text file.
I am the second sample text file.
```

Note that you should only combine *text* files. Never try to combine program files (that is, those with the file name extension .COM, .EXE, or .BAT.). If you combine program files, the resulting "program combination" file probably will not work at all, or, if it does, it might do very strange things to your computer!

If you are a DOS 4 user, return to the DOS Shell now by typing the command `DOSSHELL` and pressing Enter. (If you do not have a hard disk, be sure to insert the Shell diskette in drive A:, access drive A: by typing `A:` and pressing Enter, and then type `DOSSHELL` and press Enter). To get to the File System, select the `File System` option from the **Start Programs** screen.

Moving Files

As you gain experience in using your computer, you might occasionally decide to change the directory tree structure of the hard disk to better organize your files. When you do so, you probably will want to move, rather than copy, files from one directory to another.

The DOS 4 File System has a built-in menu option for moving files. However, earlier versions of DOS do not have a "move" command, and so you must move files using a two-step operation: 1) copy the file to the new directory, and then 2) erase it from the original directory. Let's try a simple example by moving the new COMBO.TXT file from the PRACTICE directory to the PRACTICE\TEST directory. (These steps are described for a hard disk computer, but if you created these directories on a diskette, you can follow the instructions by substituting the correct drive name.) Follow the appropriate steps for your version of DOS:

1. Select PRACTICE from the Directory Tree Area to change to the PRACTICE directory.

2. Select COMBO.TXT from the Files Area of the screen.

3. Press F10 and Enter to pull down the File menu.

4. Select `Move....`

5. Press the End key, and type \TEST to change the destination to C:\PRACTICE\TEST, as shown in Figure 8.13.

6. Press Enter to start the operation.

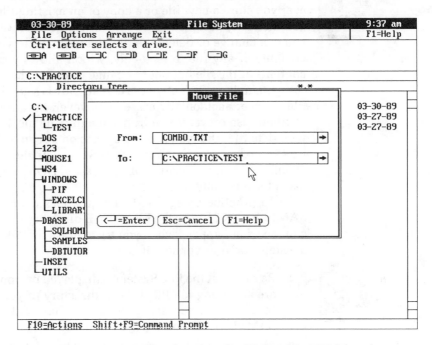

03-30-89	File System	9:37 am
File Options Arrange Exit		F1=Help

Ctrl+letter selects a drive.
⊞A ⊞B ☐C ☐D ☐E ☐F ☐G

C:\PRACTICE

Directory Tree   *.*

```
                        ┌──────── Move File ────────┐
C:\                     │                           │   03-30-89
✓ ├─PRACTICE            │                           │   03-27-89
  └─TEST                │                           │   03-27-89
  ─DOS                  │  From:   [COMBO.TXT     →] │
  ─123                  │                           │
  ─MOUSE1               │  To:     [C:\PRACTICE\TEST →]│
  ─WS4                  │                           │
  ─WINDOWS              │                           │
    ├─PIF              │                           │
    ─EXCELC            │                           │
    └─LIBRAR           │                           │
  ─DBASE               │  (←┘=Enter) (Esc=Cancel) (F1=Help) │
    ├─SQLHOM           │                           │
    ─SAMPLES           └───────────────────────────┘
    └─DBTUTOR
  ─INSET
  └─UTILS
```

F10=Actions Shift+F9=Command Prompt

Figure 8.13 Dialog box to move COMBO.TXT from the PRACTICE directory to the TEST directory.

When DOS finishes the operation COMBO.TXT is no longer displayed in the Files Area. If you move the highlight to the Directory Tree Area of the screen and select TEST to change to that directory, you'll see that COMBO.TXT is now stored on that directory.

1. Enter the command CD \PRACTICE to change to the PRACTICE directory.

2. Enter the command COPY COMBO.TXT C:\PRACTICE\TEST to copy the COMBO.TXT file to the TEST directory.

3. After DOS reports that it copied the file, verify the copy by entering the command DIR C:\PRACTICE\TEST\C*.* to view all file names on the TEST directory that begin with the letter C. Note that COMBO.TXT is listed there.

4. Because the copy was successful, you can now erase COMBO.TXT from the current directory (PRACTICE) by entering the command ERASE COMBO.TXT.

Protecting Files

Each file on your diskette or hard disk is assigned several *attributes*. Whenever you store a new file or a copy of an existing file onto your disk, DOS automatically assigns that file the attribute *read-write*, which means that you can change or delete the file at any time. However, you can reset the attribute of any file to *read-only*, which allows you to view and use the contents of the file but not to change or delete the file.

Changing a file's attribute to read-only is a good way to ensure that the file is never accidentally erased. However, because setting the read-only attribute also prevents you from changing the file, it is inconvenient to use with data files that you need to update on a regular basis (such as mailing lists, bookkeeping data, and so on). Nonetheless, files that you never change (such as application programs and DOS programs) are good candidates for read-only protection.

To practice using this technique, let's change the attribute of the SAMPLE1.TXT file on the PRACTICE directory to read-only, and then you can see what happens when you try to erase that file. Follow the appropriate steps for your version of DOS:

1. Be sure that the File System is displayed on your screen, and that you are accessing the PRACTICE directory (if you have a hard disk), or that you are accessing the drive that contains the diskette with SAMPLE1.TXT on it (if you don't have a hard disk).

2. Move to the Files Area, and select SAMPLE1.TXT (using the Spacebar or mouse, as usual).

3. Press F10 and Enter to pull down the File menu.

4. Select Change Attribute....

5. Select Change selected files one at a time. (Actually, because you only selected one file in this example, you could select either option here.)

DOS displays the Change Attribute dialog box on your screen, as shown in Figure 8.14. Note that each file has three attributes that you can change; however, for the time being let's confine the discussion to the Read only attribute. (Appendix B discusses the other options.) As instructed on the screen, to change an attribute, first highlight it and then press the Spacebar. Follow these steps to proceed:

6. Press ↓ to move the highlight to the Read only option.

7. Press the Spacebar (or click the option once with your mouse) to select the attribute. Note that a right-pointing triangle to the left of the option indicates that the read-only attribute is now turned on. (The Archive attribute may also be turned on, but you don't need to be concerned about that right now.)

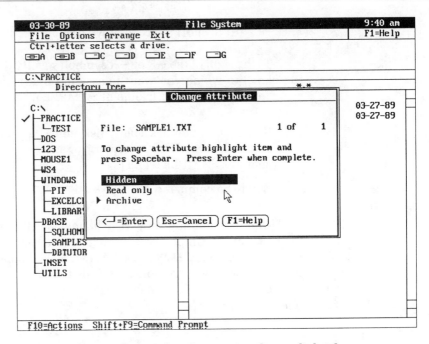

Figure 8.14. The Change Attributes dialog box.

8. Press Enter to set the attribute, leave the dialog box, and return to the File System.

Just to experiment, try to erase SAMPLE1.TXT now. Follow these steps:

1. Move the highlight to the Files Area and select SAMPLE1.TXT.
2. Press F10 and then press Enter to pull down the File menu.
3. Select Delete....
4. Press Enter when the dialog box appears.
5. Select 2. Delete this file.

Because the file has the read-only attribute assigned to it, DOS displays the error message Access denied and then offers you the option of skipping the file (that is, not erasing it) or trying to delete it again. There is no point in trying again, because the file cannot be erased. So, select option 2 (or merely press the Escape key to cancel the operation).

DOS 3 users (and DOS 4 users who prefer the command prompt) can use the ATTRIB (short for ATTRIBUTE) program to change a file's attribute. To the right of the ATTRIB command, you place the following symbols to assign or remove the read-only attribute:

+R   (to turn on the read-only attribute)

ATTRIB is not a built-in command; DOS needs to have access to the ATTRIB.EXE file to run the program.

−R   (to turn off the read-only attribute)

To the right of the +R or −R symbol, specify the file (or an ambiguous file name) to which you want to assign the attribute. Here are the exact steps for changing the attribute of SAMPLE1.TXT to read-only (+R):

1. If your computer has a hard disk, enter the command `CD \PRACTICE` to access the PRACTICE directory (or enter `B:` to access the diskette that contains SAMPLE1.TXT).

2. Enter the command `ATTRIB +R SAMPLE1.TXT`.

Although nothing appears to happen because DOS merely redisplays the command prompt, see what happens when you try to erase the file. Enter the command `ERASE SAMPLE1.TXT`. DOS displays the message `Access denied` because you cannot erase a file that has the read-only attribute assigned to it. (Enter the `DIR` command to prove to yourself that the file has not been erased.)

Resetting the Read-Write Attribute

At times you might need to change a file's attribute back to read-write so that you can modify or erase the file. Use the same basic procedure that you used to turn on the read-only attribute. Because you really do not need to protect the SAMPLE1.TXT file, follow the steps below to change it back to a read-write file:

1. Select SAMPLE1.TXT from the Files Area of the **File System** screen.

2. Press F10 and Enter to pull down the File menu.

3. Select `Change Attribute....`

4. Select `Change selected files one at a time.`

5. Highlight `Read only` and press the Spacebar (so that the triangle marker disappears).

6. Press Enter.

To reinstate the Read-Write attribute using the command prompt, use the −R option with the ATTRIB command, as in the step below:

1. At the command prompt, enter the command `ATTRIB −R SAMPLE1.TXT`.

The SAMPLE1.TXT no longer has the read-only attribute turned on, so you can change it or erase it at your convenience.

Renaming Directories

DOS 4 lets you easily change the name of a directory. Rather than work through a sample exercise to demonstrate this technique (which you probably will not use often, other than to correct a misspelled directory name), I'll merely outline the general techniques for your future reference. (You don't need to try the following steps if you do not want to change a directory name.)

Techniques for renaming directories for DOS 3 users are discussed in Chapter 9.

To rename a directory using the DOS 4 Shell, you first need to ensure that none of the file names in the Files Area are selected (otherwise DOS will rename the selected files rather than the directory). Here are the general steps you need to follow:

1. Access the **File System** screen.
2. Select the directory that you want to rename from the Directory Tree (by highlighting it and pressing Enter, or by clicking the directory name with your mouse).
3. Press F10 and Enter to pull down the File menu.
4. If the Deselect All option is available for selection, select it to ensure that no files are selected. (You would then need to press Enter to redisplay the File pull-down menu.)
5. Select Rename....
6. When the Rename Directory dialog box appears (as shown in Figure 8.15), type the new name for directory.
7. Press Enter.

After DOS completes the operation, the Directory Tree immediately displays the new directory name that you specified.

Deleting Directories

You can delete a directory at any time, provided you observe the following three rules:

- You cannot erase a directory that contains files. (You must first erase all the files.)
- You cannot delete a directory that is a parent to lower-level subdirectories.
- You cannot delete the root directory.

All of the above rules are designed to protect the integrity of your files—by making it impossible for you to inadvertently erase all the files in a directory. (Also, because the root directory contains important DOS files, you are not permitted to delete it.)

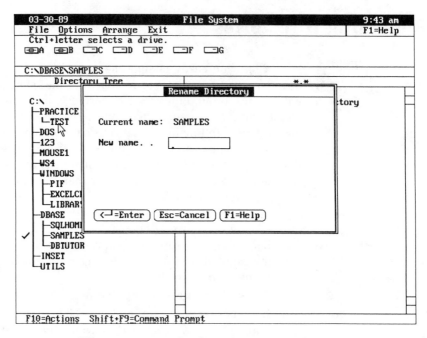

Figure 8.15. Dialog box to rename a directory.

Remember that deleting a file permanently erases it, so be sure that all the files on a directory are really expendable before you start deleting them.

To demonstrate the full series of steps that you must execute to delete a directory, let's delete the TEST directory that you created earlier. First you need to erase all the files in the directory before you can delete it, as outlined in the following steps. (If your computer does not have a hard disk, but you have created these directories on a diskette, you can follow the instructions by substituting the correct drive name for your computer.)

If you are using DOS 4, you can delete a directory (only if it contains no files) by using the Delete option from the File pull-down menu. Here are the exact steps:

1. If the File System is not already displayed, select File System from the **Start Programs** Main Group.

2. Access the TEST directory by highlighting its name (beneath PRACTICE) and pressing Enter (or by clicking the name with your mouse).

3. Press F10 and Enter to pull down the File menu.

4. Select Select All (This shortcut technique is much faster than selecting each file individually. After you select this option, note that all the files in the Files Area are indeed selected.)

5. Press Enter to redisplay the menu, and then select Delete....

6. Press Enter to confirm the command.

7. When DOS presents the options that enable you to Skip or Delete each file, select the 2. Delete this file option.

8. Continue until the Files Area displays `No files in selected directory`, indicating that the directory is now empty.

9. Press Enter to pull down the File menu.

10. Select `Delete...`.

11. When the Delete Directory dialog box appears (as shown in Figure 8.16), select `2. Delete this directory`.

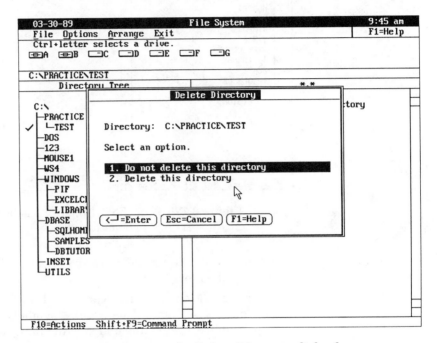

Figure 8.16. The Delete Directory dialog box.

When you return to the **File System** screen, notice that the TREE directory no longer exists beneath the PRACTICE directory, as Figure 8.17 shows.

From the command prompt, you first need to erase all the files on the directory that you want to delete. Then you need to access the parent directory and use the RMDIR or RD command (both are abbreviations for Remove Directory) to delete the directory. Here are the exact steps that enable you to remove the TEST directory:

Remember, if your command prompt does not show the name of the current directory, enter the command PROMPT PG to make it display the current directory's name.

1. First enter the command `CD \PRACTICE\TEST` to access the TEST directory (beneath the PRACTICE directory).

2. Enter the command `DIR` and be sure that only the sample files used in this chapter are stored on the directory. (You can ignore the . and .. symbols.)

3. To erase all of the files on the PRACTICE\TEST directory, enter the command `ERASE *.*`.

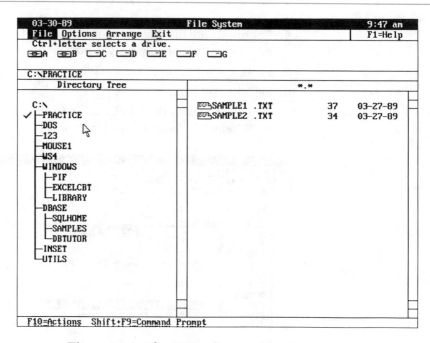

Figure 8.17. The TEST directory has been deleted
from the tree.

DOS displays the Are
you sure? (Y/N)
*warning message only
when you try to delete all
the files on a directory by
using the ambiguous file
name* *.* *(which
matches all file names).*

4. When you see the message Are you sure? (Y/N), type Y (for Yes) to erase all the files.

5. Enter the DIR command to verify that all files have been erased. (Again, you can ignore the . and .. symbols; DOS maintains sole responsibility for creating and deleting these special directories.)

6. Change to the parent directory by entering the command CD... (This shortcut method is discussed in Chapter 9.)

7. Enter the command RD TEST.

To verify that the directory was deleted, change to the root directory (by entering the command CD \), and then enter the TREE command to view the directory tree. Notice that the PRACTICE directory no longer has the TEST directory beneath it.

 Please remember to be careful when deleting your own directories. Remember, after you erase all the files on a directory, they are permanently lost.

Troubleshooting

If you make an error while managing files, DOS will most likely display one of the following error messages. Try using the suggested solutions to correct the error.

■ **Access Denied**: DOS displays this error message when one of the following problems arises:

> You tried to delete a directory that is not empty. (Erase all files in the directory first. Read-only files can be erased only after you change their attribute to read-write.)

or . . .

> You tried to create or rename a directory or file using a name that is already in use. (Use the TREE or DIR command to see if the directory or file name indeed already exists.)

or . . .

> You tried to create a file or directory using an invalid name. (Use a different name, avoiding the reserved device names and illegal characters.)

or . . .

> You tried to change or delete a read-only file. (Turn off the read-only attribute, using techniques described in the section "Resetting the Read-Write Attribute" in this chapter.)

■ **All files in directory will be deleted!--Are you sure (Y/N)?** You entered a command that will erase all of the files in a directory. Proceed with this command by typing **Y** (for Yes), or cancel the command by typing **N** (for No).

■ **Attempt to remove current directory**: You tried to delete the current directory. Enter the command **CD..** to move to the parent directory; then, try again.

■ **Bad Command or File Name**: Usually, you tried to run a program that is not in the current directory or diskette, or you misspelled a command. However, if you accidentally press Enter or double-click a file name while selecting it from the Files Area, and then you proceed after the Open File dialog box appears, this message also appears. If this is the case, press any key (as DOS instructs on the screen) and then try again, remembering to press the Spacebar or to single-click you mouse button to select the file.

This error message also appears when you try to run the ATTRIB command when the ATTRIB.EXE file is not in the current directory or diskette. (ATTRIB is a program, not a built-in DOS command.) Use the DIR command to search for the diskette or directory that contains the ATTRIB.EXE file and then try again, being sure to include the complete location and name of the file that you want to assign an attribute to. For example, the command **ATTRIB +R C:\PRACTICE\TEST\SAMPLE1.TXT** assigns the read-only attribute to the SAMPLE1.TXT file in the TEST subdirectory, regardless of your current directory.

■ **Duplicate File Name or File Not Found:** During a renaming operation, DOS either was unable to find the file that you want to rename or was unable to rename the file because the file name already exists in the current directory. Use the DIR command to check current file names to determine which error is creating the problem; then, retry the command using an acceptable file name.

■ **File cannot be copied onto itself:** The source and destination in a copy operation are identical, thus asking DOS to store two files with the same name on the same directory. Try again, being sure to specify a valid source and destination for the copy operation.

■ **File creation error:** Either there is not enough room left on a diskette to store the new file, or you exceeded the maximum number of directory entries for the disk. (See Table 6.1 in Chapter 6 for directory limitations.)

■ **File not found:** The file name specified in a command does not exist in the current directory or diskette. Either you are accessing the wrong directory or diskette, or you misspelled the file name. Check the Files Area in the DOS 4 File System, or use the DIR command to see if the file exists in the current directory or diskette.

■ **Insufficient Disk Space:** (See **File Creation Error.**)

■ **Invalid drive specification:** You specified a disk drive (such as B:, C:, or D:), but there is no such drive on your computer. Try again, using a valid disk drive name.

■ **Invalid filename or file not found:** You tried to create or rename a file using an illegal file name. (See the section "Tips on Naming Files" in this chapter.) DOS also displays this error when you try to use the wildcard characters ? or * in a TYPE command, which can only accept a single, unambiguous file name.

■ **Invalid parameter:** Most likely, you used a forward slash (/) rather than a backslash (\) in a path name.

■ **Invalid path, not directory, or directory not empty:** While attempting to remove a directory, you either misspelled the directory name, specified a directory that has subdirectories beneath it, or specified a directory that still contains files. See the section "Deleting Directories" in this chapter for more information.

■ **Invalid path or file not found:** You tried to copy a file or change a file's attributes, but you used the name of a non-existent directory or file. Use the DIR or TREE commands to determine the error, and then try again with the proper directory and/or file names.

■ **Invalid switch:** A switch specified in your command is not available with the current command. Also caused by using a forward slash (/) rather than a backslash (\) in directory names.

■ **No subdirectories exist:** You ran the TREE command from a directory that has no subdirectories beneath it. Enter the command CD \ to access the root directory, and then retry the TREE command.

- ▪ Path not found: Your command specified the name of a directory that does not exist. Check your spelling, or use the TREE command to check the directory tree for the correct path name.

- ▪ Syntax error: You used the wrong format when you typed a command. Try again, being sure to use blank spaces, backslashes, and punctuation marks carefully. Also, be sure to put file names for the command in their proper order.

- ▪ Write-protect error--Abort, Retry, Ignore (or Abort, Retry, Fail): You tried to store a new file on a diskette that is write-protected. Type A to abort the command, and then remove the write-protect tab from the diskette (as discussed in Chapter 6).

Summary

This chapter discussed the basic file-management techniques needed for viewing, copying, renaming, deleting, moving, and protecting files. The next chapter expands on these techniques to help you manage even bigger jobs. For now, let's review the basic techniques presented in this chapter:

- ▪ Regardless of which application programs you use on your computer, your file names need to conform to the rules imposed by DOS: an eight-character maximum length with no blank spaces or illegal characters, followed by an optional period and extension.

- ▪ To delete a directory, you must first erase all of the files on it.

- ▪ From the command prompt, use the general format TYPE *filename* to view the contents of a file.

- ▪ From the command prompt, you can use the wildcard characters ? and * to perform operations on groups of files.

- ▪ At the command prompt, use the general format COPY *from-source-to-destination* to copy files.

- ▪ To rename a file from the command prompt, use the general format RENAME *current-filename new-filename*.

- ▪ To erase files at the command prompt, use the general format ERASE *filename*.

- ▪ To combine files into a single new file, use the general format COPY *file1+file2+file3 new-filename* where files to be combined are joined by plus signs, and *new-filename* is the name of the resulting combined file.

- ▪ To move files from the command prompt, first use the COPY command to copy the file to the new directory, and then use the ERASE command to delete the original file from the current directory.

▓ To protect files from accidental change or erasure at the command prompt, turn on the read-only attribute using the general format `ATTRIB +R` *filename*.

▓ To delete a directory at the command prompt, first erase all of the files on the directory using the `ERASE *.*` command, then access the parent directory, and use the `RMDIR` or `RD` command to remove the directory.

▓ Select files for an operation by highlighting their names in Files Area of the File System and pressing the Spacebar (or by moving the mouse pointer to the file name and clicking once).

▓ After selecting the files for an operation, pull down the File menu, either by pressing F10 and Enter or by clicking the File option in the Action Bar with your mouse.

▓ To view the contents of a file, select a single file name from the Files Area, and then select the `View` option from the File pull-down menu.

▓ The `Copy...` option on the File pull-down menu lets you copy a selected file (or files) to a new name on the current directory, or to the same name in a different directory or disk drive.

▓ To rename a file in the File System, select the file(s) you want to rename, and then select `Rename...` from the File pull-down menu.

▓ To delete files using the File System, select the files to delete, and then select the `Delete...` option from the File pull-down menu.

▓ To move files using the File System, select the files to move, and then select `Move...` from the File pull-down menu.

▓ To protect a file from accidental change or erasure, turn on the read-only attribute by selecting `Change Attribute...` from the File pull-down menu.

▓ To rename a directory from the File System, select the directory name from the Directory Tree Area, and then select `Rename...` from the File pull-down menu.

▓ To delete a directory from the File System, first erase (or move) all of its files, then access the empty directory, and select `Delete...` from the File pull-down menu.

Power Tips for Everyone

So far, you've learned all of the basic elements of DOS that allow you to use your computer effectively. Hopefully, the hands-on exercises have helped you see for yourself how DOS operates. However, when you begin working with your own programs and data, you will be managing many more directories and files than you worked with in the previous examples.

This chapter shows you the techniques that experienced DOS "power users" use everyday to manage their files. In making the transition from "beginner" to "power-user" status, you need to keep in mind that your computer and DOS are designed to be *general purpose tools*. That is, using DOS effectively is not merely a matter of pushing the right button at the right time. Instead, using DOS effectively is a matter of knowing what tools are available to you, and how and when to use those tools to solve a particular problem.

Therefore, beginning with this chapter, you will see fewer "hands-on" exercises, because there is no way of knowing exactly what files, programs, and directories are on your computer. Instead, I'll provide general examples of how and when to use a particular tool. As you read the chapter and gain experience using your computer, you'll see that these power tips will help you to work "smarter," rather than harder, at your keyboard. The power tips are divided into two major categories, those for the DOS Shell and others for the command prompt. The usual icons mark the beginning of each section.

Power Tips for the DOS 4 Shell

The DOS 4 Shell offers many advanced features to simplify managing directories and files on your computer. The first sections of this chapter will help you take advantage of these features, and they will become even more valuable as you gain experience and your file management problems become more complex.

Arranging File Names

As you know from previous experience, the Files Area of the DOS 4 File System displays the names of files in the current directory. If a directory contains more file names than can fit in the Files Area, you can scroll through the file names using the ↑, ↓, PgUp, and PgDn keys, or you can click the scroll bar with a mouse (as discussed in Chapter 3). Figure 9.1 shows an example in which there are many more files in the current directory than can fit in the initial Files Area screen.

```
 04-05-89                        File System              12:27 am
  File  Options  Arrange  Exit                           F1=Help
  Ctrl+letter selects a drive.
  ▭A   ▭B   ▭C   ▭D   ▭E   ▭F   ▭G

 C:\WS4
       Directory Tree                              *.*

   C:\                            123PROF  .TXT      4,224   03-29-89
   ├PRACTICE                      A-T      .TXT      6,016   03-30-89
   ├DOS                           ACCOUNTS .TXT      1,920   10-20-88
   ├123                           ADDRESS  .TXT      1,152   12-15-88
   ├MOUSE1                        AGREE    .TXT      2,048   12-13-88
 ✓ ├WS4                           ANDY     .BAK      2,816   01-20-89
   ├WINDOWS                       ANDY     .LET      2,816   01-20-89
   │ ├PIF                         AR       .TXT        256   12-29-88
   │ ├EXCELCBT                    ARFILES           22,102   12-17-88
   │ └LIBRARY                     BB123    .TXT      5,248   10-04-88
   ├DBASE                         BBDOS4   .TXT      5,376   10-04-88
   │ ├SQLHOME                     BILL     .LET        512   01-03-89
   │ ├BUSINESS                    BOB      .LET      1,536   10-22-88
   │ ├SAMPLES                     BOOKNOS  .TXT        256   02-01-89
   │ └DBTUTOR                     BOOKS    .TXT        384   10-04-88
   ├INSET                         CHAP21   .TXT     82,816   09-29-88
   └UTILS                         CLIFF    .TXT      4,224   11-06-88
                                  COMPUTER .DOC      1,152   05-10-88
                                  CONVERT  .EXE     45,056   10-28-86
                                  CUSTLIST .DAT        128   03-30-89
                                  DAVID    .LET        640   02-23-89

  F10=Actions  Shift+F9=Command Prompt
```

Figure 9.1. A sample Files Area display with many files.

Refer to the inside back cover of this book if you need help making selections in the File System.

By default, DOS displays the names of all files in alphabetical order. You can rearrange the order of the display by pulling down the Options menu from the Action Bar and selecting Display options.... Doing so displays the Display Options dialog box, as shown in Figure 9.2. Initially, the cursor is in the Name: box, but you can press the Tab key (or use your mouse) to access the Sort By: option buttons.

When the cursor is in the Sort By: portion of the dialog box, you can use the ↑ and ↓ keys to access another sorting option, and then press Enter to select that option. (Mouse users merely click once on an option button and then click once on ↵=Enter.) The effects of the various options are described in Table 9.1.

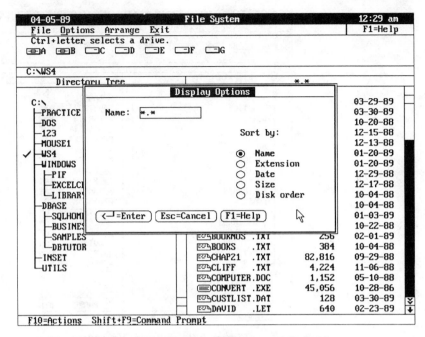

Figure 9.2. The Display Options dialog box.

These options are useful for managing files in several ways. For example, if you want to see groups of files with the same extension, select the Extension option. Because the file names are displayed in alphabetical order by extension, you can easily see all the file names in the directory that have the same extension (such as the .BAK or .COM files in Figure 9.3).

Suppose you want to see which files have been created or changed today (or recently). Merely select the Date option in the Sort By: section, and DOS displays all files in descending order by date (that is, the most recently created or modified files first).

The Disk order option displays file names in the order in which DOS

Table 9.1. Options for displaying file names.

Sort by Option	Effects
Name	File names are displayed in alphabetical order (the default selection).
Extension	File names are displayed in alphabetical order by extension.
Date	File names are displayed in descending date order (that is, the most recently created or modified files are displayed first).
Size	File names are displayed in descending (largest to smallest) order by size.
Disk order	File names are displayed in the order in which they were stored in the directory.

```
┌──────────────────────────────────────────────────────────────────────┐
│  04-05-89              File System                        12:31 am     │
│  ┌─────────────────────────────────────────────────┬────────────────┐ │
│  │ File  Options  Arrange  Exit                     │ F1=Help        │ │
│  └─────────────────────────────────────────────────┴────────────────┘ │
│  Ctrl+letter selects a drive.                                          │
│  ▭A   ▭B   ▭C   ▭D   ▭E   ▭F   ▭G                                       │
│                                                                        │
│  C:\WS4                                                                 │
│  ┌─────────────────────┐     ┌──────────────────*.*──────────────────┐ │
│  │    Directory Tree   │     │                                       │ │
│  │                     │     │                                       │ │
│  │  C:\                │     │ ▱ARFILES        22,102    12-17-88     │ │
│  │  ├PRACTICE          │     │ ▱HIPO2    .AR    4,352    12-29-88     │ │
│  │  ├DOS               │     │ ▱SMITH    .BAK     256    04-03-89     │ │
│  │  ├123               │     │ ▱GLORIA   .BAK     512    10-18-88     │ │
│  │  ├MOUSE1            │     │ ▱LABELS   .BAK     640    12-27-88     │ │
│  │ ✓├WS4               │     │ ▱ANDY     .BAK   2,816    01-20-89     │ │
│  │  ├WINDOWS           │     │ ▱DOUG     .BAK   1,664    03-15-89     │ │
│  │  │ ├PIF             │     │ ▤FIX3     .BAT     128    03-30-89     │ │
│  │  │ ├EXCELCBT        │     │ ▤FIX      .BAT     128    03-30-89     │ │
│  │  │ └LIBRARY         │     │ ▱UNTITLED .CAT   8,028    03-30-89     │ │
│  │  ├DBASE             │     │ ▤IMCAP    .COM   6,114    06-20-85     │ │
│  │  │ ├SQLHOME         │     │ ▤LIST2DAY.COM     384 ▷  05-11-85     │ │
│  │  │ ├BUSINESS        │     │ ▤LOCATE   .COM     517    06-05-86     │ │
│  │  │ ├SAMPLES         │     │ ▤WHERE    .COM     418    01-12-85     │ │
│  │  │ └DBTUTOR         │     │ ▤VTREE    .COM     512    07-31-85     │ │
│  │  ├INSET             │     │ ▤F        .COM       8    12-08-86     │ │
│  │  └UTILS             │     │ ▱CUSTLIST.DAT      128    03-30-89     │ │
│  │                     │     │ ▱INTERNAL.DCT   25,600    12-30-86     │ │
│  │                     │     │ ▱MAIN     .DCT 277,504    12-30-86     │ │
│  │                     │     │ ▱PERSONAL.DCT      529    03-29-89  ⌄  │ │
│  │                     │     │ ▱PHONE    .DIR   3,456    03-31-89  ↓  │ │
│  └─────────────────────┘     └───────────────────────────────────────┘ │
│  F10=Actions   Shift+F9=Command Prompt                                 │
└──────────────────────────────────────────────────────────────────────┘
```

Figure 9.3. Sample file names arranged by extension.

stored them on the disk. While this order might not be particularly useful in helping you find a file, it can help DOS perform operations a little more quickly, especially with operations that involve many files. When you initially select files for an operation, you should use one of the other Sort By: options to simplify the selection process; however, before you actually begin the operation, select the Disk Order option to help make DOS more efficient.

Quickly Selecting Groups of File Names

The Name option in the Display Options dialog box was previously discussed in detail in the section "Narrowing the File Name Search" in Chapter 4.

Rearranging file names is only one way of managing large groups of files. By changing the Name: section in the Display Options dialog box from *.* to a more descriptive ambiguous files name, you can quickly isolate groups of file names for an operation.

For example, suppose you want to copy some of the files with the extensions .TXT and .LET from the current directory to a diskette. Rather than painstakingly selecting each file individually, you could use the Display Options dialog box to make the procedure a quick and easy one.

Your first step would be to select the Deselect All option from the Action Bar File pull-down menu (if it is available) to cancel any currently selected files. Next, pull down the Options menu from the Action Bar, select Display options..., and change the file specifier from *.* to *.TXT. This displays only those files with the .TXT extension in the Files Area. To select all these file names for an operation, select the Select All option from the File pull-down menu.

Now, as stated earlier, you also want to include all .LET files in this operation. To isolate those file names, you again need to select Display options... from the Options pull-down menu and then change the file specifier from *.TXT to *.LET. Again, select all these files for the operation by selecting Select All from the File pull-down menu.

To verify that the appropriate files have been selected, select Display options... from the Options pull-down menu, and change the *.LET file specifier to *.* (all files). You can also select another sort order for the file names by changing the Sort By: options. In Figure 9.4, the file names are listed in alphabetical order. As you can see, all files that have the .TXT and .LET file extensions are selected. Now you can select any operation from the File pull-down menu to manage this group of files. Or, you could individually "deselect" files to exclude them from the operation. (In this example, you would select Copy....)

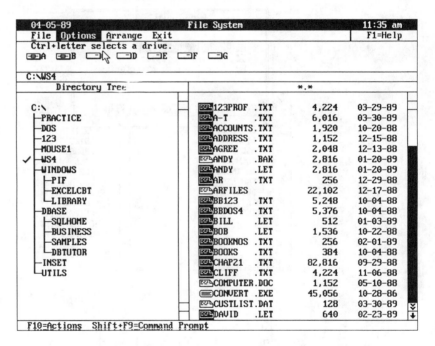

Figure 9.4. Files with the extension .TXT and .LET are selected.

Selecting Files from Different Directories

In some operations, you might need to select files that are stored on separate directories (or disk drives). To do so, you must execute two basic steps:

■ Select File options... from the Options pull-down menu and Select Across Directories from the dialog box that appears.

■ Simultaneously view the file names of two drives or directories by selecting Multiple File List from the Arrange pull-down menu.

To demonstrate the technique and capabilities of selecting files across directories, let's assume that you want to copy to drive A: all the files that have the extension .BAK from two directories, named WS4 and WINDOWS.

Your first step, assuming you are already in the File System, is to pull down the Options menu and select File options.... This displays the File Options pull-down menu shown in Figure 9.5. (Notice that the Select across directories box is not checked.)

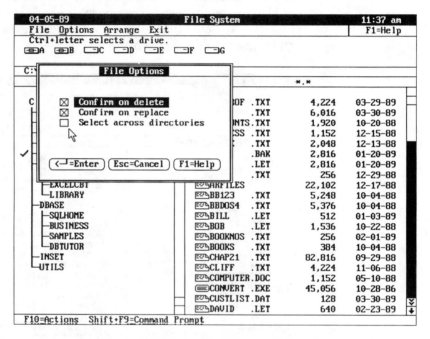

Figure 9.5. The File Options dialog box.

Next, you need to put an X in the box to the left of the Select across directories option. To do so from the keyboard, use the ↓ or ↑ key to highlight Select across directories and then press the Spacebar. If you are using a mouse, simply click the box once. (Note that both these methods act as a toggle—a single press puts the X into an empty box or removes the X if it is already there.)

The preceding step is important when you want to use files from multiple directories in a single operation. If you forget to select the Select Across Directories option, DOS automatically "deselects" files from the current directory as soon as you access another directory.

Next, to simplify your work, you can split the Files Area into two *windows*, each of which can access its own disk drive and/or directory. To split the Files Area, you need to pull down the Arrange menu on the Action

Bar, and then select Multiple file list. Immediately, the Files Area splits into two windows.

Whenever the two windows are displayed, you can use the Tab key or your mouse in the usual manner to move the highlight around the screen. Notice that each window has its own Drives Area, Directory Tree, and Files Area. Use the usual techniques to select drives, directories, and file names from each window. Figure 9.6 shows an example in which the top window is accessing the WS4 directory on drive C:, and the bottom window is accessing the WINDOWS directory on drive C:.

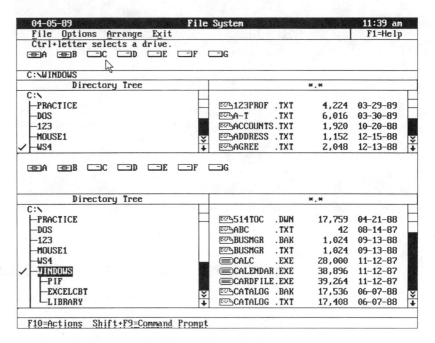

Figure 9.6. The Files Area split into two windows.

Because the Select across directories option is on, you can now use the usual techniques to select files from the Files Area of both windows. For example, to select the .BAK files from the both the WS4 and WINDOWS directories, first press F10 and select Display options... from the Options pull-down menu. Change the file specifier in the Name: box to *.BAK. The *.BAK specifier appears at the top of the Files Area for both windows, and both windows display only those file names that have the .BAK extension, as shown in Figure 9.7.

You still need to select all of the files from both windows before performing your operation. You must do this individually for each window. That is, press the Tab key until the highlight is in the Files Area of the top window; press F10 and Enter to pull down the File menu; then, select the Select All option. Press Tab a few times to move the highlight to the Files Area of the bottom window. Again, press F10 and Enter to pull down the

File menu, and then select the Select All option. Notice that all the files with the .BAK extension are highlighted, as shown in Figure 9.8.

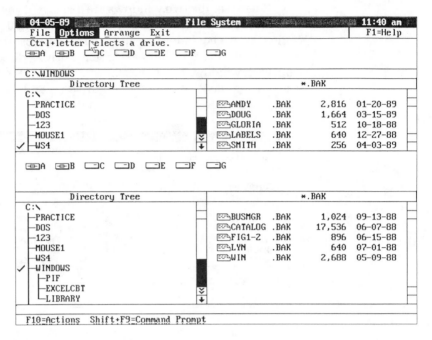

Figure 9.7. Both windows display only .BAK file names.

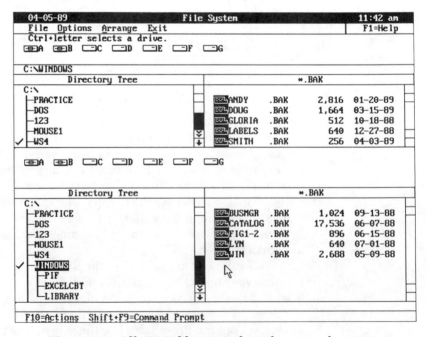

Figure 9.8. All .BAK files are selected on two directories.

*You can also use the
multiple file list to display
the source and desti-
nation directories for Copy
and Move operations.*

Now that you've selected all the appropriate files for your operation, you can pull down the File menu and select an operation (such as Copy..., in this example). The operation automatically includes all the selected files from both directories.

Selecting Files from Three or More Directories

Even though you cannot split the File System screen into more than two windows, you can still select files from more than two directories, as long as the Select across directories option is marked with an X. Using two windows isn't valuable when working with more than two directories, so switch back to the single-window view by pressing F10 to access the Action Bar and then selecting the Single file list option from the Arrange pull-down menu.

Next, select Display options... from the Options pull-down menu, and enter a file specifier in the Name: box that identifies the types of files you want to select. (Enter *.* to view all file names.) Now you can use the usual techniques to access various directories and to select files from each directory. Because the Select across directories box is marked with an X, DOS "remembers" all of the files that you select from each directory. This lets you move freely from directory to directory, so that you can select whatever files you need.

When you finish selecting files, merely pull down the File menu, and select the operation that you want to perform. (Remember, however, that the View option is available only when a single file name is selected.)

The next section discusses techniques that will help you to manage all your files and directories on a hard disk.

Searching All Directories for a File

As you add more directories and files to your hard disk, you might find it increasingly difficult to remember where every individual file is stored. You can use the DOS 4 File System to quickly and easily locate the directory that any file is stored on, even if you do not know the exact file name that you are looking for.

For example, let's suppose that you wrote a letter to a person named Smith, but you do not remember in which directory you stored the letter. Although you remember that you named the file SMITH, you aren't sure of the extension that you used after the base name. Fortunately there's a quick way to search all of the directories on your hard disk for a file beginning with the letters SMITH.

First, you must display the *System File list*, which displays all file names on all directories. To do so, press F10 to access the Action Bar, pull down the Arrange menu, and then select the Select file list option. Your screen changes slightly, but don't be concerned about that.

Next, you must change the file specifier to SMITH*.* (all files starting with the letters SMITH followed by any other characters and any extension). To do so, select Display options... from the Options pull-down menu, and change the file specified in the Name: box to SMITH*.*. Press Enter after you type the new file specifier.

As Figure 9.9 shows, the Files Area shows the names of all files that match the SMITH*.* ambiguous file name. However, notice that the area that used to show the Directory Tree now displays specific file information instead.

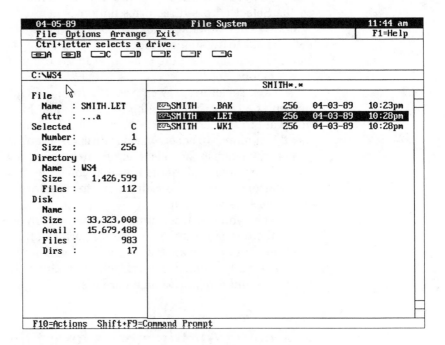

Figure 9.9. The System file list screen showing SMITH*.* files.

As you move the highlight through the file names in the Files Area, the left side of the screen displays the drive and directory that the file is stored on (as well as additional information). For example, notice in Figure 9.9 that SMITH.LET is stored on C:\WS4 (the WS4 directory on drive C:). Having located the file, you can now select Single file list from the Arrange pull-down menu and then use the Directory Tree to access both the WS4 directory and the file.

Other Features of the System File List

You can use the System file list to manage your files much like you use the "normal" single-directory file display. This can be a great tool when you want to perform an operation on all directories, such as copying or deleting a group of files.

For example, suppose you don't have much space left on your hard disk, so you decide to copy all the .BAK (backup) files to diskettes and then erase those files from your hard disk. To perform this operation quickly first select System file list from the Arrange pull-down menu to ensure that all directories are accessible. Then, select Display options... from the Options pull-down menu, and change the file specifier in the Name: box to *.BAK. (Then press Enter, as usual.)

The Files Area then displays all of the .BAK files on the entire hard disk. Next, select Select all from the File pull-down menu to select all of these files. As Figure 9.10 shows, these few simple steps selected every single .BAK file on the entire hard disk.

```
 04-05-89                      File System                    11:49 am
 File Options  Arrange   Exit                                 F1=Help
 Ctrl+letter selects a drive.
  ⌐═A   ⌐═B  ⌐═C  ⌐═D   ⌐═E   ⌐═F   ⌐═G

 C:\DBASE
 ┌─────────────────────┬─────────────────────────────────────────────┐
 │                     │                     *.BAK  ▯                  │
 │ File                │ ▨64664800.BAK       34     10-25-88   1:00pm │
 │   Name : 64664800.BAK│ ▨89743800.BAK       34     10-26-88  12:45pm│
 │   Attr :  ...a      │ ▨ANDY     .BAK    2,816     01-20-89  12:17pm│
 │ Selected        C   │ ▨AUTOEXEC.BAK       256     03-14-89   9:04pm│
 │   Number:       22  │ ▨BUSMGR   .BAK    1,024     09-13-88  10:39pm│
 │   Size  :   36,366  │ ▨CATALOG  .BAK   17,536     06-07-88   4:05pm│
 │ Directory           │ ▨CONFIG   .BAK      949     01-19-89   3:45pm│
 │   Name  : DBASE     │ ▨DOSSHELL.BAK       213     03-13-89   4:13pm│
 │   Size  :  4,077,354│ ▨DOUG     .BAK    1,664     03-15-89   1:54pm│
 │   Files :      169  │ ▨FIG1-2   .BAK      896     06-15-88  11:40am│
 │ Disk                │ ▨GLORIA   .BAK      512     10-18-88  12:29pm│
 │   Name  :           │ ▨INSERT6  .BAK    1,280     11-02-88  12:39pm│
 │   Size  : 33,323,008│ ▨LABELS   .BAK      640     12-27-88  12:02pm│
 │   Avail : 15,685,632│ ▨LYN      .BAK      640     07-01-88  10:43pm│
 │   Files :      980  │ ▨SMITH    .BAK      256     04-03-89  10:23pm│
 │   Dirs  :       17  │ ▨SYSDBS   .BAK      252     08-26-88  12:43pm│
 │                     │ ▨SYSTABLS.BAK     1,094     08-15-88   9:13am│
 │                     │ ▨TEMP     .BAK      384     11-02-88   6:09pm│
 │                     │ ▨TEST     .BAK    2,816     01-04-89   1:38pm│
 │                     │ ▨TESTUSER.BAK       348     03-31-89   2:07pm│
 │                     │ ▨WIN      .BAK    2,688     05-09-88  12:37pm│
 ├─────────────────────┴─────────────────────────────────────────────┤
 │ F10=Actions   Shift+F9=Command Prompt                              │
 └────────────────────────────────────────────────────────────────────┘
```

Figure 9.10 All .BAK files on the hard disk are selected.

See the next section, "Speeding Large Operations," for tips on speeding up copying and deleting operations.

Next, you can select any operation from the File pull-down menu as you normally would. In the current example, you would select Copy... and then specify a destination for all the selected files to be copied to. When the copy is complete, DOS automatically deselects all the file names. To erase all the files from the hard disk, again select Select all from the File pull-down menu, and then select Delete... from the File pull-down menu.

Furthermore, if your computer has multiple disk drives, you can select new drives from the Drives Area at the top of the screen, and then you can select files from the multiple drives. DOS keeps track of all the files selected on all drives and directories. After you finish selecting files, DOS lets you perform file operations that might involve several disk drives and dozens of directories.

As a bonus, the System file list screen also displays important information about your disk, as summarized in Table 9.2.

Table 9.2. Information displayed by the System file list.

Heading	Displays
File	
Name :	Name of the currently highlighted file
Attr :	Attributes assigned to the file:
	. indicates attribute not assigned
	r indicates read-only attribute is on
	h indicates hidden attribute is on
	a indicates archive attribute is on
	(See ATTRIB in Appendix B for further details)
Selected	Drives that have been accessed
Number:	Number of selected files on each drive
Size :	Combined sizes of selected files
Directory	
Name :	Directory that the highlighted file is stored on
Size :	Amount of disk space used by the files in the directory
Files :	Number of files stored on the directory
Disk	
Name :	Electronic label assigned to disk (if any)
Size :	Total storage capacity of disk
Avail :	Total available disk space remaining on disk
Files :	Total number of files stored on disk
Dirs :	Total number of directories on the disk

You can also view the information presented in Table 9.2 without displaying the System file list. To do so, move the highlight to any file name in the Files Area, and then pull down the Options menu and select Show information.... A window appears, as shown in Figure 9.11. Press Esc to leave the window, or press F1 for help.

Remember, if you want to switch between the System file list and the "standard" screens so that you can select files from both, you should first pull down the Options menu, select File options..., and be sure that the Select across directories box is checked (marked with an X, as described earlier in this chapter). Otherwise, DOS automatically deselects all files when you switch from the System file display to other displays.

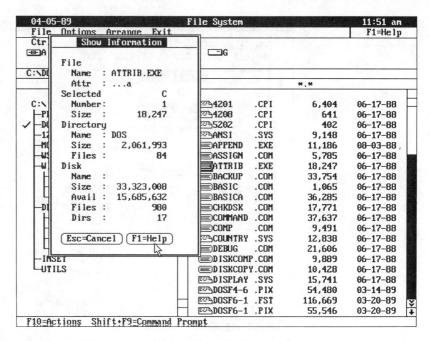

Figure 9.11 The Show Information window.

Speeding Large Operations

When you select a large group of files and then copy or erase them, DOS stops and asks for permission to erase or overwrite existing files. This safety feature is designed to help prevent you from accidentally erasing an important file. However, if you always take precautions before these operations and you are certain that you want to copy or delete the selected files, the constant "checking for permission" can become tiresome.

To prevent DOS from asking for permission before deleting or erasing a group of files, first select all the files for the operation. Then, press F10 and pull down the Options menu. Select File options... to display the dialog box shown in Figure 9.12. Note that the Confirm on delete and Confirm on replace options are marked with an X.

You can turn off either (or both) options by moving the highlight to the option and pressing the Spacebar once (or clicking the box with your mouse). Press Enter after you remove the X's; then, select the operation you wish to perform from the File pull-down menu.

Each time you start your computer, the Confirm on delete and Confirm on replace options are automatically turned on.

Note that once you turn off these options (by removing the X's), DOS leaves them off for future operations unless you turn them on again (by putting the X's back into the boxes). In addition, when you leave the DOS Shell by pressing the F3 key, DOS always turns on these options when you restart the Shell. However, if you leave the Shell by pressing Shift-F9 (as discussed in the next section), these options are not reset to "on" when you return to the Shell.

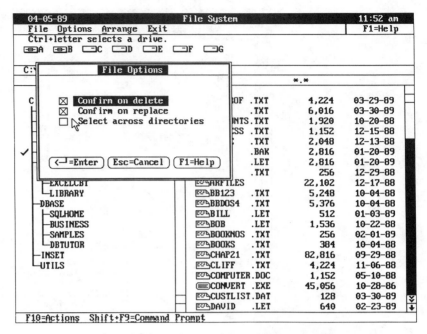

Figure 9.12 The File Options dialog box.

An Alternative Method of Leaving the Shell

In preceding examples in this book, you pressed the F3 key to leave the DOS Shell and access the command prompt. To return to the DOS Shell, you typed the command DOSSHELL and pressed Enter. When you use this technique to exit and return to the Shell, DOS always resets the File System to its original settings and automatically deselects any selected files.

The Shift+F9 =Command message prompt always appears on the screen when this exiting technique is available.

If you want to switch back and forth between the command prompt and the Shell without losing any of your current settings or file selections, press Shift-F9 (hold down the Shift key and press F9). When the command prompt appears, the top line on the screen displays the message When ready to return to the DOS Shell, type EXIT then press Enter. You can now enter any DOS commands and even change directories. When you are ready to return to the Shell, type EXIT and press Enter.

*You can also select the Command Prompt option from the **Start Programs** Main Group screen as an alternative to pressing Shift-F9.*

This alternative technique for exiting the Shell has the advantage of retaining selected files and other settings when you return. However, keep in mind that DOS accomplishes this by keeping the Shell in memory (RAM), occupying about 7KB of space. If you inadvertently enter the DOSSHELL command—rather than EXIT—to return to the shell, a new copy of the Shell is stored in RAM. If you make this mistake many times, you probably will have so many DOS Shells in RAM that you cannot run other programs, or memory conflicts "lock up" the computer, requiring that you reboot by simultaneously pressing the Ctrl, Alt, and Del keys, as discussed later in this chapter.

If you are at the command prompt, but you cannot remember whether you exited using F3 or the Shift-F9 option, just type EXIT and press Enter. If the Shell does not reappear, you must have used F3; merely type DOSSHELL and press Enter. No harm done!

Power Tips for Command Prompt Users

DOS 3 users (and DOS 4 users who use the command prompt) have many powerful shortcut techniques at their disposal. These are discussed in the sections that follow. Note that several examples involve *external* DOS commands that are stored on disk rather than in RAM. If you have a problem using any of these commands, see the Troubleshooting section near the end of this chapter.

Please keep in mind that you can also refer to the inside front cover of this book for a quick summary of DOS commands and the operations they perform. All of the commands listed on those pages are described in more detail in Appendix B.

Shortcuts to Using Directories

If your DOS prompt does not show the name of the current directory or path, enter the command PROMPT PG to change the prompt.

In previous chapters you learned the basics of using the MKDIR (or MD) command to create new directories and the CHDIR (or CD) command to change directories. As discussed previously, entering a command such as MD TEST creates a new directory named TEST beneath the current directory. Entering the command CD TEST takes you to the TEST directory *only* if you are currently accessing the parent directory.

You can get a little more control over these commands by specifying the root directory name, \, as the starting point for the operation. For example, suppose you are accessing a directory with the path name PRACTICE\TEST. If you enter the command MD FINANCES, DOS automatically creates the new directory beneath the current directory, so that the full directory path actually becomes PRACTICE\TEXT\FINANCES.

However, if you enter the command MD \FINANCES, DOS uses the root directory as the starting point, thus placing the FINANCES directory one level below root. In other words, entering the command MD \FINANCES is a shortcut for entering the following two commands:

```
CD \
MD PRACTICE
```

You can also use the root directory as the starting point for a CHDIR or CD command. The following examples show how different uses of the root directory (named \) affect the CD command:

`CD FINANCES`	Changes to the FINANCES directory only if that directory is exactly one level below the current directory.
`CD \FINANCES`	Changes to the FINANCES directory from any level, provided that the FINANCES directory is exactly one level below the root directory.
`CD \SALES\FINANCES`	Changes to the FINANCES directory (beneath the SALES directory) from any directory on the disk (that is, regardless of the "current" directory).

Keep in mind that there is no quick-and-easy way to simultaneously access both a different drive and directory in a single command. For example, if you are currently accessing floppy disk drive A:, you cannot enter the command `C:\SALES\FINANCES` to change to the SALES\FINANCES directory on drive C:. Instead, you must first change drives and then change directories, by entering the following two commands:

```
C:
CD \FINANCES\SALES
```

The . and .. Shortcuts

As you might recall from previous chapters, the DIR command always displays two "file" names (`.` and `..`) even though there are really no such files on the directory. The `.` and `..` are actually symbols: `.` is an abbreviation for the current directory, and `..` is an abbreviation for the parent directory. You can use these symbols as shortcuts in your commands.

For example, suppose your current directory path is \SALES \FINANCES. To move up to the \SALES directory from FINANCES, you need only enter the `CD..` command. Entering the command `CD..` again takes you up another level to the root directory. (Entering `CD..` from the root directory does nothing, because there are no higher-level directories.)

The `..` symbol can also be used to quickly switch between lower-level subdirectories. For example, suppose your current directory path is FI-NANCES\SALES\1989 and you want to change to the lowest subdirectory on the following path FINANCES\SALES\1990. Rather than typing out the lengthy command `CD \FINANCES\SALES\1990`, you merely need to enter the command `CD ..\1990`.

You can use the `..` symbol in any command. For example, suppose you want to copy all the files from the \FINANCES\SALES\1989 path to the lowest directory on the \FINANCES\SALES\1990 path. If \FINANCES\SALES\1989 is the current directory, you can enter either the command `COPY *.* \FINANCES\SALES\1990` or the much shorter command `COPY *.* ..\1990` (because `..` "fills in" the parent directory named \FINANCES\SALES).

In case you are wondering, experienced DOS users pronounce *. * *as "star dot star,"* .. *as "dot dot," and* . *as "dot."*

The . command can be used to specify the current directory's name. For example, suppose your current directory path is \FINANCES\SALES, and you want to copy all of SALES files to the next lower directory (on the \FINANCES\SALES\1990 path). Rather than typing in the lengthy command COPY *.* C:\FINANCES\SALES\1990, merely use . to stand for the current directory by entering the command COPY *.* .\1990.

The . symbol can also be used to specify all the files on a directory, as a shorthand way of saying *.*. For example, if you really wanted to take a shortcut, you could enter the command COPY . .\1990 rather than COPY *.* .\1990.

Furthermore, if the destination for the copy is the name of a directory that is exactly one level below the current directory, you really need not specify the parent directory, or even the .. symbol at all. Hence, if the current path is \FINANCES\SALES, and you want to copy all of its files to the \FINANCES\SALES\1990 subdirectory, the ultimate shortcut command would be simply:

```
COPY . 1990
```

In English, the command above says "Copy everything from the current directory (.) to the subdirectory named 1990, which is one level below the current directory."

For beginners, the shorthand method of entering commands can be a bit abstract. If in doubt, just use the longhand method. For example, even though the command COPY C:\FINANCES\SALES*.* C:\FINANCES\SALES\1990 takes a bit more typing than COPY . 1990, it still gets the job done, and is much more explicit and easier to understand.

Incidentally, the fact that DOS allows you to use . in place of *.* is the reason the DOS always displays a warning message when you try to erase all the files on a directory. Some users, upon seeing the . and .. symbols in the DIR display, might attempt to erase the "mysterious files" by entering the command ERASE ., which is identical to entering ERASE *.*.

Early versions of DOS displayed the message Are you sure (Y/N) before erasing the files, but many users simply typed Y, for Yes, thinking they were erasing only one file—named .! This warning has been improved in DOS 4, which adds the message All files in directory will be deleted! when you enter the ERASE ., ERASE .., or ERASE *.* commands.

Shortcuts to Specifying Files

All DOS commands make "assumptions" about the locations of files based upon the information you provide . . . and the information you omit. You can omit any information from a command, as long as you want DOS to assume that the omitted information refers to the current drive, directory, and file name. Note in the following examples how DOS makes assumptions based on omitted information:

C:\SALES\MYDATA.DAT	Assumes that MYDATA.DAT is in the \SALES directory of disk drive C:.
\SALES\MYDATA.DAT	Assumes that MYDATA.DAT is in the \SALES directory of the current drive.
MYDATA.DAT	Assumes that MYDATA.DAT is in the current drive and directory.

You can omit any *file specification* (i.e., drive name, path, and file name) in any DOS command, both to save time in moving from one directory to the next and also to shorten commands. For example, if you are currently accessing disk drive D:, and you want to see the contents of C:\SALES\MYDATA.DAT, you don't actually need to change drives or directories. Instead, merely specify the drive, the full path, and the file name in the TYPE command, as follows:

```
TYPE C:\SALES\MYDATA.DAT
```

If you completely omit the destination in a COPY command, DOS assumes the destination is the current location. For example, suppose that you are currently accessing the \SALES directory of disk drive C:, and you want to copy all the files from disk drive A: to this directory. You can completely omit the destination from the COPY command (because the destination is the current drive and directory) and specify only the source (disk drive A:), as follows:

```
COPY A:*.*
```

In English, the previous command says, "Copy all files (*.*) from drive A: to here." To copy all the .BAK files from the \MARKTNG directory to the current directory, you could enter either:

```
COPY \MARKTNG\*.*
```

or . . .

```
COPY C:\MARKTNG\*.*
```

In all of these examples, the names of the copied files have been omitted, which ensures that the copies have the same names as the originals. Suppose, however, that you want to copy all the .WKQ files from a directory named \QUATTRO to floppy disk drive A:. In addition, you want to change the extensions on the copied files from .WKQ to .BAK. Assuming that your current directory is \QUATTRO, you could enter this command to perform both operations:

```
COPY *.WKQ A:*.BAK
```

Note that *.WKQ specifies the source of the copy (all .WKQ files on the current directory), while *.BAK specifies the names of the destination files (same first name, but .BAK extension).

All these shortcuts might be a little confusing at first, but remember shortcuts are optional, not required. If you want to copy all the files from the \SALES directory to the \MARKTNG directory, the command COPY C:\SALES*.* C:\MARKTNG always works, regardless of what your current drive and directory are.

Sorting the DIR Display

The DIR command always displays file names in the order they were created, the oldest files first and the newest files later. If you prefer a more organized sort order, you can use the SORT command in combination with the DIR command. Programs such as the SORT command that rearrange output are called "filters." (Remember, as an external DOS command, the SORT.EXE file must be accessible from the current drive and directory.)

The | character, called pipe, is Shift-\ on most keyboards (hold down the Shift key and type \).

For example, to list file names in alphabetical order in the DIR display, enter the command:

```
DIR | SORT
```

To print this alphabetical list of file names, enter the command:

```
DIR | SORT > PRN
```

You can also sort file names in the DIR display by extension, size, or date. For details, see the SORT command reference in Appendix B.

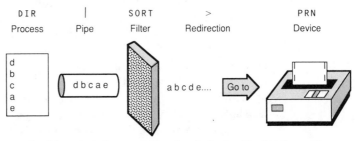

Send the output of a process through a pipeline to a filter that changes the output and then redirect that filtered output to another device instead of the screen

Figure 9.13 An illustration of how a pipe and filter work with a command.

Displaying Files from a Certain Date

You can have the DIR command display all the files on a directory that were created or last modified on a certain date. This is handy when you are looking for a file that you created earlier today or yesterday, but you cannot remember the full name of the file.

To use FIND with DIR or any other command, the DOS FIND.EXE file must be accessible from the current directory.

The first step, of course, is to use the CD command to change to the directory on which the file is stored. You then might want to enter the DATE command to check the current system date. (Press Enter at the prompt rather than entering a new date.) Next, use the DIR command followed by the pipe (|), the FIND command, and the date of interest enclosed in quotation marks. For example, to display the names of files that were created on April 30, 1990, you would enter the command:

```
DIR | FIND "04-30-90"
```

Note that the format of the date used in the command must match the format displayed by the DIR command. Most versions of DOS use the *mm-dd-yy* format used in the previous sample command. However, some foreign versions of DOS might require the *dd-mm-yy* format (that is, 30-04-89) or the *yy-mm-dd* format (89-04-30). To determine the appropriate date format for your version of DOS, merely enter the DIR command and look at the date assigned to each file.

Searching All Directories for a File

It is possible to use a single command to search all the directories on your hard disk from the command prompt. However, I must warn you that if you have an older, slower computer, the search can be quite time-consuming. Nonetheless, the technique is a valuable one, and it can come in handy in certain situations.

For example, suppose you use the Microsoft Excel spreadsheet program to prepare a budget. After spending many hours, you save the spreadsheet file with the file name BUDGET. Because Excel automatically adds the extension .XLS to any spreadsheet that you save, the file actually is stored under the file name BUDGET.XLS.

Now, suppose that the next day, when you try to bring your BUDGET spreadsheet back into Excel, Excel tells you that it cannot find a file named BUDGET.XLS. Undoubtedly, your first reaction is a sinking feeling either that you forgot to save the file or that the computer somehow failed to save the file as you'd requested. (The latter is by far the less likely of the two reasons for the missing file.)

What probably happened is that you indeed saved the file, but you were not paying attention to which directory you saved it on. Before you panic, you should first search all of the directories on your hard disk for the file. You could use the `CD` and `DIR.BUDGET.*` commands to access and search each directory, but there is an easier way.

The CHKDSK command provides an optional /V switch that displays the names of every file on the hard disk. You can see this for yourself by first changing to the directory that holds the CHKDSK.COM file, and then entering the command `CHKDSK /V`.

You can also use the CHKDSK /V command in conjunction with the FIND command to restrict the search to a particular file name or a string of characters. Remember, however, that both the CHKDSK.COM and FIND.EXE files must be on the current directory; otherwise, DOS merely displays the infamous `Bad command or file name` error message.

So now let's look at exactly how you quickly search all the directories on your hard disk for a file named BUDGET. First, change to the directory in which CHKDSK.COM and FIND.COM are located. Then, enter the command:

```
CHKDSK /V | FIND "BUDGET"
```

Notice that you must separate the two commands with the pipe character (|), you must enclose the file name you are searching for in double quotation marks, and you must enter the file name in uppercase letters. This is the basic syntax of all searches.

After a pause (which might be either a few seconds or a few minutes), your screen displays the location and name of all files that contain the name BUDGET, as in the example shown in Figure 9.14.

```
C:\>chkdsk /v | find "BUDGET"
        C:\ACCTNG\Q1BUDGET.DAT
        C:\WP\WPFILES\BUDGET.TXT
        C:\WINDOWS\BUDGET.XLS
        C:\DBASE\BUDGET89.DBF
        C:\DBASE\BUDGET89.MDX

C:\>
```

Figure 9.14. Results of searching all directories for the BUDGET file.

If your missing file appears on the list, you know exactly where to find it. For example, if you were looking for BUDGET.XLS (the spreadsheet created with the Microsoft Excel program), you now know that it is stored in a directory named WINDOWS. You now can COPY it from that directory to whatever directory you intended to store it on in the first place.

Of course, another common error is misspelling a file name while saving it, but not realizing you've made such an error. For example, you might have typed BUDHET, rather than BUDGET, when you saved the spreadsheet.

You cannot use the * and ? wildcard characters with the FIND command, but you can narrow or broaden the search by searching for more or fewer characters. For example, entering the command:

```
CHKDSK /V | FIND "BUD"
```

displays all file (and directory) names that contain the letters *BUD*.

The CHKDSK and FIND commands are also handy for finding program files that have a particular extension, such as .COM or .EXE. For example:

```
CHKDSK /V | FIND ".COM"
```

displays the names of all files on all directories that have the .COM extension. The command:

```
CHKDSK /V | FIND ".EXE"
```

displays the names of all files on all directories that have the .EXE extension.

If your search presents more files than can fit on the screen, you can channel the output to the printer instead. Merely redirect the output to the printer using the > PRN symbol, as in the following example:

```
CHKDSK /V | FIND ".EXE" > PRN
```

Or if the CHKDSK.COM, FIND.EXE, and MORE.COM files are all available from the current disk and directory, enter the command below to pause for a keypress after each screenful of information:

```
CHKDSK /V | FIND ".EXE" | MORE
```

FIND is also handy for searching for specific words or phrases within files. You can even use it to search for text or files that *do not* match some value (that is, display all files that do not have the .EXE extension). See the reference to the FIND command in Appendix B for additional applications.

Refining Your Copies

To use XCOPY, the XCOPY.EXE file must be accessible from the current drive and directory.

DOS Version 3.2 and all later versions include a program named XCOPY.EXE (for eXtended COPY) that can help you to more specifically select files for copying. Two of this command's eight optional switches are particularly handy:

/D:*date* Copies files that were created or changed on (or after) a specified date.

/S Copies all files from the current directory and all subdirectories beneath it.

To demonstrate the power of XCOPY, let's suppose that at the end of the day you want to copy new and modified files from your hard disk onto a floppy diskette in drive A:. Furthermore, you are certain that you've been working only with files on the \FINANCES and \FINANCES\SALES directories. Assuming that today's date is April 30, 1990, and that you are currently accessing the \FINANCES directory, you could enter the following command to copy only the files that were created or modified on (or after) the current date:

```
XCOPY *.* A: /D:04-30-90 /S
```

Note that the current date is specified in the *mm-dd-yy* format. However, if you are using a foreign version of DOS, you must use the appropriate format for your dates, as displayed by the DATE and DIR commands. Note also that the /S switch copies files from all subdirectories beneath the \FINANCES directory, but, because the /D switch is also set, only those files that were created or modified on or before April 30, 1990 are copied. If you start the XCOPY command from the root directory and use the /S switch, DOS copies all files from all directories on the disk.

XCOPY offers several other features that can help you speed and refine file copying. See the XCOPY command reference in Appendix B for more details.

Renaming Directories

Unlike DOS 4, earlier versions of DOS do not provide an easy way of renaming a directory. Instead, you need to create a new directory with the name you want to use, copy all the files from the old directory to the new directory, erase the files from the old directory, and then delete the old directory. Let's look at an example in which you change the name of a directory named BOOKS to BOOKS_88. (Both the new and old directories are one level below the root.)

First, you would enter the command CD \BOOKS to change to the existing directory. You might want to enter the DIR command and make a note of how many files are in the directory.

Next, enter the command MD \BOOKS_88 to create the new directory. Note the use of the backslash to ensure that the new directory is one level below the root directory. If you had entered MD BOOKS_88 DOS would have created the new directory below the current directory.

Your next step is to enter the command COPY *.* \BOOKS_88 to copy all the files from the current directory to the new directory. To verify that all the files have been copied, enter the command DIR \BOOKS_88 and be sure it contains the same number of files as the BOOKS directory.

When you are certain that all the files have been copied, enter the ERASE *.* command to delete all the files from the current directory. When DOS asks if you are sure, type Y and press Enter. Enter the DIR command to be sure all the files have been erased. (You might need to change the attributes on read-only files to erase them.)

Now you can delete the BOOKS directory. First, move up to the root directory by entering the CD \ command. Then, enter the RD \BOOKS command to remove the empty directory. Now all the files that used to be on the BOOKS directory are on a directory named BOOKS_88, and the BOOKS directory no longer exists. Use the usual CD \BOOKS_88 command to change to the new directory.

A Simple Way to Correct Errors

Aren't you annoyed when you type in a long command like COPY C\MARKTNG\BUDGET*.* C:\SALES\BUDGET and DOS responds with an error message like Path not found? You look at the command and realize that because you left out the colon after the C in the source, you have to type the whole line again. Well, guess what? You do not have to retype the entire command: DOS always remembers the last command you entered, and it provides several keys to help you change that command. The most commonly used of these special editing keys are:

F1 (or →)	Recalls one character from the previous command.
F2	Pressing F2, then any character, recalls all characters up to, but excluding, the typed character.
F3	Recalls all remaining characters from the previous command.
F4	Deletes all characters up to, but excluding, the typed character.
Ins (or Insert)	Lets you insert new characters into the command.
Del (or Delete)	Deletes one character from the previous command.
Backspace	Erases the character to the left of the cursor.
Esc	Cancels all current changes. Press Enter after Esc to redisplay the command prompt.

To fix the example command above, you would first press → six times to recall the first six characters, as follows:

```
C> COPY C
```

After you press the Ins (or Insert) key, you can insert as many characters as you need.

Next, press the Ins (or Insert) key so that you can insert a character; then, type the colon so the command now looks as follows:

```
C> COPY C:
```

Finally, press the F3 key to recall all the remaining characters from the previous command. The screen now displays the following:

```
COPY C:\MARKTNG\BUDGET\*.* C:\SALES\BUDGET
```

and you can now press Enter to enter the newly corrected command.

Let's look at a different example. Suppose you type the command DOR C:\SALES to view the names of files on the SALES directory. Of course, DOS returns the error message Bad command or file name because there is no command called DOR. To correct the error, press → (or F1) to recall the D, type the letter I (this replaces the letter O), and then press F3 to retrieve the rest of the command.

The screen now shows DIR C:\SALES, so you can press Enter to enter the command. (Note that in this example, the letter I *replaced* the letter O; it was not *inserted* before the letter O because you did not press the Ins key before typing the letter I.)

Another common error occurs when you type a path that contains a directory name that does not belong. For example, suppose you enter the command COPY C:\SALES\MARKTNG*.* A:, and DOS returns Path not found. You look at the command and remember that \MARKTNG is at the same level as \SALES, not below it. Therefore, you need to remove \SALES from the command.

To do so, press the F2 key, then the letter S to bring back all characters up to the S, as below:

```
COPY C:\
```

Next you want to delete all characters up to, but excluding, the first letter M. Press the F4 key, then type the letter M. (The deletion has no immediate effect on the screen.) Next, press the F3 key. Now the screen shows:

```
COPY C:\MARKTNG\*.* A:
```

Because the command is now correct, you can press Enter to execute the operation.

Besides being handy for correcting errors, the ability to retrieve the preceding command is valuable for entering several similar commands. For example, suppose you want to copy a file named TEMPLATE.WK1 to four different directories, named SALES\QTR1, SALES\QTR2, SALES\QTR3, and SALES\QTR4. To do so, first enter the initial command, which might look as follows:

```
COPY C:\123\TEMPLATE.WK1 C:\SALES\QTR1
```

Press Enter, and when the copy is finished, press F3 to recall the command. Press Backspace once to change the command to:

```
COPY C:\123\TEMPLATE.WK1 C:\SALES\QTR
```

Then, type 2 to change the command to:

```
COPY C:\123\TEMPLATE.WK1 C:\SALES\QTR2
```

and again press Enter. You can repeat the general procedure to copy the file to the SALES\QTR3 and SALES\QTR4 directories.

Canceling a Command

Suppose you start a process, such as copying a large group of files, but then you change your mind after DOS begins carrying out its orders. You can interrupt the command (any command) by pressing either Ctrl-C or the Break key. The "Break" key on most keyboards is Ctrl-Pause (hold down the Ctrl key and press the Pause key). On other keyboards, you press Ctrl-Scroll Lock or Ctrl-Break.

WARNING: Rebooting deletes all data stored in RAM and makes no attempt to save any data to the disk. Avoid pressing Ctrl-Alt-Del when a program other than DOS is in control of your computer.

Although it's unlikely, there may be times when your computer gets "hung up," and nothing you do at the keyboard can get it working correctly again. In such cases, you can *reboot* the system (also called a *warm boot*) by simultaneously holding down the Ctrl, Alt and Del keys. (If your computer has no hard disk, put your DOS Startup diskette in drive A: before you press Ctrl-Alt-Del.)

Your screen will go blank for a while, then DOS goes through a start-up process similar to when you first turn on the computer. Everything then should be back to normal.

Troubleshooting

If you make an error while managing files, DOS will most likely display one of the following error messages. Try using suggested solutions to correct the error.

- **Bad command or file name:** If you get this message while trying to use the ATTRIB, SORT, FIND, or XCOPY command, the appropriate file is not available on the current drive and directory. If your computer doesn't have a hard disk, you must insert the appropriate diskette into drive A: (use the DIR command to search the file names of the diskette). If you are using a hard disk, refer to the PATH command in Chapter 4 or Appendix B for information on making these *external* DOS commands more accessible.

- **Does S specify a file name or directory name on the target?:** When entering an XCOPY command, you used \S rather than /S as the switch, thereby confusing DOS. Press Break (hold down the Ctrl key and press either C or the Pause or Scroll Lock key).

- **File not found:** A specified file does not exist on the specified directory. For example, if you used only a file name, such as MYDATA.DAT, then MYDATA.DAT is not on the current disk or directory. Or, if you used a path and file name, such as C:\DBASE\MYDATA.DAT, then MYDATA.DAT does not exist in the DBASE directory of drive C:.

- **Invalid number of parameters:** You used too many optional switches with a command, or perhaps you used a backslash (\) rather than a forward slash (/) to identify a switch.

- **Invalid switch:** Either you used the wrong letter to identify a switch (as with the XCOPY command), or you used a forward slash (/) rather than a backslash (\) in a directory path (that is, you typed /FINANCES/SALES instead of the correct \FINANCES\SALES).

- **Path not found:** The path you specified in the command does not exist on your current disk. For example, you entered a command like COPY C:\SALES*.* A:, but your hard disk does not have a directory named SALES.

Summary

The power tips presented in this chapter will help you to use your computer more effectively and with much less effort. Following is a summary of the power techniques you've learned:

- To cancel an operation before DOS finishes it, press the Break key (Ctrl-Pause or Ctrl-Scroll Lock on most computers).

- At the command prompt, you can use the . symbol to refer to the current directory, and the .. symbol to refer to the parent directory.

- Enter the command DIR | SORT to view file names in alphabetical order.

- Enter the command DIR | FIND followed by a date in *mm-dd-yy* format to locate files that were created or modified on or after a particular date.

■ DOS versions 3.2 and higher offer the XCOPY command to help you gain more control over copy operations (discussed in detail under XCOPY in Appendix B).

■ The →, F1, F2, F3, F4, Ins, Del, and Backspace keys can be used as shortcuts for correcting errors in commands and for repeating a series of similar commands.

■ To rearrange the order of file names in the Files Area in the **File System** screen, pull down the Options menu and select Display options...; then, press Tab and select a sort order from the Sort by: options.

■ To quickly select all files with a similar extension from the Files Area, first pull down the Options menu and select Display options.... Then, enter an ambiguous file name in the Name: box and press Enter. Finally, pull down the File menu and select the Select all option.

■ If you want to perform an operation with files that are stored on separate directories, first pull down the Options menu, select File options..., and then, mark the Select across directories option with an X, either by highlighting and pressing the Spacebar or by clicking the option once with your mouse. Press Enter after marking the option with the X.

■ To gain access to all files on a disk—regardless of the directories they are stored on—pull down the Arrange menu, and select System file list.

■ To prevent DOS 4 from asking for permission before erasing or overwriting files, pull down the Options menu, select File options..., and remove the X's from the Confirm on delete and/or Confirm on replace options.

■ To leave the DOS Shell without disrupting current settings or selected file names, press Shift-F9.

■ To return to the DOS Shell after pressing Shift-F9, enter the command EXIT instead of the usual DOSSHELL command.

three

Customizing Your System

The next three chapters discuss techniques that let you customize many of the elements of your computer system, including the keyboard, screen displays, the printer, and the hard disk. In addition, DOS 4 users learn techniques for customizing the DOS Shell. The techniques presented in these chapters make your computer easier to use and, in many cases, simplify your work.

Topics in the following chapters include:

- *Creating and editing DOS text files with the Edlin line editor.*
- *Simplifying hard disk usage by making important programs accessible from all directories.*
- *Customizing the DOS Shell so that you can run programs merely by selecting Shell options.*
- *Important techniques for backing up your hard disk and recovering from a hard disk crash.*
- *Taking advantage of special screen features, such as color, blinking, and reverse video.*
- *Using your printer effectively.*
- *Customizing the actions of Function keys so that they perform special operations.*

Creating and Editing Files

In future chapters, there might be times when you want to use two special DOS files to configure your computer. One file, named CONFIG.SYS, tells DOS how to *configure* (set up) your hardware (described in more detail later). A second file, named AUTOEXEC.BAT, lets you customize and simplify the use of your computer.

To *edit* (change) these files, you need to use a program called an *editor*. There are hundreds of editors available for DOS microcomputers: These include word processing programs, such as WordPerfect and WordStar, and small "desktop" text editors that come with programs such as Sidekick. In addition, DOS comes with a somewhat simplified editor, named Edlin, that you can use to edit files.

This chapter focuses on Edlin because it's the only editor that your computer is certain to already have. However, if you have a more powerful word processing program, by all means use it to edit the DOS files discussed in later chapters. (You should, however, read the first few sections of this chapter.) If you don't have a word processor, or if you don't have the time to learn to use one, you can skip to the section "Using Edlin to Edit DOS Files" later in this chapter.

Using Word Processors to Edit DOS Text Files

ASCII is pronounced "AS-key."

Word processors are by far the easiest and most powerful tools for editing DOS text files. However, there is one catch to using a word processor—most assume that you are creating documents that people will be reading, rather than files that DOS will be reading. Because of this, most word processors insert special formatting characters into files. The word processor uses these formatting characters to display the document on the screen or to compose a page for the printer, but it never actually shows them on the screen, so you normally don't see them.

The Bad command or file name *error message is sometimes caused by hidden formatting characters, but other problems, such as misspelling a command, also cause this error message to appear.*

However, DOS sees the formatting characters, and it becomes quite confused by them. As soon as DOS encounters one of these formatting characters in either the AUTOEXEC.BAT or CONFIG.SYS file, it stops trying to read the file and returns an error message, such as Bad command or file name. This has been known to drive many computerists half crazy, because they cannot see the formatting characters that DOS sees, and therefore they cannot figure out what is wrong.

To show you the "invisibility" of these formatting characters, let's look at an example using WordStar as the word processing program. Figure 10.1 shows the contents of a sample AUTOEXEC.BAT file displayed on the screen by WordStar. (Don't worry if you do not understand what the items in the file mean—you will soon enough.)

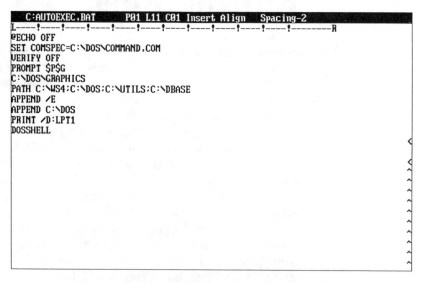

Figure 10.1. Sample AUTOEXEC.BAT file on WordStar's screen.

The WordStar screen does not appear to contain any strange-looking formatting characters in the text, just the normal letters, numbers, and punctuation symbols from the keyboard. (The top two lines are displayed by WordStar and are not part of the file. The AUTOEXEC.BAT file actually begins with the line @ECHO OFF.)

Don't worry if you cannot find your own AUTOEXEC.BAT or CONFIG.SYS file right now; your computer might not even have them yet.

Now, let's suppose that after you change the file on the WordStar screen, you save it. Later, when you restart the computer and DOS attempts to read the file, it displays an error message (such as Bad command or file name). When you use your word processing program to view the file, everything appears to be in order.

Before you waste a lot of time trying to figure out what's wrong, there is a very simple method of checking a file to see if it contains special characters: Use DOS, not the word processing program, to display the contents of the file. DOS displays *all* characters—including any special formatting characters that the word processor is hiding.

DOS 4 users can look at the contents of any file by selecting its name from the Files Area of the File System (using the Spacebar or a single mouse click) and then selecting View from the File pull-down menu. As you can see in Figure 10.2, WordStar was indeed hiding some strange-looking formatting characters, particularly at the end of each word. This is definitely *not* a plain ASCII text file, and, therefore, it is not a file that DOS can read.

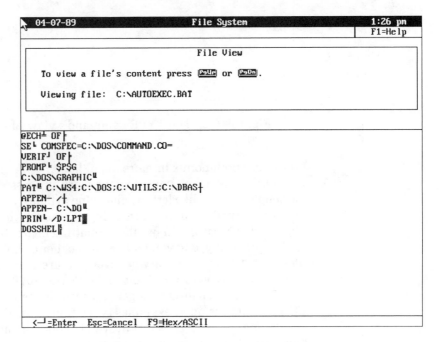

Figure 10.2. DOS's view of the WordStar file.

Command prompt users can use the TYPE command to view the contents of a file. In this example, entering the command `TYPE C:\AUTOEXEC.BAT` shows that the file is not an ASCII text file, as Figure 10.3 illustrates.

Therefore, if you use a word processor to edit DOS text files, there are two very important points to keep in mind:

■ You must take special steps to ensure that all DOS text files are saved in ASCII text format.

■ The only way you can see if a text file contains formatting codes is by using the View option in the DOS File System or the TYPE command at the DOS command prompt.

```
C:\DOS>type c:\autoexec.bat
@ECH⌐ OF├
SE└ COMSPEC=C:\DOS\COMMAND.CO=
VERIF┘ OF├
PROMP└ $P$G
C:\DOS\GRAPHIC⊔
PAT⊔ C:\WS4:C:\DOS:C:\UTILS:C:\DBAS├
APPEN─ ╱├
APPEN─ C:\DO⊔
PRIN└ ╱D:LPT▓
DOSSHEL╟

C:\DOS>
```

Figure 10.3. The TYPE command's view of a non-ASCII file.

I'll discuss both points in more detail later.

Of course, when you use your word processor to create documents for people to read, like letters, magazine articles, or books, you don't need to be concerned about the formatting characters that are saved in the file. The word processor will use the formatting characters to print your document more neatly, and you will never see them. However, you need to save files in ASCII text format whenever you are editing files that DOS must read, such as CONFIG.SYS and AUTOEXEC.BAT.

This chapter discusses general techniques for creating and editing DOS text files using as examples two popular word processing programs, WordStar and WordPerfect. However, I cannot do much more than explain how to display the file on the screen and how to save it properly. To learn the editing features of your word processor, you need to refer to that program's documentation or to a book that explains that program.

If you use a word processing program other than WordStar or WordPerfect, you need to learn how to use it to create, edit, and save ASCII text files. In particular, if you are using one of the following word processing programs, look for information describing the options listed next to each program's name:

WARNING: Never use a word processing program to edit a program file with the .COM or .EXE extension. These are not DOS text files.

Be sure to read the section "Where to Store AUTOEXEC.BAT and CONFIG.SYS" later in this chapter before using your own word processing program.

Program	Topic for ASCII files
Display Write	ASCII COPY TO FILE
Microsoft Word	Save UNFORMATTED
MultiMate	CONVERT program, or ASCII format
Sprint	File Translate, Export ASCII file

Editing DOS Text Files with WordPerfect

If you currently own a copy of WordPerfect and have installed it on your computer, you can use it to edit DOS text files. Exactly how you use WordPerfect depends on whether or not you have a hard disk. Refer to the appropriate section below for your computer.

Computers Without a Hard Disk

If your computer doesn't have a hard disk, start your computer in the usual way with the DOS Startup diskette (or the Shell diskette for DOS 4 users) in drive A:. When DOS and your computer are booted up and ready to go, remove the DOS diskette from drive A:, and insert the WordPerfect diskette. Then, put the DOS Startup diskette in drive B:.

Next, you need to start WordPerfect and tell it the name of the file you want to edit. Be sure that you are accessing disk drive A:, and then follow the appropriate steps for your version of DOS:

1. If you are using the DOS Shell, select `File System` from the **Start Programs** screen.
2. In the File System, move the highlight to the file name WP.EXE in the Files Area.
3. Press Enter, or double-click the mouse when WP.EXE is highlighted.
4. In the dialog box, type the location and name of the file you want to edit (that is, `B:\AUTOEXEC.BAT` or `B:\CONFIG.SYS`).
5. Press Enter.

1. If you are working from the command prompt, type the command `WP` followed by a blank space and the location and name of the file you want to edit (for example, `WP B:\AUTOEXEC.BAT` or `WP B:\CONFIG.SYS`).
2. Press Enter.

Computers with a Hard Disk

If your computer has a hard disk, you can run WordPerfect from its own directory and edit files on any other directory. Use the following steps for your version of DOS:

1. Select `File System` from the Shell **Start Programs** screen.
2. Select the name of the WordPerfect directory (usually `WP`) from the Directory Tree.
3. Move the highlight to the file name WP.EXE in the Files Area.
4. Run the program by pressing Enter or by double-clicking the mouse on the highlighted name.
5. Type the location and name of the file you want to edit, such as `C:\AUTOEXEC.BAT` or `C:\CONFIG.SYS`.
6. Press Enter.

1. If you are working from the command prompt, change to the WordPerfect directory (usually named WP) by entering the command `CD \WP`.

2. Type the command `WP` followed by a blank space and the location and name of the file you want to edit (for example, `WP C:\AUTOEXEC.BAT` or `WP C:\CONFIG.SYS`.

3. Press Enter.

If the file that you are editing already exists, it appears in the WordPerfect screen. If it does not already exist, most of the screen is blank, awaiting you to type new text. Figure 10.4 shows a sample AUTOEXEC.BAT file displayed on the WordPerfect screen. (Don't worry if your AUTOEXEC.BAT file looks different or if you don't understand what the commands in the file mean; you'll learn about them soon.)

```
@ECHO OFF
SET COMSPEC=C:\DOS\COMMAND.COM
VERIFY OFF
PROMPT $P$G
C:\DOS\GRAPHICS
PATH C:\WS4;C:\DOS;C:\UTILS;C:\DBASE
APPEND /E
APPEND C:\DOS
PRINT /D:LPT1
DOSSHELL
^Z




C:\AUTOEXEC.BAT                              Doc 1 Pg 1 Ln 11     Pos 3
```

Figure 10.4. A sample AUTOEXEC.BAT file on the WordPerfect screen.

Don't worry if the symbol ^Z appears at the bottom of the file. You can leave it there, or you can type over it. But do not type an extra ^Z into the file if you erased the existing one.

Now you can use any of WordPerfect's capabilities to change the file (but, again, I cannot explain how to use the program here). When you finish making changes, you need to save the file in ASCII format.

Saving An ASCII File with WordPerfect

When you save an ASCII text file that's been created or changed by WordPerfect, be sure to always follow these steps:

1. Press `Ctrl-F5` (hold down the Ctrl key and press the function key labeled F5).

2. Type the number 1 to select Save from the DOS Text File Format options.

3. Press Enter when the screen displays the Document to be saved prompt.

4. Type Y when the screen asks if you should *Replace* the original file with the new file.

5. Press the F7 function key.

6. When the message Save document? (Y/N) appears, type N (because you've already saved your changes in an ASCII text file).

7. When the Exit WP? (Y/N) message appears, type Y.

Those steps now return you to DOS.

Abandoning Your Changes

If you make errors in the file you are editing that you cannot fix, merely leave the original file intact when you exit WordPerfect. To do this, perform *only* steps 5 through 7 above (but ignore the parenthetical comment at the end of step 6).

Learning WordPerfect

Now that you know how to load and save a DOS text file with the WordPerfect word processor, you can use that program in the future when you need to change DOS files. Again, if you own WordPerfect, but don't really know how to use it yet, you should first study the documentation or a book before you try changing your DOS files.

Whether or not you plan to use WordPerfect to edit your DOS text files, be certain to read the section in this chapter called "Where to Store AUTOEXEC.BAT and CONFIG.SYS" before moving to the next chapter.

Editing DOS Text Files with WordStar

If you own the WordStar word processing program and have installed it on your computer, you can use it to edit your DOS text files. This section focuses on using Version 4 of WordStar, but the general techniques work with all versions of the program.

The exact techniques you'll use largely depend on whether or not your computer has a hard disk. Refer to the appropriate section below for your computer.

Computers with No Hard Disk

If your computer doesn't have a hard disk, start your computer in the usual way with the DOS Startup diskette (or the Shell diskette for DOS 4 users) in drive A:. When DOS and your computer are booted up and ready to go, remove the DOS diskette from drive A:, and insert the WordStar diskette. Then, put the DOS Startup diskette in drive B:.

Next, you need to start WordStar. Be sure that you are accessing disk drive A:, and then follow the appropriate steps for your version of DOS:

1. If you are using the DOS Shell, select File System from the **Start Programs** screen.
2. In the File System, move the highlight to the file name WS.EXE in the Files Area.
3. Press Enter, or double-click the mouse when WS.EXE is highlighted.
4. When the dialog box appears, leave it empty and press Enter.

1. If you are working from the command prompt, type the command WS and then press Enter to run WordStar.

Computers with a Hard Disk

If your computer has a hard disk, you can run WordStar from its own directory and edit files on any other directory. Use the following steps for your version of DOS:

1. Select File System from the Shell **Start Programs** screen.
2. Select the name of the WordStar directory (WS4 for version 4 of WordStar) from the Directory Tree.
3. Move the highlight to the file name WS.EXE in the Files Area.
4. Run the program by pressing Enter or by double-clicking the mouse on the highlighted name.
5. When the dialog box appears, leave it blank and press Enter.

1. If you are working from the command prompt, change to the WordStar directory (named WS4 for version 4 of WordStar) by entering the command CD \WS4.
2. Type the command WS and press Enter.

When WordStar first appears on the screen, it displays a menu of options. Note that one of these options is D open a document and one is N open a nondocument. When editing ASCII text files, you must *always* use the nondocument mode to create or edit a file: Type the letter N. WordStar presents the prompt Nondocument to open and waits for a file name.

You must then type the complete location and name of the file you want to edit. For example, on a computer with no hard disk, you would enter B:\AUTOEXEC.BAT or B:\CONFIG.SYS, depending on which file you want to edit. On a computer with a hard disk, you would type B:\AUTOEXEC.BAT or C:\CONFIG.SYS. Press Enter after you type the file name.

If the file that you are editing already exists, it appears on the Word-

Star screen ready for editing. If it does not already exist, most of the screen is blank, awaiting you to type new text. Figure 10.5 shows a sample AUTOEXEC.BAT file and the NON-DOCUMENT EDIT MENU displayed on the WordStar screen. (Don't worry if your AUTOEXEC.BAT file looks different or if you don't understand the commands shown in the file; you'll learn about them soon.)

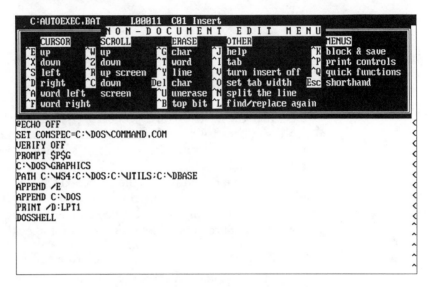

Figure 10.5. A sample AUTOEXEC.BAT file on the WordStar screen.

Now you can use any of WordStar's capabilities to change the file (but, again, I cannot explain how to use the program here).

Saving a WordStar File

When you finish changing the file, save it and exit WordStar by typing Ctrl-KX (hold down the Ctrl key and press the letter K. Then, release the Ctrl key and type the letter X).

Abandoning WordStar Changes

If you inadvertently make errors in the file, and you would prefer to abandon your changes rather than save them, press Ctrl-KQ (rather than Ctrl-KX). WordStar might ask Are you sure you want to abandon them (Y/N)?. Press Y to answer Yes. Then, type the letter X to leave WordStar and return to DOS.

Learning WordStar

Now that you know how to load and save a DOS text file with the WordStar word processor, you can use that program in the future when you need to change DOS files. Again, if you own WordStar, but don't really know how to use it yet, you should first study the documentation or a book before you try changing your DOS text files.

Whether or not you plan to use WordStar to edit your DOS text files, be certain to read the section in this chapter called "Where to Store AUTOEXEC.BAT and CONFIG.SYS Files" before moving to the next chapter.

Safety Precautions for All Word Processors

As mentioned earlier in this chapter, it is very easy to inadvertently save a DOS text file with a word processing program's formatting characters. However, because these formatting characters do not appear on the word processing program's screen, it's not so easy to realize you've actually made this error.

If you've edited one of the DOS text files in the previous examples, play it safe and view the contents of the file using DOS rather than the word processing program. That way, you can be sure the file is indeed clean of formatting characters. The general steps for checking a file are as follows:

1. If you are using the DOS 4 Shell, first access the **File System** screen.

2. Move to the Drives Area of the screen, and select the drive on which the edited file is stored.

3. Select the directory on which the file is stored from the Directory Tree. (AUTOEXEC.BAT or CONFIG.SYS are the root directory at the top of the tree.)

4. Move the highlight to the Files Area, and then move the highlight to the name of the file you just edited.

5. Press the Spacebar, or click your mouse once to select the file name.

6. Press F10 and Enter to pull down the File menu, and then select **View**.

7. After viewing the file, press Esc to return to the **File System** screen.

If you are working from the command prompt, simply enter the TYPE command followed by the location and name of the file you just edited. For example, if you do not have a hard disk, and you have just edited the AUTOEXEC.BAT file, enter the command:

```
TYPE B:\AUTOEXEC.BAT
```

If you have a hard disk, and you have just edited the AUTOEXEC.BAT file, enter the command:

```
TYPE C:\AUTOEXEC.BAT
```

Removing Embedded Formatting Codes

If you use DOS to view the contents of a file, and you discover that your text file indeed contains formatting characters, you'll need to remove those characters. If you are using WordPerfect, merely repeat all the steps that explained how to load the file and how to save the file in ASCII text format. (You don't need to make any changes while the file is displayed on the WordPerfect screen.)

If you are using WordStar, you must reformat the entire file. To do so, follow the exact steps that explained how to bring the file to the WordStar screen. Then, if you are using version 4 of WordStar, press Ctrl-QU (hold down the Ctrl key and type the letters Q then U; then release the Ctrl key). If you are using another version of WordStar (or you are not sure which version you are using), press Ctrl-QQB (hold down the Ctrl key and type the letters QQB; then release the Ctrl key). When the cursor moves to the bottom of the text, press Ctrl-KX (as described earlier) to save the reformatted file.

You might again want to use DOS to display the contents of the file, just to be sure you successfully removed the formatting characters from the file.

Using Edlin to Edit DOS Text Files

If you don't own a word processing program, and you don't want to invest the money required to purchase one, you can always use the Edlin program, which comes free with DOS, to edit DOS text files. The one advantage to using Edlin is that it always stores its files in ASCII text format, so you never have to worry about word processing characters being embedded in your files.

The main disadvantage to using Edlin is that it is a *line editor*. Whereas word processing programs are *screen-oriented*, allowing you to freely move the cursor to any position in the file and make changes, line editors, such as Edlin, allow you to work with only one line at a time. This is very inconvenient when you work with large files. Fortunately, the DOS text files that you will be editing in this book are all relatively small, so the inconvenience will be minor.

Finding Edlin

To use the Edlin program, you first need to find the diskette or directory that contains the file named EDLIN.COM. You already know many techniques for locating files, so you should be able to do this on your own by now. If you are using diskettes, EDLIN.COM is stored on one of your DOS diskettes. If you are using a hard disk, EDLIN.COM is probably stored in the same directory as your other DOS files—either the root directory or the directory named DOS. (If EDLIN.COM is not on your hard disk, copy it onto your hard disk from one of the DOS diskettes.)

Starting Edlin

After you determine which diskette or directory contains EDLIN.COM, the exact techniques for using Edlin depend on whether or not your computer has a hard disk.

If your computer does not have a hard disk, the general technique for using Edlin is to insert the DOS diskette that contains EDLIN.COM in drive A: and to insert the diskette that contains the file that you want to edit in drive B:. (Of course, if both the Edlin program and the file you want to edit are on the same diskette, you need not bother with drive B: at all. For example, if EDLIN.COM is on your DOS Startup diskette, and you want to edit the AUTOEXEC.BAT or CONFIG.SYS file, you need only place the Startup diskette in drive A: because those files must always be on the startup disk.)

If your computer has a hard disk, you might need to change to the directory that contains the EDLIN.COM file before you can use the Edlin program. DOS 4 users should use the Shell's File System to change to the appropriate drive. If you are using an earlier version of DOS, or you prefer to work from the command prompt, use the usual CHDIR or CD command to change to the directory that contains the EDLIN.COM file.

After you access the diskette or directory that contains the EDLIN.COM file, use the following general steps to start the program:

1. If you are using the DOS Shell File System, highlight the file name `EDLIN.COM` in the Files Area and press Enter (or double-click the mouse on the file name).

2. When the Open File dialog box appears, type the complete location and name of the file you want to edit, as discussed in the next section.

1. If you are working from the command prompt and are accessing the drive and directory that contains the EDLIN.COM file, type the command `EDLIN` followed by a space and the complete location and name of the file you want to edit, as discussed in the next section.

Remember that you must include the complete location (path) and file name when specifying a file to edit. For example, if you have a hard disk and want to edit the CONFIG.SYS file, specify `C:\CONFIG.SYS` as the file to edit. If you do not have a hard disk and your Startup diskette is in drive B:, specify `B:\CONFIG.SYS` as the file to edit. If both the EDLIN.COM and CONFIG.SYS files are on the same diskette or directory, you can omit the path and merely specify `CONFIG.SYS` as the file to edit.

If the file that you told Edlin to edit does not already exist on the drive and directory you specified, Edlin displays the following message:

```
New file
*_
```

If the file that you told Edlin to edit already exists on the drive and directory you specified, Edlin displays this message instead:

```
End of input file
*_
```

In either case, the asterisk and blinking cursor tell you that Edlin is ready to accept a command from you. The Edlin commands are different from DOS commands. Table 10.1 summarizes the Edlin commands discussed in this chapter, as well as their *syntax* (general format). When using Edlin, you need type only the first letter of the command (that is, L for List). Optional parts of the command are shown in angle brackets (< >). Don't type the brackets when using these options. The examples that follow will show you how to interpret the syntax properly.

Table 10.1. Summary of basic Edlin commands.

Command	Syntax
Insert text	*< line-number>* I
List lines of text	*< start-line>*,*< end-line>* L
line number	(To change a specific line, merely type the line's number and press Enter)
Delete lines of text	*< start-line>*,*< end-line>* D
Move text	*start-line,end-line,< to-line>* M
Replace text	*start-line,end-line<?>* R*oldtext^Znewtext*
Exit with save	E
Quit with no save	Q

Creating a Practice File

For some hands-on experience using Edlin, let's create a sample file named PRACTICE.TXT. If you are using a computer that doesn't have a hard disk, be sure that the DOS diskette that holds the EDLIN.COM file is in disk drive A:. Then, place a formatted diskette (perhaps the same one you used in Chapter 8 to create the SAMPLE1.TXT and SAMPLE2.TXT files) in disk drive B:. If you are using a hard disk, change to the directory that contains EDLIN.COM (usually either the root directory or the DOS directory).

Next, use the general steps described earlier to run the Edlin program and create a file named PRACTICE.TXT. If you are using a computer without a hard disk, be sure to specify `B:\PRACTICE.TXT` as the file to create. If you are using a hard disk, you can store the file on any directory. (If you want to store it on the PRACTICE directory you created earlier in this book, specify `C:\PRACTICE\PRACTICE.TXT` as the file to edit.)

Inserting New Lines of Text

To add new lines to the file, press the letter I while the asterisk and blinking cursor are displayed. Your screen displays `1:*` indicating that you are about to create the first line in the file. Now you can simply type text, using the Backspace key as necessary to make corrections. Type the sentence `Knowledge is of two kinds..`

When you finish, press Enter to mark the end of the line. Edlin now displays `2:*` indicating that it is ready for the second line (as shown in Figure 10.6).

```
C:\DOS>EDLIN C:\PRACTICE\PRACTICE.TXT
New file
*I
       1:*Knowledge is of two kinds.
       2:*
```

Figure 10.6. One line typed into the PRACTICE.TXT file.

Now, type the words `We know a subject ourselves,` (including the final comma) and press Enter. Edlin is now ready for the third line (3:*), so type the words `or we know where we can find` and press Enter again.

At the fourth line, type the words `information upon it,` and press Enter to end the line. Leave the fifth line blank by pressing Enter without typing anything.

At the sixth line, type `Boswell, Life of Johnson, 1775` and then press Enter. At this point, your file should look something like Figure 10.7.

```
C:\DOS>EDLIN C:\PRACTICE\PRACTICE.TXT
New file
*I
        1:*Knowledge is of two kinds,
        2:*We know a subject ourselves,
        3:*or we know where we can find
        4:*information upon it,
        5:*
        6:*Boswell, Life of Johnson, 1775
        7:*
```

Figure 10.7. Sample PRACTICE.TXT file typed with Edlin.

Saving a File

At the moment, all the text you've typed is stored in RAM. To save this file for future use, you must use the **E** command. First, you need to tell Edlin that you are done inserting lines. To do so, press Break or Ctrl-C (hold down the Ctrl key and type the letter **C**), and Edlin displays **^C** on the screen.

Note that after you entered the Insert command (I), the *prompt was always indented and preceded by a line number. This is Edlin's way of telling you that you are typing text, and therefore you cannot enter any commands. When you want to enter commands, you must press Ctrl-C to move back to the "un-indented" *prompt.

As Figure 10.8 shows, you enter or edit text whenever the * prompt is indented and preceded by a line number. You enter Edlin commands whenever the * prompt is not indented. Pressing Ctrl-C takes you from the text editing mode to the Edlin command mode.

Now that Edlin is ready to accept a command, enter the Exit command by typing the letter **E** and pressing Enter. This returns you to the DOS prompt (or the DOS Shell).

To verify the contents of the file, use the View option in the DOS 4 File System, or use the TYPE command at the command prompt. Figure 10.9 shows the effects of entering the command TYPE C:\PRACTICE \PRACTICE.TXT to view the file from the command prompt.

Modifying an Edlin File

To modify an existing Edlin file, you start by using the same steps (or command) that created the file. For example, from the command prompt you

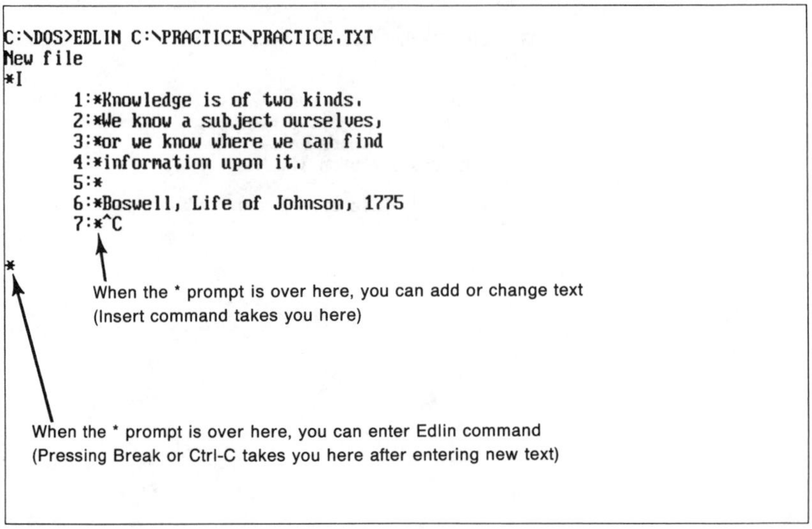

```
C:\DOS>EDLIN C:\PRACTICE\PRACTICE.TXT
New file
*I
        1:*Knowledge is of two kinds,
        2:*We know a subject ourselves,
        3:*or we know where we can find
        4:*information upon it,
        5:*
        6:*Boswell, Life of Johnson, 1775
        7:*^C
*
```

When the * prompt is over here, you can add or change text
(Insert command takes you here)

When the * prompt is over here, you can enter Edlin command
(Pressing Break or Ctrl-C takes you here after entering new text)

Figure 10.8. Two modes for using Edlin.

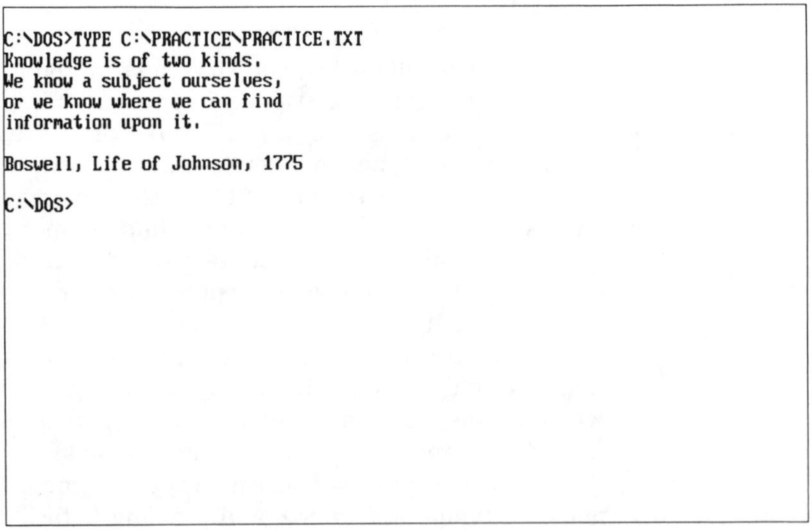

```
C:\DOS>TYPE C:\PRACTICE\PRACTICE.TXT
Knowledge is of two kinds,
We know a subject ourselves,
or we know where we can find
information upon it,

Boswell, Life of Johnson, 1775

C:\DOS>
```

Figure 10.9. Contents of PRACTICE.TXT displayed by TYPE.

enter the command `EDLIN B:\PRACTICE.TXT` or `EDLIN C:\PRACTICE` `\PRACTICE.TXT`. Edlin first displays the message End of input file and then the *prompt.

To view all the lines in the file, enter the L (List) command. Note that each line is numbered. To edit a line, type its number and press Enter. For example, to change line 4, simply type the number 4 and press Enter. Notice that the prompt is indented again, indicating that Edlin is expecting text rather than commands. Also, note that the line you want to change is displayed on the screen, followed by a blank line with the same number, as shown in Figure 10.10.

```
C:\DOS>EDLIN C:\PRACTICE\PRACTICE.TXT
End of input file
*L
        1:*Knowledge is of two kinds.
        2: We know a subject ourselves,
        3: or we know where we can find
        4: information upon it.
        5:
        6: Boswell, Life of Johnson, 1775
*4

        4:*information upon it.
        4:*
```

Figure 10.10 Line number 4 is being edited.

While you are in this "edit mode," you can make changes using the keys shown in Table 10.2 (the same keys as used for changing and correcting commands at the command prompt, as discussed in Chapter 9).

Table 10.2. Keys used while editing a line of text.

Key	Effect
F1 or →	Copies the character shown in the line above to the new line.
F2	Copies characters up to, but excluding, typed character from the preceding line.
F3	Copies the rest of line.
F4	Deletes characters up to, but excluding, the typed character.
←	Moves the cursor to the left.
Ins (or Insert)	Toggles between Insert mode and Overwrite mode.
Del (or Delete)	Deletes the character at the cursor position.
Ctrl-V	Allows the insertion of special codes.
Enter	Saves changes and returns to the * prompt.
Esc	Cancels any changes you made in the line and shows a back-slash. Press Enter to return to the * prompt.

The Ctrl-V key is included in Table 10.2 for future reference. You will learn how and when to use Ctrl-V in Chapter 14.

To demonstrate the use of these keys, let's change the word *upon* to *about* in line 4. First, press F2 then type the letter u to retrieve the first word and the space that follows it. Notice that the cursor is aligned beneath the letter "u", not the blank space:

```
4:*information upon it.
4:*information _
```

Next type the letters abou to replace the word *"upon."* Your screen now looks like this:

```
4:*information upon it.
4:*information abou_
```

Because the word *about* is longer than the word *upon*, you need to switch to "insert mode" to insert the next letter. Press the Ins (or Insert) key once; then, type the letter t so that your screen looks like the following:

After you press the Ins (or Insert) key, you can insert as many characters as you wish.

```
4:*information upon it.
4:*information about_
```

Now, press the F3 key to copy the rest of the sentence from the line above. Your screen shows the following corrected line:

```
4:*information upon it.
4:*information about it._
```

To save this change in memory, press Enter. To review the entire file to make sure the change was made, type the letter L and press Enter. Your screen should now look like Figure 10.11.

```
C:\DOS>EDLIN C:\PRACTICE\PRACTICE.TXT
End of input file
*L
        1:*Knowledge is of two kinds.
        2: We know a subject ourselves,
        3: or we know where we can find
        4: information upon it.
        5:
        6: Boswell, Life of Johnson, 1775
*4
        4:*information upon it.
        4:*information about it.
*L
        1: Knowledge is of two kinds.
        2: We know a subject ourselves,
        3: or we know where we can find
        4:*information about it.
        5:
        6: Boswell, Life of Johnson, 1775
*
```

Figure 10.11 Line 4 has been edited.

If you look closely at Figure 10.11, you'll see that line number 4 has an asterisk to its left. This asterisk is not part of the text. Instead, it's DOS's way of informing you that the line has recently been changed, and it also marks the *current line*. Some commands, such as Insert, start from the current line if you do not specify another line number in the command. This can be confusing if you are not careful. A later section titled "Inserting Lines in an Existing File" shows you how to use the I (insert) command to add new lines to a file, without regard to the current line.

Global Replaces

Another way to edit an Edlin file is to use the *global search-and-replace* feature that enables Edlin to automatically find and change a word (or words). The general syntax for the Replace command is:

*start-line,end-line***R***oldtext*^**Z***newtext*

where *start-line* and *end-line* specify the range of lines to be searched during the replacement. R is the abbreviation for the Replace command. *Oldtext* is the text you want to replace. ^Z is typed by pressing Ctrl-Z, and *newtext* is the new text to add to the file.

Let's use the procedure to tell Edlin to replace the word "know" with the word "forget" throughout the entire file. At the * command prompt prompt type 1,6Rknow^Zforget. (Remember, to type ^Z you must hold down the Ctrl key and type the letter Z.) After typing the command, press Enter. Edlin displays all the lines it changes.

Once again, to review the entire file, enter the List command by typing the letter L and pressing Enter. As you can see in Figure 10.12, Edlin changed the word "know" to "forget" in two lines.

```
      3: or we know where we can find
      4: information upon it.
      5:
      6: Boswell, Life of Johnson, 1775
*4
      4:*information upon it.
      4:*information about it.
*L
      1: Knowledge is of two kinds.
      2: We know a subject ourselves,
      3: or we know where we can find
      4:*information about it.
      5:
      6: Boswell, Life of Johnson, 1775
*1,6Rknow^Zforget
      2: We forget a subject ourselves,
      3: or we forget where we can find
*L
      1: Knowledge is of two kinds.
      2: We forget a subject ourselves,
      3:*or we forget where we can find
      4: information about it.
      5:
      6: Boswell, Life of Johnson, 1775
*
```

Figure 10.12 Edlin replaced the word "know" with "forget".

Note that the Replace command is *case-sensitive*, which means that it does not consider upper- and lowercase letters to be the same. For example, if you tell Edlin to replace SMITH with JONES, *only* SMITH (in uppercase letters) is replaced; however, *Smith* and *smith* are left unchanged. (This also explains why the "Know" in "Knowledge" was not changed to "forget" in the PRACTICE.TXT file.)

The optional ? symbol tells the Replace command to stop and ask for permission before making a change. Use this option when you want to change some, but not all, occurrences of text in a file. To try this option, type the command `1,6?Rforget^Zknow`. In English, this command says, "Starting at line one and ending in line six, replace the word "forget" with the word "know"—but ask (?) for permission first."

When you press Enter, DOS starts the replacement operation. Each time it encounters a line containing the word "forget," it displays that line followed by the prompt `O.K.?`. Type `Y` to have Edlin make the replacement in the current line, or type `N` to cancel the replacement on the current line.

Inserting Lines in an Existing File

To add new lines at the end of text in an existing file, type the command `#I` (Edlin automatically interprets the # symbol as "the next new line.") When you type `#1` and press Enter, Edlin displays the prompt showing it is ready to accept a new line number 7.

Now, press Enter to leave the new line blank; then, type the following three lines (remembering to press Enter after typing each line):

```
I MUST ALWAYS REMEMBER TO PRESS BREAK
OR CTRL-C AFTER INSERTING NEW TEXT,
TO ENTER NEW COMMANDS
```

When you finish, press Ctrl-C to return to the * prompt for entering commands. Then, type the `L` command and press Enter to review your file. It should look like Figure 10.13.

Moving Lines

You can move any lines in a text file by using the general syntax:

start line,end line,new location **M**

For example, to move lines 8 through 10 so that they start at line 3, type the command `8,10,3M` and press Enter. To see the results of the move, type the letter `L` and press Enter. Figure 10.14 shows the changes in the file.

To move a single line, use its line number as both the *start line* and *end line* number in the command. For example, to move line 10 so that it becomes line 3. you would enter the command `10,10,3 M`.

```
        6: Boswell, Life of Johnson, 1775
*1,6?Rforget^Zknow
        2: We know a subject ourselves,
O.K.? y
        3: or we know where we can find
O.K.? y
*#I
        7:*
        8:*I MUST ALWAYS REMEMBER TO PRESS BREAK
        9:*OR CTRL-C AFTER INSERTING NEW TEXT,
       10:*TO ENTER NEW COMMANDS
       11:*^C

*L
        1: Knowledge is of two kinds.
        2: We know a subject ourselves,
        3: or we know where we can find
        4: information about it.
        5:
        6: Boswell, Life of Johnson, 1775
        7:
        8: I MUST ALWAYS REMEMBER TO PRESS BREAK
        9: OR CTRL-C AFTER INSERTING NEW TEXT,
       10: TO ENTER NEW COMMANDS
*
```

Figure 10.13 New lines inserted at the bottom of
PRACTICE.TXT.

```
*L
        1: Knowledge is of two kinds.
        2: We know a subject ourselves,
        3: or we know where we can find
        4: information about it.
        5:
        6: Boswell, Life of Johnson, 1775
        7:
        8: I MUST ALWAYS REMEMBER TO PRESS BREAK
        9: OR CTRL-C AFTER INSERTING NEW TEXT,
       10: TO ENTER NEW COMMANDS
*8,10,3 M
*L
        1: Knowledge is of two kinds.
        2: We know a subject ourselves,
        3:*I MUST ALWAYS REMEMBER TO PRESS BREAK
        4: OR CTRL-C AFTER INSERTING NEW TEXT,
        5: TO ENTER NEW COMMANDS
        6: or we know where we can find
        7: information about it.
        8:
        9: Boswell, Life of Johnson, 1775
       10:
*
```

Figure 10.14 Three lines moved to a new location.

Deleting Lines

To delete lines, use the general syntax:

start line,end line **D**

For example, to delete lines 3 through 5 from the current file, type the command **3,5 D** and press Enter. Enter the **L** command to list the text and confirm that lines 3 through 5 were deleted, as shown in Figure 10.15.

```
       8: I MUST ALWAYS REMEMBER TO PRESS BREAK
       9: OR CTRL-C AFTER INSERTING NEW TEXT,
      10: TO ENTER NEW COMMANDS
*8,10,3 M
*L
       1: Knowledge is of two kinds,
       2: We know a subject ourselves,
       3:*I MUST ALWAYS REMEMBER TO PRESS BREAK
       4: OR CTRL-C AFTER INSERTING NEW TEXT,
       5: TO ENTER NEW COMMANDS
       6: or we know where we can find
       7: information about it.
       8:
       9: Boswell, Life of Johnson, 1775
      10:
*3,5 D
*L
       1: Knowledge is of two kinds,
       2: We know a subject ourselves,
       3:*or we know where we can find
       4: information about it.
       5:
       6: Boswell, Life of Johnson, 1775
       7:
*
```

Figure 10.15 Lines 3 through 5 have been deleted.

Note that you can delete a single line by specifying its line number in the command. For example, the command **7 D** deletes only line 7.

Saving or Abandoning Your Changes

After changing your file, you can either save those changes or abandon them (in case you inadvertently deleted text or made several errors). To save your changes, first be sure that the *_ prompt is displayed. (If you are still in text insertion mode, press Ctrl-C.) Then, type **E** (for Exit) and press Enter to leave Edlin and return to DOS.

If you decide that your original file was better than the edited version, type the letter **Q** (for Quit) and press Enter to abandon your changes. Edlin displays the warning prompt **Abort edit (Y/N)?**. Type **Y** to leave Edlin and return to DOS.

Learning More About Edlin

The basic Edlin editing skills you learned in this chapter are more than sufficient for you to be able to create or modify any of the files discussed later in this book. Edlin offers more advanced features that can come in handy when working with larger files (*much* larger than the examples in this book). However, as mentioned earlier, if you are going to be creating and editing large text files, you'd be wise to invest in a good word processing program. (Appendix B in this book and your DOS manual provide more information about Edlin if you want to learn the advanced features.)

Be sure to read—and remember—the information in the next section about storing your AUTOEXEC.BAT and CONFIG.SYS files. You'll need to keep in mind these important points in all your future work with these two special files.

Where to Store AUTOEXEC.BAT and CONFIG.SYS

Regardless of which editor you use to create or modify your AUTOEXEC.BAT and CONFIG.SYS files, it is extremely important to remember that both of these files *must* be stored so that DOS can automatically read them when you first start the computer. Recall from Chapter 2 that when you turn your computer on, it automatically reads the root directory of the hard disk (or the diskette in drive A:) for instructions on how to *boot up*.

After the computer gets going, DOS searches *the same diskette or directory* for two files—CONFIG.SYS and AUTOEXEC.BAT—to see if they contain any additional start-up instructions. If DOS does not find these files on the current diskette or directory, it assumes that they do not exist, and it completes its start-up operations. DOS neither searches other disk drives or directories nor displays any error messages to warn you of a problem.

In other words, if you create or modify either the AUTOEXEC.BAT or CONFIG.SYS using the wrong diskette or directory, your efforts will be fruitless. DOS will never see your changes, and you will probably find yourself at wit's end trying to figure out why DOS is ignoring your customization commands. So, read on, and remember the important points discussed in the sections that follow.

Storing AUTOEXEC.BAT and CONFIG.SYS on a Hard Disk

If your computer has a hard disk, and you always start your computer with the floppy disk drives empty, then the AUTOEXEC.BAT and CONFIG.SYS *must* be stored on the root directory of the hard disk drive that your computer boots from. On virtually all computers, this is disk drive C:.

Figure 10.16 illustrates the proper location of the AUTOEXEC.BAT and CONFIG.SYS files, using the DOS 4 **File System** screen's Directory Tree as a guide. (If you are using DOS 4, your computer probably already has these two files stored in the root directory of drive C:.)

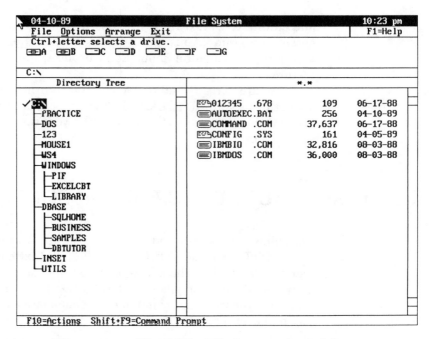

Figure 10.16. The DOS 4 File System view of the proper location of the AUTOEXEC.BAT and CONFIG.SYS files.

Figure 10.17 shows the proper location of the AUTOEXEC.BAT and CONFIG.SYS files using a hypothetical directory tree hierarchy as a guide. (If you are using DOS 3, your computer might not have these files, but if it does have them, they are stored in the root directory of drive C:.

Regardless of the version of DOS that you use, or whether you use Edlin or another text editor to edit the AUTOEXEC.BAT and CONFIG.SYS files, you must remember to specify the complete location and file name of the file you want to edit. To be safe, never assume that the root directory is the current directory. Instead, when you edit the AUTOEXEC.BAT file, be sure to specify `C:\AUTOEXEC.BAT` as the file name. When you edit CONFIG.SYS, be sure to specify `C:\CONFIG.SYS` as the file to edit. By preceding the file name with C:\, you are certain to store your changes in the root directory of drive C:.

Any changes you make to either CONFIG.SYS or AUTOEXEC.BAT take effect when you restart your computer, as discussed later in this chapter.

Storing AUTOEXEC.BAT and CONFIG.SYS on a Diskette

Usually, the root directory is the only directory on a diskette.

If you usually start your computer with a diskette in drive A:, you must be certain to save your AUTOEXEC.BAT and CONFIG.SYS files on the root directory of that diskette. Storing these files (or changes to these files) on

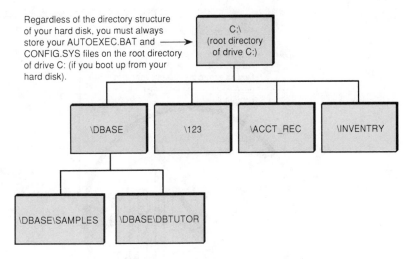

Figure 10.17 The proper location of the AUTOEXEC.BAT and CONFIG.SYS files on a sample directory tree.

any other diskette will be fruitless, because DOS doesn't look elsewhere for these files.

To clarify, let's first define the diskette that you put into drive A: before turning on your computer as your "Startup" diskette, regardless of the label you personally placed on that diskette. Figure 10.18 illustrates the importance of storing the AUTOEXEC.BAT and CONFIG.SYS files on the "Startup" diskette.

If your text editor (be it a word processing program or DOS's Edlin) is stored on a diskette other than the Startup diskette, you should start your computer as usual by placing your Startup diskette in drive A:. Then, when you create or edit the AUTOEXEC.BAT or CONFIG.SYS file, you need to be certain that you do so on the Startup diskette. If your text editor is not stored on the Startup diskette, you should use the following procedure:

Unfortunately, different versions of DOS and different diskette sizes store EDLIN.COM on different diskettes, so only you can determine which diskette that EDLIN.COM is stored on.

1. Remove the Startup diskette from drive A:, and put it in drive B:.

2. Put the diskette that contains your editing program in drive A: (so that you can run the editing program).

3. Stay logged onto drive A:, and use the proper command to run your editing program.

4. When specifying the name of the file to be edited, be sure to specify the root directory of drive B: (to edit a file on your Startup diskette). For example, if you want to edit the AUTOEXEC.BAT file on your Startup diskette, specify `B:\AUTOEXEC.BAT` as the file to be edited. If you want to modify the CONFIG.SYS file on your Startup diskette, specify `B:\CONFIG.SYS`. After making your changes, save the file using the appropriate method for your editor.

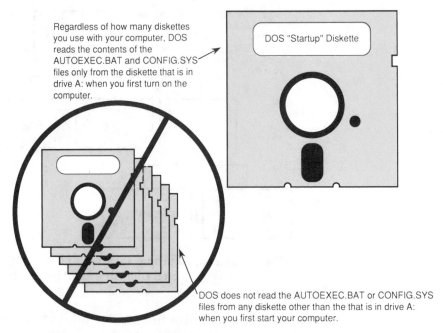

Regardless of how many diskettes you use with your computer, DOS reads the contents of the AUTOEXEC.BAT and CONFIG.SYS files only from the diskette that is in drive A: when you first turn on the computer.

DOS "Startup" Diskette

DOS does not read the AUTOEXEC.BAT or CONFIG.SYS files from any diskette other than the that is in drive A: when you first start your computer.

Figure 10.18 If you start your computer from a diskette, be sure to store your AUTOEXEC.BAT and CONFIG.SYS files on the root directory of your Startup diskette.

5. Then, remove both diskettes from their drives, and put the modified Startup diskette back in drive A:.

Your changes will take effect when you restart your computer, as discussed later in this chapter.

If your version of DOS and diskette size permits EDLIN.COM to be stored on the Startup diskette, you don't need to be concerned about using disk drive B:. Merely leave your Startup diskette in drive A:, and specify the name of the file that you want to edit after the Edlin command. For example, to edit the AUTOEXEC.BAT file, enter the command `EDLIN AUTOEXEC.BAT`. To edit the CONFIG.SYS file, enter the command `EDLIN CONFIG.SYS`. After making your changes, save the file using the usual `E` (Exit) command, as described earlier.

Your changes will take effect when you restart your computer, as discussed later in this chapter.

Special Warning for DOS 4 Users

Regardless of the editor that you use to modify your AUTOEXEC.BAT file, DOS 4 users must be aware that your AUTOEXEC.BAT file might contain the DOSSHELL command. This command automatically starts the Shell when you turn on the computer.

As soon as DOS encounters the DOSSHELL command in the AUTOEXEC.BAT file, it stops reading the AUTOEXEC.BAT file and starts the Shell. Therefore, if your AUTOEXEC.BAT file contains the DOSSHELL command, be sure that it is the last command in your AUTOEXEC.BAT file after you make changes.

When Your Changes Take Effect

After you first modify or create either the CONFIG.SYS or AUTOEXEC.BAT file on your computer, nothing new will happen. That's because DOS reads these files and executes their commands at boot-up time (that is, when you first start your computer). If you want to activate any changes you made to CONFIG.SYS, or AUTOEXEC.BAT, you must reboot.

Rebooting is a simple procedure. If you start your computer from a diskette rather than the hard disk, be sure to put the Startup diskette in drive A:. If you start your computer from a hard disk, make sure the floppy disk drives are empty. To reboot, press Ctrl-Alt-Del (hold down the Ctrl key, hold down the Alt key, and then press the Del key). Then, release all three keys. DOS reads your modified CONFIG.SYS or AUTOEXEC.BAT files (assuming that you stored them correctly, as discussed above) as it restarts the system.

Note that it is not absolutely necessary to reboot to activate commands in the AUTOEXEC.BAT file. Instead, you can simply activate the AUTOEXEC.BAT batch file by entering the command AUTOEXEC at the command prompt. You'll learn more about batch files, like AUTOEXEC.BAT, in Chapters 13 and 14.

Troubleshooting

If you make an error in some of the exercises in this chapter, locate the appropriate error message or problem description, and try the suggested solution.

- **Bad command or file name:** You tried to run a program (perhaps Edlin) that is not available on the current drive or directory. Try a different diskette, disk drive, or directory.

- *Edlin won't save your file:* (This is not a DOS error message; it's a common problem.) If you create or change a file with Edlin, but you cannot find the file later, you did one of two things wrong: either 1) you did not exit Edlin with the E (Exit) command, or 2) you saved the file properly, but you inadvertently saved it on the wrong diskette or directory.

  If the first error is your problem, you must create the file again, and remember to exit properly. If the second error is the problem, you must search for the diskette or directory that you stored the file on. Use the DOS 4 File System or the command prompt DIR command to look for the file.

■ *If DOS ignores changes in your AUTOEXEC.BAT or CONFIG.SYS file:* (Again, this is not a DOS error message, instead it's a common problem.) If DOS seems to be ignoring changes you made to either your AUTOEXEC.BAT or CONFIG.SYS file, be sure to read the section titled "Where to Store AUTOEXEC.BAT and CONFIG.SYS."

Summary

In future chapters, you might want to create or edit DOS text files, particularly the files named CONFIG.SYS and AUTOEXEC.BAT. To do so, use any text editor, word processor, or the DOS Edlin editor. In summary:

■ If you use a word processor, you must save your file as an ASCII text file.

■ The easiest way to see if a file contains word processing codes is to use the DOS 4 File System View option or the command prompt TYPE command.

■ If a text file contains formatting characters, you must remove them or DOS will not be able to read the file.

■ DOS's Edlin line editor never stores formatting characters in a file.

■ When creating or editing a file with any text editor (or Edlin) remember to accurately specify the complete location and name of the file you want to create or edit.

■ After editing either the CONFIG.SYS or AUTOEXEC.BAT file, be sure to store these files on the root directory of the appropriate hard disk drive or diskette; otherwise, DOS will ignore any changes you've made.

■ Changes that you make to the CONFIG.SYS or AUTOEXEC.BAT file do not take effect until you restart your computer.

■ If you are editing the AUTOEXEC.BAT file for DOS 4, and you want the Shell to appear automatically when you start the computer, be sure that DOSSHELL is the last command in the AUTOEXEC.BAT file.

Simplifying the Use of Your Hard Disk

 As you purchase more application programs and store them on your hard disk, you might begin to have difficulties managing and accessing all your programs. Chapter 7 presented numerous tips and techniques for organizing your hard disk and diskettes into directories so that you always have quick and easy access to files.

This chapter presents new techniques that will help you simplify using your hard disk. In particular, it focuses on techniques for making your favorite programs readily accessible from any directory on your hard disk. Of course, you can use similar techniques to manage programs on diskettes. However, since many application programs use at least one entire diskette, this chapter is really geared toward hard disks, which can store dozens of large application programs.

A Sample Directory Tree

To demonstrate ways of customizing your hard disk, we will need a sample directory tree. Needless to say, it is unlikely that your computer has exactly the same directory structure as the example; nonetheless, you can apply the general techniques that you learn in this chapter to customize *any* hard disk, regardless of the specific programs or directories stored on it.

To start, let's assume that you have a complete set of software, including a database management system, spreadsheet, and word processor. In addition, you have numerous smaller utility programs, such as an "unerase" program, an appointment scheduler, a mouse driver (for your mouse), and other useful small programs. Let's also assume that you stored all your DOS programs, such as FORMAT.COM and TREE.COM, on a directory named DOS.

To be as realistic as possible, this example uses specific brand names for the major application programs and the mouse, as listed in Table 11.1. The names of the directories that contain these programs are also included in the table.

Table 11.1. Sample software collection and directories.

Program	Product Name	Directory
Database manager	dBASE IV	DBASE
Spreadsheet	Excel	WINDOWS
Word processor	WordPerfect	WP
Utilities	(several)	UTILS
Operating System	DOS	DOS
Mouse driver	Microsoft Mouse	MOUSE1

In addition to all your programs, let's suppose that you store data for your business on two directories, named ACCTNG and SALES. Finally, let's assume that your hard disk contains numerous subdirectories of files that are used only with specific programs. Given this collection of programs and data, your directory structure might look like Figure 11.1.

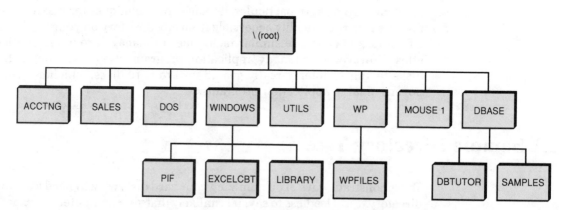

Figure 11.1. A sample directory tree.

As you can see, the sample directory tree adheres to the advice presented in Chapter 7—the tree is broad and shallow, each major application program is stored on its own directory, and each application uses the manufacturer's recommended directory name. Also, the ACCTNG and SALES directories are stored at the same levels as the major programs. Finally, subdirectories, such as PIF and DBTUTOR, contain files that pertain only to their parent directories (WINDOWS and DBASE, respectively).

Now that the directory tree is established, you need to make it easy to gain access to any and all programs. For example, while accessing the ACCTNG directory, you want to be able to run your spreadsheet, word processing, database management, utility, and DOS programs at any time.

Setting Up a Search Path

As you know from preceding chapters, if you attempt to run a program that is not in the current directory (or drive), DOS simply returns the error message `Bad command or file name` when it fails to find the program. This can indeed be inconvenient, if not outright maddening.

The solution to this problem is the all-important PATH command. This command tells DOS to look for programs in other directories if it cannot find the requested program in the current directory. The general syntax of the PATH command is:

`PATH d:pathname;d:pathname;d:pathname`

where:

> `d:` is the name of a drive
>
> `pathname` is the name of a directory on the drive
>
> `;` separates each drive and directory name

You can list as many drive and directory names or pathnames as you wish to the right of the PATH command, as long as you remember to separate each sequence with a semicolon, and you restrict the total number of characters on the line to 127 or fewer.

You can include the root directory in the search path by including its name (\) in the PATH command. For example, the following PATH command tells DOS to search both the root and DOS directories of drive C:

`PATH C:\;C:\DOS`

The order of directory names in the PATH command affects the time that DOS requires to find a particular program. A little planning can ensure that DOS locates and runs your programs as quickly as possible; that is the topic of the next section.

Planning the Perfect Path

First, it is important to remember that the PATH command searches *only* for "executable" files, which always have the file name extension .BAT, .COM, or .EXE. Therefore, it serves no purpose to include directories that contain only data files (such as ACCTNG and SALES in our sample directory tree) in the PATH command.

Second, keep in mind that DOS searches all the directories—*from left to right*—in the PATH command, until it finds the program you requested. For example, suppose you set up your PATH command as follows:

```
PATH C:\DOS;C:\WP;C:\WINDOWS;C:\DBASE
```

When you run the DBASE program from the ACCTNG or SALES directory, DOS first searches the current directory for the dBASE program; then it looks in the DOS directory, the WP directory, the WINDOWS directory, and, finally, the DBASE directory.

The DIR command shows how many files are stored on a directory, (but counts the ., .., and any subdirectories as "files", even though they are not truly files).

Therefore, you should consider two factors when ordering the directories in your PATH command: 1) How many files are on each directory, and 2) Which programs do you use most often. If a particular directory contains an exceptionally large number of files, you might want to list it as the last directory in the PATH command so that it is searched as a "last resort," when DOS determines that no other directory contains the requested program.

If you use a particular program far more frequently than other programs, you probably should list its directory (or pathname) first in the PATH command; that way, its directory is the first one searched. For example, as a writer and programmer, I use my word processing program more than any other, and therefore I always list its directory first in my PATH command.

Also, remember that you don't need to include every directory that contains a program in the PATH command. For example, the MOUSE1 directory in the example directory tree includes a program that allows you to use a mouse with some applications. However, that program needs to be run only once (at the beginning of the DOS session) to install the mouse. Therefore, you don't need to include the MOUSE1 directory in the PATH command, because it doesn't contain any programs that you need, and DOS never needs to search it.

So, let's be more specific about the sample directory tree in Figure 11.1. Let's assume that you use your DOS commands and word processing program frequently and that you use your database manager, spreadsheet, and utility programs less frequently. Furthermore, let's assume that the WINDOWS directory has, by far, the most files in it.

WARNING: Do not put any blank spaces—other than the one immediately to the right of the PATH command—in your list of directories. DOS stops reading directory names from the PATH command as soon as it encounters a blank space.

The ideal PATH command takes into consideration individual program usage. In the example situation, you could obtain maximum speed of access to all programs with this command:

```
PATH C:\DOS;C:\WP;C:\DBASE;C:\UTILS;C:\WINDOWS
```

or perhaps this one:

```
PATH C:\WP;C:\DOS;C:\UTILS;C:\DBASE;C:\WINDOWS
```

Both PATH commands commands tell DOS to first search the most frequently used directories, DOS and WP, and then to search the less frequently used directories. The crowded WINDOWS directory is always the last directory searched.

How to Enter a PATH Command

You can enter the PATH command at the command prompt at any time. (DOS 4 users need to exit the Shell using the usual F3 key.) Before you type a new path, enter the command:

`PATH`

to have DOS display the current PATH. DOS displays either the message `No Path`, if no path has been defined, or the currently defined path. (Your AUTOEXEC.BAT file might have predefined a PATH when you first started the computer.)

You define a new path simply by typing the PATH command with the proper syntax (separating each drive and directory or pathname specification with a semicolon). After you enter the PATH command, the defined path stays in effect until you turn off the computer, reboot, or define a different path. For example, when you enter the following command at the command prompt:

`PATH C:\DOS;C:\WP;C:\DBASE;C:\UTILS;C:\WINDOWS`

the programs on the DOS, WP, DBASE, UTILS, and WINDOWS directories are accessible from all directories for the remainder of the current session.

Rather than enter the PATH command each time you start the computer, you should simply include the PATH command in your AUTOEXEC.BAT file. That way, DOS automatically defines the path for you as soon as it boots the computer. (This is particularly helpful for other people who might use your computer but are less knowledgeable about DOS.)

Before you actually modify your AUTOEXEC.BAT file, look at its current contents. To do so (assuming that the DOS command prompt is on your screen), enter the following command:

`TYPE C:\AUTOEXEC.BAT`

Entering this command produces one of the following three results:

■ DOS displays an AUTOEXEC.BAT file that contains an already defined PATH (or SET PATH) command. In this case, you can always change the existing path.

WARNING: If your computer has a hard disk, it's best not to include floppy drives A: or B: in your PATH command, because if either floppy drive is empty while DOS is searching for a file, then you'll get the General Error Reading Drive error message. You would always need to put diskettes in drives A: and B: to avoid the error message.

Your AUTOEXEC.BAT file might display SET PATH *rather than* PATH, *but you can consider these to be the same thing.*

- DOS displays the AUTOEXEC.BAT file, but the file does not already contain a PATH (or SET PATH) command. In this case, you can add a PATH command to the file.
- DOS displays a message, such as File not found – AUTOEXEC.BAT. In this case, you can create your own AUTOEXEC.BAT file and then put a PATH command in it.

Regardless of the result you get when you view the contents of your AUTOEXEC.BAT file, the general editing techniques you learned in Chapter 10 now enable you to define the PATH command in your own AUTOEXEC.BAT file. Because this might be your first editing experience, let's use the Edlin editor to work through an example. However, before you begin editing, you need to know exactly where to place the PATH command in the AUTOEXEC.BAT file.

Positioning the PATH Command in AUTOEXEC.BAT

If your AUTOEXEC.BAT file already contains commands, do not remove any of the existing commands unless you know exactly what you are doing. Remember, Appendix B provides a reference to all DOS commands.

Basically, you can place the PATH command anywhere in the AUTO-EXEC.BAT file, as long as the entire command is no longer than 127 characters, and no other commands are on the same line. Always remember however, if you are using DOS 4 and your AUTOEXEC.BAT file already contains the DOSSHELL command, DOSSHELL must be the last command in the AUTOEXEC.BAT file.

Figure 11.2 shows a sample AUTOEXEC.BAT file that includes the command:

```
PATH C:\WP;C:\DOS;C:\UTILS;C:\DBASE;C:\WINDOWS
```

Notice that the PATH command includes all the directories that contain frequently used programs from the example directory tree depicted in Figure 11.1.

```
@ECHO OFF
SET COMSPEC=C:\DOS\COMMAND.COM
PATH C:\WP;C:\DOS;C:\UTILS;C:\DBASE;C;\WINDOWS
VERIFY OFF
PROMPT $P$G
C:\MOUSE1\MOUSE
APPEND /E
APPEND C:\DOS
PRINT \D:LPT1
DOSSHELL
```

Figure 11.2. A sample AUTOEXEC.BAT file with a PATH command.

Notice also that the sample AUTOEXEC.BAT file includes the command `C:\MOUSE1\MOUSE`. This line executes the mouse driver program (named MOUSE.COM in this example), which installs the mouse when the computer first boots up. Because the MOUSE1 directory is not included in the preceding PATH command, DOS must be told the exact location of the MOUSE.COM program (C:\MOUSE1 in this example) so that it can find and execute the MOUSE.COM program.

Modifying the AUTOEXEC.BAT File

If you plan to use Edlin to edit your DOS files, make photocopies of Tables 10.1 and 10.2 in Chapter 10 and keep them near your computer as a quick reference to basic commands and editing keys.

This section discusses the general steps for using the Edlin editor to create or modify an AUTOEXEC.BAT file. First, be sure to change to the directory that contains EDLIN.COM. Then, enter the command `EDLIN C: \AUTOEXEC.BAT`. Type the letter `L` (for List) and press Enter. This displays the contents of your AUTOEXEC.BAT file (if your system has such a file). Now, follow the general procedures that apply to your particular computer system in the section that follows.

Modifying an Existing PATH   If your AUTOEXEC.BAT file already contains a PATH or SET PATH command, type the PATH command's line number and press Enter. Use the →, Backspace, and F3 keys (as discussed in Chapter 10) to make changes, or merely type an entirely new PATH command. Press Enter when you finish. Then, type the `L` command again to view the entire AUTOEXEC.BAT file.

If you are satisfied with the new PATH command, type `E` and press Enter to save your changes and exit. To verify your changes from the DOS command prompt, enter the command `TYPE C:\AUTOEXEC.BAT` and press Enter. Remember, the new PATH command does not take effect until you either run the AUTOEXEC.BAT program or reboot (press Ctrl-Alt-Del) the computer.

Adding a PATH Command to an Existing AUTOEXEC.BAT file   If your computer already has an AUTOEXEC.BAT file, but it does not already contain a PATH (or SET PATH) command, you can add the PATH command yourself. It's best to put this near the top of the AUTOEXEC.BAT file, so that any other commands in the file can search the directories specified in the PATH.

For example, let's suppose that you decide to insert your new PATH command as the third line in an existing AUTOEXEC.BAT file. To do so, first type `3I` and press Enter to insert a new line number 3. Type the complete PATH command and press Enter. Then, press Ctrl-C to leave the insert mode and return to the Edlin command mode. To view the revised file, type the letter `L` and press Enter.

If the PATH command is correct, save your work and exit Edlin by typing the letter `E` and pressing Enter. If you want to verify your change from the DOS command prompt, enter the command `TYPE C:\AUTOEXEC.BAT` and press Enter. Remember, the new PATH command does not take effect until you either run the AUTOEXEC.BAT program or reboot (press Ctrl-Alt-Del) the computer.

Creating a New AUTOEXEC.BAT File that contains a PATH Command If your hard disk does yet have an AUTOEXEC.BAT file on the root directory, you can merely add the PATH command to the empty file that Edlin created when you entered the command `EDLIN C:\AUTOEXEC.BAT`. Type I and press Enter to insert a new line at the top of the file (line #1). Type the complete PATH command and press Enter. Then, press Ctrl-C to return to the Edlin command mode. Type L and press Enter to review the entire file.

If the PATH command is correct, save your work and exit Edlin by typing the letter E and pressing Enter. If you want to verify your change from the DOS command prompt, enter the command `TYPE C:\AUTOEXEC.BAT` and press Enter. Remember, the new PATH command does not take effect until you either run the AUTOEXEC.BAT program or reboot (press Ctrl-Alt-Del) the computer.

Understanding the Effects of a PATH Command

Remember, DOS refers to the PATH command *only* when you attempt to run a program that is not on the current directory. PATH has no effect on displays, such as the DOS 4 Files Area, or on the output of the DIR command.

Furthermore, DOS uses the PATH command only when searching for a program to run—it does not search for a file specified in conjunction with a command. For example, if you enter the command `TYPE MYFILE.TXT` at the command prompt to view the contents of a file named MYFILE.TXT, DOS searches PATH for the TYPE command but it searches *only* the current directory for the MYFILE.TXT file, regardless of the PATH search path. DOS "knows" that the TYPE command is merely trying to *view* the contents of the MYFILE.TXT file, and that you are not trying to *run* a program that has the .BAT, .EXE, or .COM extension.

On the other hand, when you enter a command at the command prompt that DOS does not recognize as one of its own built-in commands, such as `DBASE`, DOS "knows" that you are trying to run a program. In this case, DOS indeed searches all the directories (and pathnames) specified in the PATH command for a file named DBASE.BAT, DBASE.COM, or DBASE.EXE.

Overlays Can Disrupt a Path

I should mention one technical detail that might cause problems in some circumstances. That is, most large application programs are actually divided into several separate files—the main program, with its .COM or .EXE file, and additional *overlay* files, which often have extensions such as .OVL, .OV1, .OV2, and so on.

The main (.EXE or .COM) program for the application needs to be able to find its overlay files to run properly. If it cannot find the overlays in the current directory or disk, it usually displays an error message, such as `Cannot find overlay...`, and then it returns control to DOS.

If you are using major application programs, and you installed the programs in the directories that the manufacturers recommended, you probably will never encounter this problem. However, if you run into an overlay file problem, there is a solution: You need to use the APPEND command, in addition to (or instead of) the PATH command, to gain proper access to the program. For details, see the reference to the APPEND command in Appendix B.

A Note on DOS External Commands

You know the difference between DOS *internal* commands, which are accessible at any time, and *external* commands, which are actually stored on disk as programs. External commands are accessible only when DOS can find the appropriate file on the current directory (or in the defined PATH).

If you want to be sure that all of the internal and external DOS commands are available to you at all times, you need to take only two actions: First, be sure that all of the DOS external command programs are stored in one directory, and second, include that directory in your PATH command. Table B.1 at the beginning of Appendix B provides a quick summary of internal and external DOS commands.

Adding Your Own Commands to the DOS Shell

 DOS 4 users can further simplify the use of their hard disk by adding commands and groups to the DOS Shell. For example, notice in Figure 11.3 that the **Start Programs** Main Group screen includes a new group, named `Application Programs....`

Selecting the new `Application Programs...` option displays a new group of options, as Figure 11.4 shows. Selecting an option from this group runs a specific program (from the example programs in Table 11.1).

You can add your own groups and options to the DOS Shell at any time. To demonstrate the basic steps involved, the sections below will create a group from which you can run several application programs. This example also uses the hypothetical directory tree shown in Figure 11.1

Adding a New Group

Currently, your DOS Shell probably consists of two groups, the Main Group, which is displayed on your screen when you first start the Shell,

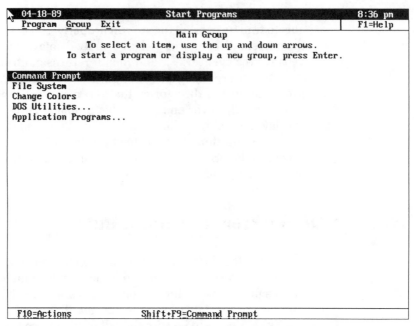

```
  04-18-89                   Start Programs                    8:36 pm
  Program  Group  Exit                                         F1=Help
                             Main Group
                  To select an item, use the up and down arrows.
                To start a program or display a new group, press Enter.

  Command Prompt
  File System
  Change Colors
  DOS Utilities...
  Application Programs...




  F10=Actions                 Shift+F9=Command Prompt
```

Figure 11.3. New group added to the **Start Programs** screen.

```
  04-18-89                   Start Programs                   10:07 pm
  Program  Group  Exit                                         F1=Help
                          Application Programs...
                  To select an item, use the up and down arrows.
                To start a program or display a new group, press Enter.

  dBASE IV
  WordPerfect
  Excel




  F10=Actions  Esc=Cancel  Shift+F9=Command Prompt
```

Figure 11.4. A new group of options for running programs.

and the DOS Utilities . . . group, which is displayed when you select DOS Utilities... from the Main Group screen. To add a new group, start by displaying the "higher level" group screen. For example, if you want the new Application Programs . . . group to be accessible from the Main Group screen, be sure that the Main Group screen is displayed.

Next, use the usual menu selection techniques to activate the Action Bar (F10 key), and pull down the Group menu, as shown in Figure 11.5.

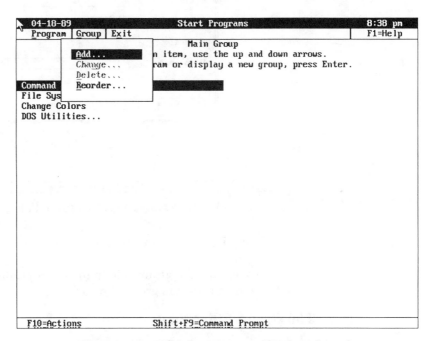

Figure 11.5. The Group menu displayed on the Main Group screen.

From the pull-down menu, select the **Add...** option to add a new group. This displays a dialog box that asks for some required and some optional information, as shown in Figure 11.6. Use the usual Tab and Shift-Tab keys to move from box to box and the usual Backspace, Ins, Del, and arrow keys to make corrections, as necessary. Each of the options in the dialog box is discussed in the sections that follow.

The Group Title

Remember that you can always press the F1 key (or click on F1=Help with the mouse) for additional help whenever you are using the DOS Shell.

The group title should briefly describe the contents of a "group" of programs. It can be as many as 37 characters long and may contain blank spaces and punctuation marks. The group title (followed by an ellipsis) appears as an option on the higher-level group screen. (For example, the Application Programs . . . option in Figure 11.3 is a group title on the Main Group screen.) The group title also appears at the top of the group's

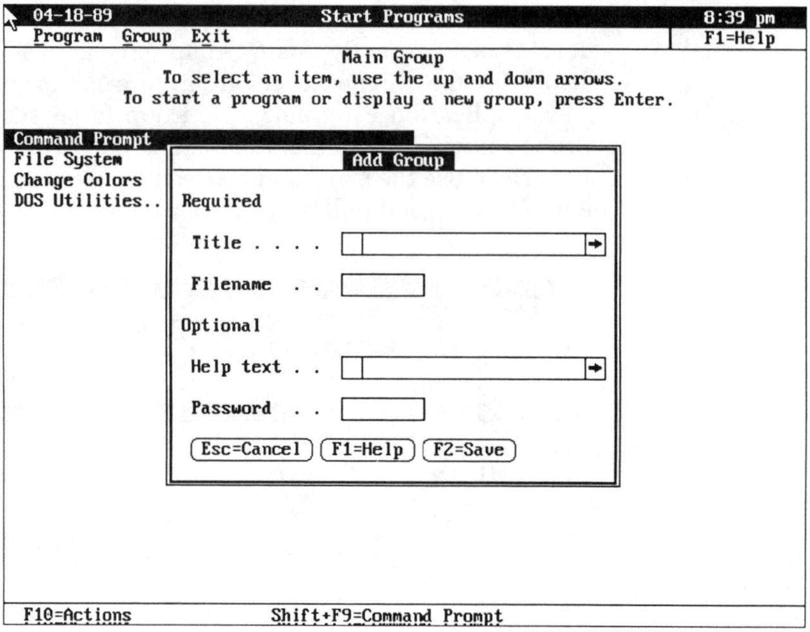

Figure 11.6. The Add Group dialog box.

screen. (In Figure 11.3, *Main Group* is the title of the currently displayed group.)

After you type the group title in the appropriate box, press Enter to move to the next box—the group file name.

The Group File Name

You must assign a valid DOS file name to each new group that you create. Follow the general rules for file names (that is, no spaces, punctuation, and so on), and do *not* include an extension. DOS automatically adds its own extension (.MEU) to the file name you provide. Press Enter after you type the file name.

The Group Help Text

You can add your own help message to a group. After you add the message, this help text appears in the help window whenever you highlight the group title and press the F1 key. You can enter as many as 487 characters, including spaces and punctuation, to the help box. Later, when DOS displays your help text, it automatically formats the text to fit inside the help window.

If you want a sentence or paragraph in your help text to begin a new line, end the preceding line with an ampersand (&). Use two ampersands if you want to add a blank line. After you enter your help text, press Enter. (You also have the option of leaving the Help Text box empty if you do not want to make help available.)

The Group Password

If you want to limit access to the new group, you can assign a password to it. The password can be as many as eight characters long, and may contain blank spaces. Keep in mind that once you enter a password, only people who know the password will be able to gain access to the group.

Be sure you write the password on a piece of paper (checking your spelling both on the screen and on the paper very carefully), and then put that piece of paper in a safe place. Otherwise, if you forget the password later, even *you* will not be able to access the new group.

If you do not want to assign a password to the group, leave this option blank.

A Sample Group

Figure 11.7 shows a completed sample Add Group dialog box. The group title is Application Programs, and its file name is APPGROUP. Only a small portion of the help text is visible. However, the entire help text is as follows (note the use of ampersands to start sentences on new lines):

```
This group lets you run the Word Processing, Spreadsheet, and
Database Management programs.&&Each program is automatically
started in its own directory.&&If you want to create or edit a
file in a different directory, be sure to specify that directory
in your file name.&&For example, use C:\SALES\QTR1.DOC to
store the QTR1.DOC file on the SALES directory.
```

In this example, the Password option in the Add Group dialog box is blank, which indicates that no password is required to access the new group.

After defining your new group, press the F2 key to save it. The group title, Application Programs . . . , then appears on the current group screen, as shown in the example in Figure 11.3.

If you add help text to your group, you can view it by moving the highlight to the group name (Application Programs . . . in this example) and pressing F1. The first lines of your custom help text appear in the help window, and you can use the usual scrolling techniques to view remaining text. Press Esc to leave the help window. Figure 11.8 shows the custom help text for the Application Programs . . . group.

Adding Programs to the Group

When you first create a new group, it doesn't contain any options. Therefore, if you select the group name from the Main Group screen (either by highlighting it and pressing Enter, or by double-clicking the group name with your mouse), DOS initially shows only the message Group is empty on the group's screen. Note, however, that the group title appears at the top of the screen, as you can see in Figure 11.9.

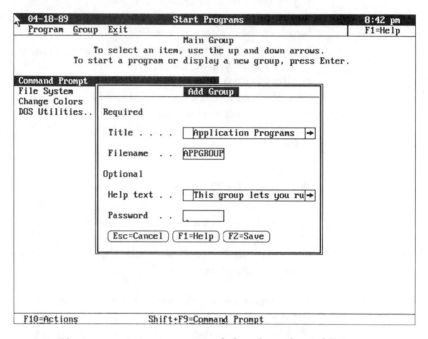

Figure 11.7. A new group defined on the Add Group dialog box.

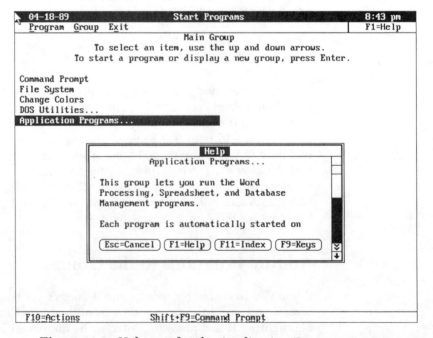

Figure 11.8. Help text for the Application Programs group.

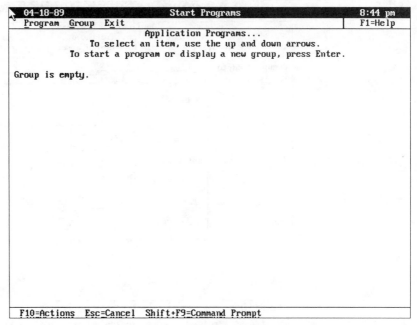

Figure 11.9. A new group before adding program options to it.

To add a new program to the group, first pull down the Program menu from the Action Bar, and then select the **Add...** option. This displays the Add Program dialog box, as shown in Figure 11.10.

Notice that the Add Program box, like the Add Group box, contains two required items and two optional items. All items are described in the following sections.

The Program Title

The program title can be as many as 40 characters long and may include blank spaces and punctuation marks. This is the title that appears on the group screen, and the one that you select to run the program. Typically, you should use either the program's commercial name here (such as dBASE IV) or merely a description of the program (such as Database Manager). After you type the program title, press Enter or Tab to move to the next item.

The Program Commands

See Chapter 13 if the program that you want to run from the Shell is a batch (.BAT) file.

In the Commands box, you need to type whatever commands DOS needs to start the program. If several commands are required, separate each command by pressing the F4 key (which generates the ‖ symbol in the box).

It is a good idea to start the Commands box with the commands neces-

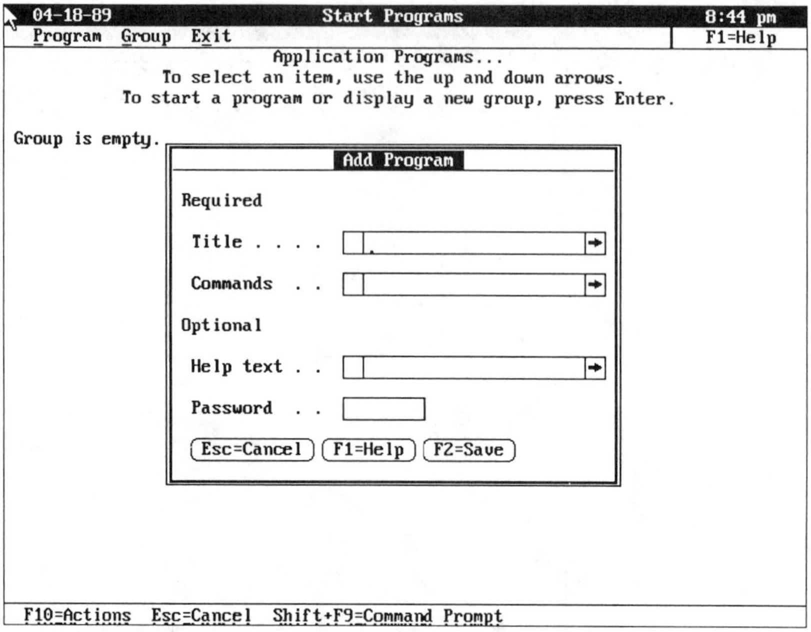

```
╔════════════════════════════════════════════════════════════════════╗
║ ▶ 04-18-89          Start Programs                      8:44 pm      ║
║   Program  Group  Exit                             │ F1=Help        ║
║                    Application Programs...                           ║
║            To select an item, use the up and down arrows.           ║
║          To start a program or display a new group, press Enter.    ║
║                                                                     ║
║   Group is empty.                                                   ║
║              ┌─────────────────── Add Program ──────────────┐       ║
║              │                                              │       ║
║              │  Required                                    │       ║
║              │                                              │       ║
║              │    Title . . . .  [ .              ]──▶     │       ║
║              │                                              │       ║
║              │    Commands  . .  [               ]──▶     │       ║
║              │                                              │       ║
║              │  Optional                                    │       ║
║              │                                              │       ║
║              │    Help text . .  [               ]──▶     │       ║
║              │                                              │       ║
║              │    Password  . .  [           ]             │       ║
║              │                                              │       ║
║              │    (Esc=Cancel) (F1=Help) (F2=Save)          │       ║
║              └──────────────────────────────────────────────┘       ║
║                                                                     ║
║   F10=Actions  Esc=Cancel  Shift+F9=Command Prompt                  ║
╚════════════════════════════════════════════════════════════════════╝
```

Figure 11.10 The Add Program dialog box.

The purpose of overlay files, which usually have file name extensions like .OVR or .OVL, are discussed in detail in Chapter 15.

sary to make the appropriate drive and directory current before running the program. Which drive and directory are "appropriate" depends on where the program is located, where its *overlay* files (if any) are located, and whether or not the program's directory is included in the PATH setting.

Use the usual DOS commands in the commands box to switch to the appropriate directory, separating the commands with the F4 key (‖) symbol. For example, in the two commands C:‖ CD \DBASE, C: makes drive C: the current drive, and CD \DBASE makes the DBASE directory the current directory. Other examples will follow.

The Program Help Text

The Help Text option for adding programs is identical to that for adding help text to a group. However, the help message that you enter here should refer only to the specific program being added, not to the group as a whole. (Leave this item blank if you do not want to add help text.)

The Program Password

The Password option on the Add Program dialog box is identical to that used with the Add Group dialog box (and the same warning still applies). However, entering a password here restricts access only to this specific program, rather than to the group as a whole. (Leave this item blank if you do not want to require a password.)

A Sample Program Definition

Figure 11.11 shows a completed sample Add Program dialog box, created to provide access to the dBASE IV program. The program title is *dBASE IV*. The program commands are `C:‖CD \DBASE‖DBASE` where:

`C:` accesses hard disk drive C:

`CD \DBASE` changes to the DBASE directory (where dBASE IV is stored)

`DBASE` is the command that starts the DBASE program

‖ separates the three commands (entered by pressing the F4 key)

The ‖ symbol that you use to separate commands actually tells DOS when to "press Enter" to enter a completed command.

You can only see a small portion of the help text. The complete help text for the dBASE IV program follows. (If you are not familiar with dBASE IV, don't let this "help" text confuse you—the message refers to dBASE menus, *not* the DOS Shell menus.)

```
Select this option to run the dBASE IV program.&&You will
automatically be changed to the DBASE directory.&&When the dBASE
Control Center appears on the screen, you can change to another
directory by selecting "DOS Utilities..." from the Tools
pull-down menu. Then select "Set default drive:directory"
from the DOS pull-down menu.
```

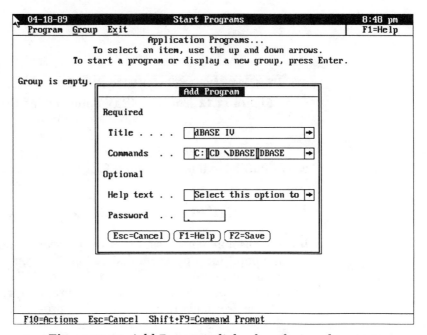

Figure 11.11 Add Program dialog box designed to start dBASE IV.

The Password option was left blank so that everyone has unrestricted access to the dBASE program. After completing the dialog box for the dBASE IV program, press F2 to save everything and return to the group screen.

You can also run a program by highlighting its option on the screen and selecting Start *from the Program pull-down menu.*

Figure 11.12 shows the Applications Programs . . . screen with the new program title dBASE IV added. Pressing F1 while this option is highlighted displays the custom help text for this option. Selecting this option, by highlighting and pressing Enter or by double-clicking with a mouse, immediately starts the dBASE IV program.

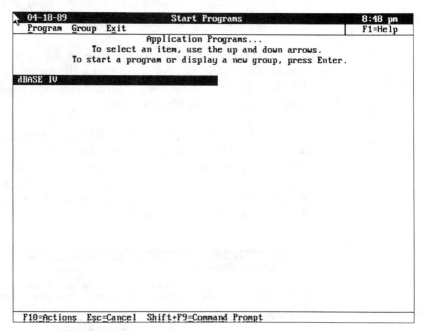

```
 04-18-89                  Start Programs                  8:48 pm
 Program  Group  Exit                                      F1=Help
                      Application Programs...
            To select an item, use the up and down arrows.
          To start a program or display a new group, press Enter.

 dBASE IV









 F10=Actions  Esc=Cancel  Shift+F9=Command Prompt
```

Figure 11.12 The dBASE IV option added to the Application Programs . . . group.

When you finish using dBASE IV and exit to DOS, you are automatically returned to the Application Programs . . . group screen.

Using a Different Default Directory

It is not absolutely necessary to use a program's "home" directory as the starting point for a program that you access from a group screen. If the program's directory is specified in the PATH command of your AUTOEXEC.BAT file, you can start the program from any directory.

A good example is the WordPerfect program, which is stored in the WP directory. As you can see in Figure 11.1, the directory tree shows a subdirectory named WPFILES beneath the WP directory. This subdirectory stores files that are used only with WordPerfect.

The reason for creating the WPFILES subdirectory is that most people (myself included) tend to save a lot of "junk" files with word processing programs, such as old letters, memos, and notes. If you do not erase these from time to time, they eventually accumulate into a huge collection of file names.

The directory tree in Figure 11.1 is designed so that the WP directory can be included in the PATH command. However, DOS shouldn't be forced to search through a lot of junk file names each time you try to run a program. Hence, the \WP\WPFILES path name leads to a directory used as a storage area for general word processing files (such as memos, letters, and notes).

To ensure that anyone who uses the computer also stores their general word processing files in this directory, you can make this the default directory that WordPerfect is started from. To do so, you must first be certain that WP is included in the PATH command (preferably in the AUTOEXEC.BAT file, so there is no chance of you forgetting to enter the PATH command at the command prompt).

Then, when you add the WordPerfect program to a group, merely specify \WP\WPFILES as the directory to start the program from. Figure 11.13 shows the appropriate Add Program dialog box for adding WordPerfect to the Application Programs . . . group. (Only a small portion of the custom help text is displayed, but you can enter any help message that you wish.)

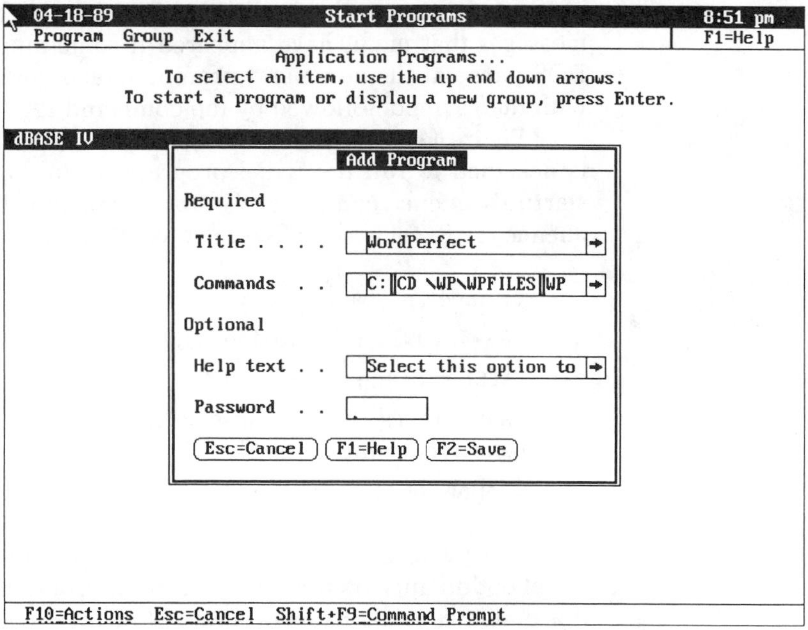

```
 04-18-89                    Start Programs              8:51 pm
 Program   Group   Exit                                  F1=Help
                      Application Programs...
              To select an item, use the up and down arrows.
          To start a program or display a new group, press Enter.

 dBASE IV
                              ┌─ Add Program ─┐

                Required

                Title  . . . .   │WordPerfect          →│

                Commands  . .    │C:║CD \WP\WPFILES║WP  →│

                Optional

                Help text  . .   │Select this option to →│

                Password  . .    │                 │

                 (Esc=Cancel) (F1=Help) (F2=Save)


 F10=Actions   Esc=Cancel   Shift+F9=Command Prompt
```

Figure 11.13 Add Program dialog box for WordPerfect.

Notice that the startup sequence C:‖CD \WP\WPFILES‖WP is actually three commands: The first accesses drive C:, the second changes to the

WP\WPFILES directory, and the third enters the program name that starts WordPerfect. This startup sequence ensures that when you "casually" save a WordPerfect file without specifying a different directory, the file will be stored on the \WP\WPFILES directory. (However, WordPerfect still *allows* you to save and edit files on other directories, if you so desire.)

As usual, after completing the Add Program dialog box, press F2 to save your changes and return to the current group screen.

Pausing Before Returning to the Shell

When you run a program from the Shell, there is a brief, almost imperceptible transition to the command prompt, and then control shifts to the program you are running. When you finish with that program and exit to DOS, there is an equally brief transition from the command prompt to the Shell. You hardly notice any of this—if everything goes right.

However, if DOS encounters a problem while trying to access a program, it displays an error message on the command prompt screen, *not* on the Shell screen. This is inconvenient because the command prompt screen is displayed so briefly that it is impossible for you to read the error message.

You can force DOS to pause and display the command prompt screen before returning to the Shell. This gives you a chance to read any error messages that might have appeared if something went wrong. To make DOS pause at the command prompt screen, end your startup sequence with the ‖ symbol followed by the command PAUSE.

When you first add a program to a group, always include the PAUSE command. That way, if you make a mistake in the dialog box, you'll be able to see the error message, which in turn might help you solve the problem.

Figure 11.14 shows an example in which the Add Program dialog box is designed to run the Excel program. Note that only a portion of the startup sequence can be seen in the Commands box. The full startup sequence for Excel is actually `C:‖CD \WINDOWS‖EXCEL‖PAUSE` where:

`C:` accesses drive C:

`CD \WINDOWS` changes to the WINDOWS directory, which contains Excel

`EXCEL` runs the Excel program

`PAUSE` forces DOS to pause so that you can read any error messages before returning to the Shell

‖ separates the commands (entered by pressing the F4 key)

After you save the dialog box shown in Figure 11.14, the Microsoft Excel option appears on the Application Programs . . . screen. Selecting this option runs the Excel program (if no errors occur) so that Excel takes control of the computer, as shown in Figure 11.15.

However, if there is a problem that prevents DOS from running the program, DOS displays an error message that briefly describes the problem. The PAUSE command you added in the dialog box gives you a chance to read that message before control returns to the Shell, as shown in Figure 11.16.

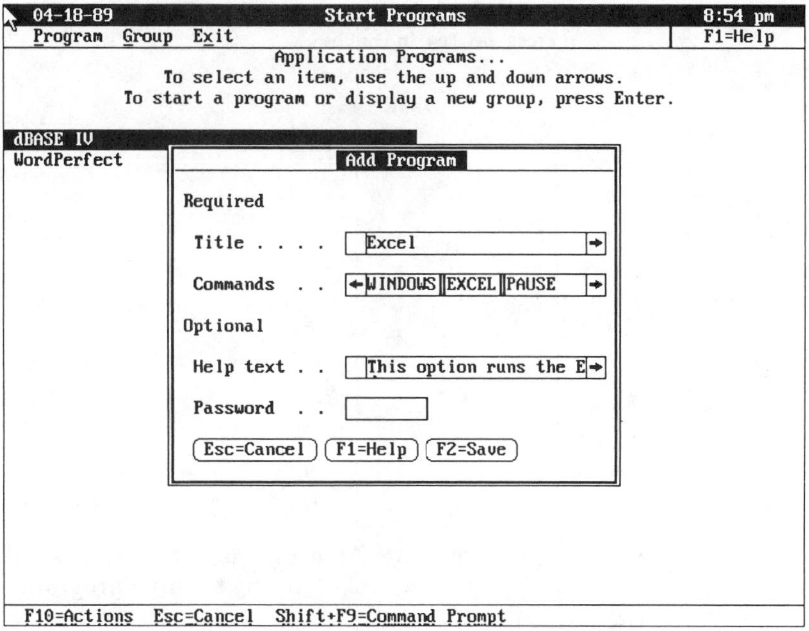

Figure 11.14 Add Program dialog box that starts Excel and pauses before returning to the Shell.

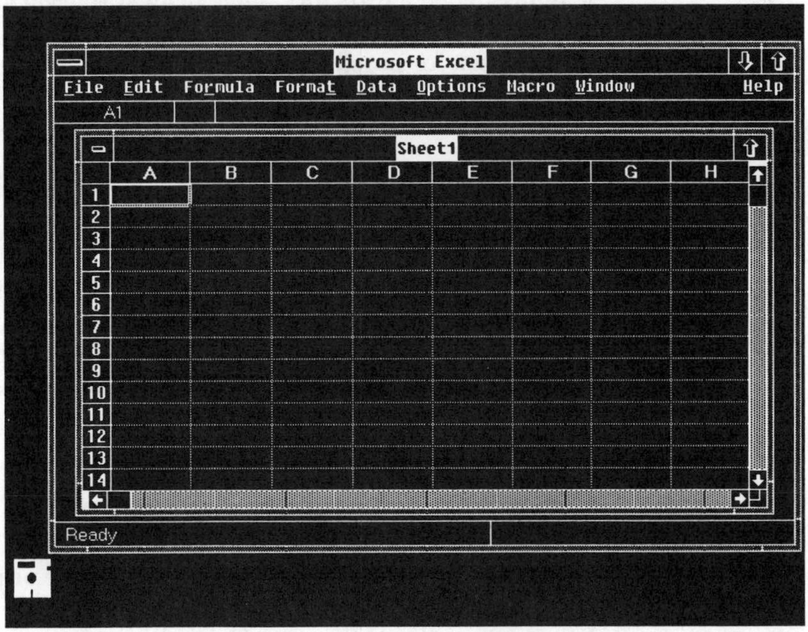

Figure 11.15 The Excel spreadsheet program is in control.

The example error messages Bad command or file name indicates either that the Excel program is not available from the current directory or that

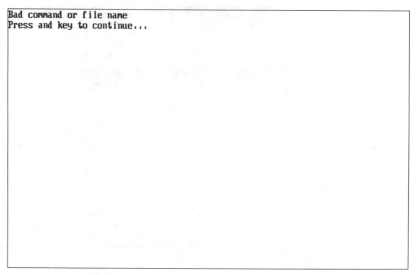

```
Bad command or file name
Press and key to continue...
```

Figure 11.16 An error message displayed after unsuccessfully
trying to run a program.

you made a mistake in the Commands portion of the dialog box. (Perhaps
you misspelled a directory name or the program startup sequence.)

After you read the error message, press a key to return to the Shell.
Then, check for possible errors in the startup sequence by using the tech-
niques described in the later section entitled "Changing a Program or
Group."

Leaving a Group Screen

To leave a group screen (other than the Main Group) and return to the Main
Group, press the Escape (Esc) key, or click your mouse once on the
Esc=Cancel option. If you press F3 to exit a group screen, DOS takes you to
the command prompt rather than the Main Group. As discussed in previous chapters, merely type DOSSHELL and press Enter to return to the Shell.

Changing a Program or Group

*If you cannot see the
cursor in the dialog box,
try pressing the Ins (or
Insert) key to make it
larger.*

You can always change the contents of a group or program dialog box. To
do so, highlight the group or program name on the screen, and then press
F10 to access the Action Bar. To modify a group definition, pull down the
Group menu. To modify a program definition, pull down the Program
menu. Then, select the Change... option.

This displays the contents of the group or program dialog box. Table
11.2 lists the editing keys that you can use to make changes. After complet-

ing your changes, press the F2 key to save the revisions, or press Esc to abandon your changes.

Table 11.2. Keys used to enter and edit dialog box entries.

Key	Effects
Tab	Moves cursor to the next option
Shift-Tab	Moves cursor to the previous option
→	Moves cursor right one character
←	Moves cursor left one character
Home	Moves cursor to the start of text in the box
End	Moves cursor to the end of text in the box
Ins (or Insert)	Toggles between insert and overwrite modes
Del (or Delete)	Deletes the character at cursor
Backspace	Moves the cursor left and erases the character
F1	Displays help
F2	Saves changes
F4	Inserts the command separator (‖)
Esc	Abandons the current changes

Deleting a Program or Group

To delete a group or program, first, highlight its name on the screen, and then press F10 to access the Action Bar. To delete a group name, pull down the Group menu. To delete a program definition, pull down the Program menu. In both cases, when you select `Delete...`, DOS presents two options:

1. `Delete this item`

2. `Do not delete this item`

Select the first option to perform the deletion; select the second option to cancel the operation.

Copying Programs to Other Groups

If you want the same program to be accessible from different groups, highlight the program's name, press F10, and then pull down the Program menu. Select `Copy....` Notice the instructions near the top of the screen:

```
To complete the copy, display the destination group, then press
F2. Press F3 to cancel copy.
```

Press Esc to leave the current group (if necessary), and select the group to which you want to copy the program. When the destination group screen appears, press F2 to complete the copy. (You also have the option of pressing F3 to abandon the copy.)

Rearranging Options in a Group

To rearrange the options in a group, first, move the highlight to the option (program title) that you want to move. Then, press F10, pull down the Group menu, and select Reorder.... The screen displays the following instructions:

```
To complete the reorder, highlight the new position, then press
Enter. Press Esc to cancel
```

As instructed, move the highlight to the new position for the current option, and press Enter. If you change your mind, press Esc to cancel the operation.

Advanced Techniques for Creating Dialog Boxes

If you've used any programs from the DOS Utilities . . . screen, you probably noticed that DOS displays a dialog box that permits you to enter additional information before DOS runs the program. For example, when you select Format from the DOS Utilities . . . screen, DOS presents the dialog box shown in Figure 11.17.

When you add your own programs to a group, you can also design a dialog box to be displayed before DOS runs the program. You can customize your program's dialog box by adding various switches in the Commands box of the Add Program or Change Program dialog box. The basic syntax for designing a dialog box is:

command [dialog box design codes] additional codes

The *command* is the command that starts the program, the *dialog box design codes* are enclosed in square brackets ([ ]), and optional *additional codes* are placed outside the brackets. Table 11.3 summarizes the dialog box design codes.

Table 11.3. Symbols used to customize program dialog boxes.

Switch	Effect
/P "*text*"	Defines a customized prompt to replace the Parameters . . . prompt (a maximum of 20 characters).

Table 11.3. (cont.)

Switch	Effect
/T *"text"*	Specifies a title line (to a maximum of 40 characters) that appears at the top of the dialog box.
/I *"text"*	Defines instructions that appear in the dialog box (a maximum of 40 characters).
/D *"text"*	Places a default value in the parameters box.
/R	Removes the default value from the parameters box as soon as a key is pressed (used in conjunction with /D).
/L *"n"*	Defines a maximum length for the prompt box entry (*n* is a number in the range of 1 to 128).
/M*"e"*	Requires that the file name entered into the parameters box exist in order to run a program.
/F *"file"*	Tells DOS to check for the existence of the named *file* before running a program. If the file is not found, the Shell beeps and redisplays the dialog box.
%n	When used inside the brackets, saves the value entered into the parameters box for future use (must be the first entry inside the [bracket). When used outside the brackets, substitutes the parameters box entry into the command. (*n* can be any number from 1 to 10.)
/D*"%n"*	Makes the previously saved parameters box entry the default entry for the current parameters box.
/C*"%n"*	Specifies the parameter box entry from the preceding dialog box as the entry for the current task.
/#	Inserts the current drive name into the startup sequence. (This option must be placed outside the brackets.)
/@	Inserts the name of the directory (without the \ characters) that contains the DOS Shell into the startup sequence. (This option must be placed outside the brackets.)

The Default Dialog Box

The simplest dialog box to design is the *default* dialog box. You can display the default dialog box simply by putting empty brackets ([ ]) to the right of the commands that start a program. For example, Figure 11.18 shows a modified startup sequence for the WordPerfect program that includes the empty brackets. (To make this change, access the Change Program dialog box by highlighting the WordPerfect option in the Application Programs . . . group screen, pressing F10, and selecting Change... from the Program pull-down menu.)

After you save the new startup sequence (by pressing F2), any future attempt to run the WordPerfect program from the screen first displays the default startup dialog box, as shown in Figure 11.19. The main problem with the default dialog box is that it does not describe what you need to type into the prompt box.

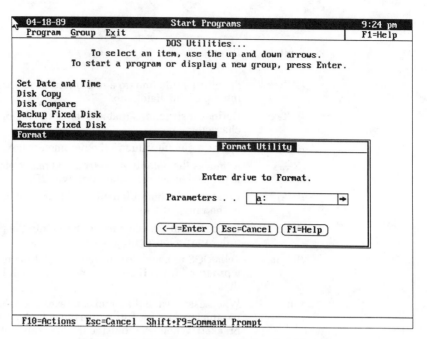

Figure 11.17 The startup dialog box for the
FORMAT program.

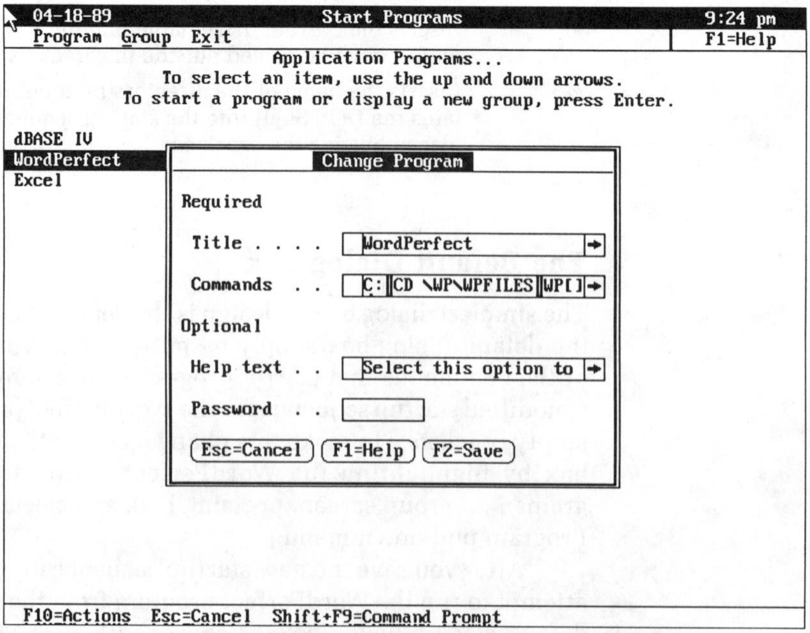

Figure 11.18 Startup sequence that displays the default
dialog box.

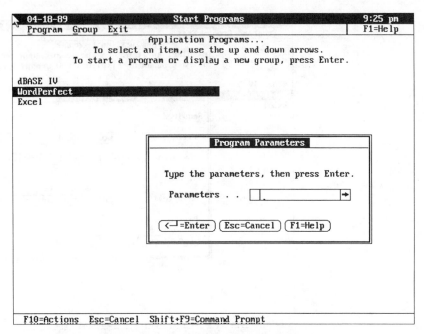

Figure 11.19 Default startup dialog box.

A Custom Dialog Box

The Change Program dialog box in Figure 11.20 shows an improved startup sequence for the WordPerfect program. However, you can only see a portion of the startup sequence in the figure. The complete startup sequence in the Commands box is:

Lengthy startup sequences are broken into several lines in this book to fit on the page, as well as to break them into more readable sections. On your screen, always type your startup sequence as one long line without blank spaces.

```
C: ||
CD \WP\WPFILES||
WP [/T"Run WordPerfect"
    /I"Enter name of file to edit"
    /P"File name... "]||
PAUSE
```

After you save the new startup code, you run the WordPerfect program in the usual manner (by selecting its name from the screen). However, now DOS immediately displays the custom dialog box shown in Figure 11.21. (Callouts indicate the codes used to design the various parts of the dialog box.)

The dialog box remains on the screen until you type an entry and press Enter or until you merely press Enter to leave the prompt box empty. Whatever you type in the dialog box is automatically added to the right of the command. For example, if you type `C:\WP\WPFILES\BOB.LET` in the dialog box, DOS executes the command `WP C:\WP\WPFILES\BOB.LET` to run

241

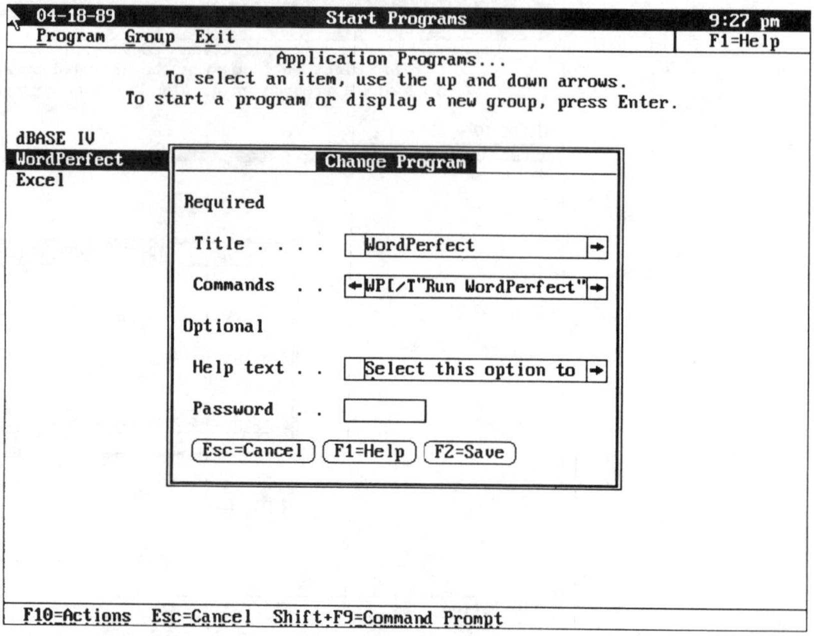

Figure 11.20 Change Program dialog box with new
WordPerfect startup sequence (partially obscured).

WordPerfect and either create or edit a file named BOB.LET on the
WP\WPFILES directory.

Multiple Dialog Boxes

You can define a dialog box for each command in a startup sequence. (Recall that the ‖ symbol, entered by pressing F4, separates multiple commands.) For example, note the following alternative startup sequence for
WordPerfect:

```
c: ‖
CD \[/T"Run WordPerfect"
   /I"Enter directory to store files on"
   /P"Directory name... "] ‖
WP [/T"Run WordPerfect"
   /I"Enter name of file to edit"
   /P"File name... "] ‖
PAUSE
```

After you save this new startup sequence and then run the
WordPerfect program from the Shell, DOS displays two consecutive dialog
boxes. The first one presents the instruction Enter directory to store
files on. After you type the directory name and press Enter, DOS executes
the CD \ command with the directory name you specified.

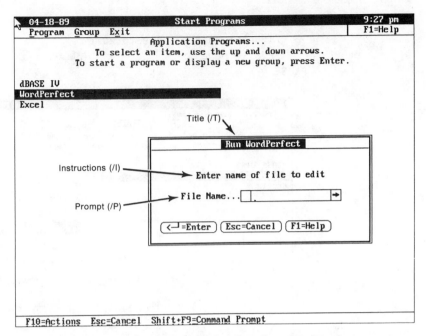

Figure 11.21 Sample dialog box for WordPerfect.

Then, a second dialog box appears and displays the message `Enter name of file to edit`. After you type a file name and press Enter, DOS issues the WP command, followed by the name of the specified file. This causes WordPerfect to create (or allow you to edit) the named file in the current directory.

Making a Suggestion in the Prompt Box

You can add a default ("suggested") value to a prompt box using the /D code. An example of this is the Format option, which suggests drive A: as the drive for the Format command (see Figure 11.17). To insert a default value, use the /D switch, followed by the suggested entry enclosed in quotation marks, in your startup sequence.

For example, note in the following program startup sequence that /D"WP\WPFILES" inserts the WP\WPFILES pathname in the prompt box as the suggested value. Now when you start the WordPerfect program, the first dialog box looks like Figure 11.22. Press Enter to accept the suggested directory name, or enter a new name by typing over the suggested directory name.

```
C: ‖
CD \[/T"Run WordPerfect"
   /I"Enter directory to store files on"
   /P"Directory name... "
   /D"WP\WPFILES"] ‖
```

```
WP [/T"Run WordPerfect"
    /I"Enter name of file to edit"
    /P"File name... "] ||
PAUSE
```

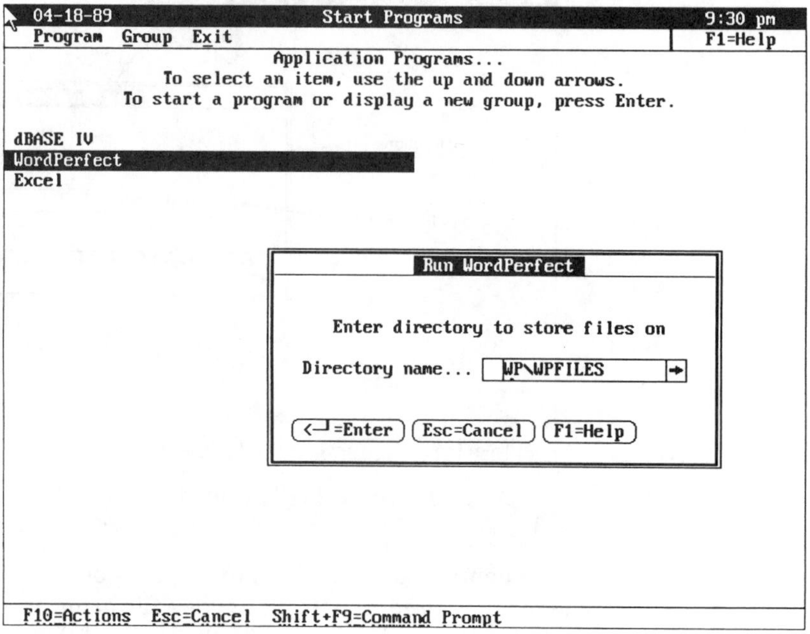

```
 04-18-89                    Start Programs                    9:30 pm
 Program  Group  Exit                                          F1=Help
                         Application Programs...
                 To select an item, use the up and down arrows.
                To start a program or display a new group, press Enter.

 dBASE IV
 WordPerfect
 Excel


                         ┌──────── Run WordPerfect ────────┐
                         │                                 │
                         │  Enter directory to store files on │
                         │                                 │
                         │  Directory name... │WP\WPFILES    │→│ │
                         │                                 │
                         │  ( ◄─┘=Enter ) ( Esc=Cancel ) ( F1=Help ) │
                         └─────────────────────────────────┘




 F10=Actions   Esc=Cancel   Shift+F9=Command Prompt
```

Figure 11.22 Dialog box with a default value.

Suppose that you decide to type a new directory name (such as SALES) while the default value is displayed in the dialog box in Figure 11.22. DOS leaves the end of the default value so that the prompt box now contains:

```
SALESFILES
```

To correct the entry, you need to press the Del (or Delete) key five times, thus erasing the last five letters of the previous entry.

If you use the /R (for *remove*) switch with a default value, DOS immediately removes the entire suggested entry from the prompt box as soon as you start typing a new entry. For example, note the addition of the /R option to the following startup sequence:

```
c: ||
CD \[/T"Run WordPerfect"
    /I"Enter directory to store files on"
    /P"Directory name... "
    /D"WP\WPFILES"]
```

```
    /R ‖
WP [/T"Run WordPerfect"
    /I"Enter name of file to edit"
    /P"File name... "] ‖
PAUSE
```

This startup sequence also displays the `Enter directory to store files` on dialog box with WP\WPFILES as the suggested drive (see Figure 11.22). However, as soon as you type one new letter or number, DOS erases the entire suggested entry in the prompt box. Therefore, if you type `SALES` as the new directory name, you end up with:

`SALES`

rather than

`SALESFILES`

Returning to the Shell Directory

You can use the /@ switch to represent the directory that contains the DOS Shell and the /# switch to represent the drive that contains the Shell. These codes can only be used *outside* of the brackets in the startup sequence.

For example, in the following startup sequence, the command /# accesses the DOS Shell drive, and the command `CD \/@` changes to the directory that contains the Shell. Only then does control return to the Shell. (Note that the two commands are separated by the ‖ symbol.)

```
C: ‖
CD \[/T"Run WordPerfect"
    /I"Enter directory to store files on"
    /P"Directory name... "
    /D"WP\WPFILES"] ‖
WP [/T"Run WordPerfect"
    /I"Enter name of file to edit"
    /P"File name... "] ‖
/# ‖
CD \/@ ‖
PAUSE
```

Using Prompt Box Entries from Multiple Commands

If you want more than one command in the startup sequence to use the entry in a prompt box, use the "% variables" to save and repeat entries. You can define as many as 10 such variables, although you can use only one per pair of square brackets.

To save an entry, the % variable must be the first item within the square brackets. To reuse the entry in a later command, the % variable must be placed outside the brackets.

For example, examine the following program startup sequence. Notice that the directory name entered in response to the instruction `Enter directory to store files on` is stored as %1. The prompt box entry in the `Enter name of file to edit` dialog box is stored as %2.

```
C: ‖
CD \[%1/T"Run WordPerfect"
      /I"Enter directory to store files on"
      /P"Directory name... "
      /D"WP\WPFILES"] ‖
WP [%2/T"Run WordPerfect"
      /I"Enter name of file to edit"
      /P"File name... "] ‖
DIR C:\%1\%2 ‖
PAUSE
```

The DIR C:\%1\%2 command in the startup sequence, retrieves the values entered into the two prompt boxes and inserts them into the DIR command. For example, if you entered WP\WPFILES as the directory to store the file on and BOB.LET as the file name, DOS actually executes the command `DIR C:\WP\WPFILES\BOB.LET`, thereby displaying the directory entry for the file returning to the Shell.

More Dialog Box Examples

To see other examples of program startup sequences, go to the DOS Utilities . . . group and move the highlight to any option on that screen. Press F10 and pull down the Program menu. Then, press Tab to move the cursor to the Commands box. To see the startup sequence for the command, scroll through the Commands box using the usual ← and → keys. (The *Getting Started with Disk Operating System Version 4* manual that came with your copy of DOS also provides additional examples.)

Designing dialog boxes can be fun; it certainly helps you customize access to your programs. However, the strange coding used in the startup sequence can be a little confusing at first. The best way to learn these techniques is to design a simple custom dialog box, test it, and then gradually add and test new features. Refer to Table 11.3 for the proper usage of these features.

Associating Data Files with Programs

Another handy technique for making programs more accessible in the DOS Shell is to *associate* file name extensions with programs. Some application programs do this automatically by assigning file name extensions to the files you create. For example, Microsoft Excel assigns the file name extension .XLS to all new spreadsheets. So, if you create a spreadsheet named INCOME, Excel automatically stores that spreadsheet in a file named INCOME.XLS.

On the other hand, some application programs do not automatically assign extensions to file names. In these cases, you can devise your own naming scheme to identify a program's data files. For example, when you use a word processor, always use the extensions .TXT (for text) and .DOC (for document) for the files that you create.

When you set up an association between an application and a file name extension, DOS automatically loads the appropriate program when you select the file name from the Files Area of the File System. The program doesn't even need to be on the same directory as the file you select.

To associate a file name extension with a program, you must first know the program name, which is the command you use to start the program followed by the extension .COM, .EXE, or .BAT. Then, select that program from the Files Area of the File System, and select Associate... from the File pull-down menu. DOS then asks you for the extension (or extensions) to associate with that program. Let's look at an example.

Suppose that you use the WordPerfect word processing program on your computer, and you typically use it to create files with the extensions .DOC and .TXT. To associate these extensions with the WordPerfect program, first use the Directory Tree Area of the File System to change to the directory that contains the WordPerfect program (usually named WP).

To ensure that only one file name is selected when associating extensions to a program, select Deselect all from the File pull-down menu before you select a file to associate.

Next, highlight the name of the file that contains the WordPerfect program (WP.EXE), and press the Spacebar (or click your mouse once) to select that file name. Press F10 and then Enter to pull down the File menu. Finally, select Associate....

This displays the Associate File dialog box in which you type in the extension(s) to associate with that program. Do not include the leading period in your assignments. If you are assigning multiple extensions, separate each with a blank space. Figure 11.23 shows an example that associates the extensions .TXT and .DOC with the WordPerfect program. (Note also that WP.EXE is selected in the Files Area.)

When you press Enter after typing the extensions, DOS provides two more options:

1. Prompt for options
2. Do not prompt for options

These options refer to what DOS does when you later select a .TXT or .DOC from the Files Area. If you select Prompt for options, DOS pauses before running the WordPerfect program and displays a dialog box that lets you add more options.

If you select Do not prompt for options, DOS immediately runs the WordPerfect program when you select a file name with the .TXT or .DOC

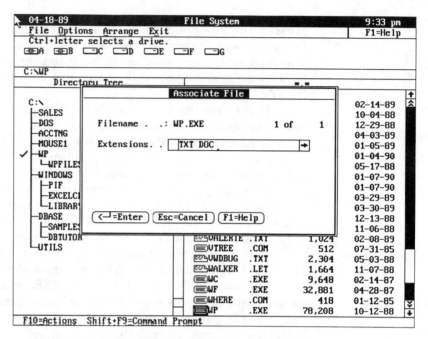

Figure 11.23 Associating the .TXT and .DOC extension with WordPerfect (WP.EXE).

extension. This is the preferred selection for most application programs because most accept only a single option—the name of a data file to work with.

After you make the association between the WordPerfect program and the .TXT and .DOC file name extensions, you'll always have quick and easy access to WordPerfect for editing files. In the future, whenever you select a file with one of those extensions from the Files Area (by highlighting its name and pressing Enter, or double clicking it with your mouse), DOS automatically runs the WordPerfect program and displays the selected file for editing.

Note that you don't need to change to the WordPerfect program's directory; DOS finds the program for you and runs it, while you remain in the current directory. For example, Figure 11.24 shows sample files stored in the WP\WPFILES directory. Selecting any file with the .DOC or .TXT extension from the Files Area automatically loads the file into WordPerfect for editing.

Figure 11.25 shows the screen after you select the hypothetical CHAP11.TXT file from the Files Area. The CHAP11.TXT file appears on the WordPerfect screen, ready for editing. After you edit the file, save your changes, and exit WordPerfect in the usual manner, DOS returns you to the Shell. Note that the edited CHAP11.TXT file is stored in the current directory, WPFILES, and not in the directory that contains the program (\WP).

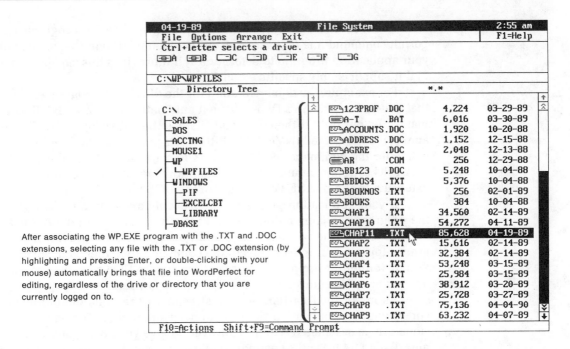

After associating the WP.EXE program with the .TXT and .DOC extensions, selecting any file with the .TXT or .DOC extension (by highlighting and pressing Enter, or double-clicking with your mouse) automatically brings that file into WordPerfect for editing, regardless of the drive or directory that you are currently logged on to.

Figure 11.24 Selecting any .TXT or .DOC file
automatically runs WordPerfect.

```
                           CHAPTER 11

                   SIMPLIFYING YOUR HARD DISK

As you purchase more application programs, and store them on your
hard disk, you'll want to have quick and easy access to all of your
computer's programs.  Chapter 7 presented numerous tips and
techniques for organizing your hard disk into directories for quick
and easy access to files.

This chapter will present new techniques for simplifying the use of
your hard disk.  In particular, we will focus on techniques for
making your favorite programs readily accessible from any directory
on your hard disk.

A SAMPLE DIRECTORY TREE

We will need a sample directory tree to best demonstrate ways to
customize your hard disk.  Needless to say, it is unlikely that your
computer will have the exactly same directory structure as the
example, but nonetheless the general techniques that you learn in
this chapter will help you to best customize any hard disk,
regardless of the programs or directories stored  on it.
C:\WP\WPFILES\CHAP11.TXT                    Doc 1  Pg 1  Ln 1      Pos 1
```

Figure 11.25 CHAP11.TXT is in WordPerfect,
ready for editing.

The associate capability works only with application programs that permit *command line options*. Consult the documentation that came with your application program to determine 1) if it provides this capability and 2) if it supports only specific extensions.

For example, the documentation for the dBASE IV program explains that you can run dBASE IV and have it automatically load a dBASE command file, but only if the command file has the extension .PRG. For example, if a file named INVENTRY.PRG exists in the current directory, you can enter the command DBASE INVENTRY to start DBASE and the INVENTRY.PRG program simultaneously. Therefore, you can associate the .PRG extension to the dBASE IV program in the DOS Shell.

If your application program supports only one option to the right of the program name, then don't select Prompt for options in the Associate menu; the program will not accept additional options anyway. If the program supports multiple options in the command line, then you can select Prompt for options to permit more options before DOS runs the program, but you are not required to do so. The choice is yours.

As mentioned earlier, you must refer to the documentation that comes with an application program to determine which file name extensions can be associated with it. However, to give you some general examples, Table 11.4 lists nine common application programs, the directories on which they are typically stored, the name of the program file, and acceptable extensions that you can associate with the program.

Table 11.4. Sample application programs and associated extensions.

Application Program	Hard Disk Directory	Program's File Name	Associated Extensions
dBASE III PLUS	DBASE	DBASE.EXE	.PRG
dBASE IV	DBASE	DBASE.EXE	.PRG
Paradox (Version 3)	PARADOX3	PARADOX3.EXE	.SC
R:BASE	RBFILES	RBASE.EXE	.CMD
Excel	WINDOWS	EXCEL.EXE	.XLC .XLM .XLS
Lotus 1-2-3	123	123.COM	.SET
Quattro	QUATTRO	Q.EXE	.WKQ
WordPerfect	WP	WP.EXE	< any >
WordStar (Version 4)	WS4	WS.EXE	< any >

Note that the WordPerfect and WordStar word processing programs do not automatically assign extensions to file names; therefore, you can associate any extension you wish to these programs. However, limit yourself to only those extensions that you use when working with these programs, such as .TXT, .DOC, and .LET.

WARNING: Never enter the extensions .COM, .EXE., or .BAT in the Associate file dialog box: Files with these extensions are programs themselves, not data files that can be associated with programs.

Refer to the sample directory tree presented in Figure 11.1. A quick examination shows that you should probably associate extensions with your dBASE and EXCEL programs, in addition to the extensions you've already associated with WordPerfect. Using the information from Table 11.3, you know that you should associate the .PRG extension with the DBASE.EXE program in the DBASE directory and the .XLC, .XLM, and .XLS extensions with the EXCEL.EXE program in the WINDOWS directory. Doing so provides quick and easy access to all three programs from the data files on *any* directory.

Simplifying Hard Disk Backup Procedures

I've discussed the importance of making copies (backups) of files to protect yourself from accidental erasures, disk problems, and so on. Backing up the files on your hard disk is especially important, because if your hard disk *crashes*, you probably won't be able to recover any of the files stored on it. A hard disk crash can be caused by any number of problems, the most common being that some moving part simply wears out or breaks.

Chapter 15 shows how a hard disk operates, and the moving parts involved.

Undoubtedly the thought of your hard disk crashing—and destroying all of your files—is unnerving. But, rest assured; this is not something that happens all the time. Personally I've had three hard disks crash in 12 years. Ironically, two of these crashes were within several days of each other. (Apparently, the new hard disk that I installed to replace the old one was defective, because a few days later, it also crashed.)

However, hard disk crashes are not the only events that can deprive you of your files. Natural disasters, such as fires and lightning-induced power surges, as well as not-so-natural disasters, such as burglars and malicious computer programs called *viruses*, can also destroy your files. If you store your backup files in the same building as your computer, some of these disasters can also ruin your backup diskettes. (You can protect valuable data by storing backups in a diskette-sized safe deposit box at the bank or in a fireproof safe.)

Speaking of disasters, even if your computer is insured, the work you put into creating your files is not. In fact, chances are that none of your software is covered by insurance. So, even if an insurance company offers you a refund for the loss of your computer hardware, you will have recouped only a small portion of your actual investment of time and money.

This section examines techniques for backing up your entire hard disk and for recovering data from the backups. Of course, backing up an entire hard disk can take quite a bit of time, so it is not the kind of task you want to do everyday. However, during the course of any single day, you will probably create or change only a few files. Because backing up these few files can be done quickly and is easily performed at the end of each day, I'll also discuss techniques for making more frequent backups.

Backing Up the Entire Hard Disk

DOS provides a command, named BACKUP, that can back up files from your hard disk onto a series of diskettes. Unlike the COPY and XCOPY commands, BACKUP stores files in a special condensed *image* format. This allows BACKUP to store copies of files that are larger than the capacity of a diskette. It is important to remember, however, that backup copies created with the BACKUP command can *only* be restored onto your hard disk using the DOS RESTORE command (discussed later in this chapter).

Calculating the Number of Diskettes Required

Backing up your hard disk is an operation that requires several diskettes. You can calculate how many diskettes you'll need by dividing the total number of bytes of data stored on your hard disk by the capacity of one diskette. To find out how many bytes of storage space are currently being used on the hard disk, use the CHKDSK command. (Remember, CHKDSK is an external command, and DOS must be able to find CHKDSK.COM when you enter the command.)

For example, suppose that you enter the command CHKDSK at the command prompt and that DOS displays the following information about your hard disk (other information that CHKDSK displays is not relevant at the moment):

```
33323008 bytes total disk space
 .
 .
 .
18071552 bytes available on disk
```

Given that your disk has a total of 33,323,008 bytes of storage space and that 18,071,552 bytes are still available, then your disk must contain 15,251,456 bytes of data (33,323,008 minus 18,071,552). To calculate the number of 360KB diskettes required to back up that much data, use the formula *data/diskette storage capacity* or, in this case:

```
15,251,456/360,000
```

which results in 42 diskettes. If you are using 1.2MB diskettes, you would calculate the number of diskettes required by using the following figures:

```
15,251,456/1,200,000
```

which results in 13 diskettes.

Sometimes the BACKUP procedure requires fewer diskettes than the calculation determines because it stores files in a somewhat compacted format. However, the data stored on your hard disk will probably grow in the future, so there is no harm in labeling a few extra diskettes for future backups.

After you determine the number of diskettes required to back up your hard disk, place labels on each diskette and number them. Be sure to number them consecutively, starting at 1. For example, you would label the first three diskettes:

HARD DISK BACKUP #1

HARD DISK BACKUP #2

HARD DISK BACKUP #3

and so on.

If you have more than one hard disk drive, you must back up each separately, and therefore you need to calculate the number of diskettes required for additional hard disks as well. Create one set of backup diskettes for each hard disk. Number each set starting with 1, and label them accordingly, as in these examples:

HARD DISK BACKUP C: #1

HARD DISK BACKUP C: #2

HARD DISK BACKUP C: #3

and so on . . .

HARD DISK BACKUP D: #1

HARD DISK BACKUP D: #2

HARD DISK BACKUP D: #3

and so on . . . .

DOS Versions 3.3 and 4 can automatically format the diskettes when you initiate the BACKUP procedure. If you are using an earlier version of DOS, you need to format each of these diskettes before you start the backup procedure.

WARNING: See the following commands in Appendix B for warnings about using them with BACKUP: APPEND, ASSIGN, SUBST, and JOIN.

After you label all the diskettes (and format them, if necessary), you can begin the backup procedure. BACKUP requires the following basic syntax:

BACKUP *drive file(s) destination switches*

drive specifies the hard disk to backup

file(s) represents a single file name or an ambiguous file name of files to back up. (For example, *.* backs up all files on the hard disk.)

destination is the floppy disk drive in which the backup diskettes are placed *switches* represents various options that control how files are backed up.

The most commonly used optional switches are listed in Table 11.5. (See Appendix B for additional, less frequently used switches.) Note that the optional switches are always preceded by a forward slash (/).

Table 11.5. Switches commonly used with the BACKUP command.

Switch	Description
/A	Adds new and modified files to existing backup diskettes
/L	Creates a log on the current directory of the hard disk that lists all backed up files
/M	Backs up new and modified files only
/S	Backs up files from all subdirectories beneath the current directory

Keep in mind that BACKUP is an external DOS command, and it requires access to a file named BACKUP.COM. Automatic formatting also requires that the FORMAT.COM file be available from the current directory. Before starting the backup procedure, either access the directory that contains these files or be sure that the appropriate directory is included in the current PATH specification.

DOS 4 users, note that the Backup option "suggests" a source, destination, and switch for backing up the hard disk. Look at the startup sequence for this option; it displays the suggestion by using the /D and /R options discussed earlier in this chapter.

To start the backup procedure, follow the appropriate steps for your version of DOS:

1. Insert backup diskette number 1 in drive A:.
2. From the Main Group screen, select **DOS Utilities....**
3. Select **Backup Fixed Disk.**
4. Press the End key, then the Spacebar, and then add the switch /L to the suggested prompt, as shown in Figure 11.26.
5. Press Enter (or click once on ⏎=**Enter**).

If you are backing up from the command prompt, follow these steps:

1. Insert backup diskette number 1 in drive A:.
2. Type the command **BACKUP C:*.* A: /S /L** and press Enter.

Regardless of whether you used the DOS Shell or the command prompt to start the backup procedure, the steps shown had you enter **C:*.* A: /S /L** as the source, destination, and switches. The **C:*.*** entry starts the backup at the root directory (that is, C:\ represents the root directory of drive C: and *.* specifies all files). The A: entry specifies drive A: as the destination. The /S switch tells DOS to include all directories beneath

```
  04-19-89              Start Programs                  12:28 am
  Program  Group  Exit                                  F1=Help
                      DOS Utilities...
             To select an item, use the up and down arrows.
           To start a program or display a new group, press Enter.

  Set Date and Time
  Disk Copy
  Disk Compare
  Backup Fixed Disk
  Restore Fixed Disk
  Format
                                 ┌───────Backup Utility───────┐
                                 │                            │
                                 │  Enter source and destination drives. │
                                 │                            │
                                 │  Parameters . .  │c:\*.* a: /s /L│→│
                                 │                            │
                                 │  (←┘=Enter) (Esc=Cancel) (F1=Help) │
                                 │                            │
                                 └────────────────────────────┘



  F10=Actions  Esc=Cancel  Shift+F9=Command Prompt
```

Figure 11.26 Dialog box for the Backup Fixed Disk option.

the starting directory (the root directory in this example), and /L creates a log file (BACKUP.LOG) on the current directory of the hard disk.

After you enter BACKUP, DOS provides instructions on how to proceed. (These instructions vary slightly in different versions of DOS.) The first message is:

```
Insert backup diskette 01 in drive A:
WARNING! Files in the target drive
A:\ root directory will be erased
Press any key to continue...
```

Double-check to be sure that you placed backup diskette number 1 in drive A:. Then, press a key to continue.

If the BACKUP command automatically formatted the diskette in drive A:, DOS displays information about the diskette, followed by the prompt Format another (Y/N)?. Type the letter N and press Enter to proceed.

Your screen now shows the directory and path of each file as it is backed up. After filling one diskette, DOS prompts you to insert the diskette you labeled number 2 and repeat the formatting and backing up process. This procedure is repeated until all the files on the hard disk are backed up. Follow the instructions as they appear on the screen; always answer N whenever DOS asks if you want to format another diskette; and be sure to place the correctly numbered diskette into drive A: when prompted.

When DOS finishes the backup, the command prompt or Shell reappears on the screen. Remove the diskette in drive A:, and write the word "Last" on the label, because DOS might require you to insert this last diskette in drive A: at some time in the future. (A later example will demonstrate this requirement.)

Printing the Log File

Refer to the section "Controlling the Printer" in Chapter 12 if you have problems printing the BACKUP.LOG file.

As soon as DOS finishes the backup procedure, you should make a printed copy of the BACKUP.LOG file. Because you won't be able to gain access to the BACKUP.LOG file if your hard disk crashes, the safest policy is to print a copy of it for future reference. To print the BACKUP.LOG file, use the following steps for your version of DOS:

1. If you are using the DOS Shell, press the Esc key to return to the Main Group.
2. Select `File System`.
3. Change to the DOS directory by highlighting its name in the Directory Tree and pressing Enter (or by clicking once with the mouse).
4. Press the Tab key to move to the Files Area.
5. Move the highlight to the BACKUP.LOG file, and press the Spacebar (or click your mouse once) to select that file name.
6. Press F10 and Enter to pull down the File menu.
7. Select `Print....`

1. If you are working from the command prompt, type `TYPE C:\BACKUP.LOG > PRN`.
2. Press `Enter`.

The printout of the BACKUP.LOG file displays the date and time of the backup, as well as the diskette number, directory, and file name of each backed-up file, as in the example shown in Figure 11.27. (Note that your printout will reflect the date, time, directories, and file names of your hard disk.)

The information in the BACKUP.LOG file might come in handy in the future if you ever need to restore a few files from your backup diskettes. Later sections will demonstrate this procedure.

Files Stored on Backup Diskettes

As mentioned earlier in this chapter, the BACKUP command stores an image of your hard disk on one or more diskettes; it does not store individual

```
4-17-90  16:30:00

001  \CONFIG.SYS
001  \012345.678
001  \AUTOEXEC.BAT
001  \DOS\COUNTRY.SYS
001  \DOS\COMMAND.COM
001  \DOS\DISKCOPY.COM
001  \DOS\DISPLAY.SYS
001  \DOS\FDISK.COM
001  \DOS\FORMAT.COM
001  \DOS\KEYB.COM
001  \DOS\KEYBOARD.SYS
001  \DOS\REPLACE.EXE
001  \DOS\SYS.COM
001  \DOS\ASSIGN.COM
001  \DOS\ATTRIB.EXE
001  \DOS\BASIC.COM
001  \DOS\BASICA.COM
001  \DOS\COMP.COM
001  \DOS\DEBUG.COM
001  \DOS\DISKCOMP.COM
001  \DOS\EDLIN.COM
```

Figure 11.27 A partial sample BACKUP.LOG file printout.

files. Therefore, you might be surprised if you look at the directory of one of your backup diskettes.

For example, if you put one of the backup diskettes into drive A: and then enter the command DIR A: from the DOS command prompt, you will see only two file names listed, as follows:

```
BACKUP     001        1,210,709      04-17-90   04:30p
CONTROL    001            3,001      04-17-90   04:30p
```

Where 001 is the number of the backup diskette label, the next column represents the size of the combined files on the diskette, and 04-17-90 and 04:30P represent the date and time of your last backup. (The DOS 4 File System screen shows the date, but not the time.)

Neither the COPY or XCOPY commands can retrieve files from these BACKUP or CONTROL files. Only the RESTORE command, discussed later, can perform this operation.

Updating the Backup Diskettes

After you initially create your backup of the *entire* hard disk, you can use a few shortcut techniques to quickly update the backups. In particular, you might want to use the /M (for *modified*) and /A (for *add*) switches to back up only modified files.

The /M switch causes BACKUP to copy only those files that have their *archive bit* turned on. The archive bit is stored with the file name and other attributes (such as read-only) in every file, and DOS automatically turns it on when you create or edit a file. When you back up a file using the BACKUP command, DOS turns off the Archive bit, and the bit remains off until you again modify the file.

The /A switch adds new and modified files to the existing backup diskettes, rather than replacing the existing backups. If you do not use the /A switch, DOS automatically reformats the backup diskette, thereby erasing all of the backup files that are already on that diskette. Basically, you want to use the/A switch whenever you want to back up only new and modified files, rather than going through the time-consuming process of backing up the entire hard disk.

DOS 4 users can select Backup from the DOS Utilities . . . screen to update the backup diskettes, but they must be sure to change the suggested entry in the dialog box to include the /M and /A switches.

To back up modified files and add new files to the existing backups, first be sure that all your numbered backup diskettes are available. Then, while still accessing the hard disk, enter a BACKUP command with the general format BACKUP C:*.* /M /A /S /L:*filename* where *filename* assigns a name other than BACKUP.LOG to the new backup log file. You might make the file name represent the current date, but be sure not to use any invalid characters. For example, if you are updating your backup diskettes on April 15, 1990, you might want to enter the command.

```
BACKUP C:\*.* A: /M /A /S /L:Apr15_90.LOG
```

When you press Enter, DOS prompts you to insert your last (highest-numbered) backup diskette in drive A:. (This is the diskette you labeled "Last" after the original backup.) Depending on the number of new and modified files that need to be backed up, DOS might prompt you to insert additional diskettes.

If backing up new or modified files requires you to use additional diskettes, write *Last* on the new highest-numbered diskette, and erase it from the label of the diskette that was previously labeled Last.

You also might want to print a copy of the new log file. Keep it handy in case you need to restore only certain files from your backup diskettes.

The XCOPY command, discussed in Appendix B, is also a useful tool for making daily backups of new and modified files.

Remember, it's a good idea to store backup diskettes off-site—away from the computer—in case of fire or theft. If you use the /A option to update your backup diskettes, you need to keep only the diskette labeled Last or better yet, a copy of that diskette) near the computer for daily updates. As you fill more backup diskettes, store them off-site with the other, lower-numbered diskettes.

Recovering from a Hard Disk Crash

If your hard disk crashes and you need to install a new hard disk, you must first format (and partition, if necessary) the hard disk and then install DOS as though you had bought a brand new computer. (See Appendix A for a detailed discussion of these topics.) Then, when the hard disk is physically ready to accept data, you can use your backup diskettes to recreate your original directory tree and copy all of your files to the new hard disk.

Appendix B discusses all the switches available for both the BACKUP and RESTORE commands.

You must use the RESTORE command to copy backup files from your diskettes to the hard disk. To ensure that all directories are recreated and that files are placed in their original directories, you must use the /S switch. In addition, you probably should use the /P switch as well. This switch causes RESTORE to pause and ask for permission before updating a file that already exists on the hard disk with an "older" copy of the file. For example, if you've upgraded to a newer version of DOS since the hard disk crashed, you do not want to replace your new DOS files with the old DOS files on the backup diskettes—the /P switch helps prevent you from doing so.

The general syntax for restoring all the files from the backup diskettes is as follows:

`RESTORE drive destination /S /P`

> *drive* is the name of the drive that will hold the backup diskette(s)
>
> *destination* is the name and the root directory of the hard disk being restored and is followed by the *.* file specifier.

There is no need to "practice" restoring a hard disk; the entire operation is "automatic." Use the RESTORE command only when necessary.

For example, to restore the entire hard disk from backup diskettes in drive A:, you would type the command:

`RESTORE A: C:\*.* /S /P`

After you press Enter to enter the command, DOS prompts you to insert the backup diskettes in sequentially numbered order. Because you specified the /P switch, DOS might stop and ask for permission before replacing an existing file with an older one. In most cases, you should answer No to keep the newer version of the file on the hard disk.

When RESTORE completes it operation it redisplays the DOS command prompt. Use the appropriate commands to examine the files on your hard disk, and notice that all your original files and directories are back in place.

Restoring Only Specific Files

In some cases, you might need to restore only a few files. For example, suppose that you tried to erase all the .BAK files on your DOS directory, but you inadvertently entered the command `ERASE *.BAT`, which erases all of your *batch files* instead. (Batch files are discussed in Chapter 13.) You need to restore these files from your backup diskettes, but you certainly do not need to restore *all* of the files on your hard disk.

In this situation, you need to restore only those files that have the extension .BAT onto the current directory (DOS in this example). To do so, enter the command:

```
RESTORE A: C:  \DOS\*.BAT /P
```

Note that the /P switch is optional; it merely helps prevent you from over-writing newer files with older files. DOS prompts you to insert your backup diskettes, in numbered order, until it has restored all of the speci-fied files.

You can speed the process of restoring only certain files by checking your printed copies of the backup .LOG files. When you locate the diskette number that contains the files you want to back up, merely insert that disk-ette into drive A: rather than the one that DOS suggests. DOS will display the message `WARNING! Diskette is out of sequence. Replace diskette or continue if OK.` Leave the diskette in drive A:, and press any key to start the restoration process from that diskette.

Troubleshooting

If you make an error while trying the techniques in this chapter, one of the following messages will probably appear on your screen. Locate the appro-priate error message, and try the recommended solution.

- `Bad command or file name`: You either misspelled a command, or the program is not available on the current diskette, directory, or in the currently defined PATH of directories.

- `General failure reading drive A`: The diskette in drive A: is probably not formatted. Type `A` to abandon the operation; then, format the disk-ette.

- `Invalid drive in search path`: Your command includes a drive name that does not exist on your computer.

- `Last backup diskette not inserted`: DOS requested that you put the last backup diskette in the destination drive, but you put in a different diskette. Try your highest-numbered diskette.

- `System files restored. Target disk may not be bootable`: Versions of DOS prior to 3.3 copy the system files during backup and restore operations. You probably need to use the SYS command (see Appen-dix B) to recopy system files from your newer version of DOS back to the root directory. (This makes your hard disk bootable again.)

■ **Target is full. The last file was not restored**: The hard disk on which you are restoring files has no more storage space, and the last-listed file name was not restored. This occurs when your backup diskettes contain more data than the hard disk can store. You probably need to manually create all new directories on your hard disk and then use the RESTORE command independently for each directory to restore only specific files.

■ **Warning! Diskette is out of sequence. Replace diskette or continue if OK**: The backup diskette in drive A: is not the one that DOS requested. Replace it with the properly numbered diskette. Or, if you are certain that you want DOS to search only the current diskette because you know it contains the files you want to recover, leave the out-of-sequence diskette in the drive. Then, press any key to continue. DOS asks to search only higher-numbered disks in future prompts.

■ **Warning! Files in the target drive A:\ root directory will be erased**: DOS is telling you that the current backup will replace previously backed up files. This message does not appear when you use the /M and /A switches to update a previous backup.

Summary

This chapter focused on techniques that help make your use of a hard disk more efficient, easier, and safer. Following is a summary of the most important points:

■ Use the PATH command to permit DOS to search specific directories for program files with the .COM, .EXE, and .BAT extensions. This lets you run programs from any directory on your hard disk and avoids the Bad command or file name error.

■ Hard disk crashes, as well as other disasters, can destroy all the files on a hard disk. Keep backup copies of files off-site so that you can recover from any type of loss.

■ The BACKUP command can back up either an entire hard disk or merely new and modified files.

■ You cannot use COPY or XCOPY to recover files that were saved with the BACKUP command; you must use the RESTORE command.

■ DOS 4 users can create, modify, and delete groups in the DOS Shell by using options in the Group pull-down menu.

■ DOS 4 users can add, change, and delete options on a group screen to provide easier access to programs. They do so by using options on the Program pull-down menu.

■ By associating selected file name extensions with programs, DOS 4 users can run programs simply by selecting file names with the associated extension from the Files Area of the DOS Shell.

Managing the Standard Devices

This chapter discusses techniques for managing the standard devices attached to virtually all computers—the screen, the printer, and the keyboard. Because you've gotten this far in the book, the devices connected to your computer are probably functioning quite well. However, as you'll see in this chapter, there are some fancy techniques that you can use to customize the features of these devices.

 Note that nearly all of the examples in this chapter use the command prompt. That's because the DOS Shell, while easy to use, does not offer as much flexibility as the command prompt in many situations. Remember, if you are using DOS 4 and want to try the command prompt examples in this chapter, you must press the F3 key to exit the DOS Shell and display the command prompt.

Directing Actions to Devices

DOS offers many commands and techniques for controlling devices. Several techniques use the redirection symbols (listed in Table 12.1) in conjunction with DOS device names (listed in Table 12.2) to manage the flow of information to and from various devices.

Table 12.1. DOS redirection symbols.

Redirection Symbol	Meaning
<	read input from *device*
>	send output to *device*
> >	send output to *file* without overwriting existing text

Table 12.2. DOS device names.

Device Name	Description
CON	The keyboard (for input) and screen (for output) (CONsole)
COM1	First serial (COMmunications) port
COM2	Second serial port
COM3	Third serial port
COM4	Fourth serial port
AUX	Another name for COM1 (AUXiliary serial port)
LPT1	First parallel printer (Line PrinTer) port
LPT2	Second parallel printer port
LPT3	Third parallel printer port
PRN	Same as LPT1 (PRiNter)
filename.ext	(Although not actually a device, a file can sometimes be used as though it were a device)

If you've followed the command prompt examples in this book, then you've already seen redirection symbols and device names. For example, the command `DIR > PRN` sends output from the DIR command to the printer. The command `TREE > PRN` sends output from the TREE command to the printer.

Note that Table 12.2 shows that some names define a *port*. You can think of a port simply as a plug on the back of your computer to which a device, like the printer, is attached. For example, if you have two printers attached to your computer on ports LPT1 and LPT2, then entering the command such as `DIR > LPT2` sends output to your second printer rather than the first.

If you use the `> PRN` symbol and device name, but it does not send output to the printer, then perhaps you have a *serial* printer attached to the COM1 port. In that case, try entering command `DIR > COM1`. In fact, if you are not sure which port your printer is hooked to, you can experiment with different device names next to the `DIR >` command until you find the device name that accesses the printer.

As you will see, DOS offers you great flexibility in using device names and redirection symbols, but the command that uses them must be logical. For example, the command:

```
DIR < PRN
```

makes no sense because the printer cannot "send" anything to the DIR command. (In fact, the printer cannot send anything *to* any device; it can only accept output *from* the computer.) However, the command `DIR > PRN` command makes sense because the DIR command can certainly send its output (text) to the printer.

This chapter demonstrates the use of several device names, but not all. Chapter 13 demonstrates the use of the other devices.

Managing the Screen

DOS 4 users have already seen how to change the colors of the DOS Shell and how to use the scroll bar and PgUp and PgDn keys to scroll through long lists of directory and file names (Chapter 3). This section focuses on techniques for managing the screen at the command prompt. These techniques work for all versions of DOS.

Clearing the Screen

You cannot clear the screen while Edlin is displaying the * prompt.

Many times when you use the DOS command prompt, the screen becomes cluttered with old command lines and the output of those commands. You can eliminate this clutter by clearing the screen. Merely enter the command CLS (short for CLear Screen), and press Enter. Everything but the command prompt (which now appears at the top of the screen) is cleared from your screen.

Controlling Scrolling

Some DOS commands show far more lines of information than the screen can display at one time, and text scrolls off the screen too quickly for you to read. You've already seen how to use the /P switch with the DIR command so that DOS pauses after each screenful of information is presented. Several more techniques for controlling scrolling are discussed in the next few sections.

Starting and Stopping Scrolling

Whenever large amounts of text are scrolling off the screen, you can always freeze the display by pressing Ctrl-S (hold down the Ctrl Key and type the letter S). Scrolling stops immediately. To resume scrolling, press any character key, or the Spacebar, or press Ctrl-S.

If your keyboard has a key labeled Pause, you can press that key instead of Ctrl-S to stop scrolling. To resume scrolling after pressing Pause, press any other key.

Using the MORE Command

In some cases, you need to be pretty quick on the keyboard to use the Ctrl-S or Pause key effectively, especially on today's high-speed computers. As an alternative, you can use the MORE command to have DOS automatically pause after each screenful of information is presented.

MORE is an *external* command. That is, it's actually a program stored in a file named MORE.COM. To use MORE, the MORE.COM file must be accessible from the current drive and directory. (If you get the `Bad command or file name` error when you first try to use the command, keep reading and try the alternative techniques discussed later in this section.)

There are two different syntaxes for using MORE. When you need to display the contents of lengthy text files, enter the MORE command, followed by the < redirection symbol, followed by the name of the file whose contents you wish to view. The general syntax for this usage is shown below (*filename.ext* is the name of the file you wish to view):

```
MORE < filename.ext
```

When you want to use MORE in conjunction with another DOS command, use the second general syntax. In this case, type the complete command, followed by the pipe character | and the MORE command. This general syntax is as follows:

```
DOS command | MORE
```

For example, let's assume that after you buy a new application program, you notice that a file named READ.ME is included on the program diskette. To read the contents of that file on your screen so that it pauses with each screenful of printed text, you can enter either this command:

```
MORE < READ.ME
```

or the command:

```
TYPE READ.ME | MORE
```

Notice how the MORE < READ.ME command uses the "input" redirection symbol to send the contents of the READ.ME file into the MORE program.

Although both commands use the MORE command in different ways, the result is the same. DOS displays one screenful of text and the prompt -- MORE --. When you see this prompt, press any key to see the next screenful. Optionally, you can press Break (Ctrl-C, Ctrl-Pause, or Ctrl-Scroll Lock) to stop viewing the file and return to the DOS prompt.

If the MORE command is not available on the current drive, directory, or PATH, change to the diskette or directory that contains the MORE.COM file (usually the DOS directory in Version 4 or the root directory in earlier versions), and specify both the location and name of the file you wish to view.

For example, if you want to view the contents of a file named README.DOC on a directory named QUATTRO, first change to the drive and directory that contains the MORE.COM file. Then, enter either the command:

```
MORE < C:\QUATTRO\README.DOC
```

or

```
TYPE C:\QUATTRO\README.DOC | MORE
```

If your computer doesn't have a hard disk, put the DOS diskette that contains the MORE.COM program into drive A:, and insert the diskette that contains the file whose contents you want to view in drive B:. Assuming that the file you want to view is named README.TXT and that the current drive is drive A:, enter either the command:

```
MORE < B:README.TXT
```

or

```
TYPE B:README.TXT | MORE
```

Remember, if you have a hard disk, you can make external commands, such as MORE, more accessible by setting up an appropriate PATH command, as discussed in Chapter 11.

As mentioned in Chapter 5, CHKDSK is also an external command, and it requires access to the program CHKDSK.COM.

You can use MORE with any command that displays data. For example, the CHKDSK /V command displays the names of all files on all directories of your hard disk. To see its output one screenful at a time, enter the command:

```
CHKDSK /V | MORE
```

Customizing the Command Prompt

In Chapter 4 you learned that you can enter the command PROMPT PG to change the DOS command prompt so that it displays the current drive and directory. There is actually quite a bit more that you can do to alter the command prompt. Table 12.3 lists all of the codes that you can use with the PROMPT command to customize your command prompt:

Table 12.3. Symbols used with the PROMPT command.

Code	Effect
$$	displays the $ character
$_	breaks prompt onto a second line
$B	displays the | character
$D	displays the current date
$e	generates an Esc (escape) character
$G	displays the > character
$H	backspaces one character

Table 12.3. (cont.)

Code	Effect
$L	displays the < character
$N	displays the current drive
$P	displays the current drive and directory
$Q	displays the = character
$T	displays the current time
$V	displays the current version of DOS
< other characters >	other characters are displayed literally

You can use these codes to change the prompt at any time. For example, the last entry in the table means that any characters other than the listed codes are displayed *literally*, or exactly as you type them in the prompt command. If at the command prompt you type:

```
PROMPT At your service -- Please enter a command:
```

and press Enter, every command prompt that DOS displays thereafter will read At your service -- Please enter a command:.

Next, Enter this command:

```
PROMPT $D $B $T$G
```

When you press Enter, the command prompt displays the current date ($D) followed by a blank space, the | symbol ($B), another blank space, the current time ($T), and the > symbol ($G), as shown below. (Note that the blank spaces in the prompt correspond to the blank spaces you typed in the PROMPT command.)

```
Thu 04-19-1990 | 10:31:42.70>
```

The $_ symbol uses the underscore character, not the hyphen. That is, it's $_ rather than $-.

To break a lengthy prompt into two lines, use the $_ character where you want to split the prompt. For example, if you now enter the command:

```
PROMPT $D$_$T$G
```

and press Enter, DOS displays a command prompt with the current date on one line and the current time and a > symbol on the second line, as follows:

```
Thu 04-19-1990
10:32:42:68>
```

The $V (version number) symbol automatically breaks the command prompt into two lines, so you don't need to use the $_ symbol. For example, if you enter the command:

```
PROMPT $V$D$G
```

and press Enter, the command prompt displays the current version of DOS on one line and the current date and the > symbol on the next, as follows:

```
IBM DOS Version 4.00
Thu 04-19-1990
```

You can use the Backspace code ($H) to erase parts of a prompt. For example, suppose you want your command prompt to display the current date *without the year* followed by the | character, the current drive and directory, and the > symbol. To do so, you must type this command:

```
PROMPT $D$H$H$H$H$H $B $P$G
```

When you press Enter, DOS displays a new prompt that resembles the following (of course, it will display today's date and your current directory):

```
Thu 04-19 | C:\DOS>
```

Note that the command uses five Backspace ($H) symbols to erase the last five characters of the current date (-1990).

You can also combine text and codes in the PROMPT command. For example, type this command:

```
PROMPT Today is $D$_Current drive and directory is $P$G
```

When you press Enter, the prompt appears as follows (with today's date displayed in place of Mon 01-01-90 and your current drive and directory in place of C:\DOS):

```
Today is Mon 01-01-90
Current drive and directory is C:\DOS>
```

If you want to return to your more familiar command prompt, enter the command PROMPT PG.

Using ANSI Codes to Control the Screen and Keyboard

Many years ago when computers were all room-size giants, the American National Standards Institute (ANSI) developed a standardized coding system for managing the interface between keyboards, computers, and monitors. They did so to make software more *portable,* that is, so programs could be used without modification on many different types of computers and monitors.

DOS comes with a *device driver,* stored in a file named ANSI.SYS, that uses the ANSI coding system to send characters and images to your screen. The file is called a "device driver" because it literally drives a device; that is, it tells a device (in this case, your monitor) what to do.

To see if your computer is currently set up to accept ANSI codes, you merely have to use the TYPE command to view the contents of your CONFIG.SYS file. Because CONFIG.SYS is always stored on the startup drive or directory, the file is easy to find—if it in fact exists.

On a hard disk, enter the following command at the DOS command prompt:

```
TYPE C:\CONFIG.SYS
```

On a computer that boots from a diskette, insert your Startup diskette in drive A:, be sure that drive A: is your current drive and enter the command:

```
TYPE CONFIG.SYS
```

If your computer can indeed accept ANSI codes, the CONFIG.SYS file contains the command DEVICE = followed by the location and name of the ANSI.SYS file. For example, on a computer that boots from the hard disk, you should see either the command:

```
DEVICE = C:\ANSI.SYS
```

or perhaps the command:

```
DEVICE = C:\DOS\ANSI.SYS
```

On a computer that starts from a diskette, you should see the command:

```
DEVICE = A:\ANSI.SYS
```

Some programs require that your CONFIG.SYS file load the ANSI.SYS file. These programs' documentation will inform you of this requirement.

If your CONFIG.SYS file does not set up the ANSI.SYS device driver, you can modify the file using the general techniques described in Chapter 10. However, it is not absolutely necessary to do so, unless you want to customize screen colors at the command prompt or redefine keys on your keyboard (as discussed later in this chapter).

To modify your CONFIG.SYS file to include the ANSI.SYS device driver, you first must be sure that DOS can find the ANSI.SYS file as soon as you turn on the computer. That is, if you boot your computer from a diskette, the ANSI.SYS file must be stored on that diskette. The CONFIG.SYS file must also contain the command:

```
DEVICE = ANSI.SYS
```

If your computer boots from a hard disk, locate the directory that contains ANSI.SYS FILE (probably the root directory or the DOS directory). When you modify the CONFIG.SYS file, be sure to specify the complete path and file name in the DEVICE command, as in the following examples:

```
DEVICE = C:\ANSI.SYS
```

or

```
DEVICE = C:\DOS\ANSI.SYS
```

After you change the CONFIG.SYS file, remember that modifications do not take effect until you reboot the computer. However, from then on, DOS automatically issues these commands every time you start your computer.

Modifying Screen Colors and Attributes

DOS 4 users already know how to change the color scheme of the DOS Shell. If you are using another version of DOS (or you prefer the DOS 4 command Prompt), you can use ANSI codes to customize the screen colors displayed at the command prompt, provided that your computer is set up to accept ANSI codes (as discussed in the preceding section).

Be sure to use the lowercase letters "e" and "m" in the escape sequences. If you make a mistake, the DOS prompt displays all characters literally from the point of the error to the right. Merely retype the command to correct it.

To color the screen, you use the PROMPT command in conjunction with special codes called *escape sequences*. An escape sequence is a series of characters that begin with the Escape (or Esc) key character. Recall from Table 12.3 that you can use the $e symbol in the PROMPT command to specify the Escape key character.

The general syntax for using an Escape sequence in the PROMPT command is as follows:

```
PROMPT $e[xxm
```

where xx is a one-digit *attribute* number or a two-digit color number. Table 12.4 lists the complete escape sequences for controlling screen colors on monitors that are capable of displaying color.

Table 12.5 lists the escape sequences for controlling special attributes on both color and monochrome screens. You can use these special attributes in conjunction with colors (on color monitors). Note that these one-digit escape sequences are similar to the two-digit codes used for coloring the screen.

Table 12.4. Escape sequences for changing screen colors

Color	Foreground	Background
Black	$e[30m	$e[40m
Red	$e[31m	$e[41m
Green	$e[32m	$e[42m
Yellow	$e[33m	$e[43m
Blue	$e[34m	$e[44m
Magenta	$e[35m	$e[45m
Cyan	$e[36m	$e[46m
White	$e[37m	$e[47m

Table 12.5. Escape sequences for changing screen attributes.

Attribute	Escape sequence
None	$e[0m
High intensity	$e[1m
Underline (monochrome only)	$e[4m
Blinking	$e[5m
Reverse video	$e[7m
Invisible	$e[8m

Let's use some of these escape sequences at the DOS command prompt. However, keep in mind that you might not see any changes until you either clear the screen or start typing again. Let's try some examples. To switch the screen display to reverse video, enter the following command:

```
PROMPT $e[7m
```

Reverse video reverses the foreground and background colors or shades used on your screen. For example, if your screen normally displays dark letters on a light background, reverse video displays light letters against a dark background.

Not much seems to happen at first (other than the fact that the command prompt disappears). However, watch what happens when you enter any command that displays text, such as "DIR". The displayed text appears in reverse video, as shown in Figure 12.1.

After changing screen colors or attributes, you can enter a new PROMPT command to redefine the command prompt, without losing the current attributes or colors. For example, to redisplay the familiar command prompt, enter the command `PROMPT $P$G`.

Now, try the blinking attribute; enter the command:

```
PROMPT $e[5m
```

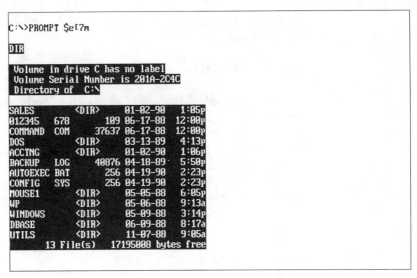

```
C:\>PROMPT $e[7m

DIR

 Volume in drive C has no label
 Volume Serial Number is 201A-2C4C
 Directory of  C:\

SALES        <DIR>     01-02-90    1:05p
012345   678        109 06-17-88   12:00p
COMMAND  COM      37637 06-17-88   12:00p
DOS          <DIR>     03-13-89    4:13p
ACCTNG       <DIR>     01-02-90    1:06p
BACKUP   LOG      40076 04-18-89   5:50p
AUTOEXEC BAT        256 04-19-90   2:23p
CONFIG   SYS        256 04-19-90   2:23p
MOUSE1       <DIR>     05-05-88    6:05p
WP           <DIR>     05-06-88    9:13a
WINDOWS      <DIR>     05-09-88    3:14p
DBASE        <DIR>     06-09-88    8:17a
UTILS        <DIR>     11-07-88    9:05a
        13 File(s)   17195008 bytes free
```

Figure 12.1. Sample display in reverse video.

To see the results, enter a command (such as DIR) that displays text on the screen. Notice that the reverse video attribute remains in effect, and now blinking has been added to that attribute.

To return to the normal screen display, remove all attributes by entering the command:

PROMPT $e[0m

Then, enter the CLS command to clear the screen and enter the PROMPT PG command to redisplay your command prompt.

If you have a color monitor, try some different color schemes. Use any combination of the foreground and background color escape sequences shown in Table 12.4. For example, to display yellow text on a blue background, enter the command:

PROMPT $e[33m $e[44m

Then, enter a command that displays text (such as DIR). If your yellow looks more like brown, switch to high intensity by entering the command:

PROMPT $e[1m

Again, enter a command to display text (such as DIR), and see the effects of these PROMPT commands.

You can use any combination of screen attributes, colors, and the command prompt style codes in a single PROMPT command if you wish. For example, to simultaneously set the screen colors to high-intensity red letters on a black background and also define the command prompt, enter the command:

```
PROMPT $e[40m$e[1m$e[31m$P$G
```

Keep in mind that DOS reads the "code strings" defined in the PROMPT command every time it displays the command prompt. Therefore, you can turn on an attribute at the beginning of the prompt and then turn it off at the end of the prompt, so that only the command prompt itself uses the defined attribute.

For example, suppose you want to display your screen in normal colors, but you want to display the command prompt in reverse video. To do so, first return to the normal screen colors and attributes by entering the commands:

```
PROMPT $e[0m$P$G
```

and

```
CLS
```

Next, enter a PROMPT command that turns on reverse video, displays the command prompt, and then turns off reverse video, as follows:

```
PROMPT $e[7m$P$G$e[0m
```

As Figure 12.2 shows, only the command prompt is displayed in reverse video.

```
C:\DOS> DATE
Current date is Wed 06-07-1989
Enter new date (mm-dd-yy): 6/7/89

C:\DOS> TIME
Current time is  8:46:36.10a
Enter new time: 8:50

C:\DOS> <--- Only the command prompt is in reverse video.
```

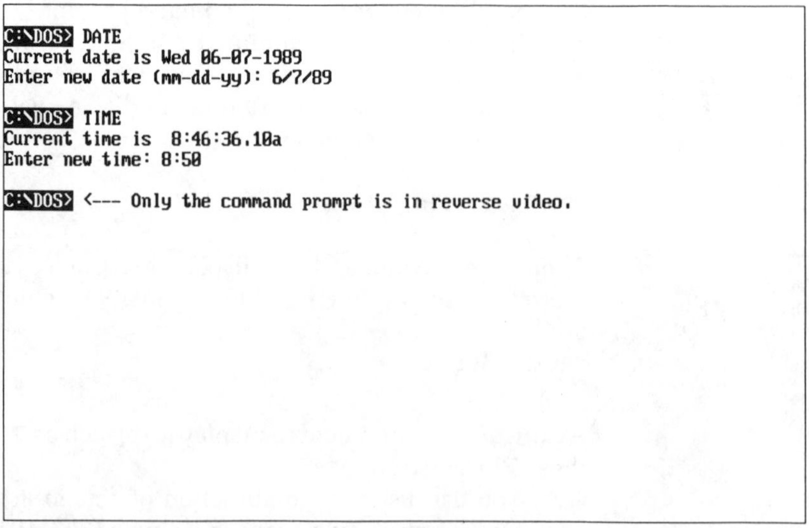

Figure 12.2. Command prompt is displayed in reverse video.

Saving PROMPT Settings

The one problem with designing a custom command prompt that uses fancy display attributes and colors is that DOS "forgets" it as soon as you turn off the computer. However, you can have DOS immediately activate your custom prompt at startup by including the PROMPT command in your AUTOEXEC.BAT file.

Remember, you can only use screen attributes and colors if your CONFIG.SYS file loads the ANSI device driver.

You can place the PROMPT command on any line within the AUTO-EXEC.BAT file. (However, DOS 4 users must remember to leave the DOSSHELL command as the last command in AUTOEXEC.BAT.) Figure 12.3 shows a sample AUTOEXEC.BAT file that contains the command `PROMPT $e[7m$P$G$e[0m`. Remember, you must edit the AUTOEXEC.BAT as a DOS text file, and you must store it in the root directory on the proper drive for your computer. Refer to Chapter 10 for details, if necessary.

```
@ECHO OFF
SET COMSPEC=C:\DOS\COMMAND.COM
PATH C:\WP;C:\DOS;C:\UTILS;C:\DBASE;C:\WINDOWS
VERIFY OFF
PROMPT $e[7m$P$G$e[0m
C:\MOUSE1\MOUSE
APPEND /E
APPEND C:\DOS
PRINT /D:LPT1
DOSSHELL
```

Figure 12.3. Sample AUTOEXEC.BAT file with a customized PROMPT command.

Controlling the Screen's Character Size

You can also use the MODE command to configure other devices. See Appendix B for details.

Normally, DOS displays 80 columns of text across the screen. However, you can double the size of the letters on the screen by telling DOS to display only 40 columns of text across the screen. To do so you must use the DOS MODE command. Table 12.6 lists the codes that you can use with the MODE command to control the display on your monitor.

Table 12.6. Options for controlling the screen display with MODE.

Code	Effect
40	Sets the display width to 40 characters on a color graphics screen. (Does not affect colors.)
80	Sets the display width to 80 characters on a color graphics screen. (Does not affect colors.)

Table 12.6. (cont.)

Code	Effect
BW40	Sets the display width to 40 characters and colors to black and white on a color graphics screen.
BW80	Sets the display width to 80 characters and colors to black and white on a color graphics screen.
CO40	Sets the display width to 40 characters and allows color on a color graphics screen.
CO80	Sets the display width to 80 characters and allows color on a color graphics screen.
MONO	Sets the display width to 80 characters and allows only a monochrome display. (The only setting available with monochrome display adapters.)

Changing the character size affects command prompt screens only, not the DOS Shell.

MODE is an external DOS program. To use MODE, the MODE.COM file must be accessible from the current diskette or directory (otherwise, DOS merely displays the Bad command or file name error message). If you are using the DOS 4 Shell, you should exit the Shell using the F3 key (not the Shift-F9 key) so that the copy of the Shell remaining in RAM does not conflict with the MODE program that will be loaded into memory.

If you have a color monitor, and you are currently at the command prompt, try the MODE command by entering the following:

```
MODE 40
```

Next, enter any command that displays text (such as DIR). As Figure 12.4 shows, the display uses much larger characters.

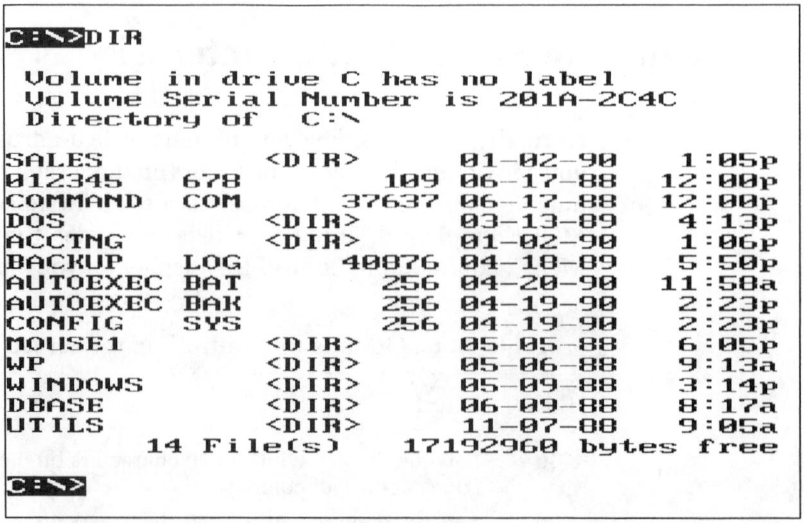

Figure 12.4. Screen displaying 40 characters per line.

To switch back to the 80-column display, enter the command:

`MODE 80`

Controlling the Printer

Any text that you display on your screen can be as easily sent to your printer. You've already used the > redirection symbol with the `PRN` device name to channel the output of some commands to the printer. For example, `DIR > PRN` prints all of the file names in a directory . The command `TYPE` *filename.ext* `> PRN` prints the contents of a file. There are other ways to send information to the printer as well, as the sections that follow describe.

Copying Screen Text

To print screen displays using the Shift-Print-Screen key combination, see the section titled "Printing Graphics" later in this chapter.

Whenever the command prompt is displayed, you can send an exact copy of whatever is on your screen (called a *screen dump*) to the printer simply by pressing the Shift-PrintScreen key (on some keyboards, PrintScreen is abbreviated Print Scrn or Prt Sc).

To try this procedure, be sure that the DOS command prompt is presently displayed on your screen, and then enter the command `DIR /W`. Then, press Shift-PrintScreen (hold down the Shift key and press the PrintScreen key).

There are two points to keep in mind about using the PrintScreen key to "dump" text from the screen to the printer. First of all, those of you who have laser printers may not see the printed results immediately. Instead, you may need to eject the current page from the printer to see the printed screen dump (as discussed in the next section).

Secondly, many printers cannot display graphics images (including the DOS 4 Shell and File System) that are displayed on your screen. Read the section titled "Printing Graphics" later in this chapter before using the PrintScreen key to print screen graphics.

Ejecting a Page

Most printers allow you to eject a page from the printer by pressing buttons on the front of the printer. However, it is often easier to let DOS do it—merely use the DOS ECHO command with the form-feed character (Ctrl-L) and the printer redirection symbol (> PRN). To use this technique, follow these steps:

1. Type `ECHO` and press the Spacebar.
2. Type Ctrl-L (hold down the Ctrl key and type the letter L; the screen then displays ^L).

3. Press the Spacebar and type **> PRN**.

At this point, your command should look as follows:

```
ECHO ^L > PRN
```

If it does, press Enter, and your printer will eject the current page.

Keeping Track of the Top of the Page

One of the most common complaints one hears about computers and printers is that the computer does not properly print text on pages. For example, your computer might start printing a new page in the middle of one piece or paper, keep printing that same page onto the second piece of paper, and then start printing the next page on the third piece of paper. This can be very irritating!

If your printer uses tractor-feed (continuous-form) paper, you can follow two simple rules to avoid this problem:

- Be sure that the page perforation is directly above the printer's printing head *before* you turn on the printer and computer.

- After you turn on the printer and computer, never manually "crank" the paper through the printer to get to the next page.

The reasoning behind these two rules is quite simple. First, whenever you start your computer, DOS "assumes" that top of a page is aligned just above the printer head. Second, DOS keeps track of the top of each page by counting the number of lines it sends to the printer.

If the paper is not properly aligned when you start the computer, DOS is "off the mark" at the outset. Even if the paper is aligned properly when you turn on the computer, DOS cannot detect you manually cranking paper through the printer. When you do that, its count of how many lines of the page have been moved through the printer becomes incorrect, and it no longer can properly align text on the page.

Ctrl-J (^J) is called the line feed character, because it "feeds" one blank line to the printer.

Now, you might be wondering how you can eject a partially printed page or insert extra blank lines without manually cranking the printer platen. Well, use the **ECHO ^L > PRN** command discussed above to eject the entire page. Or, if you only want to move the paper a few lines on the current page, use the command **ECHO ^J > PRN** (Press Ctrl-J to type the ^J symbol). After you type the command and press Enter, you can print additional blank lines by pressing F3 and Enter. (Recall that F3 repeats the previous DOS command.)

Note that some printers also provide buttons, such as "Set TOF" (Top Of Form), to help you keep track of alignment. See your printer manual for additional information about page alignment and the use of printer control buttons.

Slaving the Printer

Another way to send text to the printer is to *slave* the printer, so that it prints all text as it appears on the screen. Use the Ctrl-PrintScreen keys as a toggle to slave and "unslave" the printer.

For example, at the command prompt, hold down the Ctrl key and press the PrintScreen (or Print Scrn or Prt Sc) key; then, release both keys. Now enter any command that displays text, such as DIR. When you press Enter, the printer prints everything that appears on your screen (including the DIR command itself).

To unslave the printer, press Ctrl-PrintScreen again. Now the printer is no longer a slave to the screen. (If you've been trying the examples, type the ECHO ^L > PRN command to eject the printed page from the printer.)

Another way to slave the printer is to make it copy exactly what you type at the keyboard. Although doing so turns your computer into an overpriced typewriter, the technique is handy for quick and easy jobs like addressing envelopes. The basic procedure is to use the COPY command with CON (the DOS device name for the console) as the source and PRN as the destination.

For example, to address an envelope, first put the envelope into the printer. Then enter the command COPY CON PRN at the command prompt, as shown at the top of Figure 12.5. After you enter this command, the command prompt disappears, and you can type any text you wish. (Use the Backspace key to make corrections.) In the Figure, I inserted several blank lines by pressing Enter a few times; then, I typed a name and address, which I indented using the Spacebar.

After you type the name and address, type Ctrl-Z (which appears as ^Z) and press Enter. At this point, DOS prints the text on the printer and displays the message 1 File(s) copied on the screen. To eject the envelope from the printer, enter the ECHO ^L PRN command.

```
C:\>COPY CON PRN


                        John Q. Customer
                        1234 Silverthorne Lane
                        Anyville, CA  91234
^Z
        1 File(s) copied

C:\>ECHO ^L >PRN

C:\>
```

Figure 12.5. Using the computer to address an envelope.

Copying Files to the Printer

You've already seen how to use the TYPE command and the > PRN redirection symbol to print the contents of a file. You can also use the COPY command to copy the contents of text files to the printer. In addition, because COPY (unlike TYPE) permits ambiguous file names, you can print several files with one command.

To copy a file to the printer, use the standard COPY command syntax, specifying the name of the file you want to print as the source and the device name PRN (for printer) as the destination. For example, if you want to print all the files that have the extension .BAT from the root directory of drive C:, merely enter the command

```
COPY C:\*.BAT PRN
```

Keep in mind that you can only print text files, not programs or files that use special formatting codes. When in doubt, first view the contents of the file using the TYPE command. If the file's contents look OK on the screen, they will look fine on the printer as well.

Printing Graphics

All programs that are capable of displaying graphs are also capable of printing them on any dot matrix or laser printer, so you might never need to use the GRAPHICS program and Shift-Print-Screen keys to print a graph.

If you have an IBM, Epson, or compatible printer that is capable of displaying graphics, you can use Shift-PrintScreen to copy a graphics image from the screen to the printer *only* after you've loaded into memory the DOS GRAPHICS program. To load the GRAPHICS program, change to the directory that contains the file named GRAPHICS.COM, and then enter the command GRAPHICS at the command prompt.

After you run the GRAPHICS program, it stays in memory (RAM) until you turn off the computer. (It uses about 2KB of memory while *resident* in RAM.) For the remainder of your session with the computer (that is, until you turn off your computer or reboot), you can use the Shift-Print-Screen key to "dump" both text or graphics to your printer.

If your screen displays low-resolution graphics, graphics images are printed in the normal vertical format. If you use a high-resolution graphics screen, your graphics images will be printed sideways (horizontally) across the page. (If in doubt about low- and high-resolution graphics, just try the procedure and see what happens—you can't do any harm.)

If you always want to have the option to print graphs using Shift-Print-Screen, merely include the GRAPHICS command in your AUTOEXEC.BAT file. In fact, if you are using DOS 4, the installation process might already have performed this step for you. Use the View option or TYPE command to view the contents of your AUTOEXEC.BAT.

If you see the command A:\GRAPHICS or C:\DOS\GRAPHICS, then the graphics program is automatically loaded as soon as you start your computer. You can print graphics at any time simply by pressing Ctrl-PrintScreen (provided that your printer is capable of printing graphics).

Entering the GRAPHICS command by itself is generally sufficient for printing graphs with Ctrl-PrintScreen. However, you can use several options with the GRAPHICS command to control color printers and to reverse the colors on the printed copy. For more details, see the discussion of the GRAPHICS command in Appendix B.

Controlling Dot Matrix Print Size

If you have an IBM or Epson dot matrix printer (or any compatible printer), it is probably printing in the default setting of 80 characters per line and six lines to the inch. You can use the MODE command to change the number of characters per line to 132 and/or the number of lines printed per inch to 8.

If you have the right printer, and the MODE.COM file is available in the current drive or directory, you could use any of the following MODE commands to print files with varying line widths and line heights:

```
MODE LPT1:COLS=132 LINES=6

MODE LPT1:COLS=132 LINES=8

MODE LPT1:COLS=80 LINES=8

MODE LPT1:COLS=80 LINES=6
```

Controlling Laser Printer Print Size

If you have a Hewlett-Packard Laserjet printer, you can use a few tricks to take advantage of its special features, such as compressed print and landscape mode. However, the required codes are awkward to type at the command prompt. Therefore, in Chapter 14, you will create your own program, named JETSET.BAT, to facilitate using your laser printer's special features.

Background Printing

The main problem with using commands such as TYPE CONFIG.SYS > PRN and COPY C:*.BAT PRN to print text files is that you have to wait until the printing is done before you can use your computer again. As an alternative, you can tell DOS to print "in the background," therefore allowing you to continue using the computer while the printer is printing.

DOS accomplishes this background printing by using small *slices* of time when the computer is doing nothing else to send some text to the printer. For example, while you are reading something on the screen or thinking about what you want to do next, DOS can send quite a bit of text to the printer. Most printers, in turn, can store some text in a *buffer* (memory inside the printer) and therefore can accept data from the computer faster than the printer can print it. For example, in 2 seconds, DOS might be able to send enough text to keep your printer busy for a minute or two.

Although background printing is quite easy, each version of DOS uses a slightly different technique, so let's discuss each version separately. Note that the PRINT command offers several (rarely used) options in addition to those described in this Chapter. See Appendix B for details.

Using Print from the DOS Shell

To start background printing from the DOS 4 Shell, you use the Print option on the File pull-down menu in the File system. This is usually a very simple procedure. Use the following general steps to print one or more files:

The Print option (like the TYPE command) can only reliably print ASCII text files. If in doubt about the contents of a file, use the View option to preview the contents of the file on the screen.

1. From the **Start Programs** screen, select File System.

2. Use the Drives Area and the Directory Tree Area of the Shell to select the drive and directory that contains the file you want to print.

3. Move the highlight to the Files Area, and select as many as 10 files to print by highlighting the appropriate file names and pressing the Spacebar (or clicking once with the mouse).

4. After selecting files to print, press F10 and Enter to pull down the File menu (as shown in Figure 12.6).

5. Select the Print option.

If the Print option is shaded and unavailable on the File pull-down menu, press Esc to leave the menu, and continue reading below.

DOS immediately begins printing each file. If you selected multiple files, each file begins on a new page. Notice that you can continue to use your computer as DOS prints the files; you can even select additional files to print.

If you were unable to complete the steps above because the Print option on the menu was shaded and unavailable, yet you are sure that you selected at least one file name to print, then the PRINT command is not initialized. To initialize PRINT, press the F3 key to display the command prompt, and type PRINT /D:LPT1 and press Enter. Then, enter the command DOSSHELL to return to the Shell. Select the file(s) to print from the Files Area of the File System again; then, select Print from the File pull-down menu.

You can add the PRINT /D:LPT1 command to your AUTOEXEC.BAT file, provided that the PRINT.COM file is available from the startup directory or diskette when you first turn on the computer. For example, if you boot from a hard disk and PRINT.COM is stored on the DOS directory, add the command C:\DOS\PRINT /D:LPT1 to your AUTOEXEC.BAT file.

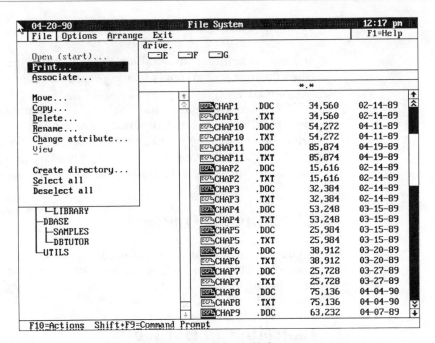

```
04-20-90                      File System              12:17 pm
 File  Options  Arrange  Exit                          F1=Help
                        drive.
  Open (start)...        ☐E   ☐F   ☐G
  Print...
  Associate...
                                                 *.*
  Move...                  ↑
  Copy...                  ⌃   📄CHAP1    .DOC      34,560    02-14-89  ⌃
  Delete...                    📄CHAP1    .TXT      34,560    02-14-89
  Rename...                    📄CHAP10   .DOC      54,272    04-11-89
  Change attribute...          📄CHAP10   .TXT      54,272    04-11-89
  View                         📄CHAP11   .DOC      85,874    04-19-89
                               📄CHAP11   .TXT      85,874    04-19-89
  Create directory...          📄CHAP2    .DOC      15,616    02-14-89
  Select all                   📄CHAP2    .TXT      15,616    02-14-89
  Deselect all                 📄CHAP3    .DOC      32,384    02-14-89
                               📄CHAP3    .TXT      32,384    02-14-89
      └LIBRARY                  📄CHAP4    .DOC      53,248    03-15-89
   ┌DBASE                       📄CHAP4    .TXT      53,248    03-15-89
   ├SAMPLES                     📄CHAP5    .DOC      25,984    03-15-89
   └DBTUTOR                     📄CHAP5    .TXT      25,984    03-15-89
  └UTILS                        📄CHAP6    .DOC      38,912    03-20-89
                               📄CHAP6    .TXT      38,912    03-20-89
                               📄CHAP7    .DOC      25,728    03-27-89
                               📄CHAP7    .TXT      25,728    03-27-89
                               📄CHAP8    .DOC      75,136    04-04-90
                               📄CHAP8    .TXT      75,136    04-04-90
                          ↓    📄CHAP9    .DOC      63,232    04-07-89  ↓
 F10=Actions  Shift+F9=Command Prompt
```

Figure 12.6. The File pull-down menu.

If you start your computer from a diskette and PRINT.COM is on the Startup diskette, add the command `PRINT /D:LPT1` to your AUTOEXEC.BAT file. Be sure to place this command before the DOSSHELL command in AUTOEXEC.BAT.

Using PRINT from the Command Prompt

To use the PRINT command from the command prompt, first be sure that the PRINT.COM file is available on the current diskette or directory (or is in a directory defined in your PATH command). Then enter the command `PRINT` followed by the location and name of the file you want to print. For example, to print a copy of the AUTOEXEC.BAT file on a hard disk, enter the command:

```
PRINT C:\AUTOEXEC.BAT
```

If this is the first time you've used PRINT in the current session, DOS displays the message:

```
Name of list device [PRN]:
```

PRN is the device name of your main printer. To use this suggested device name, merely press Enter. DOS then displays the message:

```
C:\AUTOEXEC.BAT is currently being printed
```

and begins printing. In addition, the command prompt immediately appears on your screen, ready to accept new commands while DOS is printing your file.

You can even enter additional PRINT commands while DOS is printing a file. DOS puts other files that need to be printed in the *queue*, and it prints them when the printer becomes available. You can put a maximum of 10 files into the queue for printing (unless you use the /Q switch, described in Appendix B, to expand the size of the queue).

Checking the Queue

If you want to see the names of the files that are currently lined up in the queue for printing, enter the command PRINT with no additional file names or switches.

Canceling a Print Job

PRINT provides two switches for canceling a print job: /T terminates all printing, and /C cancels the printing of a specific file or group of files. For example, suppose you enter the command:

```
PRINT C:\DOSBOOK\CHAP?.DOC
```

to print a group of files (for example, CHAP1.DOC, CHAP2.DOC, and so on). After DOS displays a message such as:

```
C:\DOSBOOK\CHAP1.DOC is currently being printed
C:\DOSBOOK\CHAP2.DOC is in queue
C:\DOSBOOK\CHAP3.DOC is in queue
```

the DOS prompt reappears, and you can type new commands. The printer then prints each file in the queue.

DOS 4 users must exit the Shell and use the PRINT /C or PRINT /T command at the command prompt to terminate a printing job.

To remove a file from the queue so that it is not printed, use the /C switch after the file name. For example, to remove CHAP2.DOC from the queue, enter the command:

```
PRINT C:\DOSBOOK\CHAP2.DOC/C
```

To cancel the printing of the current file and all remaining files in the queue, use the /T switch with the PRINT command, as follows:

```
PRINT /T
```

DOS then displays a message such as All files canceled by operator. Print queue is empty to inform you that all printing has stopped. (If your printer contains a buffer, it might continue to print for a short time.)

Using PRINT with Application Programs

PRINT might not be able to use the formatting codes, such as boldface and underlining, that your word processor offers.

Most application programs, such as spreadsheets and word processors, store special codes in the files you create. If you try to print such a file directly, using the PRINT command, the output will probably be a mess. However, virtually all application programs provide the capability to "print to a file," or to store a copy of the file in ASCII text format. (Refer to the application program's manual for specific instructions.) You can use the DOS PRINT command to print any file that has been stored in ASCII text format.

For example, let's suppose that you use the Lotus 1-2-3 program as your spreadsheet. Each month, you prepare a budgeted income statement, a portion of which appears on the 1-2-3 worksheet screen shown in Figure 12.7. Furthermore, let's assume that at the end of the year, you want to print all 12 budget sheets, but you want to use the DOS PRINT command to print in the background so that you can continue to use your computer.

```
A1:                                                                  MENU
Printer File
Send print output to file
         A         B         C         D         E         F         G
1                              ABC Company
2                         Budgeted Income Statement
3                             January 31, 1990
4
5  SALES                                              $450,000
6
7  Cost of Goods Sold:
8     Finished goods, beginning inventory             $68,500
9     Cost of goods manufactured                     $245,000
10      Cost of goods available for sale             $313,500
11    Less finished goods, ending inventory          $110,000
12     Total cost of goods sold                      $203,500
13 Gross profit on sales                             $246,500
14
15 EXPENSES
16
17    Administrative expenses                         $85,000
18    Selling expenses                                $35,000
19    Interest expenses                               $75,000
20     Total expenses                                $195,000
20-Apr-90  12:23 PM
```

Figure 12.7. A sample Lotus 1-2-3 spreadsheet.

Now, let's suppose that the spreadsheet files are stored in files named BIS_JAN.WK1, BIS_FEB.WK1, and so on to BIS_DEC.WK1. To see what format these files are in, change to the directory that contains the files and enter the command:

```
TYPE BIS_JAN.WK1
```

If your screen shows a lot of "happy faces" and other strange characters, you cannot use the PRINT command to print the file. You need to make a copy of that file that contains only ASCII text characters.

Like most application programs, Lotus 1-2-3 allows you to store a copy of a file in ASCII text format. 1-2-3 provides this capability by letting you "print" the spreadsheet to a file rather than directly to the printer. (If you actually own Lotus 1-2-3, the command is /PF, which selects Print and File from the menus.) In this example, you need to print all 12 Budgeted Income Statement spreadsheets to files. You can use the same name for the ASCII files, but you need to use a different extension, for example BIS_JAN.PRN, BIS_FEB.PRN, and so on.

When you finish that job, you would exit 1-2-3 and return to DOS. To be sure the new .PRN files contain only ASCII characters, you could enter the command `TYPE BIS_JAN.PRN` at the command prompt. Next, you would enter the command:

```
PRINT BIS_???.PRN
```

to print all 12 files. (This assumes that you used the /Q switch, discussed in the PRINT command entry in Appendix B, to initialize the PRINT command to handle more than 10 files.) Now, DOS can print all 12 files in the background, and you are free to use your computer for other jobs.

Treating Files as Devices

You've already seen how to use a file as input to the MORE command (when you used the command `MORE < READ.ME`.) You can also use file names as output devices. For example, rather than entering a command such as `DIR > PRN` to channel the output from the DIR command to the printer, you could enter a command such as `DIR > MYFILES.TXT`. This command stores the output from the DIR command in a file named MYFILES.TXT.

Storing the output from commands in files can be very handy. For example, when you use the > PRN directive to send output to the printer, you need to wait for printing to finish before you can use your computer. However, if you channel output to a file (which is much quicker than sending output to the printer), you can use the PRINT command to print the output file in the background.

Also, if you have a word processing program, you can use it to edit the output file in any way you wish. That is, you can add special printer features (such as boldface or underline), reorganize the pagination, add margins, and so on. You can even merge the output file into an existing document. In fact, virtually all application programs, including spreadsheets and database managers, let you import these DOS output files for further use.

The following example demonstrates the power of using a file as a device that accepts output from a command. Let's assume that you want to print a listing of all the files on three directories on your hard disk—the root directory, the DOS directory, and the WP directory (the last two of which your computer might not actually have).

Rather than printing the file names immediately, you decide to store them in a file so that you can print them later using the PRINT command. Let's suppose that you want to store the output from the three DIR commands in a file named MYFILES.TXT in the WP directory.

Starting at the DOS command prompt, enter the following commands to change to the WP directory and send a list of all the file names in the root directory to the file named MYFILES.TXT:

```
CD \WP
DIR C:\ > MYFILES.TXT
```

The DIR command displays nothing on the screen, because its output was sent to the MYFILES.TXT file. Now, to add the file names from the DOS directory to the MYFILES.TXT file, you need to enter the command:

```
DIR C:\DOS >> MYFILES.TXT
```

Notice that the command above used the > > redirection symbol. This symbol *adds* (or *appends*) the new output to the MYFILES.TXT file, rather than *replacing* its contents. Again, the DIR command displays nothing on the screen, but when the DOS prompt reappears you know that the output is stored in the file.

Finally, to add the list of file names from the WP directory to the MYFILES.TXT file, enter this command:

```
DIR >> MYFILES.TXT
```

Before printing the MYFILES.TXT file, take a quick look at it to be sure it actually contains the file names from all three directories. To do so, enter the command:

```
TYPE MYFILES.TXT
```

or the command:

```
MORE < MYFILES.TXT
```

Now that you are convinced that the MYFILES.TXT actually contains the text you want, you can enter the final command:

```
PRINT MYFILES.TXT
```

You are now free to use your computer while the PRINT command prints the contents of the MYFILES.TXT file in the background.

You could also preview, edit, and print the MYFILES.TXT file with your word processing program. To do so, merely run your word processing program in the usual manner, and specify C:\WP\MYFILES.TXT as the file to edit.

Customizing the Keyboard

If your CONFIG.SYS file includes the DEVICE=ANSI.SYS command (as discussed earlier in this chapter), you can customize your keyboard to perform special tasks. It's extremely unlikely that you would want to redefine one of the standard keys, such as making the A key generate the letter Z (although you *could* do so if you had the desire). A more practical application uses the procedure to assign functions to special key combinations that are not already defined by DOS, such as Ctrl-F3 or Alt-F7.

The general procedure for redefining function keys is very similar to the one used for defining screen attributes and colors. You use the PROMPT command followed by an escape sequence. However, you must also include a code that indicates the key you want to redefine, the character or characters you want the key to display (enclosed in quotation marks), the number 13 (which is the code for the Enter key), and finally, a lowercase "p" (rather than an "m"), which signals the end of the sequence. This general syntax is as follows:

```
PROMPT $e[0;key number;"characters to type";13p
```

The numbers used to specify keys that you might want to redefine are listed in Table 12.7. Those marked with an asterisk already serve useful functions in DOS (and particularly the DOS Shell), so you should avoid redefining those keys.

Table 12.7. Numbers assigned to function keys.

Key	Number	Key	Number	Key	Number	Key	Number
F1*	59	Shift-F1	84	Ctrl-F1	94	Alt-F1*	104
F2*	60	Shift-F2	85	Ctrl-F2	95	Alt-F2	105
F3*	61	Shift-F3	86	Ctrl-F3	96	Alt-F3	106
F4*	62	Shift-F4	87	Ctrl-F4	97	Alt-F4	107
F5*	63	Shift-F5	88	Ctrl-F5	98	Alt-F5	108
F6*	64	Shift-F6	89	Ctrl-F6	99	Alt-F6	109
F7	65	Shift-F7	90	Ctrl-F7	100	Alt-F7	110
F8	66	Shift-F8	91	Ctrl-F8	101	Alt-F8	111
F9*	67	Shift-F9*	92	Ctrl-F9	102	Alt-F9	112
F10*	68	Shift-F10	93	Ctrl-F10	103	Alt-F10	113

*Already assigned a function by DOS.

Suppose you want to redefine the Shift-F10 key (number 93) so that it displays the names of files when you press it. First, enter the following command at the command prompt:

```
PROMPT $e[0;93;"DIR";13p
```

After you press Enter, the command prompt is no longer visible, so merely enter the command `PROMPT $P$G` to redisplay it.

To test your new function key assignment, press Shift-F10 (hold down the Shift key and press the F10 key). Your screen now displays the names of files on the current drive or directory.

Awkward commands that are difficult to remember are especially good candidates for redefinition as function keys. For example, in order to use the DIR command to display file names sorted by date, you need to enter the command `DIR | SORT /+24` (see the SORT command in Appendix B for details). The command below assigns the appropriate command to the Shift-F8 key:

```
PROMPT $e[0;91;"DIR | SORT /+24";13p
```

After you initially enter the command, your prompt will disappear. You can enter another PROMPT command, such as `PROMPT $P$G` to bring back your original command prompt.

To view file names listed in chronological order (based on the date each file was created or last modified), you need only press Shift-F8. Note, however, that the function key will work only during the current session (before you turn off the computer), and only if the SORT.EXE program is available from the current drive and directory.

Assigning Multiple Commands to a Function Key

You can assign two or more commands to a function key, as long as you use the 13 (Enter) code to separate them. For example, the following command sets up the Shift-F7 key so that it first clears the screen (CLS) and then displays a wide directory listing (DIR /W):

```
PROMPT $e[0;90;"CLS";13;"DIR /W";13p
```

Using Function Keys to Type Text

Redefining function keys can be handy for more than entering commands. For example, let's assume that you regularly need to type your return address on envelopes. The following command sets up the Shift-F6 key to do this job for you, assuming, of course, that you substitute your own name and address for John Q. Melon's. Note that you must type the command as one long line, even if it wraps to the next screen line. (Also, the entire escape sequence cannot exceed 128 characters.) Be sure to include blank spaces only where indicated:

```
PROMPT $e[0;89;"COPY CON PRN";13;"John Q. Melon";13;"123 Oak Tree
Lane";13;"Glendora, CA 91749";13;26;13;"ECHO";12;">PRN";13p
```

After you define the key, pressing Shift-F6 displays the output shown in Figure 12.8 on your screen (which, as you may notice, looks somewhat similar to that in Figure 12.5 above). Of course, the name and address are also sent to the printer.

```
C:\DOS>PROMPT $e[0;89;"COPY CON PRN";13;"John Q. Melon";13;"123 Oak Tree Lane";1
3;"Glendora, CA 91740";13;26;13;"ECHO ";12;" >PRN";13p

PROMPT $P$G

C:\DOS>COPY CON PRN      ⎫
John Q. Melon            ⎪
123 Oak Tree Lane        ⎪
Glendora, CA 91740       ⎬   Pressing Shift-F6
^Z                       ⎪   produced all of this.
        1 File(s) copied ⎪
                         ⎪
C:\DOS>ECHO ^L >PRN      ⎪
                         ⎭
C:\DOS>
```

Figure 12.8. Result of pressing Shift-F6 after redefining the key.

Let's review this key definition to see how it works. First, COPY CON PRN;13 types the COPY CON PRN command and presses Enter, so that the following text is sent to the printer. Then, the name, address, and city, state, zip lines are typed, each followed by the Enter key code so they are placed on separate lines.

The 26 code that you see in the command causes DOS to press Ctrl-Z, the code necessary to end the COPY CON PRN command (it appears as ^Z in Figure 12.8). Then, the sequence "ECHO ;12;" >PRN";13p types the ECHO ^L > PRN command and presses Enter to eject the page from the printer.

How did I know that the 26 code would type Ctrl-Z and that the 12 code would type Ctrl-L? Easy—the Ctrl-key combinations are numbered from 1 to 26, starting at A. That is Ctrl-A is number 1, Ctrl-B is 2, and so on. Because L is the 12th letter of the alphabet, its numeric code is 12, and because Z is the 26th letter of the alphabet, its numeric code is 26.

The main problem with redefining function key definitions is that they are lost the moment you turn off your computer. Nor are key definition commands particularly good candidates for the AUTOEXEC.BAT file, because other commands may reset them during the startup procedure. However, as you'll learn in Chapter 13, you can store many key definitions in a *batch file*; then you need to type only one command to reinstate all your custom key definitions.

Also, keep in mind that many application programs, including word processors and spreadsheets, assign their own commands to the function keys. Therefore, your custom key definition might work only when the DOS command prompt is displayed.

Resetting the Function Keys

To reset a function key to its original definition, follow the 0;*key number* portion of the command with a semicolon and a repeat of the 0;*key number*. For example, to reset the Shift-F10 key (number 93) to its original definition, enter the command:

```
PROMPT $e[0;93;0;93p
```

Commercial Keyboard Customizing Packages

I must point out that there is an easier way to customize your keyboard— purchase a *keyboard macro* program. Most of these programs let you redefine a key simply be recording a series of keystrokes; therefore, you don't have to deal with long strings of strange symbols. Many can also be used in conjunction with other programs on your computer, so that your custom key definitions are not lost when you switch from one program to the next. Following are the names and manufacturers of some keyboard macro programs:

Keyworks
Alpha Software Corp.
1 North Ave.
Burlington, MA 01803
(617) 229-2924

ProKey
Rosesoft, Inc.
P.O. Box 45880
Seattle, WA 98145-0880
(206) 282-0454

SuperKey
Borland International, Inc.
4585 Scotts Valley Dr.
Scotts Valley, CA 95066
(408) 438-8400

Troubleshooting

This section lists common error message that DOS might display while trying some of the examples in this chapter. If you see one of these messages, try the recommended solution.

- `Error found, F parameter not specified. Corrections will not be written to disk`: You don't need to take any action if you see this message; see CHKDSK in Appendix B for details.

- `Errors on list device indicate that it may be off-line. Please check it`: The printer is either disconnected, turned off, or is currently off-line. Check your printer, and be sure that it is on-line (see your printer manual if necessary).

- `FIND: syntax error`: The FIND command is not phrased properly. Be sure that the characters you are searching for are enclosed in double quotation marks (for example, `FIND "BOOKS"`).

- `Invalid parameter`: A switch or option used in a command is misspelled, or the forward slash (/), backslash (\), or pipe (|) characters are used incorrectly.

- `Lost clusters found in xxx chains. Convert lost chains to files? (Y/N)`: Type Y and continue your current operation. (Refer to CHKDSK in Appendix B for an explanation of the message.)

Summary

This chapter presented commands and techniques for managing and configuring standard devices—the screen, printer, and keyboard. The main points are summarized here:

- In general, you can use the <, >, and >> redirection symbols and the DOS device names to channel output that normally appears on the screen to a different device. (File names can often be used as though they are device names.)

- The CLS command clears the screen.

- The Ctrl-S and Pause keys, as well as the MORE command, allow you to control the scrolling of text on the screen.

- The PROMPT command lets you customize the command prompt.

- If your CONFIG.SYS file loads the ANSI.SYS file during startup, you can use the PROMPT command to control screen attributes and colors and to assign text and commands to function keys.

- The Shift-PrintScreen key combination copies whatever is on the screen to your printer.

- The Ctrl-PrintScreen key combination slaves the printer so that all future screen displays are sent to the printer. (You must press Ctrl-PrintScreen again to unslave the printer.)

- To print ASCII text files in the background so that you can continue to use your computer during printing, use the PRINT command (or select the Print option on the DOS 4 File System's File pull-down menu).

P   A   R   T

Programming DOS

The next two chapters discuss DOS batch files, which are basically DOS text files that contain a group—or batch—of commands that DOS executes in sequence. In essence, batch files let you create your own DOS commands and programs. The general techniques you learned for modifying DOS text files also allow you to create and edit batch files.

The skills you will learn in these chapter include:

- How to create and run a batch file.
- How to make your batch files create useful commands that simplify your work.
- How to make batch files easy to use—for yourself and for others.
- How to create batch files that accept options from the command line.
- How to use advanced programming techniques, such as looping, decision-making, branching, and calling, to add more power and flexibility to your batch files.

Many of the powerful and practical sample batch files presented in these chapters will come in handy in your own work with your computer. In a sense, they offer new, easy-to-use commands that perhaps DOS "forgot."

Creating Your Own Commands

So far, your experience with DOS commands has consisted of typing a single command and then pressing Enter to execute that command. As an alternative to this one-command-at-a-time approach, you can store a series of commands in a single file and then have DOS automatically execute every command in the file. Files that contain multiple DOS commands are called *batch files* (because they process a "batch" of commands at one time).

All DOS batch files have the file name extension .BAT. The AUTOEXEC.BAT file you've seen in previous chapters is indeed such a batch file. However, AUTOEXEC.BAT is different from other batch files because DOS automatically executes all the commands in AUTOEXEC.BAT as soon as you start your computer.

You run all other batch files as though they were programs. That is, at the command prompt, you type the name of the batch file and press Enter. From the DOS 4 File System, you highlight the name of the batch file in the Files Area and then press Enter or double-click the mouse.

When DOS executes the commands in a batch file, it does so in first-to-last order. That is, it executes the first (top) command, then the second command, then the third command, and so on, until there are no more commands to be executed. In a sense, DOS "sees" the commands in a batch file as though each were being typed at the command prompt independently.

Creating and Storing Batch Files

Batch files must be stored as ASCII text files. Therefore, you can use any of the techniques described in Chapter 10 to create and edit your own batch files. The name you assign to a batch file must follow the basic rules of all

DOS file names—no more than eight characters in length, no blank spaces, and no punctuation other than the underscore and hyphen. The file name extension must be .BAT.

When naming a batch file, be sure not to give it the same name as a .COM or .EXE file. For example, if you have the dBASE program on your computer, do not create a batch file named DBASE.BAT. Otherwise, when you enter the command `DBASE`, DOS will run only DBASE.BAT or DBASE.EXE—but not both. (Actually, DOS runs whichever of the two files it encounters first in the current directory or in the defined PATH.)

Because batch files provide useful tools to make your work easier, they should be stored where they are easily accessible when you need them. Keep in mind, however, that if a batch file includes any DOS external commands, such as CHKDSK, TREE, SORT, FIND, or MORE, then the associated DOS program files (CHKDSK.COM, TREE.COM, SORT.EXE, FIND.EXE, and MORE.COM) must also be accessible from the current diskette, directory, or PATH.

Remember that DOS executes commands in a batch file exactly as though they were typed at the command prompt. Therefore, if your batch file contains a misspelled command, or an external program or command that is not available from the current diskette, directory, or defined PATH, DOS will display the usual `Bad command or file name` error message when it attempts to execute that command.

Creating Your Own Batch Files

You'll be creating many useful batch files in the chapters that follow, and you will probably want to use them from time to time in your own work. To ensure that these batch files are easily accessible and that they can find the DOS external programs that they require, you must know how to prepare a diskette or directory for storing batch files. Please read whichever of the two following sections is appropriate.

Preparing Batch Files for a Computer Without a Hard Disk

If your computer doesn't have a hard disk, you should store your batch files on a single diskette. Create this diskette by following these steps:

1. Start your computer in the usual manner, with the Startup diskette in drive A:.

2. If the DOS Shell appears, press F3 to display the command prompt.

3. Insert a new, blank diskette in drive B:, type the command `FORMAT B:` `/S`, and press Enter. (If DOS displays the `Bad Command or File Name`

error message, you need to insert the diskette that contains the FORMAT.COM file into drive A:, and then try again.)

4. If DOS asks for a volume label after it finishes formatting, type *UTILITIES* and then press Enter. Answer **N** when asked about formatting another diskette.

5. Using the COPY command (or the Copy option in the DOS Shell), copy all the files listed in Table 13.1 to the diskette in drive B:.

6. After you copy all of the required files to the new diskette, use the **DIR B:** command (or the DOS Shell File System) to be sure that the diskette in drive B: contains all of the files listed in Table 13.1, plus the COMMAND.COM file.

7. Remove the diskette from drive B:, and label it Custom Utilities.

DOS needs to find COMMAND.COM in order to run a batch file. When you used the /S switch in the FORMAT command, DOS automatically copied COMMAND.COM to your diskette.

Whenever you create, edit, or use a batch file, do so on the new disk that you've labeled Custom Utilities. (In later sections I will refer to this diskette as the Custom Utilities diskette.) You can use the Utilities diskette in either drive A: or B: of your computer. However, be sure that after inserting the diskette into its drive, you remember to access the appropriate drive.

If you aren't going to use the Edlin editor to create and edit your batch files, you should put your word processing diskette in drive A:, and then access drive A:. Then, insert your Custom Utilities diskette into drive B:. Whenever you create or edit a batch file, be sure to specify **B:** before the file name (for example, **B:D.BAT** to create or edit the D.BAT batch file).

Table 13.1. External DOS commands used by the sample batch files.

Command Used	File Required
CHKDSK	CHKDSK.COM
EDLIN	EDLIN.COM*
FIND	FIND.EXE
MORE	MORE.COM
SORT	SORT.EXE
TREE	TREE.COM
XCOPY	XCOPY.EXE

*Required only if you use Edlin to create and edit batch files.

Preparing Batch Files for a Computer with a Hard Disk

If your computer has a hard disk, you should store all your custom batch files in a single directory. In this example, you'll store them in a directory named UTILS. Remember, however, that your batch files require that DOS have access to the external programs listed in Table 13.1.

To give yourself maximum access to your batch files, and to give the batch files access to the external DOS commands that they need, include in your PATH command both the UTILS directory and the directory that contains the external DOS files. Follow these steps:

1. If you are using the DOS 4 Shell, press F3 to display the command prompt.
2. To create the UTILS directory, type the command `MD \UTILS` and press Enter.
3. Using the CD and DIR commands, determine which directory on your had disk contains the external commands listed in Table 13.1. (In Version 4, check the DOS directory; in earlier versions of DOS, check the root directory.)
4. Modify your AUTOEXEC.BAT file so that the PATH command includes both the new UTILS directory and the directory that contains the external DOS command.

If you are using DOS 4, remember that if your AUTOEXEC.BAT file includes the DOSSHELL command, it must be the last command in the AUTOEXEC.BAT file. Remember that the only blank space in a PATH command should be the one immediately after the word PATH.

To complete the preceding step 4, you must use techniques that were described in Chapters 10 and 11. Don't forget, if you start your computer from the hard disk, AUTOEXEC.BAT must be stored on the root directory of drive C:.

If your external DOS commands are stored in the directory named DOS, be sure that the PATH command in your AUTOEXEC.BAT file includes the DOS and UTILS directories (in addition to your other frequently used directory names), as follows:

```
PATH C:\DOS;C:\UTILS
```

If your external DOS commands are stored in the root directory, be sure that your AUTOEXEC.BAT file PATH command includes both the root and the UTILS directories (in addition to your other frequently used directory names), as follows:

```
PATH C:\;C:\UTILS
```

AUTOEXEC is an abbreviation for AUTOmatically EXECuted.

After modifying your AUTOEXEC.BAT file, be sure to save it. Doing so will bring you back to the command prompt. You can then execute the modified AUTOEXEC.BAT file using either of two methods. You can reboot the computer (by pressing Ctrl-Alt-Del), or you can enter the `AUTOEXEC` command directly at the command prompt.

If you decide to use the latter method, first enter the command CD \ to make sure the root directory is current. Then, type `AUTOEXEC` and press Enter. DOS executes each command in the AUTOEXEC.BAT file. This latter technique works because AUTOEXEC.BAT is a batch file, and any batch file can be executed simply by entering its name as a command. The only thing that makes AUTOEXEC.BAT unique among batch files is that it is the *only* batch file that DOS looks for, and executes, automatically when you first start your computer.

If your computer starts with the DOS 4 Shell displayed, press F3 to display the command prompt. To verify that AUTOEXEC.BAT has set up the proper path, type the command PATH and press Enter. DOS then shows the currently defined path.

In the future, whenever you want to create or change a batch file, either change to the UTILS directory or, if you prefer to work from a different directory, specify C:\UTILS as the location for the batch file. For example, to create or edit the D.BAT batch file from any directory, specify C:\UTILS\D.BAT as the name of the file.

A Simple Practice Batch File

A good practice batch file is one that is simple to create and use. Let's start with a batch file that contains only two simple commands—DIR /W and VER. Let's also name this simple batch file D.BAT. (Admittedly, D.BAT won't dazzle you with its power; still, it demonstrates many of the fundamental principles of batch files.)

To use the DOS Edlin editor to create this batch file, see the following steps. (If instead, you use another editor or word processor, remember to save the file in ASCII text format.)

1. Type EDLIN D.BAT and press Enter.
2. Type 1i and press Enter to insert a first line.
3. Type DIR /W and press Enter.
4. Type VER and press Enter.
5. Press Ctrl-C.
6. To save the file and exit Edlin, type E and press Enter.
7. To verify that the file was saved, type TYPE D.BAT and press Enter.

The batch file that appears on the screen consists of the following two lines:

```
DIR /W
VER
```

Running Your First Batch File

To *run* (execute the commands in) a batch file, use the same basic technique that you use to run any program—type the file name without the extension and press Enter. In this example, merely type the letter D and then press Enter.

As mentioned earlier, you can also use the DOS Shell to run the D.BAT batch file. First, use the File System to access the drive or directory that contains the file. Then, highlight **D.BAT** in the Files Area and press Enter (or double-click the mouse).

This batch file displays a wide listing of the file names on the current diskette or directory (the DIR /W command) and then the current version of DOS (the VER command), as shown in Figure 13.1. (Your screen, of course, shows different file names.) Note that the figure shows the exact series of events that took place.

```
C:\UTILS>D

C:\UTILS>DIR /W

 Volume in drive C has no label
 Volume Serial Number is 201A-2C4C
 Directory of  C:\UTILS

.                     ..              LOOKFOR  BAT    D        BAT    FF       BAT
OLDPATH  BAT    MOVE     BAT    ADDPATH  BAT    PRINTKEY TXT    LIST2DAY COM
SETKEYS  BAT    DDIR     COM    IMMGR    EXE    IMCAP    COM    IMCAP    DOC
IMSHOW   EXE    SETKEYS  BAK    LL       EXE    CONVERT  EXE    F        COM
LOCATE   COM    D        BAK    UTREE    COM    WHERE    COM    SHOWKEYS BAT
SHOWKEYS BAK
        26 File(s)    18642944 bytes free

C:\UTILS>VER

IBM DOS Version 4.00

C:\UTILS>
C:\UTILS>
```

Figure 13.1. Results of running the D.BAT batch file.

Although this is not a terribly exciting batch file, it does provide one convenience. Whenever you want to see a wide directory listing, you only need to enter the letter D at the command prompt, rather than DIR /W. So you save a few keystrokes, which is very handy if you don't like to (or can't) type.

If you made a mistake and your batch file does not work properly, use Edlin (or another text editor) to make corrections. Again, refer to Chapter 10 if you need reminders about how to edit a file.

Using ECHO to Display Text

You've already used the DOS ECHO command (with the > PRN directive) to send a special code to the printer. You can also include the ECHO command to send a message from a batch file to the screen. For the sake of practice, let's modify the simple D.BAT batch file so that it sends the (rather frivolous) message *That's all folks!* to the screen after it executes the DIR /W and VER commands. Here are the exact steps to follow if you are using the Edlin editor:

1. At DOS the command prompt, type the command `EDLIN D.BAT` and press Enter.
2. In Edlin, type `L` and press Enter to review the current contents of D.BAT.
3. To insert a new line number 3, type `3i` and press Enter.
4. Type `ECHO That's all folks!` and then press Enter.
5. Press Ctrl-C.
6. Type `E` and press Enter to save your changes and return to the DOS command prompt.
7. Type the command `TYPE D.BAT` and then press Enter to see the contents of the D.BAT batch file.

Your batch file now contains the following three lines:

```
DIR /W
VER
ECHO That's all folks!
```

To run your modified D.BAT batch file, type the letter `D` at the command prompt and press Enter. Your new batch file still displays a wide directory of file names and shows the current DOS version number. In addition, these lines appear beneath the file names:

```
C\UTIL>ECHO That's all folks!
That's all folks!
```

The ECHO command indeed displayed the *That's all folks!* message, but it did so twice, as Figure 13.2 shows. That happened because DOS automatically displays commands stored in batch files before it executes them. That is, DOS displayed the entire command `ECHO That's all folks!`, then executed that command, and then displayed the results of the command—the sentence `That's all folks!`.

Preventing Double Echoes

If you are using Version 3.3 or later of DOS, you can prevent DOS from displaying a command before executing it by preceding the command with

```
C:\UTILS>DIR /W

 Volume in drive C has no label
 Volume Serial Number is 201A-2C4C
 Directory of  C:\UTILS

.                    ..                 D        BAT    LOOKFOR BAT    D        BAK
FF        BAT    OLDPATH  BAT    MOVE     BAT    ADDPATH BAT    PRINTKEY TXT
LIST2DAY COM    SETKEYS  BAT    DDIR     COM    IMMGR   EXE    IMCAP    COM
IMCAP    DOC    IMSHOW   EXE    SETKEYS  BAK    LL      EXE    CONVERT  EXE
F        COM    LOCATE   COM    VTREE    COM    WHERE   COM    SHOWKEYS BAT
SHOWKEYS BAK
        26 File(s)    18642944 bytes free

C:\UTILS>VER

IBM DOS Version 4.00


C:\UTILS>ECHO That's all folks!
That's all folks!

C:\UTILS>
C:\UTILS>
```

Figure 13.2. Results of using an ECHO command in D.BAT.

an @ symbol. (If you are using an earlier version of DOS, you can do so by putting the command ECHO OFF at the top of the batch file, as discussed in the section "Hiding All Commands" later in this chapter.)

If you are using Version 3.3 (or later) of DOS, follow the steps below to change the ECHO command in the D.BAT batch file to @ECHO:

1. Type `EDLIN D.BAT` and then press Enter.

2. Type `L` and press Enter to review the file's current contents.

3. To access the third line, type `3` and press Enter.

4. Press the Ins (or Insert) key once to switch to insert mode.

5. Type the `@` symbol.

6. Press F3 to retrieve the rest of the command so that the line shows `@ECHO That's all folks!`. (If you made an error, use the Backspace key to erase the mistake; then, type the line correctly.)

7. Press Enter.

8. Type `E` and press Enter to save your changes and leave Edlin.

9. Type `TYPE D.BAT` and press Enter to view the contents of the new batch file.

After you complete Step 9, your screen shows the following modified D.BAT file:

```
DIR /W
VER
@ECHO That's all folks!
```

To run the new batch file, type the letter D and press Enter. This time notice that the *That's all folks!* message appears only once at the bottom of the list of file names, as in Figure 13.3.

```
C:\UTILS>D

C:\UTILS>DIR /W

 Volume in drive C has no label
 Volume Serial Number is 201A-2C4C
 Directory of  C:\UTILS

.                 ..              D        BAK   D        BAT   LOOKFOR  BAT
FF        BAT     OLDPATH  BAT    MOVE     BAT   ADDPATH  BAT   PRINTKEY TXT
LIST2DAY COM     SETKEYS  BAT    DDIR     COM   IMMGR    EXE   IMCAP    COM
IMCAP    DOC     IMSHOW   EXE    SETKEYS  BAK   LL       EXE   CONVERT  EXE
F        COM     LOCATE   COM    VTREE    COM   WHERE    COM   SHOWKEYS BAT
SHOWKEYS BAK
        26 File(s)    18642944 bytes free

C:\UTILS>VER

IBM DOS Version 4.00

That's all folks!

C:\UTILS>
C:\UTILS>
```

Figure 13.3. The @ECHO message appears only
once in D.BAT.

Using Remarks to Comment Batch Files

Although the D.BAT file is relatively simple, batch files can be quite large and complicated (as you will see in later examples). To make it easier for you—and for others who use your batch file—to understand the purpose of commands in the batch file, you should add *comments* (also called *remarks*) to the file. A comment is like a note to yourself. DOS realizes that the comment is only for humans to read, and therefore completely ignores the line.

To add a comment to a batch file, start the line with the command REM (short for "remark"). If you are using Version 3.3, or later, of DOS, you can use the command @REM to put a comment in a batch file, which prevents DOS from displaying the remark when it executes the batch file. You can test this now by adding a comment to the D.BAT batch file by following the steps below:

1. Type EDLIN D.BAT and press Enter.

2. Type L and press Enter to review your batch file.

3. To insert a comment above the third line, type 3i and press Enter.

4. If you are using DOS Version 3.3 or later, type the command @REM Show

closing message... (but if you are using an earlier version, leave off the leading @ sign). Press Enter.

5. Press Ctrl-C.

6. Type E and press Enter to save your work and leave Edlin.

7. Type TYPE D.BAT and press Enter to check your batch file.

The batch file now contains the following commands (but without the @ symbols if you are using DOS 3.2 or earlier):

```
DIR /W
VER
@REM Show closing message...
@ECHO That's all folks!
```

You can now test the D.BAT batch file by entering the command D at the command prompt. If you are using DOS 3.3 or later, and added the @REM command, you will see that the D.BAT file does its job without displaying the comment to the right of the REM command. (Again, comments preceded by REM are for "human consumption only.")

If you are using an earlier version of DOs, the REM command line will be displayed on your screen, but it will have no effect on DOS. Again, if you are using a version of DOS prior to 3.3, you cannot precede a command with @ to hide it during execution, but you will learn an alternative technique shortly.

Later examples use REM comments to label each batch file with a name and a general purpose. These comments at the top of the file will make it easier for you to determine which batch file you are viewing in a figure.

Passing Parameters to a Batch File

So far, the D.BAT file is little more than a shortcut for typing the longer command DIR /W and displaying the current DOS version number. However, it lacks one feature that the DIR command offers—the ability to specify types of files. For example, with DIR, you can enter a command such as DIR *.EXE /W to limit the listing to files that have the .EXE extension. However, if you enter the command D *.EXE, DOS still lists the names of all the files on the current diskette or directory, because it ignores the *.EXE.

Let's change the D.BAT file so that it accepts and uses a *parameter* (additional text entered at the command prompt), such as the *.EXE specifier in the previous example. The basic technique is to use *percent variables* as placeholders for additional command line entries. The first extra entry is always named %1, the second is named %2, the third is named %3, and so on. When you type a batch file name and additional parameters on the command line, each parameter passed to the % variables must be separated by a blank space.

Let's permit a single parameter to be passed to the DIR command in the D.BAT file:

1. Type EDLIN D.BAT and press Enter.

2. Type L and press Enter to review your batch file.

3. To edit the first line, type 1 and press Enter.

4. Press → four times to display the first three characters of the command (including the blank space after DIR).

5. Press the Ins (or Insert) key to enter the insert mode.

6. Type %1 and then press the Spacebar.

7. Press F3 to retrieve the rest of the command. (Be sure that %1 variable is surrounded by blank spaces; if it is not, use the Backspace key to make corrections.)

8. Press Enter.

9. Type E and press Enter to save your work and leave Edlin.

10. Type TYPE D.BAT and press Enter to check the contents of the batch file.

If you are using DOS 3.3 or later, your batch file should now contain the following commands (with all the blank spaces in the right places):

```
DIR %1 /W
VER
@REM Show closing message...
@ECHO That's all folks!
```

If you are using Version 3.2 or earlier of DOS, your D.BAT batch file should look the same, but without the @ symbol in front of the REM and ECHO commands.

Now, try using a file specifier with the D command. For example, when you enter the command D *.COM, DOS displays only the names of files (if any) on the current directory that have the extension .COM. If D.BAT is the only file on your current directory, try viewing the contents of a different directory. For example, enter the command D C:*.COM to view the .COM files on the root directory of your hard disk. Or, enter the command D C:\DOS*.COM to view the names of the .COM files on your hard disk's DOS directory.

Basically, D.BAT now has all the flexibility of the DIR command. That's because the parameter you type next to the D command gets passed to the DIR command in your batch file. For example, look closely at Figure 13.4; notice at the top of the screen that I entered the command D C:\DOS*.COM to view .COM files on the DOS directory. Also notice that the batch file *substituted* the C:\DOS*.COM parameter into its own DIR command (in place of the %1 variable).

```
C:\UTILS>D C:\DOS\*.COM

C:\UTILS>DIR C:\DOS\*.COM /W

 Volume in drive C has no label
 Volume Serial Number is 201A-2C4C
 Directory of  C:\DOS

COMMAND  COM     DISKCOPY COM     FDISK   COM     FORMAT   COM     KEYB    COM
SYS      COM     ASSIGN   COM     BASIC   COM     BASICA   COM     COMP    COM
DEBUG    COM     DISKCOMP COM     EDLIN   COM     LABEL    COM     MODE    COM
MORE     COM     TREE     COM     CHKDSK  COM     PRINT    COM     SHELLB  COM
GRAFTABL COM     GRAPHICS COM     RECOVER COM     BACKUP   COM     RESTORE COM
        25 File(s)    18642944 bytes free

C:\UTILS>VER

IBM DOS Version 4.00

That's all folks!

C:\UTILS>
C:\UTILS>
```

Figure 13.4. Results of entering D C:\DOS*.COM.

But now what happens if you merely enter the old D command without specifying a drive, directory, or file name? Well, the batch file acts exactly as it did before. DOS substitutes nothing for %1, so the command that DOS executes is once again simply DIR /W. (If you now enter the command D and examine the DIR command displayed on the screen by the batch file, you will see that this is indeed the case.)

Let's try passing two parameters to the D batch file. Notice that when you type the following command:

```
D *.* /P
```

the /P has no effect, because it is a second optional parameter on the command line (that is, a blank space separates it from the first parameter, *.*). D.BAT completely ignores this second parameter, because the batch file contains no %2 variable to handle it.

The Importance of Proper Spacing

The most common errors that people make when using % variables in batch files involve blank spaces: Sometimes, people forget to include necessary blank spaces; other times, they add spaces when they are not needed. For example, if the first line in D.BAT looked as follows:

```
DIR%1/W
```

your batch file would not work. That's because when you enter a command, such as D C:*.*, to execute the batch file, DOS substitutes the parameters into the command *exactly* as it is told to. That is, the batch file actually tries to execute the following command:

```
DIRC:\*.*/W
```

Because DOS has no idea what DIRC means, it merely displays the familiar Bad command or file name message.

Surrounding the %1 variable with blank spaces, as follows:

```
DIR %1 /W
```

ensures that blank spaces are also included during the substitution. Therefore, when you enter the command D C:*.* to execute the batch file, the parameter is substituted into the %1 variable in exactly the same way:

```
DIR C:\*.* /W
```

and DOS has no problem interpreting that command.

Hiding All Commands

Regardless of which version of DOS you are using, you can prevent batch file commands from being displayed before execution, by adding the ECHO OFF command to the top of your batch file. ECHO OFF tells DOS not to echo the commands themselves at the command prompt, but instead to display only the results of the commands.

If you are using DOS 3.3 or later, you can make the first command in your batch file @ECHO OFF, which even prevents the ECHO OFF command itself from being echoed. To test the ECHO OFF command for yourself, follow these steps:

1. Type EDLIN D.BAT and press Enter.
2. Type L and press Enter to view the file.
3. To insert a new line at the top of the file, type 1i and press Enter.
4. If you are using DOS 3.3 or later, type @ECHO OFF and press Enter (but if you are using an earlier version of DOS, omit the leading @ symbol).
5. Press Ctrl-C.
6. Type E and press Enter to save your change.
7. Type TYPE D.BAT and press Enter to view your file.

Your batch file should now contain the following commands (but without the @ signs if you are using DOS 3.2 or earlier):

```
@ECHO OFF
DIR %1 /W
VER
@REM Show closing message...
@ECHO That's all folks!
```

When you enter D to run the batch file, notice that none of the commands from the batch file are displayed—only the *results* of each command appear on the screen, as Figure 13.5 shows.

```
C:\UTILS>D

 Volume in drive C has no label
 Volume Serial Number is 201A-2C4C
 Directory of   C:\UTILS

.                    ..              D          BAT     LOOKFOR  BAT     D          BAK
FF          BAT      OLDPATH  BAT    MOVE       BAT     ADDPATH  BAT     PRINTKEY   TXT
LIST2DAY COM         SETKEYS  BAT    DDIR       COM     IMMGR    EXE     IMCAP      COM
IMCAP       DOC      IMSHOW   EXE    SETKEYS    BAK     LL       EXE     CONVERT    EXE
F           COM      LOCATE   COM    VTREE      COM     WHERE    COM     SHOWKEYS   BAT
SHOWKEYS BAK
        26 File(s)   18642944 bytes free

IBM DOS Version 4.00

That's all folks!
C:\UTILS>
```

Figure 13.5. Only the results of commands from
D.BAT are displayed

As a general rule, *don't* include the ECHO OFF or @ECHO OFF command when you first build a batch file. You are better off seeing the commands as they are executed, so that if the batch file fails to run properly, you can see which command caused the error. This is especially important when you use percent variables, because if you cannot see how the command is executed after the substitution takes place, you might have trouble figuring out what went wrong. Only after you have created, tested, and perfected your batch file, should you insert the ECHO OFF or @ECHO OFF command at the top of the file.

For the remaining batch file examples in this book, we will assume that you are using one of the later versions of DOS, Version 3.3 or Version 4. That is, we will include @ signs in front of certain commands to prevent them from being echoed on the screen.

If you are using Version 3.2 or earlier, you must remember to leave these @ signs out of your batch file. Initially, your batch file will echo commands to the screen. But, after testing and perfecting a batch file, you can add the ECHO OFF command to the top of the batch file to hide the echoes.

Now that you have some basic tools to help you create and develop batch files, you can start creating more practical, and more powerful, batch files.

A Batch File to Search for Files

As you might recall from Chapter 9, you can search every directory on a hard disk by using the CHKDSK and FIND commands. For example, entering the command CHKDSK /V | FIND "BUDGET" displays all the files that contain the name *budget*. However, wouldn't it be easier if you could perform this operation merely by entering a simple command such as LOOKFOR BUDGET? Of course, so let's create a batch file named LOOKFOR.BAT to handle the job.

The LOOKFOR.BAT batch file will use three external commands—CHKDSK, FIND, and MORE. Remember, these are external commands, and they require access to the CHKDSK.COM, FIND.EXE. and MORE.COM files. As discussed earlier in this chapter, these files must be on the same diskette as the LOOKFOR.BAT file or if you have a hard disk, in the same directory or in a directory specified in the PATH command. Now let's get started:

Actually, I wanted to name this batch file FIND.BAT, so I could enter a command like FIND BUDGET. But because DOS already includes a program named FIND.EXE, this would have created a conflict.

1. Type EDLIN LOOKFOR.BAT and press Enter.

2. Type 1i and press Enter.

3. Type @REM **************** LOOKFOR.BAT (type any number of asterisks) and press Enter.

4. Type @REM Searches all directories for a file. and press Enter.

5. Type @ECHO Did you remember to use UPPERCASE? and press Enter.

6. Type @ECHO (press Ctrl-C to cancel) and press Enter.

7. Type @ECHO Searching... and press Enter.

8. Type CHKDSK /V | FIND "%1" | MORE and press Enter.

9. Press Ctrl-C.

10. Type E and Enter to save your changes and leave Edlin.

11. Type TYPE LOOKFOR.BAT and press Enter to view the file.

Figure 13.6 shows the completed LOOKFOR.BAT batch file. The asterisks in the first line of the batch file are merely decorative: They make the name of the batch file stand out. The second line is an explanation of what the batch files does. The three @ECHO commands display messages on the screen as the batch file is executing (as you will soon see).

```
@REM *********************** LOOKFOR.BAT
@REM Searches all directories for a file.
@ECHO Did you remember to use UPPERCASE?
@ECHO (Press Ctrl-C to cancel)
@ECHO Searching...
CHKDSK /V | FIND "%1" | MORE
```

Figure 13.6. The LOOKFOR.BAT batch file.

Notice that in the last command, the %1 variable is not surrounded by blank spaces within the quotation marks of the FIND command. The reason for this is obvious: When you enter a command such as LOOKFOR BUDGET, you want the word BUDGET to be inserted into the FIND command without any blank spaces, as follows:

```
CHKDSK /V | FIND "BUDGET"
```

If you had inserted blank spaces in this example, like this:

```
CHKDSK /V | FIND " %1 "
```

during execution, the substitution would result in the following:

```
CHKDSK /V | FIND " BUDGET "
```

The FIND command would then look for the word BUDGET surrounded by blank spaces. Of course, because file names cannot contain blank spaces, the command would never find a matching name.

Notice that the CHKDSK command line includes the MORE command. This ensures that DOS pauses if LOOKFOR displays more file names than can fit on one screen. A single keypress then displays the next screenful of names. (MORE does not affect the display if all the file names fit on one screen).

Let's test this batch file. Use LOOKFOR to display the names of all files that have the .BAT extension by entering the command:

```
LOOKFOR .BAT
```

(Be sure to use uppercase letters for .BAT.) After you press Enter (and perhaps wait a while), your screen displays all file names that have the .BAT extension. Figure 13.7 shows the results on my computer.

Notice at the top of the figure that you can see where I entered the command LOOKFOR .BAT. The next three lines display messages from the ECHO commands in the batch file. The command CHKDSK /V | FIND ".BAT" |

```
C:\UTILS>LOOKFOR .BAT
Did you remember to use UPPERCASE?
(press Ctrl-c to cancel)
Searching...

C:\UTILS>CHKDSK /V ¦ FIND ".BAT" ¦ MORE

        C:\DOS\DOSSHELL.BAT
        C:\DOS\ORIGPATH.BAT
        C:\AUTOEXEC.BAT
        C:\DBASE\SAMPLES\INSTALL.BAT
        C:\DBASE\INSTALL.BAT
        C:\DBASE\DBSAMPLE.BAT
        C:\DBASE\DBTUTOR.BAT
        C:\UTILS\D.BAT
        C:\UTILS\LOOKFOR.BAT
        C:\UTILS\FF.BAT
        C:\UTILS\OLDPATH.BAT
        C:\UTILS\MOVE.BAT
        C:\UTILS\ADDPATH.BAT
        C:\UTILS\SETKEYS.BAT
        C:\UTILS\SHOWKEYS.BAT

C:\UTILS>
C:\UTILS>
```

Figure 13.7. Results of the LOOKFOR.BAT command.

MORE is the final command that the batch file executes. Note that the .BAT parameter was substituted into the command in %1 position. The remainder of the screen shows the locations and names of all the files on my hard disk with the .BAT extension.

If your LOOKFOR.BAT batch file is working properly, you might want to insert the @ECHO OFF commands as the first line. This prevents the CHKDSK command line from being displayed on the screen when you use LOOKFOR.BAT in the future. To do so, follow these steps:

1. Type EDLIN LOOKFOR.BAT and press Enter.

2. To insert a new line at the top of the file, type 1i and press Enter.

3. Type @ECHO OFF and press Enter.

4. Press Ctrl-C.

5. Type E and press Enter to save your change.

Use the TYPE command to check the contents of the file.

Because the FIND command does *not* support the wildcard characters ? and *, you cannot use these with your new LOOKFOR command. However, you can enter any partial file name to achieve the same basic result. For example, LOOKFOR MYTEXT displays all file names that contain the characters MYTEXT. The command LOOKFOR .C displays all file names that contain .C, (such as .COM, .CHK, .COS, and so on).

CHKDSK /V displays both directory names and file names, so if your search parameter includes a directory name, then all the files on that directory are displayed. For example LOOKFOR DBASE displays the names of all files on the dBASE directory. To prevent that from occurring, include the period in the file name. For example, the command LOOKFOR DBASE. displays only file names that have DBASE. in them (for example, DBASE.EXE, SQLDBASE.STR, DBASE.PIF, and others).

Interrupting a Batch File

You can stop any batch file that is being executed by pressing Ctrl-Break or Ctrl-C. DOS then displays the message `Terminate batch job? (Y/N)?`. Type `Y` to stop the batch file execution and return to the command prompt, or type `N` to resume the batch file execution. (Note that the LOOKFOR.BAT batch file displays a reminder that the batch file can be canceled by pressing Ctrl-C. This reminder is presented because the batch file can take a long time to complete on some computers, and you might get tired of waiting.)

A Batch File that Ejects a Printed Page

If you have a laser printer, you probably often need to eject pages from it. If you are tired of typing the entire `ECHO ^L > PRN` command to perform this simple task, you should create a batch file to do the job for you. Let's give this new batch file the name FF.BAT (for Form Feed):

1. Type `EDLIN FF.BAT` and press Enter.
2. Type `1i` and press Enter to start inserting lines.
3. Type `@REM **************** FF.BAT` (use any number of asterisks; they are merely decorative) and press Enter.
4. Type `@REM Send a form-feed to the printer.` and press Enter.
5. Type `@ECHO` and then press the Spacebar (*not* Enter).
6. Press Ctrl-L (hold down the Ctrl key and type the letter `L`; this appears as `^L` on your screen).
7. Press the Spacebar again.
8. Type `> PRN` so the complete line shows `ECHO ^L > PRN`.
9. Press Enter.
10. Press Ctrl-C.
11. Type `E` and press Enter to save your work and exit Edlin.

Figure 13.8 shows the complete FF.BAT file. However, if you use the TYPE command to view the contents of the file, your screen might show some character other than `^L`. That's because some screens interpret Ctrl-key combinations as graphics characters when displaying them. That is, even though Edlin shows Ctrl-L as `^L`, when the TYPE command *displays* Ctrl-L, your screen might display a graphic character, such as the Greek symbol for female. Don't worry about this. When you use Edlin in the future to look at or modify the contents of the file, it will use its usual ^L character to display the Ctrl-L character.

If your printer is hooked up and ready to go, you can now eject a page merely by typing FF and pressing Enter. Isn't that better than typing in the long, cryptic ECHO ^L > PRN command?

```
@REM *********************** FF.BAT
@REM Send a form-feed to the printer.
@ECHO ^L > PRN
```

Figure 13.8. The contents of the FF.BAT batch file.

Extending the Path

Suppose you use many different programs on your computer, and you often need to change your PATH setting. For example, suppose your AUTOEXEC.BAT file assigns the path:

```
PATH C:\DOS;C:\WP;C:\UTILS
```

and this path is adequate for your usual needs. But occasionally, you use programs that require an expanded path. Rather than force DOS to always search these seldom-used directories, you merely type the new PATH command as you require it.

Well, if you regularly need to do this, you will find it very tiring to have to retype the entire PATH command repeatedly. Wouldn't it be better if you could merely enter a command like ADDPATH C:\DBASE to add C:\DBASE to your current PATH setting? You can easily create a batch file to provide this feature. However, before you begin, you'll need to learn a few new things.

Accessing the DOS Environment

DOS stores the current settings for various commands in an area of memory called the *DOS environment* (or *environment* for short). You can examine the contents of the environment at any time—merely enter the command SET at the command prompt. DOS then displays your system's environment, as in the example below (yours will be different):

```
COMSPEC=C:\DOS\COMMAND.COM
APPEND=C:\DOS
PROMPT=$P$G
PATH=C:\DOS;C:\WP;C:\UTILS
```

A batch file can copy any information from the environment by specifying the environment *variable name* within percent signs. For example, if you insert `%PATH%` in a batch file and then later execute the file, the *current* path would be substituted for %PATH%. (You'll soon see an example of this.)

A batch file can also use the SET command to *store* information in the environment. In fact, you can even store information in the environment from the command prompt. To illustrate this, follow these steps:

1. At the command prompt, type `SET VAR1=TEST` and then press Enter.

2. Type `SET` and press Enter.

The first step above creates an environmental variable called VAR1, which contains the word TEST. The second command displays the current contents of the environment, which now includes:

`VAR1=TEST`

To remove the new variable from the environment, enter the command:

`SET VAR1=`

and press Enter. (Enter the `SET` command again to verify that the variable has indeed been removed.)

So, what are the practical implications of this? As you'll see, both the %PROMPT% variable and the SET command play an integral part in the new ADDPATH.BAT batch file. Use the following steps to create ADDPATH.BAT:

1. Type `EDLIN ADDPATH.BAT` and press Enter.

2. Type `1i` and press Enter.

3. Type `@REM *************** ADDPATH.BAT` (use any number of asterisks) and press Enter.

4. Type `@REM Extends the current path,` and press Enter.

5. Type `@REM and remembers the previous path.` and press Enter.

6. Type `SET EXPATH=%PATH%` and press Enter.

7. Type `PATH %PATH%;C:\%1` and press Enter (if you do not have a hard disk named C:, substitute a different drive name).

8. Type `@ECHO Path is now %PATH%` and press Enter.

9. Press Ctrl-C.

10. Type `E` and press Enter to save the batch file and exit Edlin.

11. Enter the command `TYPE ADDPATH.BAT` and press Enter.

The complete ADDPATH.BAT file should match Figure 13.9. To discuss how it works, let's assume that the current path is C:\DOS;C:\WP; C:\UTILS and that you run the batch file by entering the command ADDPATH DBASE. The first command following the comments substitutes the current path for %PATH%, so that the command actually becomes SET EXPATH= C:\DOS;C:\WP;C:\UTILS Then, when it executes, it stores the current path setting in the environment using the variable name EXPATH. (This variable is important in the next batch file you will create which allows you to "undo" a change made by ADDPATH.)

```
@REM *********************** ADDPATH.BAT
@REM Extends the current path,
@REM and remembers the previous path.
SET EXPATH=%PATH%
PATH %PATH%;C:\%1
@ECHO Path is now %PATH%
```

Figure 13.9. The ADDPATH.BAT batch file.

Then, the current path is again substituted for %PATH% in the next command, so that that line becomes:

```
PATH C:\DOS;C:\WP;C:\UTILS;C:\%1
```

Next, the parameter from the command line, DBASE in this example, is substituted into the position held by %1, so that the command is finally expanded to:

```
PATH C:\DOS;C:\WP;C:\UTILS;C:\DBASE
```

After both substitutions are made, DOS executes the complete command, which defines the new path as

```
C:\DOS;C:\WP;C:\UTILS;C:\DBASE
```

The last command, @ECHO Path is now %PATH% displays the new PATH setting on the screen inform you that you have selected a new path. How did %PATH% end up in containing the *new* path information? Because when you execute a command such as PATH C:\DOS;C:\WP;C:\UTILS; C:\DBASE, as this batch file did, DOS automatically adjusts the environment accordingly. So %PATH% now shows the current (altered) path.

Let's try using this batch file. First, enter the command PATH and press Enter to view your current PATH setting on the screen. Then, enter the ADDPATH command with the name of any other directory on your hard disk. For example, using the hypothetical directory tree from Chapter 11, you might enter the command:

```
ADDPATH WINDOWS
```

Your screen displays quite a bit of activity, as Figure 13.10 shows. To see if ADDPATH did its job, enter the command **SET** when the command prompt reappears. Notice that the environment now contains both the new path (next to PATH=) and the previous path (next to EXPATH=), as shown at the bottom of the figure.

```
C:\UTILS>ADDPATH WINDOWS

C:\UTILS>SET EXPATH=C:\DOS;C:\WP;C:\UTILS

C:\UTILS>PATH C:\DOS;C:\WP;C:\UTILS;C:\WINDOWS
Path is now C:\DOS;C:\WP;C:\UTILS;C:\WINDOWS

C:\UTILS>
C:\UTILS>
C:\UTILS>SET
COMSPEC=C:\DOS\COMMAND.COM
ORIGPATH=C:\WS4;C:\DOS;C:\UTILS;C:\DBASE
APPEND=C:\DOS
PROMPT=$P$G
EXPATH=C:\DOS;C:\WP;C:\UTILS
PATH=C:\DOS;C:\WP;C:\UTILS;C:\WINDOWS

C:\UTILS>
```

Figure 13.10. Results of the command ADDPATH
WINDOWS.

If your ADDPATH command is working properly, clean up its display by adding the @ECHO OFF command to the top of the batch file. Here are the steps for this procedure:

1. Type **EDLIN ADDPATH.BAT** and press Enter.

2. Type **1i** and press Enter to insert a new first line.

3. Type **@ECHO OFF** and press Enter.

4. Press Ctrl-C.

5. Type **E** and press Enter to save your changes and exit Edlin.

Restoring the Original Path

The OLDPATH.BAT batch file is the opposite of ADDPATH: It removes the last-added directory name from the path list. It's particularly handy for correcting a mistake. For example, while using ADDPATH, suppose you add the drive name, out of habit, to the directory name. Because ADDPATH

automatically adds the drive name, entering a command like `ADDPATH`
`C:\WINDOWS` produces this faulty new path:

`C:\DOS;C:\WP;C:\UTILS;C:\C:\WINDOWS`

Notice that there is an extra C:\ before the WINDOWS directory
name. DOS can't handle this, so you need to correct the path definition.
The OLDPATH.BAT batch file lets you make this correction merely by typing the command `OLDPATH` (rather than by retyping the entire PATH command). To provide feedback, OLDPATH also shows you that it has
reinstated the current path to:

`C:\DOS;C:\WP;C:\UTILS`

After running OLDPATH.BAT you need only enter the correct command, `ADDPATH WINDOWS`, for DOS to set up the new, correct PATH command.

To create the OLDPATH.BAT batch file, follow these steps:

1. Type `EDLIN OLDPATH.BAT` and press Enter.

2. Type `1i` to start inserting lines.

3. Type `@REM *************** OLDPATH.BAT` and press Enter.

4. Type `@REM Removes the latest addition to the PATH.` and press Enter.

5. Type `PATH %EXPATH%` and press Enter.

6. Type `@ECHO Path is back to %PATH%` and press Enter.

7. Press Ctrl-C.

8. Type `E` and press Enter to save your file and exit Edlin.

9. At the command prompt, type `TYPE OLDPATH.BAT` and press Enter.

Your OLDPATH.BAT batch file should match the file in Figure 13.11.
The first two lines are comments. In the next command, the previously
defined path (which, you will recall, was stored in the EXPATH environmental variable) is substituted for %EXPATH%. Therefore, the command
expands to `PATH C:\DOS;C:\WP;C:\UTILS` (using the previous example path)
when DOS executes it. This resets the PATH definition to the previous
definition. The last command displays the new current path definition.

```
@REM ********************** OLDPATH.BAT
@REM Removes the latest addition to the PATH.
PATH %EXPATH%
@ECHO Path is back to %PATH%
```

Figure 13.11. The OLDPATH.BAT batch file.

You can run the OLDPATH batch file *only* after you've used the ADDPATH batch file to add a new path (because ADDPATH creates the EXPATH variable). To test this batch file, merely enter the command OLDPATH at the command prompt. (This batch file accepts no parameters.) Notice that the path that you added with the previous ADDPATH command is now removed from the PATH definition. To further verify this, enter either the command PATH or SET.

ADDPATH for Multiple Disk Drives

As it is currently designed, ADDPATH.BAT can only be run on a computer that has a hard disk drive named C:. If you want your ADDPATH.BAT batch file to allow you to include other hard disk drives, change the following line:

```
PATH %PATH%;C:\%1
```

to:

```
PATH %PATH%;%1
```

When using this new ADDPATH batch file, you must include the drive name with the ADDPATH command. For example, to add the PARADOX3 directory from drive F: to the current PATH setting, you must enter the command:

```
ADDPATH F:\PARADOX3
```

Reinstating the Original Path

Let's develop a third related batch file, named ORIGPATH, that always resets your PATH command to its original setting in the AUTOEXEC.BAT file. First, you need to change your AUTOEXEC.BAT file to include the command SET ORIGPATH=%PATH%. Be sure to place this command beneath the PATH command in your AUTOEXEC.BAT file, because the PATH must be defined before the SET ORIGPATH command stores it in the ORIGPATH variable. Figure 13.12 shows a sample DOS 4 AUTOEXEC.BAT file with the appropriate SET ORIGPATH command in it. (This Figure includes comments that describe the purpose of its commands.)

Now you can create a simple batch file, named ORIGPATH.BAT, that looks like the one in Figure 13.13. Any time you want to reinstate original PATH definition, merely enter the command ORIGPATH. The command PATH %ORIGPATH% in that batch file resets the path to the setting defined by the original PATH command in AUTOEXEC.BAT. (Remember, however, that the SET ORIGPATH command in AUTOEXEC.BAT is not executed until you either run AUTOEXEC.BAT or you reboot your computer.)

```
@ECHO OFF
REM ************************ AUTOEXEC.BAT
REM --- Put COMSPEC in the environment.
SET COMSPEC=C:\DOS\COMMAND.COM
REM --- Set up the PATH
PATH C:\WP;C:\DOS;C:\UTILS
REM --- Store a copy of current PATH in the environment.
SET ORIGPATH=%PATH%
REM --- Turn off verification to speed processing.
VERIFY OFF
REM --- Install the mouse driver.
C:\MOUSE1\MOUSE
REM --- Make all DOS 4 files accessible.
APPEND /E
APPEND C:\DOS
REM --- Initialize PRINT.COM and design the command prompt.
PRINT /D:LPT1
PROMPT $P$G
REM --- Go straight to the DOS Shell.
DOSSHELL
```

Figure 13.12. Sample DOS 4 AUTOEXEC.BAT file.

```
@REM ************************ ORIGPATH.BAT
@REM Restores original path from AUTOEXEC.BAT.
@ECHO OFF
PATH %ORIGPATH%
ECHO Path is now %PATH%
```

Figure 13.13. The ORIGPATH.BAT batch file.

Using Batch Files to Assign Tasks to Keys

Chapter 12 showed you how to assign your own commands or keystrokes to any function key (after you installed the ANSI.SYS system via the CONFIG.SYS file). That is, you use the command PROMPT $e[0; followed by: 1) a special code for the key (see Table 12.7), 2) the keystrokes you want to display enclosed in quotation marks, and 3) the letter p, which signals the end of the sequence. There are three drawbacks to using the approach for assigning tasks to function keys:

■ As soon as you turn off the computer, your custom key definitions are lost.

■ The codes are abstract and difficult to remember, and therefore are not easy to type from memory each time you start your computer.

■ It is not always easy to remember which tasks you've assigned to which keys.

A few simple batch files can solve all these problems. The first, named SETKEYS.BAT, lets you assign tasks to any number of function keys simply by typing the command SETKEYS at the command prompt. The second batch file, named SHOWKEYS.BAT, displays the tasks assigned to each function key any time you need a reminder.

Table 13.2 shows the tasks that SETKEYS.BAT will assign to the function keys Alt-F2 through Alt-F10. (Alt-F1 is omitted because it is sometimes used by application programs to display help screens.) The third column of the table indicates the code number used in the PROMPT command to signify the key.

Table 13.2. Examples of tasks assigned to function keys.

Key	Job Performed	PROMPT Key Code
Alt-F2	DIR sorted by file name	105
Alt-F3	DIR sorted by extension	106
Alt-F4	DIR sorted by size	107
Alt-F5	DIR sorted by month/day	108
Alt-F6	DIR sorted by time	109
Alt-F7	Send linefeed to the printer	110
Alt-F8	Eject page from printer	111
Alt-F9	Shoe "clean" directory tree	112
Alt-F10	Copy new and modified files to drive A:	113

Figure 13.14 shows the complete SETKEYS.BAT batch file. Use the same techniques that you used in previous examples to create the SETKEYS.BAT file. However, to get you started and to show you a faster way of creating this batch file, let's create the first few lines together. Here are the steps:

1. At the command prompt, type EDLIN SETKEYS.BAT and press Enter.

2. Type 1i and press Enter to begin inserting lines.

3. Type @REM **************** SETKEYS.BAT (use any number of asterisks) and press Enter.

```
@REM *********************** SETKEYS.BAT
@REM Assign tasks to Alt-function keys.
PROMPT $e[0;105;"DIR | SORT | MORE";13p
PROMPT $e[0;106;"DIR | SORT /+10 | FIND /V ";34;"e";34;" |
    MORE";13p
PROMPT $e[0;107;"DIR | SORT /+14 | FIND /V ";34;"e";34;" |
    MORE";13p
PROMPT $e[0;108;"DIR | SORT /+23 | FIND /V ";34;"e";34;" |
    MORE";13p
PROMPT $e[0;109;"DIR | SORT /+33 | FIND /V ";34;"e"'34;" |
    MORE";13p
PROMPT $e[0;110;"ECHO ";10;" > PRN";13p
PROMPT $e[0;111;"ECHO ";12;" > PRN";13p
PROMPT $e[0;112;"TREE | FIND ";34;"Path";34;" | MORE";13p
PROMPT $e[0;113;"XCOPY C:\*.* A: /S /M /W";13p
```

Figure 13.14. The SETKEYS.BAT batch file.

4. Type @REM Assign tasks to Alt-function keys. and press Enter.

5. Type PROMPT $e[0;105;"DIR | SORT | MORE";13p and press Enter.

6. To save some typing, press the F1 or → key 14 times to recall the characters PROMPT $e[;10 from the preceding line.

7. Type 6 and then press F1 or → 13 times to repeat more characters from the above line. The new line now reads PROMPT $e[0;106;"DIR | SORT (including the blank space after the word SORT).

8. Press the Ins (or Insert) key once; then type /+10 | FIND /V";34;"e";34;" and press the Spacebar.

9. Press the F3 key to retrieve the rest of the previous line, so that the entire line reads PROMPT $e[0;106;"DIR | SORT /+10 | FIND /V";34;"e";34;" | MORE";13p

10. Press Enter.

11. To enter the next line, repeatedly press → to recall the characters PROMPT $e[0;10

12. Type 7 and repeatedly press → until the line reads PROMPT $e[0;107;"DIR | SORT /+1

13. Type 4 and then press F3 to repeat the rest of the preceding line.

In the previous steps, you used the F1, →, and F3 keys as shortcuts for entering the first few lines of the file. (Remember that you can use the ← and Backspace keys to "back up" if you repeat too many characters from the preceding line.) Using Figure 13.14 as your source, continue to type the rest of the commands in SETKEYS.BAT.

DOS 4 users should note that the command PROMPT $e[0;112;"TREE |
FIND ";34;"Path";34; | MORE";13p does not display anything on the screen;
DOS 4 uses a different format to display the directory tree than earlier
versions of DOS. As an alternative, you can insert the command PROMPT
$e[0;112;"DOSSHELL";13p so that pressing Alt-F9 takes you to the DOS
Shell. (The DOSSHELL.BAT and other SHELL programs stored in the DOS
directory or on the SHELL diskette must be available from the current diskette or directory for this command to work properly.)

When you have typed the entire SETKEYS.BAT file, type Ctrl-C to
stop inserting. Then, type E and press Enter to save your work and exit
Edlin. At the command prompt, type TYPE SETKEYS.BAT and press Enter to
view your file. Be sure it looks *exactly* like the screen in Figure 13.14. (If it
does not, use Edlin to make corrections.)

Before you test this new batch file, let's discuss the one new technique
presented here. Notice that several command keys use ASCII code 34 as a
character to type. If you look for this code in Appendix C, you will see that
34 is the ASCII code for the quotation mark (").

To make a function key type the quotation mark, you must place the
ASCII number 34 outside of any quotation marks used to identify specific
characters to be typed. DOS treats this character differently because of its
specialized function: "real" quotation marks always enclose the "literal"
keystrokes to be typed.

This is easier to understand when you look at an example. Suppose
that you want a function key to type the sentence Joe says "Hello". If you
set up a command such as PROMPT $e[0;105;"Joe says "Hello", DOS would
only see the first pair of quotation marks (that is, "Joe says ") and would not
know what to do about the remaining text Hello".

To differentiate between quotation marks that are used to *assign* characters to a function key and those that are actually to be *typed* by the function key itself, you must use ASCII code 34 outside of the quotation marks.
That is, if you want a function key to type Joe says "Hello", you must use
the syntax PROMPT $e[0;105;"Joe says ";34;"Hello";34. DOS interprets
this as "type Joe says, then type ASCII character 34, then type Hello, then
type ASCII character 34; all of which produces Joe says "Hello".

Assigning Graphics Symbols to Function Keys

In addition to the characters that you normally see on your screen, DOS
also can display a wide variety of graphics characters. Most of these special
characters have ASCII values greater than 127 (as you can see in Appendix
C). You can use several of these characters for drawing lines and boxes on
the screen to make your displays fancier.

The general technique for typing these graphics characters is as follows:

■ Hold down the Alt key.

■ Type the three-digit ASCII decimal code for the character *using the numeric keypad* (not the numbers at the top of the regular keyboard).

■ Release the Alt key.

Let's try this technique. The ASCII code for the double-bar horizontal line is number 205. To display that character, you must type Alt-205. Follow these exact steps:

1. Hold down the Alt key.

2. Type the number **205** *on the numeric keypad*.

3. Release the Alt key.

This produces a double-bar line next to the command prompt. (Press the Backspace key to erase it.)

The main problem with using this technique is that when you want to display, say, 30 double-bar lines in a row, you need to type 120 keystrokes (that is, press Alt-205 30 times). This can be very tedious!

It is much easier to assign these types of keystrokes to function keys. Then, you can repeatedly press that function key to draw a line of any length.

Look ahead to Figure 13.16. This is the screen displayed by the SHOWKEYS.BAT file, which you will be developing soon. Notice that the display uses double-bar lines to draw boxes. (That screen also shows you which graphics characters you will be assigning to function keys in this section.)

Adding Graphic Character Keys to SETKEYS.BAT

When you assign your graphics characters to function keys, be sure to use the decimal number— not the hexadecimal number—listed in Appendix C.

Let's first add the graphics character function-key definitions to the SETKEYS.BAT file, so that they will be available later when you develop the batch file displayed in Figure 13.16. Table 13.3 shows the correspondence between the PROMPT key number (used in the PROMPT command), the function key name, and the Alt-key combination that produces a graphics character.

To help you use the table effectively, the following steps show you how to expand SETKEYS.BAT to assign graphics characters to function keys:

1. Type **EDLIN SETKEYS.BAT** and press Enter.

2. Type **L** and press Enter to review the current contents of the file.

3. To start inserting new lines after the existing lines, type **12i** and press Enter.

Table 13.3. Alt-key Graphics Symbols assigned to function keys.

Function Key	PROMPT Key Code	Alt-key number	Graphics Symbols
Shift-F2	85	Alt-201	╔
Shift-F3	86	Alt-205	═
Shift-F4	87	Alt-187	╗
Shift-F5	88	Alt-186	║
Shift-F6	89	Alt-188	╝
Shift-F7	90	Alt-200	╚
Ctrl-F2	95	Alt-204	╠
Ctrl-F3	96	Alt-203	╦
Ctrl-F4	97	Alt-185	╣
Ctrl-F5	98	Alt-202	╩
Ctrl-F6	99	Alt-206	╬

4. Type `@REM Assign graphics characters to function keys...` and press Enter.

5. Type `PROMPT $e[0;85;"`

6. Hold down the Alt key and type the number 201. Then, release the Alt key.

7. Type `"p` so that the new line looks like line 12 in Figure 13.15.

8. Press Enter.

9. Press → 13 times to repeat the characters `PROMPT $e[0;8` from the previous line.

10. Type 6 and press → twice.

11. Press Alt-205 (hold down the Alt key, type the number 205 on the numeric keypad, and then release the Alt key).

12. Press F3 to repeat the remaining characters from the previous line.

13. Press Enter to move to the next line.

Notice in the previous steps that you assigned the Alt-201 character to function key 85 and the graphic character Alt-205 to function key 86. These correspond directly to the first two rows of Table 13.3.

To list all the lines in your SETKEYS.BAT file, enter the Edlin command 1,24L.

Using the remaining rows in Table 13.3, complete the rest of the batch file. As the last line in SETKEYS.BAT, enter the command `PROMPT $P$G`. When you are finished, your complete SHOWKEYS.BAT file should match the display in Figure 13.15. For your convenience, the entire file is shown with the Edlin line numbers. (Recall that Edlin adds the line numbers; you do not need to type them.)

```
 1: *@REM *************************** SETKEYS.BAT
 2: @REM Assign tasks to Alt-function keys...
 3: PROMPT $e[0;105;"DIR | SORT | MORE";13p
 4: PROMPT $e[0;106;"DIR | SORT /+10 | FIND /V ";34;"e";34;" | MORE";13p
 5: PROMPT $e[0;107;"DIR | SORT /+14 | FIND /V ";34;"e";34;" | MORE";13p
 6: PROMPT $e[0;108;"DIR | SORT /+23 | FIND /V ";34;"e";34;" | MORE";13p
 7: PROMPT $e[0;109;"DIR | SORT /+33 | FIND /V ";34;"e";34;" | MORE";13p
 8: PROMPT $e[0;110;"ECHO ";10;" > PRN";13p
 9: PROMPT $e[0;111;"ECHO ";12;" > PRN";13p
10: PROMPT $e[0;112;"TREE | FIND ";34;"Path";34;" | MORE";13p
11: PROMPT $e[0;113;"XCOPY C:\*.* A: /S /M /W";13p
12: @REM Assign graphics characters to function keys...
13: PROMPT $e[0;85;"▌"p
14: PROMPT $e[0;86;"═"p
15: PROMPT $e[0;87;"▐"p
16: PROMPT $e[0;88;"▟"p
17: PROMPT $e[0;89;"▙"p
18: PROMPT $e[0;90;"▄"p
19: PROMPT $e[0;95;"▛"p
20: PROMPT $e[0;96;"═"p
21: PROMPT $e[0;97;"▜"p
22: PROMPT $e[0;98;"▙"p
23: PROMPT $e[0;99;"▀"p
24: PROMPT $P$G
*
```

Figure 13.15. The complete SETKEYS.BAT batch file.

After you type the last command, `PROMPT $P$G`, press Ctrl-C to stop inserting new lines. Then, type `E` and press Enter to save your work and return to the command prompt.

Testing SETKEYS.BAT

To test your SETKEYS batch file, type the command `SETKEYS` at the command prompt, and press Enter. This causes a long list of PROMPT commands to quickly scroll past your screen. To ensure that each key works, try them. Refer to the following Figure 13.16 to see what each key is supposed to do. Note that the Alt-F7 and Alt-F8 keys require that the printer be on-line and ready to accept data.

Also, because Alt-F10 copies new and modified files from the hard disk to a diskette in drive A:, you should test this only on a hard disk system and only with a blank, formatted diskette already inserted in drive A:.

Note also that the Alt-F10 key combination is designed for you to use on a day-to-day basis for copying recently modified files. If you have not performed a BACKUP command recently (see Chapter 11), this function key probably will try to copy too many files to the diskette. If it runs out of diskette space while copying, DOS will display the message `Insufficient disk space` and then redisplay the command prompt. (No harm done, though.)

Testing the new graphics function keys at this point merely displays them next to the command prompt. If you press Enter after typing several graphics characters next to the command prompt, DOS of course displays the Bad command or file name error message. However, you will soon see that these keys can come in very handy when you use the Edlin editor.

Developing a Help Screen with Graphics Characters

Now, let's create a fancy help screen using some of the graphics characters that you assigned to function keys in the SETKEYS.BAT file. If you've turned off your computer since the last section, be sure to enter the SETKEYS command to activate the customized function keys. Then, you can begin to create the batch file that displays a help screen much like the one shown in Figure 13.16.

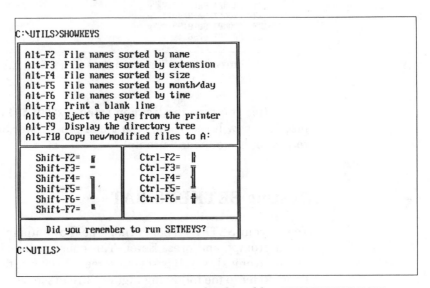

Figure 13.16. Help screen displayed by SHOWKEYS.BAT.

The following detailed steps will help get you started creating SHOWKEYS.BAT. Remember, if you make a mistake while typing a line— even if you press the wrong graphics function key—you can always press the Backspace key to erase the error:

In this case you can immediately add the ⓐECHO OFF command to the batch file. Because all of these commands actually display text, if you make an error, it will be obvious which line needs to be corrected.

1. At the command prompt, type EDLIN SHOWKEYS.BAT and press Enter.

2. Type 1i and press Enter.

3. Type ⓐRem *************** SHOWKEYS.BAT (again, type any number of asterisks) and press Enter.

4. Type ⓐREM Display a reminder about function keys. and press Enter.

5. Type ECHO OFF and press Enter.

6. Type ECHO and then press the Spacebar.

7. Hold down the Shift key and press F2.

8. Hold down the Shift key and press F3 43 times.

9. Hold down the Shift key and press F4.

10. Press Enter.

11. Press → five times to copy ECHO and the blank space from the preceding line.

12. Hold down the Shift key and press F5.

13. Press the Spacebar.

14. Type Alt-F2 and then press the Spacebar twice.

15. Type Filenames sorted by name.

16. Press the Spacebar nine times.

17. Hold down the Shift key and press F5.

18. Press Enter.

19. Press → 12 times.

20. Type 3.

21. Press → 23 times.

22. Type extension.

23. Press the Spacebar four times.

24. Press →.

25. Press Enter.

26. Press → 12 times.

27. Type 4.

28. Press the Spacebar 23 times.

29. Type size.

30. Press the Spacebar nine times.

31. Press →.

32. Press Enter.

At this point, your SHOWKEYS.BAT file should look like the first seven lines of Figure 13.17. Use these same general steps to complete the file on your own. If you forget which function key prints a certain graphic character, use the information presented in Figure 13.16 or Figure 13.17 as a reminder.

DOS 4 users might want to change line 12 to read Alt-F9 Return to DOS Shell if you made the previously discussed change to SETKEYS.BAT.

When you finish the SHOWKEYS.BAT file, remember to press Ctrl-C to stop inserting new lines. Then type E and press Enter to save your work and return to the command prompt.

To test your SHOWKEYS.BAT batch file, type the command SHOWKEYS at the command prompt, and press Enter. This displays the screen shown in Figure 13.16.

Incidentally, if you want to print a copy of the output from SHOWKEYS.BAT, enter the command CLS at the command prompt to clear the screen, and then enter the SHOWKEYS command. Then, press the Shift-

```
*L
    1:*@REM ************************** SHOWKEYS.BAT
    2: @REM Display a reminder about function keys.
    3: @ECHO OFF
    4: ECHO
    5: ECHO  Alt-F2  File names sorted by name
    6: ECHO  Alt-F3  File names sorted by extension
    7: ECHO  Alt-F4  File names sorted by size
    8: ECHO  Alt-F5  File names sorted by month/day
    9: ECHO  Alt-F6  File names sorted by time
   10: ECHO  Alt-F7  Print a blank line
   11: ECHO  Alt-F8  Eject the page from the printer
   12: ECHO  Alt-F9  Display the directory tree
   13: ECHO  Alt-F10 Copy new/modified files to A:
   14: ECHO
   15: ECHO  Shift-F2=          Ctrl-F2=
   16: ECHO  Shift-F3=   =      Ctrl-F3=
   17: ECHO  Shift-F4=   ]      Ctrl-F4=   ]
   18: ECHO  Shift-F5=          Ctrl-F5=
   19: ECHO  Shift-F6=   ]      Ctrl-F6=
   20: ECHO  Shift-F7=   l
   21: ECHO
   22: ECHO       Did you remember to run SETKEYS?
   23: ECHO
*
```

Figure 13.17. The SHOWKEYS.BAT file.

PrintScreen key (as discussed in Chapter 9). If necessary, press Alt-F8 to eject the page from your printer. If the printed graphics characters do not look the same as they do on the screen, try loading the GRAPHICS program (discussed in Appendix B); then, press Shift-PrintScreen again.

Summary

This chapter has discussed the basics of creating your own commands via batch files. The basic techniques you've learned here will allow you to create nearly any batch file that you might require. Remember, any command that you can type at the command prompt can be placed in a batch file. This includes commands that run other programs, such as DBASE, WP, or EXCEL.

In the next chapter, you'll expand your knowledge of batch files by learning about commands that are allowed *only* in batch files. But first, let's review the important points discussed in this chapter:

- Any commands that you normally enter at the command prompt can be stored as a group in a batch file.

- Batch files must have the extension .BAT and should not have the same name as any file with a .COM or .EXE extension.

- You execute all the commands in a batch file by running the file exactly as you would run any other program on your computer.

- To prevent a command from appearing on the screen before it is executed, precede the command with an @ character. (DOS 3.3 and 4 only)

■ You can pass parameters from the DOS command line to your batch file by using the names %1, %2, %3, and so on as placeholders.

■ To stop the execution of a batch file, press Ctrl-C or Ctrl-Break.

■ You can have a batch file read information from the environment by surrounding variable names with % signs. (For example, %PATH% reads the current PATH setting.)

■ You can use the SET command to store data in the environment. (When you use the SET command alone it displays the contents of the environment.)

■ If ANSI.SYS is installed on your computer, you can use the PROMPT $e[0; commands in a batch file to customize the function keys.

■ You can also assign graphics characters to function keys. Use the Alt-key and numeric keypad to display graphics characters.

Extending the Power of Your Batch Files

This chapter presents some advanced techniques that you can use to create bigger and better batch files. The sample batch files that you will develop are practical programs you will find useful in your own work.

This chapter assumes that you already know how to use the Edlin editor described in previous chapters. Therefore, I will no longer present the step-by-step instructions required to create each batch file. Remember, Chapter 10 provides general information about creating and editing any DOS text file.

Decision-Making in Batch Files

A batch file can use two commands—IF and IF NOT— to make a decision about whether or not to perform some operation. The basic syntax for the IF command is as follows:

```
IF condition command
```

where *condition* is some situation that DOS can evaluate as being either true or false. If the condition proves true, the *command* next to it is executed. If the condition proves false, the *command* next to it is ignored.

You can reverse the effects of the condition by using the IF NOT command, as shown in the following syntax:

```
IF NOT condition command
```

In this command, if the condition is *not* true, the command is executed. If the condition *is* true, the command is ignored.

The three basic techniques for using the IF command are discussed in the sections that follow.

Using IF to Check for Files

The `IF EXIST` *filename* version of IF checks to see if the file specified in *filename* exists. For example, the following command looks for a file named MYDIARY.TXT in the current directory. If the file exists, the command `TYPE MYDIARY.TXT` is executed; otherwise, the `TYPE MYDIARY.TXT` command is ignored:

```
IF EXIST MYDIARY.TXT TYPE MYDIARY.TXT
```

The next command checks to see if a file named CHAP1.TXT already exists on a directory named \BAKFILES. If the file does *not* yet exist, the COPY command copies CHAP1.TXT from the current directory to the \BAKFILES directory; if the CHAP1.TXT files *does* exist on the \BAKFILES directory, the COPY command is not executed:

```
IF NOT EXIST \BAKFILES\CHAP1.TXT COPY CHAP1.TXT \BAKFILES
```

This general syntax is useful in batch files when you want to be sure that a COPY operation does not overwrite an existing file. (You'll soon see an example of this usage.)

You also can use wildcard characters in the *filename* portion of the command. For example, the following command displays the message `No batch files here` if the current directory does not contain any files with the .BAT extension:

```
IF NOT EXIST *.BAT ECHO No batch files here
```

Using IF to Compare Strings

As you probably recall, a *string* is any character or group of characters. You can also use the IF command to compare two strings by using the general syntax:

```
IF string1 == string2 command
```

which (in English) says, "If the first string matches the second string, then do *command*." You can also use the syntax:

```
IF NOT string1 == string2 command
```

which says, "If the first string *does not match* the second string, then do *command*."

The IF command recognizes two strings as identical if they are exactly the same, including uppercase and lowercase letters. For example SMITH matches SMITH, but SMITH does not match Smith.

Typically, you use IF to see if a passed parameter or an environmental variable equals a set value. For example, the command:

```
IF %1 == Martha ECHO Hello Martha!
```

displays the message `Hello Martha` if the %1 variable contains the name Martha.

If either string is left blank, DOS returns the error message `Syntax error`. If there is a possibility that one of the strings might be left blank, follow both strings in the IF command with an extra character, such as a period. For example, suppose you create a batch file that requires you to enter a parameter at the command prompt. The following command checks to see if the parameter is blank and then displays the message `A parameter is required` if the parameter is indeed blank:

```
IF %1. == . ECHO A parameter is required
```

Remember that %1 is merely a placeholder for the first option entered at the command prompt. Therefore, if %1 contains *Joe*, then the previous command becomes `IF Joe. == . ECHO A parameter is required` before it is executed. Because *Joe.* is not the same as *.*, the ECHO command is ignored.

However, if you don't include a parameter at the command prompt, the command becomes `IF . == . ECHO A parameter is required` before execution. In this case, the two strings (*.* and *.*) are identical, so the ECHO command is executed. You'll see a practical example of this technique in MOVE.BAT and in other batch files presented in this chapter.

Testing for Command Errors

A third variation of the IF command is used in conjunction with commands such as BACKUP, FORMAT, and RESTORE. These commands all return an ERRORLEVEL value after they are executed. If the operation is completed successfully, ERRORLEVEL is zero. If the operation could not be completed, ERRORLEVEL is some number greater than zero.

The general syntax for using ERRORLEVEL in an IF command is as follows:

```
IF ERRORLEVEL number command
```

The *command* is executed only if the ERRORLEVEL value is greater than or equal to the *number*. For example, the BACKUP command returns an errorlevel value in the range of 1 to 4 when the backup operation cannot be completed. In the following sample batch file, the IF command signals DOS to display the message Backup not fully completed! if an error occurs during the BACKUP command:

```
REM ********************** QUICKBAK.BAT
REM Backs up new and modified files only.
BACKUP C:\*.* /S /M
IF NOT ERRORLEVEL 0 ECHO Backup not fully completed!
```

Many of the batch files presented later in this chapter contain practical examples of the IF command. But first, you need to learn about the GOTO command, which helps add even more decision-making power to your batch files.

Skipping a Group of Commands in a Batch File

You can use GOTO only in batch files; it is not a command prompt command.

As you know from the previous chapter, DOS usually executes commands in a batch file from the top down. However, you can force DOS to skip commands or repeat commands by using the GOTO command to perform a technique called *branching*.

The GOTO command tells DOS to skip a group of commands until it finds a *label*. When it finds the label, it resumes execution at the first command after the label. The label itself must be preceded by a colon in the batch file (but you do not include the colon in the GOTO command).

For example, the following sample batch file contains the command GOTO NearBottom, and the label :NearBottom:

```
@ECHO OFF
ECHO I'm line 1
ECHO I'm line 2
GOTO NearBottom
ECHO I'm line 3
ECHO I'm line 4
:NearBottom
ECHO I'm line 5
ECHO I'm line 6
```

If you ran this batch file, your screen would display:

```
I'm line 1
I'm line 2
I'm line 5
I'm line 6
```

Notice that the two ECHO commands between the GOTO NearBottom command and the :NearBottom label were completely ignored. That's because the GOTO command branched execution to the first command after the NearBottom label, and therefore DOS never "saw" the ECHO commands for lines 3 and 4.

Copying Files Without Overwriting

To demonstrate a practical application of the IF and GOTO commands, Figure 14.1 shows a batch file named SAFECOPY.BAT that copies files from one drive or directory to another *only* if no files at the destination will be overwritten. (This is different from the DOS COPY command, which *will* overwrite files at the destination.)

```
@ECHO OFF
REM ************************** SAFECOPY.BAT
REM Checks for overwriting before copying files.
IF EXIST %2\%1 GOTO ErrMsg
COPY %1 %2\%1
GOTO Done
:ErrMsg
ECHO Files on %2 will be overwritten!
ECHO Copy aborted
:Done
```

Figure 14.1. The SAFECOPY.BAT batch file.

Let's look at how SAFECOPY.BAT works. Assuming that you create this batch file on your own computer, you would enter the command SAFECOPY *.BAT \DOS to use SAFECOPY.BAT to copy all the .BAT files from your current directory to a directory named \DOS.

First, in the command IF EXIST %2\%1 GOTO ErrMsg, the %1 and %2 variables are replaced with the source and destination for the copy. Hence, the command becomes IF EXIST \DOS*.BAT GOTO ErrMsg before execution. This checks to see if any files on the \DOS directory have the extension .BAT. If any do, control branches to the label :ErrMsg, thereby skipping the COPY command.

If the GOTO command did not branch control to the :ErrMsg label, the command COPY %1 %2\%1 becomes COPY *.BAT \DOS*.BAT after substitution. When this command executes it copies all .BAT files to the \DOS directory.

After a successful copy, the GOTO Done command passes control to the label named :Done, so that the ECHO commands that display the error message are ignored. (These must be skipped because the batch file shouldn't display the error messages after a successful copy operation.)

The :ErrMsg label (short for *error message*) marks the location to which the GOTO ErrMsg command passes control when the IF EXIST %2\%1 command proves true. Because this label is beneath the COPY command, the COPY command is not executed when control is passed to this label.

The commands ECHO Files on %2 will be overwritten! and ECHO Copy aborted display the error message on the screen. Note that if the COPY command *is* executed, the GOTO Done command skips over these commands, so the error message is not displayed. The :Done label marks the end of the batch file, where execution ends and control returns to the command prompt.

As you will soon see, "asking questions" with IF and branching with GOTO can help you to build more "intelligent" batch files. But first, let's look at a few more optional techniques that can make your batch files even smarter.

Pausing for a Keystroke

Another useful command that you can use in batch files is PAUSE. This command temporarily stops execution of the batch file and displays the message Press any key to continue.... This pause is usually used to give a person a chance to insert a diskette in a drive. However, it can also be used to give you the option of pressing Ctrl-C to terminate the batch file in the event of an unexpected situation.

NUL is sometimes called the "garbage can" device, because anything sent to it just disappears.

You can redirect the message displayed by PAUSE to a device called NUL (for null) if you want to hide the stock message and create your own. For example, look at the following series of commands:

```
@ECHO OFF
ECHO File(s) will be overwritten!
ECHO Press Ctrl-C, then Y, to abort operation,
ECHO or any other key to proceed and overwrite...
PAUSE > NUL
COPY %1 %2
```

When executed, these commands display the following on the screen:

```
File(s) will be overwritten!
Press Ctrl-C, then Y, to abort operation,
or any other key to proceed and overwrite...
```

Pressing any key other than Ctrl-C (or Ctrl-Break) resumes processing normally, so that the COPY command below the PAUSE command is executed normally. However, pressing Ctrl-C (or Ctrl-Break) during this pause cancels execution of the batch file and displays the confirmation message:

```
Terminate batch file (Y/N)?
```

Pressing Y at this point finally terminates the batch file and returns to the command prompt. The COPY command is not executed. In essence the PAUSE command lets the user (the person who happens to be using the batch file at the moment) make a decision based on information provided by the messages on the screen.

Figure 14.2 shows a modified version of SAFECOPY.BAT that uses this alternative technique. Rather than absolutely refusing to overwrite files during a copy procedure, the batch file merely explains that files will be overwritten and asks for permission to proceed with the operation.

```
@ECHO OFF
REM ************************** SAFECOPY.BAT
REM Modified version that gives the user the
REM choice on whether to proceed or not.

REM --- If no files will be overwritten, proceed to GoAhead.
IF NOT EXIST %2\%1 GOTO GoAhead

REM --- Present message and opportunity to cancel...
ECHO File(s) will be overwritten!
ECHO Press Ctrl-C, then Y, to abort operation,
ECHO or any other key to proceed and overwrite...
PAUSE > NULL

REM --- If Ctrl-C was not pressed during pause,
REM --- execution proceeds with rest of commands.
:GoAhead
COPY %1 %2\%1
```

Figure 14.2. The modified SAFECOPY.BAT batch file.

This version of SAFECOPY.BAT begins with the command IF NOT EXIST %2\%1 GOTO GoAhead, which sends control directly to the label :GoAhead and bypasses the messages that directly follow.

The ECHO commands present the messages warning that a file (or files) will be overwritten. Then, a PAUSE waits for a keypress. Pressing Ctrl-C during the pause and then typing Y terminates execution of the batch file, so that the COPY command is never reached.

Create both versions of SAFECOPY.BAT using the Edlin editor. Test each one by trying to copy the same file to the same directory twice. On the second attempt, one batch file will not allow you to recopy the file, and the other will warn you about the operation.

Soon you will develop a similar batch file, named MOVE.BAT, that safely moves files from one drive or directory to another. But first, the next section will teach you a few tricks that you can use to make your batch files display more readable messages.

Improving Batch File Messages

If you develop batch files that display many messages and warnings on the screen, you should use some of the techniques discussed in the sections that follow.

Making Your Batch File Beep

You can easily make your batch file sound a beep when it presents an important message. If you are using the Edlin editor to create your batch files, merely type the ECHO command, followed by a blank space, and the message. However, before you press Enter to move to the next line, press Ctrl-G. Your screen now displays ^G, as in the following example:

```
ECHO Files will be overwritten!^G
```

Later, when you run the batch file, DOS will sound the beep whenever the message is displayed on the screen. (This technique is often used by programs to get your attention and warn you of a potential problem.)

Displaying Blank Lines from a Batch File

If you want a batch file to display a blank line on the screen, follow the ECHO command with a period (no blank spaces). You can try this directly at the command prompt. That is, if you enter the command:

```
ECHO
```

DOS displays the message ECHO is on (or ECHO is off). But if you enter the command:

```
ECHO.
```

DOS displays only a blank line.

A Batch File to Move Files to a New Directory

Now, let's combine most of the techniques discussed in preceding sections to develop a powerful batch file named MOVE.BAT that can move files from one directory to another. On the surface, you might think that such a batch file need only contain two commands:

```
REM ************************ MOVE.BAT
COPY %1 %2
ERASE %1
```

If this MOVE.BAT file were stored on my computer, and I wanted to move the files named CHAP1.TXT, CHAP2.TXT, and so on to CHAP17.TXT to a directory named \DONE, I would enter the command `MOVE CHAP*.TXT C:\DONE`. The first command would become `COPY CHAP*.TXT C:\DONE`, which would copy all the files from the current directory to the directory named \DONE. Then, the second command would become `ERASE CHAP*.TXT` which would erase those copied files from the current directory.

DOS 4 users already have a safe technique for moving files from one directory to another—the Move option on the File pull-down menu in the File System.

However, what if I entered the command `MOVE CHAP*.TXT C:\DONE` without realizing that I had not yet created a directory named \DONE? Because DOS would not find a directory named \DONE, it would assume I meant a file named DONE on the root directory! First DOS would copy CHAP1.TXT to the file named DONE. Then, it would copy CHAP2.TXT to the file named DONE, overwriting the current contents of the DONE file, and so on. When the COPY command was completed, the file named DONE on the root directory would contain *only* a copy of CHAP17.TXT.

This becomes a disaster when the second command in the batch file, `ERASE CHAP*.TXT`, is executed. Now I've got a problem. Not only has MOVE.BAT sent copies of the first 16 chapters to nowhere, but it has erased the originals as well!

Figure 14.3 shows a better version of the MOVE.BAT batch file, which is loaded with safety features to prevent problems. It even warns you if the MOVE operation is going to overwrite files on the destination directory, so that you can bail out before any overwriting takes place. (Blank lines are included in the batch file to help you isolate individual groups of commands, or *routines*).

Let's discuss how the improved version of MOVE.BAT works. As an example, let's suppose that you run MOVE.BAT with the command:

```
MOVE CHAP*.TXT C:\DOSBOOK
```

The first line turns off ECHO, and the next three lines are the usual comments. The first command, `IF %2. == . GOTO ErrMsg1`, checks for an initial error. This command verifies that two parameters were entered next to the MOVE command. If %2 (the second parameter) was left blank, this command passes control to the :ErrMsg1 label. In this example, the executed command would be `IF C:\DOSBOOK. == . GOTO ErrMsg1`, and because C:\DOSBOOK. is not the same as ., execution resumes with the next command.

```
@ECHO OFF
REM ********************** MOVE.BAT
REM Move file(s) to a new destination.
REM %1 is source, %2 is destination.

REM Make sure two parameters were passed.
IF %2. == . GOTO ErrMsg1

REM Make sure source exists
IF NOT EXIST %1 GOTO ErrMsg2

REM Check to see if overwriting will occur.
IT NOT EXIST %2\%1 GOTO MoveIt

REM Provide warning before overwriting.
ECHO WARNING! %1 file(s) already exist on %2^G
ECHO Press Ctrl-C now to cancel operation, or
ECHO any other key to overwrite files on %2
PAUSE > NUL

:MoveIt
COPY %1 %2\%1 > NUL
REM Double-check before erasing.
IF NOT EXIST %2\%1 GOTO ErrMsg3
ERASE %1
GOTO Done

:ErrMsg1
ECHO You must provide a source and destination, e.g.
ECHO MOVE *.BAK \BAKFILES
ECHO moves all .BAK files to the \BAKFILES directory.
GOTO Done

:ErrMsg2
ECHO %1 does not exist on current directory!
GOTO Done

:ErrMsg3
ECHO Destination directory does not exist, or source invalid
ECHO (Source may not contain a drive or directory name)
ECHO -- Operation canceled --

:Done
```

Figure 14.3. A better MOVE.BAT batch file.

The next command, IF NOT EXIST %1 GOTO ErrMsg2, checks to see if the files being copied exist in the current directory. In this example, after substitution takes place, the command becomes IF NOT EXIST CHAP*.TXT GOTO ErrMsg. If no files in the current directory match the ambiguous file name CHAP*.TXT, this command passes control to the :ErrMsg2 label. Again, this is merely a safety precaution that ensures that the command has been entered correctly at the command prompt.

The next command, IF NOT EXIST %2\%1 GOTO MoveIt, checks to see if any files in the destination directory have the same names as the files in the source directory. In this example, the command becomes IF NOT EXIST C:\DOSBOOK\CHAP*.TXT GOTO MoveIt. If none of the files on the C:\DOSBOOK directory match CHAP*.TXT, the GOTO command branches control directly to the :MoveIt label. However, if file names on the destination directory *do* match files to be moved, the next commands are executed:

```
ECHO WARNING! %1 file(s) already exist on %2^G
ECHO Press Ctrl-C now to cancel operation, or
ECHO any other key to overwrite files on %2
PAUSE > NUL
```

These commands display the message warning that files will be overwritten. After substitution, the actual message displayed is as follows:

```
WARNING! CHAP*.TXT file(s) already exist on C:\DOSBOOK
ECHO Press Ctrl-C now to cancel operation, or
ECHO any other key to overwrite files on C:\DOSBOOK
```

the PAUSE > NUL command waits for a keystroke but does not display its own message. At this point, pressing Ctrl-C cancels the batch file, so no files are moved. Pressing any other key passes control to the next commands.

:MoveIt is the label for the block of commands that perform the actual copying and erasing. First the command COPY %1 %2\%1 > NUL is converted to COPY CHAP*.TXT C:\DOSBOOK\CHAP*.TXT. (Ignore the > NUL for now; it merely hides the messages that COPY normally displays and can be omitted from the batch file if you prefer.)

Notice that the COPY command repeats the file name in the destination. This ensures that entering an invalid directory names does not lead to problems. For example, if this batch file had used the command COPY %1 %2, the command to be executed in this example would be COPY CHAP*.TXT C:\DOSBOOK. If the directory named C:\DOSBOOK does not exist, this command would copy the CHAP*.TXT files to a file named DOSBOOK on the root directory (as discussed earlier).

However, the command COPY %1 %2\%1 becomes COPY CHAP*.TXT C:\DOSBOOK\CHAP*.TXT. In this case, DOS must assume that \DOSBOOK is a directory name. Therefore, if the \DOSBOOK directory cannot be found, DOS merely cancels the operation and displays the error message Path not found. This safety procedure prevents you from inadvertently copying files to the root directory.

Before erasing any files in the current directory, the command IF NOT EXIST %2\%GOTO ErrMsg3 becomes IF NOT EXIST C:\DOSBOOK\CHAP*.TXT GOTO ErrMsg3. This command checks the destination directory to verify that it contains the files that were (presumably) copied by the preceding COPY command. If anything went wrong during the COPY operation, the destination directory will *not* contain the copied files. In that case, this command passes control to the :ErrMsg3 label, so that the ERASE command does not erase any files.

If (and only if) all went well up to this point, the ERASE %1 command expands to ERASE CHAP*.TXT. This erases all copied files from the source directory. Because every possible error has been checked, it is now safe to proceed with this ERASE command.

The next command, GOTO Done, branches control to the :Done label to bypass the error messages. Following this command are the various labels and error messages to which the preceding IF commands would have passed control in the event of an error. These are simple ECHO commands that provide information about the specific error that was encountered. As you can see below, each routine branches control to the :Done label after displaying its error message, so that the following ECHO commands are not displayed:

```
:ErrMsg1
ECHO You must provide a source and destination, e.g.
ECHO MOVE *.BAK \BAKFILES
ECHO moves all .BAK files to the \BAKFILES directory.
GOTO Done

:ErrMsg2
ECHO %1 does not exist on current directory!
GOTO Done

:ErrMsg3
ECHO Destination directory does not exist, or source invalid
ECHO (Source may not contain a drive or directory name)
ECHO -- Operation canceled --

:Done
```

In some ways, MOVE.BAT might seem almost paranoid in its concern with safety. However, considering that this batch file erases files, safety is certainly something that cannot be stressed too strongly.

Tips for Using MOVE.BAT

Keep in mind that MOVE.BAT is designed to move files *only* from the current directory to a different directory. You cannot specify a drive or another directory in the source.

For example, you cannot enter a command such as `MOVE C:\WP\WPFILES\SALEMEMO.DOC \SALES` to move the SALEMEMO.DOC file from the \WP\WPFILES directory to the \SALES directory. Instead you must first change to the \WP\WPFILES directory by entering the command `CD \WP\WPFILES` at the command prompt. Then, you can move the SALEMEMO.DOC file from that directory to the \SALES directory by entering the command `MOVE SALEMEMO.DOC \SALES`. Of course, if you make a mistake, MOVE.BAT certainly will let you know before any damage is done!

Repeating Commands in a Batch File

Another high-powered technique that you can use in batch file is *looping*. Looping allows you to repeat a command several times. The command you use for looping is FOR, which uses the following general syntax:

```
FOR %%letter IN (items) DO command
```

where *letter* is a single letter (a through z or A through Z), *items* is either a list of items separated by blank spaces or an ambiguous file name (which represents several files), and *command* is the command that is executed during each pass through the loop.

Each time the loop is executed, the %%*letter* variable assumes either the next value in the list of items or the next file name in the list produced by the ambiguous file name.

Even though you normally use the FOR command in a batch file, you can actually try an example at the command prompt. However, when using FOR at the command prompt, you use %*letter* rather than %%*letter*. Let's test the command. Assuming that the command prompt is displayed on your screen, enter this command:

```
FOR %c IN (Item1 Item2 Item3) DO ECHO %c
```

When you press Enter, your screen shows the following:

```
C:\UTILS>ECHO Item1
Item1

C:\UTILS>ECHO Item2
Item2

C:\UTILS>ECHO Item3
Item3

C:\UTILS>
```

(C:\UTILS> is simply the DOS command prompt.)

Notice what happened. In the first pass through the loop, %c was replaced by the first item in the list, so the first command executed was ECHO Item1. During the second pass through the loop, %c was replaced by the second item in the list, so the command executed was ECHO Item2. In the third pass through the loop, Item3 was substituted for %c, so the command executed was ECHO Item3. The next section examines a more practical application of looping.

LOOKIN.BAT: A Batch File to Search for a Word

LOOKIN.BAT is a batch file that can search through the contents of text files for a specific word. The more files and information you store on your computer, the more useful this batch file becomes. For example, suppose you use Edlin to create a file, named PHONE.TXT, that contains people's phone numbers, as shown in Figure 14.4. (Your file would probably contain many more names and numbers.) If you created LOOKIN.BAT, you could quickly retrieve Bonnie Baker's number by entering the command:

```
LOOKIN PHONES.TXT Baker
```

```
    Arthur Adams            (213)555-0146
    Bonnie Baker            (619)555-9302
    Charlie Charisma        (415)555-0954
    Donna Daring            (213)555-8765
    Edie Estoval            (415)555-7676
    Frankly Fastidious      (619)555-9443
    Gina Garrog             (714)555-3232
    Harry Hampton           (212)555-6543

(many more names could follow...)
```

Figure 14.4. A file containing names and phone numbers.

Your screen would display the following:

```
--------------- PHONES.TXT
Bonnie Baker            (619)555-9302

Press any key to print this list,
or Ctrl-C to abort
```

Another situation in which LOOKIN.BAT is useful is when you forget the name of a file you've created. If you know the directory in which the file is stored, and you can think of a distinctive word that is stored in the file, you can use LOOKIN to quickly search a large group of files for that word.

For example, if you wrote a letter to Albert Smith but cannot remember the name of that particular file (other than the fact that it probably had the extension .LET), you would enter the following command to search all .LET files on the current directory for the word "Albert":

```
LOOKIN *.LET Albert
```

Figure 14.5 shows sample results of running LOOKIN.BAT for the theoretical example above. Note that the name Albert appears in only the QUIKNOTE.LET file.

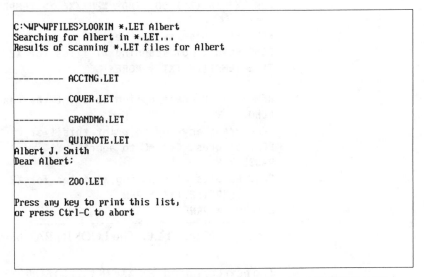

```
C:\WP\WPFILES>LOOKIN *.LET Albert
Searching for Albert in *.LET...
Results of scanning *.LET files for Albert


----------- ACCTNG.LET

----------- COVER.LET

----------- GRANDMA.LET

----------- QUIKNOTE.LET
Albert J. Smith
Dear Albert:

----------- ZOO.LET

Press any key to print this list,
or press Ctrl-C to abort
```

Figure 14.5. Sample results of a search with LOOKIN.BAT.

Figure 14.6 shows the entire LOOKIN.BAT batch file. Use the usual Edlin techniques to create LOOKIN.BAT on your own system.

LOOKIN.BAT also offers some unique features that you have not seen in previous batch files. Therefore, let's discuss the purpose of each command in LOOKIN.BAT (excluding the REM comment lines). For the purposes of example, let's assume that you executed LOOKIN.BAT with the command LOOKIN *.LET Albert.

First, the command IF EXIST TEMPFILE.TXT ERASE TEMPFILE.TXT erases the file named TEMPFILE.TXT from the current directory (if it exists). As you will see, LOOKIN.BAT channels its output to this file so that you later have the option of printing the results of LOOKIN.BAT after viewing them on the screen.

Next, the command ECHO Searching for %2 in %1 displays a message that lets you know what operation is taking place. In this example, the message on the screen would be Searching for Albert in *.LET.

```
@ECHO OFF
REM *********************** LOOKIN.BAT
REM Searches multiple text files for a word.
REM ----- %1 is file(s) to be searched,
REM ----- %2 is word to search for

REM ----- Erase TEMPFILE.TXT if it exists.
IF EXIST TEMPFILE.TXT ERASE TEMPFILE.TXT

REM ----- Search files with FIND,
REM ----- redirect output to TEMPFILE.TXT.
ECHO Searching for %2 in %1...
FOR %%c IN (%1) DO FIND "%2" %%c >> TEMPFILE.TXT

REM ----- Display the results.
ECHO Results of scanning %1 files for %2
TYPE TEMPFILE.TXT | MORE

REM ----- Present option to print the results.
ECHO.
ECHO Press any key to print this list,
ECHO or press Ctrl-C to abort
PAUSE > NUL
ECHO Results of scanning %1 files for %2 > PRN
TYPE TEMPFILE.TXT > PRN
ECHO ^L > PRN
```

Figure 14.6. The LOOKIN.BAT batch file.

The next command, `FOR %%c IN (%1) DO FIND "%2" %%c >> TEMPFILE.TXT`, executes the command `FIND "%2"` every time a new file name matches the *.LET ambiguous file name. For example, if the first file to be searched is APRIL90.LET, this command becomes `FIND "Albert" APRIL90.LET`. The >> TEMPFILE.TXT portion of the command channels the output to the TEMPFILE.TXT file without erasing existing text in TEMPFILE.TXT. This loop is repeated until all *.LET files have been searched.

The next command, `ECHO Results of scanning %1 files for %2`, displays a message on the screen: in this example, it is `Results of scanning *.LET files for Albert`. Then the command `TYPE TEMPFILE.TXT | MORE` displays the results of the search, which are stored in the file TEMPFILE.TXT. The | MORE option pauses the display after each screenful of information and waits for a keypress.

The `ECHO.` command prints a blank line on the screen. The next two ECHO commands display the message:

```
Press any key to print this list,
or press Ctrl-C to abort
```

The PAUSE > NUL command pauses without displaying a message. Pressing Ctrl-C during this pause terminates batch file execution; pressing another key resumes execution at the next command.

If you do not press Ctrl-C to cancel the operation, the next three commands send the message Results of scanning *.LET files for Albert and the contents of the TEMPFILE.TXT to the printer. The last command, ECHO ^L > PRN, then ejects the page from the printer. (Remember, ^L is entered by pressing Ctrl-L). You can omit this last command if you are not using a laser printer.

Tips for Using LOOKIN.BAT

LOOKIN.BAT can search any file, or group of files, in any directory for any single word. Remember, however, that because it uses the DOS FIND command to perform this search, the command is *case-sensitive*. That is, the command LOOKIN PHONES.TXT BAKER would *not* find Baker. (An improved version of LOOKIN.BAT, named LOOKIN2.BAT and presented later in this chapter, offers a way around this limitation.)

Also, if you use LOOKIN.BAT to search files that you created with a word processor, the results might not be accurate. The reason for this is that the word processor may use formatting codes that change the word that FIND is looking for. If in doubt, use the TYPE command to view the contents of your word processing file to see how it is stored.

If your word processor changes the last character of every word, you should use LOOKIN.BAT to search for all the characters in a word except for the last. For example, suppose you want to search through a group of files with the extension .DOC for the word "banana". However, you created these .DOC files with WordStar, which alters the last character of many words in a document. Entering the command LOOKIN *.DOC banan would yield more accurate results than the command LOOKIN *.DOC banana.

LOOKIN.BAT displays only the "Searching . . . " message while the search is taking place. Depending on the speed of your computer and the amount of text being searched, the delay might be anywhere from a few seconds to several minutes. In most cases, however, the search probably will be surprisingly fast.

COUNTIN.BAT: A Variation of LOOKIN.BAT

LOOKIN.BAT displays the name of every file searched and the lines of text in each file that contain the word you are looking for. As an alternative, you can create COUNTIN.BAT, which merely displays the names of files that contain the word you are looking for and the number of times the word appears in that file.

This can be a useful command in many situations. For example, let's assume that I've stored each chapter for a book in files named CHAP1.TXT,

CHAP2.TXT, CHAP3.TXT, and so on. If I want to see which chapter first introduced the term "reboot," I merely enter the command `COUNTIN CHAP*.TXT reboot`. The results of this search, shown in Figure 14.7, reveal that the word "reboot" is first mentioned in Chapter 3 (CHAP3.TXT). (I can also discover which other chapters contain that word.)

```
C:\WP\WPFILES>COUNTIN *.TXT reboot
Counting for "reboot" in *.TXT files
"reboot" appears in the following *.TXT files

---------- CHAP3.TXT: 2
---------- CHAP5.TXT: 10
---------- CHAP10.TXT: 1

Press any key to print this list,
or press Ctrl-C to abort
```

Figure 14.7. Results of the command
`COUNTIN *.TXT reboot`.

If you already created LOOKIN.BAT, use it as a starting point for developing COUNTIN.BAT, because the two batch files are very similar. To do so, at the command prompt, enter the command `COPY LOOKIN.BAT COUNTIN.BAT`. Then, enter the command `EDLIN COUNTIN.BAT`. Now, you need to change only a few lines, rather than create an entirely new file. Figure 14.8 shows the complete COUNTIN.BAT file.

Note that the FIND command in the line that begins `FOR %%C` . . . now uses the /C switch. This switch tells the FIND command to count, rather than display, the words being searched for.

The two lines that begin with TYPE commands have been changed to `TYPE TEMPFILE.TXT | FIND "-" | FIND /V " 0" | MORE`. The TYPE command sends the results of the search (stored in TEMPFILE.TXT) to the filters that follow the command. The first filter, FIND "-", limits the output to those lines that begin with a hyphen, because these are the only lines that contain file names (as you can see in Figure 14.7).

That output is than passed through the second filter, FIND /V " 0", which filters out all lines that contain a zero preceded by a blank space. (The leading blank space is included so that only lines with an exact count of zero are excluded, but not lines that contain a zero, such as those with a count of 10 or 20, or lines with a file name like SPRING90.TXT). The final

```
@ECHO OFF
REM ************************ COUNTIN.BAT
REM Searches multiple text files for a word.
REM ----- %1 is file(s) to be searched,
REM ----- %2 is word to search for

REM ----- Erase TEMPFILE.TXT if it exists.
IF EXIST TEMPFILE.TXT ERASE TEMPFILE.TXT

REM ----- Search files with FIND /C
REM ----- redirect output to TEMPFILE.TXT.
ECHO Counting for "%2" in %1 files
FOR %%c IN (%1) DO FIND /C "%2" %%c >> TEMPFILE.TXT

REM ----- Display the results.
ECHO "%2" appears in the following %1 files
TYPE TEMPFILE.TXT | FIND "-" | FIND /V " 0" | MORE

REM ----- Present option to print the results.
ECHO
ECHO Press any key to print this list,
ECHO or press Ctrl-C to abort
PAUSE > NUL
ECHO "%2" appears in the following %1 files > PRN
TYPE TEMPFILE.TXT | FIND "-" | FIND /V " 0" > PRN
ECHO ^L > PRN
```

Figure 14.8. The COUNTIN.BAT batch file.

output is passed through the MORE filter, which pauses the screen display every 24 lines.

A few messages and comments have also been altered slightly. After making your changes, save your work and exit Edlin in the usual manner. The basic technique for using COUNTIN.BAT is identical to that for using LOOKIN.BAT. The only difference is the format of the displayed results.

Passing Multiple Parameters to DOS Commands

Looping is also valuable for passing multiple parameters to DOS commands that usually accept only a single parameter. For example, if you want to erase the files APPLE.TXT, BANANA.DOC, and CHERRY.LET using the DOS ERASE command, you must enter three separate commands:

```
ERASE APPLE.TXT
ERASE BANANA.DOC
ERASE CHERRY.LET
```

However, the next batch file, MERASE.BAT (Multiple ERASE), lets you specify as many as nine files to erase—and any of those file names can contain wildcard characters. To erase the three files above using MERASE, you need only enter the command:

```
MERASE APPLE.TXT BANANA.DOC CHERRY.LET
```

Figure 14.9 shows the complete MERASE.BAT file.

```
@ECHO OFF
REM ************************ MERASE.BAT
REM Accepts as many as nine file names to erase.
FOR %%c IN (%1 %2 %3 %4 %5 %6 %7 %8 %9) DO IF NOT %%c. == .
    ERASE %%c
```

Figure 14.9. The MERASE.BAT batch file.

To demonstrate how the batch file works, let's assume that you created it and then entered the command MERASE APPLE.TXT BANANA.DOC CHERRY.LET to erase three files. This command stores the following values in the % variables:

%1= APPLE.TXT

%2= BANANA.DOC

%3= CHERRY.LET

%4 through %9 are empty (blank)

In the first pass through the loop, %%c assumes the value of %1, or APPLE.TXT in this example. Therefore, the command IF NOT %%c. == . ERASE %%c expands to IF NOT APPLE.TXT. == . THEN ERASE APPLE.TXT. Because APPLE.TXT and . are *not* the same, the command ERASE APPLE.TXT is executed, and the file is erased.

During the next pass through the loop, %%c takes the value of %2, or BANANA.DOC. Once again, the IF test proves true, so the ERASE BANANA.DOC command is executed, and the BANANA.DOC file is erased. In the third pass through the loop, %%c assumes the value of %3, or CHERRY.LET. Again, the IF test proves true, and CHERRY.LET is erased.

During the fourth pass through the loop, %%c takes the value of %4, which is empty. In this case, the command IF NOT %%c. == . proves false (because %%c. *does* equal .), so the ERASE command is ignored. In fact, in all remaining passes through the loop, the IF NOT command proves false; therefore, no more files are erased and the batch file ends, returning control to the command prompt.

There are no built-in safety features in this batch file: It is as immediate in its erasing as the regular DOS ERASE command. However, DOS 4 users can add the /P switch to the right of the ERASE %%c command. This forces the ERASE command to pause and ask for permission before deleting each file. Figure 14.10 shows this safer version of MERASE.BAT.

```
@ECHO OFF
REM ********************** MERASE.BAT
REM Accepts as many as nine file names to erase.
FOR %%c IN (%1 %2 %3 %4 %5 %6 %7 %8 %9) DO IF NOT %%c. == .
   ERASE %%c /P
```

Figure 14.10. Safer version of MERASE.BAT (works only with DOS 4).

You can use this general looping technique to pass up to nine parameters to any DOS command. However, it's a little trickier passing multiple parameters to a command that requires two or more parameters, such as COPY. For example, if you try to create a batch file named MCOPY that can accept multiple file names, as in the command:

```
MCOPY LETTER.TXT MYFILE.DOC A:
```

and also the command:

```
MCOPY APPLE.TXT BANANA.DOC QTRL_90.WKS ABC.LET A:
```

you might think you will have a difficult time. The reason being that in the first command, the destination (A:) is the third parameter (%3), but in the second command, the destination is the fifth parameter (%5). However, there is a simple solution to this problem. If you use a syntax that places the destination first, your batch file can always "assume" that the destination is %1.

For example, you can create a batch file named COPYTO.BAT that accepts as many as eight file names to copy, using the general syntax:

```
COPYTO destination file1 file...file8
```

where any of the eight file names can contain wildcards. That is, you could enter the command:

```
COPYTO A: *.TXT *.LET *.DOC *.BAK LETTER?.TXT
```

where A: is the destination, and the rest are file names to be copied to drive A:. Or, you could enter the command:

```
COPYTO A: APPLE.TXT BANANA.DOC CHERRY.LET
```

to copy all the specified files to drive A:.

Figure 14.11 shows the COPYTO.BAT batch file. It works on the same basic principle that MERASE.BAT does; however, the %1 variable is *not* included in the list of items for the loop command. The FOR loop processes *only* the file names (%2 through %9), while the destination (%1) is repeatedly used as the destination in the COPY command.

```
@ECHO OFF
REM ************************ COPYTO.BAT
REM Accepts as many as eight file names to copy.
REM %1 is destination, %2 through %9 are file names.
FOR %%c IN (%2 %3 %4 %5 %6 %7 %8 %9) DO IF NOT %%c. == .
    COPY %%c %1
```

Figure 14.11. The COPYTO.BAT batch file.

You can use this looping technique to pass multiple parameters to a batch file as well. However, this technique is a little different, and it also varies with different versions of DOS, as the next section explains.

Passing Control from One Batch File to Another

Because batch files are essentially customized DOS commands, they can be used like any other DOS command, either at the command prompt or in a batch file. In all versions of DOS, one batch file can pass control to another batch file; but in doing so, the first batch file relinquishes all control to the second batch file, and any additional commands in the first batch file are not executed. Let's look at a simple example.

The following BAT1.BAT file contains two ECHO commands. However, note that a command between them executes a batch file named BAT2.BAT:

```
@ECHO OFF
REM ******* BAT1.BAT
ECHO I am the first line in BAT1.BAT
BAT2
ECHO I am the last line in BAT1.BAT
```

BAT2.BAT, shown below, contains one ECHO command:

```
@ECHO OFF
REM ******* BAT2.BAT
ECHO      I am the only line in BAT2.BAT
```

If you were to create both of these batch files and then enter the command BAT1, your screen would display the following:

```
I am the first line in BAT1.BAT
    I am the only line in BAT2.BAT
```

As you can see, the second ECHO command in BAT1.BAT was never executed. That's because after the BAT2 command was executed, all control passed to BAT2.BAT. When BAT2.BAT finished its job, all execution stopped.

If you are using a version of DOS prior to 3.3, replace the CALL command with COMMAND /C in the sample batch files that follow. Be sure to follow the /C with a blank space.

With DOS versions 3.3 and later, you can have one batch file *call* another, so that when the second batch file finishes, it returns control to the first. That way, execution resumes normally, and the first batch file can finish executing its remaining commands. To use this technique, you use the CALL command.

For example, look at the following BAT1.BAT file. Notice that the only difference between this version and the previous version is that BAT1.BAT uses the command CALL BAT2, rather than simply BAT2, to pass control to the BAT2.BAT batch file:

```
@ECHO OFF
REM ****** BAT1.BAT
ECHO I am the first line in BAT1.BAT
CALL BAT2
ECHO I am the last line in BAT1.BAT
```

With this version of BAT1.BAT, entering the command BAT1 produces these messages on the screen:

```
I am the first line in BAT1.BAT
    I am the only line in BAT2.BAT
I am the last line in BAT1.BAT
```

Notice, in this example, when BAT2.BAT finished its job, it *returned* control to BAT1.BAT, and execution resumed normally at the first command beneath the CALL BAT2 command. (Versions of DOS prior to 3.3 need to use the command COMMAND /C BAT2 in place of CALL BAT2 to achieve the same result.)

This latter technique lets you easily create batch files that use other batch files. When used in conjunction with the FOR command, CALL can pass multiple parameters to batch files that normally accept only a fixed number of parameters.

For example, the previously described MOVE.BAT batch file accepts only two parameters—the source of the move and the destination of the move. Now, let's couple this batch file with a similar batch file named MOVETO.BAT, which uses this different syntax:

```
MOVETO destination file1 file2...file8
```

where *destination* is the drive or directory to which files are being moved and *file1 file2...file8* represents as many as eight file names to be moved. Therefore, this single command:

```
MOVETO C:\WP\WPFILES *.TXT *.DOC *.LET
```

moves all .TXT, .DOC, and .LET files from the current directory to the WP\WPFILES directory.

The command:

```
MOVETO A: *.BAK LETTER.TXT NOTE.TXT JUNE90.WKS
```

moves all .BAK files, plus the files LETTER.TXT, NOTE.TXT, and JUNE90.TXT, to drive A:. Again, you can list as many as eight file names, and any or all of those names can contain wildcard characters.

The real beauty of this technique is that you don't even need to modify the existing MOVE.BAT batch file to use it. Instead, you can call it from the MOVETO.BAT batch file and still get all the benefits of the safety features it offers. Figure 14.12 shows the MOVETO.BAT batch file.

```
@ECHO OFF
REM *********************** MOVETO.BAT
REM Moves multiple files
REM %1 is destination, %2 through %9 are file names.

FOR %%c IN (%2 %3 %4 %5 %6 %7 %8) DO IF NOT %%c. == . MOVE
    %%c %1
```

Figure 14.12. The MOVETO.BAT batch file.

Basically, MOVETO.BAT uses the same technique to pass multiple parameters that COPYTO.BAT used. The only real difference is the use of the CALL command in the FOR loop.

Now, let's see how MOVETO.BAT does its job. The following discussion assumes that you enter the command `MOVETO \WP\WPFILES APPLE.TXT BANANA.TXT CHERRY.TXT`.

First, the %variables immediately receive these values:

%1= \WP\WPFILES

%2= APPLE.TXT

%3= BANANA.TXT

%4= CHERRY.TXT

%5 through %9 are blank

On the first pass through the loop, %%c is replaced with %2, which is APPLE.TXT. The command `IF NOT %%c. == .` proves true, so the command

CALL MOVE %%c %1 becomes CALL MOVE APPLE.TXT \WP\WPFILES. This executes the MOVE command with these parameters, and MOVE.BAT moves the file.

When control returns to MOVETO.BAT, the next pass through the loop is executed, and %%c takes the value of %3, which is BANANA.TXT. The IF NOT %%c. ==. test proves true, so the command expands to CALL MOVE BANANA.TXT \WP\WPFILES. Once again, MOVE.BAT moves the file, and returns control to MOVETO.BAT.

On the next pass through the loop, %%c takes on the value of %4, which is CHERRY.TXT. Once again, the IF test proves true, the command CALL MOVE CHERRY.TXT \WP\WPFILES is executed, and MOVE.BAT moves the file. Again, it returns control to MOVETO.BAT.

During the next pass through the loop, %%c assumes the value of %5, which is empty. The test IF NOT %%c. ==. proves false in this case, so the CALL MOVE command is not executed. In fact, because all remaining %variables are empty, the CALL MOVE command is never again executed. After the last pass through the loop, execution ends and control returns to the command prompt.

Passing More Than Nine Parameters

As mentioned earlier, you can use up to nine %variables (%1 through %9) in a batch file. However, you can pass more than nine parameters to a batch file and gain access to those above %9 by *shifting* all other parameters to the left (that is, to a smaller %variable number). The command to shift parameters is (not surprisingly) SHIFT.

The SHIFT command is much different than the FOR . . . IN . . . DO looping method you used in previous examples to pass multiple parameters to a command. So let's stop here and discuss SHIFT in its own light.

Suppose you created a batch file named SAMPLE.BAT, and entered the following command to execute the batch file:

SAMPLE A B C D E F G H I J K

The first nine %variables would receive the following values:

%1 = A
%2 = B
%3 = C
%4 = D
%5 = E
%6 = F
%7 = G

%8 = H

%9 = I

The SHIFT command shifts all the parameters from their current positions to the next lower-numbered %variable. For example, if SAMPLE.BAT contained a SHIFT command, after that command was executed, the %variables would contain:

%1 = B

%2 = C

%3 = D

%4 = E

%5 = F

%6 = G

%7 = H

%8 = I

%9 = J

Executing the SHIFT command again would have this effect:

%1 = C

%2 = D

%3 = E

%4 = F

%5 = G

%6 = H

%7 = I

%8 = J

%9 = K

The next SHIFT command would result in the following:

%1 = D

%2 = E

%3 = F

%4 = G

%5 = H

%6 = I

%7 = J

%8 = K

%9 =

Notice that because there were no additional parameters on the command line, %9 is now blank. Each time a SHIFT command is executed in the future, the variables continue to be shifted, and the "blanks" follow accordingly. If you executed SHIFT enough times, all the % variables would eventually be empty.

To use the SHIFT command effectively, you usually couple it with the decision-making power of the IF command and the branching ability of the GOTO command. Let's look at an example of this by creating a modified version of the LOOKIN.BAT batch file, named LOOKIN2.BAT, that can accept any number of parameters.

In its current state, LOOKIN.BAT can search for only one word. Because LOOKIN.BAT is case-sensitive, a truly thorough search for all occurrences of a word such as "tomato" would require at least three commands, as follows:

```
LOOKIN *.TXT tomato
LOOKIN *.TXT Tomato
LOOKIN *.TXT TOMATO
```

With LOOKIN2.BAT, you could accomplish this same goal by entering the single command:

```
LOOKIN2 *.TXT tomato Tomato TOMATO
```

In fact, you could search for any number of words using this same basic syntax.

Figure 14.13 shows the LOOKIN2.BAT batch file. Many of the commands in LOOKIN2.BAT are identical to the commands in LOOKIN.BAT. This section will focus on those commands that are unique to LOOKIN2.BAT.

To describe the basic technique that LOOKIN2.BAT uses to search for multiple words, let's assume that you execute the batch file with the command `LOOKIN2 *.TXT Apple Banana Cherry`. This sets up the %variables as follows:

> %1= *.TXT
> %2= Apple
> %3= Banana
> %4= Cherry
> %5 through %9 are blank

First, the command `SET FileName=%1` stores the first parameter (for example, *.TXT) in the environment, using the variable name FileName. This ensures that if a later SHIFT command erases the "*.TXT" stored in %1 from the list of parameters, the batch file can still gain access to "*.TXT".

The maximum number of parameters that you can pass to a batch file is limited by the maximum allowable length of any DOS command, which is 127 characters.

```
@ECHO OFF
REM ********************** LOOKIN2.BAT
REM Searches multiple text files for multiple words.
REM ----- %1 is file(s) to be searched,
REM ----- %2 is word to search for

REM ----- Erase TEMPFILE.TXT if it exists.
IF EXIST TEMPFILE.TXT ERASE TEMPFILE.TXT

REM Put %1 in the environment for future use.
SET FileName=%1

REM ----- Search files with FIND,
REM ----- redirect output to TEMPFILE.TXT
:NextWord
ECHO Searching for %2 in %FileName%...
ECHO Search for %2 in %FileName% >> TEMPFILE.TXT
FOR %%c IN (%FileName%) DO FIND "%2" %%c >> TEMPFILE.TXT

REM Store a form-feed in TEMPFILE.TXT
ECHO ^L >> TEMPFILE.TXT

REM Shift and repeat search if more words to search for.
SHIFT
IF NOT %2. == . GOTO NextWord

REM ----- Clean up the environment.
REM ----- Display the results.
SET FileName=
TYPE TEMPFILE.TXT | MORE

REM ----- Present option to print the results.
ECHO
ECHO Press any key to print this list,
ECHO or press Ctrl-C, then Y, to abort
PAUSE > NUL
TYPE TEMPFILE.TXT > PRN
```

Figure 14.13. The LOOKIN2.BAT batch file.

:NextWord is a label that marks the beginning of the commands used for printing messages and performing the search. The next two ECHO commands display messages: The first displays its message on the screen; the second sends its message to the TEMPFILE.TXT file, where it later will be displayed as a heading for TEMPFILE.TXT. Note that both commands use %FileName% to display *.TXT, rather than %1. So, on the first search, the message displayed on the screen is:

```
Searching for Apple in *.TXT
```

The command `FOR %%c IN (%FileName%) DO FIND "%2" %%c >>`
`TEMPFILE.TXT` searches all files that match the file name *.TXT for the
word currently stored in %2. This is similar to the same command in
LOOKIN.BAT, but %FileName% is used in place of %1 so that *.TXT is
taken from the environment. This loop searches all .TXT files for the word
"Apple" and then stores the results in TEMPFILE.TXT.

The next command, `ECHO ^L >> TEMPFILE.TXT`, sends a form-feed to
TEMPFILE.TXT. (Remember, press Ctrl-L to type ^L when creating the
batch file.) This form-feed ejects the paper from the printer after the batch
file prints the contents of TEMPFILE.TXT. This ensures that the results of
each word-search start printing on a new page.

Next, the command `SHIFT` shifts all parameters to the left (or to the
next lower number). Therefore, the %variables now contain the following
values:

%1= Apple

%2= Banana

%3= Cherry

%4=

The next command, `IF NOT %2. == . GOTO NextWord`, checks to see if %2
is blank. In this example, %2 currently contains the word "Banana," so the
command `GOTO NextWord` is executed, and control branches to the
:NextWord label.

The commands below :NextWord are executed, but because %2 now
contains "Banana" (not "Apple"), the message, heading, and FIND search
are adjusted accordingly. For example, the command `ECHO Searching for`
`%2 in %FileName%` now displays the message:

```
Searching for Banana in *.TXT
```

After the FOR loop searches the *.TXT files for the word Banana and
stores the results in the TEMPFILE.TXT file, the SHIFT command is executed again. Now the %variables contain:

%1= Banana

%2= Cherry

%3=

%4=

The command `IF NOT %2. == . GOTO NewWord` once again passes control
up to the :NewWord label, and once again the message, heading, and
search are updated. However, %2 now equals "Cherry," and that is the

word that is searched for. The command `ECHO Searching for %2 in %FileName%` now displays the following message on the screen:

```
Searching for Cherry in *.TXT
```

Once again, after completing the search for the word "Cherry," the `SWITCH` command is executed. Now the %variables contain:

%1= Cherry

%2=

%3=

%4=

This time, the command `IF NOT %2. == . GOTO NewWord` does *not* pass control to the :NewWord label, because %2 *is* empty. So processing resumes with the next command in the batch file.

The command `SET FileName=` sets the FileName variable to "nothing" and thus removes it from the environment. Then, the command `TYPE TEMPFILE.TXT | MORE` displays the results of the searches, all of which have been stored in the TEMPFILE.TXT. The remaining commands print the TEMPFILE.TXT file, exactly as they did in the original LOOKIN.BAT batch file.

Including Escape Sequences in Batch Files

Many printers require that you send Escape-key sequences to activate special features. For example, the Hewlett-Packard LaserJet printers use the escape key sequences shown in Table 14.1 to activate various printing modes. The table signifies the Escape key character as {ESC}, as your printer manual might.

Table 14.1. Escape-key codes that control the LaserJet printer.

Print Mode	Escape Sequence
Portrait (normal)	{ESC}E{ESC}&l0O
Landscape	{ESC}E{ESC}&l1O
Compressed Portrait	{ESC}E{ESC}&l0O{ESC}&k2S
Compressed Landscape	{ESC}E{ESC}&l1O{ESC}&k2S
Reset to default mode	{ESC}E

Note that the characters used for portrait modes (l0O) are a lowercase "l," the number zero, and an uppercase letter "O". The characters used for

Different types of printers require different codes to activate their features; check your printer manual for a complete list of these codes.

If you use an editor other than Edlin, refer to that program's documentation for instructions on how to enter the Escape character into a file.

the landscape modes (lOO) are a lowercase letter "l," the number 1, and an uppercase letter "O".

If you want your batch file to send Escape-character sequences to the printer, you might have trouble typing them into your batch file. For example, if you use the Edlin editor, the moment you press the Esc key, Edlin assumes that you want to cancel what you've typed, and it displays a backslash character.

If you are using Edlin, you must press Ctrl-V, and then release both keys. Then, type a left square bracket ([). The characters initially appear on your screen as ^V[. Note that even though ^V[appears to be several characters, DOS interprets it as a single Escape-key character. Therefore, if you want to send to your printer an Escape key character followed by a [character, first press Ctrl-V, then press [to signify the Escape key, and then type [for the bracket. These appear on your screen as ^V[[.

The ^V symbol appears on the screen only when you first type the line. In later versions of DOS (from 3.1 up), when you use the L command to list the file in Edlin, the letter V no longer is displayed. So what originally appeared as ^V[later appears as ^[. (At the risk of further confusing the issue, I must warn you that some commands, such as TYPE, might not display the ^V characters when displaying the Esc character.)

Creating JETSET.BAT

This section shows you how to create a batch file named JETSET.BAT that allows you to set the print mode for a LaserJet printer. Figure 14.14 shows the entire JETSET.BAT file, as it appears when displayed by Edlin (in a version of DOS that hides the "V" in the ^V[sequence). Note that the line numbers are those displayed by Edlin—do not type in these line numbers yourself. Because this is a tricky batch file to type, use the following steps to get started:

1. Enter the command `EDLIN JETSET.BAT` at the command prompt, and press Enter.

2. Type i and press Enter to start inserting text.

3. Type the first 23 lines exactly as shown in the Figure. (When you come to a blank line, merely press Enter.)

4. To enter line 24, type `IF %1. == P. ECHO` and then press the Spacebar. Press Ctrl-V, release both keys, then type `[E`.

5. Press Ctrl-V again, release both keys, and type `[&lOO > PRN` (that's the lowercase letter "l", followed by the number 0, followed by an uppercase letter "O", followed by a blank space and > PRN.) Your screen now displays this as `^V[E^V[&lOO > PRN`. Press Enter.

6. To enter line 25, press the F2 key; then, type the letter P (uppercase). Type a lowercase p and then press the F3 key and Enter.

```
 1: @ECHO OFF
 2: REM *********************** JETSET.BAT
 3: REM -- Sends printer control codes to a Laserjet.
 4:
 5: REM ----- Make sure parameter passed is valid.
 6: FOR %%c IN (P p L l CP cp CL cl) DO IF %1. == %%c. GOTO Ok
 7:
 8: REM -- If parameter matches none of items checked in loop
 9: REM -- above, there must be an error. Display help below.
10:
11: ECHO JETSET requires one of the following codes:
12: ECHO.
13: ECHO     P  Portrait (normal)
14: ECHO      L Landscape
15: ECHO     CP Compressed Portrait
16: ECHO     CL Compressed Landscape
17: ECHO.
18: ECHO Example: For Compressed Landscape mode, enter JETSET CL
19: ECHO.
20: GOTO End
21:
22: REM Valid parameter was entered; send code to printer.
23: :Ok
24: IF %1. == P. ECHO ^[E^[&l0O > PRN
25: IF %1. == p. ECHO ^[E^[&l0O > PRN
26: IF %1. == CP. ECHO ^[E^[&l0O^[&k2S > PRN
27: IF %1. == cp. ECHO ^[E^[&l0O^[&k2S > PRN
28: IF %1. == L. ECHO ^[E^[&l1O > PRN
29: IF %1. == l. ECHO ^[E^[&l1O > PRN
30: IF %1. == CL. ECHO ^[E^[&l1O^[&k2S > PRN
31: IF %1. == cl. ECHO ^[E^[&l1O^[&k2S > PRN
32:
33: REM ----- Ask about performing a test to verify success.
34: ECHO.
35: ECHO Printer set -- press any key to verify,
36: ECHO or Ctrl-C, then Y, to exit...
37: PAUSE > NUL
38:
39: REM -- Proceed with test if Ctrl-C not pressed
40: ECHO This is a test. > PRN
41: ECHO ^L > PRN
42:
43: ECHO Remember that other programs might set the
44: ECHO printer back to Portrait (normal) mode!
45: :End
```

Figure 14.14. The JETSET.BAT batch file.

7. To enter line 26, press the F2 key; then, type the lowercase p. Type an uppercase C, press the Ins (or Insert key) once, and then type an uppercase P. Press the F3 key, and then press the Backspace key six times. Press Ctrl-V and release both keys; then, type `[&k2S > PRN` and press Enter.

You should be able to type the rest of the lines on your own now. Remember, you can press → to repeat any character from the preceding line, or you use the F2 key followed by a *character* to repeat lines up to, but excluding, that *character*. Be sure to pay close attention to the differences between the lowercase "l" letter and number 1, and to the uppercase "O" letter and the number 0.

Line 41 must be entered by typing `ECHO` followed by a blank space, a press of the Ctrl-L key, another blank space, and then `> PRN`. After you have typed the entire batch file, press Ctrl-C; then, type `E` and press Enter to save your work and return to the command prompt.

Using JETSET.BAT

Once you create JETSET.BAT, you can select a print mode for the LaserJet simply by entering the command JETSET followed by a one- or two-letter code (in upper- or lowercase letters) as follows:

JETSET P   Switches to Portrait mode (normal)

JETSET L   Switches to Landscape (horizontal) mode

JETSET CP   Switches to Compressed Portrait mode

JETSET CL   Switches to Compressed Landscape mode

If you enter the command JETSET without a code (or with an invalid code), the screen displays the following help message:

```
JETSET requires one of the following codes:

    P   Portrait (normal)
    L   Landscape
   CP   Compressed Portrait
   CL   Compressed Landscape

Example: For Compressed Landscape mode, enter JETSET CL
```

When you enter a valid code, JETSET displays the following message:

```
Printer set -- press any key to verify,
or Ctrl-C, then Y, to exit...
```

If you press any key other than Ctrl-C (or Ctrl-Break), JetSet sends the line This is a test to the printer and then ejects the page. This lets you verify that the proper mode has been set. If you press Ctrl-C, the newly selected print mode stays in effect, but the test sentence is not printed.

If you proceed with the test, the screen also displays the reminder message:

```
Remember that other programs might set the
printer back to Portrait (normal) mode!
```

You should test each of the possible codes that JETSET offers. If a particular command, such as JETSET CL, does not set the correct mode for your printer, you might have an error in the escape sequence in JETSET.BAT. Use Edlin to make corrections, always referring to Figure 14.14 as a guide.

How JETSET.BAT Works

When you first run JETSET.BAT, the %1 variable takes the value of the parameter entered next to the JETSET command. The command FOR %%c IN (P p L l CP cp CL cl) DO IF %1. == %%c. GOTO Ok compares %1 to each acceptable option (both uppercase and lowercase). If the %1 parameter matches one of the acceptable options, the GOTO command passes control to the label :Ok.

If the %1 variable does *not* match one of the acceptable options, the help messages beneath the FOR loop (lines 11 through 19 in Figure 14.14) are displayed instead. After the help messages are displayed, the GOTO End command skips the IF commands that send escape sequences to the printer, and therefore the print mode is not altered.

Lines 24 through 31 compare %1 to each acceptable option. When an IF command finds a match between %1 and an acceptable option, the ECHO command sends the appropriate escape sequence to the printer (that is, > PRN). Lines 34 through 37 present the message that explains the optional test, and then execution waits for a keypress. If you do not press Ctrl-C, line 40 sends a simple sentence to the printer, and line 41 ejects the page from the printer. Lines 43 and 44 display the reminder message on the screen.

Accessing Batch Files from the Shell

If you use the DOS 4 Shell, you learned in Chapter 11 how to create new groups in the Shell and how to access programs from a group. You can use those same basic techniques to create a group screen for your batch files. However, there is a difference between running programs and running batch files from the Shell. You must always use the CALL command to execute a batch file from the Shell. The reason for this is that the Shell itself is run from a batch file (named DOSSHELL.BAT). If you do not use the CALL command to execute a separate batch file, the file will not return control to the DOS Shell when it finishes.

Figure 14.15 shows the Main Group screen with the addition of a new group called Custom Utilities.... Figure 14.16 shows an example of how you could design the Custom Utilities . . . group screen. Note that the options on this screen refer to the batch files created in this and the previous chapter.

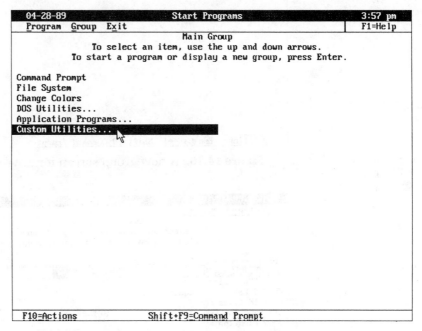

Figure 14.15. DOS Shell Main Group with a
new group added.

Figure 14.17 shows the Change Program dialog box for the JETSET printer mode option. The command you must use to run the JETSET.BAT batch file is CALL JETSET. The entire startup sequence for JETSET.BAT follows (but, remember to enter it as one long line in the Commands box):

```
CALL JETSET[/T"Run JETSET"
            /I"Enter mode (P, L, CP, or CL)"
            /P"Mode... "]
∥PAUSE
```

The startup sequence assumes that the directory that contains JETSET.BAT is listed in the current PATH setting. Therefore, the startup sequence does not change directories before running JETSET.

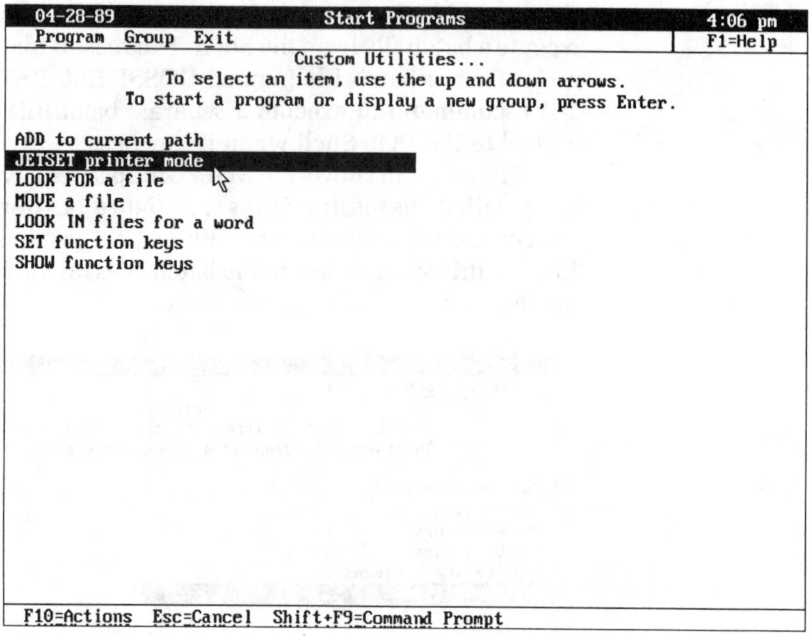

```
┌─────────────────────────────────────────────────────────────────┐
│ 04-28-89              Start Programs                    4:06 pm   │
│ Program  Group  Exit                                    F1=Help   │
│                    Custom Utilities...                            │
│           To select an item, use the up and down arrows.          │
│         To start a program or display a new group, press Enter.   │
│                                                                   │
│ ADD to current path                                               │
│ JETSET printer mode                                               │
│ LOOK FOR a file          ⌐                                        │
│ MOVE a file                                                       │
│ LOOK IN files for a word                                          │
│ SET function keys                                                 │
│ SHOW function keys                                                │
│                                                                   │
│                                                                   │
│                                                                   │
│                                                                   │
│                                                                   │
│                                                                   │
│                                                                   │
│                                                                   │
│ F10=Actions  Esc=Cancel  Shift+F9=Command Prompt                  │
└─────────────────────────────────────────────────────────────────┘
```

Figure 14.16. A new group screen for accessing batch files.

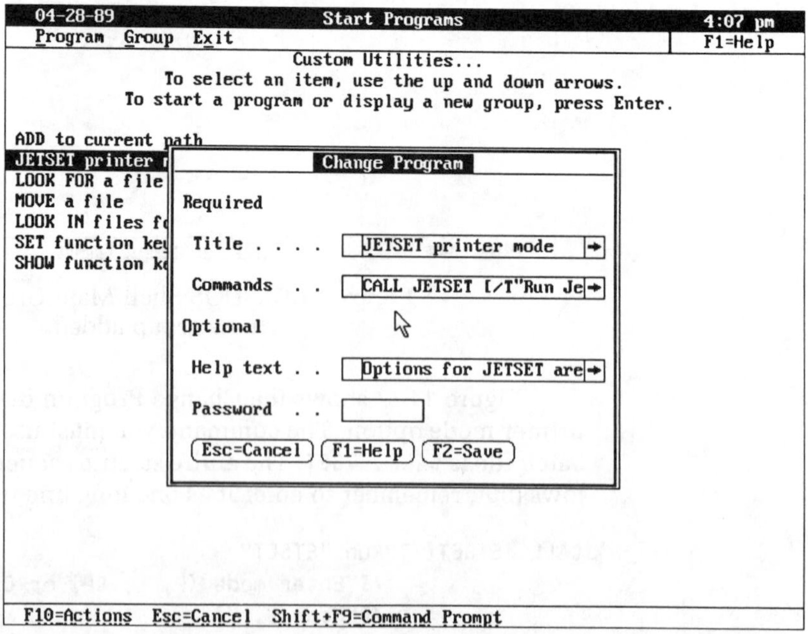

```
┌─────────────────────────────────────────────────────────────────┐
│ 04-28-89              Start Programs                    4:07 pm   │
│ Program  Group  Exit                                    F1=Help   │
│                    Custom Utilities...                            │
│           To select an item, use the up and down arrows.          │
│         To start a program or display a new group, press Enter.   │
│                                                                   │
│ ADD to current path                                               │
│ JETSET printer ┌──────────Change Program──────────┐               │
│ LOOK FOR a file│                                   │               │
│ MOVE a file    │ Required                          │               │
│ LOOK IN files f│                                   │               │
│ SET function ke│ Title . . . .  │JETSET printer mode│→│            │
│ SHOW function k│                                   │               │
│                │ Commands  . .  │CALL JETSET [/T"Run Je│→│         │
│                │                    ⌐               │               │
│                │ Optional                          │               │
│                │                                   │               │
│                │ Help text . .  │Options for JETSET are│→│         │
│                │                                   │               │
│                │ Password  . .  │      │            │               │
│                │                                   │               │
│                │ (Esc=Cancel) (F1=Help) (F2=Save)  │               │
│                └───────────────────────────────────┘               │
│                                                                   │
│ F10=Actions  Esc=Cancel  Shift+F9=Command Prompt                  │
└─────────────────────────────────────────────────────────────────┘
```

Figure 14.17. The Change Program screen for JETSET.BAT.

Figure 14.18 shows how the Run JetSet dialog box appears when you select the JETSET printer mode option. If you need reminders about how to create groups and startup sequences, refer to Chapter 11. The main point to remember here is: when executing a batch file, always begin the startup sequence with the CALL command.

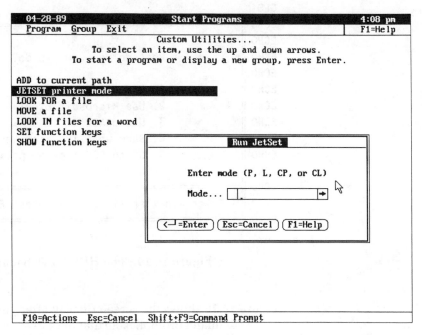

Figure 14.18. Dialog box for running the JETSET batch file.

Creating Your Own Shell

If you are the principal user of a computer that other users share, you might want to create your own "DOS Shell." this shell won't be as fancy as the DOS 4 Shell, but it can give less knowledgeable users much easier access to programs. In addition, you can also restrict beginners to certain directories (at least, until they learn how to use DOS on their own).

The basic idea is straightforward. Create a batch file (perhaps named HELP.BAT) that displays a menu of all the programs that you want to make available to other users. Label these options by assigning a number or a letter to each option. Then, create a batch file that uses the number or letter as its name, that contains the necessary commands to change to the proper directory, that runs the requested program, and, finally, that re-executes the HELP.BAT batch file when the user exits the requested program.

Figure 14.19 shows a sample HELP.BAT batch file. (The boxes were drawn using the same keys and techniques described with the SETKEYS and SHOWKEYS batch files in Chapter 13.)

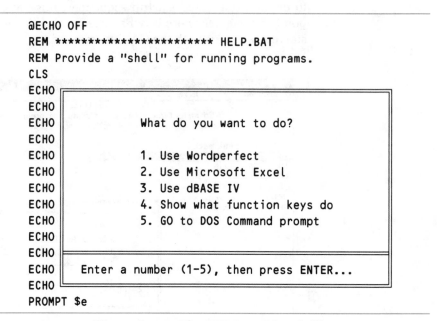

```
@ECHO OFF
REM ************************ HELP.BAT
REM Provide a "shell" for running programs.
CLS
ECHO
ECHO
ECHO                    What do you want to do?
ECHO
ECHO                    1. Use Wordperfect
ECHO                    2. Use Microsoft Excel
ECHO                    3. Use dBASE IV
ECHO                    4. Show what function keys do
ECHO                    5. GO to DOS Command prompt
ECHO
ECHO
ECHO        Enter a number (1-5), then press ENTER...
ECHO
PROMPT $e
```

Figure 14.19. The HELP.BAT batch file.

Figure 14.20 shows the screen display after you enter the command HELP at the command prompt. Note that the screen makes it appear that the usual command prompt is not even available. That's because the PROMPT $e command at the end of the HELP.BAT batch file changes the prompt to an invisible Escape character.

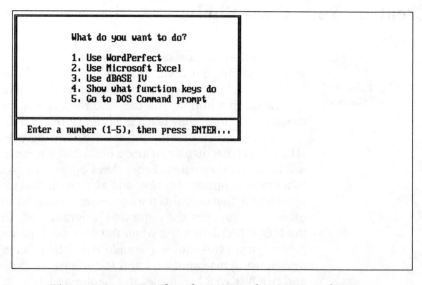

Figure 14.20. Results of entering the command HELP.

Option 1 on the Help screen lets the user run the WordPerfect program. Let's assume that you want all users at this level to store their WordPerfect files in the \WP\WPFILES directory (and, of course, the \WP directory is defined in the current PATH). Furthermore, you've stored HELP.BAT and all other batch files on the \UTILS directory. Your 1.BAT batch file must then look like the one shown in Figure 14.21.

```
@ECHO OFF
REM *********************** 1.BAT
REM Run WordPerfect from the \WP\WPFILES directory.
CD \WP\WPFILES
WP
CD \UTILS
HELP
```

Figure 14.21. The 1.BAT batch file.

When the user types 1 and presses Enter, DOS assumes that 1 is a "normal" command, and it looks for a file named 1.BAT (or 1.COM or 1.EXE). This executes 1.BAT, which first changes to the C:\WP\WPFILES directory and then runs the WordPerfect program. When the user exits WordPerfect, the CD \UTILS directory changes back to the \UTILS directory, and then the HELP command again executes the HELP.BAT batch file.

You could create similar batch files, named 2.BAT and 3.BAT, to run Microsoft Excel, dBASE IV, or any other program that is available on your system.

Option 5 uses the batch file 5.BAT, shown in Figure 14.22, to remove the HELP display from the screen and redisplay the command prompt.

```
REM *********************** 5.BAT
REM Return to command prompt from HELP.BAT.
PROMPT $P$G
CLS
```

Figure 14.22. The 5.BAT batch file redisplays the command prompt.

The reason I called this batch file HELP.BAT is because HELP is one of the first commands that comes to most peoples' minds when confronted with the command prompt. As an alternative to making users enter the command HELP, you could merely make the following two lines the last two commands in your AUTOEXEC.BAT file:

```
CD \UTILS
HELP
```

This automatically displays the help screen as soon as you start the computer. (DOS 4 users would have to delete the DOSSHELL command to do this.)

When you consider that you can customize the function keys to have them automatically enter DOS commands, and you can also create batch files such as HELP.BAT to create a type of "DOS Shell," you can see that DOS is indeed a very flexible and powerful tool. These techniques let you customize your system in just about any way you can imagine, and they make your "personal computer" very personal indeed.

Summary

This chapter presented advanced commands and techniques for creating batch files and developed several useful batch files to demonstrate their use. As you gain experience with DOS, you certainly will be able to create some interesting "customized commands" of your own.

- The IF command allows a batch file to test for a condition and then react accordingly.

- The GOTO command re-routes the normal sequence of execution in a batch file.

- The PAUSE command temporarily stops batch file execution and waits until you press a key.

- Redirecting output of a command to the NUL device hides any messages that the command normally displays.

- Type ECHO. to make a batch file display a blank line.

- To make a message in a batch file sound a beep, use the ^G character (by pressing Ctrl-G).

- The FOR command sets up a loop to repeatedly execute a command in a batch file.

- The CALL command passes execution to another batch file, but it permits execution to resume at the next command in the calling batch file.

- To use Edlin enter Escape-key sequences in a batch file, press Ctrl-V and then type [.

- To execute batch files from a DOS 4 Shell group screen, use the CALL command in the program startup sequence.

Advanced DOS Techniques

As you become more experienced in using you computer, you probably will need to start using more advanced options and capabilities, such as extended memory, expanded memory, RAM disks, and other features. Using these capabilities effectively requires a more detailed knowledge of the way things work "inside" the computer.

The next three chapters provide the technical information that you will need to understand and use the more advanced options and features of your computer. In summary, you will learn:

- *How a computer stores information.*

- *How your computer's memory is organized.*

- *Reasons for the 640KB RAM limit, and methods for overcoming that limitation.*

- *How disks store and organize information.*

- *How the computer communicates with devices and other computers through serial and parallel communications.*

- *How to get the most from your computer by using advanced features such as RAM disks, extended memory, expanded memory, and disk caching.*

- *How to resolve common problems, such as diskette, data, and program incompatibilities.*

What Makes It Tick?

You can drive a car without knowing anything about the internal workings of the transmission or voltage regulator. Similarly, you can use a computer effectively without knowing a great deal about its technical internal workings. However, if you want to use advanced options, such as extended and expanded memory, or write complex programs of your own, you must have a basic understanding about the way things work in a computer.

This chapter will explain the way your computer operates at a more technical level. The information presented here will help you better understand the techniques presented in Chapter 16, which describes how to install optional devices on your computer.

How Computers Store Information

Although you interact with your computer with the same alphabet (A to Z) and numbers (0 to 9) that you use in your daily communications, the computer actually works on a completely different principal known as the *binary* numbering system. The binary system uses only two digits—0 and 1. Why only two digits? Because all the internal workings of the computer use electronic (or in the case of disks, magnetic) switches that can be in either one of two states—"off" (0), or "on" (1).

Each of these on-off switches is called a *bit* (short for binary digit). Although "on" and "off" offer only two possible states, combining two binary digits offers four unique combinations, as follows:

00
01
10
11

A group of three bits offers eight possible unique combinations, as shown below:

000

001

010

011

100

101

110

111

Notice the progression here. One bit offers two combinations. Two bits offer four (2^2) unique combinations. Three bits offer eight (2^3) unique combinations.

Modern microcomputers use a group of eight bits to store an individual character. Using eight bits permits a total of 256 (2^8) unique combinations of bits. A group of eight bits is called a *byte*. As you might recall from Chapter 1, I pointed out that one byte equals one character; so, the word "CAT" uses three bytes of storage space.

The complete ASCII character set consists of 256 unique characters. If you look at the ASCII character set (shown in Appendix C), you will see that there are, indeed, exactly 256 unique characters, numbered 0 to 255. Each of these characters is represented by a unique set of eight bits. For example, the letter A is represented by the byte 01000001, the letter B is represented by the byte 01000010, the letter C is represented by the byte 01000011, and so on.

Hexadecimal Numbering System

If you look at Appendix C, you will notice that two numbering systems are displayed: the decimal numbers are listed in the normal sequence of 0 to 255; the Hex (short for *hexadecimal*) numbers are listed from 00 to FF. The hexadecimal numbering system is often used as a shorthand method of expressing binary numbers.

The decimal numbering system is based on 10 unique digits, 0 through 9. After you count to 9, you start using the two-digit numbers 10, 11, 12, 13, and so on to 99. Although the decimal numbering system is convenient for humans, who have 10 fingers to count on, it does not accurately reflect the computer's way of storing information, which is based on eight-bit bytes.

The hexadecimal numbering system uses 16 unique digits, 0 through 9 and A through F. In hex, you don't start using two digit numbers until you get to F, as shown below:

0
1
2
3
4
5
6
7
8
9
A
B
C
D
E
F
10

Because F is the largest single digit in hex, FF is the largest two-digit pair, just like 9 is the largest single-digit in decimal, and 99 is the largest two-digit number. Notice that the ASCII table in Appendix C conveniently ends at hexadecimal FF—the largest possible two-digit number in hex. This convenience, of course, is no accident.

Simply stated, any character in the ASCII alphabet can be represented by a two-digit hexadecimal number. In fact, the first 16 hexadecimal numbers (0, 1, 2, 3 through F) are often expressed as 00, 01, 02, 03, through 0F, to maintain the two-digit consistency.

Why Is a Kilobyte 1,024 Bytes?

The hexadecimal numbering system provides some insight into why you often encounter certain numbers, such as 64, 512, and 1,024, when working with computers. If computers were based on the decimal system, you would see the more familiar multiples of 10. For example, if you start with 1 and continue multiplying by 10, you generate the following familiar sequence of numbers:

$$1 \text{ X } 10 = 10$$
$$10 \text{ X } 10 = 100$$
$$100 \text{ X } 10 = 1,000$$
$$1000 \text{ X } 10 = 10,000$$

and so forth.

But computers are based on the number 2, and therefore the significant numbers of this base are all multiples of 2. Therefore, if you repeatedly multiply by 2, you come up with these numbers:

$$2 \times 2 = 4$$
$$4 \times 2 = 8$$
$$8 \times 2 = 16$$
$$16 \times 2 = 32$$
$$32 \times 2 = 64$$
$$64 \times 2 = 128$$
$$128 \times 2 = 256$$
$$256 \times 2 = 512$$
$$512 \times 2 = 1{,}024 \quad \text{(one Kilobyte)}$$

and so on, to . . .

$$2^{16} = 65{,}536 \ (64\text{KB})$$
$$2^{20} = 1{,}048{,}576 \ (1 \text{ Megabyte})$$

You might occasionally encounter numbers that are one or two less than a number listed above. For example, DOS allows a command entered at the command prompt to have a maximum length of only 127 characters. However, after you type a DOS command, you have to press Enter—and Enter is another character. That makes the actual length of the complete command 128 characters.

Converting Hex to Decimal

If you do not get involved in the technical aspects of DOS and your computer, you will probably never need to use hexadecimal numbers. But, in case you do, several tools are available to provide help.

To determine the hexadecimal number of an ASCII character, refer to Appendix C of this book. If you frequently make conversions between hexadecimal and decimal number, you should purchase a calculator designed for programmers. Or, you could buy a program that offers a "pop-up" calculator, such as Borland's Sidekick.

However, if you rarely make hexadecimal and decimal conversions and you don't want to spend money on such a specialized tool, you can use Table 15.1 to convert hexadecimal numbers as high as FFFF to their decimal equivalents.

To use Table 15.1, total the decimal values for each digit in the hex number. Let's try some examples. The one-digit hex number F converts to 15 in decimal. The two-digit hex number 9F is 144 + 15, or 159 decimal.

Table 15.1. Converting hexadecimal numbers to decimal.

Thousands digit		Hundreds digit		Tens digit		Ones digit	
Hex	*Decimal*	*Hex*	*Decimal*	*Hex*	*Decimal*	*Hex*	*Decimal*
0	0	0	0	0	0	0	0
1	4,096	1	256	1	16	1	1
2	8,192	2	512	2	32	2	2
3	12,288	3	768	3	48	3	3
4	16,384	4	1,024	4	64	4	4
5	20,480	5	1,280	5	80	5	5
6	24,576	6	1,536	6	96	6	6
7	28,672	7	1,792	7	112	7	7
8	32,768	8	2,048	8	128	8	8
9	36,864	9	2,304	9	144	9	9
A	40,960	A	2,560	A	160	A	10
B	45,056	B	2,816	B	176	B	11
C	49,152	C	3,072	C	192	C	12
D	53,248	D	3,328	D	208	D	13
E	57,344	E	3,584	E	224	E	14
F	61,440	F	3,840	F	240	F	15

The hex number 100 is 256 + 0 + 0, or 256 decimal. The hex number CD1 is 3,072 + 208 + 1, or 3,281 decimal. The number 1010 hex is 4,096 + 0 + 256 + 0 or 4,352 decimal. The hex number FFFF is 61,440 + 3,840 + 240 + 15 or 65,535 decimal.

Converting Decimal to Hex

Converting decimal numbers to hex involves repeatedly dividing the number (and then subsequent quotients by 16), while converting the remainder of each division to its hexadecimal equivalent, until the quotient is zero. The result of the first division produces the ones-digit in the hex number. The result of the second division produces the tens-digit in the hex number, and so on. Figure 15.1 shows an example depicting how to convert the number 751 to hexadecimal.

How Memory Is Organized

Your computer's main memory (RAM) consists of *RAM chips*. If you were to remove the cover from your computer and look inside, you would see these RAM chips as small, black, rectangular wafers plugged into a larger

```
751 / 16 = 46 remainder 15 (hexadecimal F)
 46 / 16 = 2 remainder 14 (hexadecimal E)
  2 / 16 = 0 remainder 2

751 decimal converts to...                    2EF hexadecimal
```

Figure 15.1. Converting 751 decimal to its
hexadecimal equivalent.

board. Actually, the black wafer is the *chip carrier*, and it is much larger
than the actual chip to make handling easier. If you could see through the
chip carrier, you would see that the actual RAM chip, which is actually
small enough to fit on your thumbnail (see Figure 15.2).

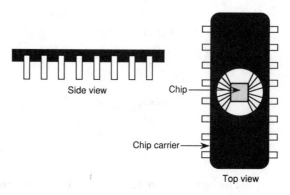

Side view

Chip

Chip carrier

Top view

Figure 15.2. A RAM chip, inside the chip carrier.

A RAM chip consists of thousands of tiny *transistors*, or switches,
each of which can be either turned on (1) or off (0). A typical RAM chip
contains 262,144 of these tiny switches (which gives you an idea of how
small each switch is). Each switch represents one bit. As you know, it takes
eight bits (a byte) to store one character, so a RAM chip that has 262,144
switches can store 32,768 bytes (or 32 Kilobytes) of information. (From a
purely technical standpoint, the bits on a single chip are not actually organized into bytes. Instead, a byte is "spread across" multiple chips.)

The switches in RAM operate very quickly, which permits the computer to operate at amazing speeds. However, these switches work only
when they receive electrical power. As soon as you turn off the computer, all
the switches go off. This is why (as Chapter 1 discussed) RAM is volatile, and
is why you need to use disks to store information permanently.

Read-Only Memory (ROM)

There is more to memory than RAM. Your computer also contains Read-
Only Memory (ROM) in addition to RAM. A ROM chip is pretty similar to a

RAM chip, except that it is pre-programmed to perform certain tasks; it cannot be used for storing data or programs. ROM occupies certain areas of your computer's total memory, as you will see in a moment.

Memory Maps

The total memory (RAM and ROM combined) in a computer is often displayed in a *memory map*. A memory map displays how memory is divided into areas that perform specific jobs. Figure 15.3 shows a sample memory map for a computer with 640KB RAM.

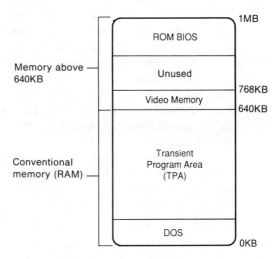

Figure 15.3. How memory is allocated in modern microcomputers.

Memory above 640KB is used for specific jobs that the computer needs to perform regularly. The first 128KB above the 640KB *address* (position in memory) (i.e., from the 640KB address to the 768KB address) is usually used for managing the video display.

The remaining 256KB at the high end of memory is partially unused, and partially used by the ROM BIOS (the Basic Input/Output System), which controls the "traffic" of data being received from, and sent to, various devices such as the keyboard, screen, and printer.

Generally, the area above 640KB is "off-limits" to the average user, because the computer reserves this area for its own "managerial" tasks. However, as you'll see later, there are some interesting things that can be done in the unused area of memory above 640KB. But first, let's focus on RAM, which is the area of memory that you have the most control over.

How DOS and Programs Use RAM

As you know, DOS is a program. When you first start your computer, a part of DOS is stored in RAM automatically (which, incidentally, explains why some DOS commands are *internal* commands, while others are *external* commands; the internal commands are already in RAM, and therefore DOS does not need to read instructions from a file stored on disk to perform an operation).

The exact amount of RAM that DOS uses is dependent on the specific version of DOS that you are using, but all versions of DOS do use some of RAM. When you enter the CHKDSK or MEM command at the DOS command prompt, DOS displays both the total memory available (for example, 655360 bytes, which is 640KB), and the total number of bytes free (for example 565552). If you subtract the free (available) bytes from the total number of bytes, the difference is the number of bytes occupied by DOS (and perhaps other programs, as discussed later).

When you run a program, a copy of that program is loaded into RAM, which ensures maximum processing speed. The largest program that you can run is determined by how much memory is available after DOS has already been loaded into RAM. This remaining area is sometimes called the Transient Program Area (or TPA), because it is used for programs that "come and go."

For example, when you use your spreadsheet program, a copy of that program is stored in RAM. When you exit your spreadsheet program, the copy in RAM is erased, and a copy of your next program is stored in RAM. This is the reason that you usually use only one program at a time. But, as discussed in the next section, not all programs are transient.

Memory-Resident Programs

Some programs remain in memory after you start them, so that you can have quicker access to the features they offer. These are often called TSR programs (for Terminate-and-Stay-Resident). Some of the DOS external commands, such as PRINT.COM and MODE.COM, stay resident in RAM if you initialize them. Also, when you activate additional devices, such as a mouse, the mouse-driver software occupies some RAM.

In addition to the DOS TSR programs, many application programs stay resident in memory after loading. These programs remain in memory so that you can access them at any time merely by pressing a key (sometimes called a "hot key"). You don't even need to be at the command prompt to run a loaded TSR program.

For example, Sidekick Plus, a TSR program from Borland International, provides handy tools such as a phone list, an appointment calendar, a calculator, and other useful tools. After you load SideKick into RAM, you can access it by pressing a special key, even while you are running another program such as your spreadsheet or word processor.

Typically, TSR programs are loaded into RAM from the top down. When you load multiple TSR programs, DOS automatically keeps track of where the current TSR program ends in memory, and stores the next TSR immediately beneath the existing TSRs.

Though the figure doesn't show it, some of DOS is actually stored near the top of the 640KB mark. But nonetheless, it occupies a specific amount of memory.

All of these TSRs use additional memory, thus reducing the size of the remaining TPA. For example, Figure 15.4 shows how much RAM remains after loading DOS's PRINT.COM, MODE.COM, the DOS 4 Shell, a mouse driver, and the Sidekick Plus program. (Though, Sidekick PLUS can be configured to use less RAM.)

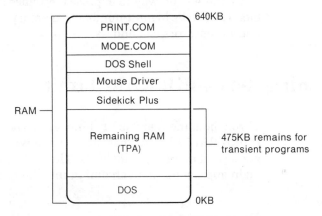

Figure 15.4. Memory after loading some TSR programs.

As you can see in the figure, only 457KB of memory remains of the original 640KB after loading several TSR programs. Any program that requires more than 457KB of RAM will not be able to run (DOS would display the message `Insufficient Memory`).

As you might recall, spreadsheet programs store *all* of the current spreadsheet's data in RAM. Even if you didn't load the additional TSRs, you simply might not have enough RAM to create the spreadsheet model you want.

You might think that you can solve this problem by buying more RAM chips. However, this is not the case. As the next section shows, for original IBM PCs, XTs, and compatibles, the 640KB RAM limitation is not so easily expanded.

Why the 1MB Memory Limit?

The reason for the 1MB (RAM plus ROM) memory limit can be traced to the microprocessor that manipulates the data and instructions that are stored in RAM. As you might remember, RAM stores data for the microprocessor, but the microprocessor actually does all the work. In order for the microprocessor (the central processing unit, or CPU) to locate and manipulate the data stored in RAM, it needs to assign each byte an *address*.

The address of a particular byte in RAM is similar to the addresses of the houses in your community. Each house has a unique address so that the Post Office can deliver the mail. Each byte in memory also has a unique address so that the CPU can transfer information to and from RAM as needed.

The CPU of computers that use the 8086 and 8088 microprocessors, such as the IBM PC, XT, and compatibles, use 20 bits for storing memory addresses. This provides for 2^{20}, or 1,048,576, directly *addressable* locations in memory. The number 1,048,576 is referred to as 1 megabyte. Because there is no way to express a number larger than 1,048,576 using 20 bits, 1MB is the highest-numbered memory location that the 8086 and 8088 microprocessors can address.

Overcoming the 640KB RAM Limit

Throughout the years, many innovations have been developed to break the 640KB RAM limit so that more space would be available for larger programs and bigger spreadsheets. The sections that follow discuss the three main approaches to overcoming this limitation.

Program Overlays

The oldest approach to running large programs in a smaller area of RAM has been to divide the program into a main file, which usually has the .COM or .EXE extension, and into separate *overlay* files, which often have extensions such as .OVL, .OVR, or .OV1, .OV2, .OV3 and so on. For example, the dBASE IV database management system program, when stripped of its optional elements, consists of the following essential files:

    DBASE.EXE
    DBASE1.OVL
    DBASE2.OVL
    DBASE3.OVL
    DBASE4.OVL
    DBASE5.OVL
    DBASE6.OVL

There are also other files, such as those containing help screens and other messages, that must be considered part of the entire program. The size of all these combined files is a massive 2,239,747 bytes—clearly larger than the 640KB (that is, 655,360 bytes) limit that DOS allows on an IBM PC or XT.

In programs that use overlays, only the .COM or .EXE file is copied into RAM when you run the program. This file typically contains the most often-used capabilities of the program so that these features are readily available when you want them. The .COM or .EXE file also reserves space in RAM, called the *overlay area*, that is meant to hold additional specialized instructions.

When you request a feature that is not currently available in RAM, the program quickly copies the overlay file that contains that feature into the overlay area, where it replaces the current overlay. That is, only one overlay file can be stored in RAM at a time. Figure 15.5 illustrates this concept, using the dBASE IV program as an example.

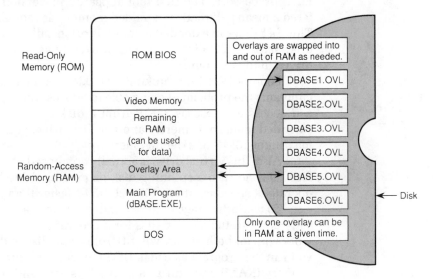

Figure 15.5. Overlays are called into RAM as needed.

Because only one overlay can be in use at a time in RAM, a program might need to swap overlays quite often, which involves copying the overlay from the disk into the overlay section of RAM. This can be a somewhat slow process (in the computer world, a two- or three-second delay is "interminable"), so it wasn't long before computer designers started seeking more efficient ways to extend the capabilities of RAM.

Extended Memory

The 80286 microprocessor, developed by Intel Corporation, offered a different solution to the 640KB memory limit—*extended memory*. This microprocessor uses a 24-bit addressing scheme that can access as much as 16MB of RAM. The IBM AT and compatible computers use the 80286 microprocessor.

The 80386 microprocessor, which uses a 32-bit addressing scheme, followed the 80286. The IBM PS/2 Model 80, the Compaq 386, and similar computers use the 80386 microprocessor. These computers also offer extended memory above the 640K limit.

Unfortunately, DOS was never designed to take advantage of the additional memory made available by the 80286 and 80386 microprocessors. DOS was designed for the earlier 8086 and 8088 microprocessors, which use the 20-bit addressing scheme. And, because most application programs were designed for use with DOS, they too were incapable of using the extended memory effectively.

DOS 3 and 4 can also use a part of "conventional" RAM memory as a virtual disk.

However, a few tools have evolved to allow DOS to at least partially take advantage of the extended memory of the 80286 and 80386 microprocessors. The first tool appeared in Version 3 of DOS, and it offered a means of treating extended memory as though it were a disk drive. This disk drive in extended memory is often called a *RAM disk*, or a *virtual disk*, because DOS interacts with it exactly as it does with all other disk drives in the computer.

Chapter 16 discusses specific instructions for using DOS 3 or DOS 4 to create a RAM disk in your computer.

Fooling DOS into thinking that extended memory is a disk drive circumvents the problem of being able to address only 1MB of memory. DOS can access as much as 32MB from a disk drive, so by telling DOS that extended memory is merely another disk drive, you can easily access the maximum 16MB of extended memory.

Also, this virtual drive is actually composed of RAM chips, and therefore does not use a spinning disk or moving drive heads. This makes it operate at speeds that are 10 to 20 times faster than a disk.

To take advantage of the extended memory as a virtual disk, you typically copy all the overlay files for a program or the data that you want to work with (or both, if they will fit) from a real disk to the virtual disk. Then, you run the program as usual. DOS still runs the program in *conventional memory* (RAM) and still swaps overlays into and out of RAM from the virtual disk. However, the swapping is much quicker because there is no slow mechanical disk drive involved.

Similarly, if the program needs to read and write data to a disk, these operations are also much quicker if the information is stored on the virtual disk. Figure 15.6 illustrates this concept.

Treating extended memory as though it were a disk does not really give you more RAM for running programs. It merely makes the movement of data into and out of RAM go more quickly, because there is no real disk drive involved. As you'll see in the next section, a different technique, called *expanded memory* was eventually devised to allow "extra" RAM to be treated as conventional RAM.

Expanded Memory

Most software developers were more interested in expanding RAM than in speeding the flow of information between RAM and a disk. This is particularly true of spreadsheet developers, because spreadsheet programs must store in RAM all the data for the current worksheet. The size of a spread-

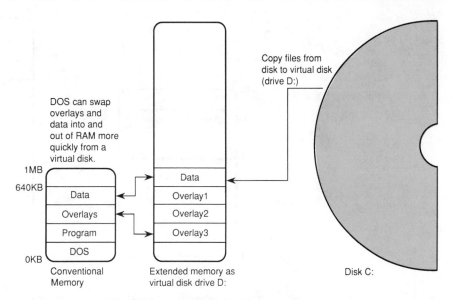

Figure 15.6. How DOS uses a virtual disk in extended memory.

sheet was therefore limited to the amount of RAM available after DOS, any TSR programs, and the spreadsheet program itself were loaded into RAM.

Many spreadsheet users complained that 640KB was simply not enough room for their spreadsheet applications. The only solution to this problem, when using DOS as the operating system, was to find a means for allowing data beyond the 640KB limit to "spill over" into additional RAM chips. Of course, data that was stored in these chips had to be as accessible as it was in conventional RAM, and this presented a tricky problem, because DOS had no way of directly addressing the data beyond the 640KB in RAM.

So three companies—Lotus Development Corporation, the maker of the 1-2-3 spreadsheet program, Intel, the maker of microprocessors, and Microsoft, the maker of DOS—joined forces to develop what is now known as the Lotus-Intel-Microsoft (LIM) standard for *expanded* memory. The word "expanded" is important here, because the LIM standard did, indeed, expand RAM beyond the 640KB limit.

From a technical standpoint this swapping of memory (also called *paging*) is trickier than you might think, because as mentioned earlier, the area of addressable memory between 640KB and 1MB is typically reserved for video memory, hard disk management, and other BIOS (Basic Input Output System) operations.

But, in most systems, a good-sized chunk of memory in this area is unused. LIM simply takes control of 64KB of this unused memory, and uses it as a "switching area" for swapping data into, and out of, expanded memory on an "as needed" basis, as Figure 15.7 illustrates.

Even though the LIM technique involves some swapping of data into and out of the 1MB of memory that DOS can address, it is very different

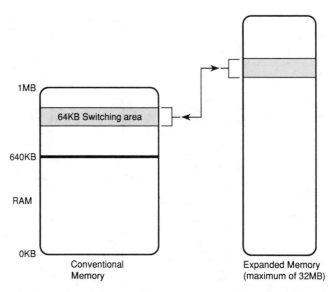

Figure 15.7. Expanded memory (EMS) uses 64KB of addressable memory as a switching area for DOS.

from the technique of using extended memory as a virtual disk. In the virtual-disk approach, DOS "sees" whatever is in extended memory as being stored on a disk. If you try to copy a file from a virtual disk into RAM, and there is not enough room in RAM to accommodate the data, DOS will deny the request with the Insufficient memory error message.

Specifically, the LIM approach sends data into memory in 16KB chunks called pages. Thus, the 64KB area in ROM can handle four pages at a time.

However, with the expanded-memory approach, the swapping is limited to the switching area memory, so DOS never issues the Insufficient memory message. That's because the EMS approach, in a sense, "tricks" DOS into thinking that it's working with data that is stored within the 1MB limit. In other words, the LIM approach lets DOS work with more RAM than it can actually handle by feeding it small chunks of data on an as-needed basis.

Spreadsheet programs that take advantage of expanded memory could now let users create much larger worksheets. As a worksheet grows in size beyond the 640KB limit, the LIM approach swaps the overflow quickly and automatically into and out of expanded memory, so that conventional RAM is no longer a constraint.

The example in Figure 15.8 shows the Microsoft Excel spreadsheet program stored in RAM accessing a huge spreadsheet that extends beyond the 640KB limit.

The Current Standards

The basic LIM standard for expanded memory has evolved and improved since Version 3.2. The two main standards used today are the EEMS (En-

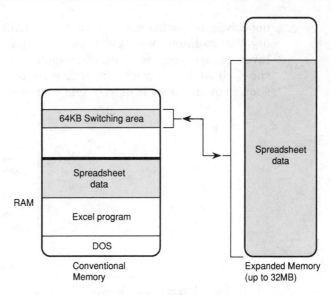

Figure 15.8. A huge Excel spreadsheet "spills over"
into expanded memory.

hanced Expanded Memory Specification), and the LIM 4.0 standard.
Whereas the original LIM 3.2 specification allowed a maximum of 8MB of
expanded memory, the current specification allows as much as 32MB of
expanded memory.

There are many alternatives available for installing expanded memory on a computer. The most common technique is to purchase a separate
EMS board (hardware), which is stored inside the computer. The board
will include a *device driver* (a program) that manages the switching of data
between expanded memory and addressable memory.

There are also EMS *emulators*, which mimic expanded memory using
extended memory, or even the hard disk. These are "software-only" products that do not require additional hardware. If you own a computer that
uses the 80386 microprocessor, chances are that you already own a program that can emulate expanded memory. Chapter 16 will discuss techniques for installing, and emulating, expanded memory in more detail.

OS/2: The Ultimate Solution

The ultimate solution to breaking the 640KB limit was the development of an
entirely new operating system, called OS/2 (for Operating System 2). Developed by Microsoft, this operating system can be used only on computers with
the 80286 or 80386 microprocessor. OS/2 offers two operating modes: *Protected mode*, which takes full advantage of memory above 640KB, and *DOS
Compatibility mode*, which runs most standard DOS programs.

The protected mode of OS/2 allows multiple programs to run simultaneously in protected memory above the 1MB limit of conventional memory. For example, with OS/2, your computer can simultaneously print invoices, age your accounts receivable, and recalculate a large spreadsheet, all while you work with your word processing program. Figure 15.9 shows how memory is used in this example.

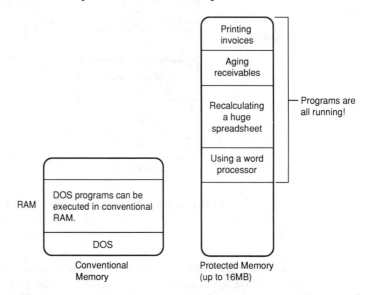

Figure 15.9. OS/2 can run several programs simultaneously in protected memory.

OS/2 includes an interface program called the Session Manager, that keeps you informed of which programs are currently running and which are available. You can easily switch from one program to the next by using simple menu selections (similar to those in the DOS 4 Shell's menu system). Conventional DOS programs can still run in RAM but not in protected memory; therefore you can still run only one standard DOS program at a time.

Since its initial release in 1988, OS/2 has not become as popular as was expected. Part of the reason for this lack of enthusiasm centers around the general lack of OS/2 application programs. Also, to use OS/2, your computer needs at least 2MB of RAM—and preferably 4MB or more—which most systems do not have. Finally, the initial version of OS/2 does not fully take advantage of all the features of the 80386 microprocessor. Apparently, DOS is here to stay for quite some time.

How Disks Are Organized

A diskette or a hard disk stores information on a surface that is coated with hundreds of thousands—or millions—of tiny magnetic particles. As you might know, magnets have a positive pole and a negative pole.

Each magnetic particle on a computer disk can have one of two states—either positive (represented as + or 1) or negative (represented as - or 0). Not surprisingly, each of these magnetic particles can represent one bit of data. And, as you know, eight bits form a byte (a character).

If you could see the positive and negative magnetic poles on the tiny magnetic particles on a diskette, the word CAT would look something like the following:

$$-+----++ \quad -+------+ \quad -+-+-+--$$

Using binary numbers, you would express the + signs as 1s, and the minus signs as zeroes, as follows:

01000011 01000001 01010100

If you check an ASCII chart that shows the eight-bit byte for each character in the ASCII character set, you'll see that these are indeed the bytes used to represent the letters CAT. Of course, the computer must convert these bytes to ASCII characters when it displays them on the screen or sends them to the printer, because the word CAT more meaningfully expresses this feline animal to humans than does 01000011 01000001 01010100.

How A Disk Drive Reads and Writes Data

Floppy disk drives and hard disk drives use the same basic principal for reading information from and writing information to the magnetic medium of a disk. As the disk spins, the *read/write head* moves across the surface (although never actually touching the disk) in much the same way that a needle on a stereo turntable moves across a spinning album. As the recording head moves above the disk, it either reads the magnetic bits, or it changes their arrangement to store information.

Some older disk drives can read only one side of a diskette, because they only have one read/write head. These drives use single-sided diskettes that can store only 160KB or 180KB of information. Figure 15.10 depicts the action of a disk drive with only one read/write head.

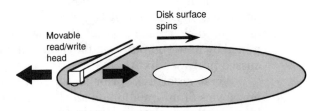

Figure 15.10. A disk drive that reads only single-sided diskettes.

Most modern disk drives have two read/write heads, one for the top of the diskette and one for the bottom. These drives use double sided diskettes, with the most popular storage capacities being: 360KB, 720KB, 1.2MB, and 1.44MB. Figure 15.11 depicts the action of a disk drive that has two read/write heads.

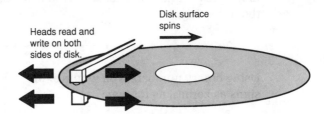

Figure 15.11. A disk drive with two read/write heads.

A hard disk usually contains several spinning disks, referred to as *platters*. Each platter typically has two heads so that data can be read from or written to both sides. Figure 15.12 shows this arrangement of platters and heads.

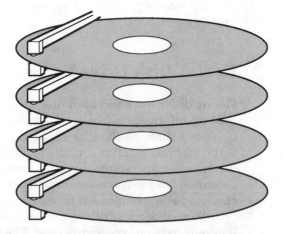

Figure 15.12. A hard disk with multiple platters.

Although the hard disk in Figure 15.12 *physically* consists of multiple platters, DOS can *logically* access the multiple platters as though they were one huge disk, named C:. How DOS logically accesses a hard disk is determined by how you *partition* the hard disk using the FDISK program (discussed in Appendix A).

Versions of DOS prior to 4.0 could only access a maximum of 32 megabytes of information on any logical hard disk. Therefore, if the combined hard disk platters offered 40 megabytes of disk storage, DOS had to do something like accessing the first 32 megabytes as drive C: and then accessing the remaining 8 megabytes as drive D:. The physical number of platters in the hard disk is not important—only the storage capacity matters.

Low-Level Formatting

When DOS first formats a disk, it performs a *low-level format*, which divides the surface of the diskette into *tracks* (rings) and *sectors* (slices), as Figure 15.13 shows. Each sector represents one *allocation unit* of data and stores a specific number of bytes, usually either 512KB or 1,024KB.

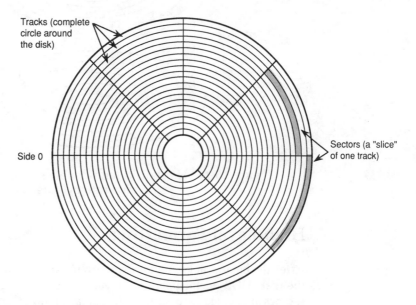

Figure 15.13. A disk divided into tracks and sectors.

Double-sided diskettes and hard disks are further divided into *cylinders*. A cylinder is the combination of all the corresponding tracks on each side of each platter, as Figure 15.14 illustrates. For example, a hard disk that has four double-sided platters contains eight tracks numbered "1." The combination of these eight tracks would be referred to as cylinder number 1.

When DOS writes a large file to a disk, it attempts to store data in a single cylinder of multiple sides (or platters), rather than in multiple tracks of a single platter. For example, when storing a file on the 10th track of a disk, DOS first fills track 10 on side 0, then track 10 of side 1, than track 10 of side 2, then track 10 of side 3, and so on. This makes reading and writing data go more quickly, because the heads are simultaneously positioned to the appropriate track (the heads always move in tandem, never independently).

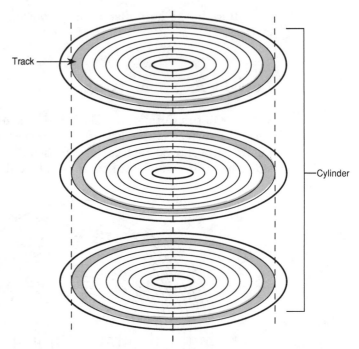

Figure 15.14. Hard disks (and double-sided diskettes) are also divided into cylinders.

High-Level Formatting

After the basic tracks, sectors, and cylinders are laid out on the surface of the disk, DOS performs a high-level format. During this phase, groups of sectors are set aside for storing information that DOS will later use to keep track of files. Each of these DOS information areas is discussed in the sections that follow.

The Boot Record

The first sector on a disk stores the *boot record*. This is where the computer looks for startup information when you first turn it on. The boot record contains information about the format of the disk, such as the number of bytes per sector, the number of sectors per track and cylinder, and so on. The boot record also lists the names of the *system files* that contain the instructions that start the computer.

The system files needed to start DOS on an IBM computer are IBMIO.COM and IBMDOS.COM. On other microcomputers, these files are usually called IO.SYS and MSDOS.SYS. In most versions of DOS, the first two files are hidden (their names do not appear when you list file names).

When you format a disk with the FORMAT /S command, DOS copies

A third file, named COMMAND.COM, is also copied to a disk that has been formatted with the /S switch. COMMAND.COM interprets DOS commands and batch files, issues prompts, and loads and executes other programs.

the two system files and COMMAND.COM to the disk, so that you can use the disk to boot the computer. If you do not use the /S switch, the system files are not copied, and the disk cannot boot the computer. Furthermore, the space that would have been occupied by the startup files is eventually allocated to other files, so you cannot copy the system files later. (Actually, you can use the /B switch to reserve space for the system files, as discussed under the FORMAT command in Appendix B.)

The Directory Sectors

Another group of sectors on the disk is dedicated to storing the directory. In the directory sectors, the following information about each files is stored in a 32-byte area:

- The name and extension of the file.
- The status of file attributes, such as Read-Only and Archive.
- The time that the file was created or last changed.
- The date that the file was created or last changed.
- The size of the file.
- The starting cluster number.

All this information is stored in binary notation. However, when you use the DIR command to view the directory sectors of a disk, DOS converts the binary numbers to decimal before displaying them on the screen.

DOS never displays the starting cluster number on your screen. Instead, DOS uses this information to find the file. It would be a waste of time for DOS to have to search the entire disk each time you requested a file. Instead, it looks up the file name in the directory sectors and finds the corresponding *starting cluster number*, which pinpoints the exact track on the disk that contains the beginning of the file.

The File Allocation Table

Every disk also reserves a group of sectors that store the File Allocation Table (FAT). This table is a map that tells DOS where to find fragments of files that have been stored in non-contiguous sectors. Files are often fragmented into non-contiguous sectors when they are altered or expanded after new files have been stored next to them.

For example, suppose you create a file named CUSTLIST.DAT that contains 50 names and addresses. Now, suppose that when you save this file, DOS stores it in sectors 5 through 10. Later, you create another file which DOS stores in sectors 11 through 15. If you then add some names to CUSTLIST.DAT, the entire file will not fit into sectors 5 through 10 anymore. And since sectors 11 through 15 are already taken, DOS must store the rest of CUSTLIST.DAT elsewhere (perhaps starting at sector 16).

The FAT keeps track of the various sectors in which a fragmented file is stored. Actually, the FAT keeps track of the *clusters* (or groups of sectors) that files are stored in. When you tell DOS to retrieve a file, it finds the starting cluster number stored with the file's name in the directory sectors. Then, it starts reading the file at that location.

After reading all the data in the starting cluster, DOS looks up the file's starting cluster number in the FAT. The FAT, in turn, tells DOS the next cluster number (if any) in which more of the file is stored. DOS then accesses this cluster and reads more of the file. This process is repeated until DOS encounters a special code in the file that says "no more clusters; the entire file has been read."

The FAT is a crucial element of a disk. If the FAT is erased or destroyed, DOS can no longer access the files, because it doesn't know where they are stored. For this reason, DOS actually keeps two copies of the FAT on the disk. If the first table is ruined, DOS uses the other copy.

The Data Sectors

The *data sectors* are the sections of the disk in which the actual files and subdirectories beneath the root directory are stored. These remaining sectors are by far the largest area on the disk.

Table 15.2 shows the total number of sectors allocated to various data areas on different types of diskettes. Figure 15.15 shows how you can envision a disk after DOS has formatted it and allocated space to specific areas.

Table 15.2. Sector allotment for various diskette sizes.

	5.25-inch		3.5-inch	
Storage capacity	360KB	1.2MB	720KB	1.44MB
Boot record (sectors	1	1	1	1
FAT sectors	4	14	10	18
Directory sectors	7	14	7	14
Data sectors	354	2,371	713	2,847
Bytes per sector	1,024	512	1,024	512
Sectors per cluster	2	1	2	1

The allocation schemes for the various sections of hard disks vary greatly from one disk to another. These are determined during formatting by taking into account the amount of available storage space, the partitioning, the number of cylinders and heads, and other factors.

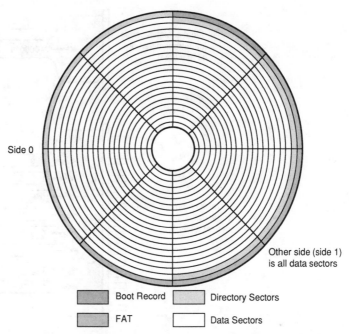

Side 0

Other side (side 1)
is all data sectors

| | Boot Record | | Directory Sectors |
| | FAT | | Data Sectors |

Figure 15.15. Space allocation on a formatted disk.

Serial and Parallel Communications

Computers use two basic techniques for sending data through wires to peripheral devices: 1) serial communication, in which bits are sent in a single-file stream, and 2) parallel communication, in which eight bits are sent in parallel through eight wires. Figure 15.16 shows the difference between these two methods, where the word CAT (binary 01000011 01000001 01010100) is being sent to a peripheral device.

Although the figure shows the parallel cable as a flat group of wires, the separate wires are usually wrapped around a core, so that the cable is actually cylindrical.

Serial communication is sometimes called asynchronous communication, because the devices involved must take turns sending and receiving; they cannot do so in a simultaneous (that is, synchronized) manner.

The serial communication technique is used when multiple wires are simply not available. For example, when sending data through phone lines via a modem, serial communication is used because the phone lines do not have the eight wires necessary for parallel communications, Serial communications are generally slower because the receiving device receives only one bit at a time.

Parallel communication is faster than serial communication because the receiving device receives one byte (that is, eight bits at a time). Most modern high-speed printers use parallel communications.

If you were to look at the back of your computer with all the plugs

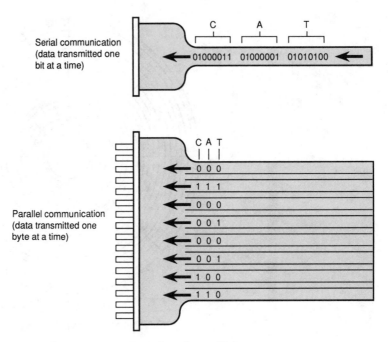

Figure 15.16. Serial and parallel communications.

removed, you would see that some of the ports are male (that is, the pins protrude from the port). These are usually serial ports. The parallel ports on the back of the computer are usually female; the pins protrude from the plug at the end of the cable.

In most situations, you do not need to do anything special with DOS to use the serial and parallel ports. Other software automatically manages the ports. However, you can configure both the parallel and serial ports, if necessary, using the DOS MODE command. (See Appendix B for details.)

Summary

When you start using the more advanced features of your computer and DOS, you need a deeper understanding of the way things work. This chapter presented a brief overview of the technical inner workings of your computer. In summary:

■ The basic unit of storage in a computer is a binary digit (bit), which can be either on (1) or off (0).

■ A single character is stored as a group of eight bits, called a byte.

■ Internally, computers use a binary (base 2) rather than a decimal (base 10) counting system. Programmers use the more convenient hexadecimal (base 16) numbering system.

- A computer's conventional memory consists of up to 640KB of RAM and 384KB of ROM, for a total of 1MB of memory.
- Extended memory can be used by DOS as a virtual disk, which "appears" to DOS as any other disk, but is much faster because there are no moving parts.
- Expanded memory can be used by DOS as though it were additional conventional RAM.
- During formatting, a disk is divided into tracks, sectors, and cylinders, which organize data for rapid storage and retrieval.
- In serial (or asynchronous) communications, data is sent one bit at a time.
- In parallel communications, data is sent one byte at a time.

Getting the Most from Your Computer

 Chapter 15 described DOS's limitations in accessing memory above the 640KB limit and outlined the solutions that have evolved to overcome this limitation. This chapter focuses on how you can use these solutions to get the maximum performance from your computer. This chapter also discusses some optional tools that you might be able to use to enhance the speed at which data is transferred between RAM and the disk.

Using a RAM Disk

As discussed in Chapter 15, a RAM disk (or virtual disk) is a portion of memory set up to simulate a disk drive. The advantage of a RAM disk is that it is 10 to 20 times faster than a *physical* (that is, "real") disk drive. The disadvantages are: 1) everything is erased from the RAM disk as soon as you turn off the computer, and 2) some programs might not have enough memory space after you assign part of memory to the RAM disk.

Later in this section, you'll learn techniques that will help you protect against the automatic erasure of your RAM disk. Also, if your computer has extended memory, you can use that memory for your RAM disk, thereby bypassing the second disadvantage and leaving conventional RAM free for programs and data.

Creating a RAM Disk in Conventional Memory

If your computer does not have extended memory, you can use conventional RAM for your RAM disk. However, you first need to realistically determine how much RAM is available for the RAM disk. Before you make this appraisal, be sure to load all of your usual memory-resident programs, such as Sidekick or Superkey, as well as any DOS memory resident programs that you use regularly, (such as PRINT.COM, MODE.COM, GRAPHICS.COM, and so on).

Next, at the command prompt, enter the CHKDSK command. The last two lines displayed show the current status of memory (RAM), as in the following example:

```
655360 total bytes memory
542832 bytes free
```

To determine how much RAM an application program requires, check that program's documentation.

In the previous example, the computer has 655,360 total bytes of memory, of which 542,832 bytes are free. (Dividing 542,832 by 1024 translates into about 530KB.) To determine a realistic size for your RAM disk, subtract the amount of RAM that your largest program requires from the amount of available memory. Remember, too, that spreadsheet programs, such as Lotus 1-2-3, store data in RAM, and therefore you must also leave enough room to include your largest spreadsheet.

For example, assuming that Lotus 1-2-3 (Version 2) requires about 179KB of RAM and that your largest spreadsheet requires 50KB of RAM, the maximum amount of RAM available for a RAM disk would be about 301KB (530KB of available memory minus 179KB for 1-2-3 and 50KB for the largest spreadsheet). Because you wouldn't want to run out of memory during a crucial operation, and because spreadsheets have a tendency to grow, play it safe, and round that number down considerably, perhaps to a nice "computer" number like 256KB.

Chapter 10 discusses techniques for creating and modifying DOS ASCII files, such as CONFIG.SYS.

To create a RAM disk, you need to use a *device driver*. The computer automatically installs this device during the startup procedure if you modify your CONFIG.SYS file to include the command DEVICE=*device-driver*. If you are using IBM PC DOS, the *device driver* for creating a RAM disk is named VDISK.SYS. Therefore, the general technique for installing a RAM disk on an IBM computer using PC DOS is to add a command to your CONFIG.SYS file that uses the following syntax:

```
DEVICE=d:\path\VDISK.SYS size sector entries
```

Some (although not all) MS-DOS users with non-IBM machines must use the RAMDRIVE.SYS device driver rather than VDISK.SYS. Check your root (or DOS) directory to see if it contains RAMDRIVE.SYS or VDISK.SYS. Use whichever device driver is available for your computer. (You might also need to check the documentation that came with your computer for additional details.)

RAMDRIVE.SYS uses the same basic syntax as VDISK.SYS, as follows:

```
DEVICE=d:\path\RAMDRIVE.SYS size sector entries
```

See the reference to
VDISK.SYS in Appendix B
for additional details
concerning restrictions
and defaults on RAM
disks.

Whether you use VDISK.SYS or RAMDRIVE.SYS, you need to replace the italicized parameters with the following information:

d:path is the name of the drive and directory that contains VDISK.SYS or RAMDRIVE.SYS

size is the size (in kilobytes) of the RAM disk (if omitted, DOS creates a 64KB RAM disk)

sector is the size of each sector on the RAM disk—128, 256, or 512 bytes (if omitted, DOS uses 128)

entries is the maximum number of file names in the root directory of the RAM disk, within the range of 2 to 512 (if omitted, DOS permits 64)

You can omit parameters only if you've specified parameters to the left. For example, if you want to allow 128 directory entries, you cannot use the command `DEVICE=RAMDRIVE.SYS 128` or `DEVICE=VDISK.SYS 128` because DOS will think that the 128 refers to the size of the disk in kilobytes. Instead, you must specify both the size of the disk and the size of each sector (even if they are equal to the defaults), as in the following examples:

```
DEVICE=VDISK.SYS 64 256 128
```

or . . .

```
DEVICE=RAMDRIVE.SYS 64 256 128
```

When DOS creates a RAM disk, it automatically assigns the next available drive name to it. For example, if your computer has one hard disk, named C:, the RAM disk is automatically named D:.

Now, suppose you want to create a 256KB RAM disk in conventional RAM. If you are using IBM PC DOS, and VDISK.SYS is stored on the \DOS directory of drive C:, you must add the following command to your CONFIG.SYS file:

```
DEVICE=C:\DOS\VDISK.SYS 256
```

If you are using MS-DOS, and RAMDRIVE.SYS is stored on the root directory, you must add this command to the CONFIG.SYS file:

```
DEVICE=C:\RAMDRIVE.SYS 256
```

After you modify the CONFIG.SYS file, DOS automatically creates the RAM disk each time you start your computer in the future. (You can install it immediately by rebooting: press Ctrl-Alt-Del.) The following information about the RAM disk appears on your screen during the startup procedure (although if your AUTOEXEC.BAT file runs the DOS 4 Shell, this message is replaced by the Shell almost immediately, unless you put a PAUSE command above the DOSSHELL command in your AUTOEXEC.BAT file):

```
xxx DOS Version x.xx: VDISK virtual disk D:
    Sector size adjusted
    Directory entries adjusted
    Buffer size:       256 KB
    Sector size:       128
    Directory entries: 64
```

In this case, DOS named the RAM disk D: and gave it a 256KB storage capacity (the "Buffer size"). DOS used its internal default values for the sector size and directory entries, because you omitted values for these parameters in the DEVICE command in the CONFIG.SYS file. Each sector is 128 bytes, and you can store a maximum of 64 files on the RAM disk.

From now on, you can use the RAM disk exactly as you would any other disk drive. (However, don't forget that everything is erased from the RAM disk as soon as you turn off the computer.) If you are using the DOS 4 Shell notice that the drive name is included in the Drives Area of the File System.

Let's assume that your computer has one physical hard disk named C:, and your RAM disk is named D:. You can switch to the RAM disk from either the DOS Shell File System or from the command prompt, by entering `D:` (as in this example). If you were to enter the command `CHKDSK D:` to check the RAM disk, your screen would show something like the following:

```
Volume VDISK V4.0 created 12-06-84 12:00p

    256896 bytes total disk space
    256896 bytes available on disk

       128 bytes in each allocation unit
      2007 total allocation units on disk
      2007 available allocation units on disk

    655360 total bytes memory
    279424 bytes free
```

As you can see, the RAM disk has about 256KB of storage space available. Actually, it has a little less—256KB is actually 262,144 (256 * 1024) bytes. However, some of the RAM disk sectors are formatted as the boot record, FAT, and directory area, and these occupy some of the disk space. DOS automatically adds the disk volume label, VDISK V4.0 in this example, when the RAM disk is created.

Notice that the CHKDSK display shows only 279,424 bytes of memory (RAM) available. That's because DOS and your TSR programs occupy memory space, and also because a large part of RAM is now dedicated to the RAM disk, as shown in Figure 16.1.

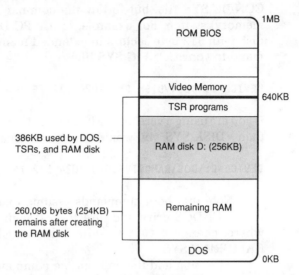

Figure 16.1. A RAM disk installed in conventional memory.

I'll discuss techniques for using a RAM disk effectively in a later section. The next section, however, explains the techniques for installing a RAM disk in extended memory, rather than in conventional RAM.

Installing a RAM Disk in Extended Memory

Even if you do use extended memory for a RAM disk, the driver that manages the RAM disk stays in conventional memory; therefore, your available RAM will decrease slightly.

If your computer has extended memory you should use that rather than conventional RAM for your RAM disk. Doing so saves precious RAM for running programs. If you are using DOS 4, you can easily determine how much extended memory is available by entering the **MEM** command (short for MEMory) at the command prompt. Your screen then shows how much conventional, expanded (if any), and extended (if any), memory is available, as in the following example:

```
655360 bytes total memory
655360 bytes available
542832 largest executable program size

4194304 bytes total extended memory
4194304 bytes available extended memory
```

None of the versions of DOS prior to 4 have a command that lets you determine how much extended and expanded memory is available. If you are using an earlier version of DOS, you must find out by referring to the documentation that came with your computer.

To convert Megabytes to Kilobytes, multiply by 1024. For example, the maximum size of a RAM disk when 4MB of extended memory is available is 4,096KB (4 * 1024).

To use extended memory as your RAM disk, activate the previously described VDISK.SYS or RAMDRIVE.SYS device driver in your CONFIG.SYS file, but follow the command with the /E (for Extended memory) switch. For example, to use PC DOS to create a 1.2MB RAM disk with 512 byte sectors in extended memory, add the following command to your CONFIG.SYS file:

```
DEVICE=C:\DOS\VDISK.SYS 1024 512 /E
```

If you are using a version of MS-DOS that provides RAMDRIVE.SYS rather than VDISK.SYS, you would add this command to your CONFIG.SYS file:

```
DEVICE=C:\DOS\RAMDRIVE.SYS 1024 512 /E
```

Note that both commands assume that the device driver is stored on the C:\DOS drive and directory. If your device driver is stored elsewhere, change `C\DOS\` to reflect the actual location of VDISK.SYS or RAMDRIVE.SYS.

After you add the appropriate command to your CONFIG.SYS file, the RAM disk is automatically installed in extended memory every time you start your computer. For example, let's suppose that your computer has one hard disk named C:. After you add the appropriate DEVICE command to your CONFIG.SYS file and boot up, your RAM disk is set up as drive D:. When you enter the following command at the command prompt:

```
CHKDSK D:
```

your screen displays information using the following general format:

```
volume VDISK V4.0 created 12-06-84 12:00p

 1042944 bytes total disk space
 1042944 bytes available on disk

     512 bytes in each allocation unit
    2037 total allocation units on disk
    2037 available allocation units on disk

  655360 total bytes memory
  541568 bytes free
```

In this example, the RAM disk has 1,042,944 bytes of storage space available. (Dividing that number by 1024 gives you 1.018MB, a little less than the 1.2MB specified. The boot record, FAT, and directory sectors of the RAM disk occupy the rest of the virtual drive.) Each sector (allocation unit) holds 512 bytes. Conventional RAM memory still has 541,568 bytes free, because the RAM disk is in extended memory, as Figure 16.2 shows.

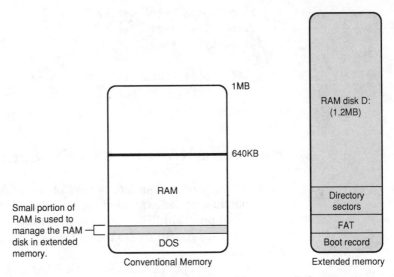

Figure 16.2. A RAM disk created in extended memory.

If you are using DOS 4, you could enter the **MEM** command to check available memory after installing this 1.2MB RAM disk in extended memory. Assuming that your computer contains a total of 4MB (4096KB) of extended memory, your screen would show (approximately) the following specifications:

```
655360 total bytes memory
655260 bytes available
541568 bytes free

4194304 bytes total extended memory
3145738 bytes available extended memory
```

As you can see, 3,145,738 bytes of extended memory remain available after you install the 1.2MB RAM disk. The rest is used by the RAM disk.

You could have used the entire 4MB (4096KB) of extended memory for your RAM disk by using one of the following commands in your CONFIG.SYS file:

```
DEVICE=C:\DOS\VDISK.SYS 4096 512 /E
```

or

```
DEVICE=C:\DOS\RAMDRIVE.SYS 4096 512 /E
```

Then, entering the **MEM** command would show different results, because all 4MB of extended memory would be dedicated to the RAM disk:

```
655360 total bytes memory
655260 bytes available
541568 bytes free

4194304 bytes total extended memory
      0 bytes available extended memory
```

Installing a RAM Disk in Expanded Memory

If your computer has expanded, rather than extended memory, you can use all, or a portion, of the expanded memory for a RAM disk. Keep in mind, however, that programs that use (or require) expanded memory will not be able to access that portion of expanded memory that you've designated for a RAM disk.

To convert expanded memory to a RAM disk, your CONFIG.SYS file must first install and activate the expanded memory (as discussed in "Installing Expanded Memory" later in this chapter). If the commands in the CONFIG.SYS file for installing expanded memory are *not* executed before the DEVICE=VDISK.SYS command used to install RAM disk, an error will occur, and the RAM disk will not be installed.

The exact command syntax required for installing a RAM disk in expanded memory depends on your version of DOS, and whether or not you are using the DOS device driver, or a particular computer manufacturer's device driver, to install the RAM disk.

If you are using DOS 4 and its VDISK.SYS device driver, you use the /X switch in the DEVICE=VDISK.SYS command to install the RAM disk in expanded memory. If you are using DOS 3.2 or later, and the RAMDRIVE.SYS device driver, you use the /A switch in the DEVICE=RAMDRIVE.SYS command. (You may need to check the DOS manual, the user's manual that came with your particular computer, or the manual that came with your expanded memory board, for specific details.)

If you are using an IBM PC AT that has one of the expanded memory boards supported by the XMA2EMS.SYS device driver, you can use up to 16MB of expanded memory as a RAM disk. The DEVICE=XMA2EMS.SYS command must precede the DEVICE=VDISK.SYS command in your CONFIG.SYS file.

For additional information on the XMA2EMS.SYS device driver, see the XMA2EMS.SYS entry in Appendix B, as well as the section titled "Installing Expanded Memory" later in this chapter.

For example, the first CONFIG.SYS command below installs all of the available expanded memory, using the XMA2EMS.SYS device driver delivered with IBM PC DOS version 4. The second CONFIG.SYS command converts 1MB (1,024KB) of the expanded memory to a RAM disk. Notice that the command for installing expanded memory precedes the command for installing the RAM disk in expanded memory. Both commands assume that the device driver files, XMA2EMS.SYS and VDISK.SYS, are stored on the \DOS directory of drive C:.

```
REM -- First install all of the expanded memory.
DEVICE=C:\DOS\XMA2EMS.SYS FRAME=D000
REM -- Then use 1,024KB of expanded memory for RAM disk.
DEVICE=C:\DOS\VDISK.SYS 1024 /X
```

Both of the DEVICE command above must be in the CONFIG.SYS file, in the order shown. (The REM commands are simply programmer comments, and have no effect on the startup procedure.)

The RAMDRIVE.SYS device driver was introduced in version 3.2 of DOS.

If your version of DOS, or computer, requires the RAMDRIVE.SYS device driver (rather than VDISK.SYS) to install a RAM disk, then you use the /A switch, rather than the /X switch, to install the RAM disk in expanded memory. Again, the DEVICE command for installing expanded memory *must* precede the DEVICE command for creating the RAM disk, so that the expanded memory is activated before the RAM disk is created.

For example, the CONFIG.SYS commands below activate expanded memory on a Compaq computer (using Compaq's CEMM.SYS device driver, discussed in more detail later in this chapter), and then install a 1MB (1,024KB) RAM disk in expanded memory:

```
REM -- First install all of the expanded memory.
DEVICE=C:\DOS\CEMM.SYS
REM -- Then use 1,024KB of expanded memory for RAM disk.
DEVICE=C:\DOS\RAMDRIVE.SYS 1024 /A
```

Installing Multiple RAM Disks

If you want to create multiple RAM disks, for example drives D:, E:, and F:, merely include multiple DEVICE=VDISK.SYS (or RAMDRIVE.SYS) commands in your CONFIG.SYS file. DOS automatically assigns the next available drive name to each RAM disk.

However, you should also include a LASTDRIVE command in your CONFIG.SYS file to prepare DOS for the multiple virtual drives. Insert the LASTDRIVE command in your CONFIG.SYS file using the general syntax:

```
LASTDRIVE=drive letter
```

where *drive letter* is the name (without the colon) of the last virtual drive. For example, if your computer has a hard disk named C:, and you want to add three 512KB RAM disks in 1.5MB of extended memory, include the following commands in your CONFIG.SYS file:

```
LASTDRIVE=F
DEVICE=C:\DOS\VDISK.SYS 512 /E
DEVICE=C:\DOS\VDISK.SYS 512 /E
DEVICE=C:\DOS\VDISK.SYS 512 /E
```

DOS automatically assigns these drives the names D:, E:, and F:.

The first command prepares DOS to support drives named A:, B:, C:, D:, E:, and F:. The first DEVICE command sets up a 512KB hard disk, named D: (because the name C: is already assigned to the physical hard disk). The second DEVICE command automatically assigns the name E: to the 512KB RAM disk. The third DEVICE command assigns the name F: to the last 512KB RAM disk.

Using a RAM Disk Safely

As mentioned earlier, a major disadvantage of using a RAM disk is that as soon as you turn off the computer, all data stored on the RAM disk is immediately erased. A virtual disk acts so much like a physical disk drive that you can very easily forget this important fact, and therefore lose all your data.

For example, suppose that your hard disk is your current drive and that you are creating a document with your word processor. When you want to quit for the day, you merely save your document, exit the word processor, and turn off the computer. The document is safely stored on the disk. However, if you use this same general procedure to save your work to a RAM disk, your work will be lost, because the RAM disk is erased as soon as you turn off the computer. It's an easy mistake to make, and can be averted only by taking extra measures to copy the data from the RAM disk to a physical disk before you turn off the computer.

The safest way to use a RAM disk is to create a batch file that automatically copies the file (or files) you want to work with onto the RAM disk and then runs your program. When you exit the program, the batch file then immediately copies all the files from the RAM disk back to the hard disk (or a diskette), in case you forget to do so. The following examples demonstrate this procedure.

Using a RAM Disk to Speed Word Processing

To best take advantage of a RAM disk when using a word processing program, such as WordStar or WordPerfect, first create a batch file that copies, in order of importance, the following files to your RAM disk:

■ The word processing file (or files) that you are editing.

■ Any overlay files that your word processing program uses.

■ The main program (.COM or .EXE) that starts your word processor.

By order of importance, I mean that you should copy as much as will fit, starting with the files you want to edit. If your RAM disk is not large enough to hold the word processing overlay files and/or the program, then merely copy the files you want to edit to the RAM disk.

For example, let's suppose that you use the WordStar word processing program (Version 4) to create and edit documents. To speed your disk transfers when working with large documents, you decide to use a RAM disk. Ideally, you should store the files you want to edit, as well as the WordStar program and its overlays, on the RAM disk.

Figure 16.3 shows a batch file named WSRAM.BAT that copies the files to be edited, the WordStar program and two of its overlays, and the main spelling dictionary to the RAM disk. The batch file assumes that the physical hard disk is named C: and that the RAM disk is named D:. You would store this batch file in any directory included in your PATH setting.

To illustrate how this batch file works, let's assume that you want to use WordStar to edit a file named CHAP1.TXT on the RAM disk. First, change to the directory that contains the file you want to edit, and then enter the command WSRAM CHAP1.TXT.

The first command, COPY %1 D: copies CHAP1.TXT to the RAM disk (drive D:). The next two commands, IF NOT EXIST D:WSMSGS.OVR COPY C:\WS4\WSMSGS.OVR D: and IF NOT EXIST D:\WSSPELL.OVR COPY C:\WS4\WSSPELL.OVR D:, check to see if the overlay files WSMSGS.OVR and WSSPELL.OVR already exist on the RAM disk. If not, those files are also copied to the RAM disk. The RAM disk must have at least 67,196 bytes free (after the file you are editing is loaded) for these to fit. Otherwise, you must omit these commands from your batch file.

The next command, IF NOT EXIST D:MAIN.DCT COPY C:\WS4\MAIN.DCT D:, copies the main spelling dictionary to the RAM disk. This file requires an additional 277,504 bytes of available space on the RAM disk. Omit this command if your RAM disk does not have sufficient memory.

The next command, IF NOT EXIST D:WS.EXE COPY C:\WS4\WS.EXE D:, copies the WS.EXE program to the RAM disk (if it has not already been copied). This requires yet an additional 78,208 bytes of free space. Omit this command if you don't have sufficient space on the RAM disk.

The next command, D:, changes to the RAM disk, and then the command WS %1 runs WordStar, automatically loading the file to be edited (CHAP1.TXT in this example). Note that if you entered a command such as WSRAM CHAP??.DOC to edit multiple files on the RAM disk, WSRAM.BAT would copy all the files that match the ambiguous file name, but WordStar would not start with a specific file to edit. Instead, you would use the usual D or N option on the WordStar opening menu to select a file to edit.

While you use WordStar, the batch file remains in a state of suspension. You can now edit and save any of the files on the RAM disk. When you finish, exit WordStar in the usual manner. Doing so passes control to DOS, which executes the remaining commands beneath WS %1 in WSRAM.BAT.

The first command, COPY %1 C:, copies the edited file (or files) back to the original directory on drive C:. The command COPY *.BAK C: also copies to drive C: the backup (.BAK) files that WordStar creates.

If your WSRAM.BAT batch file does not copy the WordStar program and its overlay files to the RAM disk, then the current PATH or APPEND setting must provide a search path to the drive and directory that the WordStar program files are stored on.

```
@ECHO OFF
REM *********************** WSRAM.BAT
REM Copies WordStar and files to edit to
REM a RAM disk, and copies them back to the
REM hard disk when done editing.
ECHO Moving files to the RAM disk.

REM -- Copy files to edit to the RAM disk.
COPY %1 D:

REM -- Copy main overlays to the RAM disk
REM -- (omit these commands if space does not permit)
IF NOT EXIST D:WSMSGS.OVR COPY C:\WS4\WSMSGS.OVR D:
IF NOT EXIST D:WSSPELL.OVR COPY C:\WS4\WSSPELL.OVR D:

REM -- Copy spelling dictionary to the RAM disk
REM -- (omit this command if space does not permit)
IF NOT EXIST D:MAIN.DCT COPY C:\WS4\MAIN.DCT D:

REM -- Copy the main program to the RAM disk
REM -- (omit this command if space does not permit)
IF NOT EXIST D:WS.EXE COPY C:\WS4.EXE D:

REM -- Move to RAM disk and run WordStar.
D:
WS %1
REM -- These commands are executed when you exit
REM -- WordStar, to copy edited files to the hard disk.
ECHO Copying edited files back to drive C:
COPY %1 C:
COPY *.BAK C:
ERASE %1
ERASE *.BAK

REM -- Return to drive C:
C:
```

Figure 16.3. WSRAM.BAT makes WordStar safe to use on
a RAM disk.

The commands ERASE %1 and ERASE *.BAK then erase the edited and
backup file (or files) from the RAM disk. Finally, the command C: returns
you to drive C:.

When you use a batch file like WSRAM.BAT to run your word processing program on a RAM disk, you will notice the greatest improvement
in speed when working with large text files that normally don't fit into
conventional RAM. You might not notice a quicker processing of smaller

files, because your word processor might always be able to handle these in RAM.

Using a RAM Disk for Database Management

When using a database management system, such as dBASE IV, you can significantly improve the speed of operations on large data files by working with a copy stored in the RAM disk. Again, the safest way to use the RAM disk is to create a batch file that automates the process of copying data to the RAM disk before processing and then back to the physical disk after exiting the database manager.

For example, the DBRAM.BAT batch file shown in Figure 16.4 copies a dBASE IV database (.DBF) file, including the index (.MDX) and memo field (.DBT) files associated with that database, to a RAM disk named D: so that operations on the entire file will be performed more quickly. This batch file requires that the directory that contains dBASE IV (usually \DBASE) be specified by the current PATH or APPEND command so that DOS can find the dBASE program while the RAM disk is the current drive.

```
@ECHO OFF
REM ************************ DBRAM.BAT
REM -- copies a dBASE IV database (.DBF),
REM -- memo field (.DBT), and index (.MDX)
REM -- files to the RAM disk.

REM -- First copy data and index files to the RAM disk.
COPY %1.DB? D:
COPY %1.MDX D:

REM -- Switch to the RAM disk and run DBASE. (Assumes that
REM -- D: is the RAM disk, and DBASE.EXE and its overlays
REM -- are available in the current PATH or APPEND setting).
D:
DBASE

REM -- These commands are executed when you exit dBASE
REM -- to copy database,index, and other dbase object
REM -- files to drive C:,and then erase them from the RAM disk.
FOR %%c IN (D F K L M P Q S U V W) DO IF EXIST *.%%c?? COPY
     *.%%c?? C:
FOR %%c IN (D F K L M P Q S U V W) DO IF EXIST *.%%c?? ERASE
     *.%%c??
REM -- Return to drive C:
C:
```

Figure 16.4. The DBRAM.BAT batch file.

To use the DBRAM.BAT batch file, first change to the directory that contains the dBASE file that you want to process. Then, enter the **DBRAM** command followed by the name of the database file (excluding the .DBF extension). For example, to work with the CUSTLIST.DBF database stored on the \SALES directory, first change to the \SALES directory, and then enter the command **DBRAM CUSTLIST**. (The DBRAM.BAT file must also be on a directory in the current PATH or APPEND setting.)

Any dBASE reports, forms, queries, applications, or programs that you create while using the RAM disk are also saved on the RAM disk. Creating these additional files on the RAM disk speeds the compilation procedure that dBASE performs. However, you must be sure your RAM disk is large enough to accommodate these additional files.

If you use your RAM disk only for dBASE databases, you can replace the complex FOR loops in DBRAM.BAT with simple COPY and ERASE commands.

When you exit dBASE, the DBRAM.BAT batch file copies all dBASE IV database, index, and object files from the RAM disk to drive C:, and then it erases them from the RAM disk. The FOR loops handle this job by copying and erasing all files that match the skeletons *.D?? *.F??, *.K??, *.M??, *.P??, and so on, which encompass all possible dBASE objects (except for catalog files, which need not be copied back to the physical disk).

The sample batch files presented here are only basic examples. There are countless other ways in which you can use a RAM disk effectively and safely. Remember that a RAM disk only speeds disk searches. If you use a RAM disk to store spreadsheet data, you will only see a significant increase in speed when you save files to and retrieve data and files from the RAM disk. dBASE operations performed on data stored in RAM, such as spreadsheet recalculation, will not be any faster.

Installing Expanded Memory

Expanded memory allows DOS programs to access RAM above the 640KB limit. Exactly how you install expanded memory on your system is determined by many factors, including your computer's microprocessor, the type of expanded memory board (or motherboard) that you have, and your version of DOS. However, the deeper your understanding of the principles of expanded memory, the easier it will be for you to install it.

As mentioned in Chapter 15, DOS uses a "switching area" in conventional memory above the 640KB RAM limit to manage data stored in expanded memory. This area is divided into four contiguous 16KB blocks of memory called *pages*. Typically, these pages are named P0, P1, P2, and P3. Combined, these four pages create the 64KB switching area which is called the *page frame*.

Some device drivers for expanded memory require that you specify the *segment* address in memory at which the page frame begins (called the page frame's *base* address). Furthermore, some of these device drivers require that you specify this segment address in hexadecimal (which can make matters even more confusing).

Figure 16.5 shows an example (and more detailed) memory map, with segment addresses expressed in hexadecimal. The base address for the 64KB page frame is usually a segment at, or above, C400.

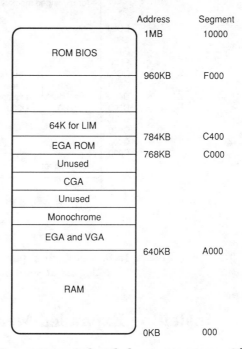

Figure 16.5. A detailed memory map, with segment addresses.

A starting address of C400 is usually considered to be the lowest "safe" starting point for the 64KB page frame that the expanded memory manager can use, because this is the first segment above RAM and video memory that is almost certainly unused.

Figure 16.6 shows a more detailed view of the 16KB segment addresses from C000 to EC00. In this example, segments D000 to DC00 are used for the 64KB page frame. Segment D000 starts the first 16KB page (P0), segment D400 starts the second page (P1), D800 starts the third page (P2), and DC00 starts the fourth page (P3).

Notice in Figure 16.6 that the segments increase in increments of 400 hex. You can use any of the segments shown in the range of C400 to EC00 as the base address for the expanded memory manager's page frame.

As mentioned earlier, your expanded memory manager may be able to find a suitable base address on its own, and therefore you may not even need to bother with these details. The sections that follow present a few general examples of installing expanded memory. But because different computers and different expanded memory adapters use different techniques, you should refer to the manual that came with your computer or expanded memory adapter for details.

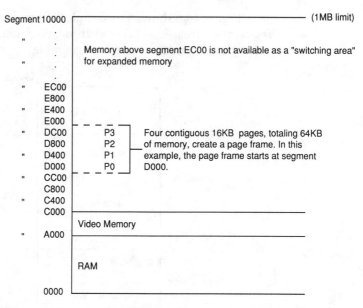

Figure 16.6. Four 16KB pages form a 64KB page frame that begins at segment D00 in memory.

Installing Expanded Memory with PC DOS 4

PC DOS 4, the version of DOS 4 that is delivered with IBM computers, contains a device driver named XMA2EMS.SYS that supports the LIM (EMS) standard for expanded memory. To use XMA2EMS.SYS on an IBM 80286 computer, your computer must be using one of the following optional expanded memory adapters (or a compatible adapter that conforms to the LIM 4.0 standard):

Computers that use the 80386 processor can emulate expanded memory without an expanded memory adapter, as discussed later in this chapter.

- IBM 2MB Expanded Memory Adapter
- IBM PS/2 80286 Expanded Memory Adapter /A
- IBM PS/2 80286 Memory Expansion Option

Use the XMA2EMS.SYS device driver as you would any other device driver: add the name to a DEVICE command in your CONFIG.SYS file. Specify a base segment address for the page frame in the range of C000 to E000, the most commonly used page frame address being D000.

For example, to use all of the memory in your expanded memory adapter, your CONFIG.SYS file must contain the command:

The strange name XMA2EMS is an abbreviation for eXpanded-Memory-Adapter-to-EMS (the LIM specification).

```
DEVICE=C:\DOS\XMA2EMS.SYS FRAME=D000
```

The expanded memory becomes active the next time you start your computer (or when you reboot). To verify that the memory is available, enter the

MEM command at the DOS command prompt. Your screen then displays a message similar to the following (your numbers, of course, will depend on memory availability in your computer):

```
655360 bytes total memory
655360 bytes available
539664 largest executable program size

1441792 bytes total EMS memory
1048576 bytes free EMS memory
```

If you want to use only a portion of expanded memory (perhaps assigning the other portion to a RAM disk), use the /X: switch at the end of the command and follow it by the number of 16KB pages of EMS. For example, let's suppose that your computer has 4MB of expanded memory, but you want to use only 2MB of it. Recall that 1 megabyte is 1,024KB; so, 2MB is 2,048KB. Dividing 2,048 by 16 gives you 128 (the number of 16KB pages). Therefore, the command to put in your CONFIG.SYS file is:

```
DEVICE=C:\DOS\XMA2EMS.SYS FRAME=D000 /X:128
```

If your expanded memory board offers 1MB (1024KB) of expanded memory, and you want to use half of that (512KB), you need to specify 32 (that is, 512/16=32) pages in your CONFIG.SYS file, as follows:

```
DEVICE=C:\DOS\XMA2EMS.SYS FRAME=D000 /X:32
```

Again, after you place the appropriate command in the CONFIG.SYS file and reboot, use the MEM command to verify that the expanded memory is available. From now on, any program that supports expanded memory, such as Microsoft Excel will automatically use the expanded memory to store data beyond the 640KB limit.

Installing Expanded Memory with MS-DOS

If you are using MS-DOS (Versions 3 or 4) on a non-IBM microcomputer, the exact techniques that you use to install expanded memory depend primarily on your expanded memory adapter. In most cases, you still need to modify your CONFIG.SYS file to include the DEVICE=*driver name* command.

The *driver name* you use is determined by the expanded memory board in your computer. For example, the AST RAMPage! board uses a driver named REMM.SYS. The Intel Above-Board uses a driver named EMM.SYS. Compaq computers that use the 80286 processor and an expanded memory adapter require a driver named CEMMP.SYS.

Refer to the documentation that came with your expanded memory adapter (or your computer) for specific instructions about modifying your CONFIG.SYS file. The documentation for a program that can use expanded memory may provide additional useful information. For example, the Microsoft Excel package contains a disk (the *Utilities Disk*) that includes device drivers for many different expanded memory adapters, as well as documentation for using the drivers.

Emulating Expanded Memory on 80386 Computers

The 80386 microprocessor can *emulate* expanded memory using extended memory, or even a disk file; you do not need to have an expanded memory adapter installed in your computer. Again, the exact techniques you use will vary from computer to computer, and you will need to refer to the documentation that came with your 80386 computer for details. However, a few examples might help you better understand the procedures outlined in your documentation.

Emulating Expanded Memory with PC DOS 4

If you have an IBM 80386 computer, such as the PS/2 Model 80, and you are using IBM PC DOS 4, you can emulate expanded memory by using the XMAEM.SYS device driver. This device driver emulates the IBM PS/2 80286 Expanded Memory Adapter/A, which conforms to the LIM 4.0 EMS standard.

Your CONFIG.SYS file must contain two DEVICE commands, each specifying a different device driver. To use all of the extended memory on an 80386 computer as expanded memory, you must add these two commands (in the order shown) to your CONFIG.SYS file:

```
DEVICE=C:\DOS\XMAEM.SYS
DEVICE=C:\DOS\XMA2EMS.SYS FRAME=D000
```

The first command, in essence, tells DOS that expanded memory must be emulated because no expanded memory adapter is installed. The second command then installs the expanded memory as though an adapter existed.

You can also set aside a specific amount of extended memory to be used for expanded memory, by specifying the number of 16KB pages. For example, you need 64 pages to specify 1MB of expanded memory (that is, 1MB is 1,024KB bytes, and 1024 divided by 16 is 64). Place this value to the right of the XMAEM.SYS driver name in your CONFIG.SYS file, as follows:

```
DEVICE=C:\DOS\XMAEM.SYS 64
```

```
DEVICE=C:\DOS\XMA2EMS.SYS FRAME=D000
```

Remember that the expanded memory is not installed until the next time you start the computer (or until you reboot). You can then verify that the expanded memory is installed by entering the MEM command at the command prompt.

Emulating Expanded Memory with MS-DOS

Most 80386-based computers come with a utilities disk that includes a device driver for emulating expanded memory. For example, the Compaq 386 computer comes with the CEMM.EXE (Compaq Expanded Memory Manager) driver. This driver is documented in the *Compaq Supplemental Software Guide* included with the Compaq 386 computer.

To use CEMM.SYS, first copy the files CEMM.EXE and CEMM.COM from the Compaq *User programs* disk onto your hard disk, either in the root directory or in a directory named \DOS (if you have one).

Next, modify your CONFIG.SYS file so that it contains a command that uses the general syntax:

```
DEVICE=d:\path\CEMM.EXE [size] [frame-address] [ON|OFF|AUTO]
```

This syntax includes the following elements:

d:\path is the location of the CEMM.EXE file.

size is the amount of expanded memory to install, from 16KB to a maximum of 8192KB (8MB). All Compaq 386 computers are delivered with at least 256KB of extended memory. Use a size greater than 256 only if you have installed additional extended memory.

frame-address is the starting memory location for the page frame. If you omit this option, CEMM.EXE automatically selects an available page frame.

ON|OFF|AUTO ON makes expanded memory available immediately; OFF disables expanded memory until you explicitly enable it again (using the CEMM command discussed later); and AUTO lets application programs turn on expanded memory as needed.

For example, suppose your Compaq 386 has 4MB of memory installed, and you want to use 1MB (1,024KB) of this memory as expanded memory. You wish to use the remaining 3MB (3,072KB) as a RAM disk. To do so, add these two lines to your CONFIG.SYS file:

```
DEVICE=C:\DOS\CEMM.EXE 1024 AUTO
DEVICE=C:\DOS\VDISK 3072 /E
```

The first command installs the 1MB of expanded memory in AUTO mode, and the second command installs the 3MB RAM disk in extended memory.

After you change the CONFIG.SYS file and reboot, you can use the CEMM.COM program to enable and disable expanded memory. Entering the command `CEMM ON` at the command prompt activates the expanded memory. Entering `CEMM OFF` disables expanded memory. Use `CHKDSK` to verify the size of the RAM disk. If you have DOS 4, use the `MEM` command to check the size of expanded memory while it is enabled. (If CEMM is set to OFF, MEM reports no available expanded memory.)

Resolving EMS Conflicts

If you add an expanded memory device driver to your CONFIG.SYS file, and then DOS won't start or displays error messages during startup, you might be having a memory conflict. These conflicts occur when two different devices attempt to use the same memory addresses within a page frame.

To resolve these conflicts, you need to modify the commands in your CONFIG.SYS file so that non-conflicting addresses are used. In some cases, your device driver displays information to help you resolve the conflict. To demonstrate this, let's discuss an example that uses the DOS 4 XMA2EMS.SYS device driver. Suppose your CONFIG.SYS file includes the command `DEVICE=XMA2EMS.SYS FRAME=D000`, which makes D000 the starting address for the page frame, as shown in Figure 16.5.

If any of the memory addresses in the segments from D000 to DC00 are already being used by other devices, DOS cannot access this area for expanded memory. You will then need to specify other addresses for expanded memory.

If the problem is a fairly straightforward one, DOS 4 displays helpful information on the screen during the startup procedure, as in the following example (*xxxx* is a hexadecimal number):

```
No page address specified
Specified page address conflicts
   with installed adapter at address xxxx
Possible 16KB page available at: xxxx
Possible 64KB frame available at: xxxx
```

These messages tell you that memory conflicts are occurring, and they recommend possible 16KB pages and 64KB frames that might be available. Write down these messages on a piece of paper (or press Shift-Print Screen to print them). If they disappear from the screen too quickly for you to read, try rebooting the system (with the Ctrl-Alt-Del key combination), and then press the Pause key or Ctrl-S as soon as the messages appear. If you still can't read the messages, modify your AUTOEXEC.BAT file by putting PAUSE commands before the DOSSHELL and any CLS commands that clear the messages from the screen; then, reboot.

If your screen displays the message `Possible 64KB frame available at: xxxx`, then you need to modify the DEVICE=XMA2EMS.SYS command in your CONFIG.SYS file to use the suggested 64KB frame address. For example, if your screen displays the message `Possible 64KB frame available at: C000`, then modify the CONFIG.SYS file by changing the FRAME portion of the expanded memory DEVICE command to C000, as follows:

```
DEVICE=C:\DOS\XMA2EMS.SYS FRAME=C000
```

Be sure to spell everything correctly, and check to see that the only blank space in the command is between .SYS and FRAME. (If you are using the /X switch, a blank space must also separate the command and the switch.) Save the edited CONFIG.SYS file in ASCII format and press Ctrl-Alt-Del to reboot so that you can see if the change corrected the problem.

If, during startup, your screen displayed the message `Specified page address conflicts with installed adapter at address: xxx`, followed by several messages such as `Possible 16KB page available at: xxx`, but no 64KB page frame address was suggested, then DOS cannot find four free contiguous blocks for the page frame. If this situation arises, you need to study the documentation that came with your devices so that you can discover where the conflicts are occurring. Then, you must reconfigure memory to prevent the conflicts. (For additional information, see the entry XMA2EMS.SYS in Appendix B.)

Using a Disk Cache to Speed Performance

Whether or not your computer has extended or expanded memory, you can use a disk *cache* (pronounced *cash*) to speed up processes that involve disk Input/Output (I/O). These processes include all operations that read data from the disk into RAM (Input) and write data from RAM to the disk (Output). The cache operates as an intermediary between the disk and RAM.

When a program requests data from the disk, DOS stores the data in the cache and then sends copies to the program (in RAM). When the program changes the data and returns it to the disk, DOS stores only the modified data in the cache. Although the program might change several items of data and send them to the disk for safe keeping, DOS actually stores these changes in the cache.

When the program finishes making changes to the data, or the cache becomes filled, *then* DOS copies all the modified data in the cache to the disk for safe storage. This single transfer is much more efficient than writing small chunks of modified data to the disk on a piecemeal basis (see Figure 16.7).

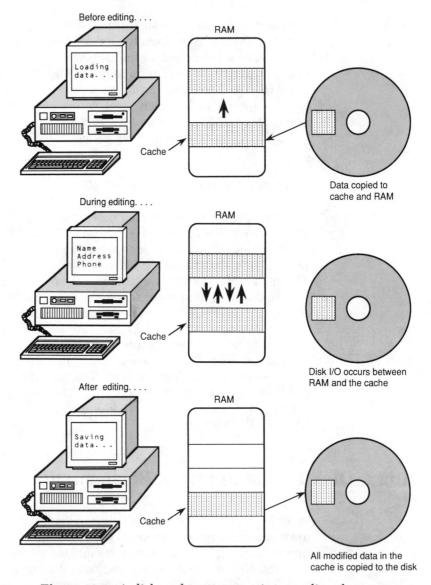

Figure 16.7. A disk cache acts as an intermediary between
RAM and a disk.

Sophisticated caching programs also keep track of how *often* data in
the cache is being used. When more space is needed in the cache to store
new data, the least-often used data is saved to disk and discarded from the
cache to make room. This method makes the cache more efficient, because
the cache tends to maintain data that is being modified frequently, rather
than only occasionally.

Some caching programs can also "look ahead" when a program requests data from the disk, reading a little more data than the program re-

quests in anticipation that the program will soon request the additional data. Later, if the program indeed requests the additional data, it's already in the cache, and therefore DOS doesn't need to access the disk.

The only disadvantage to a disk cache is that it is usually stored in RAM, thereby consuming some of your valuable memory. You *might* be able to use expanded memory for your disk cache, but this is dependent on your version of DOS and your specific disk cache program.

You can use several techniques to set up a disk cache. A simplified cache that does not provide the frequency-checking features of the more sophisticated cache programs is available in all versions of DOS. See the BUFFERS entry in Appendix B for information about using BUFFERS.

Actually, the BUFFERS command in DOS 4 provides the look-ahead capabilities, but not the frequency-checking, of a disk cache.

DOS 3.3 and 4 offer a more complete disk cache program, named FASTOPEN, which offers both frequency-checking and look-ahead. See the FASTOPEN entry in Appendix B for further information.

Some computers provide their own disk cache programs, which are separate from DOS. For example, the IBM PS/2 Models 50 through 80 provide a disk cache program named IBMCACHE. Many Compaq computers provide a program named CACHE to manage disk caching. Refer to the owner's manual, or perhaps the DOS manual, that came with your computer for information about using its unique disk caching system.

Summary

RAM disks, extended memory, expanded memory, and disk caching allow you to take full advantage of your microcomputer's potential. Many of these options are specific to a particular computer, and their features are made available to DOS through the use of device drivers. You might need to refer to the manuals that came with your computer or option board for information about using these features. In summary:

- A RAM disk simulates a physical disk drive in conventional RAM, extended memory, or expanded memory and permits quicker disk operations.

- On most computers, the device driver for installing a RAM disk is named VDISK.SYS or RAMDRIVE.SYS.

- To use extended memory, rather than conventional RAM, for a RAM disk, use the /E switch with the VDISK.SYS or RAMDRIVE.SYS device driver. To use expanded memory for a RAM disk, use the /X switch for VDISK.SYS and the /A switch for RAMDRIVE.SYS.

- Because files stored on a RAM disk are erased as soon as you turn off the computer, use the safety procedure of creating batch files that automatically copy data from a RAM disk to a physical disk when you exit a program.

- Expanded memory allows DOS to access memory beyond the 640KB

RAM limit via a 64KB page frame in the hexadecimal range of C000 to E000.

■ The specific device driver that you use for expanded memory depends on the expanded memory adapter installed in your computer, and perhaps on the version of DOS that you are using.

■ The 80386 microprocessor can emulate expanded memory using either extended memory or a disk file.

■ Disk caching is a technique that speeds disk I/O by acting as an intermediary between RAM and the disk.

■ The DOS BUFFERS device driver offers limited disk caching for all versions of DOS.

■ DOS 3.3 and 4 offer a more sophisticated caching program named FASTOPEN. Individual computer manufacturers often provide their own disk caching programs as well.

Solutions to Common Problems

This chapter, the final tutorial section of the book, discusses tips and techniques for using DOS to solve common computer problems. The seemingly unrelated topics in this chapter, in fact, represent the most commonly asked questions (in my experience) about how to use DOS to effectively handle "real-world" problems. Hopefully, the following sections will save you hours of frustration by helping you solve pesky problems that sometimes arise as you work with your computer.

Remember that Appendix B provides additional technical details about all DOS commands and options, and you can also look inside the front cover of this book for a quick reference listing of DOS commands and functions.

I hope that these topics cover any questions that you might now have. However, even if you do not have a specific question or unresolved problem at the moment, reading about the solutions to these common problems will better arm you to resolve them when they arise.

Solving Disk Format Incompatibility Problems

From the gradual extinction of the 8-inch floppy disk, in the early 1980s, until 1986, when the IBM PS/2 line of computers emerged, the 5.25-inch diskette was the standard among microcomputers. Since then, many computers, particularly laptops, come equipped with the new 720KB and 1.44MB 3.5-inch drives, thus causing compatibility problems for anyone who must use both types of machines.

There are two basic solutions to the 3.5-inch vs. 5.25-inch compatibility problem. If you own two computers—one with 5.25-inch drives and the other with 3.5-inch drives—you can solve the problem rather inexpensively using software. If you have a single computer, but you need to be able to read and write to both 5.25-inch and 3.5-inch diskettes, you'll need to use the more expensive hardware alternative.

Software Solutions

Suppose you have a laptop computer that has one or two 3.5-inch disk drives and a desktop computer that uses 5.25-inch diskettes. How do you get data from one machine to the other? Well, because you can easily transport the laptop, merely connect it to the desktop computer with a cable and use software to transfer data from a program on one machine to a similar program on the other machine.

Several software companies offer programs that make the laptop-to-desktop (and vice versa) transfers quick, easy, and uncomplicated. Some (although not all) of the programs also include the necessary cable. The following list includes the names of some of these programs and the companies that offer them. Your computer or software dealer can offer more alternatives.

> The Brooklyn Bridge
> White Crane Systems
> 6889 Peachtree Industrial Blvd., #151
> Norcross, GA 30092
> (404) 394-3119
>
> Fastwire II
> Rupp Brothers
> P.O. Drawer J
> Lenox Hill Station
> New York, NY 10021
>
> Lap-Link Plus
> Traveling Software, Inc.
> 18702 North Creek Pkwy.
> Bothell, WA 98011
> (206) 483-8088
>
> Paranet Turbo
> Nicat Marketing Corp.
> 207-788 Beatty St.
> Vancouver, B.C.
> Canada V68 2M1
> (604) 681-3421

5.25-Inch High-Density/Low Density Conversions

All disk drives can read diskettes that are the appropriate size and the same or lower density. For example, a 1.2MB high-density disk drive can read both

1.2MB 5.25-inch diskettes and 360KB 5.25-inch diskettes. A 360KB 5.25-inch drive can read 360KB diskettes, but not the higher density 1.2MB diskettes.

Similarly, a 1.44MB 3.5-inch diskette can read both 720KB 3.5-inch diskettes and 1.44MB 3.5-inch diskettes. However, a 720KB 3.5-inch diskette drive cannot read a higher-density 1.44MB 3.5-inch diskette.

DOS also allows you to format diskettes that can be used in the same types of drives or in those of lower density. For example, suppose your desktop computer uses 1.44MB 3.5-inch drives, but your laptop uses 720KB 3.5-inch diskettes drives. How would you format a diskette and copy files to it, so that you could use it with your laptop?

One solution is to use the laptop to format a 720KB diskette and then to copy files from the desktop computer hard disk to that diskette.

An alternative solution, if your laptop is not available, is merely to tell DOS to format the blank 3.5-inch diskette in the 1.44MB drive for use in a 720KB drive. Using DOS 4, the command would be FORMAT A: /F:720. (See the FORMAT entry in Appendix B for other solutions.) Then, COPY the files that you need from your hard disk to the 720KB diskette in drive A:. Your laptop will have no problem using this diskette and the copied files.

The same basic solution can be used with most 5.25-inch diskettes. To format a disk for use in a 360KB drive, using a high-capacity 1.2MB drive, you can use the /F:360 switch with the FORMAT command (in DOS 4), or the /4 switch with the FORMAT command in Versions 3.0 and later (again, refer to the FORMAT command in Appendix B if necessary).

The one exception to the use of the /F:360 and /4 switches is the IBM PC AT computer. With the AT, you can still use the FORMAT A: /F:360 or FORMAT A: /4 command to *format* the disk in drive A: as a 360KB diskette, but as soon as you *copy* a file onto that diskette, it is no longer readable in a 360KB drive!

This problem has caused much frenzied hair-pulling among IBM AT users who need to share data on computers with 360KB drives. Fortunately, there is a fairly inexpensive software solution to this problem. A program named COPY AT2PC converts files saved in the IBM AT's high-density format to low-density format so they can be read in low-density drives. For more information, contact the company below, or ask your computer or software dealer for other alternatives:

COPY AT2PC
Microbridge Computers International
655 Sky Way #125
San Carlos, CA 94070
(800) 523-8777

Hardware Solutions

You cannot reconcile the incompatibility of 5.25-inch and 3.5-inch diskettes if you have access to only one computer with only one type of drive. In this case, you must install a drive for each diskette size that you want to use. This solution is considerably more expensive than the software solutions mentioned above, but it might be the only alternative in some situations.

If there is room in your computer's main unit for an additional floppy disk drive, either above, below, or beside existing drives, then you may be able to add another *internal* drive. If there is not room for another floppy drive in the main system unit, you may still be able to add an *external* floppy disk drive. Which solution is best for your computer depends on your computer's current configuration and power supply. You'll need to consult a qualified computer technician who is familiar with your computer for advice.

Regardless of how you configure the multiple floppy drives on your computer, always remember the following two tips:

■ A computer that contains a hard disk, one 1.44MB 3.5-inch drive, one 1.2MB 5.25-inch drive, (and the previously mentioned COPY AT2PC program if you have an IBM AT) provides total accessibility to all diskette sizes and densities.

■ If you decide to install your own extra disk drive, follow the manufacturer's instructions carefully. If the manufacturer does not supply a specific device driver for activating the new drive, see the DRIVER.SYS entry (the DOS device driver for external drives) in Appendix B.

Computer dealers, manufacturers, and service technicians are all good sources for helping you determine which solution is best for you. If you specifically want to add a 3.5-inch disk drive to your existing 5.25-inch drive system, you might want to examine the following products:

Manzana Third Internal Plus
Manzana Host Powered Plus
Manzana Microsystems Inc.
7334 Hollister Ave. Suite I
P.O. Box 2117
Goleta, CA 93118
(805) 968-1387

PC Connection 3.5-inch Internal Drive
PC Connection
6 Mill St.
Marlow, NH 03456
(603) 446-3383

Sysgen Bridge-File 3.5-inch Systems
Sysgen, Inc.
556 Gilbralter Dr.
Milpitas, CA 95035
(800) 821-2151

Solving Data Incompatibility Problems

Different software products use incompatible formats for storing their data; the reason this occurs is that each product uses the most efficient storage technique for its own internal program structure. However, there are many situations in which you might want to use data from one application program within a different program. For example, you might want to use Lotus 1-2-3 to print a graph from information stored in a dBASE IV database.

Basically, whenever you want to import or export data from spreadsheet or database management programs, you can usually find a way to do so either directly or by using ASCII text files as an intermediary format. For example, dBASE III PLUS can import data from and export data to Lotus 1-2-3. Similarly, Lotus 1-2-3 can import and export dBASE III PLUS data. For information regarding data transfers between applications, you should refer to the documentation that came with the application programs (not a DOS book or manual).

In a few cases, you might not be able to directly import or export data. However, virtually all software products are capable of importing and exporting DOS text files (or ASCII text files). Some products also let you decide whether you want to use *delimited* format or *fixed-length* format for the text file. In virtually all cases, the *delimited* format is much easier to work with. (But check your program's user manual for specific advice.)

For example, suppose you want to export data from your old "Good-Base" program to dBASE IV, but GoodBase has no capability to export to dBASE IV. If GoodBase can export ASCII text files (and nearly every product can), use that capability to create an ASCII file that contains your data. Then, run dBASE IV and import the data from the ASCII text file. (To continue this example, you need to refer to the dBASE IV documentation for additional information.)

Unfortunately, importing and exporting data among word processing programs is a bit more complicated, because each uses a very different method for storing formatting codes for printer features such as underlining, boldface, and so on.

Some word processors *do* offer programs that allow you to import documents from and export documents to other word processing programs. For example, the WordPerfect word processor comes with a program named CONVERT that translates the codes in documents created on several other word processors into WordPerfect format. Similarly, the

WordPerfect CONVERT program can also translate WordPerfect documents into other formats (including ASCII text).

However, if you don't own WordPerfect, or you need to perform other types of transfers with word processing programs, you need additional help. For example, suppose you use only the WordStar program, but you need to send your document to a company that requires WordPerfect (or DisplayWrite or Microsoft Word or other) format.

Several independent software companies offer solutions to this problem. Following is a list of some of these products and the companies that manufacture them. Be sure to determine whether or not a specific program supports the word processing formats that you require. Your computer or software dealer might be able to provide additional alternatives:

R-Doc/X
Advanced Computer Innovations
30 Burncoat Way
Pittsford, NY 14534-2216
(716) 383-1939

Software Bridge
Systems Compatibility Corp.
401 North Wabash #600
Chicago, IL 60611
(800) 333-1359

Word for Word
Design Software Inc.
1275 West Roosevelt Rd.
West Chicago, IL 60185
(312) 231-4540

Using Older Programs with Newer Computers

In some cases, you can also use the simpler APPEND command (discussed in a later section) to solve problems in running programs.

Some very old ("ancient" in terms of computer age) DOS programs will not run under later versions of DOS. This is particularly true of programs that were designed to run under Version 1 of DOS, which was created for the first IBM PC computer.

You might be able to run these older programs under current versions of DOS by experimenting with several DOS commands designed to handle this situation. In particular, review the entries in Appendix B for the following commands:

ASSIGN   Reroutes program requests to a different disk drive. For example, ASSIGN lets you use a program that "insists" on reading and writing data on drive B: on a hard disk drive (even if you have no drive B:).

FCBS   Tells DOS to use the Version 1 File Control Block system of managing files rather than the "file handles" approach used by later versions of DOS. Use this command when DOS displays the error message `FCB unavailable`.

JOIN   Tells DOS to treat a disk drive as though it were a directory for a program on another drive.

STACKS   Tells DOS to allocate more "stacks" than normal (the default is 9). Use this when DOS displays the error message `Fatal: Internal Stack Failure, System Halted`.

SUBST   Forces DOS to access a subdirectory as though it were a separate disk drive. Use this command when running DOS Version 1 programs on a hard disk subdirectory rather than on a floppy disk.

Using the DOS commands in this list can be risky because these commands "trick" DOS into actions it would not normally perform; therefore, treat them with the utmost caution. Use these commands only when you have no other alternative (and heed the warnings listed in Appendix B). You should also consult the DOS manual that came with your computer for additional information about these easily misused commands.

Using Programs from Other Computers

If you import programs (not data) to your DOS computer from a non-compatible computer, such as a Macintosh or a UNIX-based microcomputer, do not expect to use these programs with DOS. All application programs are designed for use with a specific operating system and microprocessor. No amount of tinkering or translation will make your Macintosh or UNIX program run under DOS.

If you want to use a specific program, such as Microsoft Excel, on both your PC and your Macintosh, you must purchase two separate copies of that program: *Microsoft Excel* and *Microsoft Excel for the Mac*. You can then exchange Excel-created *data* between your PC and Macintosh, using special hardware and transfer programs. However, the programs themselves can run only under the operating system they were designed for.

What to Do When Programs Cannot Find Their Overlays

Most (although not all) application programs are designed to be easily accessed from a hard disk; these programs can be activated from any drive or directory, as long as the application's home directory is included in the current PATH setting. However, there is no *guarantee* that this procedure will work as expected, especially if you use a directory name other than that recommended by the manufacturer of the program.

For example, suppose you use WordStar (Version 4) as your word processing program, and you install it on a directory named \EDITOR rather than the manufacturer's recommended directory \WS4. If you include the \EDITOR directory in you PATH command, DOS can always find the main WordStar program, WS.EXE, on the \EDITOR directory.

However, the WordStar program itself will search only the current directory and the (nonexistent) \WS4 directory for its overlay files (such as WSMSGS.OVR). If your current directory is not \EDITOR, when you enter the WS command, WordStar appears to get started, but then the following error messages appear on the screen:

```
Cannot find overlay C:WSSPELL.OVR
Cannot find messages C:WSSPELL.OVR
```

Because WordStar can't find its overlay (.OVR) files in either the current directory or the (nonexistent) \WS4 directory, it "bails out" and returns control to DOS.

You might be wondering why WordStar cannot find these overlay files on the \EDITOR directory. After all, the PATH command tells DOS to search the \EDITOR directory, so why can't WordStar find these overlay files. The answer to this question is that PATH searches *only* for files with the .BAT, .COM, and .EXE extensions. The overlay files for which WordStar is searching have the extension .OVR and therefore cannot be detected by the DOS PATH command. This is not a "bug" of any kind; it's simply the way DOS, and WordStar (Version 4) operate.

Versions 3.3 and 4 of DOS offer a solution to this problem—the APPEND command. APPEND searches directories for all files *except* those with the .BAT, .COM, or .EXE extension. Therefore, the solution to the previous problem is a simple one. First, keep the \EDITOR directory in the current PATH setting so that DOS searches the \EDITOR directory for WordStar's main program WS.EXE. However, also list the \EDITOR directory in an APPEND command so that DOS searches the \EDITOR directory for the required overlay (.OVR) files.

See Chapter 10 if you need help editing your AUTOEXEC.BAT file.

All of the problems in this WordStar example can be resolved by adding these two commands to your AUTOEXEC.BAT file (assuming that all of the WordStar files are stored on a directory named \EDITOR on hard disk drive C:):

```
PATH C:\EDITOR
APPEND C:\EDITOR
```

After DOS receives these commands, you can access the WordStar program from any directory. The PATH command tells DOS to search the \EDITOR directory for the main program (WS.EXE, in this example). The APPEND command tells DOS to search the \EDITOR directory for any other files (for example, WSSPELL.OVR and WSMSGS.OVR) that WordStar requires.

For more details about using the APPEND command effectively, see the APPEND reference in Appendix B. If you are not familiar with the PATH command, see Chapter 11 first; then, study the PATH entry in Appendix B to gain a thorough understanding of this important DOS command.

Increasing Hard Disk Efficiency

As a hard disk becomes older and more packed with programs and data, you might notice a decrease in the speed at which it accesses files. A large part of this loss of efficiency is caused by *file fragmentation*, in which portions of files are scattered throughout the disk by the repeated saving, modifying, and erasing of files (as discussed in Chapter 15).

Another benefit of defragmenting files is that it reduces wear and tear on the mechanism that moves the drive head.

When a file is severely fragmented, the drive head must move around the disk a great deal to read the many scattered sectors that constitute the complete file. When this happens, you will notice that the hard disk drive in-use light remains on for a long time when reading the file. (You might also hear the drive head mechanism grinding away within the unit as it searches the disk for stray sectors.)

There are several optional file *defragmenting* programs available that can help you to rearrange your hard disk so that files are stored in contiguous sectors rather than in fragments. These programs rearrange the files so that each is stored in a continuous series of sectors, so that the drive head doesn't need to search throughout the disk to read a file.

Following is a list of popular defragmenting programs, including the names and addresses of their manufacturers. Your computer salesman or software dealer can also provide you with alternative programs.

Disk Optimizer
SoftLogic Solutions, Inc.
1 Perimiter Rd.
Manchester, NH 03103
(800) 272-9900

FastTrax
Bridgeway Publishing Co.
2165 East Francisco Blvd., Suite A1
San Rafael, CA 94912
(415) 485-0948

Mace Utilities
Paul Mace Software
123 N. First St.
Ashland, OR 97520
(800) 523-0258

Norton Utilities—Advanced Edition
Peter Norton Computing
2210 Wilshire Blvd.
Santa Monica, CA 90402
(213) 453-2361

Warnings About Using Disk Defragmenting Programs

Before you use a defragmenting program on your hard disk, pay heed to the following advice:

- Backup your entire hard disk—using either the DOS COPY, XCOPY, or BACKUP command—just in case something goes wrong.

- If your hard disk contains *any* copy-protected programs, such as earlier versions of Lotus 1-2-3, Symphony, or dBASE III, *uninstall* them before you use the defragmenting program.

If you don't follow the second item of advice before defragmenting your hard disk, you probably will no longer be able to use the copy-protected program on your hard disk without inserting the "key" diskette in drive A:.

Alternatives to Defragmenting

Remember that file fragmentation is not the only cause of inefficient hard disk accessing, nor the only solution. If your PATH command forces DOS to search directories that contain many files, extensive file searches will slow access times. As discussed in Chapter 11, putting the most crowded directories near the end of your PATH command forces DOS to search these directories only as a last resort.

Disk caching (discussed in Chapter 16) also speeds disk accessing considerably.

Defragmenting Floppy Disks

Virtually all defragmenting programs are designed for hard disks. If you need to defragment a floppy disk, the process is simple, provided that you have two compatible floppy disk drives. First, format a new, blank diskette. Then, use the DOS COPY (not DISKCOPY) command to copy all the files from one floppy to the other.

The COPY command individually copies each file into contiguous sectors on the destination diskettes. In the future, merely use the newly created disk rather than the original. You should immediately notice an increase in access speed (and hear much less drive-head noise) when using the new copy.

Vaccines for Computer Viruses

Computers don't catch diseases, but they can catch a *virus*—a program intentionally designed by "high-tech vandals" to wreak havoc on your computer. Fortunately, "virused" programs are extremely rare. No reputable software manufacturers would even consider selling virused programs, because doing so would immediately put them out of business. However, a few virused programs do find their way into the world of *public domain software* (software whose authors freely distribute their work to computer users through bulletin boards and communication networks).

Some viruses have become so widespread, and have infected so many computers, that they've earned their own titles. Some well-known virus (and similarly insidious) programs include the Pakistani-Brain Teaser, the Trojan Horse, the Time Bomb, and the Nuke.

Some viruses are relatively harmless, and simply display a comical message on a given date and time. Others may interfere with the computer's basic input/output operations, causing a severe performance slowdown, or a scrambling of data on the screen. One particularly nasty virus would just occasionally reverse two numbers on the screen (not at all funny to companies who rely on their computers for accounting and inventory management).

Some viruses are very dangerous. It's been said that a virus program actually burned out the monitors on quite a few computers. Others can damage all the files on a disk beyond any hope of recovery. One particularly famous virus, known as the Internet virus, actually crippled an entire nationwide network of computers.

Virused programs are particularly dangerous because they usually do their damage long after you use them, sometimes even after you've erased them from your disk! Most do so by modifying an important DOS file named COMMAND.COM, which is called into action whenever you run a program. A virused COMMAND.COM file can randomly erase a tiny part of your hard disk each time that you run *any* program. Eventually, these tiny erasures will cripple specific programs and perhaps even make the entire disk unusable.

One step you can take to help prevent any virused programs from damaging your own programs and data is to simply turn on the read-only attribute for the COMMAND.COM file so that no program can change it. Because no legitimate program would ever have reason to change the COMMAND.COM file, the only effect this change has is to disable virused programs.

To protect your COMMAND.COM file, first determine where it is located. A shortcut method for doing so is to enter the command SET at the command prompt. The SET command might display several lines of information, but you need only be concerned with the line that starts with COMSPEC=, because this specifies where COMMAND.COM is located.

Next, enter the ATTRIB +R command followed by the full path and name of the COMMAND.COM file. For example, if the SET command displays COMSPEC=C:\COMMAND.COM, then enter the command ATTRIB +R C:\COMMAND.COM. If the SET command displays COMSPEC=C:\DOS\COMMAND.COM, then enter the command ATTRIB +R C:\DOS\COMMAND.COM.

Although DOS merely redisplays the command prompt after you press Enter, you can rest assured that COMMAND.COM is now protected from change, which in turn protects your data from many (although unfortunately, not all) virus programs. Other executable files are also targets for viruses. (To be safe, you can apply the read-only attribute to *all* files that have the .COM or .EXE extension).

If you plan to use a lot of public domain software, you might want to take the extra precaution of investing in anti-virus software. There are several programs available on the market, including:

Flu-Shot +
Software Concepts Design
594 Third Ave.
New York, NY 10016
(212) 889-6431

Certus
Foundation Ware
2135 Renrock
Cleveland, OH 44118
(216) 932-7717

Mace Vaccine
Paul Mace Software
400 Williamson Way
Ashland, OR 97520
(503) 488-2322

Your computer salesman or software dealer might be able to provide additional virus protection packages.

Communicating with Remote Computers

If you need to communicate with remote computers via the telephone lines, you have two alternatives:

1. Install a *modem* (short for *modulator/demodulator*, which allows two computers to send and receive data and programs.

2. Buy a FAX board, which allows a computer to send and receive text and graphics (but not programs) to/from any FAX machine or any other computer with a FAX board.

The sections that follow discuss the strengths and weaknesses of each type of communication capability. Of course, you are not limited to selecting only one. However, a FAX board does require that your computer have a slot available to hold the board, as does an internal modem. The only way to know for sure how many slots are available in your computer is to remove the cover on your system unit. These hardware matters are beyond the scope of this book; so if you are in doubt, consult a computer service technician.

Modems

A modem is the most flexible means of sending data and programs from one computer to another. You also need a modem to communicate with large external database services such as The Source, Compuserve, Knowledge Index, Dow Jones, Prodigy, and the Official Airline Guides.

Perhaps the single most important feature to consider when purchasing a modem is the *baud rate*. The baud rate is the speed at which data is sent and received (measured in bits per second). The most common baud rates used in serial communications (that is, transmissions through phone lines) are 300, 1200, 2400, and 9600 baud. A modem's listed baud rate is its maximum rate of data transfer. Hence, buying a modem that can transmit and receive at 9600 baud provides the most flexibility for communicating with all other modems, both fast and slow.

A modem also requires *communications software* that manages the streams of data being sent and received by the connected computers. There are two major types of communications software available for modems. The standard communications packages allow you to perform basic communications operations, such as sending and receiving files.

Most modems are packaged with their own communications software. However, that software might only offer limited operations, especially compared to some of the more widely used communications packages available from independent software dealers. You might want to examine the following full-featured packages:

Crosstalk Mark IV
Crosstalk XVI
Crosstalk Communications
1000 Holcomb Woods Pkwy.
Roswell, GA 30076-2575
(404) 998-3998

ProComm Plus
Data Storm Technologies, Inc.
1621 Towne Drive, Suite G
Columbia, MI 65205
(314) 474-8461

If your job entails writing programs for others to use or training people to use computers, then you might need to use remote access software
with your modem rather than the standard communications packages.
These programs not only let you send and receive files, they also allow you
to control a remote computer from your own computer or watch the activity of a user on a remote computer. A few vendors of remote access software are:

Carbon Copy
Carbon Copy Plus
Meridian Technology, Inc.
7 Corporate Park, Suite 100
Irvine, CA 92714
(714) 261-1199

PC Anywhere
Dynamic Microprocessor Associates, Inc.
60 East 42nd St., Suite 1100
New York, NY 10165
(212) 687-7115

The real trick to using a modem effectively is ensuring that the two
communicating computers use the same settings for sending and receiving
files. Your communications software lets you adjust numerous settings for
communicating with other computers, as follows:

Baud Rate   Usually 300, 1200, 2400, 4800, or 9600

Parity   None, Odd, Even, Mark, or Space

Data Bits   5, 6, 7, or 8

Stop Bits   1 or 2

The *parity* setting represents the characters that are used to detect
errors during communications. The *data bits* setting establishes the number of bits that will be used to represent each character of transmitted data.
The *stop bits* setting represents the number of bits used to separate groups
of data bits.

Perhaps the most common settings used for sending and receiving
files is 1200 N-8-1, which is an abbreviated way of expressing: 1200 baud,
None (parity), 8 data bits, and one stop bit. A common setting for communicating with remote database services is 1200 E-7-1 (1200 baud, Even parity,

7 data bits, and 1 stop bit). If you're not sure of the proper settings when you first access a remote computer, either one of these settings is a good "first guess" to try.

Again, adjusting the settings for communications via modem is a matter of using your communications software correctly. For more information, consult your computer dealer or a book that specializes in communications.

FAX Boards

A second way of communicating via telephone lines is through *facsimile transmission* (FAX). The beauty of FAX is that it allows you to communicate with a worldwide network of FAX machines and other computers with FAX boards, without having to worry about settings such as baud rate, parity, and stop bits. The disadvantage of FAX is that you can only send and receive text and graphics, not programs.

The FAX standard for facsimile transmission has changed a few times throughout the years. Currently, the most widely used standard is named Group 3, although a new standard (Group 4) is emerging. When you select a FAX board for your computer, try to select one that supports at least the Group 2 and Group 3 standards.

Using a FAX board in your computer is not exactly like owning a complete FAX machine. The main reason is that a FAX board can only send and receive files, not text or graphics that are already printed on paper. If you want to be able to send printed text, as well as files, you need to invest in an additional *scanner*. Also, you could buy a FAX machine that supports both paper and computer file transmissions.

At the time this book was written, computer FAX was still in its infancy in many ways. Your computer dealer can offer up-to-date alternatives for installing a FAX board on your computer. If you want to survey the market on your own, contact the following FAX board manufacturers for additional information:

Connection CoProcessor
Intel PCEO
Mainstop CO3-07
5200 NE Elam Young Pkwy.
Hillsboro, OR 97124-6497
(800) 538-3373

JT-FAX 9600
Quadram Limited Partnership
1 Quad Way
Norcross, GA 30093
(800) 548-3420

FaxMail 96
Brook Trout Technology, Inc.
110 Cedar St.
Wellesley Hills, MA 02181
(617) 235-3026

Incidentally, a scanner is not only useful as an additional device for
FAX boards. It can be used to copy printed text directly from paper to a disk
file. You, in turn, can then use that printed text with any program; be it a
word processor, spreadsheet, or database manager. If you spend a lot of
time typing in data that's already printed on paper, a scanner might be a
worthwhile investment.

I once saw a demonstration that used a scanner connected to a computer as an input device, that also had a voice synthesizer as an output
device. As the operator fed printed text into the scanner, the voice synthesizer read each word out loud, in perfect English. As the demonstrators
pointed out, the implications of this demonstration are enormous for visu-
ally handicapped persons.

Sharing Data, Printers, and Other Devices

As a company expands its use of microcomputers, sharing resources
among computers often becomes an important issue. For example, if one
office uses four computers, it is more cost-effective to connect all four computers to one expensive laser printer than to purchase a separate printer for
each computer. If several computers need up-to-the-minute access to important data, such as a customer list or inventory, you need to link the
computers so that all users can have access to the same data.

The solutions to these resource-sharing problems are many and var-
ied, as are the costs involved. The sections that follow briefly describe
some alternatives that you may want to look into to solve these problems.

Peripheral Sharing Devices

The most inexpensive (and most limited) device for connecting several
computers and peripherals is called the *peripheral sharing device*. These
allow multiple computers to share devices, and to send files to one another.
But they do *not* allow multiple users to access the same data at the same
time.

For example, suppose you have several computers in one office, but
you do not want to spend the money to equip each computer with a printer,
plotter, and modem. A peripheral sharing device is an inexpensive means
of providing all connected computers access to a single printer, plotter,
and modem.

The names of several peripheral sharing devices, and the companies that manufacture them, are listed below. Of course, your computer dealer may be able to offer other alternatives:

The Logical Connection
Fifth Generation Systems, Inc.
11200 Industriplex Blvd.
Baton Rouge, LA 70809
(800) 873-4384

EasyLAN
Server Technology, Inc.
140 Kifer Ct.
Sunnyvale, CA 94086
(800) 835-1515

ManyLink
ManyLink for Work Groups
NetLine
2155 North 200 West, Suite 90
Provo, UT 84604
(801) 373-6000

If you need a true multiuser capability, in which several users on separate computers not only share devices but also have simultaneous access to the same data, then you need either a Local Area Network (LAN) or a multiuser operating system. These vary considerably in price and performance.

Selecting which alternative is best for your situation is a matter of assessing the potential complexity of the LAN and your requirements for operational speed and data-handling capabilities. A thorough investigation into these matters is beyond the scope of this book. Instead, you should consult a LAN consultant or study a book that specializes in local area networks. The sections that follow, however, provide an overview of the features and capabilities of these systems and can help you determine which alternatives merit further investigation.

Multiuser Operating Systems

Multiuser operating systems permit as many as 64 people to simultaneously share data stored in a single file. Typically, one 80386-based microcomputer acts as the *file server*, which stores all programs and data; multiple users then directly access this information through *dumb terminals*, which usually merely consist of a keyboard and a monitor.

Although switching to a multiuser operating system means leaving DOS behind, these systems are all designed to "mimic" DOS and run your

DOS application programs. Therefore, your knowledge of DOS (and existing DOS programs) remains useful.

The main disadvantage to some multiuser operating systems is that they do not provide adequate security for data and programs. That is, any user at any terminal can access all files on the 80386. That means, for example, that anybody can look into a payroll database to see other people's salaries or peek into files that contain their employment reviews (if they have the nerve).

If security is not a major issue, however, a multiuser operating system can be an inexpensive solution to your networking needs, provided that you have (or are prepared to buy) an expensive 80386-based computer. Some products that you might consider are:

PC-MOS/386
The Software Link
3577 Parkway Lane
Norcross, GA 30092
(800) 451-LINK

Concurrent DOS/386
Digital Research, Inc.
60 Garden Ct.
Monterey, CA 93940
(408) 649-3896

Other alternatives that you might want to consider are the UNIX and AIX operating systems. While not specifically designed to mimic DOS, newer versions of these operating systems do provide the ability for multiple users to run DOS-based application programs. Your best bet in researching these alternatives is to contact your computer dealer or a knowledgeable consultant.

DOS-Based LANs

DOS-based LANs are more expensive than multiuser operating systems, but they tend to outperform the operating systems both in terms of the number of users supported and the speed at which operations are performed. DOS-based LANs are generally less expensive than LANs that use dedicated, non-DOS operating systems (discussed in the next section). However, they provide many of the same features, including multiuser access to data, sharing of devices, and security structures that prevent access to sensitive data.

Installing a DOS-based LAN requires both hardware (a networking board in each computer and a system of cabling) and software, which manages the connections and data transfer. The expense can be considerable—as much as $600 or more per computer—and unless you feel confident about connecting a great deal of sophisticated computer hardware, you should plan on paying a consultant for the time required to install the entire network.

Some DOS-based LANs that you might want to consider are:

DNA Networks
DNA Networks, Inc.
351 Phoenixville Pike
Malvern, PA 19355
(800) 999-3622

ELS Netware II
Novell, Inc.
P.O. Box 9500
Provo, UT 84601
(801) 379-5900

LAN Smart
Localnet Communications, Inc.
3303 Harbor Blvd., Suite E-8
Costa Mesa, CA 92626-9979
(714) 549-7942

LANtastic
Artisoft Inc.
3550 N. 1st Ave. #330
Tucson, AZ 85719
(602) 293-6363

Non-DOS Based LANs

The high-end, non-DOS based LANs provide the best performance and the greatest flexibility of all the LAN alternatives. As you might expect, they are also much more expensive. Most also require that a single computer be used as the *file server*, which is dedicated to managing data, programs, and network connections. Typically, the cost of the file server alone is $3,000 to $6,000, an investment that often turns away potential office network users.

Non-DOS based LANs use their own operating systems; however, most are capable of running DOS application programs without a hitch. If you are thinking about investing in a high-powered non-DOS LAN, you should first check with a LAN consultant or your computer dealer.

Solving the "Too Many Files Are Open" Problem

Some application programs—particularly database management programs such as dBASE and Paradox—allow you to simultaneously work on several open data files. Many sophisticated "3-D" spreadsheet programs, such as Lotus 1-2-3 (Version 3), can also simultaneously manage multiple open files. In most cases, these programs can handle more open files than DOS initially allows.

When one of these application programs attempts to manage more open files than DOS allows, DOS displays an error message, such as Too many files are open. This error message can be confusing: Although your current application program displays the error message on the screen, the message is actually coming from DOS, not your application program.

If you search through the manuals that came with your application program, you will eventually discover this for yourself. However, a true "DOS whiz" knows right away that DOS, not the application program, is to blame. A true DOS whiz further knows that the only solution to this problem, regardless of the application program that presents the message, is to change the number of *file handles* allotted by FILES command in the DOS CONFIG.SYS file.

When you first install DOS 4 on your computer, it determines a "reasonable" number of files that can be open simultaneously and sets the FILES command in the CONFIG.SYS file to that number (usually about 10). to verify this for yourself, view the contents of your CONFIG.SYS file. If your computer has a hard disk, enter the following command at the DOS command prompt:

```
TYPE C:\CONFIG.SYS
```

If you start your computer from a floppy disk, put the Startup disk in drive A:, and enter the following command at the DOS command prompt:

```
TYPE A:\CONFIG.SYS
```

Your CONFIG.SYS file probably will display a line that begins with FILES= and ends with a number in the range of 8 to 255. For example, your CONFIG.SYS file might include the command:

```
FILES=10
```

which tells DOS to permit no more than 10 simultaneously open files.

Some application programs automatically adjust the FILES setting (and, in some cases, the BUFFER setting) in your CONFIG.SYS when you first install the programs. If you bypass the installation process, or you upgrade to a higher version of DOS *after* installing such a program, the FILES and BUFFERS settings might not match the number required by the application program. When this happens, the Too many files are open error message begins to appear.

The solution requires you to first refer to the documentation that came with the application program (usually the section that discusses how to install the program). Then, use Edlin or another editor (discussed in

Chapter 10), to modify the CONFIG.SYS file on your hard disk drive C: root directory or on the floppy disk that you use to start DOS. For example, if the manual states that 44 files and 22 buffers should be available to DOS, then modify your CONFIG.SYS file to contain the following instructions:

```
FILES=44
BUFFERS=22
```

Place these commands anywhere in the CONFIG.SYS file, as long as each is on a separate line. Save the edited file, and then reboot by pressing Ctrl-Alt-Del. DOS reads the new CONFIG.SYS file each time you start your computer in the future, and your application program should no longer display the Too many files are open error message. (See the FILES and BUFFERS entries in Appendix B for more details about these commands.)

Using Foreign Language Alphabets

If your work requires you to use non-English languages, and your current version of DOS uses the English alphabet, DOS contains several features that allow you to switch to a non-English alphabet and non-English formats for dates, currency, and decimal placement. The exact techniques you use depend on your version of DOS.

Rather than describe the entirely different techniques here, this section merely refers to the appropriate entries in Appendix B. if you are using DOS 3.0 through 3.2, refer to the following entries in Appendix B:

COUNTRY

KEYB

SELECT (for IBM PC-DOS only, prior to version 3.3)

If you are using DOS Version 3.3 through 4, see the following entries in Appendix B:

NLSFUNC

CHCP

SELECT

KEYBOARD

DISPLAY

MODE

GRAFTABL

COUNTRY

KEYB

DEVICE

Summary

This marks the end of the tutorial chapters in this book. By now you should be able to use the more technically detailed Appendix B without any problems. The first few pages of Appendix B discuss the best ways to use that reference section.

I hope that this book has served you well and that you are now using your computer, DOS, and favorite programs like a true computer whiz. Thanks for reading!

Installing DOS

The first time you ever sat down at a microcomputer, DOS was probably already installed on it. If you use a computer at work or school, someone else also already installed DOS. Even if your computer is fresh out of the box, and you've never even turned it on before, your computer dealer might have already installed DOS for you. (Some computer dealers often install DOS, so that they can test the computer before they ship it.)

If you are not sure whether or not DOS is already installed, read Chapter 1; then, try starting your computer, using the appropriate startup steps described in Chapter 2. If your computer refuses to start, it *might* be because DOS is not already installed. On the other hand, you might simply be using the wrong disk to start your computer (if your computer does not have a hard disk).

DOS needs to be installed only once, and re-installing DOS after it has already been installed can cause a loss of important programs and data. If you're not sure, consult your computer dealer or some other person who is knowledgeable about your particular computer before you re-install DOS.

Using DOS for the First Time

If you are upgrading your computer from an older version of DOS to a more recent version, you don't need to read this section; instead, see the section titled "Upgrading Your Version of DOS" later in this Appendix.

If you are certain that neither DOS nor any other operating system is installed on your computer, you need to install DOS yourself. Unfortunately, it is impossible for this book to give you step-by-step instructions for installing DOS on your computer, because different computers and different versions of DOS require different installation procedures.

To install DOS correctly on your computer, refer to the DOS documentation that came with your computer. However, certain aspects of these installation procedures are similar on most computers and with most versions of DOS. An understanding of the basic installation procedures presented in the following sections will help simplify matters for you.

Using DOS 3 on a Computer Without a Hard Disk

If you are using a version of DOS prior to Version 4, and your computer does not have a hard disk, you can start your computer simply by inserting the DOS System Disk (also called the Startup Disk) in drive A: before turning on your computer.

However, the documentation will recommend (and provide instructions for) making copies of your original DOS diskettes. Follow those directions immediately. In the future, always insert the *copy* of your DOS Startup diskette in drive A: before you turn on the computer. That way, if your copy is damaged, you can recreate a new copy from the original diskette.

Using DOS 3 on a Computer with a Hard Disk

If your computer has a hard (fixed) disk, and you are using a version of DOS prior to Version 4, see the DOS documentation that came with your computer for information about *preparing your fixed disk*. That section tells you how to install DOS and copy it to your hard disk, so that you can start your computer without inserting a floppy disk. You should perform the procedure for installing DOS on a hard disk *only* if you are absolutely certain that DOS is not already installed on the hard disk.

Installing DOS 4

If you are using Version 4 of DOS, you must complete the installation procedure regardless of whether your computer has a fixed disk or not. IBM computers that use PC DOS Version 4 offer this information in the manual titled *Getting Started with Disk Operating System Version 4.0*, which is included in the DOS package. Non-IBM computers that use MS DOS Version 4 offer installation information in a similarly titled manual. For example, when using MS-DOS Version 4 with a Compaq computer, refer to the manual titled *Getting Started: MS-DOS Version 4.0* that is included in the DOS 4 package.

Although it is impossible to list the step-by-step instructions for installing DOS 4 on all computers, the following example lists some general questions that the installation might ask, and provides possible responses to those questions. This example assumes that you are installing IBM PC DOS Version 4 (for the first time) on a computer that has a hard disk.

First, if you have an IBM printer attached to your computer, you should know what model it is. If you have a printer, but it is not an IBM printer, you need to know whether it is a parallel printer or serial printer. Refer to the manual that came with your printer for this information, or ask your computer dealer.

Secondly, you need a blank diskette. This must be a new diskette (not one from your DOS package). Label this diskette SELECT COPY. The installation procedure later asks you to insert this diskette into drive A: (it then copies the information on the DOS Select diskette to the blank diskette).

As per the instructions in the manual, first insert the DOS Install disk (from your PC DOS package) into disk drive A:. Then, either turn on the computer or, if the computer is already on, press Ctrl-Alt-Del (hold down the Ctrl key, then hold down the Alt key, then press the Del key, and then release all three keys).

You might be asked to remove the Install disk, and to replace it with the DOS Select disk that came with your DOS package. Do so if instructed; then, press any key (such as the Spacebar or Enter) to continue.

An introductory screen for the Select program appears and instructs you to press Enter. Press Enter, and follow any additional instructions that appear on the screen. After reading and performing the instructions on the screen, press Enter to move to the next screen. The first screen that asks you to make a decision is shown in Figure A.1.

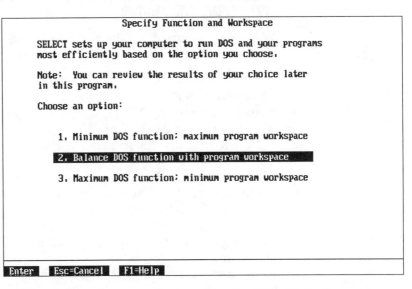

Figure A.1. A screen displayed by the DOS 4 Select program.

This first screen asks how you want to install DOS, in terms of how much memory is allotted to DOS. The highlighted selection, `Balance DOS functions with program workspace` is the best choice for all but a few specialized applications in which maximum memory is needed for programs or maximum DOS performance is required. Press Enter to select the option.

The next screen, shown in Figure A.2, asks for the drive name on which you want to install DOS. In this example (because the computer has a hard disk), you would select drive C: by leaving the highlight on the first option and pressing Enter.

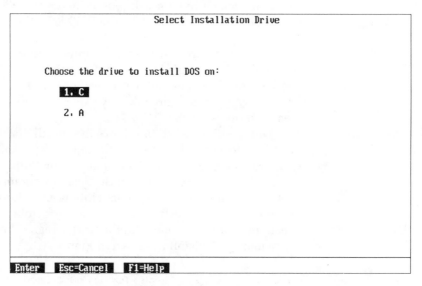

Figure A.2. The Select program asks you
to install DOS on a drive.

The next screen, shown in Figure A.3, asks for a directory in which it will install DOS (note that it suggests a directory named DOS on hard disk drive C:). To accept the suggested name, press the Tab key. To install DOS on a different directory, type a different directory name and then press the Tab key.

The options at the bottom of the screen let you decide whether or not to copy the *system files* to the hard disk. If you want your computer to start DOS 4 from the hard disk (so that you don't need to use floppy disks to start the computer), select option 1 by pressing Enter.

If you do not want to start DOS 4 automatically from your hard disk, select option 2. However, do so only if you want your computer to start with a different version of DOS (which would, presumably, already be installed).

The next screen asks you how many printers you have connected to the current computer. Type a number from 0 to 7, and then press Enter. If you type a number greater than 0, the next screen shows a list of IBM printer models, as shown in Figure A.4.

```
                     Specify DOS Location

     You can accept the DOS directory name shown or type a new
     directory name.


     DOS Directory . . . .C:\[DOS                          ]



     To select option 1 below, press Enter.  To change your
     option, press the tab key, highlight your choice and then
     press Enter.

          ┌────────────────────────────────────────────┐
          │ 1. Update all DOS files on fixed disk       │
          └────────────────────────────────────────────┘
            2. Copy non-system files to directory specified




 ███████   ██████████    █████████
  Enter     Esc=Cancel    F1=Help
```

Figure A.3. The Select program asks how and where to install DOS.

```
                     Printer Selection


     Printer.......... 1


     Choose a printer:
                                             More:   ↓

          ┌────────────────────────────────────────────┐
          │ IBM 3852 Ink Jet Printer                    │
          └────────────────────────────────────────────┘
            IBM 4201 Proprinter
            IBM 4201 Proprinter II
            IBM 4202 Proprinter XL
            IBM 4207 Proprinter X24
            IBM 4208 Proprinter XL24
            IBM 5152 Graphics Printer Model 2
            IBM 5182 Color Printer
            IBM 5201 Quietwriter Printer
            IBM 5201 Quietwriter Printer Model 2



 ███████   ██████████    █████████
  Enter     Esc=Cancel    F1=Help
```

Figure A.4. Some of the choices for installing printers.

You can press the ↓ and ↑ keys to move the highlight to any option shown. You can access additional options (beneath those shown) by repeatedly pressing the ↓ key. If you do not see your printer model listed, select Other Parallel Printer or Other Serial Printer, by highlighting the option and pressing Enter. (If you are not sure whether you have a parallel printer or serial printer, select Other Parallel Printer).

The next screen asks you to select a port for the printer. If you have only one printer port, the screen offers only one option, as shown in Figure A.5. If you have additional printers, you need to select a port for each printer (and you'll also be prompted to select the model for other printers).

```
┌─────────────────────────────────────────────────────────────────┐
│                        Parallel Printer Port                      │
│                                                                   │
│       Printer........... 1     Other Parallel Printer             │
│                                                                   │
│       Choose a parallel printer port:                             │
│         1. LPT1 - First port                                      │
│                                                                   │
│                                                                   │
│                                                                   │
│                                                                   │
│                                                                   │
│                                                                   │
│                                                                   │
│                                                                   │
│                                                                   │
├─────────────────────────────────────────────────────────────────┤
│  Enter    Esc=Cancel    F1=Help                                   │
└─────────────────────────────────────────────────────────────────┘
```

Figure A.5. The Select program asks which port to use for your printer.

After you define your printer(s) and printer port(s), the next screen asks if you want to make any changes to your preceding selections, as shown in Figure A.6. If you do not want to make any changes, press Enter. Otherwise, press ↓ to highlight the second option, and press Enter. You'll be shown a list of your current selections, with instructions about how to change them.

At this point, the Select program provides instructions for copying the DOS 4 diskettes. Follow the simple instructions as they appear on the screen, and press Enter after you insert the requested diskette. DOS displays the message Copying files... while the Select program is copying. After the operation ends, follow the new instructions to insert another diskette.

After all the diskettes have been copied, a screen appears and indicates that the installation is complete. (It also provides instructions concerning two files named AUTOEXEC.400 and CONFIG.400.) For now, you can remove the diskette in drive A:. Then, to start DOS, press Ctrl-Alt-Del.

Your computer will take a few seconds to *boot up*, and then you will see a prompt on your screen such as C>. The selections that you made in the Select program are not in effect yet. In order to make those changes take effect, follow these instructions:

1. Type COPY CONFIG.400 CONFIG.SYS and press Enter.

```
                          Installation Options

           SELECT defined a configuration based on the options
           you chose for DOS functions and program workspace.


           Choose an option:


             ┌──────────────────────────────────────────────────┐
             │ 1. Accept configuration and continue with installation │
             └──────────────────────────────────────────────────┘
               2. Review, change, or add installation choices




 ┌───────┐ ┌────────────┐ ┌─────────┐
 │ Enter │ │ Esc=Cancel │ │ F1=Help │
 └───────┘ └────────────┘ └─────────┘
```

Figure A.6. The Select program asks if you want to change any previous selections.

2. When the C> prompt reappears, type COPY AUTOEXEC.400 AUTOEXEC.BAT (on one line) and press Enter.

3. Press Ctrl-Alt-Del.

Now, every time you start your computer, DOS will read the information in the CONFIG.SYS and AUTOEXEC.BAT files and will activate the selections you made in the Select program. DOS also automatically starts the DOS 4 Shell, as discussed in Chapter 2.

Partitioning Your Hard Disk

If your hard disk is capable of storing more than 32 megabytes, you might be asked to *partition* the disk into two or more drives during the installation process. Again, you will need to refer to your DOS documentation for specific information about partitioning. Also check your manual for information about the FDISK program, which lets you partition your hard disk either before or after you install DOS.

See the SHARE command entry in Appendix B if you want to use a partition larger than 32MB with DOS Version 4.

Partitioning is required in all versions of DOS prior to Version 4 because DOS was incapable of accessing more than 32MB of data. The partitioning procedure allows you to divide a larger hard disk into several *logical* drives, none of which is larger than 32MB.

From DOS's perspective, each partition on a large fixed disk is, in essence, a separate hard disk. For example, if your computer has a 60MB fixed disk, you can partition it so that "drive C:" is 32MB and "drive D:" is 28MB.

One of these drives (usually C:) will be the *DOS partition*, in which DOS stores its own files. One partition will also be the *active partition*, in which DOS looks for instructions when you first turn on the computer. Assuming that you want to start your computer with DOS in control (which is always the case unless you've also installed another operating system), then the active partition should be the same as the DOS partition (again, usually drive C:).

Any remaining partitions (logical drives) can be used for DOS, for an entirely different operating system, or merely for storing data. If you want to use the additional logical drives with DOS, then use the FDISK program to convert the additional partitions into *Extended DOS partitions*. Optionally, you can format the extra partitions for use with another operating system (such as UNIX or OS/2), but to do this, you must follow the (entirely different) instructions that come with the other operating system.

Formatting the Fixed Disk

After you complete the partitioning process, you might need to format the hard disk before installing DOS. Be forewarned that formatting the hard disk erases all information on the disk. Therefore, **DO NOT FORMAT THE HARD DISK IF IT ALREADY HAS ANY PROGRAMS OR DATA STORED ON IT**, unless you are absolutely certain that you no longer need any of those programs.

If you share a computer that others are currently using, then you most certainly do *not* want to format the hard disk. (Otherwise, you will destroy everybody else's programs and files, which will certainly compromise your popularity. Severely.)

However, even if your computer is fresh out of the box, there is a good chance that the hard disk is already formatted. That's because, somewhere along the line, somebody should have fully tested your computer and its components. In most cases, this requires formatting the hard disk. If you are not sure that this has been done, ask your computer dealer.

After you are absolutely certain that the hard disk is *not* already formatted, follow these basic steps to format the hard disk:

1. If the computer is on, turn it off.

2. Insert the DOS Startup diskette (or the Install diskette with DOS 4) in drive A: (as discussed in Chapters 1 and 2 of this book).

3. Turn on the computer.

4. If the screen asks for the current date, merely press the Enter key.

5. If the screen asks for the current time, press the Enter key again.

6. If the DOS 4 Shell appears (as discussed in Chapter 2), press the function key labeled F3 to display the command prompt (A>).

7. Type the command FORMAT C: /S. (Be sure to use blank spaces where shown; be sure to use the forward slash / rather than the back slash \ where indicated.)

8. Press Enter.

The formatting process might take several minutes to complete. When DOS finishes, it redisplays the A> prompt on the screen.

If you used the FDISK program discussed above to create multiple DOS partitions, format these using DOS or another operating system, if you prefer. If you want to use DOS, use the FORMAT command and specify the name of the extra drive, but do not use the /S switch. For example, if you created a partition named D:, you would type the command FORMAT D: and then press Enter. Wait until the A> prompt reappears before you type any more commands. You can repeat this general procedure for any additional logical drives beyond D: (for example, FORMAT E: formats the next partition, FORMAT F: formats the next partition, and so on).

When you've finished formatting the entire fixed disk, you can start your computer without inserting a floppy disk in drive A:. To test the newly installed DOS, follow the steps in Chapter 2 for starting your computer with a hard disk.

Upgrading Your Version of DOS

If DOS is already installed on your computer, and you are experienced with that version of DOS, you can easily upgrade your current version of DOS to a newer version. For example, the installation process for upgrading from Version 3 to Version 4 is generally quite quick and simple.

Upgrading DOS on a Floppy Disk System

If you start DOS from a floppy disk, upgrading to a different version of DOS is as simple as using your new DOS Startup diskette in drive A: when you turn on the computer. Of course you still should make backup copies of your original DOS diskettes, as discussed in the manual that came with your new DOS package. Then, in the future, always use the backup diskettes of your new version of DOS when you start the computer.

Upgrading DOS on a Hard Disk System

If your computer has a hard disk, upgrading to a new version of DOS is a fairly straightforward procedure in most cases. However, to be safe, always back up your entire fixed disk (as discussed in Chapter 11) before upgrading to a newer version of DOS (just in case something goes wrong).

Generally speaking, however, you shouldn't need to reformat or re-partition your hard disk to upgrade to a newer version of DOS. If you are upgrading to Version 3 (that is, Version 3.1, 3.2, or 3.3) of DOS, use the REPLACE command (discussed in Appendix B) to replace "old" DOS files with new DOS files. You might also need to use the SYS command (also described in Appendix B) to copy the system tracks of the new version of DOS to your hard disk.

If you are upgrading to DOS 4, you need to follow the DOS 4 installation procedure. See the section "Installing DOS 4" earlier in this appendix for additional information and an example using IBM PC DOS 4.

Installing the DOS 4 Shell

If you install DOS 4 on your computer, and you start your computer from the hard disk, you should see the DOS Shell on your screen as soon as you start the computer (as discussed in Chapter 2). If your computer does not have a hard disk, you should be able to access the DOS 4 Shell by inserting the Shell diskette into disk drive A:, typing **DOSSHELL** next to the A> prompt, and pressing Enter (as discussed in Chapter 2).

If the DOS Shell fails to appear, you might have made an error during the installation procedure. Repeat the entire installation procedure, carefully following the instructions in the DOS manual that came with your computer. Then, try to access the Shell again by turning off the computer and repeating the startup procedure, as described in Chapter 2.

Modifying the DOS 4 Shell

With proper installation, DOS 4 automatically adjusts the Shell to take advantage of the devices attached to your computer. However, whenever you add a new device or change a device, you must alter the Shell configuration so that it takes advantage of the new device. In most cases, you do so by using the same program that you used to install DOS 4 the first time (for example, the SELECT program with IBM PC DOS, or the FASTART program with Compaq computers using MS-DOS). To reconfigure the DOS 4 Shell to handle your new devices, refer to the DOS manual that came with your computer for specific instructions.

As an alternative to using the SELECT, FASTART, or a similar program to add or change devices for use with the DOS 4 Shell, you can directly change the DOSSHELL.BAT file that controls the Shell. This method requires that you know how to modify DOS text files (as discussed in Chapter 10). You might need to directly modify the DOS 4 Shell in the following situations:

■ Your mouse does not work with the DOS 4 Shell, although it works with other programs.

■ Your screen displays the DOS Shell in black and white, even though your monitor is capable of displaying color.

■ You want to use the DOS 4 Shell in a network.

■ You do not want users to have access to the command prompt.

■ You do not want the Shell to produce any sounds.

If any of the above situations applies to you, see the entry for the DOSSHELL command in Appendix B for detailed instructions.

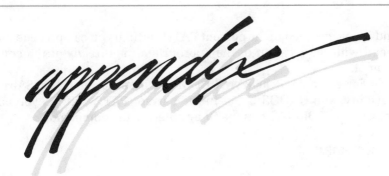

Alphabetical DOS Reference

This appendix provides a reference to all of the DOS commands and device drivers. Inside the front cover of this book is an instant reference that provides plain-English descriptions of commonly performed tasks, along with the commands required to perform those tasks.

Each entry in this appendix follows the format described below:

Entry

The command or device driver name, followed by a brief description, appears first.

Version The versions of DOS in which the command or device driver is available are listed.

Type **Command:** The type of command is described, as follows:

Internal: The command is always available from the command prompt.

External: The command uses a program that is stored on disk and is, therefore, only available if the appropriate program is available on the current disk, in the current directory, or in a directory included in the current PATH setting.

If a particular command requires an external program, that program's name is also included in this section. For example, the FORMAT command is listed as External (FORMAT.COM), which indicates that the FORMAT command requires that the file named FORMAT.COM be available on disk.

If an external DOS program is not available in the current directory and is not specified in the current PATH setting, you can precede the command with the location of the appropriate file directly at the command prompt.

For example, if FORMAT.COM is stored on the C:\DOS drive and directory, and C:\DOS is not in the current PATH setting, you can still activate the FORMAT command by entering the command:

```
C:\DOS\FORMAT A:
```

Device Driver: Device drivers must be activated by a DEVICE or INSTALL command in the CONFIG.SYS file. Device drivers are special files that allow you to install and use optional devices, such as a mouse, a RAM disk, or expanded memory.

The following table shows the DOS commands and device drivers discussed in this appendix, categorized as Internal, External, Batch File, or CONFIG.SYS commands. However, the categories are somewhat general.

For example, FASTOPEN is a command that can be used directly at the command prompt, but generally it makes more sense to install FASTOPEN through the CONFIG.SYS file. Also, all internal and external commands can be used in a batch file. Similarly, many internal commands used in batch files can also be used at the command prompt. See the individual command or device driver entries in this appendix for more specific information.

Table B.1. Categories of DOS commands and devices drivers.

Internal commands (always accessible from the command prompt)	
CHDIR or CD	PATH
CLS	PROMPT
COPY	RENAME or REN
DATE	RMDIR or RD
DEL	SET
DIR	TIME
ECHO	TYPE
ERASE	VER
EXIT	VERIFY
MKDIR or MD	VOL

External commands (used primarily at the command prompt)	
APPEND	JOIN
ASSIGN	KEYB
ATTRIB	LABEL

Table B.1. (cont.)

External commands
(used primarily at the command prompt)

BACKUP	MEM
CHCP	MODE
CHKDSK	MORE
COMMAND	NLSFUNC
COMP	PRINT
DISKCOMP	RECOVER
DISKCOPY	REPLACE
DOSSHELL	RESTORE
EDLIN	SORT
FIND	SUBST
FORMAT	SYS
GRAFTABL	TREE
GRAPHICS	XCOPY

Internal commands used solely (or primarily) in batch files

CALL	PAUSE
FOR	REM
GOTO	SHIFT
IF	

Commands and device drivers used solely (or primarily)
in the CONFIG.SYS file

ANSI.SYS	INSTALL
BREAK	LASTDRIVE
BUFFERS	PRINTER.SYS
COUNTRY	RAMDRIVE.SYS
CTTY	SHARE
DEVICE	SHELL
DISPLAY.SYS	STACKS
DRIVER.SYS	VDISK.SYS
FASTOPEN	XMAEM.SYS
FCBS	XMA2EMS.SYS
FILES	

DOS Shell Menu Access   This section explains how to use commands from the DOS Shell, if possible. All DOS Shell operations can be activated from the keyboard or with a mouse, as discussed in the earlier chapters of this book.

If the command or device driver is not immediately accessible from a menu in the DOS 4 Shell, this section displays *None*. However, although a particular command might not be directly accessible from the DOS 4 Shell menus per se, you can execute all DOS external commands from the Files Area of the File System, simply by highlighting the correct file name and pressing Enter, or by double-clicking the file name with your mouse.

For example, suppose you want to use the XCOPY command from the Shell, without using the command prompt. The entry for the XCOPY command in this appendix shows that it is an external command stored in the file XCOPY.EXE. (If you are using DOS 4, XCOPY.EXE is most likely located in the \DOS directory of your hard disk drive C:, as are all external DOS commands.)

First, select File System from the Main Group screen to access the File System. Then, select the DOS directory from the Directory Tree Area of the **File System** screen. Then, run the XCOPY.EXE program by highlighting its file name in the Files Area (as shown in Figure B.1), and press Enter, or simply move the mouse pointer to the XCOPY.EXE file name and double-click the mouse button.

```
05-24-89                      File System                    12:22 pm
  File   Options   Arrange   Exit                          F1=Help
  Ctrl+letter selects a drive.
  [=]A   [=]B   [=]C   [=]D   [=]E   [=]F   [=]G   [=]H

  C:\DOS
     Directory Tree                              *.*
                                                                       ↑
  C:\                          SHELL     .MEU      6,660   04-28-89     ↕
 √ ├─DOS                       SHELLB    .COM      3,894   04-05-89
   ├─MOUSE1                     SHELLC    .EXE    153,807   04-05-89
   ├─WS4                        SMS       .DBF    712,572   05-03-89
   │  └─WPFILES                 SMS       .DBO      1,232   01-09-89
   ├─WINDOWS                    SMS       .MDX    295,936   05-10-89
   │  ├─PIF                     SORT      .EXE      5,882   04-05-89
   │  ├─EXCELCBT                SUBST     .EXE     18,467   04-05-89
   │  └─LIBRARY                 SYS       .COM     12,600   04-05-89
   ├─DBASE                      TAPE      .EXE     45,312   04-05-89
   │  ├─SAMPLES                 TEST      .FMO      2,372   05-10-89
   │  └─DBTUTOR                 TEST      .FMT      2,302   05-10-89
   │     └─TEMP                 TEST      .SCR      4,094   05-10-89
   └─UTILS                      TREE      .COM      6,302   04-05-89
                                UNERASE   .BAT        384   10-12-87
                                UNTITLED  .CAT        969   05-11-89
                                UDISK     .SYS      7,946   04-05-89
                                WORDS                 660   04-05-89
                                XCOPY     .EXE     17,271   04-05-89
                                XMAZEMS   .SYS     29,249   08-03-88
                                XMAEM     .SYS     19,312   06-17-88

  F10=Actions   Shift+F9=Command Prompt
```

Figure B.1. The XCOPY.EXE file name is highlighted.

After you run the XCOPY.EXE program in the File System, the screen displays the Open File dialog box. Enter any parameters or options that you wish. For example, if you want to execute the Command Prompt command XCOPY C:*.WK? A: /S while the Open File dialog box is displayed, merely type all the options and switches that appear to the right of the XCOPY command in the command prompt version, as shown in Figure B.2.

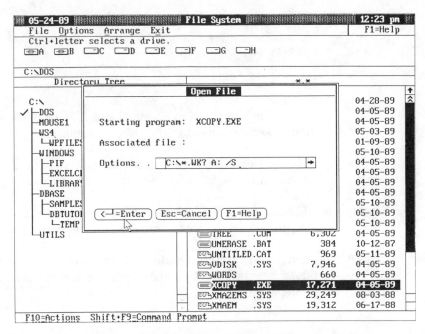

Figure B.2. DOS Shell equivalent of the command
`XCOPY C:\*.WK? A: /S.`

After you type in the options and switches, press Enter to execute the command, or click once on the ←=Enter box.

As an alternative to using the File System to run an external DOS program, you can add the program to any DOS 4 Shell group screen, as discussed in Chapter 11.

Syntax   The syntax section describes the general format of the words and options used with the command. The command itself is shown in capital letters. Optional components are enclosed in square brackets ([ ]). (Do not include the square brackets in your own DOS command.) Variable components (by which you supply appropriate information) are displayed in *italics*. The symbol [. . .] indicates that you can enter multiple options, using the same format as the options immediately preceding.

The | symbol in a syntax chart indicates that one option or the other (but not both) can be used in the command. For example, the syntax for the VERIFY command is:

`VERIFY [ON | OFF]`

The bracketed items are optional, and therefore you can omit them completely. Or, you can use either the ON or the OFF option (but not both simultaneously) with the command. Hence, all three of the following commands are valid:

```
VERIFY

VERIFY ON

VERIFY OFF
```

Clarification of the options and italicized variables used in the command section appear in the Usage section.

Usage   This section provides a general description of the command, what it does, and how to use it, including useful tips and warnings.

Examples   This section provides examples of how to use the command. Additional examples of most commands also appear throughout the book.

See Also   If there are related commands worth checking, this section either lists them or refers you to a chapter or section in the book that deals with the topic at hand.

ANSI.SYS

Controls the screen and keyboard by using standards set by the American National Standards Institute (ANSI). When installed via the CONFIG.SYS file, it allows you to customize screen displays and keyboard assignments (see Chapter 12).

Version 2 and later

Type Device driver; valid only in the CONFIG.SYS file.

DOS Shell Menu Access None

Syntax

```
DEVICE = [drive][path] ANSI.SYS [/X][/L][/K]
```

in which *drive* and *path* specify the drive and directory path to the ANSI.SYS file (required only if ANSI.SYS is not stored in the root directory).

Usage If your CONFIG.SYS file includes the command `DEVICE=ANSI.SYS`, then you can use the PROMPT command to customize the screen and keyboard (see Chapter 12).

    The following optional switches might be valid only on certain computers (see the DOS manual that came with your computer for the hardware-specific details of these features):

/X   Allows expanded keys to be remapped independently.

/L   Causes application programs to use a specific number of rows, as specified by the MODE command.

/K   Prevents the use of keyboard customization.

Examples If the ANSI.SYS file is stored on the root directory of the boot disk, then the following command, when included in the CONFIG.SYS file, activates the ANSI device driver at startup:

```
DEVICE=ANSI.SYS
```

    If the ANSI.SYS file is stored in the \DOS directory of drive C:, the CONFIG.SYS file must contain the following command to activate the ANSI device driver at startup:

```
DEVICE=C:\DOS\ANSI.SYS
```

See Also CONFIG.SYS, PROMPT

APPEND

Sets a path for searching for files.

Version 3.3 and later

Type External (APPEND.EXE) becomes internal after loaded.

DOS Shell Menu Access None

Syntax
```
APPEND [[drive]path][;[drive]path] [...] [;]
[/X:OFF] [/X:ON] [/PATH:ON | /PATH:OFF] [/E]
```

in which *drive* is a disk drive name (such as C:), *path* is a directory path (such as \123), and . . . refers to any number of additional drives and paths separated by semicolons (;).

Usage When DOS is given instructions to locate a file, it usually searches only the current disk drive and directory. If the PATH command provides additional drives and directories to search, DOS searches those additional drives and directories *only* for program files (those with the extension .BAT, .COM, or .EXE).

APPEND tells DOS to search other drives and directories for data files. You use the APPEND command to allow program (.COM or .EXE) files to find their overlay files (see Chapter 17).

Do not use the APPEND command to allow programs to find data files on separate directories; this can create confusion. For example, suppose your word processing program locates a data file on one of the drives and/or directories specified in the APPEND command. Then, you change that data file and save it. Regardless of the APPEND command setting, the new version of the data file will be stored on the current drive and directory, leaving the original (and unchanged) file on its original drive and directory.

The /X and /PATH switches are available in DOS 4 only. The APPEND command emulates the PATH command when you use the /X:ON (or /X) option. This option tells APPEND to search for and execute program and batch files. The default setting is /X:OFF.

The /PATH:OFF option prohibits the search for files when a drive and/or path is specified in the file name. The default setting, /PATH:ON, allows APPEND to search for files, whether the file name includes a path or not.

The /E option stores the APPEND list of drives and directories in the environment. This allows batch files to access the drives and directories through the use of the %APPEND% variable name. The /E option is only valid the first time that APPEND is executed.

The command **APPEND** entered with no other information displays the currently appended drives and directories (or **No Append** if none are defined). The command **APPEND ;** cancels any previous APPEND settings, and limits searches only to the current drive and directory.

Examples   Suppose you store all of your program overlay files in a directory named \OVERLAYS on drive C:. Furthermore, you store spreadsheet files in a directory named \FINANCES, also on drive C:. If you enter the command **APPEND C:\OVERLAYS;C:\FINANCES** before using any programs, those programs automatically search the directories named \OVERLAYS and \FINANCES on drive C: for overlay and spreadsheet files. (Again, however, if you save an edited spreadsheet, it might not be stored back into the \FINANCES directory.)

To ensure that all files in the directory named \DOS are accessible from any other directory, and to store the APPEND setting in the environment, add the following commands to your AUTOEXEC.BAT file:

```
PATH C:\DOS
APPEND /E
APPEND C:\DOS
```

or, to achieve the same result:

```
APPEND /E
APPEND C:\DOS /X:ON
```

If you want to use both the APPEND and ASSIGN commands, be sure to use the APPEND command first. If you use the /X switch, you must disable the APPEND command by entering **APPEND;** before issuing a BACKUP or RESTORE command.

You can use the APPEND command in a network to access data files on a remote directory (including the file server).

See Also   ASSIGN, JOIN, PATH, SUBST

ASSIGN

Reassigns the default drive specified in a program to a new drive.

Version   2 and later

Type   External (ASSIGN.COM)

DOS Shell
Menu Access   None

Syntax   `ASSIGN` *d1=d2* `[...]`

in which *d1* is the name of the drive that the program normally accesses, and *d2* is the name of the drive that you wish to use instead. The . . . refers to additional drive assignments, each using the *d1=d2* syntax.

Usage   The ASSIGN command need only be used with programs that are capable of accessing only a specific predefined disk drive. For example, suppose you have a spreadsheet program that insists on storing spreadsheet files on drive B: and offers no means for storing spreadsheet files on drive C:, where you want to store them. Entering the command `ASSIGN B=C` before using that spreadsheet program tricks the program into storing its files on drive C:.

Note that, unlike many other commands, ASSIGN does not require colons with the drive names. For example, the command `ASSIGN B=C` is legal. However, you can also use the command `ASSIGN B:=C:` if you are in the habit of using colons. Also, be sure to use only disk drive names that are valid on your computer. For example, if your computer does not have a disk drive named F:, the command `ASSIGN C=F` merely displays the error message `Invalid Parameter` and ignores your request.

The command `ASSIGN` alone reassigns drive letters to their originally designated drives. Be sure to use the ASSIGN command with no parameters before you use the BACKUP, RESTORE, LABEL, JOIN, SUBST, or PRINT commands. The commands FORMAT, SYS, DISKCOPY and DISKCOMP ignore any new drive assignments created by the ASSIGN command; they always use the original drive designations.

Never use the ASSIGN command to assign your main working disk drive to a new drive. For example, suppose you have a blank RAM disk named drive D:, but all of your important files are stored on the hard disk drive C:. The command `ASSIGN C=D` makes drive C: "invisible," and any attempt to run programs or inspect drive C: is useless: From the computer's viewpoint, only the blank drive D: exists. In this case, you can't even use the ASSIGN command (without parameters) to restore the original drive settings, because the ASSIGN program is stored on the "invisible" drive C:. The only way to recover from this error is to reboot by typing Ctrl-Alt-Del.

To use a program that requires ASSIGN, but prevent it from disrupting other DOS commands and operations, you can create a batch file that executes, then disables, the ASSIGN command.

Examples   Suppose you have a program named MYGAME.EXE that can only access disk drive B:, but you want to use it on your hard disk C:. You could create the following batch file, which activates ASSIGN, runs the MYGAME program, and then deactivates the ASSIGN automatically when you exit the MYGAME program:

```
REM **************** GAME.BAT
ASSIGN B=C
```

```
MYGAME
ASSIGN
```

To reroute all the files that a program usually stores on drives A: and B: to drive D:, use the command ASSIGN B=D A=D. Note the blank space between the two parameters.

See Also PATH, SUBST

ATTRIB

Changes the attributes of a file.

Version 3 and later

Type External (ATTRIB.EXE)

DOS Shell Menu Access Select Change Attribute... on the File pull-down menu in the File System.

Syntax ATTRIB [+R|-R] [+A|-A] [drive][path]file name [/S]

in which R determines the read/write status of the file, and A determines the archive status of the file, as follows:

+R changes a file's attribute to read-only.

−R changes a file's attribute to read/write.

+A activates the archive status of the file.

−A deactivates the archive status of the file.

The *drive* and *path* parameters specify the location of the file; *file name* is the name of the file and can contain wildcard characters.

Usage The syntax above shows options for the ATTRIB command in Versions 3.3 and later of DOS. Please be aware that Version 3.0 supports only the +R and −R switches, and does not support /S. Nor does Version 3.0 display information about a files archive bit. Version 3.2 supports +R, −R, +A, −A, but not /S.

ATTRIB lets you protect a file from accidental change or deletion. It also lets you determine whether or not a file is archived (copied) via backup commands such as BACKUP, RESTORE, and XCOPY. ATTRIB, without an A or R parameter, displays the current attributes of a file.

By default, any file can be altered or erased. To protect a file from accidental change or erasure, change its status to read-only using the +R option with the ATTRIB command. Any attempt to delete or change the file results in the error message `Access Denied`. To return a file to its normal read/write status, use the −R option with ATTRIB.

To prevent a file from being archived during a backup session, use the −A option with ATTRIB. To ensure that the file is archived during backup, use the +A option with ATTRIB.

To check the status of a file, use the ATTRIB command with only the file name. The file's status appears to the left of the file name. An `A` indicates that the file archive status is "on" and that the file has not been archived since it was last changed. An `R` indicates that the file currently has read-only status.

To include files in all subdirectories below the current directory, use the /S parameter at the end of the ATTRIB command.

The DOS 4 Shell offers a third attribute: *hidden*. When the hidden attribute is turned on, the file name is not displayed by the command prompt DIR command (however, it is still displayed by the File System).

To change file attributes using the DOS 4 Shell, go to the File System and select a file (or files) from the Files Area by highlighting and pressing the Spacebar, or by clicking once with the mouse. Then, pull down the File menu and select `Change Attribute....` You can change the attributes for selected files individually or as a group.

When the Change Attribute dialog box appears, attributes that are turned on are indicated by a right-pointing triangle. Toggle an attribute on or off by highlighting the attribute and pressing the Spacebar (or clicking the box once with the mouse).

Examples Suppose you purchase a copy of the dBASE IV program and copy its files to a directory named \DBASE on your hard disk drive C:. You want to be sure that none of these files are accidentally changed or erased. Furthermore, you do not want to include these files in backup procedures, because you know they will never be changed on the hard disk.

First, you might check the current status of the files by entering the command:

```
ATTRIB C:\DBASE\DBASE*.*
```

The resulting display shows that the files currently have read/write status (R is not displayed), and that the archive status is on (A is displayed), as shown here:

```
A              C:\DBASE\DBASE3.OVL
A              C:\DBASE\DBASE.EXE
A              C:\DBASE\DBASE1.RES
A              C:\DBASE\DBASE6.OVL
A              C:\DBASE\DBASE1.OVL
A              C:\DBASE\DBASE3.RES
```

```
A          C:\DBASE\DBASE2.OVL
A          C:\DBASE\DBASE1.HLP
A          C:\DBASE\DBASE5.OVL
A          C:\DBASE\DBASE4.OVL
A          C:\DBASE\DBASE2.HLP
A          C:\DBASE\DBASE2.RES
```

To change the program (.EXE), overlay (.OVL) and help (.HLP) files to read-only status, and to prevent them from being included in future BACKUP procedures, enter the following commands:

```
ATTRIB +R -A C:\DBASE\DBASE*.EXE
ATTRIB +R -A C:\DBASE\DBASE*.OVL
ATTRIB +R -A C:\DBASE\DBASE*.EXE
```

After making these changes, any attempt to erase the file named DBASE.EXE (for example) using the command:

```
ERASE C:\DBASE\DBASE.EXE
```

results only in the error message Access denied, and DOS refuses to erase the file.

Suppose you want to protect all .COM and .EXE files on hard disk C: from erasure. To do so, change to the root directory and use the ATTRIB command with the +R option and /S switch, as follows:

```
ATTRIB +R C:\*.COM
ATTRIB +R C:\*.EXE
```

To print a list that details the status of all files on hard disk C:, enter the command:

```
ATTRIB C:\*.* /S > PRN
```

Figure B.3 shows the Change Attribute dialog box for a file named TREE.COM. In this example, only the read only attribute is currently turned on.

See Also   BACKUP, RECOVER, XCOPY

BACKUP

Backs up files on the hard disk to floppy disks.

Version   2 and later

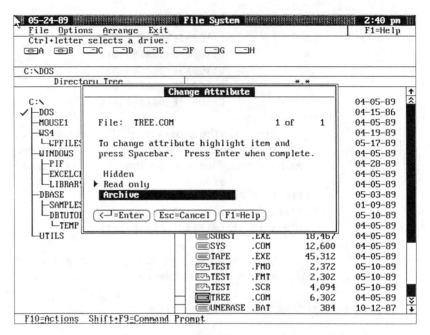

Figure B.3. The DOS 4 Shell Change Attribute dialog box.

Type   External (BACKUP.COM)

DOS Shell   Access the DOS Utilities . . . screen and select `Backup Fixed Disk`.
Menu Access

Syntax   `BACKUP [source drive][source path][source file name]`
`[destination drive] [/F] [/S] [/M] [/A] [/P] [/D:date] [/T:time]`
`[/L:logfile]`

in which *source drive*, *source path*, and *source file name* identify the file(s)
to be copied, and *destination drive* identifies the drive to which the files are
to be copied. The various switches are discussed in the following section.

Usage   The BACKUP command is used to copy files from a hard disk to diskettes.
Unlike the COPY command, BACKUP offers several options and features
that make backing up the hard disk a little faster and easier. First, BACKUP
can store a file that is larger than the capacity of a single floppy diskette by
splitting the file among multiple floppy diskettes. Second, BACKUP automatically warns you when the floppy diskette to which you are copying
files is full, and prompts you to insert a new disk.

In addition, BACKUP automatically formats a diskette (if the /F option is used), if the disk being copied to is not already formatted.

Files that are copied with the BACKUP command can *only* be retrieved with the RESTORE command. No other DOS command can access these copies.

You should label and number your backup diskettes with names such as Backup #1, Backup #2, and so on, so that you can use them in the same order during each backup session. During a BACKUP session, DOS displays the message:

```
Backing up files to drive x: ***  Diskette Number: nn
```

where *nn* is the disk number that you should write on the backup disk's label. (Later, if you ever need to recover files from these backups, DOS will ask you to insert them in the appropriate sequence.)

The various switches that are available for the BACKUP command are:

/A   By default, DOS erases all files on the target disk (the one being copied to) before copying any new files to it. If you specify the /A option, DOS *adds* new files to the target disk without first erasing the existing files. It is important to use the /A option if the diskette to which you are copying already contains backup files that you do not want to erase.

/M   The /M option tells BACKUP to copy only files that have been modified since the previous backup procedure.

/S   The /S switch tells BACKUP to include files in the subdirectories beneath the current directory.

/D:*date*   The /D switch tells BACKUP to copy only files that were created or changed on or after a specific date. The date must be entered in the format used by DOS (usually mm-dd-yy, unless modified by the COUNTRY.SYS device driver). Do not include any blank spaces in the switch.

/T:*time*   The /T switch tells BACKUP to copy only files that were created or changed on or after a specific time of day. Typically, this option is used with the /D switch to back up files that were created or changed on or after a certain time on a certain day. The time must be entered in the format used by DOS: hh:mm:ss, where *hh* is the hour (0–23), *mm* is the minutes (0–59), and *ss* is seconds (0–59). Do not include any blank spaces in the switch.

/L:*file name* The /L option stores information about the backup in a log file on the source drive and directory, using the name you specify. The log file includes the date and time of the backup, the paths and names of the files that were backed up, and the number of the disk on which the files were stored. If you specify the /L switch without a file name, DOS automatically names the log file BACKUP.LOG. If you add your own file name, be sure to use a colon (:) between the /L and *file name*. Do not include blank spaces. DOS Versions 3.3 and 4 also let you specify a path to store the log file on.

/P   Used in DOS Versions 2.0 to 3.1 to specify the "pack" option, to store files in compacted form on the backup diskette.

The BACKUP command returns a code in the ERRORLEVEL variable, which can be detected by the IF ERRORLEVEL command in a batch file. The value of ERRORLEVEL is a number between 0 and 4, with the meaning of each value as follows:

0   Backup was completed successfully, no error.
1   No files were found to back up.
2   Some files were not backed up because of file-sharing problems (occurs only on networks).
3   Backup was aborted by Ctrl-Break or Ctrl-C.
4   Backup procedure was aborted because of a system error.

Never use BACKUP when an APPEND, ASSIGN, SUBST, or JOIN command is in effect. If you do, any attempted recovery in the future will likely damage the directory structure of the hard disk.

The BACKUP command must be able to find the FORMAT.COM file in order to work correctly. FORMAT.COM must be either in the current directory or in a directory specified by the current PATH command. In DOS Versions 3.3 and earlier, you must also use the /F switch in the BACKUP command if you want it to format the backup diskette.

Examples   To back up all of the files in the root directory to floppy diskettes, change to the root directory of that disk, be sure that the BACKUP.COM program is available (either in the root directory or through a PATH command), and enter the command:

```
BACKUP C:*.* A:
```

Note that if you do not specify a file name, BACKUP assumes that you mean all files on the current directory. Hence, a shortcut for entering the command above is simply `BACKUP C: A:`.

To back up all files on drive C:, including those in directories below the root directory, specify C:\ as the starting point and use the /S switch, as follows:

```
BACKUP C:\*.* A: /S
```

To back up all files with extensions .WKS, .WK1, .WK2, and .WKQ from the directory named \SSHEETS to the disk in drive A:, enter the command:

```
BACKUP C:\SSHEETS\*.WK? A:
```

To back up all files with the extension .DBF, in the directory named \DBFILES, that were created on or after December 31, 1989, enter the following command:

```
BACKUP C:\DBFILES\*.DBF A: /D:12-31-89
```

If you wanted to limit the backup files in the above example to those created after 1:00 p.m. on December 31, 1989, you would add the /T switch to the command, as follows:

```
BACKUP C:\DBFILES\*.DBF A: /D:12-31-89 /T:13:00:00
```

You can combine as many parameters as you wish when using the BACKUP command. For example, the next command backs up every file on the hard disk, starting at the root directory C:\ and working down through all of the subdirectories (/S). The command stores information about the backup in a log file named BACKUP.LOG in the root directory of the hard disk (/L):

```
BACKUP C:\ A: /S /L
```

To repeat the above backup procedure more quickly in the future by backing up only files that have been changed, use the /A switch to add new files to the existing backup disks, and use the /M switch to limit backups to files that have changed since the previous backup procedure. The command now reads as follows:

```
BACKUP C:\ A: /S /A /M /L
```

Note that when you use the /A option with BACKUP, DOS "expects" to find the last diskette used in the previous backup in drive A:. If there is no disk in drive A:, you see the message `Insert last backup diskette in drive A:`. If you do not place the appropriate disk in drive A:, then BACKUP aborts the operation.

See Also   COPY, RESTORE, XCOPY, and Chapter 11

BREAK

Determines when DOS checks the keyboard to see if the Break key (or Ctrl-C) has been pressed.

Version   2 and later

Type   Internal

DOS Shell   None
Menu Access

Syntax   `BREAK [=] [ON | OFF]`

Usage   The BREAK command determines the frequency at which DOS checks to see if the Break (Ctrl-Break or Ctrl-C) key was pressed.

In its default configuration, in which BREAK is OFF, DOS only checks to see if Break was pressed when an operation accesses a standard device (that is, the keyboard, screen, printer, or communications port.) When BREAK is ON, DOS checks for a Break keypress before any system call, including reading or writing to the disk drives.

When BREAK is OFF, DOS can run at maximum speed. However, if you run a "calculation-intensive" program that never accesses a standard character device, and BREAK is OFF, there is no way to abort that running program.

If you set BREAK ON, DOS checks for a Break keypress more frequently, so you can interrupt a program that never accesses a standard character device. However, because DOS must check for Break keypresses more often, it runs a little slower (only about 1 or 2 percent in most cases).

In general, only enter the command `BREAK ON` before running a DOS program that will take a long time and not access any standard character device while it's running. As soon as the DOS program finishes running, enter the command `BREAK OFF` to reinstate normal checking for the Break keypress.

The command `BREAK`, with no parameters, returns the current status of the Break setting.

When using the BREAK command in the CONFIG.SYS file, insert the = sign in the command. For example, including the command `BREAK=ON` in the CONFIG.SYS file ensures that frequent Break key scanning is installed during the startup procedure.

Examples   To make DOS check for a Ctrl-Break or Ctrl-C keypress before any system call, enter the command:

`BREAK ON`

To limit Break key checking to standard character device operations, enter the command:

`BREAK OFF`

To check the current status of the BREAK setting, enter the command:

```
BREAK
```

This displays a message such as:

```
Break is off
```

BUFFERS

Defines the number of disk buffers DOS uses.

Version   2 and later

Type   Configuration (used only in CONFIG.SYS)

DOS Shell   None
Menu Access

Syntax   Versions 2 and 3:

```
BUFFERS = number
```

Version 4:

```
BUFFERS = number[,sectors] [/X]
```

in which *number* is the number of disk buffers specified in the range of 1 to 99, and *sectors* is the maximum number of sectors that can be read or written in one disk transfer, in the range of 1 to 8.

Usage   The BUFFERS command is used to set the number of buffers used by your system. DOS 4 also allows you to specify a look-ahead buffer in the range of 1 to 8 sectors.

The default values for BUFFERS are generally:

3 if any diskette drive is greater than 360KB.

5 if the computer system memory size is greater than 128KB.

10 if the computer system memory size is greater than 256KB.

15 if the computer system memory size is greater than 512KB.

Each disk buffer consumes 528 bytes (a little more than ½KB of RAM.

Each look-ahead buffer consumes as much memory as one disk sector, usually 512 bytes. Application programs that take advantage of the DOS BUFFERS setting (most database managers and some spreadsheets) usually recommend an optimal number of buffers to use. Tape backup systems also might require more buffers than the default number. Check the manual that came with the application program or tape drive unit for further information.

The /X option tells DOS to use expanded memory. If the system does not have expanded memory or if the expanded memory is in use, the BUFFERS command is ignored and the default values are used. If expanded memory is available, then the largest number of buffers is 10,000 or the total amount of expanded memory, whichever is smaller. To use /X, the device driver for the expanded memory manager must be placed above the BUFFERS command in the CONFIG.SYS file.

If you use the PC-DOS XMA2EMS.SYS device driver to install expanded memory, you must specify a page address for P255 in the `DEVICE=XMA2EMS.SYS` command before the line with the BUFFERS command in the CONFIG.SYS file. Otherwise, DOS ignores the /X switch.

Examples To allocate about 11KB of RAM to 22 disk buffers, include the command below in your CONFIG.SYS file:

```
BUFFERS=22
```

To allocate about 25KB of expanded memory (rather than conventional RAM) to disk buffers, and about 4KB to look-ahead buffers, on a Compaq 386 computer running DOS 4, include the following two commands in your CONFIG.SYS file (in the order shown):

```
DEVICE=C:\DOS\CEMM.EXE 1024 ON
BUFFERS=50,8 /X
```

The use of expanded memory in the previous example conserves space in conventional memory.

See Also FASTOPEN, FILES, XMA2EMS.SYS

CALL

Executes another batch file from within the current batch file.

Version 3.3 and later

Type Used only in batch files.

DOS Shell Menu Access	None

Syntax `CALL [drive][path]batch file name [parameters]`

in which *batch file name* is the name of the batch file that you wish to run, and *parameters* is a list of parameters that the called batch file can accept. The *drive* and *path* must be specified only if the batch file is not in the current directory or in a directory specified by the current PATH setting.

Usage The CALL command is used within a batch file to execute another batch file. When the called batch file finishes its job, the calling batch file continues with its next command. If the batch file being called can accept command line parameters, you can include them in the CALL command.

When calling another batch file, you must specify the drive and directory location of that batch file if:

1. The batch file is not in the current drive and directory, *and*

2. The batch file is not in a drive and directory specified in the current PATH.

To mimic the function of the CALL command using versions of DOS prior to 3.3, use the `COMMAND /C` command in place of CALL.

Examples Suppose a batch file named TEST1.BAT contains the following commands:

```
@ECHO OFF
REM ------- TEST1.BAT
ECHO I'm in TEST1.BAT
CALL TEST2
ECHO I'm back in TEST1.BAT now
```

A batch file named TEST2.BAT contains the commands:

```
REM ------- TEST2.BAT
ECHO Now I'm in TEST2.BAT!
```

When you enter the command TEST1, the CALL command calls (executes) TEST2.BAT. After TEST2.BAT finishes its job, TEST1.BAT resumes its tasks. Your screen displays:

```
I'm in TEST1.BAT
Now I'm in TEST2.BAT!
I'm back in TEST1.BAT now
```

The following TEST1.BAT batch file acts exactly the same as the previous TEST1.BAT; however, it can be used with versions 2 and later of DOS:

```
@ECHO OFF
REM ------- Test1.BAT
ECHO I'm in TEST1.BAT
COMMAND /C TEST2
ECHO I'm back in TEST1.BAT now
```

See Also   GOTO

CHCP

Changes the code page (character set) for all possible devices.

Version   3.3 and later

Type   Internal (after installing NLSFUNC)

DOS Shell Menu Access   None

Syntax   CHCP [code page number]

in which *code page number* is a three-digit number that defines a foreign language character set.

Usage   CHCP (an abbreviation for CHange Code Page) lets you select a character set for languages other than English for use with devices (such as the screen and a printer) that support code-page switching. Code-page options are listed in Table B-2.

Table B.2: Code page options.

Code Page Number	Alphabet
437	United States
850	Multilingual
860	Portuguese
863	French-Canadian
865	Nordic

Examples To change the code page to Portuguese, enter the command:

CHCP 860

See Also MODE, NLSFUNC, COUNTRY.SYS

CHDIR or CD

Changes to a different directory or displays the name of the current directory.

Version 2 and later

Type Internal

DOS Shell Menu Access In the File System, highlight the directory name and press Enter, or click on the directory name once with your mouse.

Syntax CHDIR [[*drive*][*path*]]

or

CD [..|\][*drive*][*path*]

in which *drive* is the disk drive name and *path* is the directory (and, optionally, subdirectory) name. The \ symbol (alone) refers to the root directory. The .. symbol specifies the parent directory, which is one level higher than the current directory.

Usage Use CHDIR (or the abbreviated form, CD) to change the current, or working, directory on the current drive or on a separate drive. If you omit the drive specification, the current drive is assumed. If you include a drive name, the current directory of the specified drive is changed, but you remain on the current drive. If you omit the path name, the command displays the name of the current directory.

If you precede the path name with a backslash, DOS searches the path starting from the root directory. If you omit the initial backslash, DOS assumes that the path begins at the current directory.

Examples Suppose you are currently in the root directory of drive C: and you wish to switch to the directory named WP, which is one level below the root directory. To do so, enter the command:

CD \WP

To return to the root directory at any time, enter the command:

`CD\`

To get to a subdirectory named DBFILES, which is stored "beneath" a directory named DBMS, enter the command:

`CD \DBMS\DBFILES`

As an alternative to the above command, you could use two steps to access the \DBMS\DBFILES subdirectory. First, enter the command:

`CD \DBMS`

to change to the DBMS directory. Then, enter the command:

`CD DBFILES`

Notice, in the second example, that the \ character was omitted, because DBFILES is only one level below the current directory DBMS and you do not want to start the search from the root directory.

If you want to switch from the DBMS\DBFILES directory to a directory named DBMS\DBTUTOR, you can use the double dot (..) symbol as an abbreviation for the parent directory. For example, you could enter the command:

`CD ..\DBTUTOR`

After you are in the DBMS\DBTUTOR subdirectory, you could enter the following command to move up one directory (to the DBMS directory):

`CD..`

When the \DBMS directory is the current directory, entering the command `CD..` will move you up a level, to the root directory. Entering the command `CD..` from the root directory does nothing, because there is no higher level.

The following command makes the directory named JULY1988 on disk drive A: the current directory for that drive (regardless of which drive is the current drive at the moment):

`CD A:\JULY1988`

Any DOS commands (such as `DIR A:` or `COPY *.* A:`) issued after this command access the directory named JULY1988 on the disk in drive A:. If you were to enter the command:

```
A:
```

at this point, to switch to the disk in drive A:, you would be accessing the JULY1988 directory of drive A:. When you enter the command:

```
C:
```

to switch back to the hard disk, you would be in the same directory from which you left the hard disk.

To display the name of the current drive and directory, enter the command:

```
CD
```

To display the current directory on another drive, specify the drive name, but not a path. For example, the following command displays the name of the current directory on the disk in drive A:

```
CD A:
```

(Note: To display the name of the current directory at all times, enter the command PROMPT PG.)

See Also   MKDIR, PROMPT

CHKDSK

Displays the status of a disk, checks for disk flaws, and optionally corrects some disk flaws.

Version   1 and later

Type   External (CHKDSK.COM)

DOS Shell Menu Access   None

Syntax   CHKDSK [drive][path][file] [/F] [/V]

in which *drive* is the name of the disk drive of interest, *path* and *file* specifies the location and name of the file to be checked, and /F and /V are optional switches.

Usage   CHKDSK (pronounced "check disk") is used to check the status of the disk and, optionally, to fix any errors on the disk. It produces a CHKDSK status report containing:

Disk volume

Date the disk was formatted

Disk volume serial number (in DOS 4)

Total disk space in bytes

Number of hidden files and the amount of disk space they occupy

Number of directories and the amount of disk space they occupy

Number of user files and the amount of disk space they occupy

Total disk space available

Number of bytes in each allocation unit (in DOS 4)

Number of allocation units on disk (in DOS 4)

Number of available allocation units

Total amount of system memory (in DOS 4)

Amount of available system memory

Because files are not always saved contiguously on disk, the number of non-contiguous areas occupied by a file is reported when the file option is specified. (If files are fragmented, their processing time is slowed down.)

If the /F option is specified in the command, and CHKDSK finds any clusters in the File Allocation Table (FAT) that are not allocated to a file, CHKDSK displays the prompt:

```
Convert lost chains to file (Y/N)?
```

If you type N in response, CHKDSK ignores the lost clusters (chains). If you answer Y, CHKDSK recovers the clusters, and places them in a file named FILEnnnn.CHK in the root directory of the disk (in which nnnn is a series of numbers beginning with 0000 and incremented sequentially with each .CHK file). After you check the files and retrieve any useful information, you can erase them.

The /V option is used to display the drive, path, and file name for all files on the disk.

You can redirect the output from CHKDSK to the printer (using > PRN) or a file (using > filename.ext). However, do not redirect output to a file when you use the /F switch with CHKDSK.

Examples   To produce a CHKDSK status report for drive C:, use:

```
CHKDSK C:
```

To check for lost clusters, use:

CHKDSK C: /F

If you want to print a CHKDSK status report that contains the names of all files and fragmentation information, use:

CHKDSK C:*.* /V > PRN

See Also Chapter 17, for information about defragmenting programs.

CLS

Clears the screen.

Version 2 and later

Type Internal

DOS Shell Menu Access None

Syntax CLS

Usage CLS clears all information from the screen and places the prompt in the upper left-hand corner of the screen. CLS clears only the screen display, it has no effect on the contents of RAM or disk files.

Examples If, after you exit a program, the screen remains cluttered with irrelevant information, clear the screen by entering the command:

CLS

COMMAND

Invokes a second copy of the command processor.

Version 1 and later

Type External (COMMAND.COM)

DOS Shell Menu Access   None

Syntax   `COMMAND [drive][path] [/P] [/C commands] [/E:size]`

in which *drive* is the disk drive where COMMAND.COM is located, *path* is the name of the directory that contains COMMAND.COM, *commands* are optional commands, and *size* is a number between 160 and 32,768, which sets the size of the environment.

Usage   COMMAND is generally used within programs to allow batch files (and other programs) to send commands directly to DOS, or to allow a temporary return to the command prompt.

    If COMMAND is used without options in a batch file, it temporarily exits the program and displays the command prompt. You can interact with the COMMAND prompt in the usual manner. To return control to the batch file, enter the command EXIT.

    The /C option lets you include a series of DOS commands that are to be executed immediately. After processing these commands, control is returned to the batch file automatically, without the need to enter the EXIT command. The /C option can also be used within a batch file to process another batch file. (This mimics the action of the CALL command used in DOS Version 3.3 and later.)

    The /P option disables the EXIT command so that the copy of the command processor remains in memory for the entire current session (that is, until you turn off the computer or reboot). If you attempt to use both the /C and /P options, the /P option is ignored.

    The /E option (available in Versions 3.2 and later) lets you set the size of the DOS environment, within the range of 160 to 32,768 bytes. By default, the DOS environment size is set to 160 bytes.

Examples   The sample batch file that follows, when typed and executed, clears the screen and displays the messages Going to DOS temporarily. Enter any DOS commands, then type EXIT to return. You can use the DOS command prompt as you normally would. When you enter the EXIT command, control returns to the batch file and the screen displays the message OK, I'm back to normal!

```
@ECHO OFF
CLS
ECHO Going to DOS temporarily.
ECHO Enter any DOS commands, then type EXIT to return.
COMMAND
ECHO OK, I'm back to normal!
```

    When you use the Shift-F9 key to exit the DOS Shell, the shell actually creates a secondary command processor, leaving the Shell "suspended" for the time being. Later, when you enter the EXIT command, the second-ary command processor ends and control returns to the Shell.

See Also   CALL, SET, SHELL

COMP

Compares two or more files.

Version   1 and later

Type   External (COMP.COM)

DOS Shell Menu Access   Select DOS Utilities... from the Main Group screen, and Disk Compare from the next screen.

Syntax   COMP [*first drive*][*first path*][*first file name*]
[*second drive*][*second path*][*second file name*]

in which *first drive*, *first path*, and *first file name* identify one set of files for comparison, and *second drive*, *second path* and *second file name* identify the second set of files.

Usage   COMP compares the contents of two files or two sets of files, to determine whether or not there are any differences. If no differences are found, COMP returns the message Files compare OK. If any differences are found, COMP displays a maximum of 10 differences. After 10 differences are found, COMP displays the message 10 mismatches--ending compare and stops comparing the two files. (COMP assumes that there is no need to compare the files any further, because there are already too many differences.)

When differences are found between the files being compared, COMP indicates the exact byte (character) location at which differences exist. The location is displayed in hexadecimal notation.

If you omit file names from the command, COMP asks you for the names of files to be compared. You can use wildcard characters in lieu of specific file names, to compare groups of files.

Do not use COMP to compare files that were backed up from the hard disk using the BACKUP command, to the originals on the hard disk. COMP will always find differences because BACKUP adds additional information to the diskette copies.

Note that when two versions of a file do not match, you can always tell which is the most recent version merely by using the DIR command to display the date and time.

When COMP finishes comparing files, it displays the message `Compare more files (Y/N)?`. Entering `Y` allows you to specify the names of other files to compare. Entering `N` returns you to the command prompt (or the DOS 4 Shell).

Unlike DISKCOMP, which can only be used to compare diskettes, COMP can compare any two files or any two groups of files on any disk.

Examples Assuming that the COMP.COM program is accessible through a predefined PATH command, enter the following command to begin a comparison:

```
COMP
```

The screen presents the prompt:

```
Enter primary file name
```

Type a file name, such as `TEST.TXT`, and press Enter. Next, the screen asks:

```
Enter 2nd file name or drive id
```

If the second file has the same name as the first, you need only enter the drive letter. You can also enter the entire file name with the drive letter. In this example, suppose you want to compare TEST.TXT with the file TEST2.TXT on drive A:. You would then enter the drive and file name at the second prompt as follows:

```
A:TEST2.TXT.
```

If no differences are found, COMP displays the following message:

```
C:TEST.TXT and A:TEST2.TXT
Files compare ok
```

If differences are found, COMP might display messages (to a maximum of 10), such as:

```
Compare error at OFFSET 18
File 1 = 67                    File 2 = 78
```

All information is presented in hexadecimal (base 16) notation, which you can translate to decimal (base 10) using an appropriate utility program, such as a programmer's calculator. In the previous example, there is a difference between the two files at the 24th character (18 hex translates to 24 decimal). File 1 contains the letter "g" (ASCII hex code 67, or ASCII decimal code 103) at the 24th character position, while File 2 contains the letter "x" at that position (ASCII hex code 78, decimal code 120). No other differences are reported.

COMP then displays the message `Compare more files (Y/N)?` before returning to DOS. Type `N` to return to DOS, or `Y` to compare more files. You'll be prompted to enter the file names, exactly as when you first ran COMP.

The names of (or wildcard characters for) files to be compared can be entered directly on the COMP command line. For example, to compare all .TXT files in the \WP directory on drive C: with all .TXT files in the \WP\WPFILES subdirectory, enter the command:

```
COMP C:\WP\*.TXT C:\WP\WPFILES\*.TXT
```

If you attempt to compare two files that are different sizes, COMP displays the message `Files are different sizes`. COMP only attempts to compare files that are the same size, because it "knows" that two files of different sizes cannot possibly be identical.

CONFIG.SYS

A file that contains commands that tell DOS how to configure the computer.

Version   1 and later

Type   Modifiable ASCII text file.

DOS Shell   None
Menu Access

Usage   CONFIG.SYS is a special file that DOS automatically reads when you first turn on your computer. You cannot actually type the command CONFIG or CONFIG.SYS. Instead, you create a file named CONFIG.SYS in the root directory of your hard disk, or in the root directory of your Startup diskette.

You can use the EDLIN editor (or any word processor or text editor capable of saving files in ASCII text format) to create and edit the CONFIG.SYS file. In addition, some computers offer special programs that simplify the creation and editing of the CONFIG.SYS file. For example, IBM PC-DOS Versions 3.3 and 4 offer the SELECT command. Compaq computers using DOS 4 use the FASTART program. See the DOS manual that came with your computer for specific information.

The configuration commands that you can include in the CONFIG.SYS file include:

BREAK=   Tells DOS how often to check for a Ctrl-C or Break keypress.

BUFFERS=   Determines the number of buffers to be set aside for disk accessing.

COUNTRY=   Specifies the date, time, and currency format to be used.

DEVICE=   Identifies a device driver (a program that controls and configures a device).

FCBS=   Specifies the number of file control blocks that can be opened at any one time.

FILES=   Specifies the number of files that can be opened at one time.

INSTALL=   Loads memory resident programs during startup.

LASTDRIVE=   Specifies the name of the highest named drive.

REM   Adds a blank line or a comment to a configuration file.

SHELL=   Specifies the name and location of the command processor (usually COMMAND.COM).

SWITCHES   Disables extended keyboard functions.

STACKS=   Specifies the number of stacks used by the system hardware interrupts.

The DEVICE and INSTALL commands are used in the CONFIG.SYS file to install device drivers. Some device drivers that your version of DOS might include are: ANSI.SYS, COUNTRY.SYS, RAMDRIVE.SYS, VDISK.SYS, PRINTER.SYS, and others discussed in this appendix. Your particular computer system might include additional device drivers for managing optional devices—for example, MOUSE.SYS to control a mouse, or Compaq Computer's CEMM.SYS to manage expanded memory.

Examples The following sample CONFIG.SYS file includes several DOS commands, as well as device drivers for both DOS and optional devices.

```
BREAK=ON
FILES=40
BUFFERS=20
DEVICE=C:\DOS\ANSI.SYS
DEVICE=C:\MOUSE1\MOUSE.SYS
SHELL=C:\DOS\COMMAND.COM /P /E:256
LASTDRIVE=D
DEVICE=C:\DOS\VDISK.SYS 3072 128 64 /E:8
DEVICE=C:\DOS\CEMM.EXE 1024 ON
INSTALL=C:\DOS\FASTOPEN.EXE C:=(50,25) /X
```

The first command, `BREAK=ON`, activates frequent checking for a Break key keypress. The command `FILES=40` specifies that a maximum of 40 files can be open simultaneously. The command `BUFFERS=20` specifies 20 disk buffers for conventional RAM.

The command `DEVICE=C:\DOS\ANSI.SYS` installs the DOS ANSI.SYS device driver for the screen and printer. The command `DEVICE=C:\MOUSE1\MOUSE.SYS` installs a mouse driver. (The MOUSE.SYS file, in this example, is stored in the \MOUSE1 directory of drive C:.)

The command `SHELL=C:\DOS\COMMAND.COM /P /E:256` specifies COMMAND.COM as the command processor. The /P switch makes the command processor permanent for the entire session, and /E:256 provides 256 bytes for the DOS environment.

The command `LASTDRIVE=D` provides for two hard disk (or RAM disk) names—C: and D:. The command `DEVICE=C:\DOS\VDISK.SYS 3072 128 64 /E:8` creates a 3MB RAM disk in extended memory. The command `DEVICE=C:\DOS\CEMM.EXE 1024 ON` activates 1MB of expanded memory (using the CEMM.EXE device driver included with the Compaq 386 computer). The command `INSTALL=C:\DOS\FASTOPEN.EXE C:=(50,25) /X` installs the DOS 4 disk caching program in expanded memory.

See Also BREAK, FILES, BUFFERS, DEVICE, ANSI.SYS, SHELL, COMMAND, LASTDRIVE, VDISK.SYS, INSTALL, FASTOPEN, SWITCHES

COPY

Copies a file or a group of files to or from a device.

Version 1 and later

Type Internal

DOS Shell Menu Access From the **Start Programs** screen, select `File System`. Then select the drive and directory, if necessary, that contains the file to be copied. Select the file(s) that you want to copy by highlighting the file names and pressing the Spacebar. Press (F10), highlight File, and press Enter. Then select `Copy....`

Modify the To: prompt in the box to specify the drive, directory, and name of the copy (if different than the name of the original). Figure B.4 shows an example in which a file named LOOKIN.BAT in the \UTILS directory of drive C: is being copied to the diskette in drive A:, using the same file name.

Press Enter after you fill in the dialog box. While copying is taking place, you see its progress on the screen. If, during the copy process, DOS discovers that a specified file name already exists on the target drive and

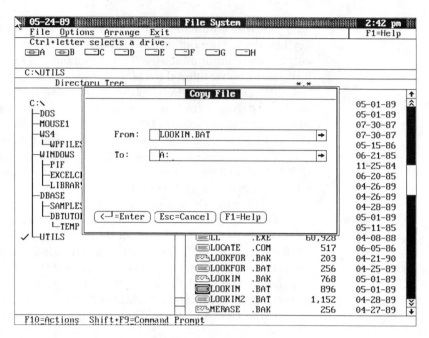

Figure B.4. The LOOKIN.BAT file on the \UTILS directory
will be copied to the diskette in drive A:.

directory, it asks if it should skip copying the current file, or overwrite the
contents of the identically named file on the target directory. You can select either option; then, DOS continues copying.

When copying is complete, you are returned to the **File System**
screen.

Syntax COPY [*source drive*][*source path*][*source file name*] [/A] [/B]
[+][...] [*destination drive*][*destination path*]
[*destination file name*] [/A] [/B] [/V]

in which *source drive*, *source path*, and *source file name* identify the location and name of the original file to be copied, and *destination drive*, *destination path*, and *destination file name* identify the target location and name
of the copy. The symbol + indicates that you can combine several separate
files to be copied to a single destination file.

Usage COPY is one of the commands that you will probably use daily in your
computer work. It allows you to make copies of files from one disk to
another, from one directory to another directory on the same disk, or from
one file to another file name on the same directory. It also allows you to
copy information from one device to another, for example from your

screen to a disk, or from a file to the printer. In addition, COPY lets you combine two or more files into a single file.

When copying files, remember that the file being copied is referred to as the *source* file. The copy is referred to as the *destination* or *target* file. Whenever you use the COPY command, the source file is always listed before the target file. Hence, you can think of the syntax of the COPY command as being COPY *source file* TO *target file*. (The one exception is when only one file description is given; in this case, the syntax is more like COPY *source file* TO HERE). The "Examples" section demonstrates all of these permutations.

Another important point to keep in mind when copying files is that COPY automatically overwrites any file with the same name *without warning* (unless you use the DOS 4 Shell to copy files). For example, suppose you have a file named BACKUP.TXT, which contains a backup of your first quarter Income Statement. You create a second quarter income statement named SECQTR.TXT.

Then, you decide to make a backup copy of SECQTR.TXT and name that backup copy BACKUP.TXT. As soon as you complete the copy, BACKUP.TXT contains the second quarter statement, and the first quarter statement backup no longer exists.

To avoid overwriting an existing file when you use the COPY command, first use the DIR command to see if a file already exists. For example, before naming your backup of the income statement file program BACKUP.TXT, enter the command **DIR BACKUP.TXT**. If DIR shows that such a file exists, simply use a different name for the new backup, such as BACKUP2.TXT.

Note that you cannot copy files to a write-protected diskette. If you attempt to do so, DOS replies with the message:

```
Write protect error writing drive A
Abort, Retry, Fail?
```

(Versions of DOS prior to Version 3.3 display the options *Abort, Retry, Ignore*.) You can remove the disk from drive A:, remove its write-protect tab, and put it back in the drive (or put a different disk in drive A:) and type the letter **R** to try again. Or, type **A** to abort the command and return to the command prompt.

When you omit the destination, DOS "assumes" that the destination is the current drive and directory. For example, if your hard disk drive C: is the current drive and you enter the command **COPY A:LETTER.TXT**, COPY copies the LETTER.TXT file from the disk in drive A: to the current drive and directory.

This works only when the source refers to a drive or directory other than the current drive or directory. For example, if you enter the command **COPY LETTER.TXT**, DOS returns the message **File cannot be copied to itself**, because you specified the current drive and directory as both the source and destination of the copy. A single drive and directory cannot contain two files with the same name.

The various switches (/A, /B, and /V) are described in the following list. In general, you do not need to use any of these switches; however, when you use COPY to combine multiple files into a single new file, the /A and /B switches can be useful. Either option affects the preceding file name and all following file names until another switch is encountered.

/A   Treats the file as an ASCII text file.

With a source file: Copies all text up to (but excluding) the EOF (end-of-file) marker, Ctrl-Z.

With a destination file: Adds the EOF marker to the end of the destination file.

/B   Treats the file as binary format.

With a source file: Copies the entire file, including any and all embedded EOF markers.

With a destination file: Does not add the EOF marker to the end of the file.

/V   Verifies that the copy is accurate.

When DOS completes a successful copy, it displays the message (*n*) file(s) copied, where *n* is the number of files that were copied.

You can also include device names, such as PRN and CON, to copy text files to devices. For example, the command COPY LETTER.TXT CON displays the contents of the LETTER.TXT file on the screen (console). The command COPY LETTER.TXT PRN prints the contents of the LETTER.TXT file.

Examples   To copy all of the files from the current directory on the hard disk to a diskette in drive A:, enter the command:

COPY *.* A:

This command works although no drive or path for the source files is given, because COPY assumes the current drive and directory. The *.* symbol refers to all files (any "first name" and any extension). Because the destination specifies only A:, files are sent to whichever directory is current on the disk in drive A:.

Suppose that your current directory is \WP on your hard disk drive C:. The diskette in drive A: contains some files that you want to copy. Furthermore, the disk in drive A: is not divided into separate directories. To copy all of the files from the diskette in drive A: to the current C:\WP drive and location, enter the command:

COPY A:*.*

The command above works although only one file name specification is given (that is, A:*.*), because COPY assumes that the destination for the copies is the current drive and directory (C:\WP in this example). The source is assumed to be all of the files on the diskette in drive A:.

You can make a copy of a file that has a different name than the original copy. This is useful for making two copies of the same file on the same disk and directory. For example, suppose you want to keep a backup copy of your spreadsheet, named DEC1988.WK3, on the same disk and directory. You decide to name this backup copy DEC1988.BAK. To make the copy, enter the command:

```
COPY DEC1988.WK3 DEC1988.BAK
```

To make copies of all of your spreadsheet files and assign the copies the extension .BAK, enter the command:

```
COPY *.WK3 *.BAK
```

This command says "Copy all of the files with .WK3 as the extension to files with the same first name, but the extension .BAK."

Suppose that the root directory of drive C: (that is, C:\) is the current directory, and you want to copy a file named MOM.LET from the directory named \WP to the diskette in drive A:. To do so, enter the command:

```
COPY C:\WP\MOM.LET A:
```

Suppose you want to perform the same operation, but you want to copy the file to a directory named \LETTERS on drive A:. Assuming that the diskette in drive A: already contains a directory named LETTERS, enter the command:

```
COPY C:\WP\MOM.LET A:\LETTERS\MOM.LET
```

If you want to do the same operation, but you want to store MOM.LET with the file name MOMLET.BAK on the LETTERS directory of drive A:, enter the command:

```
COPY C:\WP\MOM.LET A:\LETTERS\MOMLET.BAK
```

Suppose you have three ASCII text files named CHAPTER1.TXT, CHAPTER2.TXT, and CHAPTER3.TXT. You want to combine all three files into a single file named BOOK.TXT. (All of the source files and the destination file are on the same drive and directory.) To do so, enter the command:

```
COPY CHAPTER1.TXT + CHAPTER2.TXT + CHAPTER3.TXT BOOK.TXT
```

Because all three source files in this example have very similar names, you could also perform the copy using the command:

```
COPY Chapter?.TXT Book.TXT
```

To get some practice using COPY as a means of copying information between devices, you might want to try the following examples. To copy the information you type on the screen into a file named SAMPLE.TRY, use the CON device name in the COPY command, as follows:

```
COPY CON SAMPLE.TRY
```

After you enter this command, the cursor waits on the screen on the next blank line. Type the following two lines (press Enter after typing in each line):

```
This is a test
This is a test
```

Next, type Ctrl-L (hold down the Ctrl key and type the letter L). It appears as ^L on the screen. (This will force the printer to do a form feed in a later example.)

Finally, either type Ctrl-Z or press the F6 key. This displays the end-of-file marker ^Z on the screen. After you press Enter, COPY assumes that, because you entered the end-of-file marker, you have finished typing the file. You are returned to the DOS prompt.

To verify that what you typed on the screen was stored in a file, enter the command:

```
COPY SAMPLE.TRY CON
```

This displays the contents of the file (excluding the end-of-file marker, which COPY does not show).

Now, to copy the SAMPLE.TRY file from the disk to the printer, use the device name PRN as the destination for the copy, by entering the following command:

```
COPY SAMPLE.TRY PRN
```

After your printer prints the file, it ejects the entire page from the printer (in response to the Ctrl-L "form feed" that you entered into the file).

See Also   BACKUP, DISKCOPY, XCOPY, PRINT, TYPE

COUNTRY

Configures the date format, currency symbols, and other local conventions for specific countries.

Version   3 (enhanced in Versions 3.3 and later)

Type   Device driver (COUNTRY.SYS) used in CONFIG.SYS.

DOS Shell Menu Access   None

Syntax   Versions 3.0 to 3.2:

COUNTRY=*nnn*

Versions 3.3 and later:

COUNTRY=*nnn* [,*codepage*][,*drive:path*\COUNTRY.SYS]

in which *nnn* is the three-digit code for the country, *codepage* is a three-digit number for the code page (character set), and *drive* and *path*. represent the drive and directory that contain COUNTRY.SYS.

Usage   Different countries use different formats for displaying dates, times and currency. Computers built in the United States show dates in the North American formats, as follows:

Date: 12-31-90

Time: 1:50:00p

   The COUNTRY.SYS device driver lets you modify the format used to display and enter dates and times, to standards used in other countries. The COUNTRY.SYS driver was initially released with Version 3.0 of DOS, and it was revised and expanded in Version 3.3 and later versions.

   To use COUNTRY.SYS to modify the date and time format, you generally include the COUNTRY driver in your CONFIG.SYS file, followed by an equal sign and a three-digit number, which in most cases is the same as the country's telephone dialing prefix. In Version 3.3 and later, you can also specify a *code page*, which reconfigures the character set to that of the foreign language (see the entry for NLSFUNC in this appendix). Table B.3 shows the available country codes and the default code page used by each. (Those that are available only in versions 3.3 and later are marked with an asterisk.)

Table B.3. Country codes and code pages used
with COUNTRY.SYS.

Country/Language	Country Code	Default Code Page
Arabic*	785	None (requires special hardware)
Australia	061	437
Belgium	032	437
Canada—English*	001	437
Canada—French	002	863
Denmark	045	865
Finland	358	437
France	033	437
Israel	972	437
Italy	039	437
Latin America*	003	437
Netherlands	031	437
Norway	047	865
Portugal	351	860
Spain	034	437
Sweden	046	437
Switzerland—French*	041	437
Switzerland—German	041	437
United Kingdom	044	437
United States	001	437

*Version 3.3 and later only.

In Versions 3.3 and 4.0 of DOS, you can omit the three-digit country code and code page number (but you must still include the commas), in which case DOS uses the default country and code page.

Examples   Adding the following command to the CONFIG.SYS file:

```
COUNTRY=034
```

converts the date and time displays to those used in Spain. The equivalent CONFIG.SYS command, using DOS 3.3 and later versions and assuming that COUNTRY.SYS is stored on the \DOS directory of drive C:, would be:

```
COUNTRY=034,,C:\DOS\COUNTRY.SYS
```

In the future, each time you start the computer, DOS will display the date in the format 31.12.1990 (for December 31, 1990), and the time in the format 12.50.00.00 (for 12:50 PM).

The CONFIG.SYS command below specifies the United States country code and code page, and tells DOS that the COUNTRY.SYS file is on the root directory of drive C:

```
COUNTRY=001,437,C:\COUNTRY.SYS
```

The next time you start or reboot the computer, dates are displayed in *mm/dd/yy* format, the time is displayed in *hh.mm.ss* format, the decimal point is displayed as a period (.), and the currency symbol is $. The standard American keyboard is also assumed.

See Also   NLSFUNC, KEYB, MODE

CTTY

Changes the standard input and output devices.

Version   2 and later

Type   Internal

DOS Shell Menu Access   None

Syntax   CTTY [CON | *device name*]

in which CON resets the standard input and output devices to the standard monitor and keyboard, and *device name* defines another device—such as COM1, COM2, AUX, etc.—to be used as the primary input and output device.

Usage   The CTTY command is used to change the input and output devices on a system to any character-oriented device having both input and output capabilities, such as a teletype unit with both a keyboard and printer, or a remote terminal with a CRT and a keyboard.

The CTTY command can only be used for application programs that use DOS function calls. It cannot be used with BASIC and other programs that do not use DOS function calls.

Examples   To change the input and output device to a remote terminal connected to COM1, enter the following command at the DOS prompt:

```
CTTY COM1
```

To return to the standard console, use:

CTTY CON

See Also   MODE

DATE

Displays and, optionally, lets you change the system date.

Version   1 and later

Type   Internal

DOS Shell   Select DOS Utilities... from the Main Group screen, and select Set Date
Menu Access   and Time from the next screen.

Syntax   DATE [*current date*]

in which *current date* is an optional date entered in the mm-dd-yy format,
or the format specified by the current COUNTRY.SYS setting.

Usage   Use the DATE command to check the current system date (the date your
computer thinks is correct) and, optionally, to change the date. All programs that allow you to access the system date use the date defined by the
DATE command.
   The format of the date shown and the format you need to follow
to enter a new date are determined by the COUNTRY setting in your
CONFIG.SYS file. If you use United States formats for dates and times, the
date is displayed in mm-dd-yy format, although you can enter it in either
mm-dd-yy or mm/dd/yy format.

Examples   To check the system date, merely enter the command:

DATE

The screen displays the system date, and DOS gives you the opportunity to
change it, as shown below:

Current date is Wed 4-20-1990
  Enter new date (mm-dd-yy):

If the date shown is accurate, press the Enter key. To change the date, type it in the format shown on the second line (that is, mm-dd-yy in this example), and press the Enter key.

See Also   TIME

DEL

DEL is identical to the command ERASE. See ERASE in this appendix.

DEVICE

Used in CONFIG.SYS to install optional device drivers.

Version   1 and later

Type   Internal, Configuration (used only in the CONFIG.SYS file)

DOS Shell   None
Menu Access

Syntax   DEVICE=[*drive*][*path*]*file name* [*options*]

in which *drive* and *path* indicate the drive and directory location of the device driver file, *file name* represents the complete file name and extension of the device driver, and *options* represents additional parameters and switches supported by the device driver.

Usage   The DEVICE command is used only in the CONFIG.SYS file to install drivers for optional devices, such as a mouse, a RAM disk, expanded memory, or other options.

DOS offers several of its own device drivers, discussed in this appendix, such as ANSI.SYS, DISPLAY.SYS, PRINTER.SYS, VDISK.SYS, and others. Your specific computer and any optional devices that you add, such as a mouse, provide their own device drivers.

Examples   When added to your computer's CONFIG.SYS file, the following commands install the ANSI.SYS device driver, which allows for customization of the screen display and keyboard, and a 512KB RAM disk in extended memory:

```
DEVICE=C:\DOS\ANSI.SYS
DEVICE=C:\DOS\VDISK.SYS 512 /E
```

In the previous commands, the ANSI.SYS and VDISK.SYS drivers are located in the \DOS directory of hard disk drive C:.

See Also ANSI.SYS, VDISK.SYS, DISPLAY.SYS, PRINTER.SYS, RAMDRIVE.SYS, DRIVER.SYS, XMA2EMS.SYS, XMAEMS.SYS

DIR

Displays a directory of file names.

Version 1 and later

Type Internal

DOS Shell The Files Area of the **File System** screen shows the names of files in the
Menu Access current directory.

Syntax DIR [*drive*][*path*][*file name*] [...] [/P] [/W]

in which *drive* and *path* specify the disk drive and directory of interest, and *file name* is an actual, or ambiguous, file name.

Usage The DIR command is used to display the names of files on any disk drive or directory. Along with each file name, it displays the size of the file (in bytes), and the date and time of the most recent change to the file.

If there are many files in the directory, they will scroll off the screen before you can read them all. To make the display more readable, use either the /P option, which pauses for a keypress after each "page" (screenful) of information, or use the /W option, which displays the file names in as many as five columns across the screen. (The /W switch, however, does not display file information such as size and date.) You can use both the /P and /W options to display many file names in multiple columns with screen breaks.

You can also press Ctrl-S or Pause at any time while DIR is displaying file names, to temporarily stop the display. To resume the display, press any character key or the Spacebar.

You can use wildcard characters to search for specific types of files. In addition, you can use the DIR display as input to the SORT and FIND filters, to sort the display or search for particular types of files. Examples below demonstrate these uses.

If you have used ASSIGN or JOIN on a disk drive or directory, you should cancel the assignment before using the DIR command.

Examples The command:

DIR

displays all of the file names, sizes, dates, and times on the current disk drive and directory.

To view all the files on the current directory that have the .SYS file name extension, enter the command:

DIR *.SYS

Figure B.5 shows sample output from the DIR *.SYS command.

```
C:\DOS>dir *.sys

 Volume in drive C has no label
 Volume Serial Number is 201A-2C4C
 Directory of  C:\DOS

COUNTRY  SYS    12806 04-05-89   12:00p
DISPLAY  SYS    16149 04-05-89   12:00p
KEYBOARD SYS    41144 04-05-89   12:00p
ANSI     SYS     9241 04-05-89   12:00p
DRIVER   SYS     5473 04-05-89   12:00p
PRINTER  SYS    19098 04-05-89   12:00p
VDISK    SYS     7946 04-05-89   12:00p
XMAEM    SYS    19312 06-17-88   12:00p
XMA2EMS  SYS    29249 08-03-88   12:00p
REMM     SYS     9821 06-18-86    6:10p
REX      SYS     2150 04-15-86    4:26p
CEMM     SYS    64736 06-14-88    9:28a
QEMM     SYS    26100 03-29-88    4:10a
RAMDRIVE SYS     8225 03-05-88   10:51a
CLOCK    SYS     1773 04-05-89   12:00p
EMHDISK  SYS    13702 04-05-89   12:00p
        16 File(s)   15124480 bytes free

C:\DOS>
```

Figure B.5. Sample DIR display.

The command

DIR A:

shows all of the file names, sizes, dates, and times in the root directory of the diskette in drive A:.

To view the file information in the directory named \DBMS on the current disk drive, enter the command:

DIR \DBMS

To view all files with the extension .DBF in the \DBMS directory on drive C:, enter the command:

DIR C:\DBMS*.DBF

To send a copy of the directory listing to the printer, follow the DIR command with the > redirection symbol and the PRN device name, as follows:

```
DIR > PRN
```

To store a copy of the directory listing in a text file, follow the DIR command with the > symbol and a file name. For example, the following command creates a text file named DBFFILES.TXT, which contains a list of the files in the \DBMS directory that have the extension .DAT:

```
DIR C:\DBMS\*.DAT > DBFILES.TXT
```

If the SORT.EXE file is available on the current drive or in a directory included in your PATH, then the next command displays the directory sorted in alphabetical order:

```
DIR | SORT
```

If the FIND.EXE program is available, you can use it to locate files that were created on a particular date or at a particular time, or files that contain certain letters. For example, the following command locates all files that were created on September 12, 1988:

```
DIR | FIND "4-12-88"
```

You can combine as many options as you like. For example, the following command creates a text file named EXEFILES.TXT, which contains a sorted directory of files in the \UTILS directory that have the extension .EXE:

```
DIR C:\UTILS\*.EXE | SORT > EXEFILES.TXT
```

The next command displays the names of all files in the \UTILS directory that have the extension .BAT and that were created or last changed on September 12, 1988. The file names are displayed in alphabetical order:

```
DIR C:\UTILS\*.BAT | FIND "4-12-88" | SORT
```

See Also   FIND, SORT

DISKCOMP

Compares two floppy disks

Version   1 and later

Type   External (DISKCOMP.COM)

**DOS Shell
Menu Access**   Select `DOS Utilities...` from the Main Group, and then select `Disk Compare` from the Dos Utilities . . . screen.

Syntax   `DISKCOMP [first drive] [second drive] /1 /8`

in which *first drive* and *second drive* are names of two different floppy disk drives (not a hard disk drive).

Usage   DISKCOMP compares two floppy disks to see if they are identical. (DISKCOMP cannot be used with a hard disk.) Both disks must be the same size and density (that is, you cannot compare a 3.5-inch disk to a 5.25-inch disk, or a high-density disk to a double-density disk).

DISKCOMP compares all of the sectors on the disk on a byte-by-byte (character-by-character) basis. Therefore, it is best to use DISKCOMP to compare only disks that were created with the DISKCOPY command. Because COPY has the ability to defragment files, it probably will store them differently than DISKCOPY does. Therefore, DISKCOMP might think that disks created with COPY commands are "different," even though they actually contain the exact files and data.

If your computer has only one floppy disk drive, you can still use DISKCOMP to compare two diskettes. DISKCOMP will prompt you to remove and insert the disks as necessary.

If DISKCOMP does not find any differences between the two diskettes, it displays the message `Diskettes compare Ok`. If DISKCOMP does find differences, it displays the message `Compare error(s) on Track n, side y`, in which n and y are the track and side numbers.

When finished comparing disks, DISKCOMP displays the prompt `Compare more diskettes (Y/N)?` Type `N` to quit, or type `Y` to compare more diskettes.

Examples   Suppose you just used DISKCOPY to copy the diskette in drive A: to the diskette in drive B:. To verify that the two diskettes are identical, you enter the command:

```
DISKCOPY A: B:
```

Suppose you have only one floppy disk drive, named A:, and you use DISKCOPY to make a copy of a disk. To compare the two diskettes using only the one drive, enter the command:

```
DISKCOMP A: A:
```

The screen prompts you to insert and remove disks as necessary.

See Also   COMP, DISKCOPY

DISKCOPY

Makes an exact copy of a diskette onto another diskette.

Version   1 and later

Type   External (DISKCOPY.COM)

DOS Shell   Select DOS Utilities... from the Main Group, then select Disk Copy from
Menu Access   the DOS Utilities . . . group.

Syntax   DISKCOPY [source drive][destination drive] [/1]

in which *source drive* is the name of the drive containing the disk to be
copied, and *destination drive* is the drive containing the disk that is to receive the copy. The /1 switch copies only the first side of a diskette.

Usage   DISKCOPY makes an exact duplicate of a diskette, using either one or two
floppy disk drives. DISKCOPY cannot be used with a hard disk. If the disk
receiving the copy is not already formatted, DISKCOPY formats the disk
automatically. DISKCOPY is easier than COPY or XCOPY when the diskette contains many directories because it automatically copies all files in
all directories.

However, because DISKCOPY makes an exact byte-by-byte copy of a
disk, it does not consolidate fragmented files.

If you've used any of the commands JOIN or SUBST in the current
session, cancel them before using DISKCOPY. Similarly, a drive that is
shared by other users in a network should not be used for DISKCOPY.

After you complete a DISKCOPY, the screen displays the message
Copy another (Y/N)? Enter N to quit, or enter Y to perform another
DISKCOPY operation.

You can use the DISKCOMP command (discussed above) to verify
that a DISKCOPY operation was accurate.

The optional /1 switch, available in Versions 3.2 and later, copies only
one side of the diskette, regardless of the type of drive or diskettes in use.

Examples   Suppose you have purchased an uncopy-protected program that is stored
on a diskette, and you want to immediately make a backup copy of it. If you
have two identical floppy disk drives named A: and B:, you can place the
original disk in drive A: and a blank disk in drive B:, and then enter the
command:

```
DISKCOPY A: B:
```

To perform the same task, using only a single disk drive (named A:), insert the original diskette in drive A: and enter the command:

```
DISKCOPY A: A:
```

The screen prompts you to remove and insert, the source (original) disk and destination (copy) disk as necessary.

See Also   CHKDSK, COPY, DISKCOMP, XCOPY

DISPLAY.SYS

Modifies the screen to display a non-English language character set.

Version   3.3 and later

Type   Device driver, loaded by a DEVICE command in the CONFIG.SYS file.

DOS Shell   None
Menu Access

Syntax   DEVICE=[*drive*][*path*]DISPLAY.SYS CON[:]=
(*type*[,[*hardware code page*][,*additional codes*]])

or . . .

DEVICE=[*drive*][*path*]DISPLAY.SYS CON[:]=
(*type*[,[*hardware code page*][,*additional codes,sub-fonts*]])

in which *drive* and *path* are the drive and directory locations of the DISPLAY.SYS file, *type* is the display adapter type, *hardware code page* specifies the code page supported by the display device, *additional codes* represents a prepared code page, and *sub-fonts* specifies the number of sub-fonts supported for each code page.

Usage   Most computers built in the United States have the code page number 437, for the English language, built into the video display adapter. If you reside in the United States or in any other country that uses code page 437, then you should not install the DISPLAY.SYS device driver. However, if you reside in a country that uses a different code page, as listed in Table B.2

in the COUNTRY entry of this appendix, then you might need to use DISPLAY.SYS to reconfigure your screen to use a different character set.

You must also use the DISPLAY.SYS device driver if you want to use *code page switching*, which allows you to switch from one character set to another from the DOS command prompt. Note, however, that code page switching is not supported by MONO (monochrome) or CGA (Color Graphics Adapter) displays.

Most computers that support Versions 3.3 and later of DOS can help you modify your computer's character set without directly modifying your CONFIG.SYS file. For example, IBM PC-DOS offers the SELECT program. Compaq's MS-DOS Version 4 offers the FASTART program. Because code page switching capabilities vary from one computer to the next, you should refer to the DOS manual that came with your computer for specific details and capabilities. In general, however, the following acceptable parameters can be used with the DISPLAY.SYS device driver:

Type is either MONO (monochrome), CGA (Color Graphics Adapter), EGA (for Extended Graphics and VGA video adapters), or LCD (for liquid crystal display adapters).

Hardware code page is the code page supported by the video adapter, typically 437 (English), 850 (multilingual), 860 (Portuguese), 863 (French Canadian), and 865 (Norwegian).

Additional codes can be a number between 0 and 12 to support multiple code pages. If a CGA or MONO display adapter is specified as the *type*, then this value must be 0. If the *type* specified is EGA or LCD, then this value should be 1 if 437 is specified as the *hardware code page*, or 2 if a different *hardware code page* is specified.

Sub-fonts can be used only with display adapters that specifically support sub-fonts. For CGA and MONO adapters, *sub-fonts* must be omitted or set to 0. LCD display adapters support 1 additional sub-font. EGA adapters support as many as 2 sub-fonts.

Examples   The following commands, when included in the CONFIG.SYS file, set up the display adapter to use French Canadian date and time formats, as well as the French Canadian character set:

```
COUNTRY=002 863 C:\DOS\COUNTRY.SYS
DEVICE=C:\DOS\DISPLAY.SYS CON=(EGA,437,2)
```

Including the following commands in your AUTOEXEC.BAT file then prepares the French Canadian character set, and allows you to switch from one character set to another using the CHCP command:

```
MODE CON CP PREP=((863,850)C:\DOS\EGA.CPI)
MODE CON CP SEL = 863
KEYB US,863,C:\DOS\KEYBOARD.SYS
```

See Also   CHCP, COUNTRY, KEYB, MODE, PRINTER.SYS

DOSSHELL

Activates the DOS Shell.

Version   4

Type   External (DOSSHELL.BAT)

Syntax   `DOSSHELL`

Usage   The DOS 4 installation program creates a batch file named DOSSHELL.BAT, which configures the Shell to your particular computer and devices. If you install DOS 4 for use on a floppy-based system, DOSSHELL.BAT is stored in the root directory of the Shell diskette. If you install DOS 4 for use on a hard disk, the DOSSHELL.BAT file is usually created and stored in the \DOS directory of disk drive C:.

When you enter the command `DOSSHELL` at the command prompt, the DOSSHELL.BAT batch file is executed, which in turn activates the Shell. On a hard disk system, the directory that contains DOSSHELL.BAT must be included in the current PATH and/or APPEND setting, with the /X option turned on. Otherwise, you will not be able to access the Shell unless its home directory is the current directory.

You can modify the DOSSHELL.BAT batch file using any valid text editor (see Chapter 10). One lengthy line within the DOSSHELL.BAT file determines which features are to be used and which devices are available. The following command shows a typical Shell configuration command (which is stored as a single line in the DOSSHELL.BAT file):

```
@SHELLC /MOS:PCMSDRV.MOS/TRAN/COLOR/DOS/MENU/MUL/SND/
MEU:SHELL.MEU/CLR:SHELL.CLR/PROMPT/MAINT/EXIT/SWAP/DATE
```

The purpose of these options (and other possible options) are listed below:

/CLR:SHELL.CLR	Tells the Shell to look in the file named SHELL.CLR to determine which color scheme to use. (Should not be changed.)
/C01	Displays the Shell in high-resolution, 16-color, 640 x 350 graphics mode (mode 10).
/C02	Displays the Shell in 2-color, 640 x 480 graphics (VGA) mode (mode 11).
/CO3	Displays the Shell in 16-color, 640 x 480 graphics (VGA) mode (mode 12).
/COLOR	Allows color selection from the Shell. (If omitted, colors may not be changed.)

/COM2	Specifies that the serial mouse device is connected to the COM2 port. (If omitted, COM1 is assumed.)
/DATE	Displays the current date and time above the Action Bar. (If omitted, the date and time are not displayed.)
/DOS	Allows access to the File System. (If omitted, the File System is unavailable in the Shell.)
/EXIT	Allows you to exit the Shell to access the command prompt. (If omitted, you cannot exit the Shell.)
/LF	Configures the mouse for left-handed use (IBM PC-DOS only).
/MAINT	Lets you add, delete, and modify programs and groups in the Shell. (If omitted, programs and groups cannot be added, deleted, or changed.)
/MENU	Activates the **Start Programs** screen in the Shell. (If omitted, only the File System is available.)
/MEU:SHELL.MEU	Identifies the file name of the Main Group structure. This option allows a network to uniquely identify menu structures at each workstation, while sharing a single copy of the DOS Shell on the server (see the following sections for additional information).
/MOS:	(IBM PC-DOS only) Specifies the type of mouse used with the Shell; this varies with different computers. If your mouse works with other programs but not the Shell, you might need to change this setting. For the IBM PS/2 mouse, use /MOS:PCIBMDRV.MOS. For the Microsoft serial mouse, use /MOS:PCMSDRV.MOS. For the Microsoft parallel mouse, use /MOS:PCMSPDRV.MOS. (If this setting is omitted and the mouse is properly installed, the mouse will still work with the Shell, but it will use additional memory—as much as 12KB as opposed to 1KB.)
/MUL	Lets the Shell File System manipulate multiple files and directories in memory. (If omitted, performance is slowed because of increased disk accessing.)
/PROMPT	Allows a suspended (temporary) exit to the DOS command prompt with the Shift-F9 key. (If omitted, Shift-F9 is deactivated.)
/SND	Activates sound while you use the Shell. (If omitted, the Shell no longer beeps when you make an error.)

/SWAP	Allows the Shell to store directory information in a temporary file while suspended by pressing Shift-F9. (Maximizes the Shell's speed on a hard disk system).
/TEXT	Displays the Shell in text mode; slider bars and icons are not displayed.
/TRAN	Clears the Shell from memory when you exit using the F3 key. (If omitted, the Shell stays in memory after you exit.)

Transient vs. Resident Mode

The /TRAN option, when included in the SHELLC command line, configures the Shell for transient operation. On computers with a hard disk, this is generally the preferred method, because it conserves memory.

On computers without a hard disk, you should omit the /TRAN option from the SHELLC command line. That way, you can run the DOS Shell by entering the DOSSHELL command at the command prompt, then remove the Shell diskette from drive A:, and use other diskettes in that drive.

Using the Shell on a Network

There are two ways to install the DOS Shell for use on a network. You can install it so that all nodes (workstations) use the same set of Shell files, or so that each node uses its own Shell files.

To use a single set of DOS Shell files for all nodes, first install DOS 4 on the network server. Then, if you want to customize the Shell (such as adding groups or programs), do so on the server. When you finish, change the attributes of the Shell .MEU (menu), .CLR (color), and .ASC (associations) files to read-only, using the ATTRIB command. (This prevents other network users from changing these files.)

For each node in the network (and the server as well), create a new batch file that excludes the /MAINT and /COLOR options. Assign a unique name to each of these batch files (for example, SHELL1.BAT, SHELL2.BAT, SHELL3.BAT, and so on). The name of the batch file must be specified within the batch file, next to the SHELLB command.

For example, if the DOS Shell is stored in a directory named \DOS on drive F:, and the nodes are accessing the Shell on drive F:, then the batch file for node 1, named SHELL1.BAT, might look like this:

```
@ECHO OFF
REM ------------------- SHELL1.BAT
F:
CD \DOS
SHELLB SHELL1
IF ERRORLEVEL 255 GOTO END
:COMMON
SHELLC /TRAN/DOS/MUL/MENU/EXIT/PROMPT/TEXT/MEU:SHELL.MEU
:END
```

If, on the other hand, you want each node in the network to use its own set of programs, groups, and associations, you should provide each node with its own files. Install DOS 4 on the server and then customize the Shell (such as adding programs and groups) on the server.

Next, copy the Shell .MEU (menu), .CLR (color), and .ASC (association) files to each node. Assign unique file name on each node, for example node 1 might use NODE1.MEU, NODE1.CLR, and NODE1.ASC. On node 2, name these files NODE2.MEU, NODE2.CLR, and NODE2.ASC.

The Shell batch file on each node must contain the name of the batch file next to the SHELLB command, and the names of the associated SHELL files in the SHELLC command. For example, the following batch file shows how the NODE1.BAT file might look when installed on node 1:

```
@ECHO OFF
REM ------------- NODE1.BAT
F:
CD \DOS
SHELLB N1
IF ERRORLEVEL 255 GOTO END
:COMMON
SHELLC /MAINT/CLR:NODE1.CLR/COLOR/MUL/MEU:NODE1.MEU
```

Examples   When you are at the command line, you can activate the DOS Shell by typing:

```
DOSSHELL
```

DRIVER.SYS

Assigns logical names to disk drives.

Version   3.2 and later

Type   Device driver, activated by a DEVICE command in CONFIG.SYS

DOS Shell Menu Access   None

Syntax   DEVICE=[*drive*][*path*]DRIVER.SYS /D:*ddd* [/T:*ttt*] [/S:*ss*] [/H:*hh*] [/C] [/N] [/F:*f*]

in which *drive* and *path* are the location of the DRIVER.SYS file, *ddd* specifies the drive number, *ttt* specifies the number of tracks per side, *ss* specifies the number of sectors per track, *hh* specifies the maximum number of heads, and *f* specifies the form factor.

Usage   DRIVER.SYS is generally required only when you add a new external disk drive to your computer and that disk drive does not offer its own device driver. Any computer can support a maximum of twenty-six disk drives, named A: to Z:. Each partition on a single hard disk represents a drive. (For example, a 60MB hard disk that is partitioned into two drives, C: and D:, counts as two disk drives.)

Of the available switches, only /D is mandatory. You must specify a number in the range of 0 to 255 with /D. Note that floppy drive A: is referred to as drive 0 and is assumed to be internal. Floppy drive B: is already numbered 1, even if the computer does not actually have a second floppy disk drive. Therefore, you should avoid using both the number 0 and 1 with the /D option. A value of 2 represents a third floppy drive, which must be external.

The first fixed (hard) disk, usually named C:, is numbered 128. This may be either an existing internal drive or a new external drive. The second fixed disk drive is numbered 129; the third fixed disk drive is numbered 130; and so on.

The optional /T switch specifies the number of tracks per side on the disk. If omitted, the number defaults to 80. The optional /S switch specifies the number of tracks per sector, in the range of 1 to 99. If omitted, 9 is assumed. The optional /H switch specifies the maximum head number for the drive, in the range of 1 to 99. If omitted, 2 is assumed.

The optional /C switch activates the *changeline support* feature available on some disk drives. This allows the drive to detect whether or not the drive door has been opened since the last disk access. If omitted, DOS assumes that this feature is not available on the drive. Note that computers based on the earlier 8086 and 8088 microprocessors generally cannot support this feature.

The optional /N switch specifies a non-removable block device, such as a fixed disk. Never use /N when referring to a drive that uses floppy disks or a drive that supports interchangeable hard disk cartridges. The /F switch specifies the *form type* for an external floppy disk drive.

Table B.4 shows examples of the DRIVER.SYS switches for commonly used external floppy disk drives.

Table B.4. DRIVER.SYS settings used with floppy disk drives.

Drive Capacity	Disk Size	Tracks (/T)	Sectors (/S)	Heads (/H)	Form (/F)
160KB/180KB	5.25	40	9	1	0
320KB/360KB	5.25	40	9	2	0
1.2MB	5.25	80	15	2	1
720KB	3.5	80	9	2	2
1.44MB	3.5	80	18	2	7

DOS automatically names external drives using alphabetical sequencing. For example, suppose your computer already has two floppy drives, named A: and B:, and one hard disk named C:. The first time DOS encounters a `DEVICE=DRIVER.SYS` command in the CONFIG.SYS file, the newly specified drive is named D:.

To assign the highest letter names to RAM disks rather than to external disk drives, place the `DEVICE=DRIVER.SYS` command(s) *above* the `DEVICE=VDISK.SYS` commands in your CONFIG.SYS file, so that the external drives are assigned names before the RAM disks.

Remember that any changes you make to the CONFIG.SYS file are not activated until the next time you reboot. Also, be sure to check the documentation that came with your external disk drive to determine its specific requirements and whether or not it offers a device driver that can be used in lieu of DRIVER.SYS. Also, adding new disk drives to a computer often requires changing dip switch settings inside the computer. Again, only the documentation that comes with a new disk drive can provide specific information.

Examples   Suppose you have an AT-type computer with a 1.2MB disk drive named A: and a hard disk partitioned into two drives named C: and D:. The command below, when entered into your CONFIG.SYS file, adds a 720KB, 3.5-inch disk drive named E: to the computer (assuming the drive is properly connected and the DRIVER.SYS file is stored in the directory named DOS of hard disk drive C:):

```
DEVICE=C:\DOS\DRIVER.SYS /D:2 /T:80 /S:9 /H:2 /F:2
```

See Also   CONFIG.SYS, DEVICE

ECHO

Turns ECHO mode on or off, and sends characters to the screen or printer.

Version   1 and later

Type   Internal (generally used in batch files)

DOS Shell   None
Menu Access

Syntax   `ECHO [ON | OFF] [message]`

in which *message* is text or characters that you want the batch file to display.

Usage   Normally when a batch file executes its commands, it first displays the entire command on the screen. However, if you turn the ECHO off, the batch file will execute its commands without displaying them on the screen. ECHO remains off until the batch file finishes executing or the file encounters an ECHO ON command.

Regardless of whether ECHO is on or off, text to the right of an ECHO command is always displayed on the screen. When ECHO is ON, however, the command itself *and* the message are displayed. For example, if ECHO is OFF, the following command:

```
ECHO Hello friend
```

displays

```
Hello friend
```

But when ECHO is ON, the same command displays:

```
ECHO Hello friend
Hello friend
```

As an alternative to setting ECHO OFF, you can precede commands in a batch file with an @ character (Versions 3.3 and later). For example, the command `@ECHO Hello friend` displays only `Hello friend`, whether ECHO is on or off. To prevent the first ECHO OFF command in a batch file from appearing on the screen, use `@ECHO OFF` instead.

Entering the command `ECHO` directly at the DOS prompt displays the current status of the ECHO option. Entering the command `ECHO OFF` directly at the DOS prompt turns off the display of the prompt. Enter the command `ECHO ON` to recall the prompt.

ECHO affects only the display of commands within the batch file; it does not affect information messages such as `1 file(s) copied`, at the end of a COPY command. To hide such messages, redirect them to the NUL device. For example, the command `COPY *.BAK A:>NUL` copies all .BAK files from the current drive and directory to the disk in drive A:, but does not display any message during or after the copy procedure.

To redirect echoed characters to the printer, use the > PRN redirection symbol and device name. For example, to send a form feed (to eject a page) to the printer, use the command `ECHO ^L>PRN`, where ^L is typed by pressing Ctrl-L (hold down the Ctrl key and type the letter L). This command works the same whether it is included in a batch file or typed at the command prompt.

Examples   The following batch file, named GREET.BAT, clears the screen, presents a couple of greeting lines, and customizes the DOS prompt:

```
REM --------------- GREET.BAT
```

```
CLS
ECHO Welcome to DOS
ECHO Here is the prompt...
PROMPT $P$G
```

Because this batch file does not turn off ECHO, it displays the following cluttered screen when executed:

```
C>ECHO Welcome to DOS
Welcome to DOS
C>ECHO Here is the prompt
Here is the prompt
C>PROMPT $P$G
C:\>
```

The improved version of GREET.BAT includes an ECHO OFF command as the first line:

```
@ECHO OFF
REM --------------- GREET.BAT
CLS
ECHO Welcome to DOS
ECHO Here is the prompt...
PROMPT $P$G
```

When this batch file is executed, it presents this much neater display:

```
Welcome to DOS
Here is the prompt
C:\>
```

See Also   REM

EDLIN

Creates or edits a text file.

Version   1 and later

Type   External (EDLIN.COM)

DOS Shell   None
Menu Access

Syntax `EDLIN [drive][path]file name`

in which *drive*, *path* and *file name* provide the location and name of the file you want to create or edit.

Usage The EDLIN command is used to activate a line editor that can create and edit text files by deleting, inserting, editing, and displaying lines of text, and by searching for, deleting, or replacing text within one or more lines. In addition, EDLIN automatically creates a backup file of the original file, with the extension .BAK.

If the *file name* specified in the EDLIN command doesn't exist, it is created in the current directory unless the optional drive and path parameters are specified. After a new file is created, your screen displays the following message and EDLIN prompt:

```
New file
*
```

If the named file exists, it is opened and loaded into the editor and the following message and EDLIN prompt are displayed:

```
End of input file
*
```

After the file is opened, EDLIN uses fourteen commands to create and edit lines of text. These commands, used at the EDLIN prompt, can be used together to form a multiple command line.

nA (Append) is used to append n number of lines from the disk file, when the file being edited is too large to fit into the 64KB of memory used by EDLIN. For example, if the file LARGE.TXT is being edited, only those lines that fit into 64KB of memory are loaded into the editor; the rest remain stored on disk. To load the next 20 lines of text, use the command **20A** at the EDLIN prompt. Remember, however, that memory is limited. You must have room for the appended lines of text. Therefore, you should use the **nS** command to save 20 lines of text before appending 20 lines of text. If you attempt to append more lines of text than are stored on disk, EDLIN displays a message telling you that the end of the file has been reached.

first line, last line, to line [,count] C (Copy) is used to copy lines of text from one place in the file to another, in which *first line* is the first line to be copied, *last line* is the last line to be copied, and *to line* defines where the text will be inserted into the file. A line number can be any integer from 1 to 65,529. To specify the line after the last line in storage, use **#**. To specify the current line, use a period (.). Use the *,count* option to define the number of times you want the text to be copied. If *,count* is not used, the text is copied once.

[from line][,to line] D (Delete) is used to delete one or more lines of text from the file. If the command is used without the optional *from line* and *to line* parameters (for example, D), only the current line of text is deleted. If only one first line number is specified (for example, 5D), only the specified line is deleted. When only the second line number is used (for example ,4D), all text lines between the current line and the specified line are deleted.

n is used to edit a single line of text, in which n is the number of the line you want to edit. By entering a line number and pressing Enter at the EDLIN prompt, the line number and line of text are displayed. As with the D command, a line number (n) can be any integer from 1 to 65,529, # specifies the line after the last line in storage, and a period (.) specifies the current line. When editing a line:

→ displays and skips over characters you do not want to change.

← erases the last character in the line.

F2, followed by a character, displays all characters up to but not including the character.

F3 displays the remainder of the line.

Ctrl-Break or Esc, followed by Enter, cancels all changes to the line and returns you to the EDLIN prompt.

Enter accepts any changes made to the line and returns you to the EDLIN prompt. If you press Enter when the cursor is in any position other than the first character position in the line, all remaining characters on the line are erased.

E is used to Exit the EDLIN editor and save all changes to disk. If you are editing an existing file, the original file is renamed and given the extension .BAK, thus preserving it for future use. Any previously saved file with the same file name and the .BAK extension is deleted from disk. If there is not enough room on your disk to store the new file, the original file is not renamed, only the portion of the new file that fits on the disk is saved, with the extension .$$$, and all unsaved text is lost.

[n] I (Insert) is used to insert lines of text in a file, in which the optional n specifies the number of the first line to be inserted. For example, 5I inserts the new text lines after line 4. If you specify # as the line number, the new text is inserted after the last line in storage. To end the insert mode and return to the EDLIN prompt, press Ctrl-Break.

[*first line*][,*last line*] L (List) is used to list or display a maximum of 24 lines of text on your screen. If you use L without specifying line numbers, EDLIN displays 11 lines before the current line, the current line, and 12 lines after the current line. If there aren't 11 lines before the current line, EDLIN displays all of the lines before the current line and adds extra lines after the current line, for a maximum of 24 displayed lines of text.

If you specify the last line without specifying the first line (you must include the comma, as in ,22L), EDLIN displays 11 lines before the current line, the current line, and ends with line 22. If you only specify the first line (as in 10L), EDLIN displays a maximum of 24 lines beginning with line 10.

[first line][,last line][,to line] **M** (Move) is used to move lines to a new location in the text file. All lines between (and including) the *first line* number and *last line* number are moved to the *to line* number position. If you omit the *first line* and *last line* parameters, the current line (marked with an asterisk) is the only line moved. For example, the command 10,12,30M moves lines 10, 11, and 12 to line 30.

[start line][,end line] **P** (Page) displays lines in the text file one page (screenful) at a time. After each page is displayed, the prompt Continue (Y/N)? appears. Type Y to view the next page, or N to return to the * prompt. For example, the command 1,200P displays the first 200 lines in the file being edited, pausing after each screenful of text is displayed.

Q (Quit) displays the prompt Abort edit (Y/N)?. If you type Y, all changes made to the text file in the current editing session are abandoned, and you are returned to the command prompt. If you type N, you are returned to the Edlin * prompt.

[from line][,to line][?] **R** *[old string]*^Z*[new string]* (Replace) replaces the *old string* with the *new string* in all lines between the *from line* and the *to line*. If ? is included, Edlin asks for permission before replacing text in each line. To type the ^Z character, press Ctrl-Z or the F6 key. For example, the command 1,200RJane^ZMarsha searches the first 200 lines of the file for the name Jane, and replaces the name with Marsha.

[from line][,to line][?] **S** *string* (Search) searches the file, from the line number specified in *from line* to the line number specified in *to line* for the specified *string* of characters. If you do not use the optional ? parameter, the search is stopped after the first matching string is found. If you include the ? parameter, Edlin displays O.K.? when it finds a matching string and waits for a keypress, and then proceeds to search remaining lines. For example, the command 1,200SBanana searches the first 200 lines of the file for the word Banana.

[line] **T** *[drive][file name]* (Transfer) merges lines from a separate text file into the file being edited, above the *line* number specified. For example, the command 20 T C:MOVEIT.BAT merges the entire file named MOVEIT.BAT from the current directory of drive C: into the file being edited, and places all incoming text above line 20.

[lines] **W** (Write) writes the number of *lines* specified out to a disk file with the .BAK extension, starting at the first line. Generally used to add more lines of text after running out of memory.

Examples   (See Chapter 10 for practice sessions using EDLIN.)

ERASE

Removes a file from the disk.

Version 1 and later

Type Internal

DOS Shell Menu Access Access the File System in the Shell, and select the file(s) to be deleted by highlighting and pressing the Spacebar (or single-clicking with the mouse). Then select Delete from the File pull-down menu.

Syntax ERASE [drive][path]file name [/P]

in which *drive* and *path* identify the disk drive and directory of the file to erase, and *file name* is the name of the file (or group of files) to erase.

Usage The ERASE command "erases" a file from the disk. (The ERASE and DEL commands are identical.) After a file is erased, it is impossible to retrieve with DOS. However, there are a few utility programs that can "unerase" a file under some circumstances. (See the discussion of the ERASE command in Chapter 8 for more information.)

If you attempt to erase a file that is designated as read-only, DOS refuses your request and returns the message Access denied. (Use the ATTRIB -R file name command to change the file back to read/write; then, use the ERASE command to erase it.) On a network, you might get the Access denied message if you attempt to erase a file that is being used by another user.

If you attempt to erase a file on a diskette that has a write-protect tab on it, DOS returns the message Write protect error writing drive x, in which x is the name of the drive containing the diskette. To erase the file, first remove the write-protect tab.

If you attempt to erase all of the files on a disk or directory (using the command ERASE *.*), DOS asks for further confirmation by presenting the prompt Are you sure (Y/N)?. Type Y to proceed with the deletion, or N to prevent the deletion. (Note that DOS presents this warning message only when you attempt to delete all of the files on a disk or directory.)

The /P switch is available only in DOS Version 4. If specified, DOS asks for permission before erasing each file. For example, if you enter the command ERASE *.BAK /P, DOS individually presents each file on the current drive and directory that has the *.BAK extension, and displays the prompt Delete (Y/N)?. If you answer Y, the file is erased. If you answer N, the file is not erased.

Examples To erase a file named LETTER.BAK from the current drive and directory, enter the command:

```
ERASE LETTER.BAK
```

To erase all of the files with the extension .BAK from the current drive and directory, enter the command:

```
ERASE *.BAK
```

To erase a file named LETTER.BAK on the directory named \WORDS\LETTERS on drive C:, enter the command:

```
ERASE C:\WORDS\LETTERS\LETTER.BAK
```

If you have DOS 4, and you want to selectively erase files that have the .BAK extension from a directory named \WP\WPFILES, enter the command:

```
ERASE C:\WP\WPFILES\*.BAK /P
```

EXIT

Exits a secondary command processor and returns to the original.

Version   1 and later

Type   Internal

DOS Shell Menu Access   None

Syntax   EXIT

Usage   Returns control to the original command processor after you create a secondary command processor using the COMMAND command. EXIT also is used to return to the DOS Shell, if the DOS Shell is exited with the Shift-F9 key combination.

    If the secondary command processor was created with the /P switch to make that processor permanent, EXIT will not be able to leave the secondary processor.

    If no secondary processor is currently active, the EXIT command merely redisplays the command prompt and does nothing.

Examples   After pressing Shift-F9 to exit the DOS Shell, enter the command:

```
EXIT
```

to return to the Shell.

See Also   COMMAND

FASTOPEN

Installs a disk caching system that speeds disk accessing.

Version 3.3

Type External (FASTOPEN.EXE), activated by the INSTALL command in the CONFIG.SYS file.

DOS Shell Menu Access None

Syntax `INSTALL=[drive][path]FASTOPEN.EXE drive2[=n]|[=(n,m)][...][/X]`

in which *drive* and *path* represent the location of the FASTOPEN.EXE file on the disk, *drive2* specifies the drive to be accessed with FASTOPEN, *n* is the number of directory or file locations to be maintained in memory, and *m* specifies the number of look-ahead buffers.

Usage FASTOPEN installs a disk caching system in your computer's memory, to speed operations that involve disk accessing. FASTOPEN keeps track of the locations of files and directories on the disk in memory, unlike the BUFFERS command, which merely maintains a copy of the File Allocation Table (FAT). FASTOPEN actually speeds access to the FAT stored in the disk buffers, and therefore should be used in addition to, rather than in lieu of, the BUFFERS command in CONFIG.SYS.

The *drive 2* parameter can be any valid disk drive name. However, using FASTOPEN with a RAM disk generally does not speed disk accessing. Also, the *drive 2* parameter must not refer to remote drives on a network nor to any drives defined by an ASSIGN, JOIN, or SUBST command.

The *n* parameter specifies the maximum number of files or directories that FASTOPEN will maintain. The acceptable range is 10 to 999. The default value for PC-DOS is 34; the default value for MS-DOS is 10. Each file or directory location maintained in memory requires 48 bytes. Therefore, an *n* setting of 34 uses 306 (9×34) bytes, or approximately $\frac{1}{3}$KB.

If multiple drives are specified in a single FASTOPEN command, the *sum* of all *n* parameters must not exceed 999.

The optional *m* parameter specifies the number of contiguous space buffers for file operations, in the range of 1 to 999. These buffers act as look-ahead buffers. Each look-ahead buffer requires approximately 16 bytes of memory. If you omit the *m* parameter, the look-ahead feature is not activated.

The optimal setting for FASTOPEN varies from one system to the next. A good rule of thumb, however, is to use neither exceptionally large nor exceptionally small numbers for either *n* or *m*. The *n* value should be at least 10, or should reflect the number of levels of directories on your hard disk. For example, if the "deepest" subdirectory on your hard disk is named \DBASE\DBTUTOR\ALBERT, which extends down three levels, you would still want to use 10, rather than 3, as the n value.

Specifying a large m value only speeds operations that involve managing files larger than 300KB, or disks with severely fragmented files. Too large an m setting actually slows down accessing when smaller files are involved. Some systems default the m value to 34, which is an acceptable setting for general computer usage.

After FASTOPEN is activated it remains in memory for the remainder of the session and cannot be modified or deactivated. Therefore, all drives that will use FASTOPEN should be specified in a single FASTOPEN command. Also, because FASTOPEN is actually a terminate and stay resident (TSR) program, you should execute it with the INSTALL command in the CONFIG.SYS file, rather than entering FASTOPEN at the command prompt.

The /X option tells DOS to use expanded memory rather than conventional RAM for all FASTOPEN operations. This conserves conventional RAM space; however, the /X option can only be used when a preceding command in the CONFIG.SYS file has already activated expanded memory. If expanded memory is used for FASTOPEN, the total number of bytes used by FASTOPEN may not exceed a single 16KB page of memory.

Depending on the expanded memory manager you use, you might need to include P254 as a page in the command that activates expanded memory (see the "Examples" section).

Some computers offer a version of FASTOPEN with DOS versions prior to 4.0. However, these earlier FASTOPEN programs usually do not support look-ahead buffers (the m parameter) or expanded memory (the /X switch). (See the DOS manual that came with your computer for more information.)

Examples   In each of the examples that follow, the commands are presumed to be contained in the CONFIG.SYS file, not entered at the command prompt.

The following command assumes that the FASTOPEN.EXE file is stored in the directory named DOS on disk drive C:. Only disk drive C: is managed through FASTOPEN, and the default value of 34 is used for the n parameter:

```
INSTALL=C:\DOS\FASTOPEN.EXE C:
```

The next command activates FASTOPEN for two hard disk drives, named C: and D:, assigning 450 directory and file buffers and 50 look-ahead buffers to each. Note that because 450+450 equals 900, the 999 maximum sum of the n parameters is not exceeded. In this example, the FASTOPEN.EXE file is assumed to be stored in the root directory:

```
INSTALL=FASTOPEN.EXE C:=(450,50) D:=(450,50)
```

The following commands, when used on a Compaq 386 computer, activate 2MB of expanded memory (using the Compaq CEMM.EXE device driver) and establish the disk buffers and the FASTOPEN disk caching program in expanded rather than conventional memory. Because expanded memory is used, FASTOPEN is given a generous amount of memory for disk caching:

```
DEVICE = C:\DOS\CEMM.EXE 2048 ON
BUFFERS=15,2 /X
INSTALL=C:\DOS\FASTOPEN.EXE C:=(500,300) D:=(400,100) /X
```

The commands that follow assume IBM PC-DOS Version 4.0 and an IBM computer with expanded memory capability. The XMA2EMS.SYS device driver activates expanded memory and specifies page 254 (P254) for DOS buffering operations. Both the BUFFERS and FASTOPEN then use expanded memory, rather than conventional memory, for disk buffers and disk caching:

```
DEVICE = C:\DOS\XMA2EMS.SYS FRAME=D000 P254=C000 P255=C400
BUFFERS=15,2 /X
INSTALL=C:\DOS\FASTOPEN.EXE C:=(100,50) D:=(100,50) /X
```

See Also   BUFFERS, INSTALL, XMA2EMS.SYS

FCBS

Specifies the maximum number of file control blocks that can be open simultaneously.

Version   3 and later

Type   Internal (used only in CONFIG.SYS)

DOS Shell Menu Access   None

Syntax   FCBS = *max,permanent*

in which *max* is the total number of file control blocks that can be open simultaneously, and *permanent* is the number of file control blocks that are protected from automatic closure.

Usage   This rarely used CONFIG.SYS command is required only when you need to run DOS Version 1 application programs with later versions of DOS. It allows DOS to use the old-fashioned *file control blocks* (FCBS) method of managing files, in addition to the newer *file handles* approach of Version 2 and later.

The default value for *max* is 0, but any value in the range of 0 to 255 is acceptable. The value of the *permanent* parameter must be equal to or less than the value of *max*.

If you attempt to use a program that requires the older FCBS method of managing files, with a newer version of DOS, the program will simply stop running at some point, or (if you're lucky) display DOS's error message `FCB unavailable`. Either way, the solution is to use the FCBS command in your CONFIG.SYS file, and to experiment with different values.

The default setting for FCBS is 4,0 (four file control blocks, none permanent), unless the DOS SHARE program is installed, which increases the default value of FCBS to 16,8. Use these values as starting points when experimenting with larger values in the FCBS command in your own CONFIG.SYS file.

And don't forget that the FCBS command in the CONFIG.SYS file is not activated until the next time you start your computer, or reboot by pressing Ctrl-Alt-Del.

Examples The following command, when included in your CONFIG.SYS file, provides for a maximum of ten simultaneously open file control blocks, five of which are protected from automatic closure:

`FCBS=10,5`

See Also SHARE

FILES

Specifies the maximum number of open files that a program can manage simultaneously.

Version 2 and later

Type Internal (used only in CONFIG.SYS)

DOS Shell
Menu Access None

Syntax `FILES=max`

in which *max* is the maximum number of files that can be opened simultaneously.

Usage   The FILES option in the CONFIG.SYS file specifies the maximum number of file handles that DOS can simultaneously manage. DOS defaults to a maximum of eight active file handles. Five of these file handles are used by the standard input and output devices: the screen, keyboard, printer, communications devices, and the DOS error handler. (Technically, these devices are not "files" per se; however, DOS still must use file handles to manage their input and output.) This leaves three available file handles for open disk files.

Most modern programs, particularly database management and multi-sheet spreadsheet programs, can handle more than three simultaneously open files. Therefore, to use the programs (without getting a Too many files are open error message), you probably need to use a FILES command in your CONFIG.SYS file to manage more than eight file handles. (The manual that comes with a program that manages multiple files will specify the minimum setting.)

The minimum setting for FILES= is 8; the maximum is 255. Each file handle (above the default of 8) uses approximately 39 bytes of memory. Even the most sophisticated database management programs rarely require that you set FILES= to a number greater than 50.

Examples   The following command, when placed in the CONFIG.SYS file, lets your computer run programs that can manage as many as 40 simultaneously open files; the other five file handles are used by the input and output devices):

`FILES=45`

See Also   BUFFERS

FIND

Searches multiple files for specific text.

Version   2 and later

Type   External (FIND.EXE)

DOS Shell Menu Access   None

Syntax   FIND [/V] [/C] [/N] "*text*" [[*drive*][*path*][*file name*][...]]

in which *text* is the text to search for (enclosed in quotation marks), *drive* and *path* are the names of the drive and directory to be searched, and *file* name is the name of a specific file to be searched. You can specify more than one file to be searched (each separated by a blank space), but you cannot use ambiguous file names.

Usage   FIND searches specified files for a particular character string (that is, a letter, number, word, or group of words). The string being searched for must be enclosed in quotation marks. To search for a quotation mark, place three quotation marks in the string.

FIND searches only the files listed at the end of the command. These files should contain only text. Command files (such as those with .EXE, .COM, or .BIN extensions) cannot be searched. Similarly, many files created by word processing systems cannot be reliably searched, because they might contain special formatting codes.

FIND is case sensitive, which means that it considers upper- and lowercase letters as unequal. Therefore, if a file contains the word *Hello*, and you attempt to find *HELLO*, FIND will not "see" the match. FIND does not limit its search to whole words, unless spaces are included within the quotation marks. For example, a search for "*dog*" will find *dog*, *hotdog*, *doggie*, and *antidogmatic*. However, a search for " *dog* " will find only the word *dog*.

You can use the following three options with FIND:

/V   Finds lines that do *not* contain the string.

/C   Counts the number of times that the string occurs within the file, but does not display the lines.

/N   Displays the number of each line that contains the string.

The /N and /C options are incompatible, because /C displays only a total count, rather than individual lines. If you include both /N and /C in a FIND command, the /N is ignored. Note that, unlike most other DOS commands, the / options in FIND are placed before the string and file names, rather than at the end of the entire command.

FIND can accept input from any source. If you do not specify a file name with FIND, it waits for input from the keyboard. (It continues accepting text until you press F6 or Ctrl-Z and Enter). You can pipe information into FIND using the | character. You also can redirect the output from FIND to a separate device, such as to a file or the printer, using the > redirection symbol. Examples in the next section demonstrate these techniques.

Examples   Suppose you have three files, named LETTER1.TXT, LETTER2.TXT, and LETTER3.TXT, and you want to know which one is the letter to Bob. Assuming that all three .TXT files are on the current directory and that FIND.EXE is accessible through a predefined PATH command, the following command searches all three files for the string "*Bob*":

```
FIND "Bob" LETTER1.TXT LETTER2.TXT LETTER3.TXT
```

Assuming that LETTER2.TXT is the only file that contains the name Bob, the result of the FIND command looks something like this:

```
---------- LETTER1.TXT
---------- LETTER2.TXT
Dear Bob:
---------- LETTER3.TXT
```

If you include the /N option in the FIND command, the line number (corresponding to the EDLIN line number) is displayed in square brackets to the left of the matching line, as follows:

```
FIND /N "Bob" LETTER1.TXT LETTER2.TXT LETTER3.TXT
---------- LETTER1.TXT
---------- LETTER2.TXT
[1]Dear Bob
---------- LETTER3.TXT
```

If you use the /C option, only the total number of lines that contain the search string is displayed, as follows:

```
FIND /C "Bob" LETTER1.TXT LETTER2.TXT LETTER3.TXT
---------- LETTER1.TXT: 0
---------- LETTER2.TXT: 1
---------- LETTER3.TXT: 0
```

If you use the /V option, as follows, all lines that do not contain the search string are displayed.

```
FIND /V "Bob" LETTER1.TXT LETTER2.TXT LETTER3.TXT
```

The resulting output of this command would be all of the text in the LETTER1.TXT, LETTER2.TXT, and LETTER3.TXT files, except the "*Dear Bob*" line.

The next command searches for the text "*Don't go!*" *she cried* (including the quotation marks) in the files named CHAPTER1.DOC and CHAPTER2.DOC:

```
FIND """"Don't go!"""" she cried" CHAPTER1.DOC CHAPTER2.DOC
```

The following command does the same, but displays its output on the printer, because of the > PRN symbol:

```
FIND """"Don't go!"" she cried" CHAPTER1.DOC CHAPTER2.DOC > PRN
```

The next command displays file names in the current directory that contain the number 1988. Note how the output of the DIR command is used as input into the FIND command through the use of the pipe character (|):

```
DIR | FIND "1988"
```

The resulting output might look something like this:

```
Directory of  C:\
FIN1988
                <DIR>        12-29-87    5:43a
1988EST   TXT    10240       1-18-88     8:32p
1988ACT   TXT    62976      12-22-88    12:45p
1988TAX   DBF    77184      12-22-88    12:34p
QTR1988   WKS     1024       4-12-88    11:11p
```

The following command displays the names of files in the directory named \BUSINESS that were created on August 1, 1988:

```
DIR | FIND "8-1-88"
```

To exclude messages displayed by the DIR command, such as Volume in drive C has no label, use FIND to exclude lines that have a lowercase letter "e", as in the following example:

```
DIR | FIND /V "e"
```

To hide messages and directory names in a DIR command, use two FIND commands, as in this example:

```
DIR | FIND /V "e" | FIND /V "<DIR>"
```

See Also   DIR, TYPE

FOR

Sets up a loop to repeat a command.

Version   2 and later

Type   Internal

DOS Shell Menu Access   None

Syntax   At the command prompt, the syntax is:

FOR *%variable* IN (*item list*) DO *command*

In batch files, the syntax is:

FOR *%%variable* IN (*item list*) DO *command*

in which *variable* is a single character (a–z), *item list* is a list of items to process (separated by blank spaces), and *command* is the command to be repeated.

Usage   FOR repeats a command until it processes all of the items in a list. The % or %% variable (represented by a letter) assumes the value of the next item in the list with each pass through the loop. That variable then becomes part of the DO command. Examples that follow demonstrate this concept.

Examples   In the following batch file command, %%a is the variable and (LETTER1.TXT LETTER2.TXT LETTER3.TXT) is the item list. The command to be executed is TYPE %%a:

FOR %%a IN (LETTER1.TXT LETTER2.TXT LETTER3.TXT) DO TYPE %%a

When the command is first executed, the %%a variable is assigned the value LETTER1.TXT; therefore, the DO section of the command expands to become TYPE LETTER1.TXT. On the second pass through the loop, %%a is assigned the value LETTER2.TXT, so the command executed is TYPE LETTER2.TXT. On the third pass through the loop, %%a assumes the value LETTER3.TXT, so the command executed is TYPE LETTER3.TXT.

Because there are only three items in the item list, the FOR command stops after the third loop. The net result of the command, of course, is that it displays the contents of three different files: LETTER1.TXT, LETTER2.TXT, and LETTER3.TXT.

If you wanted to enter this sample command directly at the DOS prompt, type:

FOR %a IN (LETTER1.TXT LETTER2.TXT LETTER3.TXT) DO TYPE %a

See Also   SHIFT

FORMAT

Formats a blank disk.

Version   1 and later

Type   External (FORMAT.COM)

DOS Shell   Select DOS Utilities... from the Main Group screen, and Format from the
Menu Access   next screen.

Syntax   FORMAT *drive* [/1] [/4] [/8] [/0] [/B] [/F:*size*]
[/T:*tracks*] [/N:*sectors*] [/S] [/V:*label*]

in which *drive* is the name of the drive containing the disk to be formatted,
tracks is the number of tracks per side, *sectors* is the number of sectors per
track, and *label* is the optional volume label. The *size* parameter specifies
the amount of storage in kilobytes (KB).

Usage   Use FORMAT to prepare blank (empty and unformatted) disks for use with
your computer. Never format a hard disk or diskette that already has information on it; doing so completely erases all of the information. Even write-
protected files (protected with the ATTRIB +R command) are irretrievably
erased by the FORMAT command. Therefore, **be very careful when you
use the FORMAT command**.

Attempting to use a disk that has not been formatted generally produces the error message General Failure error reading drive x in which x
is name of the drive containing the unformatted disk.

Before you format a disk, the screen prompts you to insert a disk into
the appropriate drive and press Enter to proceed.

If you attempt to format a hard disk that has already been formatted,
and that hard disk already has a volume label, DOS asks that you Enter
current Volume Label for drive x: (in which x refers to the appropriate
drive). If you enter the appropriate label, FORMAT proceeds. If you do not
enter the appropriate label, FORMAT cancels the operation. (Enter the DIR
or VOL command at the command prompt to view the current volume label.)

If you are formatting a hard disk that has no label, the screen displays
the message:

```
WARNING, ALL DATA ON NON-REMOVABLE DISK DRIVE x: WILL BE LOST!
Proceed with Format (Y/N)?
```

If you are absolutely certain that you want to totally erase everything on the
hard disk, answer Y. If you do not want to lose this information, enter N.

You cannot format a diskette that has a write-protect tab on it. Nor
can you format any "virtual" disk, such as a RAM disk, or a network disk.
You also can't format a disk affected by the ASSIGN, JOIN, or SUBST
commands.

After the formatting procedure is completed, FORMAT displays the number of bytes available on the disk. If there are any flaws on the disk, these are marked as bad sectors, which are not usable. The total amount of available disk space is equal to the total space minus the bad sectors. A sample output from a FORMAT command on a 1.2MB floppy disk is shown below:

```
Format complete

   1213952 bytes total disk space

353280 bytes in bad sectors
860672 bytes available on disk

Format another (Y/N)?
```

If you enter the FORMAT command, but DOS cannot find the FORMAT.COM file on the current drive and directory, or in a directory specified in the current PATH, DOS displays the message Bad command or file name and returns you to the command prompt (or the DOS 4 Shell).

In most cases, you only need to use the FORMAT command followed by the name of the drive containing the disk to be formatted. There are several options, however, that you can use with FORMAT, as listed below:

/O   Formats a PC DOS Version 1 compatible disk (available in MS-DOS Versions 2 to 3.2).

/1   Formats one side of the diskette only, even if the diskette and drive are double-sided (Version 1, and Versions 3.2 and later).

/S   Makes the formatted disk a system disk that can be used to boot the computer. (If you use this option, it must be the last switch on the line.)

/V   Lets you assign a volume label (name) to the disk, which appears whenever you use the DIR command. The label can have as many as 11 characters.

/4   Formats a 5.25-inch diskette in a high-capacity drive as a low-capacity (360KB) diskette. (PC DOS Versions 3.0 and later, MS-DOS Versions 3.2 and later).

/8   Specifies eight sectors per track (Versions 1 and 3.2 and later).

/T   Lets you specify the number of tracks to place on the disk. Usually, you don't need to use this parameter, because FORMAT automatically generates the appropriate number of tracks for a disk. If you need to use the /T option, place the number of tracks you want to produce after the /T: symbol. Cannot be used with a hard disk. (MS-DOS Versions 3.2 and later.)

/N   Lets you specify the number of sectors per track on the disk being formatted. (MS-DOS Versions 3.2 and later, PC DOS Versions 3.3 and later).

/B   Formats a diskette, and sets aside space so that system tracks can later be copied to the diskette using the SYS command. (Unlike /S, however, this command does not automatically copy the system tracks.) Cannot be used with either /S or /V.

/F   Specifies the capacity of the diskette being formatted. (DOS 4 only)

The number of tracks per side and sectors per track of various floppy diskettes are given in Table B.3 (see the entry for DRIVER in this appendix). If you omit the /T and /N switches from the FORMAT command, DOS automatically formats the disk with the usual number of tracks and sectors.

The /F parameter is valid only on DOS Version 4. You can use /F in lieu of /T and /N to format a diskette designed for use in drives other than the current drive. The value of /F, however, must be equal to or less than the capacity of the drive. Table B.5 lists possible values for the /F switch.

Table B.5 Acceptable values for the DOS 4 /F switch.

Disk Size	Drive Capacity	Acceptable /F Values
5.25-inch	160KB	160
5.25-inch	180KB	160, 180
5.25-inch	320KB	160, 180, 320
5.25-inch	360KB	160, 180, 320, 360
5.35-inch	1.2MB	160, 180, 320, 360, 1200, 1.2
3.5-inch	720KB	720
3.5-inch	1.44MB	720, 1440, 1.44

Although DOS provides flexibility in formatting diskettes for use in lower capacity drives, the diskettes themselves do not always offer the same flexibility. For example, you cannot format a 1.2MB high-density diskette in a low-capacity drive. You can, however, format a 360KB diskette in a high-capacity drive, for use in a 360KB drive. Similarly, you will find it impossible to format a 3.5-inch, 1.44MB disk in a 720KB drive.

Some optional switches are mutually exclusive or invalid for certain types of drives. In summary:

- You cannot use /V or /S with /B.
- You cannot use both /8 and /V.
- You cannot use /N or /T with 320KB or 360KB diskettes.
- You cannot use /1, /4, /8, /B, /N, 10 or /T with a fixed (hard) disk.

Version 4 of DOS requests a volume label after formatting a disk, even if you do not use the /V switch in the FORMAT command. In earlier versions, you must use the /V switch to enter a volume label when formatting is complete. DOS displays the message Volume label (11 characters, ENTER for none)?. Type a volume label with as many as 11 characters (including blank spaces), and then press Enter. Optionally, press Enter if you do not want to add a volume label.

If you use FORMAT within a batch file, you can use the IF ERRORLEVEL command to check the results of the format. The codes returned by FORMAT are as follows:

0   Format successful

3   Format aborted by user (Ctrl-Break or Ctrl-C)

4   Format aborted due to error

5   Format aborted by user answering N to the prompt concerning a fixed disk drive.

Examples   Suppose you have a new box of blank, unformatted diskettes that you want to format for use in your computer. Change to the hard disk directory that contains the FORMAT.EXE file. Then, place one of the unformatted diskettes in drive A: and enter the command:

FORMAT A:

Follow the instructions that appear on the screen.

To make the diskette in drive A: bootable (one that you can use to start your computer), enter the following command:

FORMAT A: /S

Note that this command copies only the system tracks and COMMAND.COM to the new diskette. It does not copy your current CONFIG.SYS or AUTOEXEC.BAT files to the bootable diskette.

Suppose you want to format a 720KB, 3.5-inch disk in drive B: which is a 1.44MB, 3.5-inch drive. Using DOS 4, enter this command:

FORMAT B: /F:720

To accomplish the same result using an earlier version of DOS, enter this command:

FORMAT B: /T:80 /N:9

Suppose your computer has a 5.25-inch, high-capacity drive (named A:), but you want to format a 360KB diskette in that drive. Using DOS 4, enter this command:

FORMAT A: /F:360

Using an earlier version of DOS, enter this command:

FORMAT B: /4

See Also   GOTO, Chapter 6

GOTO

Transfers control to a new command in a batch file.

Version   1 and later

Type   Internal (used only in batch files)

DOS Shell   None
Menu Access

Syntax   GOTO *label*

in which *label* is the name of a line, preceded by a colon, in the current batch file.

Usage   Normally, the commands in a batch file are processed sequentially from top to bottom. The GOTO command lets you alter this sequential processing by passing control to a new part of the batch file. The section to which you pass control must have a name (called a label) which must be preceded by a colon (:). However, when referencing the label in the GOTO command, you omit the colon. For example, you might use the label :End in a batch file, but you pass control to that label with the command GOTO End.

GOTO is usually used in conjunction with the IF command. Be careful that your GOTO commands do not set up infinite loops. For example, the following batch file repeatedly executes the DIR command:

```
:ShowDir
DIR
GOTO ShowDir
```

The loop, in this example, is infinite, because it doesn't contain an IF command that can pass control to a command outside the loop. After a batch file begins an infinite loop, you can regain control of the system only with a Ctrl-C or Ctrl-Break keystroke, or by rebooting or shutting off the computer.

Examples   The following batch file, named NEWDISK.BAT, attempts to format the disk in drive A:. If no error occurs during formatting, the GOTO command passes control to the label named :End. If an error does occur, the batch file displays an error message:

```
@ECHO OFF
REM -------------- NEWDISK.BAT
FORMAT A:
IF ERRORLEVEL = 0 GOTO End
ECHO WARNING! The disk in drive A: cannot be formatted!
:End
```

See Also   IF, CALL

GRAFTABL

Activates the graphics characters set.

Version   3 and later (modified in Version 3.3)

Type   External (GRAFTABL.COM)

DOS Shell Menu Access   None

Syntax   GRAFTABL [*code page* | ? | /STA]

in which *code page* is a number identifying the character set to be used, ? presents available options, and /STA shows the current status of GRAFTABL.

Usage   The Color Graphics Adapter (CGA) display often distorts the images of graphics and non-English language characters that have ASCII values greater than 127. The GRAFTABL command provides an additional 1,360 bytes of memory in which "clearer" versions of these characters are stored.

GRAFTABL is not needed for systems using EGA or VGA video adapters.

If GRAFTABLE is used in a batch file, you can use the IF ERRORLEVEL command to check for an error. Error codes returned by GRAFTABL are:

0   Successful operation, new graphics character set is loaded.

1   Successful operation, but new graphics character set has replaced an existing graphics character set.

2   No new graphics character table loaded; previous graphics character set is still active.

3   Invalid parameter was entered with command; no action was taken.

4   Incorrect DOS version in use; must use DOS Versions 3.3 or 4.

Examples   The following examples assume that GRAFTABL.COM is stored on the current drive or directory, or in a directory specified in the current PATH setting. The command:

```
GRAFTABL ?
```

displays both the name of the currently loaded graphic character set table (if any) and the options available with GRAFTABL on the current computer. It uses the following format:

```
USA version of Graphic Character Set Table is already loaded.
/STA - Request Status only
?    - Display this summary of parameters
437  - USA Graphic Character Set
865  - Nordic Graphic Character Set
860  - Portugese Graphic Character Set
863  - Can. French Graphic Character Set
```

The command:

```
GRAFTABLE /STA
```

displays only the current graphics character set, as in the following example:

```
USA version of Graphic Character Set Table is already loaded.
```

The next command activates the graphic character set for the United States:

```
GRAFTABL 437
```

See Also   NLSFUNC

GRAPHICS

Allows graphics to be printed by pressing Shift-PrintScreen.

Version	2 and later
Type	External (GRAPHICS.COM)
DOS Shell Menu Access	None
Syntax	Versions 2 through 3.1:

`GRAPHICS printer [/R] [/B]`

MS-DOS Versions 3.2 to 3.3:

`GRAPHICS printer [/R] [/B] [/LCD] [/C] [/F] [/P=port]`

Version 4:

`GRAPHICS [printer] [[drive][path]file name] [/R][/B][/PB:id]`

in which *printer* is a valid printer type. In Version 4, *drive*, *path*, and *file name* represent the location and name of the *Graphics Profile* file (usually C:\DOS\GRAPHICS.PRO), and *id* represents the print box size, and *port* is a valid DOS device name.

Usage GRAPHICS is required only when you want to print graphics by pressing Shift-PrintScreen, rather than using your graphics program to do the printing. When loaded, GRAPHICS uses 6KB of conventional memory (RAM).

The first parameter after the GRAPHICS command (which is optional) must be a valid printer name. Valid printer names vary from one computer to the next. In later versions of DOS, the GRAPHICS.PRO file includes valid printer names (and additional information). You can use the command `TYPE GRAPHICS.PRO > PRN` to print this list.

The basic printer types supported by GRAPHICS are as follows:

COLOR1	IBM PC color printer with a black ribbon.
COLOR4	IBM PC color printer with an RGB (red, green, blue, and black) ribbon.
COLOR8	IBM PC color printer with a CMY (cyan, magenta, yellow, and black) ribbon.
GRAPHICS	IBM PC Graphics printer, IBM PC Proprinter, and IBM Quietwriter printer, and compatibles (the default if no parameters are listed).
GRAPHICSWIDE	IBM PC Graphics Printer with a 13.5-inch wide carriage.

THERMAL   IBM PC Convertible printer.

The /R option reverses colors on black-and-white images. It is usually used to print graphics as white on a black background, as opposed to black on a white background.

The /B switch prints a background color; however, it is only valid if the printer type is COLOR4, COLOR8, or some other printer that prints in color.

The /C switch, available in Versions 3.2 and 3.3 of MS-DOS, centers the printout on the paper. The /F switch, also available only in Versions 3.2 and 3.3 of MS-DOS, rotates the printed image by 90 degrees, so that it is printed sideways on the page. The /P= option in MS-DOS Versions 3.2 and 3.3 specifies a printer port, which can be 1 (for LPT1), 2 (for LPT2), or 3 (for LPT3). If omitted, LPT1 is assumed.

The options /PB switch, available in DOS 4, specifies a *print box*, the dimensions of the printed area on a page. The /PB switch should be followed by a colon, and a print box identifier, as listed below:

/PB:STD   Specifies the standard sized print box, with dimensions resembling a standard display monitor. (If the /PB switch is omitted, STD is assumed.)

/PB:LCD   Specifies a print area that matches the dimension of the liquid crystal display (LCD) monitors. Use this switch when you want the printed image to have the same dimensions as the LCD screen.

You can use /PRINTBOX instead of the abbreviation /PB in a GRAPHICS command if you prefer. Information about print boxes and other display and printer features are listed in a file named GRAPHICS.PRO that comes with DOS Version 4. GRAPHICS.PRO is an ASCII text file that you can view or print using the DOS TYPE and PRINT commands.

Using the GRAPHICS command and the PrintScreen key will not print graphs more quickly than a graphics program does; the delay before printing even begins can take as long as three minutes.

Note that on many enhanced keyboards you can print the contents of the screen simply by pressing the PrintScreen key, rather than pressing Shift-PrintScreen.

Examples   To print black and white graphics images, using the PrintScreen key, first enter the command:

```
GRAPHICS
```

at the DOS command prompt.

To print color graphs from the screen on a color printer, using the colors that most closely match those on the screen, first enter this command at the command prompt:

```
GRAPHICS COLOR8 /R /B
```

See Also   GRAFTABL

IF

Makes a decision in a batch file by determining whether a condition is true.

Version   1 and later

Type   Internal (used in batch files only)

DOS Shell Menu Access   None

Syntax
```
IF [NOT] ERRORLEVEL number command
IF [NOT] "string1" == "string2" command
IF [NOT] EXIST file name command
```

in which *number* is a number corresponding to an errorlevel value, *string1* and *string2* are text, *file name* is the name of a file, and *command* is a DOS command.

Usage   The IF command lets a batch file "decide" which task to perform next. If the condition on which the decision is based proves "true," then the command to the right of the IF statement is executed. If the condition proves "false," the command is not executed and processing continues normally at the next command.

The decision can be based upon a DOS error (using ERRORLEVEL), a user's entry (string1 == string2), or the existence of a file (EXIST). The NOT option is used in the same way it is used in English. For example, IF a condition does NOT occur, then do (something).

When using ERRORLEVEL, a value of 0 always indicates that no error occurred. A value of 1 or greater indicates that an error did occur. IF ERRORLEVEL returns "true" if the ERRORLEVEL value is greater than or equal to the compared value. For example, if the BACKUP command returns an ERRORLEVEL value of 1, 2, 3, 4, or 5, then the command IF ERRORLEVEL 1 GOTO End passes control to the :End label, because each of those values is greater than or equal to 1. However, if BACKUP returns a 0 ERRORLEVEL value in the previous example, the GOTO End command is completely ignored, and processing continues at the next line in the batch file.

Note that very few DOS commands return a value in ERRORLEVEL. If you use an IF ERRORLEVEL command beneath a command that does not return an ERRORLEVEL value, the batch file merely assumes there was no error (even if there was).

When comparing text strings, you typically use a parameter passed from the command line. For example, suppose you create a batch file named ME.BAT, and the user enters a command such as `ME Fred`. The command below:

```
IF "%1" == "Fred" GOTO HimAgain
```

passes control to a label called :HimAgain. If the user enters any other name, such as `ME Jane`, the `GOTO HimAgain` command is ignored and processing continues at the next line.

If either string in an IF command is null (empty), the IF command presents a `Syntax Error` message. To avoid this message, use a period at the end of each string. For example, to see if a parameter was omitted from the command line, compare the parameter followed by a period to a period. For example, using the ME.BAT example again, if the user enters *ME* without a name, the line below passes control to a label named :NoName

```
IF "%1." == "." GOTO NoName
```

The EXIST option checks to see if a file exists. For example, the command `IF NOT EXIST LOGON.BAT GOTO MakeFile` passes control to the :MakeFile label if a file named LOGON.BAT does not exist on the current drive and directory.

If the named file contains a wildcard character, then any file that matches the pattern determines a "true" result. For example, the command `IF EXIST C:\DBASE\*.DBF GOTO Done` passes control to the :Done label if any file in the C:\DBASE directory has the extension .DBF.

Examples   See Chapters 14 and 15 for practical examples of using IF in batch files.

See Also   GOTO

INSTALL

Installs DOS memory-resident programs via the CONFIG.SYS file

Version   4

Type   Internal (used only in CONFIG.SYS)

DOS Shell   None
Menu Access

Syntax   `INSTALL=[drive][path]file name [options]`

in which *drive*, *path*, and *file name* are the location and file name of the
memory-resident program to be installed, and *options* represents options
supported by the program.

Usage   INSTALL is used to install four terminate-stay-resident programs in DOS 4.
The only DOS 4 programs that can be used with INSTALL are
FASTOPEN.EXE, KEYB.COM, NLSFUNC.EXE, and SHARE.EXE.

If INSTALL is used in CONFIG.SYS to load a TSR program, the
AUTOEXEC.BAT file doesn't need to include a command to execute that
program. Furthermore, because the CONFIG.SYS file is executed before
AUTOEXEC.BAT, the AUTOEXEC file can contain commands that make
use of the already installed and active program.

Examples   The following command, when placed in your CONFIG.SYS file, loads and
activates the DOS 4 FASTOPEN disk caching system:

`INSTALL=C:\DOS\FASTOPEN.EXE C:50`

See Also   DEVICE, CONFIG.SYS, FASTOPEN, KEYB, NLSFUNC, SHARE

JOIN

Joins a disk drive to a directory path.

Version   3.1 and later

Type   External (JOIN.EXE)

DOS Shell   None
Menu Access

Syntax   `JOIN [original drive] [new drive\path][/D]`

in which *original drive* is the name of the drive that you wish to "hide," and
new drive\path is the location of the new drive and directory to be used for
storing data.

Usage   JOIN is commonly used to substitute a hard disk drive or RAM drive for a floppy disk drive. Generally, you only want to do this if you are using an older program that is not designed to run on a hard disk. By using JOIN, you can "trick" the old program into storing and accessing files on a hard disk or RAM disk rather than a floppy disk drive.

There are quite a few rules involved in using JOIN. These concern both the guest disk drive (the one being connected—that is, the floppy disk drive) and the host disk drive and directory (the one being connected to—that is, the hard disk or RAM disk). The host directory name must be included in the command, and it must refer to a level-1 directory. That is, the directory being joined to must not be a child to another directory. Hence, you can JOIN to the directory C:\TEMPFILE, but not to the subdirectory C:\TEMPFILE\TEMP2. If you specify a directory on the host drive that does not exist, JOIN automatically creates the directory.

The host directory must be empty. Attempting to use a non-empty directory on the host drive produces the error message `Directory not Empty`, and cancels the JOIN procedure.

Neither the host nor the guest drives can be virtual drives created by the ASSIGN or SUBST commands. Furthermore, neither can be network drives.

After the drives are joined, the entire guest disk, including all directories and subdirectories, becomes a part of the host directory. The guest root directory becomes the equivalent of the named host drive directory, and any subdirectories of the guest drive become subdirectories of the host directory. The guest disk drive and directory become "invisible" to DOS; any command that refers to that drive and directory returns an error message, such as `Invalid drive specification`.

After the join has taken effect, you can access files only through the new host directory. Therefore, if you join drive A: to C:\TEMPFILE, the command `DIR A:` would be invalid. Instead, you would use the command `DIR C:\TEMPFILE`.

After you've issued a JOIN command, avoid using the commands ASSIGN, BACKUP, CHKDSK, DISKCOMP, FDISK, DISKCOPY, FORMAT, LABEL, RECOVER, RESTORE, SUBST and SYS. To view the current status of any JOIN commands, enter the command JOIN with no parameters. To disengage an existing JOIN, enter the JOIN command with the /D option.

Examples   Suppose you want to treat a directory named \TEMP on drive C: as though it were disk drive B:. First, enter the command `DIR C:\TEMP` to make sure that the \TEMP directory is empty (shows only the . and .. entries). Or, if \TEMP does not exist, enter the command `MD \TEMP` at the command prompt to create the new directory.

Next, enter the command:

```
JOIN B: C:\TEMP
```

to have DOS treat the \TEMP directory as though it were disk drive B:. Now you can run your "old" DOS program, which insists on accessing drive B: for data files. However, the program will "think" that the C:\TEMP directory is drive B:, and that's where it will store, and search for, files.

When you have finished using the old DOS program, enter the command JOIN B: /D to disable the JOIN.

See Also   ASSIGN, SUBST

KEYB

Selects a keyboard layout.

Version   1 and later

Type   External (KEYB.COM)

DOS Shell
Menu Access   None

Syntax   Syntax for KEYB varies considerably among computers and some versions of DOS. The syntax for Version 3.3., at the command prompt or in a batch file, is:

KEYB [country code[,[code page][,[drive][path]file name]]]

If you are using DOS 4, you can use the previous syntax or, optionally, activate KEYB in the CONFIG.SYS file using the syntax:

INSTALL=KEYB [country code[,[code page][,[drive][path]file name]]][ID:xxx]

in which country code is a two-letter abbreviation for a country, code page is a three-digit code page number, and drive, path, file name represent the location and name of the keyboard definitions file (usually C:\DOS\KEYBOARD.SYS). The xxx option specifies a three-digit keyboard code.

Usage   KEYB changes the United States layout of your keyboard to match that of another country. Unlike earlier versions of DOS, which use commands such as KEYBUK (for United Kingdom), KEYBFR (for France), and so on,

Versions 3.3 and 4 of DOS use a space between the KEYB command and country abbreviation (that is, KEYB UK or KEYB FR).

Because KEYB is an external command, it must be on the current drive and directory, or in a directory specified in the current PATH setting, in order to be accessible.

The two-letter abbreviation used in the KEYB command must be one of those listed in the leftmost column of Table B.6. The optional three-digit code page must be one of those available for the country, as listed in the third column of the table. (If omitted, the current code page is used.)

The optional /ID: switch in DOS 4 selects a keyboard layout using the Keyboard ID number listed in Table B.6. This is used only for the countries that support more than one keyboard, France, Italy, and the United Kingdom. If /ID: is omitted, the default (first-listed) keyboard code is assumed.

Table B.6. Two-letter abbreviations and code pages for KEYB.

Two-Letter Abbreviation	Country	Acceptable Code Pages	DOS 4 Keyboard ID #
BE	Belgium	850	120
CF	Canadian (French)	850, 863	058
DK	Denmark	850, 865	159
FR	France	437, 850	189 or 120
GR	Germany	437, 850	129
IT	Italy	437, 850	141 or 142
LA	Latin America	437, 850	171
NL	Netherlands	437, 850	143
NO	Norway	850, 865	155
PO	Portugal	850, 860	163
SF	Switzerland (French)	850	150
SG	Switzerland (German)	850	000
SP	Spain	437, 850	172
SU	Finland	437, 850	153
SV	Sweden	437, 850	153
UK	United Kingdom	437, 850	166 or 168
US	U.S.A., Australia	437, 850	103

Be sure to provide the complete location and file name of the keyboard file (usually C:\DOS\KEYBOARD.SYS) as the third argument in the KEYB command.

After you activate KEYB, you use *dead keys* to type accented characters. Dead keys, when initially pressed, display nothing. However, when you press a certain letter key after pressing a dead key, the typed character appears with its appropriate accent mark. For specific maps to code pages and dead keys for your country's keyboard, refer to the DOS manual that came with your computer.

Entering the command KEYB with no parameters displays the two-letter country code and code page currently in use.

After you install KEYB, the following keys let you switch keyboard styles:

Ctrl-Alt-F1 switches to the standard U.S. keyboard.

Ctrl-Alt-F2 switches to the keyboard driver specified in the KEYB command

Examples   To configure your computer for the French Canadian language, first add the following commands to your CONFIG.SYS file (assuming that your computer has an EGA or VGA display adapter):

```
COUNTRY=002 863 C:\DOS\COUNTRY.SYS
DEVICE=C:\DOS\DISPLAY.SYS CON=(EGA,437,2)
```

Then, add these commands to your AUTOEXEC.BAT file:

```
MODE CON CP PREP=((863,850)C:\DOS\EGA.CPI)
MODE CON CP SEL = 863
KEYB US,863,C:\DOS\KEYBOARD.SYS
```

After completing the installation, you can press Ctrl-Alt-F1 to use the U.S.A. keyboard, or Ctrl-Alt-F2 to use the French Canadian keyboard.

See Also   COUNTRY, DISPLAY.SYS, MODE, PRINTER.SYS

LABEL

Assigns or changes a label to a hard disk or a floppy diskette.

Version   3 and later (PC-DOS); 3.1 and later (MS-DOS)

Type   External (LABEL.COM)

DOS Shell   None
Menu Access

Syntax   LABEL [drive] [label]

in which *drive* is the name of the disk drive containing the disk to which you want to assign a label, and *label* is the label (name) you want to assign.

Usage   The LABEL command lets you assign, view, change, or delete a disk volume label. The term *volume* merely refers to the collection of files on the disk. The label is basically a name and is entirely optional. If you choose to assign a label to a disk, that label appears as the first line of the display whenever you use the DIR, TREE, VOL, and CHKDSK commands.

The label you assign can be as long as 11 characters and can include spaces and underline characters. The label should not, however, include any of the following characters: * ? / \ or |.

You should include the disk drive name to the right of the LABEL command. (If no disk drive is specified, then the current disk drive is assumed.) If you use the LABEL command to assign a name to a disk, the new label overwrites any existing name. If you do not include a label with the LABEL command, DOS displays the existing label (if any), and prompts you to type a new label. If you press Enter without typing a new label, you'll be asked whether or not you want to delete the label. Merely answer Yes or No.

You cannot assign a label to a network drive. Similarly, you should avoid using LABEL with disk drives that are currently affected by ASSIGN, JOIN, or SUBST commands.

Note that you can also use the /V option with the FORMAT command to assign a label to a disk. The VOL command lets you view the current label, if any.

Examples   The following scenario demonstrates the ways in which you can use LABEL. To start, suppose you place a blank formatted diskette in drive A: and enter the DIR command. The first line of the output informs you that `Volume in drive A: has no label`.

Next, you decide to assign the name WPFILES to that disk. To do so, enter the command:

```
LABEL A:WPFILES
```

The disk in drive A: is now labeled WPFILES. To verify this, enter the command:

```
LABEL A:
```

and the screen displays the following information:

```
Volume in drive A is WPFILES
Volume label (11 characters, ENTER for none)?
```

As the screen explains, you can now enter a new volume label and then press Enter. (At this point, if you were to type in a new label, the new label would replace the existing one.) If you do not want to change the existing label, just press the Enter key.

If you press the Enter key, the screen then displays the prompt:

```
Delete current volume label (Y/N)?
```

If you type **Y** and press Enter, the existing label is removed. If you type **N** and press Enter, the current label is retained.

See Also   FORMAT, VOL

LASTDRIVE

Sets the maximum number of accessible disk drives

Version   3 and later

Type   Internal (used only in CONFIG.SYS)

DOS Shell Menu Access   None

Syntax   `LASTDRIVE=x`

in which *x* is a drive name specified by a letter from A to Z.

Usage   LASTDRIVE is used only in the CONFIG.SYS file. In most situations, this command is not required, because DOS can detect as many as five disk drives (drives A: through E:, including a RAM disk) after reading the CONFIG.SYS file. Three exceptions when you *would* want to use LAST-DRIVE in your CONFIG.SYS file are:

- When you have created more than one RAM disk.
- When you plan to use the SUBST command to create an artificial disk drive.
- When you will have drives with names higher than the letter E:.

Examples   Suppose your computer has a floppy disk drive named A: and one hard disk named C:. Your CONFIG.SYS file also contains two DEVICE= VDISK.SYS commands, which create two RAM disks. Furthermore, you occasionally use the SUBST command to create an artificial drive. Given this situation, you should include the command:

`LASTDRIVE=F`

in your CONFIG.SYS file. That way, DOS will be prepared to manage the two RAM disks, which automatically are named D: and E: by the

DEVICE=VDISK.SYS commands in CONFIG.SYS, as well as your artificial drive F:, when you enter a SUBST command at the command prompt.

See Also   SUBST

MEM

Displays the amount of used and available memory.

Version   4 and later

Type   External (MEM.EXE)

DOS Shell Menu Access   None

Syntax   `MEM [/PROGRAM | /DEBUG]`

Usage   MEM displays all currently used and unused conventional memory (RAM), and extended or expanded memory if available. Because MEM is external, it must be on the current drive and directory or in a directory specified in the current PATH setting, when you enter the MEM command at the DOS command prompt.

Used with no switches, MEM displays only basic memory usage. The /PROGRAM option displays programs and device drivers currently loaded into memory. The /DEBUG option presents more detailed information about programs, internal device drivers, and installed drivers in memory. Both options display memory locations and sizes in hexadecimal.

You cannot use both the /PROGRAM and /DEBUG options in a single MEM command.

Examples   Let's assume a Compaq 386 computer uses the following CONFIG.SYS file commands:

```
DEVICE= C:\DOS\CEMM.EXE 2048 ON
DEVICE=C:\DOS\ANSI.SYS
BREAK=ON
FILES=40
BUFFERS=15,2 /X
SHELL=C:\DOS\COMMAND.COM /P /E:256
LASTDRIVE=H
INSTALL=C:\DOS\FASTOPEN.EXE C:=(50,25) D:=(50,25) F:=(50,25)  /X
DEVICE=C:\DOS\VDISK.SYS 2048 /E
```

The AUTOEXEC.BAT file for this same computer contains the commands:

```
SET COMSPEC=C:\DOS\COMMAND.COM
PATH C:\WS4;C:\DOS;C:\UTILS;C:\DBASE
VERIFY OFF
C:\MOUSE1\MOUSE
APPEND /E
APPEND C:\DOS
PRINT /D:LPT1
PROMPT $P$G
DOSSHELL
```

Entering the command MEM immediately after startup might show (approximately) the following memory usage:

```
655360 bytes total memory
655360 bytes available
552912 largest executable program size

2490368 bytes total EMS memory
2064384 bytes free EMS memory

4194304 bytes total extended memory
 195584 bytes available extended memory
```

The command MEM /PROGRAM might display the following:

Address	Name	Size	Type
000000		000400	Interrupt Vector
000400		000100	ROM Communication Area
000500		000200	DOS Communication Area
000700	IO	0026A0	System Program
002DA0	MSDOS	008F00	System Program
00BCA0	IO	004760	System Data
	CEMM	001180	DEVICE=
	ANSI	001150	DEVICE=
	VDISK	000750	DEVICE=
		000820	FILES=
		000100	FCBS=
		000410	BUFFERS=
		0002C0	LASTDRIVE=
		000CD0	STACKS=

```
010410      MSDOS        000030      -- Free --
010450      MOUSE        000060      Environment
0104C0      MSDOS        000010      -- Free --
0104E0      FASTOPEN     0005E0      Program
010AD0      COMMAND      001640      Program
012120      COMMAND      000100      Environment
012230      MOUSE        002890      Program
014AD0      MSDOS        000060      -- Free --
014B40      APPEND       001E30      Program
016980      MEM          000070      Environment
016A00      PRINT        0016A0      Program
0180B0      MSDOS        0000D0      -- Free --
018190      SHELLB       000E80      Program
019020      MEM          012F00      Program
02BF30      MSDOS        0740C0      -- Free --


    655360 bytes total memory
    655360 bytes available
    552912 largest executable program size

   2490368 bytes total EMS memory
   2064384 bytes free EMS memory

   4194304 bytes total extended memory
    195584 bytes available extended memory
```

The command MEM /DEBUG might display the following information:

```
Address     Name         Size        Type
000000                   000400      Interrupt Vector
000400                   000100      ROM Communication Area
000500                   000200      DOS Communication Area

000700      IO           0026A0      System Program
            CON                      System Device Driver
            AUX                      System Device Driver
            PRN                      System Device Driver
            CLOCK$                   System Device Driver
            A: - G:                  System Device Driver
            COM1                     System Device Driver
            LPT1                     System Device Driver
            LPT2                     System Device Driver
            LPT3                     System Device Driver
            COM2                     System Device Driver
            COM3                     System Device Driver
            COM4                     System Device Driver
```

002DA0	MSDOS	008F00	System Program
00BCA0	IO	004760	System Data
	CEMM	001180	DEVICE=
	ANSI	001150	DEVICE=
	VDISK	000750	DEVICE=
		000820	FILES=
		000100	FCBS=
		000410	BUFFERS=
		0002C0	LASTDRIVE=
		000CD0	STACKS=
010410	MSDOS	000030	-- Free --
010450	MOUSE	000060	Environment
0104C0	MSDOS	000010	-- Free --
0104E0	FASTOPEN	0005E0	Program
010AD0	COMMAND	001640	Program
012120	COMMAND	000100	Environment
012230	MOUSE	002890	Program
014AD0	MSDOS	000060	-- Free --
014B40	APPEND	001E30	Program
016980	MEM	000070	Environment
016A00	PRINT	0016A0	Program
0180B0	MSDOS	0000D0	-- Free --
018190	SHELLB	000E80	Program
019020	MEM	012F00	Program
02BF30	MSDOS	0740C0	-- Free --

```
655360 bytes total memory
655360 bytes available
552912 largest executable program size
```

Handle	EMS Name	Size
DDDDDDD	DDDDDDDD	DDDDDD
0		060000
1	BUFFERS	004000
2	FASTOPEN	004000

```
2490368 bytes total EMS memory
2064384 bytes free EMS memory

4194304 bytes total extended memory
 195584 bytes available extended memory
```

See Also   CHKDSK

MKDIR or MD

Creates a directory or subdirectory.

Version 2 and later

Type Internal

DOS Shell Menu Access Access the File System, then position the highlight on the parent directory of the directory you want to create. (Use the root directory if you want to create a directory that is one level beneath root.) Press F10 and select Create Directory... from the File pull-down menu.

Syntax MKDIR [*drive*][*path*]*directory name*

or,

MD [*drive*][*path*]*directory name*

in which *drive* is the name of the disk drive, *path* is the path (if any), and *directory name* is the name of the new directory that you want to create.

Usage MKDIR (and its abbreviated form, MD) allows you to create a new directory or subdirectory on a disk. The directory you create can be either one level beneath the root (such as \UTILS), or a child directory of one or more other directories (such as \UTILS\DATA). A single directory name can consist of no more than eight characters and can include a three-letter extension preceded by a period (exactly the same format as a file name). An entire path name, consisting of several subdirectory names (such as WP\BOOKS\CHAPTERS), can contain a maximum of 63 characters.

The directory name that you assign cannot have the same path name as any other directory on the disk, nor can it be the same as any file on the parent directory.

If you use the \ character in front of the first directory name, then the directory is created in reference to the root directory. If you omit the first \ character, the directory is created in reference to the current directory (that is, as a child to the current directory). Examples in the following section demonstrate these principles.

You probably should not use the MKDIR command when using drives affected by the ASSIGN, JOIN, or SUBST commands. DOS allows you to create subdirectories when these commands are in effect, but the actual location of the directory might not be where you think it is. For example, if you enter the command ASSIGN A = C, and then enter the command MKDIR A:\TEMP, the \TEMP directory is actually created on drive C:, not drive A: as the MKDIR command implies.

If you attempt to create a directory, but you get the error message Unable to create directory, one of five things is wrong.

1. The directory already exists.
2. A file that has the same name as the directory already exists.
3. You specified a parent directory that does not exist (for example, \UTILS\DATA, but \UTILS does not exist).
4. The disk is full.
5. The root directory already contains the maximum number of files.

Examples   To create a directory named WP one level beneath the root directory, enter the following command:

```
MD \WP
```

To create a subdirectory named WPFILES beneath the \WP directory, you could use one of two techniques. If any directory *other* than \WP is the current directory you must enter the command:

```
MD \WP\WPFILES
```

If, on the other hand, \WP is the current directory, you can use a shortcut and enter the simpler command:

```
MD WPFILES
```

The following example demonstrates the importance of using the leading \ character with MKDIR. Suppose you change to the \WP\WPFILES subdirectory by entering the command:

```
CD WP\WPFILES
```

If you then enter the command:

```
MD TEXT
```

the TEXT subdirectory is created as a child to the current directory, because the command doesn't begin with the \ character, which symbolizes the root directory. Therefore, the actual path name for the new subdirectory is WP\WPFILES\TEXT.

However, if you include the leading backslash in the command, as follows:

```
MD \TEXT
```

the new directory is created as a child to the root directory only (even though your current directory is WP\WPFILES). That is, its path name is simply \TEXT, rather than \WP\WPFILES\TEXT.

Suppose you try to create a directory named \TEMP by entering the command **MD TEMP**, and DOS displays the error message `Unable to create the Directory`. Usually, this error occurs because a directory or file named TEMP already exists. To safeguard against this error, enter the **TREE** command to see if a directory named TEMP already exists on your hard disk. If not, enter the command **DIR TEMP** to see if a file named TEMP already exists in the current directory.

See Also CHDIR or CD, RMDIR or RD

MODE

Prepares devices for use.

Version 1 and later (varies among DOS versions and specific computers)

Type External (MODE.COM)

DOS Shell Menu Access None

Syntax The syntax for the MODE command depends partly on the particular device you are installing and partly on the specific features offered by your computer. The command is generally used to alter the manner in which your computer uses devices (such as the printer, screen, and keyboard), to adjust to your particular work needs. The sections that follow provide the syntax for commonly used devices.

Usage The sections that follow present some general MODE command techniques and options. To take full advantage of the features offered by your computer, refer to the DOS manual that came with your computer or to the user's manual for your specific computer.

MODE for Monitors MODE lets you define the adapter used for your monitor and the width of the screen (in characters). It can also be used to realign text on the screen.

Syntax for Monitors

MODE can use several different syntaxes to adjust your monitor, as below:

MODE *display* (Version 3.2 and later)
MODE *display,lines* (Version 3.2 and later)
MODE *[display],shift[,test]* (Version 3.2 and later)

```
MODE CON [:] COLS=cols LINES=lines (Version 4)
```

in which:

> *display* specifies the display mode as 40, 80, BW40, BW80, CO40, CO80, or MONO.
>
> *shift* can be either R (to shift right) or L (to shift left).
>
> *test* is specified by the letter T, which allows you to repeat the specified *shift* until alignment is accurate.
>
> *cols* specifies the number of columns to display, either 40 or 80.
>
> *lines* specifies the number of lines to display, either 25, 43, or 50.

Usage for Monitors

Valid options for the *display* parameter of the MODE command include:

40	Sets the display width to 40 characters.
80	Sets the display width to 80 characters.
CO40	Enables color and sets the display width to 40 characters.
CO80	Enables color and sets the display width to 80 characters.
MONO	Activates a monochrome monitor.

(See Chapter 12 for examples of these options.)

Note that defining the monitor type as color (CO) does not immediately change the color of the screen. It does ensure, however, that any programs that can use color will do so.

EGA and VGA display adapters allow monitors to display more than 25 lines of text. The *lines* parameter in the MODE command lets you change the number of lines from the default value of 25 to either 43 or 50.

The *R* and *L* options work only with a Color Graphics Adapter. If an 80-character width is used, R and L shift text two columns. If a 40-character width is used, R and L shift text one column. The *T* option should be used to help you determine when text is properly aligned.

Examples for Monitors

To double the size of the characters on your monitor, enter the command:

```
MODE 40
```

To realign your color (CGA) monitor to compensate for letters that are scrolled past the left edge of the screen, adjust the right margin by entering the command:

```
MODE CO80,R,T
```

To realign your color (CGA) monitor to view letters that are chopped off at the right edge of the screen, adjust the left margin by entering the command:

```
MODE CO80,L,T
```

Note that the last two commands display a test pattern on the screen and then question your ability to view certain characters. Answer **N** until the requested characters are visible on the screen; then, enter **Y**.

If you have an EGA or VGA adapter, or any other adapter that can display more than 25 lines of text on the screen, enter the command:

```
MODE CON LINES=43 COLS=80
```

to permit 43 lines of text to be displayed on your screen. Note that DOS commands (such as DIR) take advantage of the new line spacing and character size, but some application programs might not.

To return to the default number of lines, enter the command:

```
MODE CON LINES=25
```

MODE for Parallel Printers

MODE also allows you to configure printers attached to the parallel port. In most cases, you don't need to do this, because most programs, including DOS, take care of the printer automatically. (If you have problems with a printer, refer to the manual that came with that printer for specific information.)

Syntax for Parallel Printers

The general syntax for preparing a parallel printer for DOS Versions 1 to 3.3 is:

```
MODE printer port [cols][,lines][,P]
```

in Version 4.0, the syntax is:

```
MODE printer port [COLS=cols][,LINES=lines][,RETRY=retry
attempts]
```

in which *lines* is the number of lines per printed page, *cols* is the number of characters printed per line, and *retry attempts* determines how DOS interacts with the parallel printer.

Usage for Parallel Printers

You must specify LPT and a port number when using MODE to configure a parallel printer—LPT1, LPT2, or LPT3. Other options and valid settings are summarized as follows:

cols	80 for printers with 8-inch carriages, or 132 for wide-carriage printers or compressed print on 8-inch printers.
lines	Either 6 lines to the inch or 8 lines to the inch.
retry attempts	Usually E for network parallel printers, B for "infinite retry" (similar to specifying P in earlier versions of DOS— *not* recommended for network printers), or R to send text only when the printer is ready. This is the default setting and is recommended for most printers.

Not all printers are able to accept different characters per line or lines per inch settings. Many insist on using the default values: 80 characters per line and 6 lines per inch. (Your printer manual explains how to use special features independently of the MODE command.)

If you use the MODE command to configure a parallel port, be sure that you include exactly two commas. If you omit an optional parameter, include the comma as a placeholder.

The P option used in Versions 1 through 3.3 of DOS specifies infinite retries on a parallel printer. For example, the command MODE LPT1 ,,P uses the default column spacing and line widths, but tells DOS to wait indefinitely for the printer to be ready, should it find the printer not ready when initially sending data.

Examples for Parallel Printers

Several Espon, IBM, and other dot-matrix printers are capable of printing in densities other than the standard modes of 10 characters per horizontal inch and 6 lines per vertical inch. These printers will respond to the MODE command for parallel printers.

For example, assuming that you have a compatible printer with a wide (13.5-inch) carriage and that the printer is attached to the LPT1 (also called the PRN) port, you can enter this command to print the full width of the paper, at 8 lines to the inch:

```
MODE LPT1 COLS=132 LINES=8
```

To adjust the column width without adjusting the number of lines per inch, use this command instead:

```
MODE LPT1 COLS=80
```

MODE for the Serial Port If you use a modem, you probably use some type of communications software. This software allows you to configure your communications settings. Similarly, if you use a FAX board, it too automatically adjusts the settings for the communications (serial) port. Both of these optional devices completely override any communications port settings that you specify with the MODE command. In fact, you should avoid using MODE altogether when using a modem or FAX board (unless instructed otherwise by the documentation that came with your modem or FAX board).

On the other hand, serial printers often rely on DOS to set the communications settings. Specifically, they rely on the MODE command.

Syntax for the Serial Port

The general syntax for using the MODE command to configure a serial port for a serial printer is:

```
MODE port[:]rate[,parity[,databits[,stopbits[,P]]]]
```

or, in DOS 4:

```
MODE port BAUD=rate [DATA=databits] [STOP=stop bits]
[PARITY=parity] [RETRY=retry attempts]
```

in which:

>*port* is the name of a serial communications port: COM1 or COM2 in DOS Version 3.2 and earlier; COM1, COM2, COM3, or COM4 in DOS Versions 3.3 or later.

>*rate* is the baud rate: 110, 150, 300, 600, 1200, 2400, 4800, 9600, or 19200.

>*databits* is the number of bits per transmitted character: either 5, 6, 7, or 8. The default is 7 if omitted (only DOS 4 supports the 5 and 6 options).

>*stopbits* is the number of bits between characters: either 1, 1.5, or 2, where 1 is the default, if omitted for all baud rates except 110, which defaults to 2. (Only DOS 4 supports the 1.5 option.)

>*parity* is either NONE, ODD, EVEN, SPACE, or MARK.

>*retry attempts* is either E, B, R, or none (as discussed in the previous section pertaining to parallel communications).

Usage for the Serial Port

If you omit any of the above settings, placing only the comma in its place, the default values are used for that setting (except for baud rate, which you must specify). Default values are even parity, 7 data bits, and 1 stop bit (or 2 stop bits for 110 baud).

Examples for the Serial Port

Let's assume that you have a serial printer attached to the second serial communications port (COM2). To set that port to a baud rate of 1200 with 8 data bits, 1 stop bit, no parity, and infinite retry attempts, enter the command:

```
MODE COM2: 1200,N,8,1,P
```

or, using DOS 4 syntax:

```
MODE COM2 BAUD=1200 DATA=8 STOP=1 PARITY=NONE RETRY=B
```

at the command prompt (or in your AUTOEXEC.BAT file).

MODE for Redirecting Parallel Output

You can use MODE to tell DOS to send output that would normally go to the parallel port (usually PRN), to the serial port instead. Before doing so, be sure that the communications parameters for the serial port are ready, as described in the preceding section, "MODE for the Serial Port."

Syntax for Redirecting Parallel Output

The general syntax for redirecting parallel port output to the serial port is:

```
MODE printer[:]=port[:]
```

in which *printer* is the name of the printer port (LPT1, LPT2, or LPT3) and *port* is the name of the serial communications port (COM1 or COM2 in DOS Versions 3.2 or earlier; COM1, COM2, COM3, or COM4 in DOS Versions 3.3 or 4).

To cancel the redirection, use only the printer parameter in the MODE command.

Examples for Redirecting Parallel Output

To redirect printed output originally intended for a parallel printer to a serial printer attached to the COM2 port, first enter the MODE command required to set up the communications parameters for the serial printer. Then, enter the command:

```
MODE LPT1:=COM2:
```

Any output to LPT1 (or PRN device, in this example) is rerouted to the COM2 port. To cancel this redirection, enter the command:

```
MODE LPT1:
```

MODE for Preparing a Code Page

You can use the MODE command to prepare a non-English code page or several code pages, for use with a particular device.

Syntax for Preparing a Code Page

The general syntax for preparing a hardware device for a specific DOS code page is:

```
MODE device CP PREP= ((code page list) drive\path\file name)
```

in which:

> *device* is a DOS device name: either CON, PRN, LPT1, LPT2, or LPT3.
> *code page list* is one code page or a list of code pages, including 437, 850, 860, 863, 865, or any other that is supported by your hardware.
>
> *drive\path\file name* specifies the location and name of the Code Page Information (.CPI) file.

Usage for Preparing a Code Page

You can use CODEPAGE rather than the abbreviation CP in the MODE command. You can also use PREPARE, rather than the abbreviation PREP.
Valid code page information files for most computers include:

EGA.CPI   Code Page Information file for EGA and VGA video display adapters

LCD.CPI   Code Page Information file for liquid crystal display (LCD) screens.

4201.CPI   Code Page Information file for the IBM Proprinter II, Model 4201

4208.CPI   Code Page Information file for the IBM Proprinter II, Model 4208

5202.CPI   Code Page Information file for the IBM Quietwriter III Printer, Model 5202

Check the user manual that came with your computer for other possible code page information files.

You can use the MODE command to prepare a code page for a device only after the DEVICE=DISPLAY.SYS or DEVICE=PRINTER.SYS command in the CONFIG.SYS file has installed the appropriate device driver for the code page.

You can list one or more code pages in the MODE CP PREPARE command. Separate each three-digit code page number with a space.

Examples of Preparing a Code Page

Assuming that your CONFIG.SYS file already contains a command such as DEVICE=C:\DOS\DISPLAY.SYS CON=(EGA,437,3), the following command prepares three code pages—850, 437, and 865—for use on the screen console:

```
MODE CON CP PREP=((863,437,850)C:\DOS\EGA.CPI)
```

The command can be included in your AUTOEXEC.BAT file or can be typed in at the command prompt.

Another command, which would probably be entered at the command prompt, changes the initial MODE CON CP PREPARE command. In this example, the command changes the code pages to 850, 437, and 865. The double commas indicate that the second code page (437 in this example) remains unchanged:

```
MODE CON CP PREP=((850,,865)C:\DOS\EGA.CPI)
```

MODE for Selecting a Code Page After you have used the DEVICE command to install a device driver for a code page, and you have used the MODE CP PREPARE command to prepare a code page, you can use the MODE CODEPAGE SELECT (abbreviated MODE CP SEL) command to select a code page to be used.

Syntax for Selecting a Code Page

To use the MODE command to select a code page, use the general syntax:

```
MODE device CP SEL code page
```

in which *device* is the device name of an installed device, either CON, PRN, LPT1, LPT2, or LPT3, and *code page* is a valid code page number, usually 437, 850, 860, 863, 865, or any other number that is supported by your hardware.

Usage for Selecting a Code Page

To select a code page for the screen, the CONFIG.SYS file must already contain the proper DEVICE=DISPLAY.SYS command, and the MODE CON CP PREP command must have already prepared the code page. Similarly, to select a code page for the printer, the CONFIG.SYS file must already contain the proper DEVICE=PRINTER.SYS command, and the MODE PRN (or LPT#) CP PREP command must have already prepared the code page for the printer.

You can also use the MODE command to restore a code page, or check the status of the current code page. To display the currently active code page (in DOS 4), use the syntax:

```
MODE [device] [CODEPAGE] /STATUS
```

If you lose a code page because the printer or some other device is temporarily turned off, and then turned back on, you can re-install the current code page without rebooting. Use the MODE command with the syntax:

```
MODE device CODEPAGE REFRESH
```

Examples of Selecting a Code Page

Assuming that the CONFIG.SYS file already contains a DEVICE= DISPLAY.SYS command to install the code page device driver for your monitor, the following commands prepare code pages 863 and 850, and select code page 863 as the current code page:

```
MODE CON CP PREP=((863,850)C:\DOS\EGA.CPI)
MODE CON CP SEL = 863
```

The next command installs code page 863 into the keyboard:

```
KEYB US,863,C:\DOS\KEYBOARD.SYS
```

The command below displays the currently active code page for the display monitor:

```
MODE CON CODEPAGE /STATUS
```

The command below reactivates the current code page for the printer connected to port LPT1:

```
MODE LPT1 REFRESH
```

The DOS 4 command below displays the current status of all devices:

```
MODE /STATUS
```

See Also   KEYB, DISPLAY.SYS, PRINTER.SYS

MORE

Pauses the screen scrolling.

Version   2 and later

Type   External (MORE.COM)

DOS Shell
Menu Access   None

Syntax   MORE

Usage Normally when you use a command that displays a great deal of information, such as DIR, TYPE, or TREE, that information quickly scrolls off the screen. You can start and stop scrolling by pressing Ctrl-S or the Pause key. However, it is much easier to use the MORE filter to force the display to pause automatically at the end of each screenful.

When MORE is activated, scrolling pauses automatically after every 23 lines of text (24 lines in DOS 4), and the prompt `--more--` appears at the bottom of the screen. At that point, you can press any key to view the next screenful of information. (Optionally, you can type Ctrl-Break or Ctrl-C to return to the DOS prompt.)

MORE acts as a filter, and it must have information piped to it. There are two ways to do so. Either type in a command and follow it with `| MORE`, or enter the MORE command followed by a < symbol and the name of the file you want to view. The following examples demonstrate these techniques.

Examples The following command displays the names of all files in the current directory, pausing for a keystroke after each screenful of information:

```
DIR | MORE
```

The next command displays the directory in alphabetical order, pausing after every screenful of information:

```
DIR | SORT | MORE
```

Suppose a software package that you purchased includes a file named READ.ME that you wish to read. To pause between filled screens, enter the command:

```
MORE < READ.ME
```

You could accomplish exactly the same result by using MORE as a filter to the TYPE command, as follows:

```
TYPE READ.ME | MORE
```

If you enter the MORE command with no parameters, as follows:

```
MORE
```

it waits for input from the keyboard. To return to the DOS prompt, press the F6 key or Ctrl-Z.

See Also TYPE, SORT

NLSFUNC

Provides support for country information and the CHCP command.

Version   3.3 and later

Type   External (NLSFUNC.EXE)

DOS Shell   None
Menu Access

Syntax   `NLSFUNC [[drive][path]file name]`

in which *drive*, *path* and *file name* represent the location and name of the country information file (usually C:\DOS\COUNTRY.SYS).

Usage   The NLSFUNC command loads the extended country information from the country information file and then allows you to use the CHCP command to select a code page. NLSFUNC must be executed before the CHCP command can be used.

You can include the NLSFUNC command in your AUTOEXEC.BAT file, or you can type the command directly at the command prompt. Optionally, you can have your CONFIG.SYS file install the NLSFUNC command using the syntax `INSTALL=NLSFUNC.EXE` (or `INSTALL= C:\DOS\NLSFUNC.EXE`). If you use the INSTALL option, be sure to specify the complete path and file name, including the .EXE extension.

You can use the NLSFUNC command only once during a DOS session. For this reason, it is often best to place the command in your AUTOEXEC.BAT or CONFIG.SYS file. If you attempt to load NLSFUNC more than once during a session, DOS displays the message `NLSFUNC already installed`.

Examples   The following command, entered at the command prompt or included in an AUTOEXEC.BAT file, installs the NLSFUNC program using the usual COUNTRY.SYS country information file, which is stored on the C:\DOS directory:

`NLSFUNC C:\DOS\COUNTRY.SYS`

As an alternative to installing NLSFUNC through the AUTOEXEC.BAT file or from the command prompt, you can instead include this command in your CONFIG.SYS file:

`INSTALL=NLSFUNC C:\DOS\COUNTRY.SYS`

See Also   CHCP

PATH

Specifies multiple directories to be searched for programs.

Version 2 and later

Type Internal

DOS Shell Menu Access None

Syntax `PATH [drive][path][;...]`

in which *drive* is the name of the drive to search, and *path* is a directory name or directory/subdirectory sequence. Multiple drive and directory specifications must be separated by semicolons, with no blank spaces.

Usage PATH sets up a series of disk drives and directories that DOS will search for program files if those files are not on the current drive or directory. This is a valuable capability, because it allows you to access DOS external programs, such as ATTRIB, CHKDSK, FIND, PRINT, and others, from any drive and subdirectory. Note, however, that PATH only searches for executable program files (including batch files) that have the extensions .BAT, .COM, and .EXE. (The APPEND command searches for other types of files.)

Whenever you attempt to run a program, DOS searches the current drive and directory for the appropriate file. If the file cannot be found on the current drive and directory, DOS checks the PATH setting and searches the specified directories and subdirectories in the order in which they are listed. As soon as the file is located, it is loaded into memory and the program (or batch file) is executed.

It's a good idea always to include in your PATH command the drive and directory that contains your word processor or text editor. That way, you can use it at any time, on any drive or directory, to create or change files. Because PATH is such an important and frequently used command, it is nearly always included in the AUTOEXEC.BAT file.

The current PATH setting is always stored in the DOS environment. It can be accessed from a batch file using the variable name %PATH%, or it can be displayed by entering the command `SET` at the command prompt.

Examples Suppose you have stored all of your DOS programs—such as CHKDSK.COM, FIND.COM, and so forth—in a directory named \DOS on drive C:. You've stored some additional utility programs in a directory named \UTILS on drive C:. Finally, you've stored your word processor in a directory named \WP.

To ensure that all of the DOS commands, your utility programs, and your word processor are accessible at all times from any drive or subdirectory, enter the command:

```
PATH C:\DOS;C:\UTILS;C:\WP
```

Note that each directory specification is separated by a semicolon, without any blank spaces.

To include the root directory in a PATH command, specify its name simply as the drive name followed by a backslash (\). For example, the following command adds the root directory to the previous PATH command example:

```
PATH C:\;C:\DOS;C:\UTILS;C:\WP
```

To view the current PATH setting at any time, enter the command:

```
PATH
```

without parameters. To cancel a previously defined path, enter the command:

```
PATH ;
```

See Also   APPEND, Chapter 11

PAUSE

Pauses a batch file and waits for a keypress.

Version   1 and later

Type   Internal (used in batch files and in the DOS 4 Shell)

DOS Shell   None
Menu Access

Syntax   `PAUSE [comment]`

Usage   The PAUSE command temporarily halts a batch file and presents the message `Strike a key when ready....` or `Press any key to continue...` in DOS 4. When you press a key, processing continues normally at the next line in the batch file. However, if you press Ctrl-Break or Ctrl-C, the batch file immediately terminates.

You can use an ECHO command above a PAUSE command to present a more descriptive error message. For example, if the batch file needs to wait for the user to insert a diskette in drive A:, you can use an ECHO command to present the message *Insert diskette into drive A:*.

To hide the message that PAUSE normally displays, redirect the output to the NUL device. Precede the PAUSE command with your own descriptive messages, as in the example that follows.

Examples   The following batch file uses three ECHO commands to display messages, and a PAUSE command to temporarily halt processing:

```
@ECHO OFF
ECHO Place a diskette in drive A:
ECHO Then press any key to copy.
ECHO (or press Ctrl-Break to cancel the operation)
PAUSE > NUL
COPY %1 A:
```

When executed, the batch file displays the messages:

```
Place a diskette in drive A:
Then press any key to copy.
(or press Ctrl-Break to cancel the operation)
```

The PAUSE > NUL command then interrupts command execution and waits for a keypress. (PAUSE does not display its own message in this example, because its output is redirected to the NUL device.)

If the user presses Ctrl-Break or Ctrl-C during the pause, DOS displays the message Terminate batch job (Y/N)?. Enter Y to terminate the batch file or N to proceed. If you press any other key during the pause, the COPY command proceeds normally.

See Also   ECHO

PRINT

Activates background printing.

Version   2 and later

Type   External (PRINT.COM)

DOS Shell   Access the File System and select a file (or files) to print by highlighting and
Menu Access   pressing the Spacebar (or by single-clicking with the mouse). Then, select
Print from the File pull-down menu.

Syntax   The syntax for initializing the PRINT command is:

```
PRINT [[/D:printer port] [/Q:queue size] [/B:buffer size]
[/U:busytick] [/M:max ticks] [/S:time slice]]
```

The syntax for using the PRINT command after it has been installed is:

```
PRINT [[drive][path][file name] [...]] [/C] [/T] [/P]
```

in which *drive*, *path*, and *file name* identify the file (or files) to be printed.

Usage   PRINT lets you print files "in the background," thus allowing you to use your computer while the printer is active. PRINT allows you to specify several files to be printed, and then it places all the files in a queue (in which they await their turn to be sent to the printer). When PRINT finishes printing one file, it automatically begins printing the next file in the queue.

PRINT can only be used to print ASCII text files (files that do not contain "strange" graphics characters when displayed with the TYPE command). It cannot print files created by spreadsheet, database management, or word processing programs, unless those files have already been converted to ASCII text format. PRINT cannot print executable program files, such as those with the extensions .BIN, .COM, or .EXE.

A portion of the PRINT command (called the *resident portion*) must be loaded into RAM before you can use the command. To load the resident portion from your AUTOEXEC.BAT file without actually printing a file, use the /D option. (Failure to do so when using DOS 4 makes the Print option inaccessible from the DOS 4 File System.)

If you do not load PRINT into memory *before* using the command, DOS asks you to specify a print device and suggests PRN. Usually, this is the correct device, so you can merely press Enter.

You can use wildcard characters in file names. For example, the command **PRINT *.BAT** prints a copy of all batch files in the current directory. However, unless you use the /Q option to extend the length of the queue, the PRINT command prints only the first ten batch files accessed.

The optional switches used with PRINT during initialization are described in more detail in the list that follows. These options can be used only once during a session—when you initialize the PRINT command. You can use any of these switches in the PRINT command in your AUTOEXEC.BAT file.

/D:*device*   Must be the first listed switch, if several are used. The *device* name can any valid DOS device name, such as LPT1, LPT2, LPT3, PRN, COM1, COM2, COM3, COM4, or AUX.

/Q:*queuesize*   Specifies the maximum number of file names that can be stored in the queue. *Queue size* can be any number in the range of 4 to 32. If omitted, DOS uses the default queue size of 10.

/B:*buffer size*   Sets the size of the internal buffer used to store text to be printed. *Buffer size* can be any number in the range of 512 bytes to 16KB. If omitted, the default of 512 is used.

The other options require an understanding of how the PRINT command works. Basically, your computer contains a clock that "ticks" about 18.2 times per second (with most computers). Each "tick" is called a *time slice*. When DOS simultaneously performs multiple operations, such as printing in the background while running a spreadsheet program, it allocates a certain percentage of time slices to each operation.

Because the clock ticks so quickly, it appears (to humans) that DOS is doing both jobs simultaneously, although in reality it's switching back and forth (very quickly) from one job to the other.

The PRINT command uses a certain percentage of clock ticks to manage background printing. You can use the default percentage simply by omitting the following optional switches. Or you can customize PRINT by using these switches in your initial PRINT command.

/S:*time slice*   Specifies the number of time slices that PRINT allocates to other operations. The *time slice* parameter can be any value between 1 and 255. If omitted, DOS uses a default value of 8. A higher *time slice* value slows the background printing and speeds the foreground task.

[/M:*max ticks*]   Specifies the maximum number of time slices that PRINT can use to pass characters to the printer. *Max ticks* can be any value in the range of 1 to 255. If omitted, DOS uses the default value of 2. A higher *Max ticks* number means faster background printing, but slower execution of the foreground task.

/U:*busytick*   Specifies the number of clock ticks that PRINT will wait for the printer to become available. This option is called into play only if the printer is busy (unable to accept text) when PRINT is ready to send some characters. *Busytick* can be any value in the range of 1 to 255. If omitted, DOS uses the default value of 1. If PRINT waits for the printer longer than the number of time slices specified in *busytick*, it surrenders its current time slice to the foreground operation.

To calculate the actual percentage of time that is allocated to PRINT, use the formula:

$$\frac{max\ ticks}{(time\ slice\ +\ busytick)} \times 100$$

By default, PRINT uses a /M:*max ticks* value of 2, a /S:*time slice* value of 8, and a /U:*busy tick* setting of 1. Therefore, PRINT actually gets (2/(8+1))*100, or 22 percent, of all time slices. Because the printer is usually the slowest device on the computer, 22 percent of the time slices is usually sufficient to keep it running at top speed. (The foreground operation runs at 78 percent of its normal speed.)

If the /U (busytick) setting is too high, PRINT spends a lot of time waiting for the printer to become available, and the foreground task does nothing. Generally, the default setting of 1, or perhaps a small value such as 2 or 3, is the best setting for the /U option, unless your printer is extraordinarily fast and you want your background print operations to have top priority.

Ideally, getting the maximum performance from the PRINT command is a matter of allocating exactly the right amount of time to PRINT to make your printer run at full speed, without allocating more time than the printer can actually use. However, experimenting with these options is a laborious and time-consuming task, and unless your printer or foreground task is unbearably slow, you should probably use the default settings.

Switches that you can use with the PRINT command, after it has been installed and PRINT is currently printing some files, include:

/T   Terminates the entire print queue, including the current file

/C   Removes specified files from the print queue

/P   Adds specified file names to the print queue

Entering the command `PRINT` with no options or file names displays the names of files currently in the queue.

While PRINT is in control of the printer, attempting to use another program to print a file displays an error message such as `Device not ready` or `Printer out of paper`. You must either wait until PRINT finishes or use PRINT /T to cancel the background printing.

Never use MODE PREPARE or MODE SELECT to switch printer code pages while PRINT is printing text.

PRINT cannot be used in a network. Use the NET PRINT command instead.

Examples   The following command initializes the PRINT program, specifying the first parallel printer port (LPT1) and a maximum of 20 files in the queue:

```
PRINT /D:LPT1 /Q:20
```

DOS then displays the messages:

```
Resident portion of PRINT loaded
PRINT queue is empty
```

Note that loading PRINT with a maximum of 20 file names in the queue consumes about 6.3KB of conventional RAM.

Assuming that PRINT.COM is available on the current disk and directory, or in a directory specified in the PATH setting, the following command places in the queue as many as 20 files with the extension .DOC, from the current directory, and starts printing the first listed file:

```
PRINT *.DOC
```

After printing starts, the command prompt reappears. You can now use your computer to run any program you want. (However, you cannot access the printer while PRINT is printing in the background.)

To see a list of the file names currently in the queue (in the order in which they will be printed) enter the command:

```
PRINT
```

The next command removes the file CHAP11.DOC from the print queue and inserts the file CHAP11.TXT into the queue:

```
PRINT CHAP11.DOC /C  CHAP11.TXT/P
```

To stop all background printing and empty the queue, use the command:

```
PRINT /T
```

See Also   TYPE

PRINTER.SYS

Allows code page switching with printers that support the capability.

Version   4

Type   External device driver (PRINTER.SYS) activated by DEVICE in the CONFIG.SYS file.

DOS Shell Menu Access   None

Syntax
```
DEVICE=[drive][path]PRINTER.SYS port=
(type[,(hardware code page list][,max pages])
```

in which *drive* and *path* indicate the location of the PRINTER.SYS file. Other options are described in the following section.

Usage PRINTER.SYS can be used only with printers that support code page switching. Users in the United States do not need to use the PRINTER.SYS device driver unless they want to print text written in a foreign language. Parameters used in the DEVICE=PRINTER.SYS command include:

port	Specifies the port to which the printer is connected: either LPT1, LPT2, LPT3, or PRN (same as LPT1).
type	Specifies the model number of the printer. Most versions of DOS support the following printer models, but your computer might support others (see either the DOS manual that came with your computer or your printer manual):

4201	IBM 4201 Proprinter family
	IBM 4202 Proprinter XL
4208	IBM 4207 Proprinter X24
	IBM 4208 Proprinter XL24
5202	IBM 5202 Quietwriter III

hardware code page list	Specifies one or more code pages that are supported by the printer (usually 437, 850, or both).
max pages	Specifies the maximum number of code pages that can be prepared with the MODE PREPARE command. The maximum value is 12, although most printers can support only 1 or 2.

Examples The following command, when added to the CONFIG.SYS file, prepares an IBM model 4201 printer, connected to parallel port LPT1, for use with the 437 (English language) code page and one code page that can be installed by the MODE command. The command assumes that the PRINTER.SYS file is stored in the \DOS directory of disk drive C:

```
DEVICE=C:\DOS\PRINTER.SYS LPT1=(4201,437,1)
```

The next command, entered at the command prompt or stored in the AUTOEXEC.BAT file, then copies the fonts for the 850 (multilingual) code page from the 4201.CPI file to the device driver for the printer:

```
MODE LPT1 CP PREP=((850) C:\DOS\4201.CPI)
```

The following command then selects code page 850 for current use with the printer:

```
MODE LPT1 CP SEL=850
```

See Also DRIVER.SYS, KEYB, MODE, your printer or computer manual

PROMPT

Changes the system prompt and activates ANSI features.

Version 2 and later

Type Internal

DOS Shell Menu Access None

Syntax `PROMPT codes`

in which *codes* are special codes preceded by the $ symbol that define the system prompt and, optionally, configure the screen and keyboard.

Usage Many versions of DOS display the command prompt as simply the current drive followed by a greater than sign:

`C>`

You can change the prompts to include any text, merely by typing the text after the PROMPT command. In addition, you can use the codes listed in Table B.7 to display special features in the prompt.

Table B.7. Command prompt codes used with the PROMPT command to display special features.

Code	Displays
$D	Current date
$T	Current time
$N	Current drive
$P	Current drive and directory
$V	Version of DOS in use
$_	Carriage Return/Line Feed
$e	Escape character
$H	Backspace
$Q	= symbol
$G	> symbol
$L	< symbol

Table B.7. (cont.)

Code	Displays
$B	| character
$$	$ symbol
$C	(character
$F	) character
$A	& character
$S	Blank space

Note in the table that the $_ code, which displays a Carriage Return/Line Feed combination, actually breaks the prompt into two lines.

The $H character is a backspace that erases the preceding character. For example, $T displays the system time in the format 12:29:03.25. However, THHH erases the last three characters and displays 12:29:03 instead.

If you use the $P option to display the current drive and directory, the current drive must always be ready. If you attempt to switch to an empty floppy disk drive when the PROMPT command uses $P, the screen displays the message:

```
Not ready reading drive
Abort, Retry, Fail?
```

To return to the command prompt, type F.

The $e character, which represents the Esc key, can be used with display control codes offered by ANSI.SYS to control the screen colors and to customize function keys. These work only if your CONFIG.SYS file contains the command `DEVICE=ANSI.SYS`. Note that the "e" must always be lowercase. See Chapter 12 for additional information.

Examples Entering the following command from the DOS directory of your hard disk:

```
PROMPT Current location - $P -$G
```

changes the system prompt to display

```
Current location - C:\DOS ->
```

Entering the command

```
PROMPT $D $T$H$H$H $B
```

displays a prompt containing the current date, the current time (erasing the hundredths of a second), and a trailing | character, as follows:

```
Mon  4-25-1988 22:29:56 |
```

Entering the PROMPT command:

```
PROMPT $D$H$H$H$H$H$_$T$H$H$H$_$V$P:
```

displays the system prompt with the current date, time, version of DOS, and drive/directory broken into four separate lines, as follows:

```
Mon  4-25
12:35:00
MS DOS Version 4.01
C:\DOS:
```

The command:

```
PROMPT Say the magic word $G
```

changes the system prompt to display

```
Say the magic word >
```

Entering the command:

```
PROMPT
```

with no parameters cancels the newest PROMPT setting and redisplays the default prompt.

See Also   Chapter 12

RAMDRIVE.SYS

See VDISK.SYS.

RECOVER

Attempts to recover files from a disk with damaged sectors.

Version   2 and later

Type   External (RESTORE.COM)

DOS Shell Menu Access   None

Syntax   `RECOVER [drive][path][file name]`

in which *drive*, *path*, and *file name* specify the location and name of the file to be recovered, or

`RECOVER disk drive`

in which *drive* is the name of an entire disk drive to recover.

Usage   Occasionally, a disk sector goes bad and loses some information. The effect of this loss can be anything from a nuisance to a catastrophe. For example, if the bad sector wipes out your Christmas card list of 10 people, you probably can live with that. However, if the bad sector wipes out the File Allocation Table (FAT, the "map" that tells DOS where to find all of the files on the disk), you could lose everything on the disk, and that is indeed unpleasant.

The RECOVER command attempts to recover as much of a lost file as possible. However, it can only recover portions of simple text files that were stored in the bad sector. Never use RECOVER to attempt to recover program files (that is, those with .COM or .EXE extensions). If you recover one of these programs, then run it, there is no telling what the recovered program might do. (Murphy's Law dictates that the recovered program probably will make matters worse.)

RECOVER is a drastic measure that should only be used as an absolute last resort. If you make backups of your files regularly, you probably will never need to use the RECOVER command. If a bad sector wipes out a file or directory, you can merely copy the backup files back onto the disk.

Never use RECOVER on a networked disk drive, nor on a drive that is affected by an ASSIGN, JOIN, or SUBST command. Don't try to use RECOVER to retrieve a file that was accidentally deleted with the DEL or ERASE command—it won't work. In general, only use RECOVER when all else fails!

Examples   Suppose you attempt to access your only copy of the file FORMLET.TXT, which is an ASCII text file. However, the disk drive whirs and buzzes for a moment, and then finally stops to report that it cannot access the file because of a bad sector. A few experiments with DIR and TYPE indicate that most files seem OK, so the damage is isolated to FORMLET.TXT. To recover FORMLET.TXT, enter the command:

```
RECOVER FORMLET.TXT
```

If RECOVER is successful, you should be able to access the information in FORMLET.TXT in the newly created file FILE0001.REC. However, any information that was stored in the disk sector that went bad will not be in the file.

In a more drastic situation, you attempt to use a disk and cannot access any information. Even the DIR command tells you that it cannot display file names because of a bad sector. Don't panic (yet).

First, try to find someone who knows a lot about computers and ask for help. This person might be able to diagnose the problem and fix it without using the drastic RECOVER command.

If you can use XCOPY to copy files off the damaged disk, do so. Save any files that can be saved. After you've copied files to good diskettes, erase them from the damaged disk. Check to see if you have backups of the files that you cannot copy from the damaged disk.

After you've salvaged what you can from the damaged disk, enter the RECOVER command with only a drive specification (for example, `RECOVER C:`. RECOVER attempts to recover as much information as it can from the disk. Unfortunately, it places the recovered information in files named FILEnnnn.REC, in which nnnn is a number starting at 0001; you won't have access to the original file names.

Next you need to figure out exactly what RECOVER did to your files. Use a word processor or text editor to examine the files. When you see data that you recognize, save it under an appropriate file name on a different disk. You might have to spend quite a long time untangling the mess that RECOVER has created, so be prepared for some unpleasant work.

When you finish recovering whatever information you can, remember how unpleasant the experience was, and make backups frequently in the future.

REM

Identifies a remark in a batch file.

Version   1 and later

Type   Used only in batch files and in CONFIG.SYS.

DOS Shell   None
Menu Access

Syntax   `REM comment`

in which *comment* is a line of text.

Usage   REM is generally used to write remarks (notes to yourself) within a batch file that remind you of what various commands do. If ECHO is on, any text to the right of the command appears on the screen while the batch file is running. If ECHO is off, the text is not displayed while the batch file is running.

Examples   The AUTOEXEC.BAT file shown in Listing B.1 includes several comments used to describe the purpose of various commands.

Listing B.1. Sample batch file with comments.

```
@ECHO OFF
REM *********************** AUTOEXEC.BAT
REM --- Put COMSPEC in the environment.
SET COMPSEC=C\DOS\COMMAND.COM

REM --- Set up the PATH.
PATH C:\WS4;C:\DOS;C:\UTILS;C:\DBASE

REM --- Turn off verification to speed processing.
VERIFY OFF

REM --- Install the mouse driver.
C:\MOUSE1\MOUSE

REM --- Make all DOS 4 files accessible.
APPEND /E
APPEND C:\DOS

REM --- Initialize PRINT.COM and design the command prompt.
PRINT /D:LPT1 /Q:20
PROMPT $P$G

REM --- go straight to the DOS Shell.
DOSSHELL
```

See Also   ECHO

RENAME or REN

Changes the name of a file.

Version   1 and later

Type Internal

DOS Shell Menu Access Access the `File System`; then select a file (or files) to rename by highlighting them and pressing the Spacebar, or by clicking once with the mouse. Then, press F10, pull down the File menu, and select `Rename....`

Syntax `RENAME [drive][path]currentfilename newfilename`

in which *drive* and *path* specify the location of the file you want to rename, *currentfilename* is the name of the file you want to rename, and *newfilename* is the new name for the file.

Usage RENAME (and its abbreviated form, REN) allows you to change the name of a file or group of files. It has no effect on the contents of the file. RENAME cannot be used to change the location of a file (that is, you cannot rename C:\UTILS\UNERASE.COM to A:\UNERASE.COM). RENAME always assumes that the file will still be stored on the same disk and directory.

You cannot rename a file to a name that already exists on the specified drive or directory. For example, if you have a file named LEDGER.TXT, and a file named LEDGER.DOC, the command `RENAME LEDGER.TXT LEDGER.DOC` returns the error message `Duplicate file name or File not found`. Both LEDGER.TXT and LEDGER.DOC remain unchanged. (The same error message appears if you attempt to rename a file that does not exist on the specified drive and directory.)

You can also use wildcard characters in the file names. For example, entering the command `RENAME CHAPTER?.TXT CHAPTER?.DOC` attempts to rename all files that begin with CHAPTER and one other character, followed by the extension .TXT, to the same file name, but with the extension .DOC. However, if a duplicate file name is encountered during the renaming process, DOS displays the error message `Duplicate filename or File not found`, and no other files are renamed. You need to enter the commands `DIR *.TXT` and `DIR *.DOC` to figure out which files were renamed and which were not.

Note that the existing file name is always listed first, and the new name is listed second. Hence, the "English" syntax for the RENAME command is RENAME <*existing file name*> TO <*new file name*>. If the file being renamed is not on the current drive and directory, you need only specify the drive and directory for the original file name. RENAME assumes that you intend the same drive and directory for the new file name.

Examples To change the name of the file named FORMLET.TXT to FORMLET.DOC in the current directory, enter the command:

```
RENAME FORMLET.TXT FORMLET.DOC
```

To change the extension of all files in the current and directory from .TXT to .DOC, enter the command:

```
REN *.TXT *.DOC
```

To change the name of the file TEMP.TXT to JUNK.OLD in the directory named \LETTERS on drive C:, enter the command:

```
RENAME C:\LETTERS\TEMP.TXT JUNK.OLD
```

The JUNK.OLD file is automatically stored on the C:\LETTERS drive and directory.

Entering the command:

```
RENAME TEMP.TXT
```

generates the error message Invalid number of parameters, because no new name for the file is specified. TEMP.TXT remains unchanged.

If a command such as:

```
REN INTRO.TXT INTRO.DOC
```

returns the error message Duplicate filename or File not found, then either there is no file named INTRO.TXT in the current directory, or there is already a file named INTRO.DOC in the current directory. The command DIR INTRO.* would show you which problem was causing the error message.

See Also COPY, XCOPY

REPLACE

Replaces files on a disk, or adds new files.

Version 3.2 and later

Type External (REPLACE.EXE)

DOS Shell Menu Access None

Syntax REPLACE [*source drive*][*source path*][*source file name*]
[*destination drive*][*destination path*][*destination file name*]
[/S] [/A] [/P] [/R] [/W] [/U]

in which *source drive*, *source path* and *source file name* indicate the location and names of new files, and *destination drive*, *destination path*, and *destination file name* are the location and name of files to be replaced.

Usage   The REPLACE command replaces existing files with new files of the same name. It is generally used to update existing files, typically replacing old versions of programs with new ones. However, it can be used to add new files to a disk without replacing any files. REPLACE can also search directories on a destination disk for files that need to be replaced.

The syntax of REPLACE might seem backward from what the English equivalent of the command might be. The actual English syntax would be REPLACE <*new files*> OVER <*old files*>.

The various options that you can use to control REPLACE include:

/A   Adds source files that do not already exist on the destination disk, to the destination disk. Cannot be used with /S or /U.

/P   Prompts you before replacing or adding each file; lets you select whether or not to replace or add the file.

/R   Replaces read-only files as well as read/write files.

/S   Searches all subdirectories beneath the destination directory for matching file names.

/W   Tells REPLACE to pause before transferring files, so that you can change diskettes.

/U   (DOS 4 only) Replaces files on the target directory that have a more recent date.

You can combine switches at the end of the REPLACE command.

When REPLACE finishes its job, it returns a value in the ERRORLEVEL variable, so that you can build batch files that make decisions based on an IF ERRORLEVEL or IF NOT ERRORLEVEL statement to respond to possible errors. The ERRORLEVEL values returned by REPLACE are:

0   REPLACE completed normally.

1   REPLACE was aborted because of an error in the command line.

2   No source files were found.

3   A non-existent source or destination path was given.

5   A read-only file was encountered on the destination drive, and no /R option was provided to permit an overwrite.

8   Not enough memory exists to perform the REPLACE.

11   An invalid command was entered; too few or too many parameters.

15   An invalid drive name was specified in the command.

22   An incorrect version of DOS is in use.

Examples   Suppose drive A: contains a diskette with files named LETTER1.TXT, LETTER2.TXT, LETTER3.TXT, and NEWFILE.TXT. The directory named \WPFILES on drive C: contains the files LETTER1.TXT, LETTER2.TXT, and LETTER3.TXT. To replace the files in C:\WPFILES with files of the same name on the disk in drive A:, enter the following command while the \WPFILES directory of drive C: is current:

```
REPLACE A:*.* C:
```

In response to the command, DOS shows the following information:

```
REPLACE Version x.xx (C) Copyright 19xx
Replacing C:\WPFILES\LETTER1.TXT
Replacing C:\WPFILES\LETTER2.TXT
Replacing C:\WPFILES\LETTER3.TXT
3 file(s) replaced
```

Note that only the LETTER1.TXT, LETTER2.TXT, and LETTER3.TXT files on drive C: are replaced. The NEWFILE.TXT file on drive A: is not copied or replaced because there is no file by that name on the destination directory (that is, there is no C:\WPFILES\NEWFILE.TXT to replace).

You could use the /P option in the previous example to have DOS ask you for permission before each replacement. For example, if you entered the command:

```
REPLACE A:*.* C: /P
```

you would see a prompt such as:

```
Replace C:\WPFILES\LETTER1.TXT? (Y/N)
```

Type Y to replace the file; type N to cancel the replacement. After you answer Y or N, REPLACE proceeds, asking for permission before replacing any other files.

If you wanted to add new files from drive A: to drive C:, without replacing any existing files, use the /A option as follows:

```
REPLACE A:*.* C: /A
```

This command displays the message:

```
Adding C:\WPFILES\NEWFILE.TXT
1 file(s) added
```

In this case, LETTER1.TXT, LETTER2.TXT, and LETTER3.TXT remain unchanged on both drives A: and C:. However, because drive C: does not contain a file named NEWFILE.TXT, that file is copied from the source drive A: to the destination drive C:.

You can use the /A and /P options together. For example, the command below:

```
REPLACE A:*.* C: /A/P
```

asks for permission before copying any files from drive A: to drive C:.

Suppose that you copy several files from several different directories from your computer at work. You take the files home for the weekend and make some changes. When you get back to work on Monday, you need to replace all the old files with your new copies. Rather than individually copying each file to the appropriate subdirectory, you can use the /S option with REPLACE to have it automatically locate the appropriate subdirectories and replace the files.

To ensure that REPLACE has access to all the subdirectories on the destination disk, you must run the REPLACE command from the root directory. For example, assuming you want to replace old files on drive C: with new copies of those files stored in drive A:, enter the following command:

```
CD\
REPLACE A:*.* C: /S
```

Note that unless you use the /R switch at the end of the command, REPLACE will not overwrite files that are marked read-only by an ATTRIB +R command. Therefore, the command:

```
REPLACE A:*.COM C: /R
```

replaces all files on drive C: that have the extension .COM with copies of files (with the same name) from drive A:. Even those files defined as read-only are replaced.

If you use the /W switch, REPLACE pauses to allow you to place a source diskette in the disk drive. For example, if you enter the command:

```
REPLACE A:*.* C: /W
```

REPLACE displays the prompt Press any key to begin replacing file(s) before going to work. You can insert a new disk and press any key to begin the replacement.

See Also   COPY, XCOPY

RESTORE

Restores backup files from floppy disks.

Version 2 and later

Type External (RESTORE.COM)

DOS Shell Select DOS Utilities... from the Main Group screen, and Restore Fixed
Menu Access Disk from the DOS Utilities group screen.

Syntax
```
RESTORE backup drive [destination drive]
[destination path][destination files]
[/S] [/P] [/B:date] [/A:date] [/E:time] [/L:time] [/M] [/N]
```

in which *backup drive* is the name of the drive containing the backup diskettes; *destination drive*, *destination path* and *destination files* identify the
location and names of the files to be restored; and *date* and *time* represent
dates and times when files were created or last changed.

Usage RESTORE retrieves files created with the BACKUP command from diskettes to the hard disk. (RESTORE cannot access files that were copied or
created with any command other than BACKUP.) You can use RESTORE
to recover a single file, a group of files, or all of the files on a disk.

When you use RESTORE, it requests that you insert backup diskettes
into a floppy disk drive in the same order in which they were created during BACKUP. For this reason, it is vitally important that you number your
BACKUP diskettes clearly as you create them. If you insert a disk out of
order, DOS displays the prompt Warning! Diskette is out of sequence and
prompts you to remove that diskette and replace it with the appropriate
one.

RESTORE provides several options to help you clearly specify the
exact files that you want to restore. Note that options that use the date and
time parameters require you to specify a date or time in valid DOS format.
For example, if you are using the default United States settings, the valid
format for dates is mm-dd-yy (for example, 12-31-88), and the valid
format for times is hh:mm:ss (for example, 13:30:00 for 1:30 in the afternoon). The
options for RESTORE are as follows:

/A:*date* Restores all files that were created or modified on or after the
specified *date*.

/B:*date* Restores all files that were created or modified on or before the
specified *date*.

/L:time	Restores all files that were created or modified on or later than the specified *time*.
/E:time	Restores all files that were created or modified on or earlier than the specified *time*.
/S	Restores all files in the specified directory and in all subdirectories.
/P	Causes RESTORE to display a prompt requesting permission to restore read-only files, hidden files, or files that have been modified since the last BACKUP.
/M	Restores only files that have been modified or deleted since the last BACKUP.
/N	Restores only files that no longer exists on the destination disk.

When using either /L or /E to specify a time, be sure to also use /A or /B to specify a date.

Never attempt to use RESTORE when an ASSIGN, JOIN, or SUBST command is active. Doing so might damage the directory structure of your hard disk and cause a loss of data.

When RESTORE is finished, it sets the ERRORLEVEL variable to one of the values below:

0 RESTORE completed successfully.

1 No files to restore were found.

2 Some files were not restored because they were in use by others (on a network).

3 RESTORE procedure was canceled because the user typed Ctrl-Break or Ctrl-C.

4 RESTORE was aborted due to a system error.

You can use the IF ERRORLEVEL command in a batch file to determine whether or not a RESTORE command was successful.

PC DOS Versions 2 to 3.2 support only the /S and /P switches. Versions 3.3 and 4 do not restore the system files, nor COMMAND.COM. These must be copied using the SYS command. In PC DOS, the system files are named IBMBIO.COM and IBMDOS.COM. In MS-DOS, these are named MSDOS.SYS and IO.SYS.

Examples   Suppose you use BACKUP regularly to back up all of the files on your hard disk. Then you accidentally erase all files on the C:\UTILS directory. To restore those files, insert you first BACKUP diskette in drive A:, and from the drive C: prompt enter the command:

```
RESTORE A: C:\UTILS\*.*
```

DOS presents the instructions:

```
Insert backup diskette nn in drive A:
Strike any key when ready
```

in which *nn* represents the backup disk number that you are to insert in drive A:. Once you insert the disk and press Enter, DOS displays the following prompts and proceeds with the restoration:

```
*** Files were backed up 09/26/1989 ***
*** Restoring files from drive A: *** Diskette: nn
```

Referring to the above situation, suppose you accidentally erase some, but not all, of the files that are on the \UTILS subdirectory. In that case, use the /N switch to limit the restoration to only files that no longer exist on the \UTILS directory. Enter the command:

```
RESTORE A: C:\UTILS\*.* /N
```

See Also   BACKUP

RMDIR or RD

Removes an empty directory.

Version   2 and later

Type   Internal

DOS Shell Menu Access   Access the File System, and select the directory that you want to delete from the Directory Tree. If the Files Area shows that the directory contains files, these must be moved to another directory, or erased. Then press F10 to pull down the File menu, and select Delete....

Syntax   RMDIR [*drive*][*path*]*directory name*

The command can be abbreviated as:

RD [*drive*][*path*]*directory name*

in which *drive* is the name of the disk drive containing the directory, and *path* is the name of the directory (or subdirectory), that you wish to remove.

Usage   RMDIR (and its abbreviated equivalent, RD) lets you remove a directory from a disk. You cannot remove the root directory, the current directory, or a directory that contains files. Attempting to remove any such directories displays the error message Invalid path, not directory, or directory not empty and leaves the directory intact.

To delete a directory, first switch to that directory using the `CHDIR` or `CD` command. Then, use `DIR` to see if it contains any files. `COPY` any files that you want to keep to another directory or a diskette. Then use `ERASE *.*` to erase all files. Enter `DIR` again to be sure that all files have been erased. Any files that DOS refuses to erase are probably set to read-only status. Use the command `ATTRIB -R *.*` to set the files to read/write status, and then enter the `ERASE *.*` command again.

After the DIR command indicates that there are no files left on the subdirectory (except for `.` and `..`), use the `CD` or `CHDIR` command to change to another directory. Then, enter the `RMDIR` or `RD` command with the appropriate directory name to remove the subdirectory.

Examples   This example offers a typical scenario that demonstrates how to remove a directory. Suppose you need to free some storage space on your hard disk, so you decide to remove a directory named \TEMP that you have not used in a long time.

First, change to that directory using the command `CD \TEMP`. Then, enter the command `DIR` to display the files in that directory

You decide that only one file, named IMPORTNT.TXT, is worth saving, so you enter the command `COPY IMPORTNT.TXT C:\WP\WPFILES` to copy the file to the \WP\WPFILES directory (for example).

Then, enter the command `ERASE *.*` to erase all files on the directory. When you enter `DIR` again, you discover that not all of the files have been erased. Therefore, enter the command `ATTRIB -R *.*` to set all remaining files to read/write status. After you enter the `ERASE *.*` and `DIR` commands, you see that the only files remaining on the subdirectory are `.` and `..`.

Now you are ready to remove the subdirectory. First, enter the command:

`CD\`

to move to another directory. Then enter the command:

`RD \TEMP`

to remove the directory.

When you enter the TREE command or return to the DOS Shell File System, note that the \TEMP directory no longer exists.

See Also   MKDIR, CHDIR

SET

Enters and displays environment settings.

Version   2 and later

Type   Internal

DOS Shell   None
Menu Access

Syntax   SET [*variable[=value]*]

in which *variable* is a variable name and *value* is the value you want to store in that variable.

Usage   The environment is an area in RAM reserved for storing certain settings, such as the drive and directory location of the command processor (COM-MAND.COM), the customized PROMPT in use (if any), and the current search PATH.

Parameters defined in the environment can be accessed from within batch files. To do so, use a variable name surrounded by percent signs (no blank spaces), as follows:

%COMPSEC%   Returns the location of the command processor.

%PROMPT%   Returns the current customized prompt setting.

%PATH%   Returns the path used to search for program files.

%APPEND%   Returns the path used to search for non-program files, assuming that an APPEND /E command stored the APPEND setting in the environment.

To view the environment settings from the DOS prompt, enter the command SET with no parameters.

You can also use SET to store your own information in the environment, which is sometimes handy with batch files. Be careful not to use the variable names COMSPEC, PROMPT, PATH, or APPEND for your own variables, because these are already used by DOS. Also, the variable name may not contain spaces. Because the size of the environment is limited, try to use short variable names.

By default, DOS sets aside 127 bytes for the environment. You can use the COMMAND command to increase the size of the environment; however, you should do so early in your CONFIG.SYS file, using the SHELL command, because as soon as DOS loads a memory-resident program, you can no longer expand the size of the environment.

The named variable can be accessed from any batch file using the syntax %*variablename*%. Examples are provided in the discussion of the SHIFT command in this appendix, and in Chapters 13 and 14.

Examples   To store the name "Janice" in an environmental variable named Name, enter the command:

```
SET NAME=Janice
```

To view the current status of the environment, enter the command:

```
SET
```

See Chapters 13 and 14 for examples of batch files that use environment variables.

See Also   PATH, PROMPT, SHIFT, COMMAND

SHARE

Provides support for file sharing and diskette change protection.

Version   3 and later

Type   External (SHARE.EXE)

DOS Shell Menu Access   None

Syntax   `SHARE [/F:filespace] [/L:locks]`

in which *filespace* sets the amount of memory space to be used for file sharing, and *locks* sets the maximum number of file and record locks.

Usage   SHARE allows two or more programs that are running simultaneously on one computer to share files. (This is different from a network, in which multiple computers share files and other resources.)

After SHARE is loaded, all programs that support SHARE must check to see if a file is in use by another program before modifying data in that file. If another program has exclusive use of the file (that is, the file is locked), then the current program is denied access. If the other program has a record or several records locked, the current program can view but not change the locked records. (However, a particular program that uses SHARE might impose other rules.)

SHARE is also used with Version 4 of DOS to support hard disk partitions larger than 32MB. If you use partitions larger than 32MB with DOS 4, then the SHARE.EXE file must be in the root directory of the hard disk or in the directory specified by the SHELL command in your CONFIG.SYS file.

Some floppy disk drives can keep track of whether or not the disk in the drive has changed since the last access. DOS does not take advantage of this feature until you load the SHARE program.

You can load the SHARE program in your CONFIG.SYS file using the INSTALL (not DEVICE) command. Optionally, you can load SHARE directly from the command prompt.

If you do not use the /F: switch in the SHARE command, DOS sets aside 2,048 bytes of memory to manage file sharing. If you do not use the /L: switch, DOS defaults to a maximum of 20 locks.

Specifying /F: and /L: values larger than the default values increases the amount of memory usage proportionately.

Examples To install SHARE (using the default settings) directly from the command prompt, enter the command:

```
SHARE
```

To install SHARE during system startup (specifying 4,096 bytes of RAM for file sharing management and specifying a maximum of 40 locks), include the following command in your CONFIG.SYS file (assuming that the SHARE.EXE file is stored in a directory named \DOS):

```
INSTALL=C:\DOS\SHARE.EXE /F:4096 /L:40
```

See Also DRIVER.SYS

SHELL

Installs the command processor.

Version 3 and later

Type Internal (used in the CONFIG.SYS file)

DOS Shell Menu Access None

Syntax `SHELL=[drive][path]file name`

in which *drive*, *path*, and *file name* identify the location and name of the command processor.

Usage SHELL installs the program that DOS uses to process commands. Except in very rare cases in which a programmer develops his own command processor, you must use COMMAND.COM with DOS.

SHELL does not affect the COMSPEC environment variable. Therefore, if you use the SHELL command to install the command processor from a disk file, your CONFIG.SYS file should also use the SET COMSPEC command to set the COMSPEC variable to the same directory.

Examples   The following command, when included in your CONFIG.SYS file, installs the DOS COMMAND.COM command processor from the C:\DOS directory in memory:

```
SHELL=C:\DOS\COMMAND.COM /P /E:256
```

The next command, included in the AUTOEXEC.BAT file, sets the COMSPEC environment variable to point to the same command processor:

```
SET COMSPEC=C:\DOS\COMMAND.COM
```

See Also   COMMAND

SHIFT

Shifts parameters in a batch file.

Version   2 and later

Type   Internal (batch files only)

DOS Shell Menu Access   None

Syntax   SHIFT

Usage   SHIFT moves the parameters passed to a batch file one position to the left. That is, if %1 is LETTER1.TXT and %2 is LETTER2.TXT, then after the SHIFT command, %1 becomes LETTER2.TXT and %2 no longer has a value. SHIFT is used mainly to create batch files that can accept more than the usual limit of nine parameters (or an unknown number of parameters).

Examples   The sample batch file below, which we'll assume is named TEST.BAT, can be used to demonstrate how SHIFT works on your own computer.

```
ECHO OFF
:Top
```

```
ECHO 1= %1
ECHO 2= %2
ECHO 3= %3
ECHO 4= %4
ECHO 5= %5
ECHO Shifting now...
ECHO.
SHIFT
IF NOT .%0 -- . GOTO Top
ECHO Demo over
```

If you create this batch file, you should then execute it, passing at least two parameters to it. For example, the command below:

```
TEST Dog Cat Mouse Fish
```

passes four parameters.

After entering the command, the screen shows:

```
1= Dog
2= Cat
3= Mouse
4= Fish
5=
Shifting now...
```

Then, the SHIFT command shifts the parameters values, and the batch file shows the contents again, as below:

```
1= Cat
2= Mouse
3= Fish
4=
5=
Shifting now...
```

After the next SHIFT, the batch file shows:

```
1= Mouse
2= Fish
3=
4=
5=
Shifting now...
```

This process continues until all the parameters are empty.

See the section titled "Passing More than Nine Parameters" in Chapter 14.

See Also FOR, SET

SORT

Sorts lines of text which are input from a command, device, or file and outputs the sorted text to a file or device.

Version 2 and later

Type External (SORT.EXE)

DOS Shell Menu Access None (although in the File System, you can select a sort order for file names by selecting Display Options... from the Options pull-down menu).

Syntax SORT [/R] [/+start column]

in which *start column* is the column on which the sort is based.

Usage SORT can act both as a command and as a filter for other commands. Because it is an external program, it must be accessible for use. Typically, SORT.EXE is stored in a directory that is included in your PATH command, so that you always have access to it.

As a filter, you can use SORT to the right of a command and | character. For example, the command DIR | SORT displays the directory sorted alphabetically by file name. As a command, SORT can be used to sort an ASCII text file. For example, the command SORT ASCII.TXT sorts the rows in a file named ASCII.TXT into alphabetical or numerical format.

The /R option causes a file to be sorted in reverse order (that is, Z to A). The /+ option specifies that the sort begin at a certain column in the file or display.

Note that SORT performs its sort in a very "literal" manner; it does not "process" the information that it is sorting. For example, when sorting dates, SORT considers 12/31/87 to be later than 1/1/88, because 12 is larger than 1 (it does not take the year into consideration). When sorting times, 5:00 p.m. is considered earlier than 8:00 a.m., because 5 is smaller than 8.

Numbers are sorted properly only if they are correctly aligned. For example, the following column of numbers would be sorted properly:

1.0

223.3

1234.5

99

But the next column of numbers would not be sorted properly, because it is not right-aligned:

```
1.0
223.3
1234.5
99
```

SORT provides only a rudimentary sorting capability. For more realistic sorts (and sorts within sorts) you need a more powerful program, such as a database management system or a spreadsheet.

Examples   The output from a DIR command displays the file name, extension, size, and date and time of creation of the most recent change. The information is consistently displayed in the following columns:

Section of DIR	Column
Filename	1
Extension	10
Size	15
Date	24
Time	34

To display the files in a directory in alphabetical order, enter the command:

```
DIR | SORT
```

To display the files sorted by size (smallest to largest), enter the command:

```
DIR | SORT /+15
```

To display the files sorted by date, and to display the output on the printer, enter the command:

```
DIR | SORT /+24 > PRN
```

Suppose you have a file named NAMELST.TXT, which contains the following information:

```
Zorro  Albert  123 A St.
Moore  Renee   P.O. Box 2800
Adams  Arthur  988 Grape St.
```

Entering the command:

```
SORT < NAMELST.TXT
```

displays the names in alphabetical order, as follows:

```
Adams   Arthur   988 Grape St.
Moore   Renee    P.O. Box 2800
Zorro   Albert   123 A St.
```

Entering the command:

```
SORT < NAMELST.TXT /R
```

displays the contents of the file sorted in reverse order (Z– A), as follows:

```
Zorro   Albert   123 A St.
Moore   Renee    P.O. Box 2800
Adams   Arthur   988 Grape St.
```

The following command displays the contents of the NAMELST.TXT file sorted by street address (which begins in the sixteenth column in the file):

```
SORT < NAMELST.TXT /+16
```

The resulting display from this command is:

```
Zorro   Albert   123 A St.
Adams   Arthur   988 Grape St.
Moore   Renee    P.O. Box 2800
```

Note that when sorting a column that contains both numbers and letters, as in the previous example, the numbers are listed before the letters (that is, 988 comes before P.O. Box).

To actually sort a file, as opposed to just displaying its contents in sorted order, use an output redirection symbol and a new file name. For example, the following command creates a new copy of the NAMELST.TXT file, sorted by last name, in a file called NEWLIST.TXT:

```
SORT < NAMELST.TXT > NEWLIST.TXT
```

If you were to enter the command TYPE NAMELST.TXT after entering this command, you would see that the file does indeed contain the same information as NAMELST.TXT, but in sorted order, as follows:

```
Adams   Arthur   988 Grape St.
```

```
Moore   Renee   P.O. Box 2800
Zorro   Albert  123 A St.
```

To replace the contents of NAMELST.TXT with the contents of NEWLIST.TXT, and then erase NEWLIST.TXT, enter the command:

```
COPY NEWLIST.TXT NAMELST.TXT
```

and then the command:

```
ERASE  NEWLIST.TXT
```

See Also DIR

STACKS

Changes the number of stacks used by hardware interrupts

Version 3.2 and later

Type Internal (used only in CONFIG.SYS)

DOS Shell Menu Access None

Syntax STACKS=*number,size*

in which *number* specifies the number of stacks (in the range of 8 to 32), and *size* specifies the size (in bytes) of each stack (in the range of 32 to 512).

Usage Very few computers need to use the STACKS directive. It is only required when a particular program brings the entire system to a halt, displaying the message Fatal: Internal Stack Failure, System Halted. You must turn off the computer at this point (you cannot do anything else).

When you turn on the computer again, do not run the problem program. Instead, examine your CONFIG.SYS file to see if it already contains a STACKS command.

If your CONFIG.SYS file contains the command STACKS=0,0, then the computer might not support dynamic stacks. You should not change the STACKS setting (and, therefore, you cannot use the program that caused the Fatal error).

If no STACKS command is listed, then your system is using the default of 9 stacks with 128 bytes each. Try increasing the number of stacks, rather than the size; then, reboot (press Ctrl-Alt-Del) and try running the program that halted the system. You might need to experiment, raising the number of stacks a little each time, until the program runs successfully.

Examples   The following command, when included in the CONFIG.SYS file, sets the number of stacks to 12, each using the default of 128 bytes:

STACKS=12,128

SUBST

Substitutes a subdirectory for a disk drive.

Version   3.1 and later

Type   External (SUBST.EXE)

DOS Shell   None
Menu Access

Syntax   SUBST [*original drive new drive new path*] [/D]

in which *original drive* is the drive that you wish to "hide," and *new drive* and *new path* specify the drive and path that are to replace the drive being hidden.

Usage   SUBST lets you use a directory in place of a disk drive. It is generally used to "trick" programs that are incapable of using directories into using them. For example, suppose you have an old accounting package that can only store its data on a diskette in drive B:. You prefer that the program store its data on the subdirectory named \ACCT\DATA on your hard disk drive C:. The SUBST command allows you to "trick" the accounting program into doing just that.

The original drive specified in the SUBST command need not really exist on your computer. For example, if your accounting package insists on storing data on drive B:, and your computer does not even have a drive B:, SUBST still allows you to substitute a directory for drive B:.

The original drive that you are attempting to substitute cannot be the current drive. For example, if you want to use subdirectory C:\WPDATA as a substitute for drive B:, drive B: cannot be the current directory when you enter the SUBST command.

The new drive can be any drive from A: to E:, or higher if you've used the LASTDRIVE option in your CONFIG.SYS file to specify a larger highest-drive name (see the LASTDRIVE entry in this appendix).

After a substitution is in effect, it affects all DOS commands, which can make things a bit confusing. For example, if you set up drive and path C:\TEMP as the substitute for drive D:, then a command such as DIR D: will actually show you the files stored on C:\TEMP.

SUBST cannot be used with a network disk drive. When a substitution is in effect, do not use the ASSIGN, BACKUP, CHDIR, CHKDSK, DISKCOMP, DISKCOPY, FDISK, FORMAT, JOIN, LABEL, MKDIR, PATH, RESTORE, or RMDIR commands. Before using any of these commands, cancel the substitution. To do so, use the syntax:

```
SUBST original drive /D
```

To see if a substitution is in effect at any time, enter the SUBST command without any parameters.

Examples The following series of steps shows how to set up, use, and then delete a substitution. Suppose your computer does not have a drive B:, and you want to use a program that can only use a drive B:. You decide to create a directory named \FAKE_B on your hard disk drive C: to store the information that the program usually stores on drive B:.

First, be sure the hard disk is the current drive, and enter the command:

```
MD \FAKE_B
```

to create the new directory (if it does not already exist).

Next, use the SUBST command to substitute C:\FAKE_B for drive B: by entering the command:

```
SUBST B: C:\FAKE_B
```

As a test, enter the following commands at the command prompt to store a simple file on this phony drive B: (the ^Z character is entered by pressing the F6 key or by typing Ctrl-Z):

```
COPY CON B:TEST.TXT
This is a test
^Z
```

To verify that the file TEST.TXT is stored on "drive B," enter the following commands at the command prompt:

```
DIR B:
TYPE B:TEST.TXT
```

You can see from the results of these commands that the TEST.TXT file actually exists on the fake drive B:. If you enter the command:

```
SUBST
```

the screen shows you that C:\FAKE_B is being used to act as drive B:, as follows:

```
B: => C:\FAKE_B
```

You can now run the old program that stores and reads files only on disk drive B:. When you finish using that program, return things to normal. To cancel the substitution, enter the command:

```
SUBST B: /D
```

Now if you enter the command:

```
DIR B:
```

you receive only the error message Invalid drive specification, because there is no longer a fake drive B:. Where are the files that were being stored on this fake drive B:? They are on the substitution drive and directory, C:\FAKE_B. To verify this, enter the command

```
DIR C:\FAKE_B
```

and display the files in the directory.

For added safety, you can create a batch file that sets up the substitution, runs the "old" program, and then automatically cancels the SUBST command. That way, you don't need to worry about inadvertently leaving the SUBST command active when you've finished using the program that requires the fake drive. The following batch file presents an example that runs a program named OLDACCT:

```
REM **************** FAKEIT.BAT
C:
IF NOT EXIST C:\FAKE_B\*.*: MD \FAKE_B
SUBST B: C:\FAKE_B
CD \OLDACCT
OLDACCT
SUBST B: /D
```

See Also   ASSIGN, JOIN

SWITCHES

Disables extended keyboard function.

Version   4

Type   Internal (used only in CONFIG.SYS)

Syntax   `SWITCHES = /K`

Usage   Disables extended keyboard functions on the enhanced keyboard, to provide compatibility with programs designed for use on conventional keyboards.

Example   To mimic a conventional keyboard, even though an enhanced keyboard is attached to the computer, include the command:

`SWITCHES=/K`

in your CONFIG.SYS files. This disables extended keys, like F11 and F12, thereby providing compatibility with programs the "expect" a conventional keyboard.

See Also   CONFIG.SYS

SYS

Makes a bootable DOS system disk.

Version   1 and later

Type   External (SYS.COM)

DOS Shell   None
Menu Access

Syntax   `SYS drive`

in which *drive* is the name of the drive that contains the diskette to which you copy the DOS system tracks.

Usage   Whenever you start your computer, it automatically reads the DOS system files from the disk to "pull itself up by its bootstraps" (or "boot" for short). If the computer cannot find the system files that it needs, DOS displays the error message `Non-system disk or disk error` and waits for you to insert a diskette that contains the system files (also called the system tracks).

    If your computer has a hard disk, it most likely boots from the root directory of the hard disk. You only see the Non-system disk error if you turn on your computer without first opening the drive door or removing the disk from drive A:

If your computer does not have a hard disk, drive A: must contain a bootable diskette when you turn on the computer; otherwise the Non-system disk error message is displayed. To make additional bootable diskettes for your computer, you can use either the FORMAT /S command, or the SYS command.

Generally, you use the SYS command to make a bootable diskette from a diskette that is already formatted and already contains files. (If you use the alternative FORMAT /S command, it erases all files in the disk!) There are several rules that you must follow before using SYS:

- The diskette in the current drive must be a system (bootable) diskette itself.

- The diskette to which you are copying the system tracks must already be formatted.

- The diskette to which you are copying the system tracks must have sufficient space to store the system tracks, otherwise DOS displays the error message No room for system on destination disk.

Keep in mind that the SYS command copies to the diskette only the files necessary to start the computer, which are usually hidden. SYS does not copy the COMMAND.COM file to the new disk. Nor does it not copy your CONFIG.SYS or AUTOEXEC.BAT files, so the new bootable disk might not behave exactly as your original Startup diskette (unless you copy CONFIG.SYS and AUTOEXEC.BAT to the new Startup diskette yourself).

You cannot use the SYS command to write on a network drive, nor on a pseudo-drive created with the ASSIGN or SUBST commands.

When formatting your own diskettes, you can use the /S switch with the FORMAT command to perform the same operations that the SYS command does. Optionally, you can use the /B switch with the FORMAT command to reserve enough space so that SYS can be used later to store the system tracks.

Examples   Suppose you purchase a new word processing program for use on your laptop computer, which does not have a hard disk. However, you want to be able to boot from the word processing program's disk.

To do so, start your computer with your usual Startup diskette in drive A:. Then, put the new word processing disk in drive B:, and enter the command:

```
SYS B:
```

at the command prompt. If there is sufficient room on the word processing disk, DOS displays the message System transferred.

Actually, a better (and more reliable) technique would be to make a bootable diskette, and then copy the word processing programs to the new disk. That way, you can store the original word processing diskette in a safe place, in case the copy becomes lost or damaged.

To use this technique, start your computer in the usual manner, with your Startup diskette in drive A:. Then put a new, blank, unformatted diskette (*not* the word processing diskette!) in drive B:, and enter the command:

```
FORMAT B: /S
```

at the command prompt.

After DOS finishes formatting the new diskette, and the command prompt reappears, you can enter the following commands to copy your CONFIG.SYS and AUTOEXEC.BAT files to the new bootable diskette:

```
COPY CONFIG.SYS B:
COPY AUTOEXEC.BAT B:
```

Then, remove the DOS diskette from drive A: and put the original word processing diskette in its place (in drive A:). Enter the command:

```
COPY *.* B:
```

When copying is complete, remove all diskettes, and label the new disk something like "Bootable Word Processing Diskette." To test the new diskette, turn off the computer, and then use the new "Bootable Word Processing Diskette" in drive A: to start the computer. Your computer should start correctly.

You can use the DIR command to verify that the diskette contains all the word processing programs, or merely enter the command required to start your word processing program.

See Also   FORMAT

TIME

View or change the system time.

Version   1 and later

Type   External in Version 1.0; Internal in all later versions

DOS Shell   Select DOS Utilities... from the Main Group screen, and Set Date and
Menu Access   Time from the DOS Utilities . . . screen.

Syntax   `TIME [hh:mm:ss.hn][A|P]`

in which *hh* is the hour (0 to 23), *mm* is the minutes (0 to 59), *ss* is the seconds (0 to 59), and *hn* is hundredths of seconds.

Usage   TIME lets you view or change the system time. The time is expressed on a 24-hour clock, where 0 is midnight, 12 is 12:00 noon, 13 is 1:00 in the afternoon, and 23 is 11:00 p.m. Hence, the time 23:59:59.99 is one hundredth of a second before midnight, and 00:00:00.00 is exactly midnight.

On most computers, the time is kept accurate by a small internal clock, which runs even when the computer is turned off. The clock, however, isn't perfect, and it sometimes can lose track of time. The TIME command lets you see what time the computer "thinks" it is, and, optionally, lets you change that time.

The system time displayed by the TIME command is the one that is used to time-stamp files on disk. It is also the time used by other programs, such as spreadsheets and database managers.

Only DOS 4 supports the A and P options; which can be used to specify A.M. or P.M.

Examples   To check the current system time on your computer, enter the command:

`TIME`

The screen replies with a message such as:

`Current time is 13:47:58.68  Enter new time:`

If you merely press the Enter key at this point, the time remains unchanged. Optionally, you can type a new time, using the hh:mm:ss.hh format. (Actually, you need to enter only hh:mm.) For example, to change the current time to 1:50 p.m., type 13:50 at the `Enter new time:` prompt and press Enter.

To enter the current time as 1:50 in the afternoon, using DOS 4, you could enter the command:

`TIME 1:50p`

See Also   DATE

TREE

Displays the directory structure.

Version   2 and later

Type   External (TREE.COM)

DOS Shell Menu Access   None (DOS displays the directory tree whenever you access the File System).

Syntax   Versions 2 through 3.3 use:

TREE [*drive*] [/F]

Version 4 uses:

TREE [*drive*][*path*] [/F] [/A]

in which *drive* is the name of the drive whose directory structure you want to display, and *path* is the starting directory for the TREE display.

Usage   TREE displays the names of all directories on a disk. If you include the /F option, TREE also shows the names of all the files on each directory and subdirectory. If you do not specify a drive name in the command, the current drive is assumed.

All versions of DOS prior to 4 display all directories on the disk, regardless of which directory is current. In DOS 4, only the current directory and directories beneath are displayed, unless you specify the root directory as the starting directory.

DOS 4 displays the directory in a vertical tree structure, similar to the way it appears on the File System screen. In DOS 4, you can also specify the /A option to use only ASCII characters in the display, which provides for universal code page acceptance, and speeds printing slightly.

Examples   To view the names of all directories on the current drive, enter the command:

TREE

or, if you are using DOS 4, enter the command:

TREE \

To view the names of all files on each directory, enter the command:

TREE /F

or, in DOS 4:

TREE \ /F

To pause the information displayed by the TREE command, use the MORE filter as follows:

```
TREE | MORE
```

or

```
TREE /F | MORE
```

To sort the list of directory names and pause the display (using DOS 3.3 or earlier), enter the command:

```
TREE | SORT | MORE
```

To print a copy of the directory tree, enter the command:

```
TREE > PRN
```

or in DOS 4:

```
TREE \ > PRN
```

To print a list of all files in all directories, using DOS version 3.3 or earlier, enter the command:

```
TREE /F > PRN
```

or, in DOS 4:

```
TREE \ /F > PRN
```

In DOS Versions 3.3 and earlier, you can display a summarized TREE structure without all the blank lines and redundant subdirectory listings and limit the display to lines that contain the word "Path" by entering the following command:

```
TREE | FIND "Path"
```

or, to control scrolling:

```
TREE | FIND "Path" | MORE
```

See Also   DIR, MKDIR, FIND, MORE

TYPE

Displays the contents of a file.

Version 1 and later

Type Internal

**DOS Shell
Menu Access** Access the File System and select one file from the Files Area by highlighting the file and pressing Enter, or by clicking once with the mouse. Then, press F10 and select View from the File pull-down menu. (Press Esc when you finish viewing the file.)

Syntax TYPE [*drive*][*path*]*file name*

in which *drive* and *path* specify the location, and *file name* is the name of the file you want to view.

Usage TYPE provides a quick and easy way to look at the contents of a file. If the file that you display contains only ASCII text characters, the output is quite readable. However, if you use TYPE with a program, spreadsheet, database, or some word processing files, the contents seem to consist of strange graphics characters (such as happy faces) and the computer might even occasionally beep.

   If you need to stop the TYPE command before it is finished, press Ctrl-Break (or Ctrl-C).

Examples To view the contents of a file named READ.ME on the current drive and directory, enter the command:

TYPE READ.ME

To pause the TYPE command so that it displays only a single screenful of information at a time, use the | MORE filter, as follows:

TYPE READ.ME | MORE

To send the output of the TYPE command to the printer, use the > PRN symbol and device name, as follows:

TYPE READ.ME > PRN

Before printing a file, use the TYPE command without > PRN to preview the file's contents on the screen. If the file contains strange characters, don't use > PRN to print it.

If the file that you want to view is not on the current drive and/or directory, specify the drive and directory before the file name, as follows:

```
TYPE C:\NEWWARE\READ.ME
```

See Also   PRINT, MORE

VDISK.SYS

Creates a RAM disk. (Also called RAMDRIVE.SYS in versions of MS-DOS)

Version   3 and later (RAMDRIVE.SYS: 3.2 and later of MS-DOS only)

Type   Device driver (installed with a DEVICE command in CONFIG.SYS)

DOS Shell Menu Access   None

Syntax   DOS Version 3.2:

```
DEVICE=[drive][path]VDISK.SYS [size] [sectors] [entries] [/E]
```

DOS Versions 3.3 and 4:

```
DEVICE=[drive][path]VDISK.SYS [size] [sectors] [entries]
[/E:max] [/X:max]
```

Some non-IBM computers use RAMDRIVE.SYS rather than VDISK.SYS, with the general syntax:

```
DEVICE=[drive][path]RAMDRIVE.SYS [size] [sectors] [entries] [/E]
[/A]
```

in which *drive* and *path* are the location of the VDISK.SYS or RAMDRIVE.SYS file, and *size*, *sectors*, *entries*, and *max* are described in more detail below.

Usage   VDISK.SYS and RAMDRIVE.SYS both function in the same way. They create a RAM disk, or virtual disk, in memory. Check your computer's DOS manual, or the root directory or DOS directory on disk, to determine whether VDISK.SYS or RAMDRIVE.SYS is available on your computer. This section focuses on the more common VDISK.SYS device driver, most of which is directly relevant to RAMDRIVE.SYS as well. Any important differences are noted.

A RAM disk formats memory—either conventional RAM, extended memory, or expanded memory—as though it were a disk drive. DOS treats the RAM disk as though it were a real (physical) disk; all the operations that you normally use to manage disk files work with the RAM disk as well.

The major differences between a RAM disk and a physical disk are:

1. The RAM disk is 10 to 20 times faster than a physical disk.

2. Everything is erased from the RAM disk as soon as the power is cut off.

The first optional parameter, *size*, specifies the size of the RAM disk in kilobytes. If omitted, the default value of 64KB is used. The range of acceptable values is 1 to the maximum amount of available memory on your computer. If you specify a size that leaves less than 64KB of conventional memory available, VDISK automatically adjusts the size of the RAM disk so that it leaves 100KB of conventional RAM for programs.

Because part of the RAM disk is used for the boot record, File Allocation Table (FAT), and directory (exactly as on a physical disk), the actual amount of available storage on the RAM disk is somewhat less than the *size* specified in the DEVICE command.

The second optional parameter, *sectors*, specifies the sector size in bytes. Acceptable values are 128, 256, and 512. If you omit this option or specify an invalid sector size, DOS uses the default value of 128.

In general, the larger the sector size, the faster the performance of the RAM disk. However, because files are stored in entire sectors and never in parts of sectors, a large sector size wastes disk space if you want to use the RAM disk to store many small files.

The third optional parameter, *entries*, specifies the maximum number of files that can be stored on the RAM disk. Any number in the range of 2 to 512 is acceptable. If omitted, the default value of 64 is used.

Each directory entry uses 32 bytes of the RAM disk (including empty entries). If the value you specify in the *entries* parameter is not a multiple of the sector size, VDISK adjusts your entry parameter upward. For example, if you specify 9 directory entries and a 128-byte sector size, DOS adjusts the parameter upward to allow 12 directory entries. The reason is that $9 \times 32 = 288$, which is not evenly divisible by 128. However, $12 \times 32 = 384$, which *is* evenly divisible by 128.

If the size of the RAM disk is too small to hold the boot record, FAT, directory, and two additional sectors, the number of *entries* specified in your DEVICE command is rounded down until these conditions can be met. If VDISK cannot round down far enough to meet these conditions, DOS displays an error message and the RAM disk is not installed.

Versions 3.2 through 4 of DOS offer the /E switch, which allows you to specify extended memory, rather than conventional RAM, for the RAM disk. The /E switch also lets you specify the maximum number of sectors that DOS can pass to the RAM disk at one time. To do so, follow the /E switch with a colon and a values of 1 through 8. If you omit a value, DOS assumes an 8 (the largest setting).

DOS Version 4 also offers the /X switch, which installs the RAM disk in expanded memory. Many versions of RAMDRIVE.SYS also allow you to install the RAM disk in expanded memory, but RAMDRIVE.SYS requires that you use the /A switch, rather than /X.

You can specify the maximum number of sectors that can be passed in each access using /X (or /A), followed by a colon and a value between 1 and 8. If you omit this value, DOS uses the largest (and fastest) setting of 8.

Storing a RAM disk in extended or expanded memory conserves conventional RAM for program execution. However, each RAM disk created in expanded or extended memory uses about 800 bytes of conventional RAM to manage the RAM disk. You can use as much as 16MB of extended or expanded memory for one (or several) RAM disks.

Each `DEVICE=VDISK.SYS` or `DEVICE=RAMDRIVE.SYS` command in your CONFIG.SYS file creates a separate RAM disk. DOS automatically names each one in alphabetical order, starting with the first available disk drive name. For example, if you have one hard disk, named C:, and your CONFIG.SYS contains two DEVICE commands that install RAM disks, the RAM disks are automatically named D: and E:.

If your RAM disk (or disks) extend beyond the name E:, you must include the LASTDRIVE directive in your CONFIG.SYS file to specify a drive name beyond the last RAM disk. For example, if your computer has a drive C:, and you plan to create three RAM disks, named D:, E:, and F:, your CONFIG.SYS file must contain the command `LASTDRIVE=G`.

Examples   The following command, when included in the CONFIG.SYS file, creates a 64KB RAM disk in conventional memory. It assumes that the RAM disk device driver, named VDISK.SYS, is stored in the \DOS directory of drive C:. Assuming that the computer has a single hard disk, named C:, the RAM disk is named D:

```
DEVICE=C:\DOS\VDISK.SYS
```

If your computer uses RAMDRIVE.SYS rather than VDISK.SYS, and the RAMDRIVE.SYS file is stored in the \DOS directory of drive C:, the following CONFIG.SYS command performs the same installation as the previous command:

```
DEVICE=C:\DOS\RAMDRIVE.SYS
```

The next command creates a 720KB RAM disk in extended memory, with 512KB sectors and a maximum of 128 directory entries:

```
DEVICE=C:\DOS\VDISK.SYS 720 512 128 /E
```

The equivalent command using most versions of RAMDRIVE.SYS is:

```
DEVICE=C:\DOS\RAMDRIVE.SYS 720 512 128 /E
```

If your computer has expanded memory and your CONFIG.SYS file contains a device driver to activate expanded memory, you can use the /X switch with VDISK.SYS (or the /A switch with RAMDRIVE.SYS) to use all or some of the expanded memory for the RAM disk. The DEVICE command that activates the expanded memory in your CONFIG.SYS file must precede the DEVICE command that creates the RAM disk, so that expanded memory is already installed and active when the RAM disk is installed.

The following command assumes that at least 1MB of expanded memory is installed and active, and that the VDISK.SYS device driver is stored in the root directory of drive C:. The command then creates a 1MB RAM disk in expanded memory, with 512-byte sectors and a maximum of 128 directory entries:

```
DEVICE=VDISK.SYS 1024 512 128 /X
```

The equivalent command using RAMDRIVE.SYS, which is assumed to be stored in the root directory of drive C:, is:

```
DEVICE=RAMDRIVE.SYS 1024 512 128 /A
```

The following commands divide 4MB of extended memory into four 1MB RAM disks. If the computer already has physical disks named D: and E:, these four RAM disks are named F:, G:, H:, and I:. The LASTDRIVE command, also included in the CONFIG.SYS file, prepares DOS to handle at least this many drives:

```
LASTDRIVE=J
DEVICE=C:\DOS\VDISK.SYS 1024 512 64 /E
DEVICE=C:\DOS\VDISK.SYS 1024 512 64 /E
DEVICE=C:\DOS\VDISK.SYS 1024 512 64 /E
DEVICE=C:\DOS\VDISK.SYS 1024 512 64 /E
```

See Also Chapters 15 and 16, XMA2EMS.SYS, XMAEM.SYS, LASTDRIVE

VER

Displays the version of DOS in use.

Version 3 and later

Type	Internal
DOS Shell Menu Access	None
Syntax	VER
Usage	The VER command displays the version number of DOS that is currently running on your computer.
Examples	Suppose you call a software dealer to get some help, and they ask you which version of DOS you are using. To find out, merely enter the command:

VER

at the command prompt.

If you see the message Bad command or file name, you either spelled the command incorrectly or you are using a version of DOS prior to 3.0

VERIFY

Displays or sets file-writing verification

Version	2 or later
Type	Internal
DOS Shell Menu Access	None
Syntax	VERIFY [ON | OFF]
Usage	Commands that store data on disks do not normally double-check to ensure that the correct information is written. Because disk-writing errors are quite rare, double-checking every character that is stored on disk is counterproductive—it takes time and needlessly slows DOS.

However, there might be cases in which you want to be sure crucial information or large programs are stored correctly. When such circumstances arise, you can set the VERIFY status ON. Doing so slows DOS operations, but it gives you piece of mind.

To view the current status of the verification option, enter the VERIFY command with no parameters. To turn on verification, use the command VERIFY ON. To turn off verification, use the command VERIFY OFF.

Note that turning on the verification feature is the same as using the /V option in a COPY command.

Examples   Let's assume you are preparing to send some important information, stored on diskettes, to a company in Istanbul. It isn't easy to get information to and from Istanbul, so you want to be sure that the data you send is accurate the first time.

First, check the status of the verification feature by entering the command:

```
VERIFY
```

The screen informs you that VERIFY is off. Therefore, enter the command:

```
VERIFY ON
```

Now you can use COPY, or some other program, to store the necessary information on the diskette in drive A:. Because verification is on, the copy takes a little longer than usual.

When you finish making the copy, enter the command:

```
VERIFY OFF
```

to turn off verification and permit DOS to run at top speed.

See Also   COPY

VOL

Displays a volume (disk) label.

Version   2 and later

Type   Internal

DOS Shell Menu Access   In the File System, pull down the Options menu and select Show Information.... The disk's volume label, if any, is shown as the Disk Name.

Syntax   VOL [*drive*]

in which *drive* is the name of the drive whose label you want to see.

Usage   You can use the LABEL command (or the /V option with the FORMAT command) to assign a name (label) to a disk. This name can be as many as 11 characters and is displayed whenever you view the directory of the disk with a DIR command or use the TREE or CHKDSK commands.

The VOL command also displays the label assigned to the disk. Unlike the other commands, however, VOL displays only the label and none of the other information.

Examples   Suppose you place a diskette in drive A: to see if it has been assigned a label. Enter the command:

```
VOL A:
```

If there is no label assigned to the disk, DOS displays the message Volume in drive A has no label. If there is a label assigned to the disk, DOS displays the message Volume in drive A is followed by the name.

See Also   LABEL, FORMAT

XCOPY

Copies files.

Version   3.2 and later

Type   External (XCOPY.EXE)

DOS Shell Menu Access   None

Syntax   XCOPY [*source drive*][*source path*][*source file name*]
[*destination drive*][*destination path*][*destination file*]
[/S] [/E] [/P] [/V] [/A] [/M] [/D:*date*] [/W]

in which *source drive*, *source path*, and *source file name* identify the file (or files) to be copied, and *destination drive*, *destination path*, and *destination file* identify the destination of the copy. The *date* option is a date in mm/dd/yy format (or the appropriate format for a foreign country).

Usage   XCOPY is an extended version of the COPY command, offering many additional features and options. It allows you to automatically copy only files that have been changed since the last XCOPY command or only files that have been changed since a particular date. XCOPY also can copy files from subdirectories beneath the current directory (creating subdirectories as needed on the destination disk). The features that XCOPY offers are available as the following switches:

/A	Copies only files that have been changed (that is, files with the archive bit on), but does not turn off the archive bit.
/D:*date*	Copies files that were created or modified on or after a specified date.
/E	Copies subdirectories, creating the subdirectories on the destination disk if they do not already exist.
/M	Copies modified files (that is, files with the archive bit on) and turns off the archive bit.
/P	Prompts you for permission before copying each file.
/S	Copies files from the current directory and from all subdirectories beneath the current directory.
/V	Verifies that the copy was 100 percent successful.
/W	Waits for a source disk to be inserted.

When using the /D option, be sure to enter the date in the appropriate format, as specified by your computer's COUNTRY setting. In the United States, you can use either the mm/dd/yy format, or the mm-dd-yy format. For example, both 12/31/89 and 12-31-89 are valid dates.

The /A and /M options both limit copying to files whose archive bit is set to ON. The archive bit is ON whenever a file is first created, or changed. The /A option leaves the bit set on after the copy takes place. The /M option turns off the archive bit after copying the file. Therefore, the /M option is similar to the BACKUP command, which copies only files that have the archive bit set, and then it turns off the archive bit.

The /S option copies all files in all subdirectories that are children of the current directory on the source drive. Therefore, if you are copying from the root directory, XCOPY copies all disk files, creating subdirectories on the destination disk as necessary. However, empty subdirectories are not created on the destination disk unless you specify the /E option. You can only use /E if you've already specified the /S option.

Examples   To copy all of the spreadsheet files with the extension .WK? from all directories on hard disk drive C: to the diskette in drive A:, first switch to the root directory or drive C:, then enter the following XCOPY command:

```
CD\
XCOPY *.WK? A:\ /S
```

Because the /S option is used and the copy was initiated from the root directory, all files with the .WK? extension are copied, regardless of the directory on which they are stored.

To repeat this XCOPY command in the future, but include only spreadsheet files that have been changed since the last XCOPY or BACKUP command, use the /M parameter, as follows:

```
XCOPY *.WK? A:\ /S /M
```

To copy all files with the extension .DBF, which were created or modified on or after December 1, 1988, from the directory named \DBASE on drive C: and all subdirectories beneath \DBASE, to drive A:, enter the command:

```
XCOPY C:\DBASE\*.DBF A:\ /S /D:12/1/88
```

To copy all files and the directory structure (including empty subdirectories) from the diskette in drive A: to the diskette in drive B:, enter the command:

```
XCOPY A:\*.* B:\ /S /E
```

In this example, the \ characters are included after the drive names to ensure that all subdirectories are referenced from the root directory. Note that, in this case, the *.* is optional. If you do not specify a file name after a drive and directory specification in an XCOPY, *.* is assumed. Therefore, the following command performs exactly the same operation as the previous one:

```
XCOPY A:\ B:\ /S /E
```

To force XCOPY to pause for a disk change before beginning the copy process, to ask permission before copying each file, and also to verify the accuracy of each copy, use the /P, /W, and /V options as follows:

```
XCOPY *.TXT A: /P /W /V
```

See Also   COPY, BACKUP

XMAEM.SYS

Emulates the expanded memory on IBM 80386 computers using IBM PC-DOS Version 4.

Version   IBM PC DOS 4 and later

Type   Device driver activated by a DEVICE command in CONFIG.SYS

DOS Shell Menu Access	None

Syntax `DEVICE=[drive][path]XMAEMSYS size`

in which *drive* and *path* specify the location of the XMAEM.SYS file, and *size* specifies the amount of expanded memory to allocate.

Usage All computers that use the 80386 microprocessor support *virtual memory*, which enables any type of memory (including disk storage) to "act like" extra RAM (or expanded memory). IBM computers that use the 80386 microprocessor (such as the PS/2 Model 80) and DOS 4 include the XMAEM.SYS device driver that uses extended memory to emulate expanded memory.

Non-IBM 80386 computers offer the same capabilities as IBM 80386 computers, but the device driver for emulating expanded memory usually has a different name. Furthermore, the device driver is described in the computer's manual—not the DOS manual--and probably exists on a separate diskette (often labeled "Supplemental Programs" or "Device Drivers") that came with your computer.

For example, the Compaq computer provides the CEMM.SYS device driver, which emulates expanded memory. CEMM.SYS is stored both on the Compaq Supplemental Programs disk and in the Compaq MS-DOS4 disks. (If you have two copies of the device driver for emulating expanded memory, use the one on the DOS diskettes to ensure that you are using the correct device driver for your version of DOS. Otherwise, when the computer attempts to install the device driver, DOS might display the error message `Incorrect DOS version`.)

The XMAEM.SYS device driver specifically emulates the IBM Personal System/2 80286 Expanded Memory Adapter/A, which conforms to the LIM EMS standard 4.0 and uses extended memory to do so. The `DEVICE=XMAEM.SYS` command must precede the `DEVICE=XMA2EMS.SYS` command in your CONFIG.SYS file, so that the expanded memory is emulated before the XMA2EMS.SYS device driver activates it.

If you do not use the optional *size* parameter in the DEVICE=XMAEM.SYS command, all extended memory is converted to expanded memory. If you use the *size* parameter, it must specify the size of expanded memory in 16KB pages. For example, 1MB of expanded memory is 1,024 kilobytes. Furthermore, 1,024 divided by 16 is 64. Therefore, to emulate 1MB of expanded memory in extended memory, you must specify 64 as the *size* parameter.

Examples If the XMAEM.SYS file is stored in the \DOS directory of drive C:, and you want to use all of the extended memory as expanded memory, include this command in your CONFIG.SYS file (above the DEVICE=XMA2EMS.SYS command):

```
DEVICE=C:\DOS\XMAEM.SYS
```

If you want to use 1MB of extended memory for expanded memory, include this command in your CONFIG.SYS file (above the DEVICE=XMA2EMS.SYS command):

```
DEVICE=C:\DOS\XMAEM.SYS 64
```

If you are using a Compaq 386 computer and you want to use 2MB of extended memory as expanded memory, be sure the CEMM.SYS file is stored in the \DOS directory of drive C:, and include this command in your CONFIG.SYS file:

```
DEVICE=C:\DOS\CEMM.SYS 2048 ON
```

With the CEMM.SYS device driver, you do not need to use a second DEVICE command to activate the expanded memory. The ON option in the DEVICE command activates the expanded memory immediately.

See Also   Chapters 15 and 16, XMA2EMS.SYS

XMA2EMS.SYS

Installs expanded memory in IBM PC-DOS Version 4:

Version   IBM PC-DOS version 4

Type   Device driver (activated by a DEVICE command in CONFIG.SYS)

DOS Shell Menu Access   None

Syntax
```
DEVICE=[drive][path]XMA2EMS.SYS
[FRAME=hex address] [Pxxx=hex address [...]] [/X:size]
```

in which *drive* and *path* specify the location of the XMA2EMS.SYS file, *hex address* is a memory address specified in hexadecimal notation, *xxx* is a page number, and *size* specifies the amount of expanded memory in 16KB pages.

Usage   The XMA2EMS.SYS device driver is included with IBM PC-DOS Version 4. Other computers and versions of DOS usually offer similar device drivers. For example, the COMPAQ CEMMP.SYS device driver installs expanded memory on Compaq 80286-based microcomputers.

The XMA2EMS.SYS device driver can be used to install expanded memory on an IBM 80286 or 80386 computer that has one of the following EMS adapters installed:

- IBM 2MB Expanded Memory Adapter
- IBM Personal System/2 80286 Expanded Memory Adapter/A
- IBM Personal System/2 80286 Memory Expansion Option

or on an IBM Model 80 or other IBM 80386-based computer with the XMAEM.SYS device driver already loaded

The optional parameters that you can use with the XMA2EMS.SYS device driver include:

hex address   When used with the FRAME= option, the *hex address* must refer to a starting address that specifies four contiguous 16KB page frames. Acceptable values are in the hex range of A000 through E000 (although a range of C000 to E000 is safer because it avoids conflicts with video memory).

xxx   Refers to a page frame number, in which *xxx* can be 0, 1, 2, or 3 for expanded memory switching, or 254 or 255 for DOS functions. The *hex address* specified with the P*xxx*= option must refer to the starting point of a 16KB page frame, in the hexadecimal range A000 through E000 (although a range of C000 through E000 is safer because it avoids conflicts with video memory).

size   Represents the size of expanded memory to install in 16KB chunks. The minimum is 4 (4 × 16KB = 64KB of expanded memory). If you specified a *size* in the `DEVICE=XMAEMS.SYS` command when emulating expanded memory in extended memory on an 80386 computer, the /X:*size* parameter in the DEVICE=XMA2EMS.SYS command is ignored.

If you use the FRAME= option to specify four contiguous 16KB page frames, you cannot individually set pages P0 through P3. However, you can still set pages P254 and P255 individually, as long as you use memory locations that are not already in use by the FRAME= option.

If you want to install a RAM disk (using the VDISK.SYS device driver) or the FASTOPEN disk caching system in expanded memory (using the /X option with these device drivers), you must specify a 16KB page block of memory in the DEVICE=XMA2EMS.SYS command for P254. If you want to use the /X option with the BUFFERS command in CONFIG.SYS to install the disk buffers in expanded memory, you must specify a starting address for P255 in your DEVICE=XMA2EMS.SYS command.

The memory addresses for P254 and P255 must not conflict with the 64KB page frame specified in the FRAME= option, or with the 16KB blocks of memory that have been assigned individually to P0, P1, P2, and P3.

If you merely want to see which memory addresses are available for a page frame or individual pages, use the DEVICE=XMA2EMS.SYS command in your CONFIG.SYS file, but do not include the FRAME= or Pxxx= options. DOS displays available frames and pages when you reboot (but it does not install the expanded memory). Write down or print these suggested frame and page addresses; then, modify the DEVICE=XMA2EMS.SYS command in your CONFIG.SYS to use the available frames and pages.

Examples   Suppose you want to activate all of your expanded memory, and you also want to use expanded memory for the disk buffers and FASTOPEN disk caching program in order to conserve conventional RAM. If your XMA2EMS.SYS file is stored on the \DOS directory of drive C:, and if you have an expanded memory adapter installed in you computer, your CONFIG.SYS file should contain commands similar to the following (in the order shown):

```
DEVICE=C:\DOS\XMA2EMS.SYS FRAME=D000 P254=C000 P255=C400
BUFFERS=15,2 /X
INSTALL=C:\DOS\FASTOPEN.EXE C:=(50,25) /X
```

In this example, the FRAME=D000 option allocates memory addresses from D000 to one byte beneath E000 for expanded memory switching. Therefore, pages 254 and 255 are installed at the non-conflicting addresses C000 and C400.

If your computer does not have an expanded memory adapter, but does use the 80386 microprocessor, you can achieve the same results by including these commands (in the order shown) in your CONFIG.SYS file:

```
DEVICE=C:\DOS\XMAEM.SYS
DEVICE=C:\DOS\XMA2EMS.SYS FRAME=D000 P254=C000 P255=C400
BUFFERS=15,2 /X
INSTALL=C:\DOS\FASTOPEN.EXE C:=(50,25) /X
```

If you are using a non-IBM computer, you must use other device drivers to activate and emulate expanded memory. For example, suppose you have a Compaq 386 computer with 4MB of extended memory. You want to use 2MB of that memory as expanded memory, part of which is used to manage the disk buffers and FASTOPEN disk caching program. You also want to use 1MB of extended memory as a RAM disk and reserve the remaining 1MB of extended memory for programs that can use it directly (such as Lotus 1-2-3 Version 3).

Assuming that all of your device drivers are stored in the \DOS directory of drive C:, include the following commands in your CONFIG.SYS file (in the order shown):

```
DEVICE=C:\DOS\CEMM.EXE 2048 ON
BUFFERS=15,2 /X
INSTALL=C:\DOS\FASTOPEN.EXE C:=(50,25) D:=(50,25) /X
DEVICE=C:\DOS\VDISK.SYS 1024 512 128 /E
```

For specific information about using extended and expanded memory adapters designed for your computer, see the DOS manual that came with your computer, or see your computer's Technical Reference Guide.

See Also   BUFFERS, FASTOPEN, VDISK.SYS, XMAEM.SYS, Chapters 15 and 16

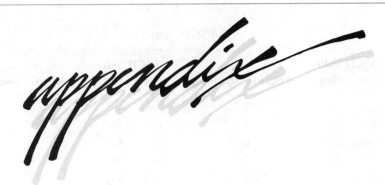

ASCII Code Character Set

(including IBM extended character codes)

ASCII Value Dec	Hex	ASCII Character	ASCII Value Dec	Hex	ASCII Character
000	00		023	17	↕
001	01	☺	024	18	↑
002	02	☻	025	19	↓
003	03	♥	026	1A	→
004	04	♦	027	1B	←
005	05	♣	028	1C	FS
006	06	♠	029	1D	GS
007	07	●	030	1E	RS
008	08	◘	031	1F	US
009	09	○	032	20	SP
010	0A	■	033	21	!
011	0B	♂	034	22	"
012	0C	♀	035	23	#
013	0D	♪	036	24	$
014	0E	♫	037	25	%
015	0F	☼	038	26	&
016	10	►	039	27	'
017	11	◄	040	28	(
018	12	↕	041	29	)
019	13	‼	042	2A	*
020	14	¶	043	2B	+
021	15	§	044	2C	,
022	16	▬	045	2D	-

ASCII (cont.)

ASCII Value			ASCII Value		
Dec	Hex	ASCII Character	Dec	Hex	ASCII Character
046	2E	.	085	55	U
047	2F	/	086	56	V
048	30	0	087	57	W
049	31	1	088	58	X
050	32	2	089	59	Y
051	33	3	090	5A	Z
052	34	4	091	5B	[
053	35	5	092	5C	\
054	36	6	093	5D	]
055	37	7	094	5E	^
056	38	8	095	5F	_
057	39	9	096	60	`
058	3A	:	097	61	a
059	3B	;	098	62	b
060	3C	<	099	63	c
061	3D	=	100	64	d
062	3E	>	101	65	e
063	3F	?	102	66	f
064	40	@	103	67	g
065	41	A	104	68	h
066	42	B	105	69	i
067	43	C	106	6A	j
068	44	D	107	6B	k
069	45	E	108	6C	l
070	46	F	109	6D	m
071	47	G	110	6E	n
072	48	H	111	6F	o
073	49	I	112	70	p
074	4A	J	113	71	q
075	4B	K	114	72	r
076	4C	L	115	73	s
077	4D	M	116	74	t
078	4E	N	117	75	u
079	4F	O	118	76	v
080	50	P	119	77	w
081	51	Q	120	78	x
082	52	R	121	79	y
083	53	S	122	7A	z
084	54	T	123	7B	{

ASCII (cont.)

| ASCII Value | | ASCII Character | ASCII Value | | ASCII Character |
Dec	Hex		Dec	Hex	
124	7C	¦	163	A3	ú
125	7D	}	164	A4	ñ
126	7E	~	165	A5	Ñ
127	7F	DEL	166	A6	ª
128	80	Ç	167	A7	º
129	81	ü	168	A8	¿
130	82	é	169	A9	⌐
131	83	â	170	AA	¬
132	84	ä	171	AB	½
133	85	à	172	AC	¼
134	86	å	173	AD	¡
135	87	ç	174	AE	«
136	88	ê	175	AF	»
137	89	ë	176	B0	░
138	8A	è	177	B1	▒
139	8B	ï	178	B2	▓
140	8C	î	179	B3	│
141	8D	ì	180	B4	┤
142	8E	Ä	181	B5	╡
143	8F	Å	182	B6	╢
144	90	É	183	B7	╖
145	91	æ	184	B8	╕
146	92	Æ	185	B9	╣
147	93	ô	186	BA	║
148	94	ö	187	BB	╗
149	95	ò	188	BC	╝
150	96	û	189	BD	╜
151	97	ù	190	BE	╛
152	98	ÿ	191	BF	┐
153	99	Ö	192	C0	└
154	9A	Ü	193	C1	┴
155	9B	¢	194	C2	┬
156	9C	£	195	C3	├
157	9D	¥	196	C4	─
158	9E	P_t	197	C5	┼
159	9F	ƒ	198	C6	╞
160	A0	á	199	C7	╟
161	A1	í	200	C8	╚
162	A2	ó	201	C9	╔

ASCII (cont.)

ASCII Value			ASCII Value		
Dec	*Hex*	ASCII Character	*Dec*	*Hex*	ASCII Character
202	CA	⊥	229	E5	σ
203	CB	⊤	230	E6	μ
204	CC	⊩	231	E7	τ
205	CD	=	232	E8	Φ
206	CE	⧈	233	E9	Θ
207	CF	⊥	234	EA	Ω
208	D0	⊥	235	EB	δ
209	D1	⊤	236	EC	∞
210	D2	⊤	237	ED	ϕ
211	D3	∟	238	EE	ϵ
212	D4	⊢	239	EF	$\cap$
213	D5	⊨	240	F0	$\equiv$
214	D6	┌	241	F1	$\pm$
215	D7	╫	242	F2	$\geq$
216	D8	╪	243	F3	$\leq$
217	D9	┘	244	F4	$\lceil$
218	DA	┌	245	F5	$\rfloor$
219	DB	█	246	F6	$\div$
220	DC	▬	247	F7	$\approx$
221	DD	▌	248	F8	$\circ$
222	DE	▐	249	F9	$\cdot$
223	DF	▬	250	FA	$\cdot$
224	E0	α	251	FB	$\sqrt{}$
225	E1	β	252	FC	η
226	E2	Γ	253	FD	^{2}
227	E3	π	254	FE	■
228	E4	Σ	255	FF	

Index

P

The Best Book of: WordStar® Features Release 5
Vincent Alfieri

With the release of WordStar Professional Release 5, this book will help word processors and computer operators access all of the more than 200 new features and improvements in this "classic" software package.

The book provides in-depth explanations of Professional Release 5 features such as the new advanced page preview, the ability to display font styles and sizes exactly as they appear, the new pull-down menus and additional information on fonts, telecommunications, outlining, and merge printing.

Topics covered include:

- Revisions
- Print Effects, Page Preview and Printing
- Formatting Essentials
- Blocks and Windows
- Finding and Replacing
- Macros and Other Shortcuts
- Working with DOS and File Management
- Controlling the Page and the Printer
- Boilerplates, Format Files, and Document Assembly
- Conditional Printing
- Working with Laser Printers
- Appendices: The Files Used in This Book, Quick Reference Guide

768 Pages, 7½ x 9¾, Softbound
ISBN: 0-672-48434-X
No. 48434, $21.95

WordPerfect® Version 5.0: Expert Techniques for Power Users
Kate Barnes

This book provides the experienced word processor with a quick guide to basic features and a detailed reference to advanced features such as application techniques and macros. Its "keystroke summaries" provide a reference for the everyday user accomplishing typical word-processing tasks.

The book includes never-before-published tips, tricks, macros, forms, and applications and shows how to give documents a finished look with the advanced features of electronic publishing.

Topics covered include:

- Customizing and Starting
- Refreshing the Basics
- Spelling, Thesaurus, and Hyphens
- Creating and Using Macros
- Using Footnotes, Endnotes, Automatic Referencing, and Indexes
- Organizing Lists, Master Documents, Outlines, Paragraphs, and Tables
- Working with Columns
- Merging and Sorting
- Using Math
- Style and Graphics
- Printing and "Electronic Publishing"
- Converting Files
- Using the Library

432 Pages, 7½ x 9¾, Softbound
ISBN: 0-672-22649-9
No. 22649, $19.95

The Best Book of: OS/2™ Database Manager
Howard Fosdick

This is a complete, self-contained introduction to the Database Manager component of IBM's OS/2 operating system. It covers such topics as how to install the Database Manager, how to query tables and write reports, and how to update data in tables.

A comprehensive tutorial, it guides the reader in the use of the Query Manager through numerous screen pictures and examples. The book shows how to define tables, build databases, develop queries and reports, update databases, load tables, run utilities, and design systems with the Database Manager.

Topics covered include:

- Using the Query Manager
- Maintaining Your Data
- Developing Tailored Reports
- Designing Your Applications
- An Example Design
- Database Implementation
- Using the Customized Interface
- Defining the School Administration Application
- Panels for Data Maintenance
- Altering Applications
- Procedures
- More on Variables and Query Manager Commands
- Maintaining Your Applications and Data
- Advanced Features

300 Pages, 7½ x 9¾, Softbound
ISBN: 0-672-48436-6
No. 48436, $24.95

Understanding Lotus® 1-2-3®, Release 3.0
Alan Simpson

Understanding Lotus 1-2-3, Release 3.0 is designed for the computer novice who wants a quick, practical guide to putting 1-2-3 to work immediately. Its brief, concise, and nontechnical approach makes the book ideal for those readers who do not have a lot of spare time to learn about "theory".

The book covers all of the most important features of 1-2-3, including the worksheet, graphics, database management, and macros. Includes margin notes which provide important tips, hints, and cautions, "Quick Steps" to step-by-step keystroke sequences for performing specific tasks, and includes margin icons to help experienced 1-2-3 users quickly locate new information.

Topics covered include:

- Getting Started with 1-2-3
- Creating a Worksheet
- Using Functions and Formulas
- Working with Groups of Cells
- Formatting Your Worksheet's Appearance
- Printing Your Worksheet
- Managing Linked Worksheets
- Creating Graphs
- Printing Graphs
- Building a Database
- Sorting, Searching, and Printing
- Creating Macros
- Creating Your Own Menus
- Installing and Configuring 1-2-3
- Interfacing 1-2-3 with Other Programs

350 Pages, 7 x 9, Softbound
ISBN: 0-672-27282-2
No. 27282, $19.95

Visit your local book retailer or call
800-428-SAMS.

The Waite Group's OS/2™ Programmer's Reference
Asael Dror

This intermediate-level programming book provides a complete look at the unique capabilities of this powerful multitasking operating system. With more than 120 examples and explanations of the syntax for all the system's functions, the book organizes and simplifies the information contained in the OS/2 Software Developer's Kit.

The functions are divided into related categories, each beginning with its own tutorial. Within each catagory, functions are presented alphabetically with the purpose, syntax, and a real-world example, including explanations of error codes, common uses, cautions and pitfalls, and references to related APIs.

Topics covered include:

- API Jump Table
- OS/2 Programming Philosophy and Functions
- OS/2 and the Different Programming Languages
- Creating and Using Dynamic Link Libraries
- Using LINK, IMPLIB, BIND, MKMSGF, and MSGBIND
- Task Manager
- IPC Semaphores, Pipes, and Queues
- Memory Management, Dynamic Load, File and Device I/O
- Signal Processing and Error Handling
- Environment and Timer
- National Language Support
- Keyboard, Mouse, and Video

800 Pages, 7½ x 9¾, Softbound
ISBN: 0-672-22645-6
No. 22645, $24.95

Advanced MS-DOS®: Expert Techniques for Power Users & Programmers
Carl Townsend

Written for the intermediate to advanced programmer familiar with C and assembly language, this is a comprehensive guide to the MS-DOS operating system. Compatible with version 4.0 and filled with programming examples and illustrations, the book details terminate and stay resident programs, shows how to write device drivers, and discusses program "viruses"—what they are and how to avoid them.

Topics covered include:

- The Structure of MS-DOS
- Introduction to the MS-DOS File Management System
- Disk Organization and Management
- The MS-DOS Program Structure
- Compilers and Utilities
- Debuggers and Disassemblers
- Using BIOS Interrupts
- Using the DOS Interface
- Using the Display Video
- Using the Keyboard
- MS-DOS File Input and Output
- Parallel and Serial Communication
- Writing Installable Device Drivers
- Creating Terminate and Stay Resident Programs
- Memory Management in MS-DOS
- Executing Child Programs
- Introduction to Windows
- Programming with Windows

544 Pages, 7½ x 9¾, Softbound
ISBN: 0-672-22667-7
No. 22667, $24.95

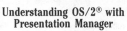

Understanding OS/2® with Presentation Manager
Daniel and Kathleen Paquette

This book is for novice users of this new operating system for 80286 and 80386 microprocessors from Microsoft® and IBM®, and those interested in understanding the differences between the new system and older versions. Students, business users, and programmers will benefit from its broad, general coverage.

Divided into two distinct parts, the first part of the book is a general overview of the system that also explains concepts and terms. The second part provides greater detail by highlighting the specific commands by functionality, such as disk usage and file manipulation.

Topics covered include:

- Overview and Getting Started
- The Presentation Manager
- Disks, Directories, and Files
- Redirection
- Setting up the Computing Environment
- Batch Files

236 Pages, 7 x 9, Softbound
ISBN: 0-672-27281-4
No. 27281, $19.95

Visit your local book retailer or call
800-428-SAMS.

The DOS 4 Start Programs Screen (Main Group)

Action	Options	See Pages	Action	Options	See Pages
① To move the highlight bar	Press ↑ or ↓ keys; or position the mouse pointer and click once	31–34	④ To position the mouse pointer	Move the mouse	31–34
② To select an option	Move the highlight bar to the option and press Enter, or position the mouse pointer and double-click	31–34	⑤ To get help	Press F1, or position the mouse pointer to the F1 = Help box and click once	34–38
③ To activate the Action Bar	Press F10, then press Enter, or position the mouse pointer and click once	39–40	⑥ To access the File System	Move the highlight bar to the File System option, and press Enter, or double-click File System with your mouse	51–52
			To access the DOS command prompt	Press F3	42–43

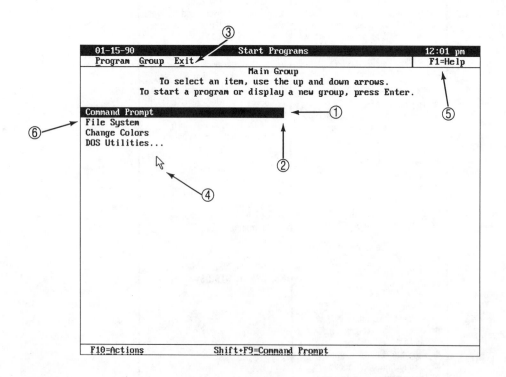